ENCYCLOPEDIA OF COMPUTERS AND COMPUTER HISTORY

ENCYCLOPEDIA OF COMPUTERS AND COMPUTER HISTORY

VOLUME TWO, M–Z

Raúl Rojas, Editor in Chief

FITZROY DEARBORN PUBLISHERS
CHICAGO • LONDON

339 Fifth Avenue, New York, New York 10016
www.mosgroup.com

Produced by The Moschovitis Group, Inc.

Publisher:	Valerie Tomaselli
Executive Editor:	Hilary W. Poole
Assistant Editor:	Jenna Brinning
Editorial Coordinator:	Sonja Matanovic
Design and Layout:	Annemarie Redmond
Illustrations:	Richard Garratt
Photo Research:	Gillian Speeth
Editorial Assistants:	Stewart Rudy, Colleen Sullivan
Copyediting:	Zeiders & Associates
Proofreading:	Joseph Reilly, Paul Scaramazza
Index:	Robert Elwood

For more information write to:

Fitzroy Dearborn Publishers
919 N. Michigan Avenue, Suite 760
Chicago, Illinois 60611
United States

or

Fitzroy Dearborn Publishers
310 Regent Street
London W1B 3AX
United Kingdom

British Library and Library of Congress Cataloging-in-Publication Data are available

ISBN 1-57958-235-4

First published in the USA and UK 2001

Contents

List of Entries

Volume Two

MACH

MACH is an **operating system** derived from **Unix** but different in its implementation philosophy. Instead of using a large "kernel" in which all main features of the system are contained, as of version 3.0, MACH works with a microkernel, a lightweight process that provides only essential functionality. Other services, such as the user interface, drivers for peripherals, or support of certain functions, are started as new user processes only when they are needed. For example, the pager, which swaps blocks from the **hard disk** to main memory, is not part of the kernel and can be replaced by the user. In this way the central part of the operating system is lean and portable. Functionally, MACH is more of a platform on which to build operating systems than a fully grown operating system.

Work on MACH started at Carnegie Mellon University (CMU) in 1985 and continued until 1994. MACH's most interesting feature is that it supports multiprocessing through its **object-oriented** approach. In MACH, the memory allocated to processes is treated as objects. The processes communicate with the memory by sending messages. The operating system can reroute these messages to another computer in a network and receive the response. Threads (i.e., portions of code running in parallel) are treated in the same way and can be transferred to another processor. Therefore, MACH makes the allocation of computing resources invisible for the programmer and includes interprocess communication functionality at the kernel level.

The MACH kernel supports different machines and is a truly distributed operating system, with provisions for handling different network speeds. MACH has six primitive abstractions: task, thread, port, port set, message, and the memory object. A *thread* is the basic execution unit and runs inside a *task*. Tasks communicate through *ports*, and several of them form a *port set. Threads* communicate using *messages*.

Other **software** vendors have adopted MACH's philosophy. For example, the operating system for the **NeXT** workstation (NeXTSTEP), the first object-oriented operating system commercially available, was written using MACH as its basis. MACH was also adopted by the Open Software Foundation for OSF/1 and by **IBM**, which used it to develop **OS/2** for RS6000 machines. The MACH project also contributed to the development of other operating systems by way of a brain drain. Avie Tevanian, who worked in the MACH project at CMU, later became the principal scientist at NeXT and **Apple Computer**. Richard Rashid, MACH's principal investigator, became director of research at **Microsoft** and was involved in the design of **Windows NT**. It was Rashid who started MACH after having worked in a project called RIG (Rochester Intelligent Highway) at the University of Rochester in the 1970s.

Further Reading

Boykin, Joseph, David Kirschen, Alan Langerman, and Susan LoVerso. *Programming Under MACH.* Reading, Mass.; Menlo Park, Calif.; Don Mills, Ontario; Harlow, England; Amsterdam; Bonn; Sydney; Tokyo; Madrid; San Juan; Paris; Seoul; Milan; Mexico City; Taipei: Addison-Wesley, 1993.

Coulouris, George F. *Distributed Systems: Concepts and Design.* Wokingham, England, and Reading, Mass.: Addison-Wesley, 1988; 2nd ed., 1994.

Rashid, Richard F. "MACH: A Case Study in Technology Transfer." In *Computer Science: A 25th Anniversary Commemorative.* Anothology Series. New York: ACM Press, 1991.

Silberschatz, Abraham, and James L. Peterson. *Operating Systems Concepts.* Reading, Mass.: Addison-Wesley, 1988.

—*Raúl Rojas*

Machine Language

Computers execute programs, sequences of commands that have been written by a programmer. There are several levels of abstraction for the description of those instructions. High-level languages such as **Fortran** or **Pascal** operate with powerful instructions that are easy to grasp and remember; they can be interpreted more easily by the human intellect than by the computer. Machine language, on the other hand, is the lowest level of abstraction: It is just another name for the elementary binary sequences that can be executed by a processor. They are difficult for people to understand but are directly interpretable by the processor.

In a high-level language one can just write "A = B + C" to compute the sum of two variables B and C and store the result in variable A. To express the same operation in machine language the computer must be told what to do, step by step. The programmer uses a symbolic notation called ***assembler*** for the elementary machine instructions. In assembler, the processor is ordered to load variable B to a register in the processor, to load variable C to another register, to perform the addition, and to store the result in variable A. The following set of instructions of a hypothetical assembler, where R1, R2, and R3 denote three registers in the **central processing unit** (CPU), would deliver the desired result:

```
LOAD   B, R1
LOAD   C, R2
ADD    R1, R2, R3
STORE  R3, A
```

The symbolic instructions above are transformed into binary numbers by the special assembler program, so-called because it puts together the binary program. In a 32-bit machine, each of the instructions above would be transformed into a 32-bit number and the complete program would consist of four 32-bit numbers.

To transform the instructions in the example into binary numbers, the instructions need to be coded. Some bits in the 32-bit binary number are reserved to code the name of the command. These bits are the *opcode* (operation code) of the instruction. The rest of the bits are used to code the numbers of the registers used and/or the address of the variable loaded from or stored to memory. Since the processor only understands machine language and the programmer writes in a high-level language, it is necessary to translate one into the other. A compiler does exactly that: It transforms source code, written in Pascal or **LISP**, into object code, ready to be executed by a specific processor. Since processors have dissimilar instruction sets and therefore different machine languages, a compiler is needed for each computer.

Compiled programs that have been transformed into object code are also called *binaries*. In many cases the original programmer leaves a company and the source code of a program is lost. Only the binaries remain, but they are very difficult to understand, since they consist simply of long sequences of binary numbers. They can be disassembled by a special program that recovers the symbolic assembler code from the binary file. Such difficulties were very common when companies had to inspect old programs to ensure that they would handle dates correctly in the year 2000.

An executable program is object code stored on a **hard disk**. In **DOS**, the original operating system for the IBM **personal computer** (PC), binaries use the extension EXE. Any file with this extension is presumably an executable program. Other operating systems have different conventions to mark files that contain executable files.

Programming in assembler has always been an arcane science and the domain of **hackers**, and it is becoming increasingly unfashionable because modern **microprocessors** are so complex. They work by looking ahead in the instruction stream trying to locate instructions that can be executed in parallel, and also making predictions about the result of branches and reassigning registers to increase the performance of the machine. A computer can do this complex optimization better than a human programmer. Therefore, code written in **C** or Pascal can be translated by an optimizing compiler, and the resulting program runs faster than machine language code written by the average programmer.

FURTHER READING

Blaauw, Gerrit A., and Frederick P. Brooks, Jr. *Computer Architecture: Concepts and Evolution*, Reading, Mass.; Menlo Park, Calif.; Don Mills, Ontario; Harlow, England; Amsterdam; Bonn; Sydney; Tokyo; Madrid; San Juan; Paris; Seoul; Milan; Mexico City; Taipei: Addison-Wesley, 1997.

Gill, Arthur. *Machine and Assembly Language Programming of the PDP-11.* Englewood Cliffs, N.J.: Prentice Hall, 1978; 2nd ed., 1983.

—*Raúl Rojas*

Macintosh

Few computers have inspired quite so much devotion as **Apple Computer**'s Macintosh (or "Mac"). Introduced in 1984, it has influenced the "look and feel" of all modern computers, spawned the industry of **desktop publishing**, and constantly set performance standards to which other personal computers have aspired. But although the Macintosh has always been an innovative machine, successive improvements in **Microsoft**'s **Windows** software and the turbulent history of Apple Computer have gradually undermined its technical lead. Despite the introduction of new models, it remains unclear exactly what the future holds for the Macintosh in a Windows-dominated world.

What made the Macintosh so revolutionary in 1984 was its **graphical user interface** (GUI). The world's most popular computer at this time was the industry-standard **personal computer** (PC) from **IBM**, a cumbersome box that ran Microsoft's Disk Operating System (**DOS**). For most people, DOS was difficult to use, because it required them to memorize and type long strings of arcane commands onto a text-based display screen. The Macintosh worked in a totally different way: Instead of typing in commands, the user simply dragged pictures of objects (icons) around the "desktop" (the computer screen) using a handheld **mouse**. On a Macintosh, a document could be deleted simply by dragging its icon onto a picture of a trashcan; in DOS, deleting a file involved typing in a command such as

Thousands of Macintoshes at a factory in Fremont, California, on 28 March 1984. (AP/Wide World Photos)

"delete c:\myfile.txt." All this made the Macintosh much more friendly and much easier to use. Where the IBM PC came with thick manuals, the Macintosh came with just a thin booklet; indeed, one Macintosh advertisement was based on just this comparison.

But the Macintosh was not just easier to use. It ran a unique **operating system**, which was faster than DOS because its design was closely tied to the design of the Macintosh **hardware**. It was also incompatible with DOS for the same reason, so the Macintosh could not run programs written for the IBM PC. Despite having a fast 8-megahertz **Motorola** 68000 processor, early Macintoshes were slower than comparable PCs, due to the intensive processing required by the graphical user interface. There were other drawbacks, too. The first Macintosh had a memory of just 128 kilobytes (kB), equivalent to 131,072 characters or approximately 30 pages of text. It also lacked a hard-disk drive; programs were stored on **floppy disks** and users had to keep swapping these over to run different applications or store their own files.

Although the Macintosh was released in 1984, its history dates back almost two decades before that. In 1967, Ph.D. researcher Jef Raskin was writing his thesis on graphical user interfaces at Pennsylvania State University. Some years later, he was doing similar research at the influential **Xerox Palo Alto Research Center** (PARC). In 1978, he joined Apple, the California-based microcomputer company that had been started two years previously by **Steve Wozniak** (1950–) and **Steve Jobs** (1955–). One of his first jobs, before running the Macintosh project, was to write a proposal for an easy-to-use machine called the Person in the Street (PITS) computer. Soon afterward, following an investment in Apple by Xerox, Steve Jobs visited Xerox PARC himself and saw a U.S.$40,000 workstation called the **Alto computer**, which had many innovative features including a **graphical user interface** operated by a **mouse**. Jobs resolved that future Apple computers would work this way, too.

The Macintosh was not the first Apple computer to make use of the Alto's groundbreaking technology. By March 1980, a machine known as the Apple Lisa was being developed by a team that included 15 employees from Xerox PARC; that team did *not* include Jobs, who took over the Macintosh project from Raskin and worked his engineers beneath a pirate flag in a "battle" against the Lisa. Released in January 1983, more than a year before the Macintosh, the Lisa sold for an enormous U.S.$10,000 at a time when an industry-standard IBM PC cost less than U.S.$3500.

Although the Lisa failed in the marketplace, it was an important milestone on the road to the Macintosh, which was finally released in January 1984. Enthusiasts still fondly remember the commercial produced by Apple for this occasion, in which a female runner sends an athlete's hammer hurling through a huge video screen playing a lecture from a menacing Big Brother figure. The message: "On January 24, Apple Computer will introduce Macintosh. And you'll see why 1984 won't be like *1984*." Described by Steve Jobs as "the computer for the rest of us" and an "insanely great" machine, the U.S.$2495 Macintosh was designed to be a direct challenge to the dominance of the small business and home markets by "Big Brother" IBM.

Even with such dramatic advertising, the Macintosh was not an immediate success. Apple had forecast some 2 million sales by 1985 but achieved only a quarter of that target, largely because the Macintosh lacked a **killer application** (a piece of software so useful that it alone justifies the purchase of a machine). This was partly because the first Macintoshes were very difficult to program; there was not even a decent programmer's handbook. The lack of software prompted Apple to set up its "evangelism" program in which enthusiastic and technically knowledgeable employees were given the job of persuading software vendors to produce applications to help sell its new machines.

Hundreds of Macintosh applications soon followed. Jobs also found his killer application in the shape of Aldus PageMaker, which helped the Macintosh to pioneer and dominate what is still its most significant market: desktop publishing. All this paid off when the much more powerful Macintosh Plus, with its 1 million-byte memory, was launched in January 1996. By the end of 1987, annual sales had climbed to U.S.$2.7 billion.

Despite this, the Macintosh failed to take over from the IBM PC and its compatibles as the industry-standard desktop computer; Microsoft's DOS (and later Windows software) was already securing a position of dominance. As early as 1985, **Bill Gates** (1955–) had proposed to Apple that they license the Macintosh technology to other manufacturers, whom he argued would boost Apple's market overall by producing **clone** machines. But following the departure of Steve Jobs earlier in 1985, Apple's chief technologist, Jean-Louis Gassée (1955–), insisted that market share was irrelevant and that the Macintosh should be sold as a high-end product. He resisted the plan to license the Macintosh because he believed that cheap Macintosh clones would undermine Apple's own enormously profitable Macintosh business instead of undermining the competition. Apple continued to wrestle with the idea of licensing until 1995, when it finally granted licenses to Power Computing, Motorola, IBM, and other manufacturers. But the plan was controversial, and one of the first things Steve Jobs did when he returned to Apple in the late 1990s was to cancel all clone manufacturing.

There was only one reason why the Macintosh had not become the desktop standard: Microsoft Windows. While the Apple Lisa and Macintosh were still under development, Microsoft was already trying to add a graphical user interface (originally called Interface Manager) on top of DOS. Later, after seeing a demonstration of the prototype Macintosh, Gates offered to develop software for the new machine but also incorporated a similar "look and feel" into his new Windows software. Following a dispute between Apple CEO John Sculley (1939–) and Bill Gates in 1985 over whether Microsoft had stolen ideas from the Macintosh, Apple granted Gates a license to use elements of the Macintosh's user interface in return for Microsoft continuing to develop software for the Macintosh. But increasingly sophisticated versions of Windows seemed to Apple to be too similar to its own products, and Apple launched a disastrous U.S.$5.5 billion copyright lawsuit in 1988. Four years later, the case finally collapsed, confirming that Microsoft could use the Macintosh look and feel, at no cost, in all "present and future" versions of Windows.

Despite its turbulent business history, Apple has continued to refine the Macintosh throughout the 1980s and 1990s, often confusing customers with a plethora of different models. These included the low-cost Performa, the PowerBook **laptop**, and the Power Mac based on a fast microprocessor using a technology known as **RISC** (reduced instruction set computing, a technique for speeding up microprocessors by restricting them to just a few simple programming instructions). More recent additions have included the Power Mac G3, based on Motorola's PowerPC G3 processor chip, and the consumer-friendly iMac, designed mainly for use as an Internet machine. Significantly, just under half the iMac's buyers are entirely new to the Macintosh; they are customers who would otherwise have bought Windows-based PCs.

Even with the near dominance of *Wintel* (Windows–Intel) PCs at the end of the 1990s, the Apple Macintosh retains a small but significant (less than 10 percent) share of the personal computer market. But the overall significance of the Macintosh, the world's first affordable computer designed with a graphical user interface, is much more important than this would suggest. Whatever the outcome of the legal disputes between Microsoft and Apple, the Macintosh has undoubtedly had a significant influence on the development of Microsoft Windows; indeed, former Apple employees believe that the Macintosh really "lives on" through Windows. The Macintosh remained the only real alternative to IBM-compatible PCs throughout the 1980s and 1990s and by constantly setting better performance standards than Wintel PCs, helped to drive forward the performance of all PCs. Whatever the future holds for the Macintosh, this influential past ensures that it will always occupy an important place in the history of personal computing.

FURTHER READING

Carlton, Jim. *Apple: The Inside Story of Intrigue, Egomania, and Business Blunders*. New York: Harper Business, 1998.

Cringely, Robert X. *Accidental Empires: How the Boys of Silicon Valley Make Their Millions, Battle Foreign Competition, and Still Can't Get a Date*. Reading, Mass; Menlo Park, Calif; Don Mills, Ontario; Harlow, England; Amsterdam; Bonn; Sydney; Tokyo; Madrid; San Juan; Paris; Seoul; Milan; Mexico City: Addison-Wesley, 1992.

Levy, Stephen. *Insanely Great: The Life and Times of Macintosh, the Computer That Changed Everything*. New York: Penguin, 1995.

Linzmayer, Owen W. *The Mac Bathroom Reader*. Alameda, Calif.: SYBEX, 1994.

—*Chris Woodford*

Magnetic Drum

Magnetic drums are used to store digital information for computers. The **bits** are recorded on the surface of the rotating drum, which is coated with a magnetic material. The magnetic drum was the precursor of the **hard disk**.

Valdemar Poulsen (1869–1942) invented the first magnetic drum in 1898 as a voice recording device. It was a hollow brass cylinder wound with wire, mounted vertically inside a bell jar; as the drum rotated, the "speaking magnet" head followed the spiral wire, moving parallel to the drum from top to bottom. The advantage of the drum was that it did not twist like wire or stretch like tape. However, the magnetic signal was so weak that Poulsen's invention failed to win acceptance.

In 1937, Poulsen's drum was considered by **John Atanasoff** (1903–95) as a possible memory device for his electronic computer. However, he could not afford the **vacuum tubes** necessary to amplify the magnetic pulses, and decided to use nonmagnetic capacitors on the drum. During World War II, magnetic recording was improved by the Germans and by Semi Begun (1905–95) at the Brush Development Company. These developments were studied by Engineering Research Associates (ERA) after the war as part of the U. S. Navy's Project Goldberg, to develop a computer that could solve cryptographic problems. In 1947, William C. Morris led a group of engineers at ERA in Minneapolis that built the first magnetic drum out of recording tape from a captured German Magnetophone recorder and heads from a Brush wire recorder. The strips of tape would not stick to the aluminum drum, so they spray-painted directly onto the surface of the drum an iron oxide emulsion obtained from 3M in Minneapolis. John Coombs reported their success at the Chicago National Electronics Conference in November 1947. The drum was 5 inches in diameter and revolved at 3000 revolutions per minute, recording at a density of 230 bits per inch with a rigid head mounted only 0.001 inch from the surface of the drum.

Howard Aiken (1900–73) was also experimenting with a magnetic drum for the Mark II computer in 1947, and he would make the drum the key feature of his improved Mark III computer in 1948. Harry Huskey (1916–) would use a magnetic drum in his design of the Standards Eastern Automatic Computer for the National Bureau of Standards in 1948. Arnold D. Booth (1918–) in Britain built a magnetic drum for the Automatic Relay Computer in 1948 and would install a drum in the **Manchester "Baby"** computer in 1949. ERA would build the **Atlas** computer in 1948 with a magnetic drum 8.5 inches in diameter with 200 read/write heads and a capacity of 16,384 words of 24-bit length. ERA would patent its drum design in 1948, including the *sprocket track*, a control track to map the addresses of data in the storage tracks. The access speed and large capacity of magnetic drums exceeded all other forms of computer memory in use during the decade after World War II, such as the **cathode ray tube** and the mercury delay line. It would remain the preferred computer memory until the faster, magnetic **core memory** devices became available in the late 1950s.

ERA produced a survey of the computer technology that was published in 1950 as *High-Speed Computing Devices*. It described the magnetic drum as an improved transfer medium over punched cards and mercury delay lines. A drum 10 inches long and 34 inches in diameter could store 16,384 numbers or words of 30 bits each, with 74 magnetic read/write heads for 74 tracks, and a cycle time of 64 milliseconds. The magnetic recording could be permanent (or *nonvolatile*) and immune to power failures, or it could be continually rerecorded with new data. The cycle time was faster than that of other forms of memory, and drums were durable as long as the heads did not touch the drum surface. The survey did not mention magnetic core memories, being developed at Harvard as part of the **Whirlwind** project, or the hard disk and magnetic tape drives that **IBM** would soon develop.

IBM decided in May 1948 to improve the Model 604 with magnetic drum storage, using engineers from the **Selective Sequence Electronic Calculator** project, led by Frank Hamilton, at the North Street Lab in Endicott, New York. The Endicott Lab had been working on magnetic recording since the late 1930s. James W. Bryce (1880–1949) filed a patent application in 1938 (granted in 1943) for recording on magnetic cards. Hamilton in 1943 built an attachment for the 405 Accounting Machine to read and write binary data on the magnetically coated edge of a ledger sheet. In January 1947 Hamilton had attended a symposium at Harvard on recording techniques, including a presentation by a representative of the Brush Development Company.

At the November 1947 National Electronics Conference, Hamilton heard a report on magnetic drum development at ERA. In March 1948, Arnold Cohen of ERA presented a paper on magnetic drums at the New York meeting of the Institute of Radio Engineers. By the summer of 1948, Hamilton believed that his team at Endicott could build a drum to hold 1000 words of 10-digit length and make possible dynamic instruction modification as had been described by **John Mauchly** (1907–80) at the Harvard symposium in January 1947. With sufficient internal storage space, instructions could be stored as well as data, and the computer could execute an unlimited number of instructions by reading and writing instructions at different locations recorded by a special three-digit instruction location number.

By 19 April 1949, the specifications for the Magnetic Storage Calculator were completed, including drum storage for 2000 ten-digit words. For the first time in IBM history, the machine was not driven by punched cards. Instead, instructions were added to the magnetic drum to make the machine read and punch cards. The Type 650 Magnetic Drum Calculator would finally be manufactured in July 1953. However, IBM quickly decided to add magnetic drum storage to the existing Model 604 punched card computer. By June, Hamilton's engineers had made an inexpensive magnetic drum by winding a copper-nickel-iron alloy wire around a drum and using a lathe to cut away half of the wire, leaving a smooth surface. However, the drum proved to be incompatible with the fixed stored-programming design of the Model 604. By November 1949, IBM asked ERA for help in designing a workable drum, but ERA proposed a parallel bit storage method versus IBM's serial method, and the cost was too high to adapt to the Model 604.

The 650 MDC would become one of IBM's most popular computers. Three hundred machines were installed by 1956, far more than the new Model 701 mainframe introduced in 1952, and the 650 continued to be manufactured until 1962. IBM developed the computers for the **SAGE** air defense system after 1956 that used magnetic **core memory** and magnetic drum storage. SAGE had a great effect on pushing IBM ahead of Remington Rand and making it a world leader in computer research. Remington Rand's UNIVAC computer stayed with magnetic drum memory throughout the 1950s, even when it became clear that disk drives would be the storage medium of the future.

FURTHER READING

Bashe, Charles J. *IBM's Early Computers.* Cambridge, Mass.: MIT Press, 1986.

Burks, Alice R. *The First Electronic Computer: The Atanasoff Story.* Ann Arbor, Mich.: University of Michigan Press, 1988.

Engineering Research Associates. *High-Speed Computing Devices.* Los Angeles: Tomash Publishers, 1983.

Gray, George. "Engineering Research Associates and the Atlas Computer (UNIVAC 1101)." *Unisys History Newsletter,* Vol. 3, No. 3, June 1999.

Lee, John A. N. "Howard Aiken's Third Machine: The Harvard Mark III Calculator or Aiken-Dahlgren Electronic Calculator." *IEEE Annals of the History of Computing,* Jan.-Mar. 2000, pp. 62–81.

Williams, Michael R. *A History of Computing Technology.* Englewood Cliffs, N.J.: Prentice Hall, 1985; Los Alamitos, Calif.: IEEE Computer Society Press, 1997.

—*Steven Schoenherr*

Mainframes

The traditional classification of computers according to computational power and cost divides the computer world into **microcomputers**, **minicomputers**, mainframes, and **supercomputers**. Microcomputers used to fit on a desktop; minicomputers, one or two large cabinets; a mainframe, a room; and a supercomputer, a very large room. With the miniaturization of electronic components, these clear-cut boundaries have gradually disappeared. From the perspective of performance, the borderlines have also become blurred: The **Pentium** III processor, for example, delivers more computational power than a small **IBM** business minicomputer. Furthermore, supercomputers are built now

Design model for the IBM System/370, which dominated the mainframe industry in the 1970s. (Courtesy of IBM)

using off-the-shelf microprocessors. However, the term *mainframe* has not disappeared and applies to large computers used by corporate users in their data processing centers. Historically, the paradigmatic mainframe is the IBM 360/370 family.

Almost all early computers were rather large, in terms of both size and cost. They were mainframes in the best sense of the word. The first commercial computer in the United States, the **UNIVAC** I, was built by **John Mauchly** (1907–80) and **J. Presper Eckert** (1919–95) while working for Remington-Rand. It was first delivered in June 1951 and sold for U.S.$250,000. Forty-eight machines were built. IBM entered the computer market in 1953 with its first electronic computer, the 701, of which 18 machines were sold.

In the early 1960s, IBM was already the main computer company, having introduced several successful machines. However, they were all incompatible and consisted of two families: business computers, with built-in decimal arithmetic, and scientific computers, geared toward floating-point computations. A decision was made to concentrate IBM's efforts not on isolated machines, but on a family of computers that would be upward compatible. Programs for the smaller machines could be executed unchanged in the largest machines in the family. Such a family of computers possess the same instruction set, which is cast in stone for the life of the computer family. The new system was called IBM 360 because it would cover all applications ("360 degrees") with a single instruction architecture. The standardization of IBM computers in a single family was a bold move at the time, but the ensuing years would confirm that customers preferred compatibility to any other feature. IBM started down the long path of step-by-step evolution that still characterizes the company's policy.

In 1965, IBM was so dominant that the other mainframe companies were collectively called the "seven dwarfs." Their respective market shares at the time were: IBM, 65.3 percent; Sperry Rand (formerly Remington Rand), 12.1 percent; **Control Data Corporation**, 5.4 percent; **Honeywell** (formerly a division of Raytheon), 3.8 percent; **Burroughs**, 3.5 percent; General Electric, 3.4 percent; RCA (Radio Corporation of America), 2.9 percent; NCR (National Cash Register), 2.9 percent; and the oft-forgotten eighth dwarf, Philco, 0.7 percent. The last four eventually abandoned the computer business. The other four dwarfs survive in different forms, after various mergers and acquisitions.

Having frozen the instruction set for the IBM 360 family, IBM's computers were no longer a moving target for the competition; other firms could try to contend in IBM's own strongholds. **Gene Amdahl** (1922–), a former engineer at IBM and co-designer of the 360 family, introduced the first IBM clones in 1975, after founding the company that bears his name in 1970. Amdahl's firm, more flexible and entrepreneur driven, was even able to beat IBM in both price and performance. Although Amdahl could never take a large portion of the market away from IBM, the company was independent until 1997, when it was bought by **Fujitsu**.

Until the late 1960s, mainframes were computers confined to the data processing centers of large companies. Even programmers had little contact with the hardware proper: Their programs were punched on cardboard cards and a computer operator fed them to the computer. The programmer could pick up his results several hours later, only to discover that the program had been aborted due to a slight programming error. Therefore, from the point of view of the computer user, the next significant advance after the invention of compatibility was the introduction of **time-sharing**.

Time-shared systems allow programmers to sit in front of terminals and type commands into the computer. A time-shared operating system allocates portions of computation time to each user, giving each of them the illusion of having his or her own computer. The first time-sharing operating system was **Multics**, developed at the Massachusetts Institute of Technology in the mid-1960s.

The first successful commercial mainframe built around a time-sharing operating system was the legendary PDP-10 delivered by **Digital Equipment Corporation** (DEC) in 1967. The PDP-10 was a computer with 36-bit word length. IBM's own 360 family had a word length of 32 bits, which would become standard in the years to come, but DEC's PDP-10 was more flexible and was installed at many universities and research institutions. The PDP-10 operating system, TOPS-10, influenced **Gary Kildall** (1942–94), the creator of the **CP/M** operating system in the 1970s. CP/M, in turn, influenced Tim Paterson (1956–), the creator of MS-DOS. Some MS-DOS commands resemble TOPS-10 commands, so that the legacy of the PDP-10 mainframe is still alive in millions of microcomputers all over the world.

Today's microcomputers make use of many technological advances introduced in mainframes. Such is the case with the floppy disk, invented to store the microcode of IBM's mainframes. When the IBM 370 system (successor to the 360 family, with a compatible instruction level) was introduced, IBM engineers decided that the computer would load its microcode at startup. The microcode reconfigures the microoperations inside the machine so that an instruction behaves in any desired way. The standard microcode could be loaded, making the 370 just a faster 360, or alternatively, the user's microcode could be installed. The user could then redefine the entire instruction set to fit his needs. This microcode was stored in a small interchangeable floppy that was loaded in the floppy drive.

The market for mainframes has undergone all phases of the product cycle by now: childhood (the 1950s), adolescence (1960s), and maturity (1970s and 1980s). The market peaked in the 1970s, but soon afterward, minicomputers and microcomputers were cannibalizing mainframes. IBM was the undisputed leader in the mainframe arena but reacted too slowly to the emergence of new business opportunities. The minicomputer was invented by Digital Equipment, not IBM. Subsequently, IBM and DEC both missed the microcomputer market, which was started by new companies such as **Apple Computer**.

A serious challenge for mainframes came from the widespread introduction of computer networks in the 1990s. In a network, each user has a computer but keeps the illusion of an integrated system. Special dedicated servers stored the data that can be accessed by many users. In most cases, networks of microcomputers are more cost-effective than mainframes.

Although its demise has been forecasted relentlessly, the mainframe has not disappeared, because although networks of microcomputers are more cost-effective, data integrity and software upgrades remain a significant problem. With so many computers in a network it is difficult to back up data and to install new software releases. In a mainframe, on the contrary, everything is stored in the same system and upgrades are a one-off action. Data are kept at a central location and can be backed up regularly.

The desire for both the flexibility of computer networks and the security and convenience of mainframes is the driving force behind the idea of **network computers**. Network computers, also called *thin clients*, are "dumb" terminals that are connected to a centralized location where data and programs are stored. The market for mainframes is still dominated by IBM and its IBM 3090 machines. In the late 1990s, IBM had yearly revenues of more than U.S.$6 billion in this market segment.

FURTHER READING

Amdahl, G., A. Blaaw, and F. Brook. "Architecture of the IBM System 360." *IBM Journal of Research and Development*, Vol. 8, No. 2, 1964.

Bell, Gordon. "The Mini and Microindustries." *IEEE Computer*, Vol. 17, No. 10, 1984.

Goldstine, Herman H. *The Computer from Pascal to von Neumann*. Princeton, N.J.: Princeton University Press, 1972.

Pugh, Emerson, Lyle Johnson, and John Palmer. *IBM's 360 and Early 370 Systems*. Cambridge, Mass.: MIT Press, 1991.

—*Frank Darius*

MAN See Metropolitan Area Networks.

Management Information System

A management information system (MIS) is an integrated human–machine system that provides information to support operations, management, analysis, and decision-making functions within an organization. The system utilizes computer **hardware** and **software**; manual procedures; models for analysis, planning, control, and decision making; and a database. Although this is a general theoretical definition of a MIS, in practice it is more often a federation of loosely integrated systems used to supply, manipulate, and process one of an organization's most important resources: information. A properly implemented MIS becomes an extension to organizational functions such as managerial accounting, operations research, finance, purchasing, and so on.

An MIS is physically composed of software, hardware, database, procedures, and personnel. Some users see an MIS as a collection of **mainframes**, **personal computers** (PCs), and **minicomputers**, sometimes linked through **local** or **wide area networks** (LANs or WANs). The machinery uses software—custom written or purchased—to process transactions, store information, provide ad hoc query support, and build reports. The database is viewed as a software package loaded with specific instances of corporate data and information. Procedures and written policies govern the use of the software, equipment, and information.

Another practical view of MIS involves its place in a business. A pyramid can be used to represent various functions that map to the organizational level. The bottom level of an MIS consists of transaction processing. Operational planning, decision-making, and control functions form the next level. The third level provides information resources to aid in tactical planning and decision making. The top level represents MIS support for strategic planning and decision making. This view can be extended throughout an organization. Each of these subsystems is designed to fulfill a business need. A subsystem might not be entirely independent (one program or database may be used by several subsystems). This structure of an MIS can be divided into four major information processing groups: transaction processing, operational control, managerial control, and strategic planning. Each of these areas has unique information and shared information. In addition, shared software and databases may also exist. Within the three management function areas (excluding transaction processing), applications can be classified according to the type of support they provide. The support can be broken into three areas: monitoring information, action information, and decision support information.

MIS is a broad field that developed along many fronts simultaneously. In general terms, MIS started with the automation of transaction processing systems. One of the first business-specific, computerized transaction processing systems was offered by IBM in 1957. This machine, the 305 random access method of accounting and control (**RAMAC**), which had the first computer disk storage system, became a standard storage medium. In the years that followed, organizational computing was dominated by large mainframe computers such as **IBM**'s System/360, the first large family of computers to use interchangeable software and peripheral equipment. Although a variety of hardware platforms were available, much of the transaction processing software was developed using **COBOL**. Additional layers of software were developed on top of the transaction processing systems to enable management to receive summary reports of business activity. Throughout the following decade, organizational MISs continued to advance in terms of computing power, database technology, and decision support capability. Business forecasts, planning, and strategic uses of information were developed. Eventually, the concepts of **data warehousing** and **data mining** emerged as more sophisticated uses of organizational information were required.

Recent pressures on traditional MISs—brought about by year 2000 concerns and the growth of the **Internet**—have resulted in a variety of new software and hardware products specifically aimed at replacing older COBOL-based systems with newer client–server and **electronic commerce** systems. The most successful of these products, holding a 32 percent market share, is SAP's R3, which revisited the current computing environment and developed software to help companies of all sizes link their disparate business processes. All the traditional functions of MIS were tied together under a common system. In addition, the software was developed to work on a multilingual/multinational level, ideal for the new Internet-worked environment of the late 1990s. Applications in the area of accounting, production, human resources, marketing, and finance have been streamlined and reengineered to take advantage of new technology and innovation.

Other organizations, such as **Oracle**, have focused on linking transaction processing systems over the Internet through distributed databases and other mechanisms to create seamless e-commerce systems. Traditional business systems are becoming linked networks of distributed databases and applications that work together. This innovation has allowed Oracle to challenge IBM's dominance in the database marketplace.

FURTHER READING

Gorry, G., and M. Scott Morton. "A Framework for Management Information Systems." *Sloan Management Review*, 1989, pp. 49–61.

Stair, Ralph, and George Reynolds. *Principles of Information Systems*, Boston: Boyd and Fraser, 1992; 4th ed., Course Technology, Cambridge, Mass.: 1999.

—*Roger McHaney*

Manchester Mark I and the Baby

In the years 1947-50 a small team at the University of Manchester was responsible for a series of key pioneering steps in the birth of the electronic computer. By the autumn of 1947 they had built an electronic memory that could hold up to 2048 bits. To test this they built the Small Scale Experimental Machine, nicknamed the Baby, which first worked on 21 June 1948. This was the first working stored-program computer. By October 1948 they had designed a full-sized computer, the Manchester Mark I, with a two-level store. By April 1949 they had completed everything but the peripheral equipment, and the machine was made available to outside personnel for research, and so became the first available full-sized computer. In June 1949 a successful nine-hour run was recorded, doing mathematical research. By about October 1949 the full machine was complete, the first machine with a fast random access two-level store (in modern parlance, with both random access memory [**RAM**] and a **hard disk**). This machine was used as the prototype for the **Ferranti Mark I**, the first production electronic computer, first delivered in February 1951.

The team was led by Freddie C. Williams (1911–77) of the Department of Electrical Engineering, appointed in December 1946 from the Telecommunications Research Establishment. At first there were just two engineers working full time, both seconded from TRE and able to draw equipment from TRE. There was no other funding for the Baby project. The senior engineer, Tom Kilburn (1921–2001), was responsible for most of the detailed design of the series of machines. Max H. A. Newman (1897–1984) of the Department of Mathematics acted as consultant on programming and mathematical matters. In October 1948 the team was

Manchester Mark I, 1949. (Courtesy of the Computer Museum History Center)

expanded with three research students, and Newman recruited **Alan M. Turing** (1912–54) to lead the software development part-time.

The Williams-Kilburn memory, for the main store of the Baby, used a standard radar **cathode-ray tube** (CRT). Charge was placed on the phosphor dielectric inside the face of the tube by a scanning electronic beam, in a 32 by 32 array. Charge was placed at each position by firing either a short burst of electrons, a dot representing a 0, or a slightly longer burst, a dash, for a 1. A wire mesh was placed against the outside of the face, and the difference between a dot or a dash at any given position could be detected by the changes in potential on the mesh at the instant a new burst was fired at the position. The charge would decay over time, so the charge at each position would need to be refreshed at regular intervals. The key to this was that it was possible to detect a position's value in time to fire the longer burst for a dash if needed. The standard procedure was to refresh one row (i.e., a word) at a time in a regular cycle, interleaved with the store accesses for instructions and numbers.

The Baby used two other CRT memory tubes, one for a 32-bit accumulator A, and one to hold both the address of the current instruction C and the instruction itself. An ordinary CRT was placed on the console, which could be switched to display the current contents of any of the storage tubes. This was the only form of output, with input achieved using hand switches to identify a particular word in store and 32 buttons to set its value in binary. The order code was minimal, seven instructions, sufficient to allow a variety of long-running short programs to test the store fully. There were two instructions to copy between the accumulator and a word in store, one to subtract the contents of a store word from the accumulator, two unconditional jump instructions, a conditional jump on the sign of the accumulator, and an instruction to stop the program. The only redundant instruction was the second unconditional jump. Subtraction was chosen as the arithmetic operation rather than addition, as addition can be achieved using subtraction (e.g., $x + y = x - [0 - y]$), but not vice versa. Addition was added to the Baby within a couple of months. Each instruction was obeyed in around 1.2 milliseconds, four times the random access time for a main store word.

The reliability of the Baby was impressive, and the design permitted up to 256 main store CRTs. Within a few months they could have extended the Baby to, say, 512 words of main store, to allow substantial programs to be run, using a subroutine for multiplication. However, separate projects were already well in hand to build a multiplier and experiment with a random access secondary store; so, since the Baby had so clearly demonstrated the power and potential of the von Neumann computer model, Williams decided to go straight for a full-sized machine. By October the main design was completed, and the government had contracted Ferranti Ltd. to manufacture a line of computers based on it.

The Manchester Mark I was built as a physical extension of the Baby, using much of its circuitry. The main store was increased to 128 words of 40 bits each, with an 80-bit accumulator, but instructions were condensed to 20 bits, allowing two instructions per word. The four control instructions were retained. But there were now 20 arithmetic instructions, including multiplication. An operand could be treated in four ways: signed or unsigned, integer or fraction of 1. Multilength arithmetic was supported. Input and output were by reading and punching five-hole paper tape as used with teleprinters.

Further instructions provided two major advances over the von Neumann model: instruction modification and a two-level store. Two special registers were provided, which could be loaded from the store, and the contents of one or the other added to the current instruction code. The random access secondary store, the drum (nowadays, a disk), was a rotating cylinder coated with magnetic material. Given a unit of store as a page of thirty-two 40-bit words, the drum held a set of parallel circular tracks each holding two pages (i.e., 2560 bits). Transfers could be programmed to or from any page in main store from or to any page on drum. The capacity was around 3000 words, and on average it took around 16 instruction times to read a 32-word page from drum.

In the summer of 1949 the main effort was switched to completing an enhanced design for the Ferranti Mark I. Storage was increased; the arithmetic instructions were enhanced a bit; the control instructions and instruction modification machinery were enhanced a lot. The Manchester Mark I was dismantled in the summer of 1950 to make way for the first Ferranti Mark I. This provided a successful computing service for the university and a number of other organizations for seven years.

The Manchester team did not invent the stored-program electronic computer. The principles were already established in the United Kingdom and the United States. Existing projects were struggling to get an effective electronic store working, with the mechanism closest to working being the awkward mercury acoustic delay line store, which was not random access. The team did invent the first working electronic store and as a result realized the first working stored-program electronic computer. Along with delay line store, their CRT store was the mainstay of computers worldwide until core store became generally available in the mid-1950s. The team did not refer to existing computer designs, as the store being used greatly affected the detailed design. They quickly made two major advances on the von Neumann model, inventing instruction modification and providing a random access two-level store. Instruction modification meant that it was no longer necessary to program alterations to instructions in store. Without it, every instruction that contained an address not known before the run started would have to be altered before it was obeyed.

In the Ferranti Mark I the idea was refined by providing eight modification registers and permitting simple arithmetic and testing on them, thus providing the first index registers for handling loop control and array access. The team's other main achievement was the engineering skill displayed in building the machines so quickly and (relatively) reliably, with a wealth of detailed innovation.

The software operation was less successful. Programs were written using an ingenious but primitive mechanism devised by Turing, and the two-level store also made life more complicated for the programmer. In contrast, the University of Cambridge **EDSAC** computer, first working in May 1949, had a more user friendly system, with innovative software and a larger main store, but no drum.

FURTHER READING

Croarken, Mary. *Early Scientific Computing in Britain.* Oxford: Oxford University Press, 1990.

Kilburn, T. "The University of Manchester Universal High-Speed Digital Computing Machine." *Nature*, Vol. 164, 22 Oct. 1949.

Lavington, S. H. *A History of Manchester Computers.* Manchester, Lancashire, England: NCC Publications, 1975.

Napper, B. "The Manchester Mark I Computers." In R. Rojas and U. Hashagen, eds., *The First Computers: History and Architecture.* Cambridge, Mass.: MIT Press, 2000.

—*Brian Napper*

Mandelbrot, Benoit

1924–

French–U.S. Mathematician

Benoit Mandelbrot showed how a class of mathematical objects, which he named **fractals**, could help us to understand natural and social phenomena, from the shape of clouds to the behavior of the stock market. He is popularly known for the mathematical object that bears his name, the Mandelbrot set, which is also a good example of the application of computers as tools of mathematical investigation. Furthermore, fractals have had considerable application in digital imaging.

Mandelbrot was born in Warsaw in Poland in 1924, immigrated with his family in 1936 to France, where his uncle Szolem Mandelbrojt became professor of mathematics at the Collège de France. Szolem was responsible for much of Benoit's early education, and in 1945 introduced him to Gaston Julia's (1893–1978) paper "Mémoire sur l'itération des fonctions rationnelles" (1918), which contains examples of the strange behavior of iterated functions that Mandelbrot would later rediscover in the Mandelbrot set.

His early life was much disrupted, and he attended the Lycée Rolin in Paris sporadically until the outbreak of World War II and the Ecole Polytechnique from 1944 to 1947, where he worked under Paul Lévy (1886–1971). In the 1950s, Mandelbrot held positions in both France and the United States, before finally joining **IBM**'s research laboratories at Yorktown Heights in 1958, a fertile association that would last more than three decades.

At IBM, Mandelbrot investigated a curious feature found in the noise afflicting electronic data transmission. The noise pattern was self-similar: If one section of noise was examined in detail, a smaller cluster could be found, and so on. This self-similarity in apparent randomness recalled to Mandelbrot similar phenomena he noticed in economics, financial fluctuations, turbulence, and statistical thermodynamics, as well as the pathological mathematical cases of Giuseppe Peano (1858–1932), Richard Dedekind (1831–1916), Helge von Koch (1870–1924), and Gaston Julia (1893–1978). Mandelbrot's achievement was to bring these disparate topics together as fractals, a term he popularized in *Les Objets fractals: forme, hasard et dimension* (1975) and *The Fractal Geometry of Nature* (1982).

The *Mandelbrot set* is the best known fractal, popularized in the "fractalmania" of the late 1980s. Mathematically, it is a set of points on the complex plane. If a complex number is of the form $c = a + bi$, it can correspond to a point (a,b) on a two-dimensional flat surface. Complex numbers can then be represented and visualized. Mandelbrot asked what happened to the iterative sequence: $z_{n+1} = z_n^2 + c$, where c is a complex number. For some starting values of c, with $z_0 = 0$, this sequence diverges away from the origin, while for others it stays nearby. The boundary between the two is extremely complex—a fractal, in fact.

At IBM Mandelbrot had the computational facilities to investigate this equation, but he also had access to expertise in computer graphics. Novel programs were needed to visualize the fractals, first achieved for the Mandelbrot set in 1980. Mandelbrot has continued to publish prolifically on self-similarity and apparent randomness, including the collections *Fractals and Scaling in Finance* (1997) and *Multifractals and 1/f Noise* (1999). Having been discovered through improved computer graphics, fractals have returned the compliment: finding application, for example, in new techniques of data compression and texture definition.

BIOGRAPHY

Benoit B. Mandelbrot. Born 20 November 1924, in Warsaw, Poland. Immigrated to France, 1936. Studied engineering at the Ecole Polytechnique, Paris, France, 1944–47; studied at the California Institute of Technology, 1947–49. Received Ph.D. in mathematics from the University of Paris while working at the electronics firm Philips, 1952. Held a series of academic positions: at the Institute for Advanced Study, Princeton, New Jersey; the Institut Henri Poincaré, Paris, France; the universities of Geneva and Lille; and a return to the Ecole Polytechnique, 1957. Joined IBM, 1958. Has held numerous visiting positions at Harvard, Yale, and MIT, as well as a seven-year stint with the National Bureau for Economic Research.

SELECTED WRITINGS

Mandelbrot, Benoit B. *The Fractal Geometry of Nature.* New York: Freeman, 1982.

———. *Les Objets fractals: forme, hasard et dimension.* Paris: Flammarion, 1975; 3rd ed., 1989.

———. *Fractals and Scaling in Finance: Discontinuity, Concentration, Risk: Selecta Volume E.* New York: Springer-Verlag, 1997.

———. *Multifractals and 1/f Noise: Wild Self-Affinity in Physics (1963–1976): Selecta Volume N.* New York: Springer-Verlag, 1999.

FURTHER READING

Briggs, John. *Fractals: The Patterns of Chaos: A New Aesthetic of Art, Science, and Nature.* New York: Simon and Schuster, 1992.

Peitgen, H.-O., and P. H. Richter, eds. *The Beauty of Fractals: Images of Complex Dynamical Systems.* Berlin and New York: Springer-Verlag, 1986.

—*Jon Agar*

"A Mathematical Theory of Communication"

By Claude Shannon

Information theory is the mathematical study of information transmission and reception. It underlines all modern communications systems, including the telephone network and the **Internet**. Its origins can be traced back to a single paper, "A Mathematical Theory of Communication," written by **AT&T** engineer **Claude Shannon** (1916–2001) and originally published in the *Bell System Technical Journal* in 1948.

Shannon's theory grew out of a desire to remove the hiss of static and interference from phone conversations, which at the time were very noisy. His insight was to treat information as a physical quantity, borrowing many of the ideas and equations in his theory from the field of thermodynamics. He developed a theory that allowed engineers to calculate the maximum capacity and expected error rate of any given communications channel, such as a cable or a wireless link.

Shannon defined the basic quantity of information as the ***bit*** (binary digit). There is an exponential relationship between the number of bits in a message and how much information it contains; for example, a message of two bits can represent four choices, one of three bits can represent eight, and so on. This means that for each bit that is subject to uncertainty, the useful information content of the message is halved.

The most important equation of the paper, *Shannon's theorem*, shows how to calculate the capacity of a channel from its *signal-to-noise ratio* (SNR) and ***bandwidth***. SNR is a measurable physical quantity, and bandwidth is the range of frequencies available. This relationship between capacity and bandwidth is now so well known that many engineers and writers use the term *bandwidth* when they mean *capacity*. Written mathematically, this is expressed as

$$C = W \log_2 (1 + S/N)$$

where C is the capacity in hertz, W the bandwidth in bits per second, and S/N the signal-to-noise ratio.

Individual messages can also have their information content calculated using Shannon's theories, by working out how many bits would be needed to convey the same content. This is the basis of **data compression**, which seeks to fit a message into as few bits as possible. It is also useful in **cryptography**, an area in which Shannon himself worked, where the aim is to reduce the apparent information content of a message.

FURTHER READING

Bray, John. *The Communications Miracle: The Telecommunication Pioneers from Morse to the Information Superhighway*. New York: Plenum Press, 1995.

Pierce, John R. *An Introduction to Information Theory: Symbols, Signals and Noise*. New York: Dover, 1980.

Shannon, Claude E., and Warren Weaver. *A Mathematical Theory of Communication*. Urbana, Ill.: University of Illinois Press, 1998.

—*Andy Dornan*

Mauchly, John

1907–80

U.S. Scientist

John Mauchly and **J. Presper Eckert** (1919–95) were among the designers of the **ENIAC**, the first large-scale electronic computer, and together they founded the company that built the **UNIVAC**, the first computer to be offered for commercial sale in the United States. Mauchly also played a key role in the early development of programming languages.

While working as an instructor at Philadelphia's Ursinus College in the 1930s, Mauchly became interested in weather prediction, but found that the amount of computation involved exceeded the capacity of calculators available at the time. He began to consider ways to increase the speed of calculation and did some experimentation with **flip-flop** circuits. These used bistable **vacuum tubes** as electronic counters, getting their name from the fact that they could switch quickly from the "off" to the "on" state, and vice versa. Mauchly built some counters using neon tubes, which were less expensive than vacuum tubes.

In December 1940, Mauchly met **John Atanasoff** (1903–95), a professor at Iowa State College, who was designing an electronic computer intended to solve systems of simultaneous equations. With the help of

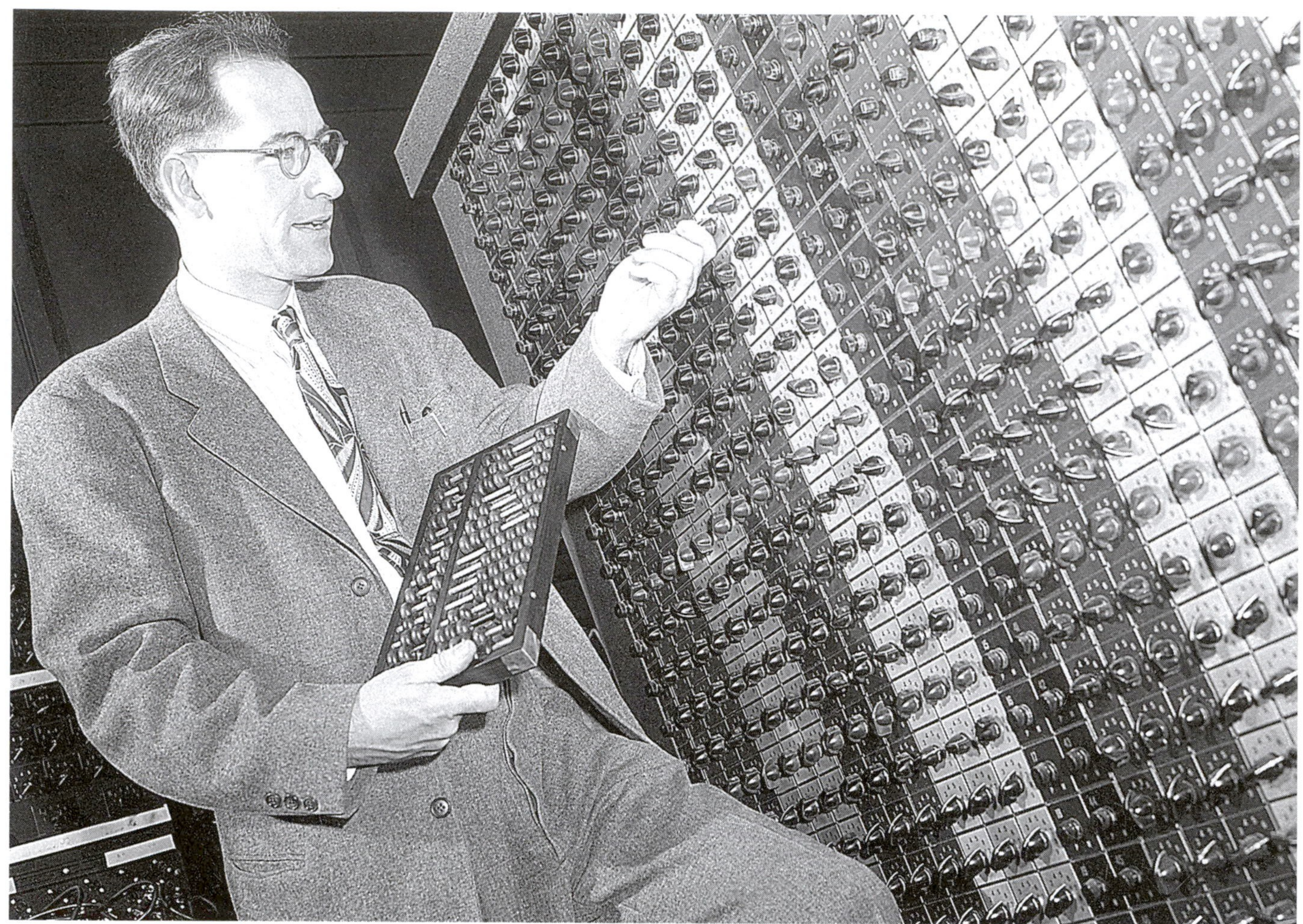

John Mauchly in front of the control panel of the ENIAC computer, 2 February 1946. (Bettmann/CORBIS)

Clifford Berry (1918–63), a graduate student, Atanasoff started to build the machine in 1941. Mauchly visited Atanasoff in June of that year and saw Atanasoff's computer under development. This visit would be at the heart of a later patent dispute concerning the true inventor of the first automatic **digital computer**.

During the summer of 1941, Mauchly enrolled in a 10-week course on electrical engineering for defense industries offered by the **Moore School of Electrical Engineering** at the University of Pennsylvania. He then became an adjunct instructor at the Moore School. After discussions with J. Presper Eckert, another staff member, Mauchly wrote a memo proposing the construction of an electronic computer that could be used to compute ballistic trajectories. U.S. Army Ordnance accepted the proposal, and the project to build the Electronic Numerical Integrator and Computer (ENIAC) began in July 1943. John Brainerd (1904–88) was the project supervisor, with Eckert as chief engineer and Mauchly as principal consultant.

After the ENIAC's completion, Mauchly and Eckert resigned from the Moore School in March 1946 because of a dispute over patent rights, but stayed in Philadelphia to form a partnership named the Electronic Control Company, later incorporated as the Eckert-Mauchly Computer Corporation. Their goal was to produce computers for both scientific and business use. This was a bold—some said foolhardy—move, since hardly anyone besides Eckert and Mauchly believed that there would be a large demand for computers. Always desperate for money, the company was able to build the Binary Automatic Computer (BINAC) in 1949 for Northrop Aircraft Corporation and to work on the Universal Automatic Computer (UNIVAC) for the U.S. government. Unable to attract enough investment capital, Eckert and

Mauchly sold their company to Remington Rand in February 1950. The UNIVAC was completed in March 1951 and turned over to the U.S. Census Bureau.

While work was under way on the BINAC, Mauchly had conceived the idea of a program language for expressing algebraic equations, which he called Brief Code. The interpreter for Brief Code was written by William Schmitt under Mauchly's supervision during the summer of 1949, but there was no time to try it out before the BINAC was shipped to Northrop. Mauchly kept the idea alive, although the name was changed to Short Code, and Schmitt rewrote it for the UNIVAC in 1950. Short Code used two-character codes to designate operations and variables. It had about 30 operations, including floating-point arithmetic, logarithms, integral roots and powers, parentheses for grouping expressions, and input/output. Although it was very primitive, Short Code was essentially a high-level language, since its statements related to the problem to be solved, and there was no direct correspondence between the statements and the machine code of the UNIVAC.

Mauchly stayed with Remington Rand and Sperry Rand until 1959, when he resigned, frustrated by the feebleness of its marketing program for the UNIVAC. He formed his own consulting firm, Mauchly Associates, and worked primarily in the areas of project planning and management.

The attempt by Sperry Rand to enforce the ENIAC patent led to a lawsuit from Honeywell. After a trial, the judge ruled that the ENIAC patent was invalid, because it had been filed too late, and went on to state that Atanasoff was the true inventor of the computer. This started a controversy that has continued ever since. Partisans of Eckert and Mauchly point out that Atanasoff's computer was never really completed and that the ENIAC was much faster and more capable than Atanasoff's computer.

BIOGRAPHY

John William Mauchly. Born 30 August 1907 in Cincinnati, Ohio. Attended McKinley Technical High School in Washington, D.C. and Johns Hopkins University, 1925; Ph.D. in physics, 1932. Instructor at Ursinus College and University of Pennsylvania in the 1930s. Consultant on ENIAC project, 1943–46. Cofounder of Eckert-Mauchly Computer Corporation, 1946; consultant on UNIVAC computer. Founded his own company, Mauchly Associates, 1959. Received various awards, including NAM Modern Pioneer Award, 1965; AFIPS Harry Goode Memorial Award for Excellence, 1968; and IEEE Computer Society Pioneer Award, 1980. Died 9 January 1980 in Ambler, Pennsylvania.

SELECTED WRITINGS

Eckert, J. Presper, Jr., John W. Mauchley, Herman H. Goldstine, and J. C. Brainerd. *Description of the ENIAC and Comments on Electronic Digital Computing Machinery. Contract W/670/ORD 4926.* Philadelphia: Moore School of Electrical Engineering, University of Pennsylvania, Nov. 30, 1945.

Mauchly, John W. "The ENIAC." In N. Metropolis, J. Howlett, and Gian-Carlo Rota, eds., *A History of Computing in the Twentieth Century.* New York: Academic Press, 1980, pp. 541–550.

———. "Preparation of Problems for EDVAC-Type Machines." Reprinted in Brian Randell, ed., *Origins of Digital Computers: Selected Papers.* Berlin: Springer-Verlag, 1982, pp. 393–398.

———. "The Use of High Speed Vacuum Tube Devices for Calculating." Reprinted in Brian Randell, ed., *Origins of Digital Computers: Selected Papers.* Berlin: Springer-Verlag, 1982, pp. 355–358.

FURTHER READING

Berkeley, Edmund C. *Giant Brains or Machines That Think.* New York: Wiley, 1949.

Costello, John. "As the Twig is Bent: The Early Life of John Mauchly." *Annals of the History of Computing,* Vol.18, Spring 1996, pp. 45–50.

Schmitt, William F. "The UNIVAC Short Code." *Annals of the History of Computing,* Vol. 10, 1986, pp. 7–18.

Shurkin, Joel. *Engines of the Mind.* New York: Norton, 1984, 1996.

Stern, Nancy. "The BINAC: A Case Study in the History of Technology." *Annals of the History of Computing,* Vol. 1, July 1979, pp. 9–20.

———. *From ENIAC to UNIVAC.* Bedford, Mass.: Digital Press, 1981.

Tropp, Henry S. "Mauchly: Unpublished Remarks." *Annals of the History of Computing,* Vol. 4, No. 3, July 1982, p. 245ff.

—George Gray

MBONE

The MBONE is the *multicast backbone*, a virtual network overlaid on a subset of the physical network of wires and switches that make up the **Internet**. The MBONE was created in 1992 as an experimental network to support multicast extensions to the Internet Protocol (IP) that were not implemented in the production Internet.

The IP multicast service delivers information to multiple destinations more efficiently than is possible with the basic unicast (point-to-point) service. The information source sends only a single copy of each packet of data; then the network replicates those packets only where necessary at branching points along the tree of paths to the multiple destinations. No network link carries more than one copy of the data, resulting in large **bandwidth** savings compared to unicast transmission of separate copies from the source to many destinations. IP multicast was invented by Stephen Deering for his thesis at Stanford in the late 1980s.

Although multicast transmission may be utilized in many different applications, the most significant impact of the MBONE has been in the transmission of audio and video programs simultaneously to hundreds of receivers around the world. These programs included small teleconferences and large symposia as well as U.S. Space Shuttle missions and other newsworthy events. The MBONE may have received its greatest notoriety with the transmission of a Rolling Stones concert in November 1994.

The MBONE grew out of an idea to transmit audio from a meeting of the Internet Engineering Task Force (IETF) at San Diego in March 1992, for the benefit of some participants who could not attend in person. Deering and Stephen Casner operated the audio equipment and coordinated the construction of a temporary network of virtual point-to-point links called *tunnels* to reach participants at 20 sites on three continents. The tunnel endpoints were workstation-class computers with operating system support for IP multicast and running the "mrouted" multicast routing daemon to forward the multicast packets onto local area networks such as **Ethernet** that support multicast directly. Mrouting was developed by Deering and later enhanced by a number of others, in particular Bill Fenner.

At the following IETF meeting in November 1992, the temporary network was again constructed but with more nodes and links. Slow-frame-rate video was transmitted along with the audio. At that meeting arose the idea to make the virtual network a permanent, experimental facility supported as a cooperative, volunteer effort, and it was given the name MBONE. At each of the 23 IETF meetings since then, two channels of audio and video have been transmitted over the MBONE.

The number of nodes in the MBONE grew exponentially to about 1000 in 1994 (see map) and 1400 in 1996. Some Internet service providers participated and provided MBONE connections to their customers, but usually on an unsupported basis because the service was experimental.

For the IP multicast service, the destination **IP address** in each packet is of a special type called a *group address*. Receivers interested in a particular multicast transmission join the group. **Routers** (the switch nodes in the network) exchange information with their neighboring routers using a multicast routing protocol to determine a tree of network paths emanating from the source and branching where necessary to reach all the receivers that have joined the group.

In the MBONE, workstation-class computers served as the IP multicast routers. To pass multicast packets through tunnels across the production Internet routers that didn't implement multicast, each packet was encapsulated with a normal unicast destination address identifying the far end of the tunnel. The tunnel endpoint would remove the encapsulation and then add a new one if needed to forward the packet onto the next tunnel.

The audio, video, and shared whiteboard applications running on the MBONE became known as the "MBONE tools." The most popular ones included the Visual Audio Tool (vat), the vic video tool, and the wb shared whiteboard tool developed by Van Jacobson and Steven McCanne, and an earlier video tool named nv developed by Ron Frederick. These applications were used for both interactive teleconferences among small groups and for workshop and symposium transmissions. A session directory tool named sdr, developed by Mark Handley, displayed a list of sessions or programs that could be received; the information describing those programs was also distributed using multicast.

A significant difference between the MBONE audio and video tools and the more recent paradigm

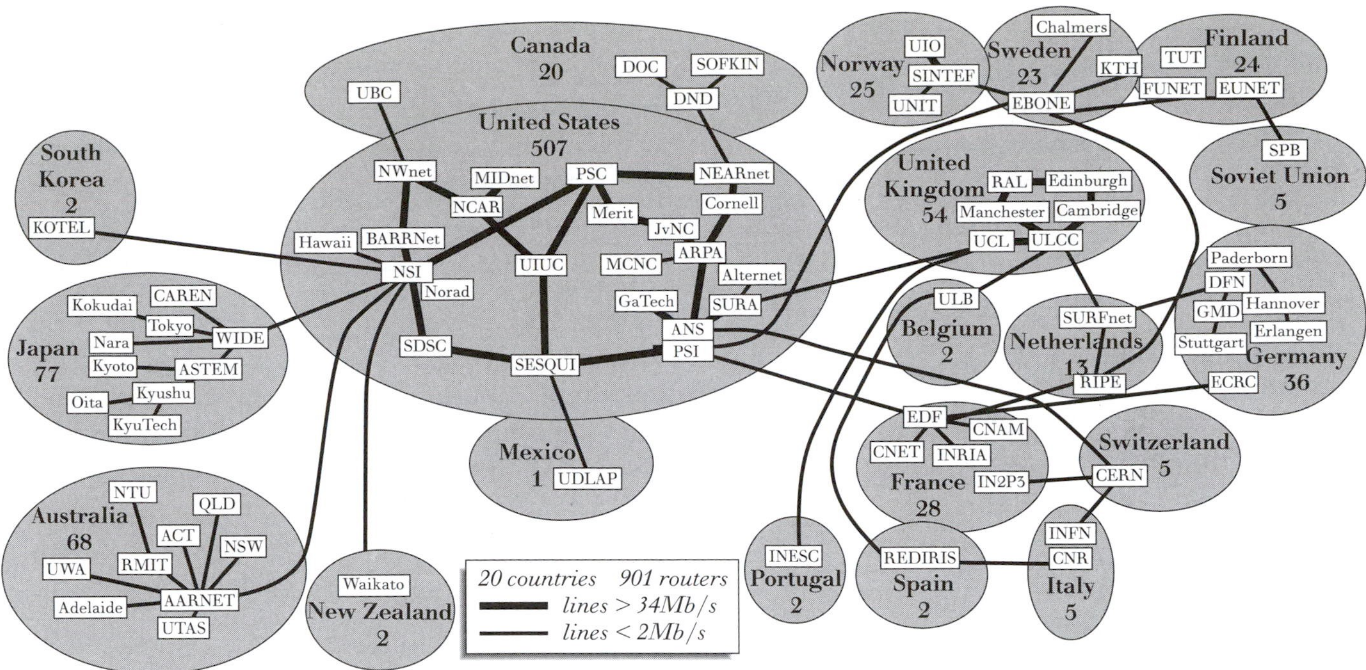

Major MBONE routers and links as of 1994.

of streaming video servers and players is that remote participants in IETF meetings could transmit back to the meeting room as well as the other remote participants. At least one IETF presentation was given by a remote presenter over the MBONE, and there were a few instances where key meeting decisions could not have been made without the remote participation. Such interactivity is provided by production videoconferencing systems, but they typically support only a few participants, compared to the hundreds of participants that the MBONE-based audio and video applications supported.

The MBONE also provided the gathering place for a new community to form. In the early days, many of the participants would leave their workstations always tuned in to a session named "MBONE Audio." That session was used for coordinating the development of the MBONE and for resolving problems. Usually it was quiet, but if you said "Hello" you might get a response from someone in Australia, the United States, or Europe. Later, a session called "Places all around the world" was established. On that session there was no audio, but video cameras operating continuously at a low data rate would show the view out the window at locations all around the world, allowing viewers to watch the progression of sunrises and sunsets. This session foretold the popularity of "Web cams" as the Internet and **World Wide Web** became a global phenomenon.

Networking engineers comprised a significant fraction of the MBONE community, but there were other users as well. In a telemedicine demonstration, an unusual liver operation performed in San Francisco was viewed live by doctors in London and Sweden, who were able to ask questions of the surgeon as the procedure was performed.

The MBONE also supported applications other than audio and video. It has carried multicast distribution of **Usenet** news (text messages) and distributed simulation and visualization. In 1993, MBONE participants running a visualization program were able to monitor in real time the telemetry data transmitted from an undersea vessel operating off the coast of Baja California as part of the Jason Project.

The MBONE and the applications developed to use it demonstrated to the Internet community that IP multicast routing would work and that transmission of audio and video over the Internet was, in fact, quite feasible. This advance was enabled by the conjunction of several enabling technologies: the introduction of built-in audio input–output devices in the endpoint computers, sufficient processing power for compressing audio and video, and increasing bandwidth in the network.

The quality of signals transmitted across the MBONE was often quite good, but sometimes (and in some places) pretty poor. The primary cause of reduced quality was congestion induced by excess traffic on the Internet, which resulted in dropped packets. In those places where MBONE virtual links were carried across high-bandwidth physical links, congestion was not a problem. Bandwidth was not unlimited, of course. As an experimental system, the design bandwidth of the MBONE was 500 kilobits per second. Clearly, this was not enough to support all the possible uses and users.

The separate overlay network of the MBONE was always expected to fade away as "native" IP multicast routing became available in the production routers of the Internet itself. That has happened to some degree, but not as seamlessly as was anticipated. Some of the production implementations of multicast routing use different routing protocols than the Distance Vector Multicast Routing Protocol (DVMRP) that was used in the experimental MBONE. DVMRP was never intended to scale up to support a large, global network. However, interoperation of multiple different routing protocols has proven difficult and somewhat error prone. As a result, a separate infrastructure of interconnected networks supporting native multicast using the Protocol Independent Multicast (PIM) routing protocol has formed. There are connections between the overlay network of the MBONE and the native multicast infrastructure, but the transfer of data and routing information is not sufficiently reliable. As a result, the experimental MBONE will probably come to an end, replaced by native multicast routing.

Because multicast was and is not implemented everywhere in the Internet, commercial products have been developed to enable **streaming audio and video** over the Internet using a separate unicast stream for each receiver, usually at very low bandwidth. In some cases, the inefficiency of sending the same information many times has been accommodated simply by increasing the capacity of the network. In other cases, a form of application-specific multicast distribution has been implemented in which audio–video "splitters" are installed at points around the network to receive a stream and replicate it to multiple destinations.

This approach requires that new application-specific replicators be deployed each time a new application is developed, rather than deploying the general-purpose IP multicast replication service in the network once. Time will tell which method proves more effective.

Further Reading

Casner, Stephen, and Stephen Deering. "First IETF Internet Audiocast." *ACM Sigcomm Computer Communication Review*, July 1992.

Hafner, Katie. "The MBone: Can't You Hear It Knocking?" *Newsweek*, 5 Dec. 1994, p. 86.

Kumar, Vinay. *Mbone: Interactive Multimedia on the Internet.* Indianapolis, Ind.: New Riders, 1996.

Macedonia, M., and D. Brutzman. "MBone Provides Audio and Video Across the Internet." *IEEE Computer*, Apr. 1994.

Savetz, Kevin, Neil Randall, and Yves Lepage. *MBONE: Multicasting Tomorrow's Internet.* Foster City, Calif.: IDG, 1996.

—*Stephen Casner*

McCarthy, John

1927–

U.S. Computer Scientist

John McCarthy named and cofounded the field of **artificial intelligence** research, initiated the field of mathematical theory of computation and invented computer **time-sharing**. His work has emphasized epistemological problems: what information and modes of reasoning are required for intelligent behavior. He also originated the **LISP** programming language for computing with symbolic expressions and pioneered the use of mathematical logic to prove the correctness of computer programs.

McCarthy coined the term *artificial intelligence* in 1955 and organized the first major conference in that field, the Dartmouth Conference, the following year. At the Massachusetts Institute of Technology (MIT) in 1958, he and **Marvin Minsky** (1927–) organized and directed the Artificial Intelligence Project, where much pioneering work took place in a wide range of fields, from robotics to theory of computation to the development of human–computer interfaces. In 1958, McCarthy also developed the LISP (List Processing) language, which has been the principal language used in artificial intelligence ever since. He was also a leading participant in the development of the **ALGOL** 58 and ALGOL 60 languages.

In 1959, he was the first to propose a way to create general-purpose time-sharing systems that would allow a number of people to share a computer interactively without interfering with each other. By 1962 he had demonstrated the practicality of this scheme by overseeing development of a time-sharing system as a consultant to **Bolt, Beranek and Newman** (BBN), concurrent with other time-sharing implementations based on his ideas. This work led to the initiation of **Project MAC** at MIT and the development of a number of time-sharing systems elsewhere, giving rise to widespread use of interactive computing long before it became practical to build workstations or personal computers.

In 1962, McCarthy went to Stanford University and started an Artificial Intelligence Project there, including new work in speech recognition and robotics, and continued his work on mathematical theory of computation. He also initiated the development of the first display-oriented time-sharing system, called THOR, which included many of the features found in modern **personal computers** and workstations. By the early 1970s he had begun to think about the potential of networks of personal home computers, and in 1972 presented a paper on "The Home Information Terminal."

Since the 1950s McCarthy has pursued the goal of developing a logical formalism that will permit the construction of a large commonsense knowledge base. His recent work includes formalization of nonmonotonic reasoning whereby people and computers draw conjectural conclusions by assuming that complications are absent from a situation. His work in 2000 involves the formalization of context in mathematical logic and the notion of elaboration tolerance.

In addition to his intellectual leadership, McCarthy has long been active in support of the human rights of computer professionals, especially those from Eastern Europe and the former Soviet Union.

Biography

John McCarthy. Born 4 September 1927 in Boston, Massachusetts. Served in U.S. Army, received B.S. in mathematics from California Institute of Technology, 1948. Ph.D. in mathematics from Princeton University, 1951. Lecturer at Princeton University, 1951–53; Stanford University, 1953–55; Dartmouth College, 1955–58; Massachusetts Institute of Technology, 1958–62; and again at Stanford since 1962. Director of the Artificial Intelligence Laboratory, 1966–80. Recipient of many honors and prizes, including ACM Turing Award, 1971; Research Excellence Award of the International Conference on Artificial Intelligence, 1985; Kyoto Prize, 1988; and National Medal of Science, 1990.

Selected Writings

McCarthy, John. "Programs with Common Sense." *Proceedings of the Teddington Conference on the Mechanization of Thought Processes*, 1958.

———. "The Home Information Terminal." *Man and Computer, Proceedings of the International Conference, Bordeaux, France, 1970.* Basel: S. Karger, 1972, pp. 48–57.

———. "Applications of Circumscription to Formalizing Common Sense Knowledge." *Artificial Intelligence*, April 1986.

———. "Philosophical and Scientific Presuppositions of Logical AI." In H. J. McCarthy and Vladimir Lifschitz, eds., *Formalizing Common Sense: Papers by John McCarthy*. Norwood, N.J.: Ablex, 1990.

Levesque, Hector J., and Fiora Pirri, eds. *Logical Foundations for Cognitive Agents: Contributions in Honor of Ray Reiter.* Berlin and New York: Springer-Verlag, 1999.

Shannon, Claude, and John McCarthy, eds. *Automata Studies.* Princeton, N.J.: Princeton University Press, 1956.

Further Reading

Levin, Michael. *Lisp 1.5 Programmer's Manual: The Computation Center and Research Laboratory of Electronics, Massachusetts Institute of Technology.* Cambridge, Mass.: MIT Press, 1965.

Lifschitz, Vladimir, ed. *Artificial Intelligence and Mathematical Theory of Computation: Papers in Honor of John McCarthy.* Boston: Academic Press, 1991.

—*Les Earnest*

McCulloch, Warren S.

1898–1969

U.S. Psychiatrist and Neurophysiologist

Warren S. McCulloch was an American psychiatrist and neurophysiologist who cofounded the field of **cybernetics**. His greatest contributions to computer science include an early existence proof for universal computers (**Turing Machine**) and a model of artificial **neural networks**, which explains how a biological brain could perform logical calculations and which serves as the basis of **artificial intelligence** (AI).

After receiving his master's degree in psychology from Columbia University, McCulloch soon became disappointed by the division of psychology into behavioristic, psychoanalytic, and introspective camps, and with the antagonism that existed among them. He decided that all three could be replaced by a complete neurophysiological theory of the human mind. Believing that a proper understanding of psychology would have to be made formally rigorous by treating mental concepts as logical propositions, McCulloch felt that the only place to begin this formal theory of the mind was by empirical inquiry into the nervous system. He continued his studies and received an M.D., with specialties in psychiatry and the physiology of the brain, from Columbia University in 1927.

He then turned to the study of the neurological basis of mental disorders as a physician at Bellevue Hospital from 1928 to 1930, and at Rockland State Hospital for the Insane from 1930 to 1932. In order to study the structural properties of nervous activity, McCulloch moved to the Yale Medical School. There he began research under Dusser de Barenne (1885–1940) to map neuronal projections of the sensory and motor cortex areas of live animal brains, by observing the electrical activity stimulated by localized injections of strychnine. In 1940 he moved to Chicago to accept a position as professor of psychiatry and clinical professor of physiology and direct the new Research Laboratory at University of Illinois Medical School's Neuropsychiatric Institute.

There, McCulloch met two students, Jerome Lettvin and Walter Pitts (1923–69), who would become his closest colleagues, collaborators, and friends. Lettvin was a young medical student interested in the use of mathematics in biology and in the electrical properties of the brain. Pitts was a polymath who had never graduated from high school or enrolled in college but began studying logic with the Vienna Circle philosopher Rudolph Carnap (1891–1970) at the University of Chicago after running away from home at the age of 14. In 1941, the 18-year-old Pitts began working with McCulloch on a theory of the mind that would show how neurons in the brain could represent logical propositions.

In their 1943 paper, McCulloch and Pitts demonstrated that a suitably configured network of mathematically idealized neurons could represent any well-formed logical proposition and compute any function representable in their logical calculus. Any such network could simulate a "memory" if its outputs were fed back into its inputs. Thus, their neuron nets were a kind of universal computer (see **"On Computable Numbers"**).

While mathematically idealized, the logical neurons they devised simulated what was then known of the electrical behavior of biological neurons. They took advantage of the fact that neurons exhibited an "all-or-none" property of firing or not firing to set up a crucial analogy to the binary "true-or-false" property of propositions in Boolean logic. This mathematical model of artificial neural networks thus provided a compelling basis for a theory of how the brain, by being formally equivalent to a computer at the level of synaptic transmission, was capable of performing sophisticated logical reasoning.

This paper became one of the foundations of the new field of cybernetics, and McCulloch became one of its principal leaders. In 1952, McCulloch moved to the Research Laboratory of Electronics at the Massachusetts Institute of Technology (MIT) to join the other prominent leader of the movement, **Norbert Wiener** (1894–1964), and to set up a research group to study the circuit theory of the brain. The two men had a falling out by the end of that year, but McCulloch remained at MIT for the rest of his career. During that time many noteworthy students came to his lab to study the mathematical properties of natural and artificial neurons, including **Benoit Mandelbrot** (1924–), who later developed **fractals**, and the computer scientists Manuel Blum (1938–), Stuart Kaufmann (1921–), **Marvin Minsky** (1927–), and **Seymour Papert** (1928–).

Even though his work formed the basis of the field of AI and its subfield of artificial neural networks,

McCulloch maintained a somewhat ambiguous relationship with these areas of research. Initially, McCulloch saw the mechanical simulations of AI as a means of experimenting with theories of how the brain worked. But in the 1950s, as computer programs were being developed that could play checkers and do other forms of logical problem solving, McCulloch began to reject many of these projects as efforts aimed at developing toys rather than a greater understanding of the mind. He believed that much of this research merely *assumed* that the mind was a computer, instead of showing how the brain performed particular calculations, and merely sought to demonstrate the mental-like tasks that computers could perform, rather than attempting to propose or test empirical theories of the mind.

Much of McCulloch's dissatisfaction with AI may have been a reaction to **John von Neumann**'s (1903–57) 1951 paper "A General and Logical Theory of Automata." The paper was addressed directly to McCulloch and Pitts's 1943 paper, and issued a serious challenge to it as a theory of mind that McCulloch would never feel had been fully answered. The problem von Neumann articulated was that the logical network could only represent concepts that were specified completely and precisely, whereas, in fact, most of our ideas and knowledge are not specifiable in this way. Worse, if they *were* so specified, it might require more bits of information than there are atoms in the universe to represent them. Thus, merely showing that some limited domain of mental performance could be specified completely and precisely, as most AI projects sought to do, did not really answer this fundamental challenge. McCulloch's preoccupation with this problem led him to investigations of multivalued higher-order and probabilistic logics.

In 1947, Pitts and McCulloch had written another influential paper, "How We Know Universals: The Perception of Auditory and Visual Forms." This paper outlined a theory of how an artificial neural network can perform a kind of abstraction or statistical induction. That is, it could obtain a representation of a *universal* concept such as "apple" by seeing many instances of *particular* apples. This idea laid the groundwork for the use of neural networks as models for learning generalized rules from specific instances, and as models of sensory perception in pattern recognition and classification tasks. Through the 1950s, McCulloch still held out hope that a better understanding of the behavior of artificial neural networks would be able to elucidate the inner workings of the brain in experiments.

Research on neural networks exploded during the 1960s after the psychologist Frank Rosenblatt introduced his Perceptron model in 1958. Whereas research during the 1940s and 1950s had been primarily mathematical, with just a few analog neural circuits being built, the Perceptron was a learning rule for a statistical simulation of neural computation run on a mainframe computer. It became the basis of the modern neural network. As **digital computers** became more readily available in the 1960s, research in machine learning turned away from logic circuits and toward building statistical simulations in digital computers. These networks essentially solve the problem of class membership, as in "Which class of things is this object a member of?" Many kinds of problems can be reduced to this problem, and many neural network simulations were constructed during this period to solve all sorts of pattern recognition problems involving the classification of handwritten characters, speech, and visual forms. The Perceptron became the paradigm for a vast amount of research done during the 1960s.

This research abruptly halted when the U.S. military stopped funding these projects, and resources were shifted toward research into the methods of symbolic logic and the development of expert systems during the 1970s. A commonly cited cause of this shift was the 1969 publication of a lengthy criticism of the Perceptron model by two long-time neural network researchers and students of McCulloch, Minsky and Papert. Their criticism amounted to a mathematical observation that the only functions that a single-layer network of Perceptrons can learn is a line that divides a plane (or a plane that divides a hyperplane) into multiple regions, where each region represents a classification and each observed example is a point in the region. For his own part, McCulloch was impressed by the work that led up to this book and hoped that it would discourage many of the "charlatans" who had taken up research in neural networks. Ultimately, he believed that neural networks could explain only some of the phenomena of sensory perception, but not the whole of the mind.

After becoming disenchanted with these two fields of research he had inspired, McCulloch spent the remainder of his career searching for a neurological theory of a much more obscure faculty of the mind: consciousness. He was dissatisfied with notions of consciousness that made it into the central authority of a hierarchically organized mind. His efforts involved detailed studies of the reticular formation of the brain stem, the part of the brain responsible for the most basic vital functions, such as breathing and metabolic control. He believed that consciousness was related to the ability of an organism to switch rapidly between a small number of basic modes of interacting with the world: eat, drink, sleep, fight, flee, hunt, and so on. He used as his operative metaphor the decentralized control of naval fleets, in which any ship in the fleet can come to be in command of the entire fleet if it comes into contact with the enemy before the others or is in the best position to take command. He theorized that one specialized substructure of the brain could wrest control from the others when its functions became imperative to the survival of the organism, as when swallowing automatically shuts off breathing to prevent choking. Thus, knowledge and necessity become the basis of the shifting authority of mental command.

Biography

Warren Sturgis McCulloch. Born 16 November 1898 in Orange, New Jersey. Studied at Haverford College, Pennsylvania and Yale University, 1917–21. Served as an officer in U.S. Naval Reserves, 1919–21. Received M.A. in psychology from Columbia University, 1923, and M.D. from Columbia Medical School, 1927. Practicing physician at Bellevue Hospital, 1928, and at Rockland State Hospital for the Insane, 1930. Became director of the Research Laboratory at University of Illinois Medical School's Neuropsychiatric Institute, 1940. Chairman of the Macy Conferences on Circular Causal and Feedback Mechanisms in Biological and Social Systems, 1946–53. Moved to the Research Laboratory of Electronics at the Massachusetts Institute of Technology (MIT) to study the circuitry of the brain, 1952. Continued teaching, researching, and publishing on the mind, brain, and cybernetics at MIT and from his farm in Old Lyme, Connecticut. Died 26 September 1969.

Selected Writings

Lettvin, Jerome Y., Humberto R. Maturana, Warren S. McCulloch, and Walter Pitts. "What the Frog's Eye Tells the Frog's Brain." *Proceedings of the IRE,* Vol. 47, No. 11, Nov. 1959. Reprinted in Rook McCulloch, ed., *The Collected Works of Warren S. McCulloch,* Vol. 4. Salinas, Calif.: Intersystems Publications, 1989, pp. 1161–1172.

McCulloch, Warren S. *Embodiments of Mind.* Cambridge, Mass.: MIT Press, 1965.

———. *The Collected Works of Warren S. McCulloch,* Vols. 1–4. Edited by Rook McCulloch. Salinas, Calif.: Intersystems Publications, 1989.

McCulloch, Warren S., and Walter Pitts. "A Logical Calculus of the Ideas Immanent in Nervous Activity." *Bulletin of Mathematical Biophysics,* Vol. 5, 1943, pp. 115–133.

Pitts, Walter, and Warren S. McCulloch. "On How We Know Universals: The Perception of Auditory and Visual Forms." *Bulletin of Mathematical Biophysics,* Vol. 9, 1947, pp. 127–147.

Further Reading

Anderson, James, and Edward Rosenfeld, eds. *Talking Nets: An Oral History of Neural Networks.* Cambridge, Mass.: MIT Press, 1998.

Lindgren, N. "The Birth of Cybernetics–An End to the Old World: The Heritage of Warren S. McCulloch." *Innovation,* Vol. 6, 1969, pp. 12–15.

Minsky, Marvin, and Seymour Papert. *Perceptrons: An Introduction to Computational Geometry.* Cambridge, Mass.: MIT Press, 1969.

Moreno-Diaz, R., and J. Mira-Mira, eds. *Brain Processes, Theories and Models: An International Conference in Honor of W. S. McCulloch 25 Years After His Death.* Cambridge, Mass.: MIT Press, 1996.

Perkel, D. H. "Logical Neurons: The Enigmatic Legacy of Warren McCulloch." *Trends in Neuroscience,* Vol. 11, No. 1, 1988, pp. 9–12.

Rosenblatt, Frank. *Principles of Neurodynamics: Perceptrons and the Theory of Brain Mechanisms.* Washington, D.C.: Spartan Books, 1962.

Rumelhart, David, John McClelland, and the PDP Research Group. *Parallel and Distributed Processing: Explorations in the Microstructure of Cognition,* Vol. 1: *Foundations.* Cambridge, Mass.: MIT Press, 1986.

Turing, Alan M. "On Computable Numbers, with an Application to the Entscheidungsproblem." *Proceedings of the London Mathematical Society,* Vol. 42, 1937, pp. 230–265.

Von Neumann, John. "The General and Logical Theory of Automata." In L. A. Jeffress, ed., *Cerebral Mechanisms in Behavior, The Hixon Symposium.* New York: Wiley, 1951. Reprinted in William Asprey and Arthur Burks, eds., *Papers of John von Neumann on Computers and Computing Theory.* Cambridge, Mass.: MIT Press, 1987, pp. 391–431.

—*Peter Asaro*

MCI WorldCom

MCI WorldCom operates as a global provider of facilities-based and fully integrated local, long distance, international, and **Internet** services in more than 65 countries. In 1999, revenues exceeded U.S.$37 billion.

The company was founded in September 1983 as a long-distance reseller. The idea for the corporation was conceived over iced tea in a Hattiesburg, Mississippi coffee shop, where Murray Waldron and William Rector met to discuss a business plan. With the help of a waitress, the fledgling company was given the name LDDC (long-distance discount calling). Later, the name was changed to LDDS (long-distance discount service).

In November of that same year, LDDS was given permission to operate as a long-distance carrier. The University of Southern Mississippi signed on as the first customer. By 1985, LDDS had named investor Bernie Ebbers (1943–) as chief executive officer. Over the next few years, LDDS continued to grow rapidly and expanded out of Mississippi.

LDDS acquired Advantage Companies, Inc. and went public in August 1989. It began buying up small telecommunications firms and expanding its customer base, culminating in the purchase of Advanced Telecommunications Corporation for approximately U.S.$850 million.

LDDS kept up its rapid pace of acquisition by purchasing six large organizations over the next four years. In 1993, two full-service long-distance companies, Metromedia Communications Corporation (MCC) and the Resurgeons Communications Group, were purchased with cash and stock for approximately U.S.$1.25 billion. In 1994, the IDB Communications Group was acquired for their international communications network. The value of this stock transaction was U.S.$936 million. In 1995, WilTel network services, including all fiber optics and microwave transmission facilities, was purchased from the Williams Group. This gave LDDS the ability to provide large corporations with both voice and data services. In May 1995, LDDS renamed itself WorldCom, Inc.

1996 marked WorldCom's resolve to invest heavily in the growing use of networking to support Internet applications and growth. In a U.S.$12 billion stock-for-stock transaction, WorldCom acquired the MFS Communications Company, Inc. and their recent acquisition, **UUNET** Technologies, Inc.

WorldCom again embarked on a series of mergers in 1998. This time, Brooks Fiber Properties, Inc., **CompuServe** Corporation, Advanced Network Services (ANS), and MCI Corporation were all involved in the transactions. The MCI merger alone was valued at approximately U.S.$40 billion. WorldCom was now MCI WorldCom.

The integration of MCI and WorldCom resulted in an organization able to reduce costs and offer lower rates on leased lines and other networking services. The CompuServe merger and purchase of ANS from AOL resulted in greater strength in Internet services and additional systems integration capability.

MCI WorldCom was built through acquisition and mergers, a growth philosophy that is still being pursued. In 1999, MCI WorldCom announced that it would be merging with Sprint. Provided that regulators approve the transaction, analysts believe the event will occur sometime late in the year 2000.

Further Reading

Semilof, Margie. "MCI WorldCom Mantra: We Do More Than Just Sell Pipes." *Computer Reseller News,* No. 890, 17 Apr. 2000, pp. 7, 14.

—Roger McHaney

McLuhan, Marshall

1911–80

Canadian Media Theorist

Theorist Marshall McLuhan achieved recognition for his visionary explorations in the field of media and his pioneering research into the relationships between technology, society, and culture.

Underlying McLuhan's general approach was a belief that social changes are intimately connected to developments in technology and communication media, and thus we can approach an understanding of society and culture through an understanding of media. His view has since been labeled by some as *media determinism*, reflecting the view that new media are among the causes of social change. A typically McLuhanesque aphorism, "the medium is the message," highlights that it is the forms, properties, and effects of communications media that should be the objects of study rather than the content. In his writings, McLuhan described the properties and social effects of media and technologies through the ages: from the spoken word and the resulting oral cultures, through print and visual culture, to the electronic technologies of the twentieth century, such as television, radio, and cinema.

In 1962, McLuhan published *The Gutenberg Galaxy: The Making of Typographical Man*, an attempt to trace the links between media and society from the advent of printing technology up to the present day. He observed that for several centuries the printed page has been a dominant communication medium in Western society, creating the conditions necessary for the development of Western culture since the Renaissance. Properties of the print medium, McLuhan argues, have shaped Western intellectual development, resulting in a tradition of linear thought, specialization, and rationalism. McLuhan further observed that the electronic technologies of the twentieth century are leading to a return to a way of life resembling that which existed in village communities prior to the invention of print, widespread literacy, and early mass media. For this new mode of living—as part of a community where relations are mediated by electronic communication technologies—McLuhan coined the term **global village**.

Marshall McLuhan, Canadian philosopher and media theorist, circa 1966. (Bettmann/CORBIS)

In his 1964 book *Understanding Media: The Extensions of Man*, McLuhan introduced a number of important ideas that were to become highly influential in media and culture theory. One of these is to characterize media as extensions of human faculties, especially the senses. Thus the telephone extends the sense of hearing, the printed page extends the visual sense, and media such as television involve a mixture of visual and auditory sensory experiences. Extending a particular sense, or altering the "ratios of sense perception," alters in turn the way we perceive the world and how we think and act within it.

Another well-known idea of McLuhan's is the categorization of media as being "hot" or "cool." *Hot media* are those that extend a single sense in high definition, are rich in information, and require relatively little active participation from the audience. *Cool media*, on the other hand, are relatively low-definition and demand greater audience participation in order to "fill in the details." Use of the terms *hot* and *cool* in this context derives from the jazz slang used to contrast a brassy and scripted big-band sound (hot) with more improvised styles (cool). The printed text, for example, is a highly defined visual medium, permitting the reader a relatively passive role and is therefore hot. By contrast, oral communication requires much more active participation on the part of the listener in order to make sense of a conversation and is thus termed a cool medium. The cinema is seen as a high-definition and therefore hot medium, which viewers may passively consume. Television, by contrast, with its smaller screen, lower definition, and its many channels, as well as its ability to transmit distant events rapidly into our living rooms, is a much more cool medium. As an example of how the cool medium of television is characterized by more audience participation and a stronger sense of involvement and community, McLuhan cites the TV coverage of President Kennedy's funeral. The coverage was far more than simple reportage, creating a situation where an entire population was involved in a collective ritual.

McLuhan's 1967 book was entitled *The Medium Is the Massage: An Inventory of Effects*, combining a pun on his own aphorism—"the medium is the message"—with a pun on the "mass age," or possibly a recognition of the way media massage and shape the audience. In this volume many of the themes of McLuhan's earlier work, such as the effects of media on society, the huge impact of printing technology, and media rather than content as an object of study, are restated and reinforced. The book, which became a best-seller, was produced as a mosaic of text and images, rich with the witty, punning, aphoristic style so characteristic of McLuhan. Its significance lies not so much in its content but in the way it aims to stretch and redefine our very understanding of the book medium at the beginning of the era when print seemed to be giving way to computer-based technologies.

McLuhan died at the very dawn of the personal computer age, and when he wrote about electronic technology, he was referring primarily to media that now seem like unremarkable parts of everyday life: television, telephone, radio, and so on. However, since computers, the **Internet**, and the **World Wide Web** have become ubiquitous, McLuhan's ideas have found renewed acclaim among those seeking to interpret and comment on the new technologies and accompanying social changes. McLuhan's concept of hot and cool media has been used to characterize the Web as a cool—some would say freezing—medium. **Hypertext** and hypermedia involve a mixture of ways in which information can be presented (text, hyperlinks, graphics, animation, and sound), and they provide many ways in which a particular collection of information may be read. A hypertext, therefore, is not a linear medium like conventional writing or print, but allows the reader far greater flexibility in navigating documents and constructing interpretations. The number and variety of pathways through the Web demands a relatively high degree of participation from a reader in order to construct any particular pathway.

McLuhan's views and work seem especially relevant in the Internet era, and it has often been said that the Web and related technology mean that the global village is closer than ever to becoming a reality. Other commentators have pointed out that the acceptance of such phrases as "global village," and the ubiquity of new technologies such as the Internet would probably have led McLuhan to say that the time has come to reevaluate such metaphors and look for new ones to describe the technologies of the new millennium.

An important message to be drawn from McLuhan's writings concerns the idea that because technologies and media shape society, they cannot be considered morally neutral. For McLuhan, therefore, being aware of how technologies affect individuals and cultures is an important prerequisite to making judgments about the value of our technological achievements. To quote from *The Medium Is the Massage*: "There is absolutely no inevitability as long as there is a willingness to contemplate what is happening."

Biography

Herbert Marshall McLuhan. Born 21 July 1911 in Edmonton, Alberta, Canada. Studied literature at the University of Manitoba and Cambridge University. Received Ph.D. from Cambridge University, 1943. Held teaching posts at the University of Wisconsin, St. Louis University, Fordham University, and Assumption College. Became a full professor of English at the University of Toronto, 1954; director of the Center for Culture and Technology at the University of Toronto, 1963-1979. Appointed to the Vatican as a consultant to the Pontifical Commission for Social Communications, 1973. Recipient of many awards and honorary degrees. Published many articles and books, some of which achieved best-seller status. Appeared in Woody Allen's movie *Annie Hall*, 1977. Died 31 December 1980.

Selected Writings

Carpenter, E., and Marshall McLuhan. *Explorations in Communication*. London: Jonathan Cape, 1970.

McLuhan, Marshall. *The Mechanical Bride: Folklore of Industrial Man*. New York: Vanguard, 1951.

———. *The Gutenberg Galaxy: The Making of Typographical Man*. Toronto, Ontario, Canada: University of Toronto Press, 1962.

———. *Understanding Media: The Extensions of Man.* London: Routledge and Kegan Paul, 1964.

McLuhan, Marshall, and Quentin Fiore. *The Medium Is the Massage: An Inventory of Effects.* London: Allen Lane The Penguin Press, 1967.

Further Reading

Ebersole, S. "Media Determinism in Cyberspace." *Regent Online Journal of Communication*, 1996. *http://www.regent.edu/acad/schcom/rojc/ecspring96.html*

Guay, T. *WEB Publishing Paradigms*, 1995. *http://hoshi.cic.sfu.ca/~guay/Paradigm*

Levinson, P. *Digital McLuhan: A Guide to the Information Millenium.* London: Routledge, 1999.

McLuhan, E., and F. Zingrone, eds. *Essential McLuhan.* London: Routledge, 1995.

The McLuhan Program in Culture and Technology, University of Toronto, Toronto, Ontario, Canada. *http://www.mcluhan.utoronto.ca*

Wolf, G. "The Wisdom of Saint Marshall, the Holy Fool." *Wired*, 4.01, Jan. 1996. *http://www.wired.com*

— *Bob Fields*

Mead, Carver

1934–

U.S. Engineer

Carver Mead's inventions played a crucial role in modern design and production of **very-large-scale integrated** (VLSI) circuits, which are themselves the basis of the computing and communications industries. He has also created important specific electronic devices, had notable success as a teacher, and now, in his 60s, is concentrating on electronic embodiments of the functions of living systems.

Mead found a congenial academic environment at the California Institute of Technology (Caltech), with which he has maintained affiliation throughout his scientific career. His first work in the late 1950s was on the physics of insulators and charge-carrier tunneling. In 1965, he invented the gallium arsenide metal-semiconductor field-effect **transistor** (MESFET). This was a milestone on the path from the discrete high-temperature devices then required for amplification at very high frequencies, to current mass production of efficient, low-noise solid-state elements.

In 1969, Mead launched *scaling theory*, with an analysis of the constraints on the physical dimensions of silicon circuits. He famously postulated the importance of oxide substrate reliability and 0.15 micron as an industrially achievable characteristic dimension. His predictions were rather controversial, although by the 1990s, engineering practice had finally advanced to the point of confirming them to a remarkable degree.

The standard amplifying device in contemporary microwave communications systems, crucial in essentially all satellite and many ground-based links, is the high electron mobility transistor (HEMT). Mead invented the original form of the HEMT in the mid-1960s.

The considerations led in a natural way to his first course in 1970 on VLSI design. His fundamental motivation in this work was his realization that craft habits of circuit analysis and design were inadequate for the million-device chips he foresaw. *Introduction to VLSI Systems* is the classic textbook on this subject that he coauthored in 1980 with student Lynn Conway (1938–). These accomplishments initiated the field of electronic design automation (EDA). In Mead's conception, EDA's "silicon compilers" provide the abstractions that allow designers to manage underlying physics and electronics efficiently.

Currently, *structured custom design* is the methodology used at all major semiconductor companies to create new chips. Mead invented this in the decade of the 1970s; after several years of opposition, it has nearly replaced the previous "manual" traditions of circuit layout, validation, and construction. Moreover, his textbooks are the standards for this area of electronics.

Mead presently focuses on *neuromorphic electronics,* systems modeled on the nervous systems found in nature. His Physics of Computation laboratory at Caltech has already generated several patents in the areas of machine vision, hearing, and learning. Through his enthusiastic teaching, sound engineering, and deep insight, Carver Mead has profoundly affected the electronic theory and practice of the last 40 years.

Biography

Carver Andress Mead. Born 1 May 1934 in Bakersfield, California. B.S., 1956; M.S., 1957; Ph.D., 1960; all from Caltech and all in electrical engineering. Professor at Caltech from 1957; Gordon and Betty Moore Professor of Engineering and

Applied Sciences from 1980. Member of board of directors of Synaptics, Inc. and Aptix Corp. Recipient of many awards, including Centennial Medal of IEEE, 1984; Phil Kaufman Award, 1996; Lemelson–MIT Prize, 1999. Also the recipient of many honorary degrees, and membership in numerous scholarly societies, including the National Academy of Engineering, National Academy of Sciences, Royal Swedish Academy, and Franklin Institute.

SELECTED WRITINGS

Hutchinson, James Christof Koch, Jin Luo, and Carver Mead. "Computing Motion Using Analog and Binary Resistive Networks." *IEEE Computer*, Vol. 21, No. 3, 1988, pp. 52–63.

Mead, Carver. "VLSI and the Foundations of Computation." *IFIP Congress*, 1983, pp. 271–274.

———. *Analog VLSI and Neural Systems.* Reading, Mass.: Addison Wesley Longman, 1993.

Mead, Carver, and Lynn Conway. *Introduction to VLSI Systems.* Reading, Mass.: Addison-Wesley, 1980.

—*Cameron Laird*

Mechatronics

Mechatronics is a discipline that combines *mechan*-ical engineering and elec*tronics*. It is a way of designing automated machines and robots in which the techniques of mechanical engineering are completely integrated with those of electronics, **computer science**, and control theory (a theoretical approach to monitoring machines and industrial processes).

Machines were not always designed using the mechatronic approach. Once, devices such as automated washing machines were designed by separate teams of engineers. Mechanical engineers specialized in designing the basic moving mechanisms, while electrical and electronic engineers took the finished machine from the mechanical engineers and designed a control system to automate it. The term *mechatronics* was coined in Japan in 1969 by the Yaskawa Electric Company, a pioneer in using electronic circuits to control electric motors, and Japanese engineers and designers remain at the forefront of mechatronics. Today, the term reflects the way that a single design team will design a machine all at once, not necessarily starting from the mechanical components.

Mechatronics is closely related to **robotics**, and there is a considerable overlap between the two fields. But whereas robotics is generally concerned with the design of computer-controlled robotic devices, such as the robot arms used in car-assembly plants, mechatronics generally has a wider application to any electronically or computer-controlled machine with some moving mechanical parts.

Control theory forms the basis of mechatronics. The simplest machine, a device such as an electric fan, exists in two states—it is either on or off. When it is switched on, it blows cool air around a room; when it is switched off, less air circulates, and the room warms up. Suppose the fan incorporates a mechanical thermostat that switches on the electric current when the temperature rises above a certain value and switches it off when the temperature falls below a different value. The fan will then cycle on and off, regulating the room temperature between the two values. This is known as a *control system* because it controls an output (the temperature of the room) according to an input (the temperature on the thermostat).

The most important element of control theory is the principle of *feedback*, which means that the output from a machine is monitored constantly and forms part of its input. In the cooling fan, for example, the thermostat detects changes in room temperature and feeds these back to switch the fan on or off. A device that uses feedback is also known as a *closed-loop system*; the thermostatically operated fan is an example. A device with no feedback is called an *open-loop system*—a fan with no thermostat, for example.

There are four main components in any mechatronic system: sensors, actuators, controllers, and control software. *Sensors* are the key component of the feedback loop, because they measure the current state of the system and so influence its future state. Although sensors can be purely mechanical (e.g., simple make/break switches in a burglar alarm system that detect whether a window has been opened), they are more often transducers: devices that change one kind of energy (e.g., a temperature or pressure change) into another (usually, an electrical signal).

Actuators are usually mechanical components that move in some way. A robot arm or the electrically operated drawer of a compact disk player would be operated by actuators. Mechanical actuators include cogs, cams, and gears; electrical actuators include switches, solenoids, electric motors, and stepper motors (electric motors that can be made to turn through a precise angle).

Controllers are the parts of a mechatronic system that detect the difference between a system's current state (as measured by one or more sensors) and the state the system should be in and take action to correct the difference between the two (by operating one or more actuators). Although controllers can be mechanical or electrical, today they commonly take the form of **microprocessors** preprogrammed to perform one or more specific tasks (such as controlling the different movements of a paint-spraying robot or the different operating modes of a videocassette recorder [VCR]). These contain the final component of the system: the software that operates them according to control theory.

As microprocessors have replaced many forms of mechanical control since their popularization in the early 1970s, so the balance of mechatronics has shifted away from mechanical and toward electronic. In the 1970s, mechatronic devices were typified by automatically operated shop doors and relay-controlled vending machines. In the 1980s, microprocessor-controlled toasters, washing machines, VCRs, and antilock braking systems (ABS) on cars represented the state of the art.

During the 1990s, mechatronic devices incorporated a greater proportion of optical-electronic components, such as charge-coupled devices (CCDs), the light-sensing elements used in digital cameras and scanners, and greater use of computer networks to enable remote operation. The twenty-first century is likely to see more sophisticated mechatronic machine vision systems and an even greater use of mechatronic devices in remote and hostile environments such as space.

FURTHER READING

Åström, Karl J., and Björn Wittenmark. *Computer-Controlled Systems: Theory and Design*. Englewood Cliffs, N.J.: Prentice Hall, 1984; 3rd ed., Upper Saddle River, N.J.,1997.

Bolton, W. *Mechatronics: Electronic Control Systems in Mechanical Engineering*. Harlow, Essex, England, and New York: Addison Wesley Longman; 2nd ed., 1999.

Fraser, Charles, and John Milne. *Integrated Electrical and Electronic Engineering for Mechanical Engineers*. London and New York: McGraw-Hill, 1994.

Histand, Michael, and David Alciatore. *Introduction to Mechatronics and Measurement Systems*. Boston: WCB/McGraw-Hill, 1999.

—*Chris Woodford*

Memory Hierarchy

A computer stores data in different types of media: fast static memory chips, slow dynamic memory chips, **hard disk**, or tape. Usually the fastest devices are also the most expensive. Therefore, optimizing the cost of a computer system means that the memory has to be organized hierarchically: Starting with the processor, the devices are connected in a chain going from the fastest to the slowest. The fastest devices are smaller, since they are so expensive; the slower devices have a larger storage capacity. This is the memory hierarchy and moving information across the different levels is called *memory hierarchy management*.

The fastest "data containers" available in a computer are the registers. Data can be stored and retrieved from them in a few nanoseconds. Current **microprocessor** generations have cycle times of 2 nanoseconds (ns) (at a 500 megahertz [MHz] clock rate), and ideally, a piece of data should be retrievable in each cycle. Registers are constructed of the fastest logic elements available, and a microprocessor can have just a few or several hundred.

The next element in the memory hierarchy is the data **cache**, which can be divided in up to three levels, and then we have the main memory. Usually, dynamic random access memory (**RAM**) chips are used for main memory, which can be as large as hundreds of megabytes. The cache is made of fast and expensive chips. Data present in the main memory are replicated in the cache so that the processor can access it from the faster medium, but since the cache is smaller than main memory, special circuits must decide which data must be kept in the cache and which can be overwritten.

When the processor needs data from a memory address, it looks in the first-level (L1) cache. If it is there, the data are transferred to a register. If not, the electronic looks in the second-level (L2) cache. If the data are found there, they are transferred to the first-level cache, then to the processor. Additional cache levels only extend this strategy using more access levels. When the data are not present in any of the cache levels, they are read from main memory.

The figure provides a more detailed view of a possible memory hierarchy organization. The processor accesses only the first-level cache, which is divided into two units: The instruction cache contains only instructions; the data cache, as the name implies, contains only data. The purpose of this division is to allow the processor to access one instruction at the same time that a data word can be read or written. The first-level cache is not connected directly to the L2 cache; there are three buffers between both. The first *miss buffer* connected to the L1 instruction cache holds any data coming from the slower-level caches, until the L1 cache can absorb it. Any speed mismatches between the cache units are absorbed in this way by the stream buffer. The two other stream buffers between the L1 and L2 data cache are used to read and write data, respectively, from and to the lower-level cache. The buffers between the third-level and second-level caches have the same purpose.

The next level in the memory hierarchy is main memory itself, and then the hard disk. Almost all modern operating systems use **virtual memory**. This means that although the computer may have only 64 megabytes (MB) of memory, the **operating system** simulates that it has more by using part of the hard disk to extend main memory. To avoid having to read single words from the hard disk (which would be too slow), entire pages are transferred between main memory and the hard disk. Called *swapping*, this extends the available memory for programs.

However, between the **bus** and the hard disk, we could also have a *disk cache*. A disk cache is composed of memory chips, which hold the latest sectors read from the hard disk. Just as in the case of the L1, L2, L3 caches, the purpose of the disk cache is to avoid having to retrieve often-used data from the slower unit each time these data are needed. Many hard disk controllers for PCs include a hard disk cache on the same expansion card.

The last level in the memory hierarchy depicted in the diagram is constituted by magnetic tapes stored in a special room and handled by a robotic arm. Data that have not been accessed in the last year, for example, can be copied from hard disk to tapes. The tape device has hundreds of times the storage capacity of the hard disks, but accessing the information can take several minutes.

The "distance" from the hierarchy of different elements to the processor is measured according to the number of cycles that it takes to bring a piece of data to a register, the *data retrieval latency*. According to this definition, the distance of the various elements of the memory hierarchy could be the following: L1 cache, 2 cycles; L2 cache, 5 cycles; L3 cache, 8 cycles; main memory, 30 cycles; disk cache, 1000 cycles; hard disk, 1 million cycles; tape, 300 billion cycles (10-minute access time at 500 MHz).

The size of each element of the memory hierarchy is lower when the distance to the processor is smaller. The L1 and L2 caches could hold several kilobytes, the L3 cache several megabytes. Main memory and a disk cache are measured in hundreds of megabytes, and the hard disk in gigabytes. The tape device can hold terabytes of data.

Management of the memory hierarchy is based on the *principle of locality*. This means that when programs access data from a specific address, it is highly probable that neighboring addresses will also be accessed to read or store numbers (spatial locality). It is also likely that a piece of data that has been read will be reused afterward (temporal locality). Finally, programs are written as sequences of instructions and data are stored in arrays, so that if an address is read, it is probable that the addresses immediately following will

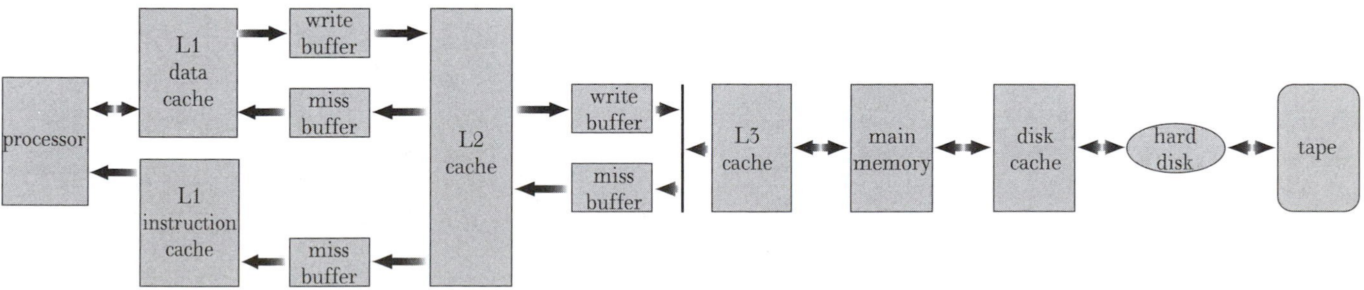

Memory hierarchy.

also be needed (sequential locality). Therefore, whenever an address is read from main memory into a cache, an entire block (i.e., several consecutive addresses) are loaded at the same time. When these extra addresses are needed later, they will already be loaded in the cache. The same happens when a piece of data is read from the hard disk: One or more sectors are brought into the hard-disk cache, anticipating that the additional data will be needed later.

Although all computers built since 1945 had several levels of faster or slower storage, the first person to suggest the automatic management of caches (i.e., the loading of data into the faster devices without explicit programmer's intervention) was **Maurice Wilkes** (1913–) at Cambridge University, who gave credit for the idea to Gordon Scarott. The Titan, an experimental computer built from 1961 to 1964, was the first to implement *slave memory*, as Wilkes called caches. The **Atlas**, built by **Tom Kilburn** (1921–2001) in Manchester in 1962, was the first to provide virtual memory (i.e., the automatic mapping of memory pages to a magnetic drum). The **IBM** 360/86, introduced in 1967, is credited with having been the first commercial computer to include a cache. A modern microprocessor such as the **Pentium** III from **Intel** provides two levels of cache on-chip with an L2 cache of 256 MB.

The largest single problem that computer architects will have to face in the near future is the widening gap between the clock rate of the processor and the cycle time of memory elements. There are already commercial microprocessors running at 1 gigahertz, that is, 1 ns of cycle time, whereas commercial memory chips have access times between 30 and 60 ns. Also, since the **transistor** budget (the number of transistors that can be accommodated on a single chip) has increased and is expected to reach several hundred million units, the question arises if it is better to integrate main memory into the same chip as the processor. This has been called *intelligent RAM* and is one of the options being investigated to solve the processor–memory bottleneck.

FURTHER READING

Intel. *Pentium III Processor Data Sheet.* San Jose, Calif.: Intel, 2000.

McNutt, Bruce. *The Fractal Structure of Data Reference: Applications to the Memory Hierarchy.* Boston: Kluwer Academic, 2000.

Przybylski, Steven. *Cache and Memory Hierarchy Design: A Performance-Directed Approach.* San Mateo, Calif.: Morgan Kaufmann, 1990.

Wilkes, M.V. "Slave Memories and Dynamic Storage Allocation." *IEEE Transactions on Electronic Computers,* Vol. EC-14, No. 2, Apr. 1965.

—*Raúl Rojas*

Metcalfe, Robert

1946–

U.S. Electrical Engineer and Journalist

As the inventor of **Ethernet**, the world's most popular method of connecting computers to one another and to the **Internet**, Robert Metcalfe has been one of the most important figures in the computer revolution of the late twentieth century. He founded the highly successful **3Com Corporation** in the 1970s to take advantage of his invention and in the 1990s became a noted computer journalist and technology pundit.

Bob Metcalfe traces his interest in computers to an eighth-grade science project in 1959, when he constructed a primitive electronic calculator out of his model railroad controller. His other formative computer experience involved programming an **IBM mainframe** in Saturday morning science classes for high school students hosted by Columbia University. But the pattern of his life was really sealed by an earlier episode at school. Faced with an imminent deadline to write a book review, the 9-year-old Metcalfe picked out one of his father's electronics textbooks almost at random and concluded his review with a prophetic sentence indicating that he planned to go to Massachusetts Institute of Technology (MIT) to study electrical engineering.

Almost a decade later, as he had promised, Metcalfe began his studies at MIT. He was soon exposed to a variety of powerful **mainframe** computers, including the college's IBM 7094 (IBM's first transistorized mainframe) and a military-grade **Univac** that he used for an after-hours' programming job. Just as Metcalfe had benefited from Saturday morning programming classes at Columbia during his high school years, so he found himself teaching similar classes in his final year at MIT. This led to one of the more unusual incidents of his colorful career. **Digital Equipment Corporation** (DEC) had loaned the college a U.S.$30,000 minicomputer and teletype to help with the teaching program, but the machine was stolen while it was in Metcalfe's care. Metcalfe finally plucked up the courage to call DEC to break the news, but he was astonished—and relieved—when the company decided to turn the incident into a news story that this was the first computer small enough to steal.

After completing his studies at MIT, Metcalfe took another degree in management, then moved on to Harvard to take his Ph.D. in **computer science**, outlining a modified version of the University of Hawaii's **AlohaNet** network that he called "EtherNet." But he moved back to MIT when Harvard refused to let him connect the college's computer system to the new Advanced Research Projects Agency Network (**ARPANET**), the early network of mainframe computers that subsequently developed into the Internet. Back at MIT, he designed a vital piece of packet-switching hardware called an *integrated message processor* (IMP) that successfully linked the college's DEC PDP-10 computers to the ARPANET. He also wrote an influential conference pamphlet called *Scenarios for the ARPANET*, outlining the benefits of highly networked computer systems for nontechnical users; today, he refers to it as "the first *Internet for Dummies*."

Later that year, Metcalfe went to work for the prestigious **Xerox Palo Alto Research Center** (PARC). Faced with the problem of connecting hundreds of powerful computers to a laser printer in such a way that high-resolution documents did not take hours or days to print, he combined earlier ideas from AlohaNet and the ARPANET and proposed a new method of networking, Ethernet, in an internal memo he circulated on 22 May 1973.

Ethernet was based on three simple ideas: nodes in the network would be linked across the "ether" (empty space) by ordinary coaxial cable; information could be sent between nodes by **packet switching** (breaking large files into small packets); each node would remain silent unless it was transmitting or receiving packets. Importantly for the problem of high-resolution printing, Ethernet allowed data to flow between computers and their peripherals at up to 10 megabits per second. With the help of his colleague David Boggs (1950–), Metcalfe had produced a working prototype of Ethernet by November 1973. The two researchers announced the development in an important 1976 paper and Ethernet was patented on 13 December 1977.

Xerox PARC has long been known as an institution where groundbreaking products were invented but never marketed successfully. Ethernet was destined to follow in this tradition when Metcalfe left Xerox in June 1979 to set up his own company. **3Com**, which stood for "computer communication compatibility" and operated for its first year out of Metcalfe's apartment, was intended to exploit the market for Ethernet devices. Initially helping blue-chip companies such as General Electric and Exxon to use Ethernet, Metcalfe proposed what has since become known as *Metcalfe's law*: The value of a computer network increases with the square of the number of its users; in other words, bigger networks are vastly more useful than smaller ones.

With the help of Xerox, DEC, and **Intel**, and with encouragement from **Steve Jobs** (1955–) at Apple, Metcalfe's 3Com soon established Ethernet as the standard method of linking **personal computers** (PCs) and workstations in **local area networks** (LANs). But despite trying on two separate occasions in 1980, Metcalfe failed to persuade IBM to use Ethernet as its PC networking technology. He now believes that the corporation's decision to develop its rival networking system, token ring, played a major role in its downfall in the mid-1980s: Instead of adopting Ethernet in 1980, they did not perfect token ring until 1986, and Metcalfe believes that critical delay cost them the market.

In 1982, venture capitalists who controlled 3Com's board of directors refused to allow Metcalfe to continue running his own company. But in a decision he describes as "the hardest thing I ever did," he remained as vice-president of sales and marketing. Within two years, his charismatic zeal, belief in Ethernet, and hard work had dramatically increased the company's revenue, from nothing to more than U.S.$1 million per month. Soon ready to go public, 3Com offered its shares on 21 March 1984 at U.S.$6 per piece, earning Metcalfe a considerable personal fortune. But in August 1990, 3Com's board snubbed its founder once more, choosing a young engineer called Eric Benhamou (1955–) as the company's new chief executive officer (CEO). Benhamou would go on to turn 3Com into a U.S.$5 billion company; Metcalfe decided to leave.

So, in the 1990s, Metcalfe's career took a new direction. After spending a year as an academic at Cambridge University in England, he returned to California as publisher of the *InfoWorld* computer journal and chief technology officer (CTO) of its parent company, International Data Group (IDG). His new ambition to be a journalist found an outlet in *InfoWorld*'s infamous "From the Ether" column, which was published weekly until September 2000.

Using *InfoWorld* as his platform, Metcalfe reinvented himself as a self-proclaimed "technology pundit." But his views and analysis have frequently ruffled feathers—never more so than in December 1995, when he predicted that massively increasing traffic would cause the Internet to "go spectacularly supernova and in 1996 catastrophically collapse." The statement attracted considerable media attention, but despite teething troubles, the Internet backbone survived 1996 intact. The following year, in front of a delighted conference of industry professionals, Metcalfe delivered on a promise to eat his own words if his prediction was wrong by shredding his column in a blender and drinking the pulp.

The experience did little to temper Metcalfe's outspoken views. More recent predictions have been closer to the mark, notably his suggestion in fall 1999 that so-called "dot.com" Internet stocks have been massively overvalued and would soon see dramatic falls in their share price. Metcalfe's *InfoWorld* columns have made him an important commentator on contemporary issues, while his role as the inventor of Ethernet and the founder of 3Com ensure an important place for him in the history of computer networking.

Biography

Robert Metcalfe. Born 1946 in Brooklyn, New York. Graduated from Massachusetts Institute of Technology (MIT) in 1969 with a B.S. in electrical engineering and a B.S. in management from Sloan School of Management. Received M.S. in applied mathematics (1970) and Ph.D. in computer science (1973) from Harvard University. Worked at MIT, 1970–72. Joined Xerox Palo Alto Research Center (PARC) in 1972 and on 22 May 1973 wrote memo outlining Ethernet. Founded 3Com in June 1979, serving as chairman, chief executive officer, and in various other positions before retiring in 1990. Visiting academic at Wolfson College, Cambridge University, 1991-92. In 1992, became publisher of *InfoWorld* journal and chief technology officer of parent company, International Data Group. Recipient of many awards, including Association for Computing Machinery (ACM) Grace Murray Hopper Award, 1980; Institute of Electrical and Electronics Engineers (IEEE) Alexander Graham Bell Medal, 1988; San Francisco Exploratorium Public Understanding of Science Award, 1995; and IEEE Medal of Honor, 1996.

Selected Works

Metcalfe, Robert. "How Ethernet Was Invented." *Annals of the History of Computing*, Vol. 16, 1994, p. 81.

———. "From the Ether: Predicting the Internet's Catastrophic Collapse and Ghost Sites Galore in 1996." *InfoWorld*, 4 Dec. 1995.

———. *Internet Collapses and Other InfoWorld Punditry*. IDG Books Worldwide, 2000.

Metcalfe, Robert, and David Boggs. "Ethernet: Distributed Packet-Switching for Local Computer Networks." *Communications of the ACM*, Vol. 19, No. 7, July 1976, p. 395.

Further Reading

Ceruzzi, Paul E. *A History of Modern Computing*. Cambridge, Mass.: MIT Press, 1999.

Leiner, Barry, Vinton Cerf, David Clark, et al. "A Brief History of the Internet." *http://www.isoc.org/internet-history/brief.html*

Segaller, Stephen. *Nerds 2.0.1: A Brief History of the Internet*. New York: TV Books, 1998.

—*Chris Woodford*

Metropolitan Area Networks

Metropolitan area networks (MANs) support two-way communication over a shared medium, such as an **optical fiber** cable, and may offer point-to-point high-speed circuits or packet-switched communication. They were originally oriented exclusively toward data, but now often carry voice and video traffic as well. MANs do not have the large traffic-handling capability of a switched exchange network, such as the existing telephone system or the future broadband integrated-services digital network (BISDN), which will offer worldwide service. A cable television (CATV) network, which is essentially a broadcasting system, is not ordinarily classified as a MAN but can be modified to support two-way MAN service.

MANs for residential users are building out from the CATV mode, in parallel with the public telephone network, to accommodate a highly asymmetric traffic mix and the public thirst for visual distribution services, including entertainment. Most of the capabilities of these nearer-term models may some day be available in all-services optical network architectures. Ultimately expected to transmit data at rates of 1 megabit per second (Mb/s) or more within areas 50 kilometers or so in diameter, MANs serve industry and education as well as business and the home.

MAN topologies are derived from both the star topology of the telephone system (a central station connected to all single users) and the tree-and-branch configuration of the cable TV system. The star topology permits the transfer of data in the kilobit-per-second (kb/s) range between any two sites equipped with modems and at megabit-per-second rates between sites equipped with special 1.544-Mb/s circuits (2.048 Mb/s outside North America and Japan). The latter is costlier, typically requiring the equivalent of 24 voice circuits versus the modem's one voice circuit. In fact, with the existing twisted-pair local loops, even the much-discussed **ISDN** will provide ISDN basic service only at 144 kb/s.

Current CATV systems are not set up to transfer megabits per second between arbitrary sites. But their tree-and-branch topology is less to blame than their allocation of **bandwidth**. The two or three reverse channels available for transmission from the home are grossly outnumbered by the 50 or so forward channels (i.e., to receive information) on a typical cable system using subsplit allocation of channels, in which the reverse band occupies 5 to 30 megahertz (MHz), and the forward band 50 to 500 MHz. However, the bandwidth could be allocated using midsplit (5 to 116 and 168 to 400 MHz) or high-split (5 to 174 and 232 to 400 MHz) channels.

The forward and backward channels, used for upstream and downstream communication, do not have to be symmetrical in size. If asymmetrical data transfer is expected (e.g., if more data will be sent to the user than the user will send to the network), the forward channel out to the user should be larger in bandwidth size, in order to deliver the data to the user efficiently. One example of an application that would be well suited for a large outbound channel to the user and a relatively small inbound channel from the user to the source would be Web browsing, where the size of the data delivered to the user far exceeds the size of the data block sent in from the user.

FURTHER READING

Morreale, P., and G. Campbell. "Metropolitan Area Networks." *IEEE Spectrum*, Vol. 27, No. 5, May 1990.

—*Patricia Morreale*

Microcomputer

A microcomputer is generally defined as a computer based on a **microprocessor**. The term contrasts with the larger (and previously available) **minicomputers** and **mainframe** computers. Microcomputers provided the first truly portable computer affordable by individuals. A single-user microcomputer is normally known as a **personal computer** (PC). The phrase *home computer* has also sometimes been used for a microcomputer intended for utilization in the home. Workstations are traditionally more powerful single-user computers, but the distinction between PCs and workstations has become more blurred as microcomputers have increased in power.

The term *microcomputer* is also sometimes used to describe a complete computer implemented on a single chip (**central processing unit** [CPU], memory, and interface circuitry, compared to a microprocessor, which includes just the CPU). For example, as part of its 6800 microprocessor family, **Motorola** included the 6801, a microcomputer on a chip with 128 bytes of internal random access memory (**RAM**), 2 kilobytes (kB) of internal read-only memory (**ROM**), and four 8-bit input–output ports.

In January 1975, a photo of the Micro Instrumentation and Telemetry Systems' (MITS, based in Albuquerque) **Altair 8800** computer kit, often considered the first microcomputer, appeared on the front cover of *Popular*

Electronics in the United States. This was based on a 2-megahertz (MHz) **Intel** 8080 microprocessor, together with a tiny 256 bytes of RAM, available as a kit or assembled. No monitor or **keyboard** was included. Input was achieved using switches, and light-emitting diodes (LEDs) were used as a means of output. **Bill Gates** (1955–), then 19, with his high school friend **Paul Allen** (1953–), developed a version of **BASIC** for the Altair 8800, the first high-level microcomputer programming language, although this required the use of 4-kB memory boards.

In 1976, **Steve Jobs** (1955–) and **Steve Wozniak** (1950–) developed the **Apple I** microcomputer in a **Silicon Valley** basement. Its 1977 successor, the **Apple II**, became the first popular home computer; it had a monitor, **keyboard**, 16 kB of RAM, and 16 kB of ROM. The CPU was MOS Technology's 6502 microprocessor, first made available in 1975. In 1978, Apple added 5.25-inch floppy disk drives to the Apple II. Competing U.S. computers such as the Commodore PET (Personal Electronic Transactor, with an integral display screen, keyboard, and cassette tape drive), Tandy TRS-80, and Atari 400/800 games-oriented machines were also available in the late 1970s.

The first popular microcomputer application software was released in 1979: WordStar for **word processing**, **dBase** for **database management**, and most innovatively, VisiCalc for spreadsheets. These were the first major microcomputer programs of interest to non-programmers. In particular, VisiCalc encouraged business use of microcomputers.

In 1981, the first IBM personal computer (PC), based on the Intel 8088 microprocessor running at 4.77 MHz, and with a 160-kB floppy disk drive, was launched, including the MS-DOS operating system. DOS was developed by Microsoft, the company that Bill Gates started around his version of BASIC. In 1982, Compaq developed an IBM PC **clone**, providing the first of many alternative sources for PCs. The increasing popularity of PCs meant that alternative microcomputer operating systems such as CP/M were discontinued. Many companies, such as **Dell**, **Hewlett-Packard**, and **Sony**, subsequently manufactured PCs, ensuring their long-term survival.

Commodore continued producing successful microcomputers such as the VIC 20 (1981), **Commodore 64** (1982; containing the first audio chip for a home computer), and Amiga 1000 (1985; an early multimedia computer). Meanwhile, in the early 1980s, the U.K. microcomputer market was dominated by a succession of locally produced and relatively cheap microcomputers, notably the Z80 microprocessor-based ZX80 (1980; at less than £100), ZX81 (1981), and Spectrum (1982), produced by Sinclair, as well as the Atom (1981), followed by the BBC microcomputer (1982) from Acorn. All supported BASIC programming but not much else, with program storage on cassette tape and display on a standard television screen. At the time, the United Kingdom had more computers per head of population than anywhere else in the world. The availability of the much more practically useful IBM PC meant that this initial lead was not maintained.

Based on the Motorola 68000 microprocessor, with 128 kB of RAM and the first 3.5-inch 400-kB floppy disk drive, the Apple **Macintosh** became the first serious competitor to the IBM PC in 1984. Unlike the DOS-based PC, the Mac offered a **graphical user interface** (GUI). Microsoft realized the advantage of the Mac GUI and later produced **Windows**, the operating system that was to come to dominate microcomputers, as a GUI.

In terms of numbers, microcomputers have been much more successful than the previous generations of minicomputers and mainframes because they have become both increasingly useful and increasingly affordable. Although there have been promises of next-generation **network computers** (with functionality moved largely to the network), microcomputers have remained extremely popular since their inception in the 1970s. They have become even smaller with the advent of highly portable **laptop** computers in the 1990s.

FURTHER READING

Campbell-Kelly, Martin, and William Aspray. *Computer: A History of the Information Machine*. New York: Basic Books, 1996.

Ceruzzi, Paul E. *A History of Modern Computing*. Cambridge, Mass.: MIT Press, 1998.

Freiberger, Paul, and Michael Swaine. *Fire in the Valley: The Making of the Personal Computer*. Berkeley, Calif.: Osborne/McGraw-Hill, 1984; 2nd ed., New York: McGraw-Hill, 2000.

—*Jonathan Bowen*

Microprocessor

A microprocessor is an **integrated circuit** housed in a **semiconductor**, often known as a *chip* (or rarely, a set of chips), that implements the **central processing unit** (CPU) of a computer. Sometimes known as a *micro* for short, the semiconductor is normally manufactured of **silicon**, hence the term *silicon chip*. The invention of the microprocessor in the early 1970s has revolutionized the computer industry by allowing dramatically decreasing physical size and costs of computing and increasing the power of computing over the years.

In 1968, **Robert Noyce** (1927–90) and **Gordon Moore** (1929–) resigned from **Fairchild Semiconductor** and set up a new company called **Intel**, specializing in memory chips. In the summer of the following year, a Japanese calculator manufacturer called Busicom asked Intel to develop a set of chips for a new range of programmable electronic calculators. An initial design included 12 chips of 3000 to 5000 transistors each, advanced for the time. Marcian E. Hoff, Jr. (1937– ; "Ted" to his friends) was assigned to the job. Hoff held a B.S. in engineering from Rensselaer Polytechnic Institute in Troy, New York and a doctorate from Stanford University, in the heart of **Silicon Valley**. A consummate engineer, he concluded that Busicom's design was too complicated to be cost-effective. Most of the design was implemented in hardwired logic that was inflexible, although some of the calculator's functions were to be controlled by a read-only memory (**ROM**). Although Intel could have produced the chips, their complexity meant that yields would be low.

Hoff's solution was to develop a general-purpose logic chip that, like the CPU of a computer, could perform any of the tasks required. The *microprocessor* would be programmable like a conventional CPU, reading instructions and data from ROM and random access memory (**RAM**). To produce a different calculator, a new program could be written and placed in the ROM; thus Intel could produce general-purpose chips for a variety of customers. The design for the Busicom calculator was reduced from 12 chips to four (consisting of a microprocessor, ROM, RAM, and an input–output chip). The simpler design resulted in decreased cost and size, as well as increased reliability and flexibility. It was an innovation with great benefits and no significant drawbacks. Busicom accepted the design, albeit with little appreciation of its potential, and the first microprocessor, designated the 4004, was produced by Intel in late 1970.

Repair of a microchip was considered a problem, but Hoff suggested, much to the surprise of his colleagues, that a microprocessor could just be thrown away and replaced by a new one. This was a revolutionary idea for a computer at the time, since they were thought of as very expensive items. This is a small example of Hoff's tremendous insight.

The 4004 microprocessor was developed under exclusive contract with Busicom and thus could not be offered on the open market initially. However, Busicom requested a price reduction, and in exchange, Intel negotiated the right to market the 4004. But even Intel did not realize the potential of the microprocessor, assuming that it would be used primarily in calculators and **minicomputers**. It was released to the world in the 15 November 1971 issue of *Electronic News* as "a micro-programmable computer on a chip" and "a new era of integrated electronics."

The Intel 4004 was a 4-bit microprocessor in that its data **bus** was 4 bits wide, although its 45 instructions were 8 bits long. It was just part of the MCS-4 **microcomputer** system, consisting of four chips. The program and permanent data were to be held in one or

Intel 4004 microprocessor. (Courtesy of the Computer Museum History Center)

more 4001 mask-programmable (permanent) ROMs. For temporary storage, the 4002 RAM was available and output ports could be expanded using the 4003 register chip. This chip set made 4096 8-bit bytes of ROM storage (addressable by a 12-bit program counter) and 5120 bytes of RAM storage available. There were sixteen 4-bit (or eight 8-bit) general-purpose registers, an accumulator, a 4-bit parallel adder, and a pushdown four-level stack (e.g., for subroutines). The 4004 was implemented in a 16-pin dual in-line package (DIP) using only 2300 transistors. It was originally intended to run at a clock rate of 1 megahertz, but actually ran at 740 kilohertz (eight clock cycles per CPU cycle of 10.8 microseconds). The lack of power for general-purpose computing disguised the great potential of the microprocessor to many at this stage.

In 1972, Intel produced the 4040, an enhanced version of the 4004, that added 14 instructions, larger (eight-level) stack, 8 kilobytes (kB) of program space, and interrupt facilities (including copies of the first eight registers). An 8-bit 8008 was developed but not widely used. Subsequently, they produced the highly successful 8-bit 8080 microprocessor, which was sufficiently powerful to be useful as a basis for a simple microcomputer. The chip was packaged in a 40-pin DIP, as were many other microprocessors in the 1970s. The 8080 really brought the potential of microprocessor technology to wider attention. A slightly enhanced version, the 8085, was also widely used.

The obvious progression for microprocessors was to increase data and address bus widths (normally by powers of 2 for the data bus at least) and also to improve clock frequencies. Intel introduced the 16-bit 8086 (with 20 bits of addressing), together with an 8-bit version, the 8088. This developed into the 80186, 80286, 80386, 486, and **Pentium**. These were developed in a backwardly compatible manner and formed the basis of the highly successful IBM **personal computer** (PC) and subsequent clones that have come to dominate the world of computing. Hence Intel has maintained a leading role in the world of microprocessors throughout their development.

However, there have naturally been competitors in the field. Other manufacturers quickly followed Intel's lead once the potential for the technology was realized. Soon after the development of the 8080, the rival company Zilog was formed, including ex-Intel employees. The 8-bit Z80 was a significantly enhanced microprocessor that was backwardly compatible with the 8080. It formed the basis for many early microcomputers, such as the Sinclair ZX80, which brought the possibilities of the microprocessor to the attention of the public by making low-cost personal computing widely available. Zilog also produced the 16-bit Z8000, a very complex microprocessor for its time. Perhaps it was too complicated, since Zilog did not manage to keep up with Intel in the development of microprocessors subsequently.

Motorola produced important microprocessor families that included the 8-bit 6800 series in a standard 40-pin DIP. As well as the basic 6800, the family included the 6801, a microcomputer on a chip with 128 bytes of internal RAM, 2 kB of internal ROM, and four 8-bit input–output ports. The 6809 provided a more sophisticated instruction set. Even more influential was the 8- to 32-bit 68000 family. The 68000 formed the basis for the original **Sun Microsystems** and **Silicon Graphics** workstations with a 16-bit data bus and 24-bit address bus in a 64-pin DIP. The original **Macintosh** also used 68000 technology. The smaller and less widely used 68008 had an 8-bit data bus in a 48-pin DIP. The 68010 added virtual memory, important in the advancement of early workstations, and the 68020 provided a 32-bit data bus. Although many engineers regard Motorola microprocessors as better designed than the equivalents from Intel from a technical stance, they have not achieved the same market penetration.

Rockwell produced the important 8-bit 6502 that formed the basis of a number of early home computers, including the very successful **Apple II** and the BBC microcomputer that was popular in the United Kingdom. The RCA 8-bit CMOS microprocessor was used in early specialist low-power applications. Other microprocessors include the National Semiconductor 16-bit NS16000 and 32-bit NS32000, **Texas Instruments** 16-bit 9900 series, ARM, MIPS, PowerPC (the basis of the Power Mac from **Apple**), and the Inmos Transputer family. Sun Microsystems produced microprocessors based on the SPARC architecture for use in its workstations. Even the successful minicomputer manufacturer **Digital Equipment** produced 16-bit J-11 and the smaller T-11 microprocessors based on its well-known PDP-11 computer architecture. However, it failed to capitalize on the microprocessor revolution.

A single-chip microprocessor may include other components, such as memory (RAM, ROM, PROM [programmable read-only memory]), memory management, caches, floating-point unit, input–output ports, and timers. Such devices are also known as *microcontrollers* or sometimes *microcomputers*, although the latter term can confusingly refer to a computer based on a microprocessor as well.

The important characteristics of a microprocessor are the widths of its internal and external address bus and data bus (and instruction), its clock rate, and its instruction set. Processors are also often classified as either **RISC** (reduced instruction set computer) or CISC (complex instruction set computer). The more traditional microprocessors, from Intel and Motorola, for example, are CISC in style with many complex instructions, often designed to be backwardly compatible with previous generations from the same manufacturer. Later processors, such as SPARC, ARM, and MIPS, are RISC in style, with a smaller number of simpler instructions designed to run very fast. The burden is moved to the software writers to combine these instructions in efficient ways to produce a potentially faster system overall.

With the exponentially increasing number of transistors in a top of the range microprocessor, reliability and correctness are of increasing concern to microprocessor manufacturers. For example, a mistake in an Intel microprocessor **floating-point** unit caused the company's stock to drop significantly; Intel hardware is used in critical applications where an error could be very expensive. Manufacturers have increasingly moved to techniques allowing the correctness of hardware to be demonstrated mathematically. The FM8501 was an early, if little used microprocessor that was verified in its entirety by Computational Logic, Inc. Other partially verified microprocessors include the Viper and the Transputer floating-point unit. Model-checking tools now allow exhaustive scrutiny of significant parts of microprocessors.

Although the calculator manufacturer Busicom provided the original application that brought the microprocessor into being, they have since gone out of business. On the other hand, Intel has gone from strength to strength, becoming one of the major integrated-circuit manufacturing corporations, largely on the back of the personal computer revolution. They have worked in partnership with **Microsoft**, which produced the **DOS** and **Windows** operating systems to run on successive generations of Intel microprocessors.

The microprocessor has had a profound effect on the development of computing, since its introduction to the world in 1971. Speeds and complexity have increased exponentially, while size and cost have decreased similarly. The vast majority of computers in the world are based on microprocessors, and many more electronic devices have microprocessors embedded in them. Microprocessors range from simple devices costing a few cents, capable of undertaking a dedicated task (e.g., as a controller in an embedded system), to sophisticated processors capable of significant computation, especially when used in parallel. The impact is still being felt and developments continue apace. Eventually, the limitations of physics will be reached, and alternative technologies and parallelism will be required for further improvements.

FURTHER READING

Chandor, Anthony. *The Penguin Dictionary of Microprocessors.* Harmondsworth, Middlesex, England, and New York: Penguin Books, 1981.

Evans, Christopher. *The Mighty Micro: The Impact of the Computer Revolution.* London: Gollancz, 1979; new ed., 1982.

Hutcheson, G. Dan, and Jerry D. Hutcheson. "Technology and Economics in the Semiconductor Industry." *Scientific American*, Jan. 1996, p. 40.

Jackson, Tim. *Inside Intel: Andy Grove and the Rise of the World's Most Powerful Chip Company.* New York: Dutton, 1997.

Mayall, W. H. *The Challenge of the Chip.* London: Her Majesty's Stationery Office, Science Museum, 1980.

—*Jonathan Bowen*

Microprogramming

Microprogramming is a systematic technique of designing the control unit of a computer. Before describing how a microprogrammed computer is implemented, it would be helpful to explain how a computer works.

A modern computer consists of four main components: the input, output, memory, and processor. Memory stores data and program code. Input and output provide an **interface** between memory and physical devices. The processor retrieves and executes program instructions from memory.

The processor contains a data path and a control unit. The data path has the ability to access and alter information stored in memory. It includes a set of registers and an arithmetic-logic unit (ALU). The control unit issues *control signals* that direct the actions of the data path, memory, input, and output. Each signal tells its recipient what operation to perform and indicates when to perform it.

The basic operation of the data path, called here a *data path cycle*, consists of sending the contents of one or two of the registers to the ALU, performing an operation on the data with the ALU, and storing the result back into a register. The control unit determines which register or registers are gated to the ALU inputs, what operation the ALU performs, and to which register the result is stored. The control unit can also cause values from memory to be copied to registers in the data path, and vice versa. Using these two very basic operations, data path cycles and memory access, the control unit can fetch and execute instructions of a program stored in memory.

For example, the control unit issues control signals to memory, telling it to copy the next program instruction into a data path register. The control unit then determines (through a mechanism described later) that the instruction is an ADD instruction. The control unit will then fetch the two numbers to be added. It copies one, then the other, to data path registers using the same process that it used to fetch the instruction. Prompted by control signals, the registers holding the addends deliver their values to the ALU. The ALU then responds to control signals that tell it to add its inputs together. The sum is then stored in a register determined by the control unit. The control unit can then send control signals to cause the value of this register to be copied to memory. The next program instruction can now be fetched and executed in much the same manner.

Notice that the description of steps taken to run a program instruction resembles the description of the steps in a normal program. Much like a regular program, what takes place above is a sequence of basic operations that need to take place in order to complete a more complicated task: in this case, the execution of a program instruction. Each step (load from memory, data path cycle, store to memory) is described by a set of control signals, or *microinstruction.* The sequence of microinstructions needed to execute a set of program instructions, or *macroinstructions*, is called a *microprogram.* The microprogram is stored in a *control store*, a block of memory contained within the control unit.

Each microinstruction is responsible for two actions, issuing control signals to the hardware components and determining the next microinstruction to be executed. This is represented in the microinstruction as two fields, a word containing the control signals and a next address field. Each **bit** in the word corresponds to a single control signal, and its value is gated to the appropriate component. After the control signals are issued, the control unit fetches from the control store the microinstruction indicated by the next address field. Some microinstructions have more than one next-address field. The decision of which address to use is based on the state of data path components. For example, one address may be selected if the result of an ALU operation is zero, a second if the result, nonzero. This allows the microprogram to perform conditional branches as in a normal program.

A microprogram runs in an infinite loop, continually fetching, decoding, and executing macroinstructions. The main part of the microprogram fetches and decodes the macroinstruction, then jumps to the appropriate microprogram subroutine. The subroutine contains the sequence of microinstructions that run the specific macroinstruction.

In many computers, the opcode (operation code, the numerical representation of the instruction) of the macroinstruction is actually the address of a microinstruction. After an instruction has been loaded from memory into a register, the microprogram will jump to the control store address stored in the register instead of an explicitly defined next address. Thus a macroinstruction is merely a pointer to the first microinstruction in a microprogram subroutine.

In the early days of computing, the control unit of a computer was hardwired. In a hardwired control unit, the logic for control signal generation is implemented directly by permanent hardware circuitry. The early hardwired controls were designed in an ad hoc manner. The designer would draw block diagrams until one was created that satisfied functional requirements and looked reasonably economical. The result was a complex and unsystematic control unit.

While developing the **EDSAC**, **Maurice Wilkes** (1913–) of Cambridge University began to realize that the sequencing of control signals resembled the execution of a normal program. He developed the idea that the sequence of control signals could be represented in a stored program. This technique of control unit design, which Wilkes called *microprogramming*, was introduced in 1951 during a presentation at Manchester University. In this presentation, Wilkes described a control store consisting of a diode matrix. In the matrix were stored the control signals that comprised each microinstruction, followed by the address of the next microinstruction to be executed.

In 1953, Wilkes and colleague J. B. Stringer wrote a paper, "Microprogramming and the Design of the Control Circuits in an Electronic Digital Computer," that further described microprogramming. This paper explored some of the capabilities of microprogramming, including pipelining, exploiting parallelism of the data path, upgradable control stores, and the implementation of multiple **instruction sets**. Wilkes went on to build the EDSAC2 in 1957, which was the first microprogrammed computer.

Although it was immediately appreciated by theoreticians interested in a flexible, systematic control unit, microprogramming was not used by commercial computer manufacturers for nearly a decade. This was due primarily to the lack of a reliable, cheap, and fast control stores. By the 1960s, technology had caught up and microprogrammed computers were being developed for the consumer market.

In the early 1960s, **IBM** investigated microprogramming as a way to design a compatible line of computers. Wilkes had recognized in his papers that microprogramming could allow a single computer to implement several instruction sets with no change to the **central processing unit** (CPU) design. IBM was interested in the fact that the inverse was also true, that microprogramming allowed computers with vastly different CPUs to implement the same instruction set. Previous IBM computers were implemented with their own instruction sets, which proved to be a liability for consumers wishing eventually to upgrade their systems. At the time, most programs were written in low-level languages and were not compatible across different machines. Porting software to another architecture often meant rewriting the programs. Convinced that microprogramming would allow compatibility across an entire line of computers, IBM stepped up its development of memory technology. In 1964, after an investment of U.S.$5 billion, IBM announced the System/360 family of computers, the first series of computers compatible at the instruction set level. This was a development that was well received by consumers, and the 360 dominated the market.

Due to the large amount of incompatible **legacy software** in use at the time, IBM researched ways to run old programs on the 360. An initial solution was the use of software simulators, programs that would interpret the instructions of the incompatible programs. This approach invariably resulted in poor performance. Stewart Tucker of IBM presented the idea of implementing simulators in microcode. Tucker coined the term *emulation* to describe complete simulation at the microprogramming level. The new 360s were able to emulate the instruction sets of the older 1400 and 7000 series of IBM computers, sometimes offering better performance than the original hardware.

After IBM embraced microprogramming, many other manufacturers followed suit. Microprogramming quickly grew in popularity, and by the end of the 1960s, it was a common feature in control unit design. With the growing popularity of microprogramming came larger and more sophisticated instruction sets. These *complex instruction set computers* (CISCs) contained microcode implementations of certain large, complicated functions. The CISC design technique offered some significant economic and performance enhancements. The large set of powerful instructions supported by CISC architectures produced smaller programs, since more and more processing was being performed by the hardware. In these days of limited, expensive memory, this was a clear advantage. Memory was also slow. A simple fetch or store request could take tens of clock cycles. Smaller programs also meant fewer instructions had to be fetched from memory and decoded during execution. Also, a call to a microprogrammed subroutine was much more efficient than a call to a software subroutine. It was demonstrated that the performance of certain operations (e.g., polynomial multiplication and character scan operations) could be improved dramatically when implemented directly by hardware components. The DEC VAX-11/780, one of the most complicated of the CISC computers, supported over 300 different macroinstructions and over a dozen memory-addressing modes, and had a 500-kilobit control store.

There was also a growing interest in high-level programming. It was easier to compile high-level code to large instruction sets. Microprogrammers could even implement alternative architectures, such as stack-based architectures, that made the job of compiler designers easier yet. Control stores were initially read-only, but eventually writable control stores were developed to allow field modifications of the microprogram. IBM developed the 8-inch floppy diskette to distribute microcode patches.

During this time, technological advances were being made that would allow major changes in the way that control units could be implemented. More reliable memory could be produced much more cheaply than before. System cache, small memory units running near or at the internal frequency of the CPU, were becoming available, making memory access times closer to control store access times. CPU designers were also developing more disciplined methods of implementing hardwired control, which attracted much attention, as hardwired control units are much faster than microprogrammed control units. Improved compilers and the interest in high-level languages meant that fewer programs were being written at the instruction set level.

In 1980, David Patterson (1947–) and David Ditzel proposed a new model for CPU design, which they called the **reduced instruction set computer** (RISC). A RISC architecture is characterized by two features, a simplified hardwired control unit and a streamlined instruction set. The term *reduced instruction set* was intended to clearly establish the differences between RISC and CISC architectures and does not necessarily indicate a severely diminutive instruction set. The proposed RISC instruction set was comparable in size to earlier, more modestly sized instruction sets. More important to the RISC model than the size of the instruction set is its style. RISC instructions fall into two categories: instructions that transfer data between memory and CPU registers, and instructions that pass the contents of one or two registers to the ALU and store the result back into a register. These instructions tend to have fixed widths (fixed number of operands) and short execution times. Instructions of the second category can, after necessary decoding time, be executed in a single clock cycle.

One could point out that these simplified instructions tend to resemble highly encoded microinstructions, and thus RISC could be viewed as an alternative implementation of a microprogrammed control. Rather than having a fixed microprogrammed interpreter stored on the CPU, programs are compiled directly to microcode stored in memory.

The reduced amount of control circuitry in RISC-based computers yielded CPUs with simpler designs and smaller packaging. Despite these advantages, the computer community as a whole was initially hesitant to adopt RISC design principles. The fact that a program written for a RISC architecture used several times more instructions than a CISC program to complete certain tasks was a source of criticism from RISC skeptics. However, since the instructions are not interpreted, RISC machines could execute instructions several times as quickly as could CISC machines, resulting in an overall performance advantage.

Today, most high-performance CPUs are RISC-based, the notable exception being the Intel x86 family and compatibles. These processors use microprogramming to maintain compatibility to older computers, not because of any technological advantage of microcode. In fact, the **Intel** processors have become a hybrid of sorts, containing a RISC core that executes the simplest instructions in a single clock cycle and CISC circuitry that executes more complicated instructions by microprogram. Even though the use of mircrprogramming has diminished in recent years, its principles have influenced computer design in a way that continues to fulfill Wilkes's original goal of simple and systematic control circuitry.

FURTHER READING

Agrawala, Ashok K., and Tomlinson G. Rauscher. *Foundations of Microprogramming.* New York: Academic Press, 1976.

Husson, S. H. *Microprogramming: Principles and Practice.* Englewood Cliffs, N.J.: Prentice Hall, 1970.

Patterson, David A., and John L. Hennessy. *Computer Architecture: A Quantitative Approach.* San Mateo, Calif.: Morgan Kaufmann, 1990; 2nd ed., San Francisco, 1996.

———. *Computer Organization and Design: The Hardware/Software Interface.* San Mateo, Calif.: Morgan Kaufmann, 1994; 2nd ed., San Francisco, 1998.

Tanenbaum, Andrew S. *Structured Computer Organization.* Englewood Cliffs, N.J.: Prentice Hall, 1976; 4th ed., Upper Saddle River, N.J., 1999.

Wilkes, Maurice V. "The Genesis of Microprogramming." *Annals of the History of Computing,* Apr. 1986, pp. 116–126.

———. *Computing Perspectives.* San Francisco: Morgan Kaufmann, 1995.

Wilkes, Maurice V., and J. B. Stringer. "Microprogramming and the Design of the Control Circuits in an Electronic Digital Computer." *Proceedings of the Cambridge Philosophical Society,* Vol. 49, 1953. Reprinted in *Annals of the History of Computing,* Apr. 1986.

—*Dan Stone*

Microsoft

Under the visionary leadership of **Bill Gates** (1955–), Microsoft has become the largest and most influential **software** company in the world. Microsoft developed the industry standards for personal computer **operating systems** and graphical **interface** software with MS-DOS (Microsoft Disk Operating System) and **Windows**. They also developed widely used applications, including Microsoft Word, Excel, and PowerPoint. As the company grew, it expanded into desktop publishing, **CD-ROM**, **Internet**, and interactive television products.

The company was founded in 1975 by Gates and **Paul Allen** (1953–) in Albuquerque, New Mexico. During the early years, Microsoft specialized in developing software programming languages for personal computers, including **Fortran**, **BASIC**, and **COBOL**. In 1979, Microsoft moved to Bellevue, Washington, and the following year Gates hired his college friend Steve Ballmer to help recruit new employees.

By 1981, Microsoft had 129 employees and the number kept growing each year. They had a reported 21,298 employees by 1997. The company has a reputation for hiring people based on intelligence, or *intellectual bandwidth,* rather than industry experience. When most U.S. corporations were downsizing, Microsoft was hiring. Gates views reorganizations as vital to keeping company employees creatively challenged and efficient. Employees frequently move back and forth between product development and customer-related jobs.

Microsoft's early history is tainted by stories of manipulation and deceit over its development of **DOS** and its relationship with **IBM**. When IBM approached Digital Research, the leading supplier of disk operating software, to supply them with software for the IBM **personal computer** (PC), the two companies could not come to an agreement and a deal was not made. During a following visit to Microsoft to inquire about programming languages, the IBM representatives revealed that they needed operating system software. Allen knew about an operating system program called QDOS being developed by Tim Paterson (1956–) at Seattle Computer Products (SCP). Allen contacted Rod Brock, the president of SCP, and told him that a customer—whom Allen did not identify—was interested in sublicensing QDOS. The same day that they reached a verbal agreement with Brock, Microsoft submitted a preliminary proposal to IBM to supply them with operating system software. Brock later sued and received a settlement from Microsoft.

For a variety of reasons, IBM licensed the MS-DOS software instead of buying it outright from Microsoft. As a result, Microsoft could license the software to all PC-clone manufacturers, such as Compaq and Dell, when they entered the personal computer market. The IBM PC and PC clones running Microsoft's Disk Operating System (DOS) later became the industry standard for business and personal computers. Eventually, IBM lost control of the personal computer market while Microsoft dominated its software.

After creating MS-DOS, Gates decided that Microsoft would start developing **spreadsheet** and **word processing** programs that could be ported to as many different computers as possible. This was a unique idea at the time. In February 1981, Microsoft hired Charles Simonyi (1948–) away from the **Xerox Palo Alto Research Center** (PARC) to take over its applications development. Gates and Simonyi shared the same vision of creating software that would make computers easier to use. Gates wanted applications to become more important to Microsoft than its operating system software.

After Simonyi joined Microsoft, Gates met with **Steve Jobs** (1955–) about developing software applications for the new **Macintosh** with its **graphical user interface**. Gates agreed to develop three software applications: a spreadsheet, a business graphics program, and a database. Then, less than three weeks after Gates signed the agreement with **Apple Computer**, he and Allen started developing their own graphical user interface environment for DOS-based computers called Windows.

By 1983, Microsoft was the second-largest software company in the personal computer industry. At this point, Allen resigned as executive vice-president because he had Hodgkin's disease and needed immediate treatment. However, he remained on Microsoft's board of directors.

As a market leader, Microsoft employed a technique (also favored by IBM in its heyday) to keep customers from flocking to a competitor's product by announcing that their product, when finished, would be significantly better. Consequently, they announced Windows before the product was ready. But the delay of Windows became an embarrassment for Microsoft, and it was seen as another example of *vaporware*, an industry term that is used to describe a product that has been announced but that does not actually seem to exist.

Throughout the development of Windows, Microsoft maintained its relationship with IBM. During the summer of 1985, they announced a new pact called the Joint Development Agreement (JDA) to codevelop a new version of DOS. Microsoft called this new version DOS 5 and IBM turned the project into **OS/2**. After the announcement of this agreement, Microsoft's stock was traded publicly on the New York Stock Exchange for the first time and it hit U.S.$90.75 a share. Shortly afterward, Gates became a billionaire. But cultural clashes emerged between the programming styles of Microsoft and IBM employees, making it difficult for them to develop jointly. In the spring of 1988, IBM joined the Open Software Foundation (OSF) along with numerous other companies to develop a unified version of the **Unix** operating system. This move angered Gates and contributed to the tensions growing between the two companies.

In 1989, Microsoft began focusing on Windows as a new interface for DOS. This would be the third version of the Windows product. Over the years, Microsoft had followed a three-step software development pattern. The first version of a new product generally worked badly and it let Microsoft find out what customers really wanted. The second was a more serious attempt, but it still was not quite right. The third time proved to be the charm; on 22 May 1990, Microsoft launched Windows 3.0 amid a fanfare of publicity.

But the success of Windows 3.0 started a final separation process between Microsoft and IBM. The companies negotiated an agreement leaving DOS and Windows with Microsoft and OS/2 with IBM. On 17 September 1990, it was announced that they would no longer work together, but they would be able to sell the products developed by each other, and IBM decided to license Windows from Microsoft. After the break, Microsoft continued to upgrade and refine its Windows software.

Again, like IBM, the U.S. government began to investigate Microsoft for monopolistic practices. In 1994, Microsoft signed a consent agreement with the U.S. Department of Justice and the European Union regarding potential antitrust violations, but it was appealed successfully the following year. Nonetheless, Microsoft's antitrust troubles had only begun.

With the August 1995 release of Windows '95, Microsoft had achieved dominance in the marketplace and overwhelmed the competition. Gates was quickly becoming the richest man in the world. Microsoft's strategy for the 1990s was to make Windows the standard interface for all types of digital devices. But they were caught offguard by the popularity of **Netscape** and the **World Wide Web**. As a result, they immediately began developing their own Web browser, called Internet Explorer; the decision to include (or bundle) the browser with the Windows operating system would become the cornerstone of the government's future antitrust case against the company.

During the 1990s Microsoft began to expand beyond operating system and application software programs, and it appeared that there was no software domain that could be beyond their control. Microsoft established its own internal research groups in computer science and expanded into the online services and Internet markets. Hired in 1991, Nathan Myhrvold (1960–), a Ph.D. in theoretical physics, quickly rose through the ranks of Microsoft as head of the company's research and advanced development work. By 1995, he was a group vice-president and a member of Microsoft's Office of the President. Moreover, Myhrvold has been an influential counsel in the strategic planning of the company. Microsoft is currently exploring new opportunities in *media convergence*, the merging of computers, television, and telecommunications in a digital communication environment.

One opportunity that the company has explored is developing an online service. Microsoft conceived the MSN network as an information and service network using proprietary software. But by the time it was launched, Microsoft's primary competition was the World Wide Web rather than other online services. The Web had become popular because of its openly published standards. As a result, Microsoft was forced to rethink its networking strategies.

In 1995, Microsoft joined with General Electric's NBC television network to create multimedia products and interactive television programs. They have also made investments in companies involved with the integration of the Internet and television. In software development, Microsoft focused on its Windows NT operating system to attempt eventually to displace the Unix system as the preferred choice for corporate computer networking. In 1999, Microsoft launched Microsoft Office 2000, viewed by the company as a tool to support "Knowledge Workers Without Limits," and they announced Windows DNA (Distributed interNet Architecture), an integrated platform for building and operating distributed Web applications.

By the year 2000, Microsoft Windows was the technology standard, utilized by almost 90 percent of all personal computers. After years of legal battles, Judge Thomas Penfield Jackson (1937–) ruled that Microsoft was a monopolistic predator and that they had repeatedly violated U.S. antitrust laws. (See **Microsoft, United States v.** for more information on the case.) Gates appealed the decision and contended that Microsoft harnessed the power of personal computers to make lives better and that, as he states in a widespread advertising campaign, the "best is yet to come."

FURTHER READING

Cringely, Robert X. *Accidental Empires: How the Boys of Silicon Valley Make Their Millions, Battle Foreign Competition, and Still Can't Get a Date.* New York: Harper Business, 1996.

Cusumano, Michael A., and Richard W. Selby. *Microsoft Secrets: How the World's Most Powerful Software Company Creates Technology, Shapes Markets, and Manages People.* New York: Free Press, 1995.

Gates, Bill, with Nathan Myhrvold and Peter Rinearson. *The Road Ahead.* New York: Viking, 1995; rev. ed., New York: Penguin Books, 1996.

Rohm, Wendy Goldman. *The Microsoft File: The Secret Case Against Bill Gates.* New York: Times Business, 1998.

Stross, R. E. *The Microsoft Way: The Real Story of How the Company Outsmarts its Competition.* Reading, Mass.: Addison-Wesley, 1996.

—*Susan B. Barnes*

Microsoft, United States v.

In May 1998 the U.S. government, along with a number of U.S. states and the District of Columbia, filed complaints against **Microsoft** in the U.S. District Court. The complaints asserted that Microsoft had violated a number of federal and state antitrust laws, including a claim of illegal maintenance of a monopoly. Two years later, District Court Judge Thomas Penfield Jackson (1937–) entered a judgment against Microsoft, ordering that Microsoft be broken into two companies: **operating systems** and applications. The breakup and other remedies ordered against Microsoft were all stayed (put on hold) by the judge until Microsoft has the opportunity to complete all its appeals.

The May 1998 filing of the complaints against Microsoft was not the first time U.S. antitrust authorities had filed an enforcement action against this leading American technology company. In 1994, Microsoft and the government agreed to a consent decree to end one such investigation. A consent decree is a court order that is the result of agreement between a government enforcement agency and a company or person that the agency is investigating. If a company can reach agreement with the government, it can avoid the time and expense of defending itself against a government investigation without admitting that it did anything wrong. Microsoft and the Justice Department reached an agreement in 1994 that resulted in a consent decree being entered in 1995.

Under the 1995 consent decree, Microsoft agreed to change the way that it priced its **Windows** operating system software. Microsoft also agreed that it would not force any buyer who wanted to purchase Microsoft's operating system software to purchase other Microsoft software.

In October 1997, the U.S. government, through the Justice Department, filed a proceeding in U.S. District Court asserting that Microsoft had violated the 1995 consent decree and was forcing buyers who wanted its operating system software to take its **World Wide Web** browsing software, known as Internet Explorer. The Justice Department asked Judge Jackson to find Microsoft in contempt of court for violating the court-ordered 1995 consent decree and impose severe monetary fines against Microsoft for these actions.

In December 1997, Judge Jackson refused to find Microsoft in contempt of court but agreed with the Justice Department that Microsoft's actions were in violation of the 1995 consent decree. Judge Jackson issued a new court order, a preliminary injunction, that specifically prohibited Microsoft from requiring purchasers of its Windows software to take Microsoft's Internet Explorer software.

Microsoft promptly made available versions of its Windows software that it believed complied with the preliminary injunction. The Justice Department disagreed and again, in January 1998, asked Judge Jackson to find Microsoft in contempt of court, this time for failure to comply with the December 1997 preliminary injunction. On the eve of an important hearing on that request, Microsoft and the Justice Department reached an agreement that Microsoft would make available a new version of Windows that the Justice Department accepted as in compliance with the preliminary injunction.

The filing of the two complaints in May 1998 opened up a broad set of new claims against Microsoft and also continued the government's assertion first made in the fall of 1997 that Microsoft was illegally tying, or **bundling**, its Internet Explorer software to its Windows software. Bundling is a complex concept in U.S. antitrust law that at its most basic level involves an assertion that a buyer who wants one product that is highly desirable is being forced to buy a second product that the buyer would otherwise not want. The complaints asserted that the alleged bundling of Explorer with Windows was in violation of antitrust law. This was an important difference from the proceeding started in the fall of 1997, where the government asserted that similar actions were a violation of the 1995 consent decree but did not assert the claim that the antitrust laws were also violated.

The May 1998 complaints also included other claims. One of the most important claims was that Microsoft was engaging in illegal activities to maintain a monopoly. Simply having a monopoly is not a violation of U.S. antitrust law; engaging in illegal activities to obtain or maintain that monopoly is. Under U.S. antitrust law a company that sells a certain percentage, usually 75 percent or more, of the products in a specific product market has a monopoly. The Justice Department asserted that Microsoft had more than 75 percent of the market for personal computer operating system software. The complaints also asserted that Microsoft was engaging in illegal activities in an attempt to monopolize the market for Internet browsers, essentially leveraging its operating system monopoly to monopolize the browser market.

In June 1998, the Court of Appeals for the District of Columbia issued a ruling in Microsoft's favor, ruling that Judge Jackson had been in error in ruling against Microsoft in December 1997. What was before the Court of Appeals at that time was only Judge Jackson's preliminary injunction that prohibited Microsoft from requiring purchasers of its Windows software to take Microsoft's Internet Explorer software as well. Judge Jackson's decision was based on his reading of the provisions of the 1995 consent decree. The broader antitrust tying claims made in the May 1998 complaints were not part of that decision and were therefore not before the Court of Appeals in June 1998.

Nevertheless, the Court of Appeals decision contained discussions of general antitrust law principles that, although not yet binding law, raised serious questions in the minds of many observers about the strength of the bundling theories in the May 1998 complaints. Potentially very damaging to the government's claims was broad language in the June 1998 Court of Appeals decision that suggested that judges were very ill equipped to apply current law to the complexities of designing high-technology products such as software.

The trial against Microsoft began in October 1998 in front of Judge Jackson. It involved thousands of pages of written testimony, thousands of pages of documents and other exhibits, and over 60 days of live testimony in court, and it concluded in June 1999. Most observers consider the case to have been tried quite fast given the complexities of the legal and factual issues. Microsoft asserted at various times that the case had moved too quickly, depriving it of the right to defend itself fully.

Judge Jackson issued his Findings of Fact in November 1999. Because there was no jury, it was part of Judge Jackson's responsibilities to determine which evidence he believed and what that evidence established. His Findings of Fact were a major victory for the government, agreeing with many parts of the government's evidence and setting the stage for the judge's Conclusions of Law that were issued in April 2000.

The Conclusions of Law found against Microsoft on many critical points. The judge concluded that (1) Microsoft's Windows family of personal computer operating system software was a monopoly; (2) Microsoft had engaged in illegal activities to protect that monopoly; (3) Microsoft had illegally tied browser software to its monopoly Windows software; and (4) Microsoft had engaged in illegal activity in an effort to obtain a monopoly over browser software. However, the judge rejected some of the government claims, including the claim that Microsoft had entered into illegal contracts with Internet service providers and others that required them to promote Microsoft's Internet Explorer browsing software exclusively.

On 7 June 2000, Judge Jackson entered his judgment against Microsoft. In the memorandum issued by the judge at that time, he called Microsoft "untrustworthy," mentioning that one reason he reached this conclusion was the way that Microsoft had behaved in the prior proceeding when he issued the December 1997 preliminary injunction against Microsoft.

The case then moved into the phase where Microsoft hopes it will reverse Judge Jackson's judgment against it—the appeals process. As of January 2001, the U.S. Court of Appeals was overseeing the appeal of Judge Jackson's ruling. Many observers have suggested that the changing of the presidential guard will bring with it a change in Justice Department priorities; some have suggested that a Bush administration might drop the case entirely. Meanwhile, the attorneys general of numerous states have vowed to continue the fight.

When this case is finally concluded, it will provide valuable lessons on how the Sherman Antitrust Act, passed by Congress at the close of the nineteenth century, will be applied to the complex twenty-first-century world of software, hardware, biotechnology, and the Internet.

FURTHER READING

Brinkley, Joel, and Steve Lohr. *U.S. v. Microsoft: The Inside Story of the Landmark Case.* New York: McGraw-Hill, 2000.

Edstrom, Jennifer, and Marlin Eller. *Barbarians Led by Bill Gates: Microsoft from the Inside.* New York: Holt, 1998.

Leibowitz, Stan J., and Stephen E. Margolis. *Winners, Losers & Microsoft: Competition and Antitrust in High Technology.* Oakland, Calif.: Independent Institute, 1999.

Rivlin, Gary. *The Plot to Get Bill Gates: An Irreverent Investigation of the World's Richest Man... and the People Who Hate Him.* New York: Times Business, 1999.

—*Rich Gray*

MIDI

MIDI, an acronym for musical instrument digital **interface**, is the standard protocol and interface for communication between computers, synthesizers, and other digital instruments, such as

MIDI sound modules, samplers, and MIDI flute or guitar controllers.

A MIDI message consists of a status **byte** that is usually followed by one or two data bytes. There are many different MIDI messages, such as "key on," "key off," "pitch bend change," "program change," "channel aftertouch," and so on. Such messages tell the instrument which note to play and for how long.

MIDI specifies 16 separate channels: That is, with a single cable up to 16 different instruments can be controlled. Channel messages are sent only to one instrument, whereas system messages are sent to all instruments at once. The most basic channel message is "note on," which starts playing a note, while a "note off" message releases the key. MIDI messages are processed by MIDI sequencers. MIDI sequencer software can record, play back, and edit MIDI data and usually present it in some sort of note layout.

Before MIDI was introduced, different manufacturers used their own proprietary methods to communicate between musical instruments. The MIDI specification was written in 1984 and the first MIDI processing unit, the MPU-401, was later introduced by the Ronald company. Since 1984 there have been many enhancements and updates to the MIDI protocol, such as the inclusion of new controller messages. Although MIDI has many limitations (e.g., 16 channels and relatively slow communication speed), it has remained the de facto standard for digital musical instruments.

The standard MIDI file format is used to exchange complete MIDI music files between programs. A MIDI music file can sound different if played on different MIDI instruments because the same MIDI program number can be assigned to any instrument voice, and the same instrument can be assigned to different channels. The General MIDI System Level 1 (GM) was introduced in 1991 to give a standard configuration to MIDI systems.

General MIDI uses a fixed assignment of the first 10 channels; for example, channel 10 is used for percussion. All 128 program numbers are preassigned to specific sounds; for example, program 1 corresponds to "acoustic piano" and program 17 to "drawbar organ." General MIDI System Level 2, which was defined in 1999, is an extension of the original General MIDI standard.

Further Reading

Roads, Curtis. *The Computer Music Tutorial.* Cambridge, Mass.: MIT Press, 1996.

Rossing, Thomas D. *The Science of Sound.* Reading, Mass.: Addison-Wesley, 1982; 2nd ed., 1990.

—*Petri Kuittinen*

MIME

MIME is an acronym for *multipurpose Internet mail extension*. The MIME standard is useful for the transmission of multimedia and other kinds of data files using **electronic mail** messages.

Part of the success of e-mail is that it borrows from physical mail a loose coupling between addressing and content. Users can send many kinds of content to the same address, and the same content to many addresses, and they can read content generated on many different platforms and send to an equal variety. The technical vehicle for the universality of content is the **ASCII** character encoding, which can be assumed readable on any modern computer. Moreover, any modern e-mail system can transmit and receive ASCII messages.

Although adequate for several billions of e-mail messages annually, ASCII is limiting in some respects. It makes no provision for diacritical marks (e.g., the umlaut), for typeface formatting, for the glyphs of languages not written with the Roman alphabet, and certainly not for images, sound, executable content, or other richly structured data. In fact, many otherwise healthy e-mail systems simply reject messages that include such simple extensions to ASCII as accented characters.

MIME addresses these constraints. Five documents, designated RFC 2045-2049, issued by the Internet Engineering Task Force (IETF) in November 1996, define standard extensions to ASCII applicable to e-mail. These provide technical definitions that allow new types of content to be encoded as ASCII, so that existing e-mail systems can be used to transport the extended content, including images and sounds. They replace earlier and more limited forms of MIME published officially in 1993.

With this background, MIME can be understood in terms of three dimensions: the varieties of extended content that it recognizes, its specific technical encoding, and the transport mechanisms, including but not limited to e-mail, that respect MIME. MIME makes it possible to handle message bodies in non-ASCII character sets such as accented characters, which most e-mail systems can process without modification; alphabets such as the cyrillic, which most e-mail systems can deliver, although fewer display it properly; and Arabic, Hebrew, oriental ideographic scripts such as Chinese, and all other human languages, which few e-mail systems handle at all.

MIME specifies that *binary data*—anything other than ASCII—may be encoded as ASCII using either the "quoted printable" or "base64" transforms. Standard libraries that perform these encodings and corresponding decodings are widely available.

Finally, it is important to realize that the MIME specification can apply to any transport that accommodates ASCII content. In fact, MIME might already be in more widespread use for Web (Hypertext Transport Protocol [**HTTP**]) content than it is for e-mail messages. It is also common to see MIME used with the Network News Transport Protocol (NNTP, the basis of **Usenet**), and MIME frequently is adopted for a wide variety of networking transmissions, including proprietary ones. This takes MIME far afield from mail or multimedia. When programmers think of MIME in the year 2000, it is simply a standard definition for encoding extended content to deliver across a channel constrained to handle only ASCII.

FURTHER READING

Rhoton, John. *Programmer's Guide to Internet Mail: SMTP, POP, IMAP, and LDAP.* Boston: Digital Press, 2000.

Rose, Marshall T., and David Strom. *Internet Messaging.* Upper Saddle River, N.J.: Prentice Hall, 1998.

—*Cameron Laird*

Minicomputer

From the mid-1960s, the introduction of reliable, inexpensive **transistors** and then **integrated circuits** made it possible to build smaller, less costly computers. **Mainframe** computers, which often were so expensive that they were shared by more than one university or company, increasingly were replaced by minicomputers owned by a single school, research institution, or business. Thus minicomputer refers to a computer of relatively modest size and price compared to early mainframe computers, although larger and more expensive than present-day **microcomputers**.

The minicomputer came out of U.S. universities; it was not developed by existing computer companies. One of the earliest, best known, and most successful minicomputer firms was **Digital Equipment Corporation** (DEC), founded in 1957 by **Kenneth H. Olsen** (1926–) and Harlan Anderson, two former staff members of the Massachusetts Institute of Technology's Lincoln Laboratories. DEC initially sold circuit modules, but by 1960 DEC was ready to sell its first programmed data processor, the PDP-1. The design of this machine resembled that of an early transistorized computer, the TX-0, which Olsen and other DEC personnel had worked on at Lincoln Labs.

DEC built relatively small, less costly machines by using transistors instead of **vacuum tubes** for electronic components, by having smaller memories, and by using word lengths of 18 bits (on the PDP-1) or only 12 bits (on the PDP-8) instead of the 36-bit word used on many mainframe computers. This limited the number of memory addresses and the number of digits available in calculations. Early minicomputer manufacturers also provided only **hardware**, leaving it to customers to develop **software**. Only a few peripherals were available and marketing was not extensive. DEC was willing to sell customers its machines outright, rather than renting them on a monthly basis as mainframe computer makers did at the time. It also provided detailed descriptions of the computer's circuits and charged only a fraction of what a larger computer would cost.

About 50 PDP-1's were produced, and their success persuaded DEC to develop several smaller computers in the **PDP** series, most notably the PDP-8, introduced in 1965. The PDP-8 sold for only U.S.$18,000 (compared to U.S.$120,000 for the PDP-1), and occupied much less space than its predecessors. DEC manufactured some 1200 PDP-8's in the original form of the machine and continued to make improved versions, at lower cost and smaller size, through the 1970s. Some 40,000 units of the PDP-8 series eventually sold.

By the late 1960s, integrated circuits were sufficiently cheap and durable to be incorporated in minicomputers. New companies, as well as new divisions of older computer companies, rushed to take advantage of the new market. About 100 such firms introduced minicomputers between 1968 and 1972. Successful companies included Data General, Prime Computer, Interdata, and Varian Associates. By this time, minicomputer makers generally settled on using a 16-bit word length (the word length would increase over time, but remained a power of 2). From the introduction of Data General's "Super Nova" in 1971, integrated circuits came to replace magnetic cores as the random access memory of minicomputers. DEC's PDP-11, introduced in 1970, offered another innovation. In most earlier computers, the central processing unit continually monitored and controlled interactions between memory and input/output devices. However, the PDP-11 had a standard set of wires, each carrying one bit of data, that served as a data bus, sending, receiving and exchanging data without processor intervention.

The first minicomputers were designed for relatively sophisticated users. But although scientists and engineers remained important users of minicomputers, their use expanded as the price went down. Minicomputers were increasingly incorporated into other instruments, as microprocessors might be today. Moreover, in 1969, with funding from the U.S. Department of Defense's Advanced Research Projects Administration (**ARPA**), large computers at four separate locations were linked together to form the first four nodes of the **ARPANET**, the forerunner of the Internet. At each of these four sites, a DDP-516 minicomputer made by **Honeywell** served as an interface message processor (IMP), handling incoming and outgoing data.

From as early as 1962, minicomputers were configured so that they could be used simultaneously by more than one person. By the time DEC introduced the PDP-11, it offered software designed specifically for time-sharing. In so doing, it developed a version of the **BASIC** programming language, which would greatly influence early companies selling software for microcomputers, particularly Microsoft. In the late 1970s, Wang Laboratories extended the use of time-sharing to the office, introducing systems of word processors linked to a central minicomputer. With these machines, which were designed specifically to require no knowledge of programming, minicomputers had moved very far indeed from their original status as devices sold primarily as hardware. In this same period, more powerful minicomputers such as DEC's **VAX** had many of the capabilities of a mainframe computer of the 1960s.

The markets developed by minicomputers—in the laboratory, within other instruments, in networking, and in the office—have expanded greatly since the 1970s. However, in the last 20 years microcomputers and special software have come to play many of the roles once held by minicomputers.

FURTHER READING

Ceruzzi, Paul. *A History of Modern Computing*. Cambridge, Mass., and London: MIT Press, 1998.

Kidder, Tracy. *The Soul of a New Machine*. New York: Modern Library, 1997.

Pearson, Jamie. *Digital at Work: Snapshots from the First Thirty-Five Years*. New York.: Prentice Hall, 1992.

—*Peggy Aldrich Kidwell*

Minsky, Marvin Lee

1927–

U.S. Scientist

Respected now as one of the "fathers" of **artificial intelligence** (AI), together with **Claude Shannon** (1916–2001), **John McCarthy** (1927–), and others, Minsky built in 1951what was effectively the first artificial **neural network** as part of his Ph.D. work. Minsky initially studied psychology at Harvard, but unhappy with the behaviorist approach prevalent there, he switched to mathematics, which allowed him to explore more formally a cognitive approach to psychology, and hence brain function.

The principle underlying artificial neural networks (ANNs) is that a number of simple elements (neurons), which individually have extremely limited capability, may achieve considerably greater power when interconnected as a network. This idea is loosely modeled on the structure of the brain, in that the network's properties emerge as a consequence of highly complex, and evolving, structure. Although his machine had limited success, Minsky continued his work in attempting to describe psychological processes in computational terms, and with John McCarthy he founded the **MIT Artificial Intelligence Laboratory** in 1959.

The period from about 1945 to the late 1960s is the time when what is sometimes called the first generation of ANNs were developed. Warren McCulloch (1898–1969) and Walter Pitts (1923–69), two of Minsky's mentors, developed the first artificial neuron in 1943, and in 1957 Rosenblatt's *perceptron* appeared. Minsky then achieved international prominence with publication of his report *Perceptrons* (with **Seymour Papert** [1928–], 1969), which was a response to the work of Rosenblatt and others in this field.

In *Perceptrons*, Minsky showed that certain fundamental elementary logical operations were not possible with the topology and **algorithms** available. In practice, this meant that perceptron networks were unable to classify as different certain very simple distinct inputs. The importance of Minsky's paper was that his criticism was based on scrupulous mathematical argument, demonstrating the serious theoretical shortcomings in the capability of the perceptron model to distinguish two similar objects. The force and elegance of Minsky's argument were such that funding for research into ANNs was effectively ended for almost 20 years until the backpropagation algorithm was devised by Rumelhart and McClelland. Arguably, however, Minsky and Papert's work had much to do with AI subsequently having a serious, respectable theoretical foundation.

All his academic life, Minsky has been at pains to point out that what we call consciousness, or feelings, are not impenetrable mysteries. His primary interest has been in computational neuroscience; that is, how mental processes can be formally described. However, he is concerned not just with how the brain works, but with how cognitive processes (including emotions) arise.

The publication in 1986 of *The Society of Mind* represented the culmination of almost 20 years of work. This book proposes that "mind" is an emergent property of the brain, by virtue of the interaction of a vast number of diverse agents. He has said that "minds are simply what brains do." According to this view, the brain is an immensely complex machine, but in principle our lack of current understanding is due simply to its complexity. For instance, there was no understanding, 200 years ago, of the distinct but interacting chemical and biological processes that enable our physical body to regulate temperature, repair tissue, or manage electrolyte balance. There was a view that living beings demonstrated the existence of some invisible "vital force." Similarly, Minsky argues, we will one day understand how the brain's processes give rise to mind, and there will be no need for speculation about a spiritual or psychical force. Emotions will also be viewed as cognitive processes—that is, special ways of thinking. Minsky is thus one of the most outspoken proponents of "hard AI," the notion that building artificially intelligent beings will someday be possible.

In addition to this work in the theoretical foundations of AI, Minsky has been active in many other areas. He developed a revolutionary microscope with exceptional resolution, has been active in many areas of **robotics**, and retains interest in musical synthesis, education, and **computer science**. He developed frames, which allow the currently fashionable notion of object orientation in AI research. Since 1990, Minsky has been Toshiba Professor of Media Arts and Sciences, and Professor of Electrical Engineering and Computer Science at the Massachusetts Institute of Technology.

BIOGRAPHY

Marvin Lee Minsky. Born 9 August 1927 in New York City. Attended Bronx High School of Science and Phillips Academy, Massachusetts. Joined Navy, 1945. B.A. in mathematics from Harvard, 1950. Ph.D. in mathematics from Princeton University, 1954. Founder and co-director of Massachusetts Institute of Technology AI Laboratory, 1959–74. Co-authored *Perceptrons*, 1968. Became the Donner Professor of Science, MIT, 1974; became the Toshiba Professor of Media Arts and Sciences, and Professor of Electrical Engineering and Computer Science, MIT, 1990 to present. Recipient of numerous honors and awards including ACM Turing Award, 1969; Science and Technology Foundation Japan award, 1990; International Joint Conference on Artificial Intelligence Research Excellence award, 1991; and Dickinson College Joseph Priestley award, 1995.

SELECTED WORKS

Minsky, Marvin. *Semantic Information Processing.* Cambridge, Mass.: MIT Press, 1968.

———. *The Society of Mind.* New York: Simon and Schuster, 1986.

Minsky, Marvin, and Seymour A. Papert. *Perceptrons: An Introduction to Computational Geometry.* Cambridge, Mass.: MIT Press, 1969; expanded ed., 1988.

FURTHER READING

Dennett, Daniel C. *Kinds of Minds: Towards an Understanding of Consciousness.* New York: Basic Books, 1996.

Franklin, Stan. *Artificial Minds.* Cambridge, Mass.: MIT Press, 1995.

Pinker, Steven. *How the Mind Works.* New York: Norton, 1997.

—*David Brunskill*

MIT Artificial Intelligence Laboratory

The Artificial Intelligence Laboratory at the Massachusetts Institute of Technology (MIT) was founded in 1959 by **Marvin Minsky** (1927–) and **John McCarthy** (1927–), two young professors who would later become highly renowned in the **artificial intelligence** (AI) field. The lab continues to exist, with the stated objective to "understand human intelligence at all levels, including reasoning, perception, language, development, learning...and to build useful artifacts based on intelligence." Academic surveys in the United States consistently rank the MIT AI lab as first in its class, followed by the AI labs at Stanford and Carnegie Mellon University.

The strength of the MIT AI lab arose from its willingness to face "grand challenge" problems at every stage of its history. Some important ideas that would later become incorporated into the mainstream of **computer science** were actual MIT AI lab projects. This is the case, for example, with bit-mapped displays, computer algebra programs, the **Connection Machine** architecture, and **operating systems** research. Such undertakings, despite their thin connection to cognitive science, were started at the lab because they pertained to the frontiers of knowledge, and AI has always been at the frontier of computer science.

There is no other AI laboratory as legendary as the one at MIT, and no other that has produced so many world-class researchers in the field. There are even songs composed by former students, always ready to poke fun at the LISP tradition of the lab:

Sung to the tune of "Alice's Restaurant" by Arlo Guthrie.

You can hack anything you want on MIT LISP machines
You can hack anything you want on MIT LISP machines
Walk right in and begin to hack
Just push your stuff right onto the stack
You can hack anything you want on MIT LISP machines
(But don't forget to fix the bug...on MIT LISP machines!)

LISP and LISP machines figure high in the list of accomplishments of the AI Lab at MIT (see box). John McCarthy developed the first versions of the language, and other variants, such as Scheme, were also designed there. The first LISP machines were built at the lab and were especially developed to speed up the language and make more ambitious applications possible. Two companies spun off from MIT to market LISP machines, the most important being Symbolics, which was founded in the early 1980s, but faltered 10 years later.

The MIT AI Lab has been traditionally strong in **robotics** and **computer vision**. Members of the lab take pride in having developed methods for finding the shape of objects from video images and the microworld approach to AI. In this setting, a robotic hand could be directed, using natural language commands, to place or remove blocks from a pile of objects. This was a dramatic achievement for a vision and robotic system in the 1970s.

Currently, the MIT lab pioneers a different approach to AI that has been called *nouvelle AI.* Rodney Brooks (1954–), the director of the lab, has developed a new methodology for building intelligent systems, which consists not in trying to emulate human intelligence first but lower and more specialized "intelligences," such as those of insects. Brooks builds robots and lets them move in a real environment. This is the "situated" and "embodied" approach to AI. Only by letting the program have a body and move in the real world, that is, only by letting the program control a robot, is there an immediate feedback to the researcher on the adequacy of his theories. In Brooks's *subsumtion architecture*, intelligence consists in developing reactive layers of **software** that build on each other. A walking machine, for example, can learn to move its legs in coordination, and then the next software layer can take care of handling rough terrain. Intelligence, under the *nouvelle* AI approach, is not a zero-sum problem; there are many shades of intelligence and a robot that can navigate in an office already exhibits some of them.

Inspired by the situated approach to robotics, many of the current projects have to do with walking machines and humanoids. The Cog project in particular has received much attention from the media. Cog is half a humanoid, from the waist up, capable of recognizing objects, grasping them, and reacting to new situations. The idea behind Cog is that "humanoid intelligence requires humanoid interaction with the world." The robot has led to many new ideas about visual maps and saccadic movements that could not have been obtained from a software simulation.

FURTHER READING

Brand, Stewart. *The Media Lab: Inventing the Future at MIT.* New York: Penguin, 1988.

Brooks, Rodney. *Cambrian Intelligence: The Early History of the New AI.* Cambridge, Mass.: MIT Press, 1999.

McCorduck, Pamela. *Machines Who Think: A Personal Inquiry into the History and Prospects of Artificial Intelligence.* San Francisco: Freeman, 1979.

—*Raúl Rojas*

MIT Media Laboratory

The MIT Media Laboratory is a research and academic facility at the Massachusetts Institute of Technology (MIT) committed to the development of innovative media technologies. Founded in 1985 by Nicholas Negroponte (1943–) and Jerome Wiesner (1915–94) of MIT, the Media Lab is a renowned think tank sponsored by several international corporations. Over 100 projects are being pursued in such diverse areas as video, holography, cognitive computing, human–machine **interfaces**, electronic music, and graphic design.

Negroponte himself studied at MIT, where he specialized in the emerging field of **computer-aided design** (CAD) during his graduate studies. After joining the MIT faculty in 1966, he founded the Architecture Machine Group in 1968, a combination of lab and brainstorming pool that attempted to approach the human–machine interface problem in a new way. Later in 1980, Negroponte was involved for one term as founding chairman of the **International Federation of Information Processing** "Computers in Everyday Life" program. Negroponte started the Media Lab with Wiesner, who was president of MIT until 1980 and was also a former scientific advisor of U.S. presidents John F. Kennedy (1917–63) and Lyndon Johnson (1908–73). One of Wiesner's own areas of research was human–machine communication. After his presidential tenure at MIT, he devoted his work to the application of new technologies in the arts and media.

The educational wing of the Media Lab offers graduate degrees through its Media Arts and Sciences Program and undergraduates can participate in project-oriented courses. Media Arts and Sciences is conceived of as a multidiscipline field at MIT: The humanities, communications, and **computer science** merge in an academic program in which the core is the development and creative implementation of breakthrough technologies for human–machine interaction.

Digital Life, one of the three central divisions of the lab, is concerned with the interconnection of humans, objects, and **bits** in an online world. News in the Future is another research consortium and serves as a forum for the Media Lab and its sponsors, exploring new technologies for journalism. The News in the Future group concentrates not only on the analysis of news consumers, but also on interface design, data management, and on improving the efficiency of news production.

One of the most exciting areas of research at the Media Lab is the Things That Think consortium, originally initiated by Negroponte. In his book *Being Digital,* Negroponte prophesizes the end of atomized information. He proclaims the era of physical objects to be over and the future to be one of bits. Physical information requires an enormous organizational infrastructure that becomes obsolete in a virtual world. Indeed, the main focus of the Media Lab is on "how bits meet atoms," and the research group Things That Think studies computational intelligence for everyday objects: doors that can recognize the house occupants and automatically let them in; carpets that automatically load the freshest news into the user's shoes, which then project them into the eyeglasses; toasters that know their owner's habits and are able to communicate with other appliances.

Many special-interest groups (SIGs) also make their homes at the MIT Media Lab, such as those studying broadcasting, toys, health, the elderly, and cognitive machines. Some of the research accomplishments of the late 1990s included a new **Java**-based application called Hive, which should link together everyday "thinking" objects (see above), intelligent net **agents**, and the development of a wireless digital town, to provide remote areas with digital communication access. One SIG, Cognitive Machines, is trying to better understand human cognition by constructing computational examples of infant development and aims at building machines with intelligence akin to that of human beings. Such computers should be able to learn from speech and video as we learn from our experience.

Ninety percent of the Media Lab's approximately U.S.$35 million annual budget is provided by corporate sponsors. Private individuals and the U.S. government also contribute funding. About half of the firms that sponsor the lab are U.S.-based; the other half are European and Asian corporations. The sponsors come from a wide diversity of branches: from high-tech corporations such as **Motorola**, to toy companies such as Lego, telecommunication giants such as Telecom Italia and Deutsche Telekom, and entertainment companies such as Nickelodeon. The sponsors gain insight and are involved in research that might otherwise be too expensive or unusual to be pursued within their own company.

Around 2003, the MIT Media Lab will expand its facilities to encompass the new Okawa Center for children, learning, and developing nations, as well as two other centers specialized in art and expression, and the fusion of atoms and bits.

Further Reading

Brand, Stewart. *The Media Lab: Inventing the Future at MIT.* New York: Penguin, 1988.

Negroponte, Nicholas. *Being Digital.* New York: Knopf, 1995.

—*Jenna L. Brinning*

Modem

A modem is an electronic device used to send and receive **digital** computer data, most often using telephone lines. Inexpensive modems, popularized by companies such as Bell, **Hayes**, and US Robotics (now part of **3Com**), have been available since the early 1970s, but their use has become much more widespread with the explosive growth in **Internet** use.

When Alexander Graham Bell (1847–1922) used electromagnetism to send the sound of his voice by telephone in 1877, he could never have imagined that people would be transmitting images and data by essentially the same means a century later. The telephone network designed around Bell's invention was designed to carry continuous human speech using analog (continuously varying) electrical signals, not discrete packets of digital computer data. The modem is an ingenious compromise for ordinary telephone lines, designed around the physics of wave transmission, that allows digital data to be reliably encoded in analog form and transmitted as though it were a kind of "conversation" between two computers.

Strictly speaking, a modem is two devices in one: a modulator and a demodulator. At the sending location, a computer feeds its digital data (information taking only certain fixed values) through a modulator, which uses a process called *modulation* to produce analog signals (information continuously varying in a wave-shaped pattern) that can be sent over the ordinary telephone network (sometimes called Plain Old Telephone Service, or POTS). At the receiving end, a demodulator turns the analog signals back into digital data that can be understood by the receiving computer. Because most communication between computers is two-way, a modulator and a demodulator are needed at both ends of the telephone line. These are packaged conveniently into a single modem, often fitted as a self-contained circuit board inside the case of a computer or packaged in a small box connected to the **central processing unit** by a standard **interface** (such as an RS-232 cable). For greater portability, **laptop** computers may use modems packaged in the form of compact, plug-in cards (such as those designed to PCMCIA standards).

Many of the world's long-distance telephone networks have been upgraded substantially to transmit digital data using fiber optic cables and communications satellites. However, because of the huge cost of replacement, the connection known as the *local loop* between a typical home or office and the local switching center (called an *end office* in the United States and an *exchange* in the United Kingdom) is still usually based on **analog** technology—specifically, four metal wires known as a **twisted pair**. In practice, this means that data sent from one computer to another by a long-distance telephone connection may be changed from digital to analog form several times during the course of its journey. At the sending end, a modem changes the computer's digital data into analog signals that travel over the local loop. At the end office, the analog signals may be turned back into digital data to travel over fiber optic trunk lines using a device called a *codec* (coder–decoder), which carries out the opposite job to a modem. The digital signals may then be sent over hundreds or thousands of miles, perhaps even bouncing into space and back using a satellite. Eventually, at the other end of the journey, another codec at another end office will turn the signals back into analog form for transmission over the local loop that leads to the receiving computer. There, a second modem will turn the analog signals back into a digital form that the computer can understand.

The key to converting digital data into analog signals is the process known as *modulation*, a general technique for transmitting information using a continuously varying sine waveform called a *carrier wave*. Modulation is perhaps best known as the method by which radio signals are sent from a broadcasting station to a transistor radio. A signal (the radio program) is embedded in the carrier wave by constantly changing (modulating) either its amplitude (the size of the wave peaks) or its frequency (how often the wave peaks occur). These two techniques lend their names to amplitude modulation (AM) and frequency modulation (FM) radio stations.

The objective of data communication is to send as much data as possible as quickly (and reliably) as possible. In practice, this means sending as many bits of data as possible on each carrier waveform, or maximizing the "number of bits per symbol," as this is technically known. Modems can encode digital data using AM, FM, or phase modulation (PM), which encodes information by shifting the phase (the relative position of the wave peaks) in the carrier wave. Typically, modems use a combination of different modulation techniques to increase the number of bits per symbol. Two common methods are quadrature amplitude modulation (QAM) and trellis-coded modulation (TCM), which combine amplitude and phase modulation to achieve higher data transmission rates.

Another method of increasing the transmission rate is to compress data before they are sent. Instead of sending data as binary-encoded **ASCII** characters (or the **EBCDIC** equivalent), some modems use a technique called *Huffman encoding*, which uses fewer bits to transmit common characters (such as the letters "e" and "t") and more bits to transmit uncommon characters (such as "z" or "%"). Another standard compression method used by modems is V.42bis (based on a mathematical technique called Ziv–Lempel encoding), which reduces the amount of data transmitted to around a quarter of its size. MNP5 compression (also known as *run-length encoding*) reduces data by eliminating long strings of

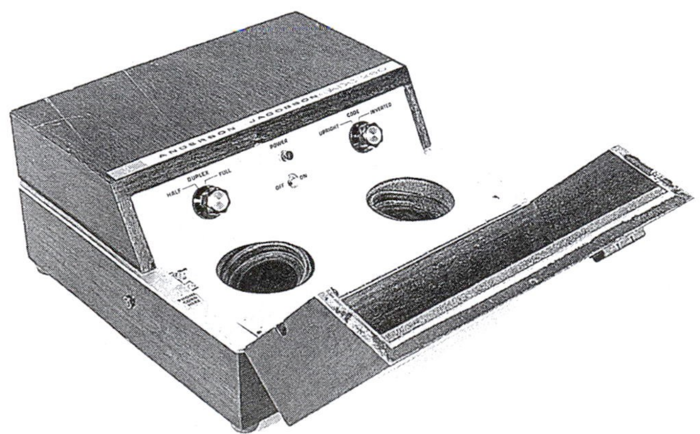

Modem made by Anderson-Jacobsen in 1966. (Courtesy of the Computer Museum History Center)

repeated bytes. Fax machines use this technique to transmit large areas of white paper (such as blank pages) more efficiently.

Modems are versatile devices that can be used in a range of different ways according to the application software running on their host computer. Apart from providing *dial-up connections* to Internet servers, they can be used to send and receive fax messages at up to 14,400 bits per second (bps) according to one of the three internationally standard "groups" of fax communication. They can also be used to store and dial numbers like an ordinary telephone handset. The features of a modern modem can be operated through a command language, originally developed by the Hayes company, using strings of ASCII control characters. For example, the command ATD18001234 means "Attention: dial number 1-800-1234."

Like any form of communication, sending data between computers by telephone means using two modems that speak the same "language." As modems have become more sophisticated, newer international standards have evolved to help achieve better transmission rates, but many older modems remain in use and the latest designs are almost always upwardly compatible with their predecessors. The start of any data exchange between two modems is marked by a process called *handshaking* in which the two devices compare capabilities and agree on a speed of data transmission that both can understand. Importantly, this means that the exchange of data can never exceed the speed of the slower modem.

Any modem must be able to talk to potentially any other type of modem that it could encounter on the end of a telephone line, so international standards are among the most important parts of modem design. Bell modems, the first widely available devices of their kind, set the de facto standard in the 1970s, and Hayes modems established the widely used AT command language. International modem standards have since been established by a regulatory body known as the ITU-T (**International Telecommunications Union**–Telecommunications). The main standards include V.22 (1200 bps), V.32 (9600 bps), V.32bis and V.33 (14,400 bps), V.34 (28,800 bps), V.34+ (33,600 bps), and V.90 (56,000 bps). V.90 evolved out of two incompatible rival standards: X2, promoted by US Robotics/3Com, and K56flex, promoted by Rockwell.

Unlike earlier modem standards, which assumed the telephone network to be mainly analog, the latest internationally agreed standard, V.90, assumes that the network is mainly digital. Internet service providers (ISPs) may be connected directly to the digital part of the network, bypassing their analog local loop. This means data can be downloaded from an Internet server to a client (such as a Web browser) at the fastest speed the digital part of the network allows, which turns out to be a maximum rate of 56,000 bps. But at this very high rate of transmission, noise (unwanted electrical signals) on the telephone line becomes a critical issue and limits the effective downloading speed typically to somewhere between 33,600 and 48,000 bps. Data transmission in the opposite direction (uploading) is restricted by the analog local loop at the client end of the connection and uses the older V.34+ standard to achieve speeds up to 33,600 bps.

The future of networking will see an increasing shift away from analog to digital communication. **ISDN** (Integrated Services Digital Network) enables digital data to be transmitted at high speeds from one computer to another down digital lines, so no modem is required, but ISDN lines are still relatively expensive and uncommon. A technique called **digital subscriber line** (DSL/ADSL) connects the ordinary analog telephone connection at a home or office to a high-speed digital link, bypassing the normal voice-telephone network, and achieving download speeds of up to 1.5 megabits per second.

FURTHER READING

Bingham, John. *The Theory and Practice of Modem Design.* New York: Wiley, 1988.

FitzGerald, Jerry, and Alan Dennis. *Business Data Communications and Networking.* New York: Wiley, 1984; 6th ed., 1999.

Forouzan, Behrouz. *Introduction to Data Communications and Networking.* Boston: McGraw-Hill College, 1998.

Stallings, William, and Richard van Slyke. *Business Data Communications.* New York: Macmillan; London: Collier Macmillan, 1990; 3rd ed., Upper Saddle River, N.J.: Prentice Hall, 1998.

Stamper, David, and the Saratoga Group. *Essentials of Data Communications.* Menlo Park, Calif: Benjamin-Cummings, 1997.

Tannenbaum, Andrew. *Computer Networks.* Upper Saddle River, N.J.: Prentice Hall, 1996.

—*Chris Woodford*

Modula-2

The programming language Modula-2 is a descendant of **Pascal**. Its main additional feature is the module structure. Whereas Pascal programs are monolithic pieces of program text, a Modula system typically consists of several interconnected modules. Therefore, Modula is suitable for the development of large systems by groups of people.

Each module specifies from which other modules it imports which entities (i.e., data types, constants, functions, procedures, and perhaps variables). The module hides additional details that are of no concern to other modules. The specification of externally visible entities is given in a separate text, called a *definition module*, which effectively constitutes the module's interface to other modules. This facility is particularly valuable for the construction of large systems, because modules can be compiled separately. Most important, type consistency is fully checked across module boundaries during compilation.

Modula's features include co-routines and low-level facilities. They made the language popular for the design of embedded systems for data acquisition and machine control, because they allow access to (memory-mapped) registers of peripheral devices. A controversial feature was omitted from Modula: the GO TO statement. Its absence forces the programmer to confine the design to well-structured formulation of conditional and repetitive executions, and thereby facilitates the verification of programs very considerably, contributing to reliability and early detection of possible mistakes. Modula is thus a language that promotes and encourages the disciplines of structured and modular programming.

Modula-2 was designed by **Niklaus Wirth** (1934–) at the Swiss Federal Institute of Technology (ETH) in Zurich in 1976–79, following a year's visit to the **Xerox Palo Alto Research Center** (PARC). It incorporates ideas, including the module, from PARC's language Mesa, while preserving the style and much of the simplicity of Pascal. Modula was first implemented (as a five-pass compiler) for the DEC PDP-11 computer with 32 kilobytes of storage.

Parallel to this effort the Personal Workstation Lilith was designed and built at ETH in Zurich. In many ways it resembled PARC's **Alto computer**. Lilith directly interpreted the M-code (byte code) generated by the compiler. Lilith's software was programmed exclusively in Modula-2, including drivers for the **mouse** and the high-resolution raster scan display, demonstrating that entire systems can be built without using code written in **assembler** language.

Further Reading

Wirth, Niklaus. *Programming in Modula-2.* Berlin and New York: Springer-Verlag, 1982; 4th ed., 1988.

—*Niklaus Wirth*

Moore, Gordon

1929–

U.S. Electronics Engineer and Co-founder of Intel

Gordon Moore is chairman emeritus of **Intel**, the California-based **semiconductor** manufacturer he cofounded in 1968. His significant stock holding in the company has made him one of the richest men in the world, with an estimated wealth of over U.S.$8 billion. Moore is better known as the person who devised **Moore's Law**.

After completing his Ph.D. in 1954, Moore took a job in the Applied Physics Laboratory at Johns Hopkins University in Maryland, where he carried out basic chemical research. After calculating how much taxpayers were paying per word for his published articles, he questioned whether society was really benefiting from his work. But later innovations in which Moore was involved ensured that society would be more than fully repaid.

Soon afterward, in an attempt to do something more practical, Moore tried to join the research staff at Lawrence Livermore Laboratory. Following his interview, he came to the attention of **William Shockley** (1910–89), the brilliant but temperamental physicist who had worked at **Bell Labs** with **John Bardeen** (1908–91) and **Walter Brattain** (1902–87) and turned their invention of the **transistor** into a commercially successful device. Shockley hired Moore as a chemist to work at his new company, Shockley Transistor, in 1956.

Attracted by the idea of working on a practical, cutting-edge project to design a **silicon** transistor, Moore jumped at the chance to return to his home state of California. Moore described Shockley as having "phenomenal intuition" for physics, but Shockley proved to be a poor and insensitive manager, and eventually, eight of his best staff, including Moore, mutinied and founded their own company, **Fairchild Semiconductor** in 1958.

During his 11 years at Fairchild, Moore forged his profitable partnership with another of the "Fairchild eight," **Robert Noyce** (1927–90). Although, like Shockley, Fairchild's initial goal had been to devise an improved form of silicon transistor, it soon came up with the *planar process*, a revolutionary method of manufacturing integrated circuits. Moore initially managed Fairchild's engineering department, then in 1959 became director of research and development when Noyce became general manager of the company.

In 1965, *Electronics* magazine invited Moore to contribute to its 35th anniversary edition by speculating on how semiconductor technology might develop over the following decade. Looking back on how **integrated**

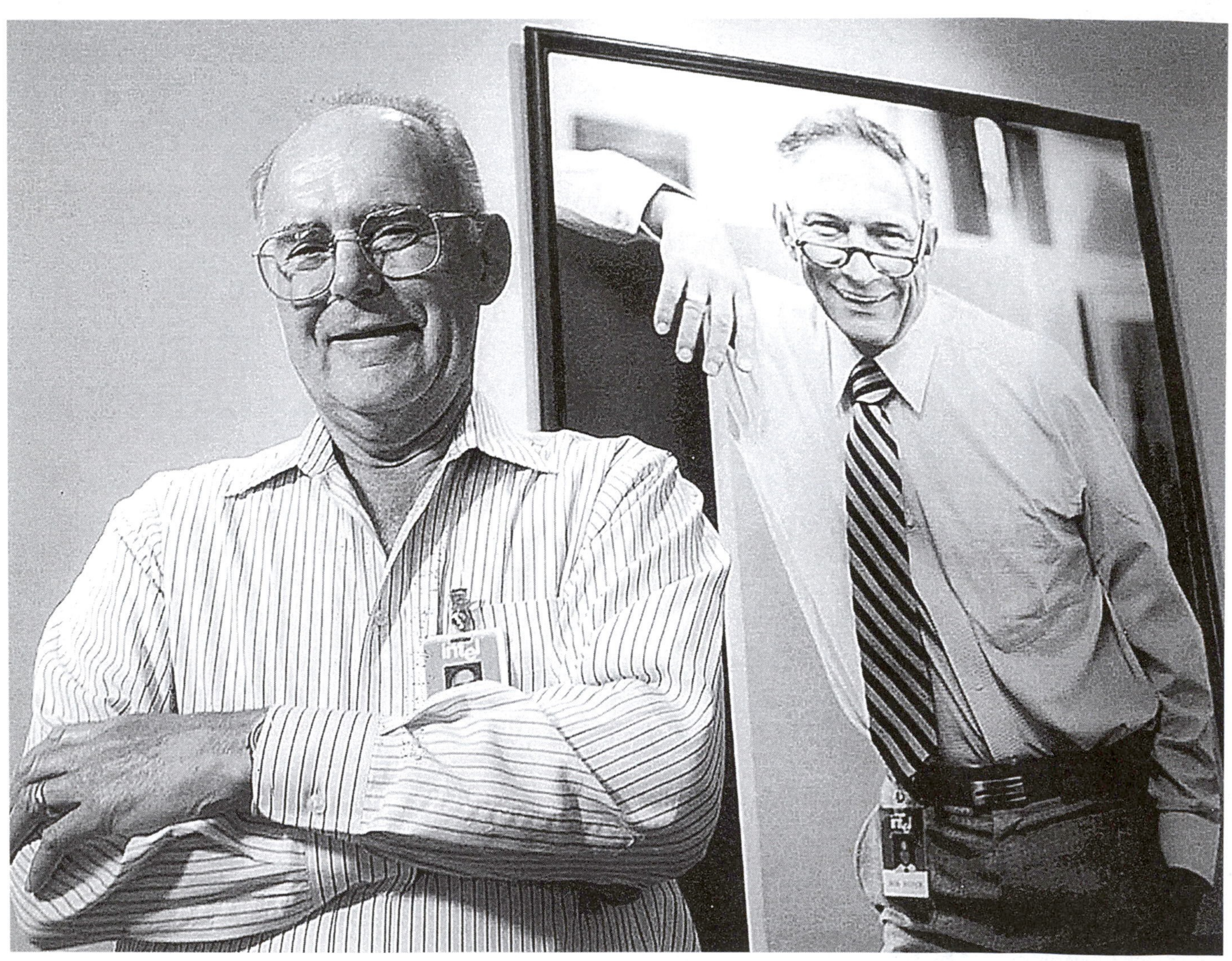

Gordon Moore with photo of Robert Noyce at Intel headquarters, 16 July 1998. (AP Photo/Paul Sakuma)

circuits had enabled the number of transistors to double virtually every year since their invention, he made a rough prediction that the same trend might continue. This idea became known as Moore's law, although Moore later revised the period over which doubling would occur to 18 months.

Fairchild Semiconductor gradually fell victim to the departure of its brightest engineers and disputes with its parent company in New York. When Robert Noyce was passed over for the job of chief executive officer (CEO), he and Gordon Moore decided to leave to form their own company. In 1968, they set up Intel and decided to concentrate on developing semiconductor memories. But the company soon stumbled across a much better invention, the **microprocessor**, the single-chip computer on which its remarkable success has been built for the last 30 years. Moore initially served as executive vice president, ran the company from 1975 through 1979 as president and CEO, was chairman and CEO from 1979 through 1987, and stepped down as CEO in 1987 when **Andy Grove** (1936–) replaced him.

Although Moore was largely responsible for steering Intel toward its commercial success, he nevertheless recalls his early mistakes with some amusement. Convinced that it had to find applications for the microprocessor, it invested around U.S.$15 million in digital watchmaker Microma without making the business profitable. Moore is still woken up each morning by what he describes as his "$15 million Microma watch," a memento of the episode. But the opportunity cost of Intel's focus on simple microprocessor appliances may have been much greater. As Moore now recalls, he was approached in the early 1970s with a proposal for a home **personal computer**. Unable to imagine that there would be a market for such a device, he passed on the deal.

Despite his wealth and his status in the computer industry, Moore still works regularly at Intel's Santa Clara headquarters in a cubicle no different from thousands of others in the building.

BIOGRAPHY

Gordon Moore. Born 3 January 1929 in San Francisco, California. B.S. in chemistry from University of California at Berkeley, 1950; Ph.D. in chemistry and physics from California Institute of Technology, 1954. Research scientist at Applied Physics Laboratory, Johns Hopkins University, 1954–56. Worked at Shockley Semiconductor, 1956–57. Cofounded Fairchild Semiconductor, 1957, becoming director of research and development in 1959. Co-founded Intel with Robert Noyce in 1968; initially executive vice-president, then president and chief executive officer, 1975; chairman and chief executive officer, 1979; chairman, 1987; and chairman emeritus, 1997. Recipient of numerous awards, including the AFIPS Harry Goode Award for Leadership in Science, 1978; American Society of Metals Medal for Advancement of Research, 1985; Founders Award from the National Academy of Engineering, 1988; National Medal of Technology, 1990; and several awards from the Institute of Electrical and Electronic Engineers (IEEE).

SELECTED WRITINGS

Moore, Gordon. "Cramming More Components onto Integrated Circuits." *Electronics*, Vol. 38, No. 8, 19 Apr. 1965, pp. 114–117.

———. "The Microprocessor: Engine of the Technology Revolution." *Communications of the ACM*, Vol. 40, No. 2, Feb. 1997, pp. 112–114.

FURTHER READING

Gwennap, Linley. "Birth of a Chip." *BYTE*, Dec. 1996, p. 77.

Jackson, Tim. *Inside Intel: Andy Grove and the Rise of the World's Most Powerful Chip Company*. New York: Dutton, 1997.

Wagner, Peter. "How Microchips Shook the World." *BYTE*, Dec. 1996, p. 69.

Walker, Rob. "Silicon Genesis: Oral Histories of Semiconductor Industry Pioneers: Interview with Gordon E. Moore: March 3, 1995." Transcription by Dag Spicer, Department of History, Stanford University Libraries, 1996.

—*Chris Woodford*

Moore School of Electrical Engineering

The University of Pennsylvania in Philadelphia created a Department of Electrical Engineering in 1914. The department was renamed the Moore School of Electrical Engineering when Alfred Fitler Moore, the head of a large Philadelphia cable manufacturing company, donated a large endowment. The department quickly became well known for training students with superior abilities; many of them contributed enormously to the history of computing.

In 1935 the Moore School, in an effort to solve large electrical engineering problems, constructed a differential analyzer. The design was based on that of a similar machine created by **Vannevar Bush** (1890–1974) a few years earlier at the Massachusetts Institute of Technology (MIT). At this time there were very few large differential analyzers available and the Moore School machine was one of the largest and most accurate. They also produced a copy of this machine for use by the U.S. Army Ballistic Research Laboratory (BRL), which was located in Aberdeen, Maryland. The possession of a fine differential analyzer and their relationship with the BRL put the Moore School in a strategic position when, upon the outbreak of World War II, there was a pressing need for the production of ballistic artillery tables. The school was enlisted by the BRL to assist with the creation of these tables.

The Moore School found it difficult to meet the demands for all types of military calculation. Although this difficulty was due in part to the fact that many of the staff had left for military service, in truth the amount of calculation required would not have been possible even under ideal staffing conditions. In an effort to replace the missing professors, junior research associates, such as **J. Presper Eckert** (1919–95), and staff of nearby institutions, including **John Mauchly** (1907–80) from Ursinus College, were recruited. It was the chance combination of these two men that led directly to the creation of the first large-scale general-purpose digital computing machine—the **ENIAC**. Mauchly had the ability to see what might be needed in the design of a high-speed calculating machine, and Eckert was one of the finest electrical engineers of his generation. When the BRL approached the Moore School requesting any suggestions for speeding up the ballistic calculations, Eckert and Mauchly presented their ideas and the Army provided the funding to proceed. Later, after they had realized the shortcomings of the ENIAC, the concept of the modern stored program computer emerged from that same group. Although the U.S. Army, at first, refused to fund another project, the intervention of **John von Neumann** (1903–57) changed their minds, and they provided additional funds for research on the new concept for a machine called **EDVAC**.

Just after the end of World War II, when the ENIAC was up and running and the EDVAC was still in a very preliminary phase of research, a dispute arose among the staff of the Moore School; one of the main issues was a dispute over patent rights to the new devices that had been created. The conflict resulted in the breakup of the research team in the spring of 1946, with some leaving to form commercial firms (the Eckert-Mauchly Computer Company, later **UNIVAC**, being the main one), and others returning to various academic institutions. The Moore School was able to reunite the group once more in the summer of 1946 when they put on an 8-week high-level course: Theory and Techniques for the Design of Electronic Digital Computers (always simply called the Moore School Lectures). It was during these lectures that the concept of the stored program was first explained publicly. The majority of the first generation of modern computers were constructed by groups who were either present at these lectures or influenced by those who were.

After the Moore School Lectures the exodus of the core of the computer development group resulted in great difficulties in the contract to build the EDVAC computer. The EDVAC may have been the prototype design for the new stored program computer, but it was not actually fully functional until 1952, long after it had been superseded by more advanced machine designs.

FURTHER READING

Brainerd, J. G. "Genesis of the ENIAC." *Technology and Culture*, Vol. 17, No. 3, July 1976, pp. 482–491.

Campbell-Kelly, Martin, and Michael R. Williams, eds. *The Moore School Lectures*, Vol. 9 in the Charles Babbage Institute Reprint Series for the History of Computing. Cambridge, Mass.: MIT Press, 1985.

Goldstine, H. H. *The Computer from Pascal to von Neumann*. Princeton, N.J.: Princeton University Press, 1972.

—*Michael R. Williams*

Moore's Law

From 1958, when the **integrated circuit** (IC) was invented, until about 1972, the number of transistors per chip doubled each year. In 1972, the number began doubling only every year and a half, or increasing at 60 percent per year, resulting in a factor of 100 improvement each decade. Consequently, **semiconductor** memory capacities have increased fourfold every three years. This phenomenon is known as Moore's law, after **Intel**'s cofounder, **Gordon Moore** (1929–), who first observed and posited it. Moore's law is not a law that is defined by a collection of physical phenomena; instead, it is an observation about the behavior of the entire industry that builds and uses semiconductors.

Density increases enable chips to operate faster and cost less, for two primary reasons. First, the smaller everything gets, approaching the size of an electron, the faster the system behaves. Second, miniaturized circuits produced in a batch process tend to cost very little once the factory is in place. The price of a semiconductor factory appears to double each generation (three years); nevertheless, the cost per transistor declines with new generations because volumes are so enormous.

The semiconductor industry makes the analogy that if cars evolved at the rate of semiconductors, today we would all be driving Rolls-Royces that go a million miles an hour and cost 25 cents. The difference here is that computing technology operates Maxwell's equations defining electromagnetic systems, whereas most of the physical world operates under Newton's laws defining the movement of objects with mass.

Moore's law is nicely illustrated by the number of bits per chip of dynamic random access memory (DRAM) and the year in which each chip was introduced: 1 kilobyte (kB) (1972), 4kB (1975), ..., 64 megabytes (MB) (1996). This trend is likely to continue until 2010. The National Semiconductor road map calls for 128 MB in 2001 and 8 gigabytes (GB) in 2010.

Just as increasing transistor density has improved the storage capacity of semiconductor memory chips, increasing areal density has directly affected the total information-storage capacity of disk systems. **IBM**'s 1957 disk file, the **RAMAC** 350, recorded about 100 bits along the circumference of each track, and each track was separated by 0.1 inch, giving an areal density of 1000 bits per square inch. In early 1990, IBM announced that one of its laboratories had stored 1 billion bits in 1 square inch and shipped a product with this capacity in 1996. This technology progression of six orders of magnitude in 33 years amounts to a density increase at a rate of more than 50 percent per year.

Increases in storage density have led to magnetic storage systems that are not only cheaper to purchase but also cheaper to own, primarily because the density increases have markedly reduced physical volume. Smaller disks store much more, cost much less, are much faster and more reliable, and use much less power than their ancestors. Without such high-density disks, personal computers would be impossible.

In 1992, electro-optical disk technologies provided 1 GB of disk memory at the cost of a compact audio disk, making it economically feasible for **personal computer** users to have roughly 400,000 pages of pure text or 10,000 pages of pure image data instantly available. Similarly, advances in video compression using hundreds of millions of operations per second of processing power permit VHS-quality video to be stored on a single compact disk. By 2000, one disk will hold 20 GB, and by 2047 we might expect this to grow to a minimum of 20 terabytes.

It is safe to predict that the computers in 50 years will be at least 100,000 times more powerful than those of today. However, if processing, storage, and network technologies continue to evolve at the rate of Moore's law, in 50 years computers will be 10 billion times more powerful than those today. A probable outcome is the creation of thousands of specialized, essentially zero cost, system-on-a-chip computers. These one-chip, fully networked systems will be everywhere, embedded in everything from phones to light switches to motors to building walls. They will serve as eyes and ears for the blind and deaf. Onboard networks of them will "drive" vehicles that communicate with their counterparts embedded in highways and other vehicles. The only limits will be our ability to interface computers with the physical world (i.e., the interface between **cyberspace** and physical space).

FURTHER READING

Moore, Gordon. "Cramming More Components onto Integrated Circuits." *Electronics*, Vol. 38, No. 8, 19 Apr. 1965, pp. 114–117.

Schaller, Robert R. "Moore's Law: Past, Present, and Future." *IEEE Spectrum*, Vol. 34, No. 6, 1997, pp. 53–59.

Walker, Rob. "Silicon Genesis: Oral Histories of Semiconductor Industry Pioneers: Interview with Gordon E. Moore: March 3, 1995." Transcription by Dag Spicer, Department of History, Stanford University Libraries, 1996.

—*Gordon Bell*

MOS/CMOS

Metal oxide semiconductor (MOS) and complementary MOS (CMOS) refer to the technology used in the fabrication of certain **integrated circuits**. MOS and CMOS transistors are not built out of individual components—they are etched on a **silicon** plate by carving the different components out of a metallic and silicon oxide substrate. A silicon plate is used because its oxide is a good insulator.

Transistors are basic electronic elements that can be used to amplify signals, as **digital** switches, or to provide a given resistance. There are two basic types of MOS transistors: *n-doped* and *p-doped*. The first type is negatively doped at the source and drain, the second positively—hence the n and p prefixes.

A bipolar transistor is built on top of a silicon wafer by sandwiching a p-type layer between two n-type regions, or vice versa. Silicon is a crystal with a regular atomic structure. When some elements are added to the material (using diffusion, for example), electrons can be set free (n-doping) or *holes* arise, that is, positions in the atomic bindings that are more stable when an electron is captured (p-doping). Adding arsenic, for example, creates n-doped silicon and adding boron produces p-doped silicon. Figure 1 is a diagram of an n-MOS transistor. The metallic gate is not in contact with a p-doped layer. A layer of silicon dioxide isolates the metal from the p-doped semiconductor.

The purpose of the n-MOS transistor is to implement a digital switch with two states, open or closed. If the voltage at the gate is low, electrons cannot flow from the drain to the source, because the p-doped material acts as a barrier, and therefore the switch is open. But if the gate is set to a higher voltage (higher than a certain threshold), electrons are attracted to the gate, forming a conducting channel that allows electricity to flow from the n-doped drain to the n-doped source. The switch is now closed. A p-MOS transistor has a similar structure, but the n-doped and p-doped regions are interchanged, and the gate voltage must be inverted. The design with an insulated gate is called a field-effect transistor (FET).

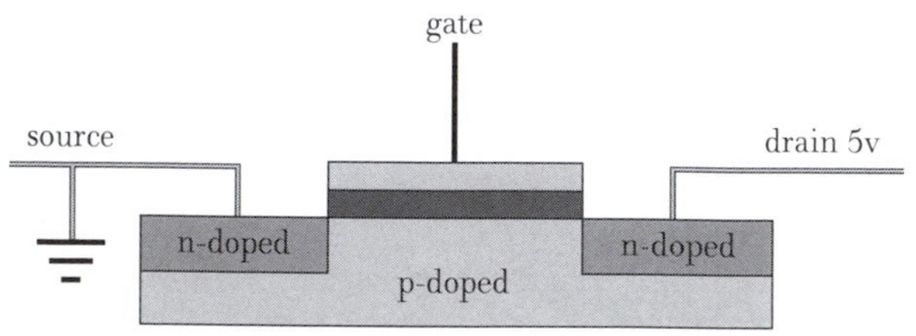

Figure 1 *n-MOS transistor.*

When an n-MOS or p-MOS transistor is closed, there is a flow of electricity between source and drain. MOS transistors are fast but consume too much energy in their 1 state. CMOS components provide a solution. A CMOS switch is built out of two MOS transistors, an n-MOS and a p-MOS transistor, placed side by side. CMOS design is now the dominant technology for the implementation of **microprocessors**, memories, and other chips, because of its lower power dissipation. CMOS circuits consume energy only when they switch state, not in their static modes.

The operation of a CMOS element can be illustrated by considering a CMOS inverter. Figure 2 shows a schematic design of such a circuit. The p-type transistor has been drawn connected to the 5-V line and with a gate that receives the inverted input (the small circle means *inversion*). The n-type transistor is connected to ground. Note that there is no direct connection between the 5-V line and ground. When the input is negative, the p-type transistor closes, the n-type transistor is open, and the output line is connected to 5 V. When the input is positive (a

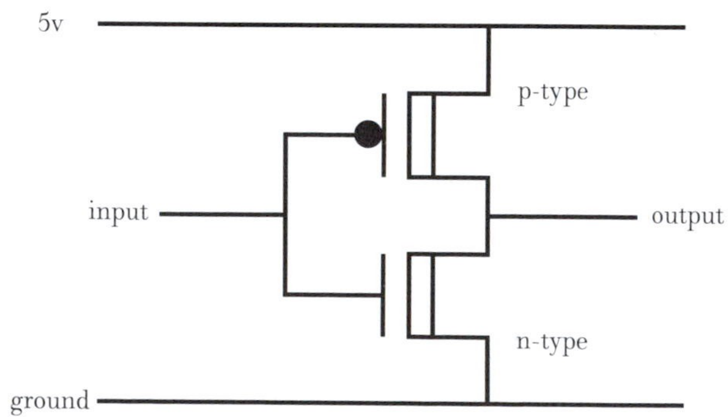

Figure 2 *CMOS design.*

	Electron-tube era	
1901	J. C. Bose	Vacuum rectifier
1902	Ambrose Fleming	Vacuum tube (diode)
1906	G. W. Pichard and L. W. Austin	Crystal detector
1907	Lee de Forest	Audion three-electrode tube (triode)
1918	Czochralski	Method of pulling crystals from the melt
1925	Julius Edgar Lilienfeld	Principle of the field-effect transistor
1934	Oskar Heil	Structure of the junction field-effect transistor
1938	W. Schottky	Schottky-barrier diode
	Bipolar transistor era	
1947	J. Bardeen, W. H. Brattain, and W. Shockley	Germanium point contact transistor
1948	W. Shockley	Germanium junction transistor
1950	W. J. Pietenpohl and R. S. Ohl	Silicon bipolar transistor
1951	G. K. Teal and E. Buehler	Germanium single crystal
1952	G. K. Teal and E. Buehler	Silicon single crystal
1952	Texas Instruments	Commercial production, silicon bipolar transistor
1953	Keck, H. C. Theuerer, and Emeis	Float-zone processing
1957	R. C. Sangster	Vapor-phase epitaxial growth
	Integration era	
1959	Jack S. Kilby	Monolithical integrated circuit
1959	Robert N. Noyce	Planar junction field-effect transistor
1958	Jean A. Hoerni	Planar surface field-effect transistor
1959	Gordon E. Moore and Robert N. Noyce	Planar technology
1960	H. C. Theuerer, J. J. Kleinach, H. H. Lour, and H. Christensen	Epitaxial diffused transistor
1960	J. A. Hoerni	Silicon planar process
1960	D. Kahny and M. M. Atalla	MOS field-effect transistor
1961	Fairchild Semiconductor	First commercial digital integrated circuit
	MOS transistor era	
1962	Fairchild Semiconductor	MOS integrated circuits
1963	Frank Wanlass, Fairchild Semiconductor	CMOS integrated circuits
	Application era	
1967	Dalbergh Hearing Aids	First hearing aid worn in the ear
1968	Hodges et al.	MOS 64-bit RAM memory
1968	Fairchild Semiconductor	μmA709 operational amplifier
1970	Dennard, IBM	One-transistor dynamic memory cell
1970	Marcian E. Hoff, Intel	1103 4-kbit DRAM
1971	Intel	4004 4-bit microprocessor
1972	Intel	8008 8-bit microprocessor
1974	Intel	8080 8-bit microprocessor
1981	J. W. Beyers et al., Hewlett-Packard	450,000-transistor microprocessor
1984	[several contributors]	Megabit memory chip
1995	[several contributors]	Experimental gigabit memory chip

Figure 3. *Timetable of the electronic era.*

1 in the input), the n-type transistor closes, the p-type transistor opens and the output line is therefore connected to ground. The circuit thus transforms a 0 into a 1 and a 1 into a 0. Many other logical operations, such as OR and AND, can be implemented using CMOS designs.

When comparing this circuit with a simple n-MOS or p-MOS transistor, the important point to notice is that the only time when there is a flow of electricity between the 5-V line and ground is when the state of the transistors is switched. This is the only moment in which energy is consumed. When the output has been set and the circuit has stabilized, there is no energy consumption except for charge leaks at the gate. In this design the gate is like a small capacitor that has to be replenished or depleted at each change of state.

In 1963, Frank Wanlass and C. T. Sah, engineers at Fairchild, applied for a patent on CMOS technology. Although CMOS electronic elements are slower than bipolar transistors, they consume 10 times less power, and many more transistors can be integrated on a chip when the power requirements are reduced. The introduction of CMOS technology therefore paved the way for VLSI (very large scale integration) chips. In 1991, Frank Wanlass received the Solid-States Circuits Award from the **Institute of Electrical and Electronics Engineers** for "pioneering contribution to high-speed dynamic memory design and cell technology."

Further Reading

Baker, Jacob, Harry Li, and David Boyce. *CMOS Circuit Design, Layout, and Simulation.* New York: IEEE Press, 1998.

Morris, P. R. *A History of the World Semiconductor Industry.* London: Peregrinus IEE, 1990.

Riordan, Michael, and Lillian Hoddeson. *Crystal Fire: The Birth of the Information Age.* New York: Norton, 1997.

—*Raúl Rojas*

Motherboard

In a **personal computer** (PC), the motherboard is the base onto which the main electronic components, such as the processor and memory, are soldered. Expansion boards are connected to the motherboard by inserting them into expansion slots. Motherboards for **IBM** PC–compatible computers are dominant in the microcomputer industry.

The figure shows an example of a commercial motherboard. The processor (a **Pentium** II) is inserted in a special slot. Having a slot for the processor is very convenient, since it can be replaced when a better model becomes available. In this way the rest of the **hardware** investment can be preserved. The DIMM sockets are used to plug-in memory chips in DIMM (dual-in-line memory module) packages. In this example there are also some connectors for floppies, hard drives, and parallel and serial ports.

The **BIOS** (basic input output software) is stored in a **ROM** (read-only memory) chip that contains the basic code to control the computer. The battery in the figure is used to keep the computer clock running. Expansion slots are quite prominent in this motherboard: three ISA (industry standard architecture) and three PCI (peripheral component interconnect) slots are present. The AGP (accelerated graphics port) chipset is used to speed up the display of computer graphics on the screen, especially three-dimensional images.

The USB (universal serial bus) is a new kind of "**plug and play**" interface that makes it possible to connect peripherals without having to add an expansion card to the motherboard. USB is a standard developed by several companies, which have made it available to other computer manufacturers free of charge. The power connector takes a set of different voltage levels from the power source and delivers them to all components using metallic lines etched on the motherboard, possibly in several layers. Other types of boards include the daughter card (those that connect to a motherboard), controller cards (used to interface a peripheral to the motherboard), a network interface card (NIC, used to connect the computer to a **local area network**), and video cards (used to control the screen).

There are many parameters that differentiate motherboards, such as the number of processors that can be plugged in, the clock speed, the maximum data transfer rate of the local bus, the BIOS used, and the amount of maximum memory that can be added to the system. Although, in theory, upgrading a computer by buying a new motherboard should be easy, in practice it can be very difficult because there are so many available options, and very detailed knowledge of all the hardware is needed.

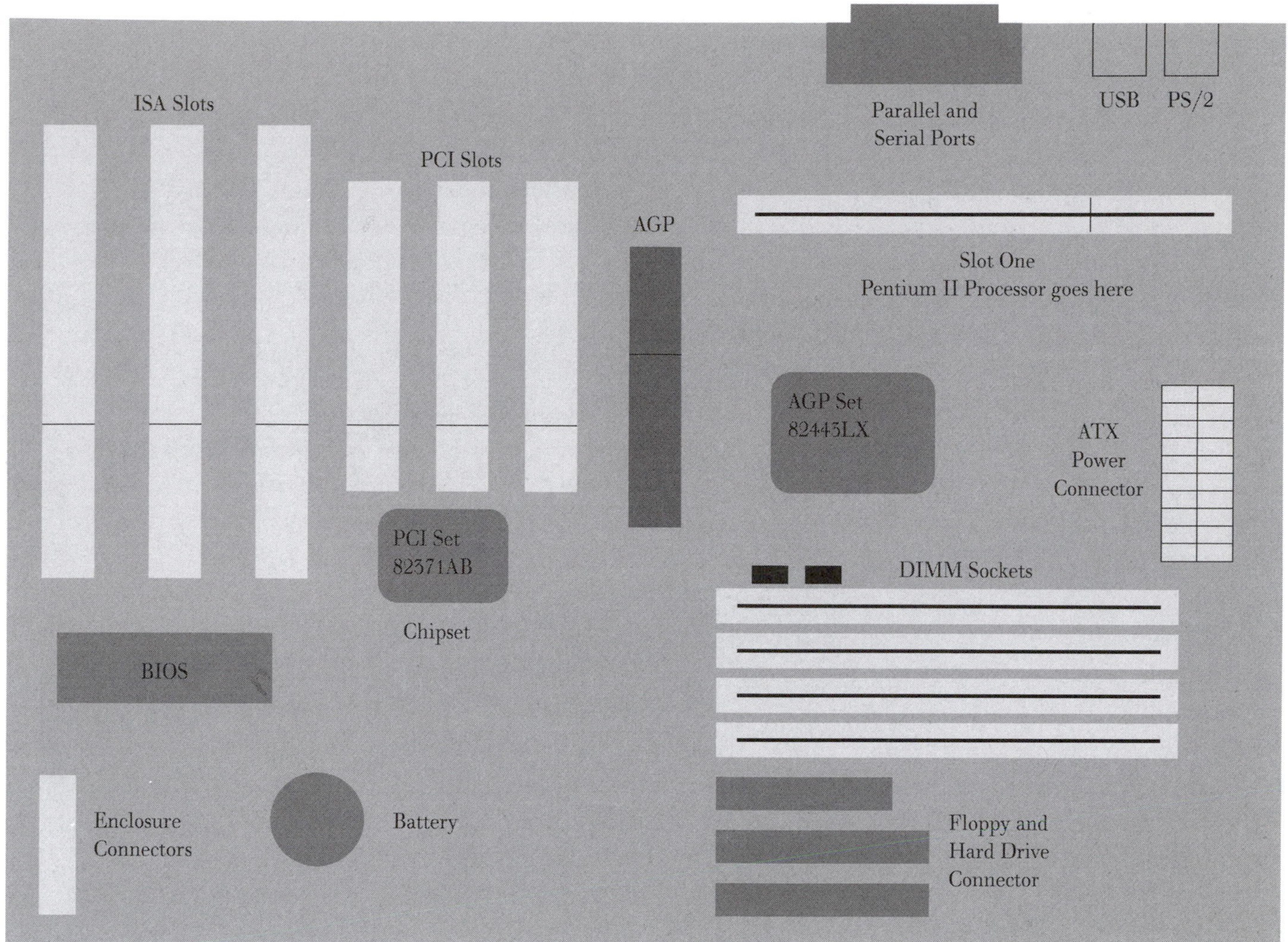

Commercial motherboard with a Pentium II processor.

FURTHER READING

Brenner, Robert C. *IBM PC Advanced Troubleshooting and Repair.* Indianapolis, Ind.: Sams 1988.

Chambers, Mark. *Building a PC for Dummies.* Foster City, Calif.: IDG Books, 1998.

—*Raúl Rojas*

Motorola

Motorola is one of the leading **semiconductor** companies in the United States. It sells a wide variety of electronic products, such as **microprocessors**, cellular telephones, networking equipment, and embedded **analog** and **digital** systems.

When Paul and Joseph Galvin bought out a bankrupt battery firm and founded the Galvin Manufacturing Company on 25 September 1928, they probably never dreamed that they had just begun what was to become a global leader in electronics. The Galvin brothers set up shop in Chicago with five employees and total assets of around U.S.$1300. Their first product was a battery eliminator, but it was with automobile radios that they made a fortune. Car radios were not available directly from the manufacturer, and the Galvins's radios were sold and installed through car dealerships. In 1930, the Galvin Manufacturing Company had a net revenue of over U.S.$287,000. Paul then coined the name *Motorola*, mixing *motion* and *radio*, for the company's line of new products. By 1936, Motorola was well established in the U.S. market as a brand name, and home radios were introduced into the product line shortly thereafter.

During World War II, Galvin Manufacturing Corporation was a supplier of electronics for the war effort. In fact, the first hand-held two-way AM radio, the *handie-talkie*, was developed for the U.S. Army. In 1943 the *walkie-talkie*, a two-way FM radio for the backpack, followed. These two innovations became a standard in war communications on the front. After the end of the war, the company once again switched to consumer electronics, and as the brand name Motorola had become so widely accepted, the Galvins changed the company's name to Motorola Inc. in 1947.

In the years to follow, Motorola concentrated on the development of semiconductors, led successfully by its head researcher Daniel Noble. The first Motorola product utilizing **transistors** was a small auto radio (1956). A pager was introduced shortly thereafter, and Motorola soon began supplying other manufacturers with semiconductors, becoming the first company to produce them en masse. Many innovations followed in the 1960s, such as the first rectangular tube for color television, and eight-track tape players for cars. Motorola continued to grow, and eventually expanded internationally, adding production plants worldwide. By 1970, Motorola had more than 30,000 employees, and even the National Aeronautics and Space Administration relied on its products to communicate with astronauts.

After introducing its first microprocessor in 1974, the 6800 chip holding 4000 transistors, Motorola continued development and released a 16-bit microprocessor, the popular 68000, in the late 1970s. A few years later, a 32-bit chip followed, which by the mid-1980s more than 100 companies were using for their own products. The original **Macintosh** and the first SUN workstation were two famous computers built around the 68-kilobyte architecture.

By the early 1990s, Motorola was turning over yearly net sales of more than U.S.$10 billion. The third-generation 68000 chip, the 68040 with 1.2 million transistors, went into production. It was fast, yet still compatible to software developed for the 68000.

Motorola continues its activity in the semiconductor branch, competing against **Intel**, as well as offering a broad range of commercial products, including mobile phones, pagers, two-way radios, and embedded electronics for automobiles, broadband communication devices, and so on. The company is split up into various units that concentrate on these different sectors of Motorola's commerce, and family tradition thrives: Christopher B. Galvin (1951–) is president of Motorola as of this writing.

FURTHER READING

Antonakos, James L. *The 68000 Microprocessor: Hardware and Software Principles and Applications.* Columbus, Ohio: Merrill, 1990; 4th ed., Upper Saddle River, N.J.: Prentice Hall, 1999.

Dye, Norman, and Helge Granberg. *Radio Frequency Transistors: Principles and Practical Applications.* Boston: Butterworth-Heinemann, 1993.

Moorthy, R. S., et al. *Uncompromising Integrity: Motorola's Global Challenge.* Schaumberg, Ill.: Motorola University Press, 1998.

—*Jenna L. Brinning*

Mouse

The computer input device known as the mouse was first developed by **Douglas Engelbart** (1925–) and his team working on the Augmentation System at the Stanford Research Institute (SRI). The team experimented with a variety of methods of interacting with the computer system, including a lightpen, a joystick, knee controls, and head cursor controls. But muscles would cramp, and they discovered that the mouse was the best input device. In addition to the mouse, the Augmentation System utilized a traditional **keyboard** and a five-key, one-hand chord keyset to input information. Simple commands were input with the keyset, including I (insert), D (delete), and M (move or rearrange). After the commands were typed, the user pointed with the mouse to tell the system where on the screen the command should be executed.

The Engelbart mouse was a little box with hidden wheels underneath and a cable to the terminal. As it rolled, the wheel's turns signaled the computer and the computer moved the cursor on the screen. The cursor is a symbol on a display screen that indicates the active position at which the next character or action will be executed. By rolling the mouse over a flat surface, users could move quickly around the screen by pointing the cursor at target areas, and clicking the buttons on the keyset to enter commands. With a few hours of practice, a person could learn to operate the mouse and chord keyset together.

In the early 1970s, a number of researchers left Engelbart's project and went to work at **Xerox Palo Alto Research Center** (PARC). Scientists at PARC were designing the **Alto**, a small **microcomputer** with a graphical display screen. To manipulate the images displayed on the screen, the Alto team hired Jack S. Hawley to convert the **analog** mouse into a **digital** device, reduce its size, and simplify its handling. In contrast to Engelbart's mouse, which used variable resistors and an A/D conversion circuit, Hawley's mouse was digital. Much of Hawley's basic design has been applied to today's mouse that comes with most personal computers.

In December 1979, **Steve Jobs** (1955–) and a group from **Apple Computer** toured Xerox PARC and saw the graphical display screens with the mouse input device. Jobs immediately went back to Apple and began developing graphical interfaces for their computers, the Lisa and **Macintosh**. In 1984 the Macintosh was introduced and it became the first commercially successful **personal computer** to utilize the mouse.

FURTHER READING

Barnes, Susan B. "Douglas Carl Engelbart: Developing the Underlying Concepts for Contemporary Computing." *IEEE Annals of the History of Computing*, Vol. 19, No. 3, 1997, pp. 16–26.

Nelson, Theodor H. *Computer Lib-Dream Machines*. Redmond, Wash.: Microsoft Press, 1987.

Rheingold, Howard. *Virtual Reality*. New York: Summit Books, 1991.

—*Susan B. Barnes*

MPEG

MPEG, the Moving Picture Expert Group, is a working group established under the joint direction of the **International Organization for Standardization** (ISO) and the IEC (International Electrotechnical Commission). Its goal is to develop standards for the binary representation of moving pictures, audio, and their combination. The acronym is also used as a nickname for the family of standards the group has produced.

The Moving Picture Expert Group was formed in January 1988. Its first meeting was held in May 1988, and 25 experts participated. Today it has grown to a large committee with about 350 experts from 200 companies, as well as academic organizations from 20 countries. As a rule, the group meets in March, July, and November each year, although if the workload so demands, it meets more frequently. In 1998, for example, it came together five times.

The standards produced by the group are structured in phases and divided in layers. The phases are normally noted in Arabic numerals (e.g., MPEG-1, MPEG-2, MPEG-4) and the layers are noted in Roman numerals (layer I, layer II, layer III). Quality and bitrate differ from phase to phase, whereas each layer represents a different family of coding algorithms. Layer I has the weakest complexity but suppresses less redundant signals than layer II, which is more complex, or even layer III, which has the highest complexity.

The compression **algorithms** used by MPEG are based on *perceptual coding*. Perceptual coding means that the coder does not try to maintain every bit of the original signal, but tries to ensure that the output signal seems identical to human perception. This is achieved by suppressing details of a picture or audio signal that cannot be perceived by human beings.

The audio encoding algorithms use the *psychoacoustic model*, which is a set of empirical mathematical formulas, diagrams, and tables describing the inaccuracies of the human auditive system. For example, a tone of a specific frequency and amplitude makes another tone of similar frequency inaudible. This is called *masking effect*.

The video coder encodes the signal by dividing the pictures into three different types: I-frames, P-frames, and B-frames. *I-frames* (intracoded frames) are encoded using JPEG, a still image compression algorithm. They are self-contained and independent of the other two types of frames. Using only these frames would work but would not eliminate the repetition that occurs in successive pictures. *P-frames* (predicted frames) are frames that contain only the data that differs from an I-frame. *B-frames* (bidirectional frames) are predictions of pictures that come between I- and P-frames. B frames use I- and P-frames to interpolate and predict the content they should contain. For example, a typical MPEG compressed video clip would contain the following types of frames: I,B,B,P,B,B,I. This method of coding only the differences between successive pictures is called *motion compensation*.

All MPEG standards have a five-digit ISO number. An additional sixth digit represents the part. For example: 1 represents the part that describes the system (this means how to combine video and audio), 2 represents the video part, and 3 represents the audio part. Higher numbers are used for descriptions of conformance testing methods or for addendums.

MPEG-1 (ISO 11172), published in 1993, is a video and audio streaming format that targets a bandwidth of 1 to 1.5 megabits per second (Mbps) offering home VCR-quality video at a resolution of 352 by 288 pixels (smaller than a regular NTSC TV-screen) and 30 pictures per second. It requires special hardware for real-time encoding. Decoding is easier, so it can be done by software, but most implementations still consume a large fraction of processor time. MPEG-1 does not offer resolution scalability, and the video quality is highly susceptible to packet losses. One application is video playback from **CD-ROM**.

MPEG-2 (ISO 13818) was published in 1995 and extends MPEG-1 by including support for higher-resolution video and increased audio capabilities. The targeted bit rate for MPEG-2 is 4 to 15 Mbps, providing broadcast-quality full-screen video, which can be used by television stations. It does offer scalability, which means that the compression-to-quality ratio can be adjusted. It is more complex than MPEG-1, so real-time encoding and decoding requires even more expensive hardware. MPEG-2 is also very sensitive to packet losses. It is used primarily for satellite broadcasts.

A first version of MPEG-4 (ISO 14496) was released in October 1998. Its intention is to provide a compression suitable for video conferencing with data rates lower than 64 kilobytes per second, which would be usable for the Internet or mobile networks. It follows a slightly different approach as it standardizes a number of *media objects* (such as video, audio, text, etc.), which are then combined. MPEG-4 offers the possibility to better manage and protect content owner rights.

The next standards planned are MPEG-7, which aims to be a multimedia content description interface, and MPEG-21.

FURTHER READING

Orzessek, Michael, and Peter Sommer. *ATM & MPEG-2: Integrating Digital Video into Broadband Networks.* Upper Saddle River, N.J.: Prentice Hall, 1998.

Poynton, Charles A. *A Technical Introduction to Digital Video.* New York: Wiley, 1996.

Symes, Peter. *Video Compression: Fundamental Compression Techniques and an Overview of the JPEG and MPEG Compression Systems.* New York: McGraw-Hill, 1998.

Watkinson, John. *MPEG-2.* Oxford and Boston: Focal Press, 1999.

—*Gerald Friedland*

MP3

MP3, which stands for *MPEG-1 Audio Layer* 3, is a file format for compressing sound. Since MP3 files are considerably smaller and produce better quality output than other formats, the MP3 format has gained in popularity in recent years.

In 1987 the Institut für Integrierte Schaltungen of the Fraunhofer Institute, Germany, embarked on a project to define a standard for digital audio broadcasting. Since **bandwidth** has always been the limiting factor, the goal was to produce highly compressed audio streams while retaining a level of quality close to that provided by compact disks (CDs). CDs sample an audio stream 44,100 times a second (44.1 kilohertz [kHz]) and are thus able to capture frequencies up to 22.05 kHz. This easily covers the range that a typical person can perceive. The accuracy of the sample is stored in 16 bits, so that one hour of stereo CD quality music takes up 630 megabytes (MB).

Initial work at the Fraunhofer Institute, in conjunction with scientist Dieter Seitzer, led to the Moving Picture Expert Group, Level 1 algorithm (**MPEG** 1 or simply MP1), which reduced the necessary space to 25 percent of the original size. Level 2 achieved compression rates of up to one-eighth, and level 3 of up to one-twelfth of the original size. This has become the current MP3 standard.

These high compression rates are achieved through complex psychoacoustic models, which are able to identify and eliminate frequencies from recordings that the human ear is unable to hear. The resulting file is consequently much smaller than a music CD, but when the audio signal is reconstructed on an MP3 player, the reproduction is virtually undistinguishable from the original.

The encoding algorithm can produce output using constant or variable bit rates. The latter adjusts the resolution of the digital sample to the complexity of the input, while the former sacrifices this feature for reduced complexity.

Since the MP3 decoder does not require extensive processing power, these files can be reproduced not only on any personal computer (PC) but also on dedicated MP3 players. These small devices commonly have 32 MB of random access memory (**RAM**) and are loaded from a **personal computer** (PC) with a simple cable with over 30 minutes of audio data, usually music. Their popularity is closely related to the number of sites that offer MP3 music files, whose numbers have recently increased dramatically. The AltaVista internet search engine, for example, found over 1.4 million hits for the term MP3.

MP3 players have no moving parts, weigh a fraction of the weight of a Walkman or minidisk player, are completely skip free, and last many hours on a single battery. Numerous vendors have announced newer models with more RAM and removable RAM disks, making the older portable audio player technology obsolete.

Making an MP3 file from any audio input requires the corresponding encoder software. Many such shareware and freeware applications can be loaded from the **Internet** so that any PC with a sound card is capable of generating these files. Given a CD-ROM drive, a user can convert entire CDs to this compressed format and post them on the Internet.

Not surprisingly, the exchange of copyrighted material and bootleg music has skyrocketed—for example, through music swapping Internet sites such as Napster. This is a matter of great concern to the music industry, and many lawsuits have been instigated on behalf of copyright holders. On the other hand, this new technology provides a means for unknown musicians to distribute their music to a wide audience, effectively bypassing the need of support from a big record label. Similarly, established musicians can use this medium to sell their music directly to the consumer by circumventing all intermediaries. In 1999, rap musician Ice-T, for example, signed an exclusive marketing agreement with the Web site MP3.com. The consequence is a reduced retail price for his albums, with higher margins per sale for the artist, due to faster distribution and the fact that no medium needs to change hands.

Meanwhile, the Fraunhofer Institute continues to advance this technology and has defined the standard for MP4 and presented it at the Audio Engineering Society Conference in 1997. This advance promises further compression with less reduction in quality compared to standard CDs and will be backwardly compatible to MP3.

Further Reading

Behar, Michael. "It's Playback Time! A Wired Special Report on Downloadable Music, Video, and More." *Wired*, 7.08, Aug. 1999. *http://www.wired.com/wired/archive/7.08/dl_opener_pr.html*

Fries, Bruce, and Marty Fries. *The MP3 and Internet Audio Handbook*. Silver Spring, Md.: TeamCom, 1999.

Hacker, Scot. *MP3: The Definitive Guide*. Sebastopol, Calif.: O'Reilly, 2000.

Robertson, Michael, and Ron Simpson. *The Official MP3.com Guide to MP3*. San Diego, Calif.: MP3.com, 1999.

—*Thomas Schwerk*

MUDs and MOOs

MUDs (Multiuser Dungeons or Dimensions) are software programs that allow multiple users to connect at the same time and interact with each other. MOOs (MUDs object oriented) add additional features to the database, such as rooms, exits, and notes.

MUDs started as "Dungeons and Dragons"–style adventure games. The first MUD was created by Roy Trubshaw and Richard Bartle in England in 1979. In the mid-1980s most MUDs were dial-up systems that existed as databases on proprietary networks; players connected to them with a modem and online service. Since the spread of the **Internet**, MUDs have evolved into a variety of forms. The release of the software for games, such as AberMUD and Monster in 1988, prompted the creation of many imitators. MUD communities began to emerge that were based on "families" of MUDs, including the DikuMUD and TinyMUD communities. Users often played in several MUDs at the same time, forming communities that spanned several MUDs.

There are three basic types of MUDs: adventure, social, and educational. In early adventure MUDs, players gained levels based on their experiences of killing computer-controlled creatures and solving puzzles. These MUDs were combat-oriented and featured complex interactions between players and the computer-maintained world. In social MUDs, people focus on building a new world together rather than engaging in combat. These MUDs are infinite games that continue to develop as players add new objects. MUD software is also utilized by educators to conduct classes or foster discussion. For example, some students studying Western literature have created Dante's five levels of hell in MUD space. Similarly, MUDs have been set up as serious social spaces for the intellectual exploration of topics such as postmodern theory.

MOOs support an embedded programming language that enables players to describe objects and create types of behavior for the objects they create. MOO software gives each user access to a shared database of "rooms," "exits," and "objects." Users navigate the database from "inside" the rooms and they see only the objects that are located in the particular room that they are in. Users move from room to room through the exits that connect them together. For example, in LambdaMOO visitors enter through a coat closet and exit into a living room. MOOs can be thought of as a form of text-based virtual reality because commands are typed into a keyboard, and feedback is displayed as unformatted text on the computer screen.

In MOOs and MUDs, players create their own characters, worlds, social structures, and hierarchies. New players must learn how to use simple software commands to communicate with others: MUDs can be very disorienting for new players because the conversation is chaotic and text scrolls by at a fast rate. MUDs also have rules and regulations that players must learn, including being polite to other players and not wasting computing resources. Players who do not follow the rules are sometimes locked out of the MUD.

Central to MUD interaction is the notion that people can experiment with their behavior. For example, it is not unusual for players to approach a complete stranger and start up a conversation in a manner that they would never use face to face. Some researchers believe that MUD interaction can be beneficial for adolescent identity-formation because it allows young people to experiment with their identity without suffering real-world consequences. However, the real-life anonymity of players can also lead people to behave in socially unacceptable ways. As social laboratories, MUDs are places where people can experiment with both identity formation and developing social structures.

MUDs are not for everyone. Good typing skills are a requirement for this type of interaction because typos and spelling mistakes can reflect on the character. Moreover, people who interact in these online environments must be able to handle three or four conversations at the same time. People who are used to doing one thing at a time can find MUDs very stressful. In contrast, people who enjoy role-playing and fantasy games tend to like this type of socializing.

Further Reading

Bennahum, D. "Fly Me to the MOO." *Lingua Franca,* May/June 1994, pp. 1, 22–36.

Curtis, P., and D.A. Nichols. *MUDs Grow Up: Social Virtual Reality in the Real World.* Palo Alto, Calif.: Xerox Palo Alto Research Center, 1993. *http://www.rrz.uni-koeln.de/themen/cmc/text/curtis.93.txt*

Dibbell, Julian. *My Tiny Life: Crime and Passion in a Virtual World.* New York: Henry Holt, 1999.

Turkle, Sherri. *Life on the Screen: Identity in the Age of the Internet.* New York: Simon and Schuster, 1997.

—*Susan B. Barnes*

Multics

Multics (multiplexed information and computing service) is a **time-sharing** operating system for **mainframe** computers. Multics was intended to be the prototype of a "computer utility," providing computing service on demand to many users simultaneously. The system met its goals, although not as rapidly as originally hoped.

Developed in 1965 as a joint project between the Massachusetts Institute of Technology's (MIT) **Project MAC**, **Bell Labs**, and General Electric's Large Computer Products Division, the Multics project was led by Fernando J. Corbato (1926–) of MIT. At the 1965 Fall Joint Computer Conference, the system was introduced in a series of six papers describing the ambitious project, one of the largest **software** development efforts of its day.

Multics has several notable features. Its memory addressing system, called *segmented virtual memory*, organizes memory into segments. Each segment has addresses from 0 to 256k words (1 megabyte). The file system is integrated with the memory access system so that programs refer to files by making memory references. Multics also uses paged memory in the manner pioneered by the **Atlas** system. Addresses generated by the **central processing unit** (CPU) are translated by **hardware** from a virtual address to a real address. A hierarchical three-level scheme, using main storage, paging device, and disk, provides transparent access to the **virtual memory**.

Multics uses a tree-structured, hierarchical file system, providing directories that contain files, directories, and links. It was the inspiration for file systems in most modern systems. Multics also provided the first commercial relational database product, the Multics relational data store (MRDS), in 1978. The Multics hardware **architecture** features symmetric multiprocessing, meaning that it supports multiple CPUs sharing the same physical memory. Multics also has multiple language support: In addition to **PL/I**, Multics supports BCPL, **BASIC**, **APL**, **Fortran**, **LISP**, **C**, **COBOL**, **ALGOL** 68, and **Pascal**. Routines in these languages can call each other.

Multics was designed to be able to run 24 hours a day, seven days a week. CPUs, memory, I/O controllers, and disk drives can be added to and removed from the system configuration while the system is running. Multics was also designed to be secure. In the 1980s, the system was awarded the B2 security rating by the U.S. government, the first (and for years only) system to get a B2 rating. As part of its computer utility orientation, high-level-language implementation, design and code review, structured programming, modularization, and layering were employed extensively to manage the complexity of the system.

MIT started providing time-sharing service on Multics to users in the fall of 1969. That same year, Bell Labs withdrew from the development effort. **Ken Thompson** (1943–), **Dennis Ritchie** (1941–), and several other Bell Labs researchers who had worked on Multics went on to create the **Unix** operating system. In 1970, GE sold its computer business to **Honeywell**, which offered Multics as a commercial product and sold about 80 multimillion-dollar systems to the government, automakers, universities, and commercial data processing services. In the 1980s, Honeywell's partner, Bull, sold a total of 31 Multics sites in France. In 1985, Honeywell decided not to create a new hardware generation for Multics and stopped developing the operating system. A few Multics systems are still in use.

FURTHER READING

Corbato, F. J., and V. A. Vyssotsky. "Introduction and Overview of the Multics System." *AFIPS Conference Proceedings*, Vol. 27, 1965.

Daley, R. C., and P. G. Neumann. "A General-Purpose File System for Secondary Storage." *AFIPS Conference Proceedings*, Vol. 27, 1965.

David, E. E., Jr., and R. M. Fano. "Some Thoughts About the Social Implications of Accessible Computing." *AFIPS Conference Proceedings*, Vol. 27, 1965.

Glaser, E. L., J. F. Couleur, and G. A. Oliver. "System Design of a Computer for Time-Sharing Applications." *AFIPS Conference Proceedings*, Vol. 27, 1965.

Organick, E. I. *The Multics System: An Examination of Its Structure*. Cambridge, Mass.: MIT Press, 1972.

Ossanna, J. F., L. Mikus, and S. D. Dunten. "Communications and Input-Output Switching in a Multiplexed Computing System." *AFIPS Conference Proceedings*, Vol. 27, 1965.

Vyssotsky, V. A., F. J. Corbato, and R. M. Graham. "Structure of the Multics Supervisor." *AFIPS Conference Proceedings*, Vol. 27, 1965.

—Tom Van Vleck

Multimedia

The term *multimedia* describes a wide variety of **software** application products, such as desktop video, animation, Web design programs, and content packages, including electronic books, games, educational software, and encyclopedias. Multimedia content products add dynamic characteristics to information that was previously distributed on static printed pages; for example, multimedia databases enable text, graphics, video, and audio to be combined on **CD-ROMs** through which people interactively navigate.

Early computer-based multimedia products were distributed on videodisk and often had an educational focus. Many of these products utilized an encyclopedia model of multimedia design that featured a structured approach to information access. Detailed information is organized by subject category and textual data are supplemented with images, video clips, and sound files. Students were able to access segments and to receive feedback and analysis from the laser disk. Some products also enabled students to create their own multimedia documents by editing video and audio clips into their own unique story sequence.

HyperCard was an early multimedia authoring program that was developed by Bill Atkinson in 1987. It was envisioned as a software "erector set" to enable **Macintosh** owners to mix on-screen animation, digitized and prerecorded compact disk audio, and live motion video into artistic and educational documents. After HyperCard, a variety of authoring programs became available, including ToolBook, Macromind Director, and Authorware.

With the dynamic growth of the **World Wide Web** in the 1990s, designing and developing multimedia content emerged as an important industry. As a result, new models for designing multimedia products were developed. Many of these new approaches have borrowed heavily from existing media, incorporating elements of documentary and film production, music recording, and magazine journalism. These newer types of multimedia designs tend to follow a film style of production because the product is developed and organized under the leadership of a director who has control over the overall vision and execution of the project.

By adding multimedia features to the formerly text-oriented **Internet**, the Web became a hybrid medium, combining elements of television, newspapers, and magazines. The Web merges the visual excitement of television with the in-depth reporting found in a printed newspaper. With the introduction of higher levels of **bandwidth** and the development of **streaming audio and video** technologies that deliver data in real time, multimedia promises to be a key feature of the Internet's future. Some authors also use the word monomedia because, they argue, all past vehicles of communication will eventually be reduced to a single form: data on computers.

FURTHER READING

Cotton, B., and R. Oliver. *Understanding Hypermedia from Multimedia to Virtual Reality*. San Francisco, Calif.: Chronicle Books, 1993.

Pavlik, John V. *New Media Technology: Cultural and Commercial Perspectives*. Needham Heights, Mass.: Allyn and Bacon, 1998.

Von Wodtke, Mark. *Mind over Media: Creative Thinking Skills for Electronic Media*. New York: McGraw-Hill, 1993.

—*Susan B. Barnes*

Multiprocessor

A multiprocessor is a computer with multiple instruction processors (**central processing units** [CPUs]). Originally, a multiprocessor consisted of four basic elements: two or more central processing units; a memory that can be shared by all processors (called a *shared memory multiprocessor*) or can be distributed so that each processor has its own private local memory (called a *distributed memory processor*); shared input/output access to all peripheral devices; and a single **operating system** in overall control of all **hardware** and **software**. The multiprocessor concept has subsequently been broadened to include multiprocessors with distributed operating systems. A multiprocessor is contrasted with a uniprocessor (or unit processor) where there is only one central processor. When all CPUs are of equal capability, the system is known as *symmetric multiprocessing*, as opposed to *asymmetric multiprocessing*, where processors have different capabilities.

The computers of the early 1950s, such as the UNIVAC I or the IBM 701, had only one processor, which carried out the execution of programs and controlled input/output operations. Computer designers realized that the processor could be utilized more efficiently if the input/output tasks were turned over to some other entity. In 1958 the IBM 709 and UNIVAC 1105 introduced I/O channels (special-purpose processors) that could control input/output independently. The CPU created channel programs and placed them in memory for the channels to execute. This concept was carried further by the UNIVAC LARC of 1960, which had a CPU and a separate I/O processor. This was not called multiprocessing, however, because there was just one CPU.

The first multiprocessor computer was the **Burroughs** D825, introduced in 1962 for military applications. It used a crossbar switch arrangement where switch modules (distinct from processors or memory modules) contained circuitry to accommodate and queue simultaneous memory requests. The D825 could have up to four processors, 16 memory modules, and 10 input/output controllers. Burroughs delivered the B5000, the first multiprocessor for the commercial market, in 1963. It had a maximum of two processors.

The CDC 6600, released by **Control Data Corporation** in 1964, is an example of asymmetric multiprocessing. It contained multiple arithmetic/logic units and 10 smaller peripheral processors that were used to control the input/output, the system console, and the flow of tasks to the arithmetic/logic units.

The development of multiprocessor computers accelerated during the late 1960s. In 1965, Sperry Rand delivered a multiprocessor computer for the U.S. Army's Nike-X antiballistic missile (ABM) project that consisted of three processors, two memory units, and two input/output controllers (IOCs). The following year this architecture was adapted for its commercial UNIVAC 1108 computer. IBM's time-sharing 360/67 (1967) was enhanced to have a two-processor capability, and a two-processor version of the 360/65 was announced in 1969. In the area of scientific computation, the development of **parallel processing** architectures started at this time.

Multiprocessor computers became commonplace during the 1970s and 1980s. The concept was applied in the microprocessor realm during the late 1980s. Intel's 8086 main processor combined with the 8087 math coprocessor was an example of asymmetric multiprocessing. Symmetric multiprocessor systems for both **Unix** and **Windows** operating environments are now widely available.

FURTHER READING

Enslow, D. H., Jr., ed. *Multiprocessors and Parallel Processing.* New York: Wiley, 1974.

Rosen, Saul. "Electronic Computers: A Historical Survey." *Computing Surveys,* Vol. 1, Mar. 1969, pp. 7–36.

—George Gray

Multitasking

Simply defined, multitasking is doing more than one thing at a time. In the case of computers with a single CPU (**central processing unit**, the "brain" of the computer), multitasking actually consists of switching back and forth between multiple programs ("tasks") quickly enough that it *looks* like the computer is doing more than one thing at a time. In systems with more than one CPU, tasks can be spread out over the processors, so that the computer actually *is* doing more than one thing at a time. This is called **parallel processing**.

Because the CPU of a computer is much faster than the physical devices surrounding it, the CPU must spend much of its time waiting. It waits for data to be transferred to or from a disk drive, for the user to type on the **keyboard**, for a response to arrive from a **modem**, or for a page to print on a **printer**. All of these tasks are known as *input–output* (I/O). During these waiting times, a multitasking **operating system** (OS) can allow the computer to work on something else.

This concept works well when most of the tasks running are *I/O intensive*, meaning that they use devices other than the CPU the majority of the time. When one or more tasks are *computation intensive*, performing intensive calculations without giving up control to the operating system, everything else on the computer can grind to a halt.

This brings us to the two main classifications of multitasking: cooperative and preemptive. In *cooperative multitasking*, each program running on the computer is responsible for giving up control voluntarily every so often so that other programs have a chance to run. Since most programs make extensive use of the OS, much of the cooperation can happen at that level. Even if the programmer neglects to take multitasking into consideration when writing the program, each time the program calls an OS function, such as to read data from a disk or communicate with the user, the OS has an opportunity to give control to another task. Still, though, programmers must look for sections of the program that are computation intensive and give up control voluntarily during those times. Operating systems such as the **Macintosh** (before OS/X) and early versions of **Windows** use cooperative multitasking.

In *preemptive multitasking*, the CPU has a way of taking control away from each task on a schedule, triggered by a clock that generates processor interrupts. Programs are allocated time slices, and when the program's slice is up, the CPU will save the state of the program and move on to the next task. Operating systems such as **Unix**, Windows NT, Windows 2000, and OS/2 use preemptive multitasking.

Traditionally, multitasking was used in **mainframe** computers to allow them to handle more than one user at a time—this was known as **time-sharing**. When **microcomputers** were introduced, they were intended to work for a single user, and multitasking became a way to make a single user more productive rather than a way for multiple users to share a computer. Today, some level of multitasking exists in virtually every computer.

Both preemptive and cooperative multitasking work well when all programs are behaving as expected. The great danger in cooperative multitasking is when a program bug causes a task to loop indefinitely, continuing to perform calculations without giving up control to the OS or another task. If the OS cannot get control, the rogue program forces the entire system to be restarted. When a program in a preemptive multitasking OS goes into an indefinite loop, the OS can continue to allow other tasks to run, and the user can intervene, shutting down the "hung" task without interfering with any other tasks running at the same time.

Thus far, we have considered only systems in which all tasks are equally important. Another benefit of preemptive multitasking is that tasks can be assigned priorities, with important tasks given more of the system's time. A process that interacts with the user, for example, is considered to be higher priority than one that handles background processes such as printing, so that the user will not be forced to wait for the system.

In a simplistic multitasking system, the OS would take control every fraction of a second on a fixed schedule. The tasks would be arranged in a round-robin list, and each time the OS took control, it would move on to the next task in the round robin. If there were 20 tasks running, each would get one-twentieth of the processor's time (less the overhead of the actual task switching). A more realistic implementation would check each process to make sure it was ready to run before giving it control, so that the CPU wouldn't waste time on a process that was waiting for user input when another process needed the time.

In priority systems, each task is assigned a priority that determines how much time it gets. Rather than following a straight round-robin approach, the OS gives control to the highest-priority task that is ready to run. Various **algorithms** exist to handle priorities, including creating multiple round-robin lists (one for each priority level) and not passing control to any task until all higher-priority tasks have been given a chance to run.

Alternatively, the OS can continue to give control to tasks in round-robin order, but change the length of time assigned to the task based on its priority. With this approach, high-priority tasks do not get more time slices, but the time slices they get are longer. Some operating systems allow the user or system administrator to control aspects of the priority system, to fine-tune performance. Even in a preemptive multitasking environment, well-written programs should be made "nice," giving up control periodically during heavy computation-intensive routines so that they do not monopolize the processor.

A key element of any multitasking system is a component of the operating system known as the *task switcher*. It is the responsibility of the task switcher to save the state of the current task and give control to the next task with all resources in place exactly as they were when the task gave up control (or when control was taken from it). Task switchers change memory maps, save and restore registers and stacks, and swap task memory from disk to random access memory (**RAM**) in a **virtual memory** system. All of the processing done by the task switcher must be done as quickly as possible to avoid unnecessarily bogging down the system, as task switches happen many times per second.

For this reason, the task switcher is carefully designed and tuned for performance.

Multitasking should not be confused with *multithreading*. In multitasking, an operating system allows a number of programs to run independent of each other. Although these tasks may be able to communicate through pipes and other interprocess communication methodologies, each task has a separate environment, including its own memory space and variables. Generally speaking, tasks can be started and stopped independent of each other.

In multithreading, on the other hand, a single program splits apart into two or more concurrently operating "threads," which run as parts of the same program, sharing memory space and variables. These threads can communicate among themselves in ways that separate programs cannot, including shared variables. Typically, threads cannot be stopped by anything other than the task that created them, and the operating system assigns CPU time and priority to all of the threads in a task as a single unit rather than giving each thread its own time slices.

Even simple single-tasking operating systems can perform some basic multitasking through the use of **interrupts**. In MS-DOS, for example, the hardware or firmware in an I/O controller can be given a task to perform, and it will interrupt the CPU when that task is complete. This allows such programs as print queues to run in the background while the foreground task interacts with the user.

FURTHER READING

Bach, Maurice J. *Design of the Unix Operating System.* Englewood Cliffs, N.J.: Prentice Hall, 1990.

Comer, Douglas, and Timothy V. Fossum. *Operating System Design.* Englewood Cliffs, N.J.: Prentice Hall, 1988.

Nutt, Gary J. *Kernel Projects for Linux.* Boston: Addison-Wesley, 2000.

Stallings, William. *Operating Systems: Internals and Design Principles,* 3rd ed. Upper Saddle River, N.J.: Prentice Hall, 1997.

Tanenbaum, Andrew. *Modern Operating Systems.* Englewood Cliffs, N.J.: Prentice Hall, 1992.

Tanenbaum, Andrew, and Albert S. Woodhull. *Operating Systems: Design and Implementation.* Englewood Cliffs, N.J.: Prentice Hall, 1987; 2nd ed., Upper Saddle River, N.J., 1997.

—*Gary Robson*

Multithreaded Architecture

A computer with a multithreaded architecture usually has a single processor that executes numerous instruction streams (**threads**), switching among them with the help of multiple register sets. One can think of a multithreaded processor as a parallel execution unit based on a single processor. In the late 1990s and early 2000s, several prototypes of multithreaded processors were built.

Computer architects are constantly looking for different ways to extract more performance from the "transistor budget" provided by modern VLSI (**very large scale integration**) chips. Since the 1980s, *pipelining*, which is a form of parallel execution, has been used and has become almost universal in all current processors. In a pipelined processor, the execution of each instruction is divided into several stages and the instruction goes sequentially through each. A common scheme, for example, consists of using five stages, such as instruction fetch (retrieving the instruction from memory), instruction decode, instruction execution proper, memory access, and write back (the result is stored in a register). Once the stages have been defined, they are isolated electrically from each other in such a way that when an instruction has gone through the first stage, a new one can be inserted into the pipeline, and so on. When the pipeline is full, up to five instructions are in the processor and have achieved different degrees of completion. Pipelined execution resembles assembly lines in manufacturing plants—every worker (every stage) receives a new piece of work as soon as the last one has been completed and passes the completed work on to the next worker in the line.

The advantage of pipelining is that instructions can be started faster since each stage is shorter than the full execution path. Under ideal conditions, a pipeline of five stages provides a fivefold performance gain over a similar sequential processor without pipelining. The challenge of pipelining is keeping the pipeline full with normal programs, which is very difficult. Conditional branches in the code can lead to a situation where the execution path has to be changed (retrieving instructions from another place in memory) after other instructions located below the branch have already been loaded into the pipeline. In this case the pipeline has to be *flushed*, clearing and restarting it with instructions from the new instruction stream. *Data hazards* are another common problem. These are conflicts between instructions loaded back to back into the pipeline. It could be the case that the result of an instruction is needed by the next instruction, which has to stop the pipeline until the first instruction writes back its result into the registers, so that it can be used by the instruction waiting. Such waiting cycles lead to *pipeline bubbles,* in which no useful work is done in some pipeline stages.

An elegant solution to the problem of pipeline bubbles is to execute several threads simultaneously. Threads can be thought of as programs running in parallel in a computer. The name *thread* is used because a single program (e.g., the text processor) can start parallel activities (checking grammar at the same time that text is formatted); since these parallel pieces of code belong to the same program, they are called threads of execution of the mother program.

Consider again the example with a pipeline made of five stages, and assume that five threads are running. The first instruction for the pipeline could be taken from thread 1, the second instruction from thread 2, and so on, until the pipeline is full. Then the loading process is repeated cyclically (taking one instruction from each thread) each time an instruction is complete and abandons the pipeline. The advantage of this scheme is that a new instruction from a thread is fetched only after the previous instruction has finished executing. There are no ambiguities, no problems with conditional branches, and no conflicts between back-to-back instructions in the code.

There is, however, a drawback: Switching between the different threads can be done rapidly only if each thread uses a different set of registers to hold information temporarily in the processor. In our example, we would need five sets of, say, 32 registers each. Each thread can manage its 32 registers as desired. The processor then needs a grand total of 5 times 32 registers (i.e., 160 registers). Some other internal registers also have to be replicated: for example, the program counter, which keeps track of the position in memory of the next instruction to be executed.

Multithreaded processors can therefore keep the pipeline full and achieve the full performance gain of the pipelined processor, under the assumption that there are enough threads waiting for attention by the processor. This requires new compilation techniques, in order to make programs parallel automatically, even if the programmer wrote sequential code.

The type of multithreading described above is called *interleaved multithreading.* When a block of instructions (not a single instruction) is taken from each thread, this is called *block multithreading.* The processor can switch between threads synchronously, according to a clock, or asynchronously (i.e., only when a conflict would generate a pipeline bubble).

One example of a commercial multithreaded system is the one being built by Tera Computers, a supercomputing company. In the Tera architecture, the **central processing unit** switches context every 3 nanoseconds among 128 different threads. The machine can contain up to 256 processors. **Sun Microsystem**'s SPARC architecture, with up to 512 registers and several register windows, has also been used experimentally to implement multithreaded systems.

FURTHER READING

Bokhari, Shahid H., and Dimitri J. Mavriplis. *The Tera Multithreaded Architecture and Unstructured Meshes.* Hampton, Va.: Institute for Computer Applications in Science and Engineering, NASA Langley Research Center; Springfield, Va.: National Technical Information Service, distributor, 1998.

Iannucci, Robert A., et al. *Multithreaded Computer Architecture: A Summary of the State of the Art.* Boston: Kluwer Academic, 1994.

Moore, Simon W. *Multithreaded Processor Design.* Boston: Kluwer Academic, 1996.

—*Raúl Rojas*

Music, Computer

Music has seen some of the most creative and productive applications of computer technology thus far. Computer-based synthesizers have spawned previously unimaginable electronic orchestras; techniques such as **virtual reality** have blurred the distinction between composer and performer, mind and machine; and computer-inspired models have enabled psychologists to better understand how human brains process musical information. Computers have revolutionized music as much as any other field of human endeavor.

Although the history of computer music faithfully follows the history of computing through much of the twentieth century, its beginnings date back earlier than the modern computer age. Around 1860, German physicist and psychologist Hermann Helmholtz (1821–94) published his influential *Sensations of Sound: Psychological Basis for Theory of Music.* This demonstrated how musical sounds were built up by combining independent sound tones, a theory on which all computer-based musical instruments and synthesizers are now based.

The invention of the **vacuum tube** in 1906 by the"father of radio" Lee de Forest (1873–1961) produced several notable early instruments. These included de Forest's own Audion Piano, the Theremin (an antenna connected to a vacuum tube, which emitted a noise that varied in pitch and intensity when the performer's hand moved toward or away from it) and the Ondes Martenot of 1928 (a sophisticated keyboard instrument that produces eerie swooping noises and features prominently in Olivier Messiaen's [1908–92] *Turangalîla Symphony*).

During the 1950s, composers came to technology, rather than the other way around, and the technology, such as it existed, was available only through experimental studios attached to radio stations. Notable among these was the Electronic Music Studio founded in 1953 in Cologne, where pioneering German composer Karlheinz Stockhausen (1928–) painstakingly assembled his early electronic works. In the United States, Harry Olson and Herbert Belar of the Radio Corporation of America (RCA) used computer technology to produce the RCA MkI and MkII synthesizers. Sounds were created using vacuum tubes (12 in the MkI and 24 in the MkII) and could be preprogrammed using punched paper tape inputs or recorded by an internal lacquer disk-cutting system.

The invention of the **transistor** in 1947 and the **integrated circuit** (IC) in 1958 produced little benefit for musicians until the 1960s. But their arrival revolutionized computer music as much as the wider computer industry. Early synthesizers, such as the RCA, had been comparable in size, usability, and reliability (or lack of) to early computers such as the **ENIAC**. But semiconductors enabled engineers such as Donald Buchla and Robert Moog (1934–) to produce much more compact instruments. Buchla produced the first commercial synthesizers, but Moog's influence proved more far reaching. His machines, manufactured from 1964 onward, became hugely popular following the release in 1968 of an album by Wendy Carlos (1939–) called *Switched-On Bach.* Moog's compact and portable Minimoog synthesizer, produced in 1969, finally moved synthesizers from the studio to the stage. Modern, keyboard-style synthesizers using ICs and **microprocessors** were commonplace by the mid-1970s, due partially to competition between manufacturers and partially to the enthusiastic patronage of musicians such as Stevie Wonder (1950–), German groups Tangerine Dream and Kraftwerk, and French composer Jean-Michel Jarre (1948–).

Until the 1970s, computer music was little more than a spin-off of electronics technology. But the development of affordable desktop **microcomputers** (later standardized in the form of **personal computers** [PCs]) and affordable tabletop synthesizers led to a more productive synergy between the two fields. Groundbreaking machines such as the New England Digital Synclavier of 1975 and the Fairlight Computer Musical Instrument (CMI) of 1979 were hybrid computer–synthesizers that combined the best of both technologies. They were fully fledged musical instruments that could be played on stage, but they were also powerful computers that could sequence (play back preprogrammed sounds, such as a bass rhythm) and sample (e.g., allowing the sound of a dog barking to be played up and down the scale of a piano keyboard). With the exception of its twin keyboards, the Fairlight CMI looked much like any microcomputer of its era. Unlike other synthesizers, it featured a green-screen monitor on which sounds could be edited or manipulated directly using a light pen. Inside, it was powered by two 8-bit Motorola 6800 microprocessors.

Another major development happened completely by chance. **Human–computer interaction** (HCI) pioneer **Raymond Kurzweil** (1948–) began applying computer technology to synthesizer design in 1982 after developing a computerized reading machine for blind people and becoming friendly with Stevie Wonder. Their collaboration spawned a synthesizer that married the control and versatility of computer technology with the rich sound of traditional instruments. When the Kurzweil Music Systems K-250 was released in 1984, musicians could accurately mimic grand pianos, strings, drums, and other instruments using a synthesizer keyboard. Its secret was to use **ROM** memory to store complex sound models of traditional instruments and microprocessors that manipulated sounds in real time according to those models.

If computers made synthesizers into powerful musical instruments, synthesizers worked the same magic in reverse on personal computers. Where music was concerned, early microcomputers and PCs were little more than toys. Some contained polyphonic voices (multiple sound generators that could be combined and shaped in various ways to produce richer effects, such as the sound of a piano), but most were let down by poor-quality speakers and an inability to interface to other electronic musical instruments. That changed in 1984 with the introduction of **MIDI** (Musical Instrument Digital Interface), a standard interface for connecting computers and musical instruments. Using MIDI, a PC could be used as a sequencer to play a repetitive pattern of notes through a synthesizer, for example. Computer games and multimedia prompted the addition of increasingly sophisticated sound-generating electronics to PCs during the 1990s. Popular soundcards such as the Creative Laboratories Sound Blaster have turned PCs into complete synthesizers, with polyphonic voices, CD-quality recording and playback, sampling, and MIDI interfaces.

Conceptually, synthesizers lie somewhere between computers and musical instruments. A traditional instrument such as a violin or a trumpet takes its characteristic sound from the way that sound waves resonate inside its uniquely shaped body. But a synthesizer creates sound waves artificially with individual tone generators, combining them and changing their shapes using processes called modulation and envelope shaping, based on the physics of sound and the psychology of hearing. This makes computer music an abstraction of traditional music and explains why a synthesizer player may be less of a traditional musician and more of a programmer, psychologist, and physicist.

This provides a clue to the numerous, rather disparate directions into which computer music research has ventured in recent years. Much of that research continues to focus on ways of producing better synthesizers and how to develop them beyond simple mimics of traditional instruments or generators of space-age novelty sounds. Some researchers see producing a synthetic singing voice as the holy grail of synthesizer development. Perry Cook of Princeton University has produced a somewhat limited but surprisingly realistic sounding computerized opera singer called Sheila.

Computers offer not just better ways of synthesizing music, but also simpler and more creative interfaces to musical instruments. Acquiring virtuosity with a traditional instrument takes many years of practice and is not transferable: A world-class concert pianist cannot become a world-class flautist overnight. But synthesizers and MIDI interfaces put virtuosity into the reach of almost anyone. For example, a flautist can play piano using an electronic flute, a MIDI interface, and a synthesizer.

Virtual reality (VR) has provided the most interesting avenue for this research. VR pioneer and musician Jaron Lanier (1961–) has devised a range of virtual instruments that are played by a musician using standard VR props such as head-mounted displays (HMDs) or datagloves. His virtual orchestra includes the Rhythm Gimbal (a type of gyroscope that emits sound as the musician spins it around), the Pianobeam (a piano played by the musician's hands moving though empty space), and the Cybersax (a virtual saxophone that can play two melodies at the same time).

Computers are used not just in musical performance but increasingly in the act of musical composition. A popular piece of software called Sibelius can transcribe a composition automatically and print out a musical score if the composer plays the notes on a synthesizer keyboard. But an increasingly productive field of research is examining what happens when computers are allowed to compose music according to preprogrammed rules or parameters. One notable avenue is fractal music, which uses mathematical chaos and **artificial intelligence** theories to compose music that evolves recursively into complex and beautiful patterns. Popular PC programs such as Gingerbread mean that anyone can compose fractal music with just a few minutes of training.

Beyond performing and composing music, computers have become indispensable in studies of music cognition and acoustics. Since the 1950s, cognitive psychology has produced scientifically productive models of the human brain based on the idea that it processes information as a computer does. Music cognition, by analogy, seeks to advance our understanding of music perception using the idea that the brain processes sound using some cerebral combination of computer, synthesizer working in reverse, and MIDI interface. Computer models have also proved indispensable in auditory research. Researchers at institutions such as IRCAM (Institut de Recherche et Coordination Acoustique/Musique) in Paris have long used computer models to study sound production and perception: for example, how the sounds produced by an orchestra combine to form a three-dimensional soundscape.

Music and computers have proved mutually beneficial throughout the twentieth century. The twenty-first century may herald an equally fruitful synergy between the two fields, for example, through the use of the **Internet** for collaborative real-time musical composition and performance or through the use of VR in teaching children to play musical instruments.

Further Reading

Abbott, C., ed. Special Issue on Computer Music. *ACM Computing Surveys*, Vol. 17, No. 2, 1985.

Cook, Perry R., ed. *Music, Cognition, and Computerized Sound: An Introduction to Psychoacoustics.* Cambridge, Mass.: MIT Press, 1999.

Dodge, Charles, and Thomas Jerse. *Computer Music: Synthesis, Composition, and Performance.* New York: Schirmer, 1985; 2nd ed., 1997.

Griffiths, Paul. *Modern Music: A Concise History.* London: Thames and Hudson, 1985; rev. ed., 1994.

Jourdain, Robert. *Music, the Brain, and Ecstasy: How Music Captures the Imagination.* New York: Morrow, 1997.

Kurtz, Michael. *Stockhausen: A Biography.* Translated by Richard Toop. Boston: Faber, 1992.

Manning, Peter. *Electronic and Computer Music.* Oxford: Clarendon Press, 1985; 2nd ed., 1993.

Mathews, Max V., and John R. Pierce. *Current Directions in Computer Music Research.* Cambridge, Mass.: MIT Press, 1989.

Moore, F. Richard. *Elements of Computer Music.* Upper Saddle River, N.J.: Prentice Hall, 1998.

Neesham, Claire. "Digital Diva." *New Scientist,* 7 Sept. 1996, p. 36.

Rubin, David M. *The Desktop Musician.* Berkeley, Calif.: Osborne/McGraw-Hill, 1994.

Von Foerster, Heinz, and James W. Beauchamp. *Music by Computers.* New York: Wiley, 1969.

—*Chris Woodford*

MVS

MVS, multiple virtual storage, is an **operating system** (OS) for the **IBM** 370/390 series of computers that has gone through many different incarnations. The initial MVS release was an upgrade for the OS of the 370 series. It was called MVS because it managed multiple 16-megabyte address spaces, in contrast to the previous version of the OS, which could manage only a single virtual address space. MVS became MVS/SP, then MVS/XA (with 31-bit addressing), and finally, MVS/ESA. This version was repackaged later as OS/390.

In 1972, IBM announced the new 370 series of **mainframes**, which used **virtual memory**. Shortly afterward, a new OS release was announced that could manage the virtual address space. It was named OS/VS2 SVS (single virtual space) because at first it did not contain multiple virtual spaces. In 1974, OS/VS2 MVS was shipped. After Release 3 of MVS in 1975, users could customize the operating system by including only those modules actually needed. This gave the end user greater flexibility but made it more difficult for IBM to provide service. Therefore, IBM started including the selectable units as default options in later releases of MVS.

With the introduction of the 390 series of computers, MVS migrated to the new **architecture** and became MVS/ESA (Enterprise Systems Architecture) in 1991. Marketing support for the 370 version of MVS was discontinued, but the operating system continued evolving, handling all new features of the IBM mainframes, such as support for several processors and extremely large address spaces.

One interesting feature of MVS/ESA is that it allows the loading of "guest" OSs. A **Unix** user, for example, can start IBM's version of Unix as a guest OS under

MVS/ESA and run any Unix utility or program. The latest release of MVS/ESA allows loading even older versions of MVS/ESA as guests, in this way preserving 100 percent compatibility of legacy software in new machines under new releases of the OS. This is one of the few features of mainframes that has not yet found its way into the world of **personal computers** and workstations.

FURTHER READING

Bambara, Richard. *MVS and UNIX: A Survival Handbook for Users, Developers, and Managers in a Multiplatform Environment.* New York: McGraw-Hill, 1998.

IBM. *Virtual Machine/Enterprise Systems Architecture,* Version 2, Release 4, Handbook, May 1999.

—*Frank Darius*

N

Nasdaq

Nasdaq is a computer-networked securities market owned by the National Association of Securities Dealers (NASD), a regulatory organization of U.S. investment banking, mutual fund, and over-the-counter (OTC) securities brokerage firms. Unlike exchange or auction securities markets such as the New York Stock Exchange (NYSE), Nasdaq is an OTC market, has no trading floor, and does not rely on a single specified market maker to set quotations. Instead, many dealers serve the market-making function by placing "bid" and "ask" orders on a computer **network**.

From the late nineteenth century to the early 1970s, OTC securities trading was fragmented and often characterized by low volume and inefficiency. In 1963 the Securities and Exchange Commission (SEC) sought to address this problem by enlisting NASD to investigate the creation and adoption of an automated quotation system. In December 1968, NASD signed a contract with the Bunker Ramo Corporation to develop the Nasdaq (National Association of Securities Dealers Quotation) System, the defining feature and namesake for the new OTC securities market. A team of approximately 50 engineers, systems analysts, and programmers, most of whom were from Bunker Ramo, soon began work on the project. On 8 February 1971 the Nasdaq system became operational, revolutionizing over-the-counter trading by displaying quotations for more than 2500 corporate securities on networked terminals nationwide.

The initial system consisted of two **UNIVAC** 1108 multiprocessing computers that were housed in a new 40,000-square-foot facility in Trumbull, Connecticut; more than 20,000 miles of high-speed communications circuitry; four regional **Honeywell** DDP-516 computers with Bunker Ramo–designed communication control units placed in New York, Chicago, Atlanta, and San Francisco to direct network traffic; and hundreds of Bunker Ramo model 2217 terminals in the offices of subscribing OTC market-making firms. The **software** for the system included an enhanced UNIVAC Exec 8 operating system. In its first iteration, the Nasdaq system was capable of serving 2000 brokerages, processing and updating price and volume information added from any of the system's networked terminals within five seconds 95 percent of the time.

The initial growth of Nasdaq was constrained by the struggling economy of the early 1970s, but by middecade the market had grown substantially. In 1975, Nasdaq established listing standards, segregating qualifying firms from the rest of the OTC market. By this time, an increasing number of rapidly growing technology firms, including **Intel Corporation** and **Apple Computer**, were listed on Nasdaq. The success of such companies led Nasdaq to separate its highly successful firms from many smaller speculative OTC companies, or penny stocks, by establishing the Nasdaq National Market in 1982. Smaller firms meeting less stringent qualifications were listed on the Nasdaq Small Capitalization market. In 1986 the Federal Reserve granted brokerages the right to give customers margin trading privileges on Nasdaq issues, further fueling growth of the market. During 1994 the Nasdaq passed a major milestone by surpassing the NYSE in annual trading volume.

The growth of Nasdaq precipitated a series of upgrades to the system's computing and networking equipment to improve efficiency and handle rapidly expanding volume. By the mid-1980s the Nasdaq system had grown from its initial two mainframes to 30 far more powerful machines and was capable of handling trading volume of 125 million shares per day. In addition to the Trumbull facility, a U.S.$17 million backup processing center was set up in Washington, D.C. Technology for the system was coming increasingly from Nasdaq-traded firms, as **Sun Microsystems**, **MCI WorldCom**, Intel, and Apple became major equipment suppliers. Further upgrades in the 1990s brought the Nasdaq trading capacity to well over 1 billion shares a day.

By the mid-1990s accusations of widespread collusion between Nasdaq market-making firms became a frequent topic of financial journalists and academics. Critics argued that market makers had been artificially widening bid/ask spreads in order to boost their profits. Evidence of collusion remains inconclusive, while attention to the issue has been directly proportional to the continually accelerating amount of adulation and scrutiny that the Nasdaq market has received in the latter part of the 1990s as an increasing amount of capital is held in Nasdaq-traded firms.

During the 1990s, Nasdaq substantially outperformed historical stock market averages. The Dow Jones Industrial Average grew by roughly 300 percent in the 1990s (composed of all NYSE issues until it added several Nasdaq firms at decade's end), while Nasdaq advanced 685 percent. Leading large-capitalization high-technology Nasdaq-traded firms of the new economy, such as **Cisco Systems**, **Oracle**, and **Microsoft**, have contributed strongly to the growth of Nasdaq, which in turn has become a barometer for the continued high expectations for the technology sector of the U.S. economy.

FURTHER READING

Barclay, Michael J. "Bid–Ask Spreads and the Avoidance of Odd-Eighths Quotes on Nasdaq: An Examination of Exchange Listings." *Journal of Financial Economics*, Vol. 45, No.1, 1997, pp. 35–60.

Goodyear, W. Frederick. "The Birth of the Nasdaq." *Datamation*, Vol. 18, No. 3, 1972, pp. 42–45.

Leffler, George Leland. *The Stock Market*. New York: Ronald Press, 1951; 7th ed., by Richard J. Teweles and Edward S. Bradley, New York: Wiley, 1998.

Mills, N. "NASDAQ: A User-Driven, Real-Time Transaction System." *AFIPS Conference Proceedings 40, 1972 Spring Joint Computer Conference*, 1972, pp. 1197–1206.

Schwartz, M., R. R. Boorstyn, and R. L. Pickholtz. "Terminal-Oriented Computer-Communications Networks." *Proceedings of the IEEE*, Vol. 61, Nov. 1972, pp. 1408–1423.

—*Jeffrey R. Yost*

National Telecommunications and Information Administration

The National Telecommunications and Information Administration (NTIA) is an agency of the U.S. government. It is within the administrative structure of the U.S. Department of Commerce (DoC) and headed by the assistant secretary for Communications and Information. The NTIA advises the president on issues of telecommunication and information and manages the use of the radio-frequency spectrum by the federal government.

The NTIA was created in 1979 by combining the functions of the White House's Office of Telecommunications Policy and the U.S. DoC Office of Telecommunications. In addition to its advisory role, it presents the president's views on communications matters to the Federal Communications Commission (FCC), which has regulatory powers in this area, and the U.S. government's position on international telecommunications issues. The NTIA has significant technical expertise to serve its policy and advisory roles, which is housed in the Institute for Telecommunications Sciences (ITS). ITS conducts research on advanced telecommunications and information technology in cooperation with private industry.

The overall approach of the U.S. policy in this area gives the private sector leadership in developing and building telecommunications and information infrastructure while ensuring that it will be consistent with universal service. In other words, the government tries to make sure that it does not become an unnecessary obstacle for private enterprise in the domestic markets for telecommunications and information and leads the charge to open foreign markets and enhance the international competitiveness of U.S. business in this industry.

The main regulatory effort of U.S. policy intends to ensure that most U.S. customers will have access to telecommunication and information services at reasonable prices. For example, the NTIA has devoted significant effort to the development of schemes that will make services available in underserved markets, such as rural regions or segments of the population with lower economic status. This issue is sometimes referred to as the *digital divide.*

The policy issues addressed by the NTIA reflect the convergence of communications and computing that has occurred over the last decades. Along with allocation of spectrum resources, ownership of broadcast stations, and the introduction of high-definition TV, the NTIA addresses issues such as domain name management and the detailed vision of the administration on the national and global **information infrastructures**.

FURTHER READING

D'Udekem-Gevers, M., and C. Lobet-Maris. "Non-profit Applications of the Information Highways: Comparing Grant Programs of the European Commission and the National Telecommunication and Information Administration." *Cybernetica*, Vol. 39, No. 4, 1996, pp. 347–356.

Information Infrastructure Task Force. *The National Information Infrastructure: Agenda for Action.* Washington, D.C.: National Telecommunications and Information Administration, U.S. Department of Commerce, 1993.

———. *Global Information Infrastructure: Agenda for Cooperation.* Washington, D.C.: National Telecommunications and Information Administration, U.S. Department of Commerce, 1995.

National Telecommunications and Information Administration. *The NTIA Infrastructure Report: Telecommunications in the Age of Information.* Washington, D.C.: U.S. Department of Commerce, 1991.

—*Juan D. Rogers*

Natural Language Processing

The goal of natural language processing (NLP) is to enable human beings to communicate with a computer much as they do with another person, using the languages that humans use naturally (such as English or Japanese). This includes talking to computers, getting computers to understand written messages and articles, and having computers assist in interpreting and translating between different languages.

The first focus of NLP research was machine translation. In 1949 a memorandum written by Warren Weaver (1894–1978), who had been involved in code breaking in World War II, inspired several groups in the United States, the United Kingdom, France, and the Soviet Union to attempt to develop systems to translate between human languages (e.g., Russian to English). These early systems were not terribly successful. It became apparent that language was much more complex than had been anticipated; imagine trying to translate from an unknown language simply with the aid of a dictionary. This is likely to result in extremely poor translations: Different languages use different grammatical constructions and word order; a word in one language may have several interpretations in another, and so on.

Help came in 1957 with the linguistic theories of **Noam Chomsky** (1928–). He showed how the syntactic structure of language could be formalized in a rule-based manner. This provided a formal basis for automating the processing of natural language, for machine translation, or other applications. Although many other theories have followed, Chomsky's has probably had the most influence.

However, knowledge of the structure of language (syntax) is not enough. Whether translating a text or understanding a question in natural language, it is necessary to think about what it *means*, not just whether it is a legal, grammatical construction. But how do we represent the meaning of a sentence—we are used to defining meaning using natural language, but for processing using a computer we require a formal notation. In the 1970s there were many attempts to come up with formal representations of meaning based on logic, but none were as expressive as natural language, nor were they easy to reason with using a computer.

It has also become increasingly apparent that working out what something really means requires knowledge of the world—more than mere knowledge of language: It is necessary to have knowledge about the objects and actions mentioned in the text. For example, proper understanding of a political news article requires some knowledge of the events and characters involved.

From the mid-1960s through the 1970s, researchers came to a common understanding of the problems that needed to be solved and the basic framework for processing natural language. The key stages of processing included syntactic analysis (structure), semantic analysis (meaning), and pragmatic analysis (using world knowledge and information about the context). An important system at that time was SHRDLU, developed in 1972 by Terry Winograd (1946–). This system simulated a robot that manipulated blocks on a table top. It could handle instructions such as "Pick up a big red block" and answer questions such as "Which cube is on the table?" SHRDLU could handle language only in this very limited domain, but it did attempt to combine knowledge of syntax, semantics, and pragmatics.

Attempts to scale up the kind of approach used in SHRDLU have met with only limited success. It is too difficult to capture and represent all the knowledge that we need to understand arbitrary natural language. In the late 1980s and 1990s, with the advent of bigger, faster machines, researchers have therefore turned to statistical methods, based on analyzing huge numbers of online texts. To illustrate this approach, consider the following sentence: "John likes flying planes." One problem in determining what this means is deciding whether *plane* refers to a woodworking tool, an airplane, or a tree. In the classic approach to NLP we would need to have represented somewhere the fact that airplanes fly but trees generally do not. But using statistical methods we just analyze many texts, find all the sentences that mention planes, and find out how often the word *flying* occurs in each one and how that varies according to which type of plane is mentioned. This requires that someone has annotated the texts to indicate what meaning of the word is intended in each case, but after that the process can be automated. We might find that in (say) 95 percent of cases where *plane* occurs in the same sentence as *flying*, it means an airplane.

These statistical techniques, based on analyzing large corpora (rather than hand-authoring rules and knowledge) have proved successful for a range of practical NLP tasks. Speech recognition is based almost entirely on statistical models. Other tasks, such as determining the right *part of speech* (noun, verb, etc.) of words, or determining the correct word sense (as in the plane example), can also be done efficiently and effectively using simple probabilistic models. NLP is still some way off from full, robust, general language understanding, but we now know how to do some useful language-related tasks well. While statistical models may be used, these are based on our evolved understanding of the structures and processes involved in making sense of language. These techniques are now being exploited in (for example) speech interfaces, and to help us find and make sense of the vast quantities of natural language texts now available on the **World Wide Web**. The vision of talking to computers in everyday language may still be in the distant future, but our understanding of language processing has matured to enable a wide variety of practical NLP applications.

Further Reading

Allen, J. *Natural Language Understanding.* Redwood City, Calif.: Benjamin/Cummings, 1987; 2nd ed., Menlo Park, Calif., 1995.

Hutchins, W. J., and H. Somers, eds. *An Introduction to Machine Translation.* London and San Diego, Calif.: Academic Press, 1991.

Jurafsky, Daniel, and James H. Martin. *Speech and Language Processing: An Introduction to Natural Language Processing, Computational Linguistics, and Speech Recognition.* Upper Saddle River, N.J.: Prentice Hall, 2000.

Russell, S., and P. Norvig. *Artificial Intelligence: A Modern Approach.* Englewood Cliffs, N.J.: Prentice Hall, 1995.

—*Alison Cawsey*

NEC Corporation

NEC Corporation is a leading manufacturer in the world of communications equipment, **semiconductors**, and computer technology. The company was founded in Tokyo in 1899 as the Nippon Electric Company and was originally a joint venture with a U.S. partner. Only nine years later, NEC founded its first international office in Korea. One hundred years after its foundation (i.e., in 1999) NEC had total yearly sales of U.S.$40 billion, 155,000 employees worldwide, and 125 manufacturing plants in 21 countries.

The largest Japanese computer technology companies today are Matsushita, **Toshiba**, NEC, **Fujitsu**, and Mitsubishi, in that order. All of them produce a wide range of computer products, from **liquid-crystal displays**, to **laptops**, semiconductors, and even **supercom-**

puters. Almost one-fourth of NEC's revenue comes from the sale of computer chips, making NEC the second largest producer of semiconductors (**Intel** is first).

The emergence of NEC as a major computer company was partially the result of the Japanese government's strategy of subsidizing strategic industrial sectors in the 1960s. Companies such as NEC, Fujitsu, and **Hitachi** could sell computers in Japan regardless of **IBM**'s world dominance. In the 1970s, the Japanese also subsidized chip design and production, with the result that Japanese producers displaced American traditional semiconductor companies in the 1980s. American companies could maintain an edge in the market only for **microprocessors**. The close relation of the NEC executives with the Japanese government, however, led to a major scandal in the 1990s, when it was discovered that NEC had profited illegally from government contracts.

One sector in which NEC has been very successful is the production and marketing of supercomputers. NEC's machines are of the type called *vector processors* and are specially suited for scientific computations. In the 1990s, almost all major U.S. supercomputer companies went bankrupt. NEC, however, flourished in Japan and started selling more machines in the United States and Europe. This led to conflicts with the U.S. Commerce Department, which accused NEC of using unfair tactics in pricing.

In an effort to get a foothold in the U.S. personal computer market, NEC bought Packard-Bell, at one time the largest producer and distributor of **personal computers** in the United States. However, the manufacturing plant in Sacramento was closed in 1999 and the brand name disappeared.

FURTHER READING

Anchordoguy, Marie. *Computers Inc.: Japan's Challenge to IBM.* Cambridge, Mass.: Council on East Asian Studies, Harvard University, distributed by Harvard University Press, 1989.

—*Raúl Rojas*

Netiquette

Every culture has its own rules or guidelines for good conduct. On the **Internet**, those rules are called *netiquette*—that is, network etiquette. Rules of netiquette are not rules of law. They are enforced only by the threat of social disapproval. Like nonvirtual etiquette, netiquette is based on self-restraint. It says, essentially, that the mere fact that the Internet gives you the ability to do something does not necessarily make it a good idea.

Netiquette has developed along with the Internet. One of the first published netiquette guides, Chuq von Rospach's "A Primer on How to Work with the Usenet Community," was written in 1984 in response to an influx of new users. It, like many other netiquette guides, was published on the Internet rather than in printed book form, and is still updated periodically.

Advice given by different netiquette guides may vary, and what constitutes good netiquette varies among the many subcultures of the Internet; and, of course, netiquette issues change with time and technology. In 1994, a huge netiquette controversy grew up around the emergence of **spam**—mass, unsolicited commercial postings to newsgroups and **electronic mail** addresses. Spammers experienced every form of electronic retaliation imaginable, from *flames* (angry e-mail harangues) to *mail-bombing* (sending reams of data to an e-mail address, thus overloading the culprit's server and forcing it to shut down). But spam has proved unstoppable. In 2000, spamming, although still generally disliked, is a fact of life. Because netiquette proved inadequate to the task of preventing spam, several groups are pursuing legislative remedies to make spam illegal.

In the year 2000, new netiquette issues have been created by the popularity of *instant messages,* real-time messages that pop up on the computer screens of friends and family members. Unlike e-mail, which can be read at the recipient's convenience, instant messages demand one's attention immediately. The technology has created some new netiquette dilemmas: How does one refuse an instant message that comes at a bad time, or discourage friends and family members from sending instant messages to the workplace without offending them? This was not an issue in 1994, because instant messaging technology didn't exist. It is likely that new netiquette issues will arise with new Internet technology in years to come. Still, despite changes in culture and technology, respect and consideration for

CORE RULES OF NETIQUETTE

Some basic principles of netiquette remain valid across the Internet. These 10 rules form a good guide:

1. Remember the human. Although you are looking at a computer, you are still communicating with real people. If you're not sure whether to send or post something you've written, ask yourself whether you'd say it to a person's face. If the answer is no, hit the delete key.
2. Follow the same standards of behavior online that you use in real life. Unethical behavior is no more acceptable on the Internet than in your home or office.
3. Know the customs of your corner of cyberspace. Netiquette varies from domain to domain, so lurk (i.e., quietly check out new areas of cyberspace before participating) before you leap. You'll win far more respect by following the local customs than by flouting them.
4. Respect other people's time and bandwidth. It's fine if you think what you're doing at the moment is the most important thing in the universe, but don't assume that others will, too.
5. Make yourself look good online. Before you post, check your grammar, spelling, and most important, your logic. Your e-mail, Web site contributions, and discussion group postings may be around for a long, long time, so make sure that they represent you as you want to be represented.
6. Share your knowledge. Despite the rise of electronic commerce, the Internet's existence as a community still depends on individuals who share their information and experience.
7. Help maintain a civil atmosphere online. Passionate discourse is often appropriate; verbal abuse almost never is.
8. Respect the privacy of others.
9. Don't abuse your power.
10. Be forgiving of other people's mistakes.

Adapted from Netiquette *by Virginia Shea. Reprinted with permission.*

other people in the online universe remain the guiding principles of good conduct online.

FURTHER READING

Rinaldi, Arlene. "The Net: User Guidelines and Netiquette." 1993.
http://www.fau.edu/netiquette/net

Shea, Virginia. *Netiquette.* San Francisco: Albion, 1994.
http://www.albion.com/netiquette/index.html

Templeton, Brad. "Emily Postnews Answers Your Questions on Netiquette." 1986.
http://www.templetons.com/brad/emily.html

Von Rospach, Chuq. "A Primer on How to Work with the Usenet Community." 1984.
http://wrk.chuqui.com/publications.html

—*Virginia Shea*

Netscape Communications Corporation

Netscape Communications Corporation is a U.S. company based in Mountain View, California, that develops **Internet** and **intranet** software. Best known for its **browser**, Netscape Navigator, it was acquired by **America Online** (AOL), in November 1998 for U.S.$4.2 billion.

Netscape Navigator is described by the corporation as "the world's most popular PC application." It is a **multimedia** browser, a piece of software on a local computer that provides access to text, images, video, animations, and sound files stored on remote computers (**World Wide Web** servers) anywhere else on the Internet. Navigator runs on no fewer than 17 operating system platforms, including **Windows**, **DOS**, **Macintosh**, and **Unix**. This makes it particularly useful for enterprises that want to share information between different machines using a small-scale private version of the Internet known as an intranet. Designed for intranet use, its latest version of Navigator, called Netscape Communicator, includes an **electronic mail** program and tools to enable users to share calendars, **spreadsheets**, and word-processed documents. Netscape also produces **electronic commerce** and Web server software.

Netscape (originally Mosaic Communications Corporation) was formed in April 1994 by Jim Clark

(1944–), founder of **Silicon Graphics**, and **Marc Andreessen** (1972–), developer of the user-friendly Web browser, Mosaic. It released its first products in December 1994 and leapt to world attention in August 1995, when its stock market initial public offering (IPO) valued the company at over U.S.$2 billion. Industry analysts saw Netscape as a potential challenger of **Microsoft** domination, and that fall Microsoft's share price plunged by 7 percent. In the months that followed, **Bill Gates** (1955–) declared that Microsoft would place the Internet at the center of its business, giving away its Internet Explorer Web browser at no cost with its Windows operating system in a direct challenge to Netscape Navigator.

An aggressive battle for Internet domination ensued, at the height of which Andreessen commented: "Everybody in the software industry just takes it for granted that Microsoft wants to put us out of business." In August 1996, Netscape complained to the Department of Justice with allegations of "anticompetitive" behavior, and the following month the department announced an investigation of Microsoft's practices. A lengthy trial followed, during which the U.S. government claimed that Microsoft had threatened to "cut off the air supply" of Netscape, an allegation Gates dismissed as "an unbelievable lie." In October 1996, Netscape announced it planned to concentrate on the lucrative intranet market (forecast to be worth U.S.$8 billion in 1998). But the damage was done. By January 1998, Netscape had posted an U.S.$88 million loss and fired 400 of its employees. It was subsequently taken over by AOL in November 1998. Its share of the browser market stood at the end of 1999 at around 35 percent (compared to Microsoft's Internet Explorer, which has approximately 60 percent of the market).

Further Reading

Clark, Jim, with Owen Edwards. *Netscape Time: The Making of the Billion-Dollar Start-up That Took on Microsoft.* New York: St. Martin's Press, 1999.

Quittner, Joshua, and Michelle Slatalla. *Speeding the Net: The Inside Story of Netscape and How It Challenged Microsoft.* New York: Atlantic Monthly Press, 1998.

Reid, Robert H. *Architects of the Web: 1000 Days That Built the Future of Business.* New York: Wiley, 1997.

—*Chris Woodford*

NetWare

There was a time in the mid-1980s when the only high-quality networking **software** for the **IBM personal computer** (PC) and compatible computers was provided by **Novell**. The Novell NetWare system has gone through many releases and still exists, although its importance has been greatly reduced by the incorporation of networking functionality into the **operating systems** for PCs. From the beginning, NetWare was not an operating system but rather, a *network operating system.*

NetWare was introduced in 1983. The first versions were written by a four-person team: Drew Major, Kyle Powell, Dale Niebaur, and Mark Hurst. The name of the product was accidental, because the first name they had selected (Sharenet) was already taken, so they opted for another. NetWare 4.0 was the first commercial release. Coming from the mainframe and minicomputer world, with its centralized administration of resources, the four programmers tried to give the data sharing functionality of larger computers to **networks** of PCs.

NetWare was initially a proprietary system that ran using **Motorola** processors. Later, the IBM PC was made a client of the system. This meant that users wanting to install a network could use PCs as clients but had to buy the server machine from Novell. Later, NetWare-X was introduced, which also allowed the IBM PC-XT to function as server. The proprietary server product was renamed NetWare-S.

Novell made sure that each new release of NetWare would run using the most popular networking cards available, especially **Ethernet** boards. A kind of symbiosis resulted from this strategy, because Ethernet networks became an option in the PC world due to NetWare, while NetWare itself became popular due to the high transmission speed of Ethernet cards.

Releases of NetWare began with 1.0 again when Advanced NetWare was introduced in 1985. Many new features were added in the next releases, such as the option to network **Macintosh** computers and the use of nondedicated servers, that is, machines that could do other useful work.

In 1998, **intra-** and **Internet** features were added to NetWare. Later, **Java** was incorporated and better integration with the Web was achieved. For example, using a **browser,** network administrators can manage a Novell network from any other computer in the Internet. The latest version of NetWare is the 5.1 release.

The market share of Novell networking software began falling steadily once PC operating systems started incorporating network functionality, management of users, and providing some security features. From its 70 percent of the market in 1993, Novell's market share fell to less than 57 percent in 1997. Its adoption of Internet technology happened rather late, and some ill-advised acquisitions added to a climate of uncertainty about Novell's future. In 1994 Novell bought WordPerfect Corporation for U.S.$855 million, a company that at the time produced and marketed the highly popular WordPerfect text processor. However, only a few months later WordPerfect was divested and the product disappeared.

Novell has been struggling in the last years trying to focus again on the networking arena, which has been transformed so profoundly by the Internet. The main asset of the company is a set of software protocols called Novell Directory Services (NDS). The main purpose of NDS is to provide the end user a structured view of all documents in a network. Every computer has its own tree of subdirectories, but they are integrated into a global tree accessible by other computers according to rules that specify security levels and bind together subdirectories of different groups. NDS is more than having links between computer directories—it helps manage the network and enforce security policies. Network managers, accessing the network from many distributed geographic points, can collaborate and modify the structure and policies of the global directory easily.

NDS is the main directory service for networks of PCs, but other alternatives have been put forward, notably by **Microsoft** and **Cisco**. The latest release of **Windows**, Windows 2000, integrates many networking functions in the operating system and is based on Microsoft's own brand of directory services, called Active Directory.

Novell has been repositioning itself vigorously as an Internet company, and NetWare and NDS have become just part of its long-time strategy to provide global networking services. In 1999, 3.8 million servers in the world, with 80 million users, were using Novell software.

Further Reading

Currid, Cheryl C., and Mark A. Eggleston. *Novell's Introduction to Networking*. Indianapolis, Ind.: IDG Books Worldwide, 2000.

Kearns, David, George Sheldon, and Brian Iverson. *The Complete Guide to Novell Directory Services*. Almadea, Calif.: Sybex, 1996; 2nd ed., San Francisco: 1998.

Shafer, Kevin. *Novell's Encyclopedia of Networking*. San Jose, Calif.: Novell Press, 1997.

—*Raúl Rojas*

Network Computer

A network computer (NC) is a simple machine optimized for electronic communication. It can not be used without a **network**, as the **software** is not stored in a local **hard disk**. Programs are loaded directly onto the network from a **file server**.

Lawrence Ellison (1944–), chief executive officer of **Oracle**, announced the first NC in 1995. His aim was to bypass the personal computer and increase computer sales into U.S. homes with a sealed, appliance-style computer that did not require software installation or **hardware** upgrades. The NC should be capable of running **word processing** software, and **spreadsheet** and database programs, to send and receive **electronic mail**, and to allow **Internet** browsing using a low-cost processor, 4-megabyte (MB) random access memory (**RAM**), television or computer monitor, **keyboard**, **mouse**, and connection to the Internet.

Microsoft countered with the announcement of a *simply interactive personal computer* (SIPC), which would bundle a television set and a videocassette recorder with a **Pentium**-based computer and **multimedia** applications. This was also a sealed unit, but with expansion through a *universal serial bus* (USB) for slow devices, and IEEE 1394 (Firewire) to connect video devices. Separately, **Intel** planned a *networked PC* (NetPC) with capabilities similar to those of the NC. The NetPC *Systems Design Guidelines* were written in association with **Dell**, **Compaq**, **Hewlett-Packard**, and Microsoft (which quietly dropped its plans for the SIPC).

At the time, **Sun** had started developing the platform-independent language **Java** and the JavaStation NC based around the *microSPARC* processor. Java applications, including a word processor and spreadsheet, could be loaded from the network.

In an effort to reduce customer confusion, **Apple**, **IBM**, Oracle, Microsoft, **Netscape**, and Sun formed the *Network Computing Management Group* (NCMG) and prepared an *NC Reference Profile*, which specifies the protocols to start the computer from a network, additional industry standards to manage e-mail, images, sound, and security, and new standards for user mobility and software licensing. The protocols do *not* specify a processor type and do not limit additional features. They allow all shades of hardware, from a JavaStation, with its operating software in *read-only memory* (**ROM**), to a standard **personal computer** (PC) using the network.

The NC with the most work to do at booting is the one with the least preconfiguration. Its user presses the power button; a boot monitor in ROM is started and does some basic tests, such as sizing memory and identifying the network interface. The only piece of information it can use may be the unique *medium access control* (MAC) address manufactured into the network interface. The boot monitor reads this and makes a *bootstrap protocol* (BOOTP) message, which it transmits (i.e., *broadcasts*) to everyone on the network, communicating its *MAC address* and requesting its own **IP address**, the server IP address, and bootstrap file name. A *BOOTP server* on the network receives the request and matches the *MAC address* to its configuration databases. It can then send a BOOTP reply and give the NC an identity.

At this point the NC can actually begin with a *Trivial File Transfer Protocol* (TFTP) *read request* (RRQ) sent to its newly acquired *server IP address*, requesting its *bootstrap file name*. The server addressed starts sending TFTP data packets, which the NC loads into memory and responds to with TFTP acknowledge packets (or possibly error packets) until the entire operating system kernel is loaded.

Now the kernel can establish normal network connectivity and retrieve additional configuration files created for the machine and indexed by its IP address. Window background images can be loaded and initial applications started.

This sequence will vary between manufacturers and according to different underlying network types. For example, the BOOTP exchange may be preceded by *Dynamic Host Configuration Protocol* (DHCP) messages to obtain a temporary IP address. The initial configuration could be entered in nonvolatile memory in the NC to bypass the BOOTP stage entirely. Also, TFTP may be replaced by the *network file system* (NFS) before the kernel is established because it is faster than TFTP and allows security checks. If the system is booted through a serial interface using the *Point-to-Point Protocol* (PPP), details will change again.

Although several manufacturers announced the availability of network computers in the late 1990s, they have not yet become the overnight sales success predicted.

FURTHER READING

Croft, W., and J. Gilmore. "Bootstrap Protocol (BOOTP)." *IETF Request for Comments: RFC* 951, Sept. 1985.

Droms, R. "Dynamic Host Configuration Protocol (DHCP)." *IETF Request for Comments: RFC* 2131, Mar. 1997.

Finlayson, R. "Bootstrap Loading Using TFTP." *IETF Request for Comments: RFC* 906, June 1984.

Friedrichs, Jürgen, et al. *Java Thin-Client Programming for a Network Computing Environment.* Upper Saddle River, N.J.: Prentice Hall, 1998.

—*John Deane*

Networks

Networks of computers have been developed and deployed since the 1960s, culminating in today's global computer network—the **Internet**. During that founding decade, the U.S. government invested heavily in research and development that led to today's networking technology, which is based on the **TCP/IP** protocol. Other organizations in Europe and Asia pursued similar opportunities; the French Cyclades network was one of the first experimental packet networks to be deployed.

There are many networking technologies, and listing all of them is beyond the scope of this article. One of the most significant is the **packet-switching** technology used in the Internet, which uses **routers** to forward packets from source to destination along paths that are defined in the routing tables; the particular path used may change from one packet to the next. By contrast, the **IBM** Corporation promoted a networking architecture (System Network Architecture) based on forwarding data along predefined paths (as is done in "plain old telephone systems," or POTSs, for voice traffic). In standards committees, the telephone industry (both in the United States and abroad) defined a standard for packet-based services called X.25, and in the 1980s defined a new high-speed service called Frame Relay. The phone companies also developed and promoted a new digital phone service for voice and data called **ISDN** (Integrated Services Digital Network). The television industry became the driver for the cable-TV industry, which first used analog technology to provide television images to homes and is now rapidly moving to digital technology.

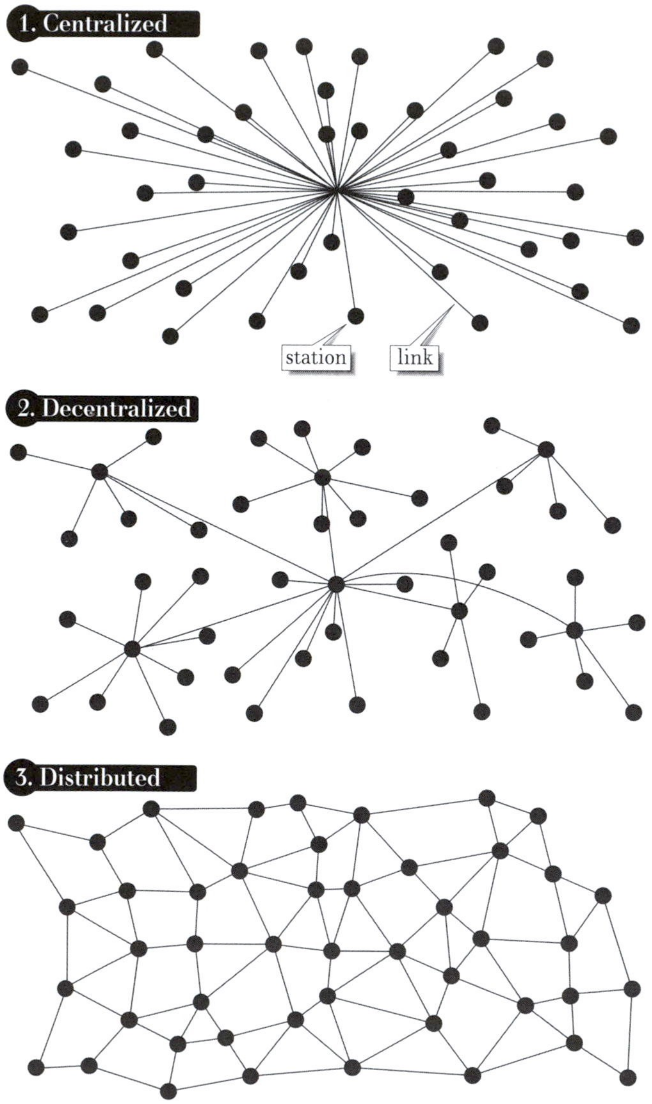

Certain common concepts pervade all networking technologies. First, there is the concept of traffic, which is used to describe the network's payload. In early networks, traffic was described principally in terms of a specified rate, such as calls per second for a telephone network, packets per second for a packet-switching network, or cells per second for an **asynchronous transfer mode** (ATM) network. Other common metrics to describe traffic include **bits** or other data units per second. However, as networks become more complex, it becomes customary to describe traffic not only in terms of the amount being transmitted but also in terms of its nature and requirements. Thus the *burstiness* of traffic is an important characteristic: Traffic is said to be bursty if it can be described in terms of alternating quiet and very active intervals. The so-called *quality-of-service* (QoS) requirements of network traffic are also very important. Some types of traffic require very short delays between sender and receiver, whereas other forms of traffic are very sensitive to any occurrences that can cause some of the traffic to be lost.

Another basic concept in networks is that of sources and destinations. These are locations in the network that generate messages, and that are receivers or consumers of traffic. Thus all traffic in a network has some source and may have one or more destinations. *Multicasting* is a technique that allows a given source to convey traffic through the network to several destinations.

It is quite common to discuss a network in terms of its *topology*. This refers to the structure that links the various components of the network. Since the function of a network is to convey traffic from sources to destinations, this must be accomplished over physical *links*. The manner in which these links are structured is usually called the **topology** of the network. The network links are the basic data-carrying connections, and one often talks about *full-duplex* links if these are able to carry data in both directions. Links are said to be *half-duplex* if they carry data in only one direction.

Three types of network: centralized, decentralized, and distributed.

Network topology is composed of both links and nodes. The term *node* is used loosely to characterize processing units that have the ability to switch data through the network. Thus a network is composed of nodes, each of which has many incoming and outgoing links and is connected to other nodes via these links. A very simple network topology is a *star*, where a single node is connected via radial links to a set of other nodes. In this topology, *N* peripheral nodes are all connected to the same central node; they communicate with each other via this central node.

Another simple topology is the **bus** structure; in this case, all nodes communicate via a single shared link that runs through all the nodes. A bus structure is common to many local network architectures, discussed later in this article. On the other hand, networks that cover wide geographical areas (**wide area networks** [WANs]) will often adopt a *meshed* topology. In this case nodes are interconnected with each other in an irregular grid, with one particular node being directly linked with several other nodes, and so on.

It is common to refer to network nodes as *switches* since their role is to decide how to route traffic. Nodes can serve as sources of traffic, as destinations, or simply as switches whose role is to select an outgoing link for the traffic they receive so that it may head toward its destination. Switches are very common in telephone systems, where the terminology first originated. However, the term *switch* is also used for other kinds of networks. In many modern networks the terms *switch* and *router* may be used interchangeably.

The function of routing traffic through a network is complex and requires information about the instantaneous state of the network. To carry out this routing function, nodes or switches have to maintain routing tables that store information about the path that traffic must take in going from a source node to a destination. These routing tables need to be updated constantly or periodically, and the table-updating activity is a significant source of additional work for the nodes and an additional source of network traffic. Routing tables need to be updated whenever changes occur in the network topology. These changes may be the result of adding new nodes and links to the network or of removal of certain nodes. Changes can also result from network failures or interruptions of service at certain nodes or links. In a large network, as a result of the large number of nodes and links that make up the network, the collective frequency of such events can be very high even though any individual changes or failures may be infrequent. Routing can be done in a fixed mode, with a predetermined assignment of a set of possible paths from source to destination, or it may be carried out adaptively by the routers to optimize certain performance functions.

Another important concept pertaining to networks is that of *protocols*. These are typically the rules that are used in a network to make sure that data are transmitted and received with a minimum amount of data loss or errors, as well as to control the flow of traffic.

Although the following distinction is slowly losing some of its importance, it is customary to describe networks as being *connectionless* if data are transferred from a source to a destination without having established a physical destination between the two. Telephone systems have traditionally established a connection between source and destination. Similarly, when we connect our home computer to our office computer via a telephone connection using a **modem**, we are physically establishing a connection between the two computers. On the other hand, when we first dial up an **Internet service provider** from home, and then remotely connect into our office computer, our communication between our home computer and the office computer is being established in a connectionless fashion via the Internet. In this case, our office computer is receiving packets that contain the data we generate on our home computer (and vice versa), without a physical continuous connection being established between the two.

Nodes in many networks also play the role of intermediate storage devices for the data that are transiting through the network. This is particularly true in the Internet, where the network routers are known as *store-and-forward switches*. Packets arriving at a node are stored in the node's buffers while the node determines how the packets should be routed. Packets are then placed in output queues, which correspond to the appropriate output links of the node. In networks that try to minimize the transit delay, the input and output buffer queues of a node are either nonexistent or are very small, so that the delay incurred by the data as they travel through each node is correspondingly small.

It is common to classify networks as either **local area networks** (LANs) or as **wide area networks** (WANs), although this classification based on distance may be somewhat misleading. As an example, random access–based networks such as the widely used **Ethernet** are essentially used over short distances of a few kilometers. However, other technologies, such as ATM, can be deployed over short distances within a building or a laboratory, or can be used to cover distances of several hundred kilometers. Similarly, wireless networks can be used both to cover short ranges and deploy over very long distances with the help of a hierarchical or cellular architecture.

LANs are designed to interconnect a limited number of computers, from a few to several hundred, in a geographically constrained environment where the physical problems of data connections, such as propagation delays, do not constitute a major roadblock to efficient communications. Typically, a LAN uses a simple physical interconnection scheme (i.e., coaxial cable or **twisted pair cable**) and relies on a unique set of communication rules.

LANs are typically grouped into two classes: Ethernet-like systems that use some form of random access, and rings. Rings are in turn grouped into slotted rings and **token rings**. Ethernet is a very popular LAN technology whose major advantage is to allow for a decentralized control of communications. On the other hand, rings provide strong control over the manner in which communications are being conducted.

Slotted rings have a number of *slots* or spaces that circulate constantly around a physical loop. This loop is implemented using technology that may consist of a twisted pair, a coaxial cable, or an optical fiber. A node or computer that needs to send data will observe the passing slots, grab the first empty slot it sees, and fill it with the data it wishes to send; as it does so it will provide the address of the intended destination node. All the nodes on the loop will constantly monitor the passing slots and copy into their memory the data in a slot if they see that the destination address corresponds to their own identity. Typically, the slot is then emptied by the sender node, which uses this mechanism as a way to verify that the transmission has been carried out correctly. *Token rings* have similar behavior, except that empty slots are not actually carried around the ring. A special data sequence known as the *token* is used to signify a permit to transmit. If a node sees a passing token, it grabs it and transmits a data sequence to a destination node placed around the ring. When the same data sequence (or some acknowledgment of receipt) returns to the sender, the source node will release the token so that it may be "grabbed" by some other source, and so on.

Because of the large investments made in network infrastructure, and the major stake that users and society have in their proper and efficient operation, there has always been a major effort in the development and application of techniques used to evaluate network performance. These techniques are based essentially on queuing theory and are being used constantly to design and improve local or wide area networks, which are now a vital component of our economy.

FURTHER READING

Gelenbe, Erol, and Israel Mitrani. *Analysis and Synthesis of Computer Systems.* New York: Academic Press, 1980.

Gelenbe, Erol, and Guy Pujolle. *An Introduction to Queueing Networks.* New York: Wiley, 1987; 2nd ed., 1998.

Tannebaum, Andrew S. *Computer Networks.* Englewood Cliffs, N.J.: Prentice Hall, 1981; 3rd ed., Upper Saddle River, N.J.: 1996.

—*Erol Gelenbe and G. A. Marin*

Neural Network

A neural network is an adaptive, parallel, and distributed information processing system. Neural network research is generally considered to be a branch of the **artificial intelligence** (AI) field, and its techniques have found a broad range of application in many engineering and programming domains, from signal processing to financial analysis. These systems are called *neural* because they draw on an analogy to information processing in the brain, which is achieved by networks of cells called *neurons.* The art of building neural networks, sometimes called *neurocomputing*, *connectionism*, or *parallel and distributed processing* (PDP), actually consists of a varied range of techniques that differ in many ways and can take the form of programs or specialized hardware.

Neural networks were first conceived by **Warren S. McCulloch** (1898–1969) and Walter Pitts (1923–69) in 1943. The McCulloch–Pitts neuron is a binary switch, or **logic gate**, which could be linked into networks in order to compute logical functions. In 1949, Donald Hebb (1904–85) first proposed a mechanism for learning in networks of logic gates based on conditioned response. In *Hebbian learning*, a connection strength between two neurons is increased whenever the two neurons fire at the same time, and decays over time otherwise. Thus, subnetworks involved in a shared function will become more tightly coupled.

The first neural network computer, the SNARC, was built in 1951 by **Marvin Lee Minsky** (1927–), the future founder of the **MIT Artificial Intelligence Laboratory**, for his doctoral thesis at Princeton. Frank Rosenblatt's Perceptron (1958) was the first adaptive threshold-gate neuron model and was proven to have the ability to learn any function that it could represent. The Perceptron was studied in both the form of Cornell University's Mark I Perceptron and in various digital computer simulations throughout the 1960s. Another early **algorithm** for which iterative convergence on a good answer could be proven was the *least mean squares algorithm*, developed by Bernard Widrow (1929–) and Theodore Hoff (1937–) at Stanford in 1959. Widrow and Hoff constructed the ADALINE (adaptive linear neuron) **analog computer** as a realization of this algorithm, and Hoff later went on to invent the microprocessor at the **Intel Corporation**. **Carver Mead** (1934–) has also done a great deal of work on **very large scale integration** (VLSI) designs for implementing neural networks.

What all neural networks have in common is that they can be represented by a set of computational elements—mathematically idealized neurons—that are linked together by weighted connections. A more formal way to represent a neural network is as a graph, where the information processing capacity rests in the weights of the edges and each node computes its own function. The differences among the various neural network techniques consist of the different connective architectures of networks, mathematical functions that the neuronal elements compute, and means of training the networks to get them to perform as desired. There are two main types of architectures: *feedforward networks*, which can be represented by a directed acyclic graph, and *recurrent* or *feedback networks*, whose graphs contain loops or cycles.

In general, *feedforward neural networks* perform one version or another of statistical pattern analysis and classification; that is, they induce statistical patterns from training data to learn a representative function, then apply this function to classify future examples. A *classification* is simply a mapping function from inputs to outputs; in other words, it maps the objects to be classified into their types or classes. Consider, for example, the problem of classifying all two-dimensional geometric shapes into one type of set: [*square, circle, triangle, other*]. A total mapping function would assign every member of the set of two-dimensional geometric shapes to one of these four types. There are many possible mapping functions, however, and only a few of these will classify the inputs in a desirable way.

Supervised learning offers a way to learn a good mapping function automatically by presenting the network with correctly classified examples. A network is typically trained until it is able to classify correctly most of the examples it has seen, up to a desired percentage. The accuracy of a trained network on new examples will depend on the size of the training data set, the number of times it sees the training set or number of training *epochs*, the learning algorithm used to modify the network after each epoch, the complexity of the classification space, the complexity of the example space, and how representative of the real world the training data are. A network can also be *overtrained* if it is trained for too many epochs and begins to lose the ability to generalize to new examples when they do not look exactly like training examples.

Other learning techniques simply help in discerning statistical patterns in the data—such techniques include grouping data points into clusters and learning to map examples to key or prototypical examples that represent the center of a class. These techniques are called *unsupervised learning* because they provide representations of the data without receiving corrections from a supervisor.

The first feedforward networks contained a single layer of neurons connected to inputs; more recent multilayer network architectures contain an input layer, output layer, and one or more hidden layers. Single-layer networks such as the Perceptron are limited to learning mapping functions for data that are *linearly separable*—if the data points for two classes were plotted on a two-dimensional plane, it would be possible to divide the classes using a straight line. The concept of *linear separability* can be extended to many-dimensional spaces using a measure called the *VC-dimension* (Vapnik, 1998). The addition of hidden layers greatly increases the complexity of the possible mapping functions a network can "learn"—such networks can classify data even when they are not linearly separable. Multilayer networks were made possible only by introduction of the error backpropagation algorithm, which propagates output errors back through multiple hidden layers. Backpropagation was discovered independently at least three times (Amari, 1967; Werbos, 1972).

Recurrent networks were introduced by the physicist John Hopfield (1933–) in 1982. The two principal types of recurrent neural networks are Boltzmann machines and Hopfield networks. Both architectures draw on the mathematics of thermodynamics and physical dynamics respectively to define a phase space. This phase space contains points that are attractors and represent equilibria points for the network. Once configured, the network is allowed to run as a dynamic system with quantities of energy cycling through the network repeatedly until the network settles into a stable equilibrium state. In these networks the inputs are represented by the initial configuration parameters, and the output is represented by the final steady state.

Both types of neural networks can be viewed as optimization techniques: Feedforward networks find optimal mapping functions between inputs and outputs, while recurrent networks find the lowest energy state of a physical system. Unfortunately, all neural network architectures are prone to finding only local maxima or minima rather that global optimizations, and special mathematical techniques are employed by the various architectures to increase their chances of finding better optimizations.

Neural networks are *distributed* in the sense that what the network represents is distributed over all the elements of the network. Consider, for example, a neural network that classifies geometric shapes into circles and squares. In such a network, there will not be a single node that represents squares and another that represents circles. Instead, there will be many nodes, all of which together represent both squares and circles—each node might represent something more like the flatness, roundness, or cornerness of a small geometric region. On its own, the information processed by each node is not particularly useful or interesting; it is only when the outputs of all the nodes are taken together that a useful result can be obtained.

Similarly, these networks are *parallel* in the sense that each of the nodes acts on its own and (at least in theory) simultaneously. Whereas most programming techniques employ algorithms that work by proceeding in sequential steps, the computational elements of a neural network depend only on the information they receive as inputs and their local memory, and affect only those elements that receive their outputs. In the case of a network that classifies circles and squares, the flatness nodes and the roundness nodes for all the various regions can compute their functions independently and simultaneously—in parallel—without depending on knowing the judgments of their neighbors. Thus each neuron acts on its own and on local information, while the network as a whole performs a useful function.

Neural network systems are argued to be superior to traditionally programmed systems because they do not require the programmer to completely understand the processes the system carries out, and the systems can be quite flexible and robust. Since neural networks learn from training data, the programmer does not have to discover the underlying patterns of the data, since the network can learn these for itself. Because neural network representations are distributed, they can give good results even if some nodes are removed or are faulty; and by providing a mapping of every possible input to some output, they offer a robust form of generalizing from training data to new data. Thus, even though a network has not seen a particular example, as long as it is sufficiently similar to previous examples from the same class, the network will classify this new example correctly.

The most notable applications of neural networks involve various forms of pattern recognition and control systems. The neural networks of the 1960s were able to recognize handwritten characters and digits as well as spoken phonemes and words, although not very robustly. NETtalk was a neural network that learned to read written text aloud by finding a mapping from text to phonemes (Sejénowski and Rosenberg, 1987). It is said to have sounded like a babbling baby as it learned, and did much to popularize neural network research in the media. ALVINN (autonomous land vehicle in a neural network) is a neural network that learned to map images of a road from a video camera to control signals for a steering wheel, accelerator, and brake of a car (Pomerleau, 1993). ALVINN's successor drove a car across the United States successfully in 1995 (the neural net was in control 98 percent of the way). An enormous amount of effort has been put into building neural networks to predict financial trends in stock and commodities markets. These networks can perform quite well but are still susceptible to the great uncertainties and capriciousness of economic markets. More practical applications have included forgery analysis of signatures on credit card purchases, the analysis of a person's credit risk, credit and insurance fraud detection, and the visual inspection of manufactured parts for flaws.

FURTHER READING

Amari, S. "A Theory of Adaptive Pattern Classifiers." *IEEE Transactions on Electronic Computers,* Vol. 16, 1967, pp. 299–307.

Anderson, James A., and Edward Rosenfeld, eds. *Neurocomputing: Foundations of Research.* Cambridge, Mass.: MIT Press, 1988.

———. *Talking Nets: An Oral History of Neural Networks.* Cambridge, Mass.: MIT Press, 1998.

Anderson, James A., A. Pellionisz, and Edward Rosenfeld, eds. *Neurocomputing 2: Directions for Research.* Cambridge, Mass.: MIT Press, 1993.

Hopfield, John J. "Neural Networks and Physical Systems with Emergent Collective Computational Abilities." *Proceedings of the National Academy of Sciences,* Vol. 79, 1982, pp. 2554–2558.

McClelland, John, David Rumelhart, and the PDP Research Group, eds. *Parallel Distributed Processing: Explorations in the Microstructure of Cognition,* Vol. 2. Cambridge, Mass.: MIT Press, 1986.

McCulloch, Warren S., and Walter Pitts. "A Logical Calculus of the Ideas Immanent in Nervous Activit." *Bulletin of Mathematical Biophysics,* Vol. 5, 1943, pp. 115–133. Reprinted in Rook McCulloch, ed., *The Collected Works of Warren S. McCulloch,* Vol. 1. Salinas, Calif.: Intersystems Publications, 1989, pp. 343–361.

Minsky, Marvin, and Seymour Papert. *Perceptrons: An Introduction to Computational Geometry.* Cambridge, Mass.: MIT Press, 1969.

Pitts, Walter, and Warren S. McCulloch. "On How We Know Universals: The Perception of Auditory and Visual Forms." *Bulletin of Mathematical Biophysics,* Vol. 9, 1947, pp. 127–147. Reprinted in Rook McCulloch, ed., *The Collected Works of Warren S. McCulloch,* Vol. 2. Salinas, Calif.: Intersystems Publications, 1989, pp. 530–550.

Pomerleau, D. *Neural Network Perception for Mobile Robot Guidance.* New York: Kluwer Academic, 1993.

Rosenblatt, Frank. *Principles of Neurodynamics: Perceptrons and the Theory of Brain Mechanisms.* Washington, D.C.: Spartan, 1962.

Rumelhart, David, John McClelland, and the PDP Research Group, eds. *Parallel and Distributed Processing: Explorations in the Microstructure of Cognition,* Vol. 1: *Foundations.* Cambridge, Mass.: MIT Press, 1986.

Sejénowski, T., and C. R. Rosenberg. "Parallel Networks That Learn to Pronounce English Text." *Complex Systems,* Vol. 1, 1987, pp. 145–168.

Vapnik, Vladimir N. *Statistical Learning Theory.* New York: Wiley, 1998.

Werbos, P. "Beyond Regression: New Tools for Prediction and Analysis in the Behavioral Sciences." Ph.D. dissertation, Harvard University, 1972.

Widrow, B., and M. A. Lehr. "30 Years of Adaptive Neural Networks: Perceptron, Madeline, and Backpropagation." *Proceedings of the IEEE,* Vol. 78, No. 9, 1990, pp. 1415–1442.

—*Peter M. Asaro*

Neuromancer

By William Gibson

William Gibson's (1948–) **cyberpunk** novel *Neuromancer* (1984) introduced the word **cyberspace** to the English vernacular. In the novel, cyberspace is used in reference to the "Matrix," a parallel **virtual**

reality of information, a consensual hallucination, which, we are told, had historical roots in arcade games and military simulation **software**. Cyberspace can be accessed directly by "jacking in" via a computer.

The story's hero, Henry Dorsett Case, was once a talented thief in cyberspace but was caught stealing from his employer, and maimed to prevent him accessing the Matrix. *Neuromancer* opens with Case being pursued around squalid, crime-infested Tokyo. He is picked up by Molly, a mirror-eyed retainer of Armitage, a mysterious war veteran. Armitage pays for the repair of Case's damaged neural system, the replacement of his pancreas (with a new pancreas genetically modified to screen out amphetamines and cocaine), but also the implantation of poison capsules. Since only Armitage has the antidote, Case is forced to work for his team.

In their first job, Molly and Case raid the Sense/Net corporation for a program that contains the personality and skills of Dixie Flatline, a famous but dead **hacker**. The story takes the team to the Sprawl (a megalopolis stretching between Boston and Atlanta), Istanbul, and into space, including a Rastafarian space station and an expensive resort called Freeside. Case and Molly find out that Armitage is being directed by an **artificial intelligence** called Wintermute. But artificial intelligences are prevented by law from becoming too powerful, so Case is soon in trouble with the Turing police.

The story's climax involves an assault on the orbiting mansion of an ancient, powerful, and inbred family, Tessier-Ashpool. Again the attack is partly in cyberspace and partly in the real world: Case and the construct of Dixie Flatline use a Chinese computer virus to break through the 'intrusion countermeasures electronics' (or "Ice") protecting Tessier-Ashpool, while Molly takes the direct real route to interrogate the surviving family member, Lady Jane Marie-France Tessier-Ashpool. The attack succeeds and results in Wintermute merging with another artificial intelligence, Neuromancer, to form a Godlike being capable of communicating with alien artificial intelligences. Case, Molly, and the Rastafarian Maelcum are paid off.

Neuromancer was greatly influenced by the *noir* fiction of Dashiell Hammett (1894–1961) and Raymond Chandler (1888–1959), and the stateless, anarchic situations described by William S. Burroughs (1914–97), J. G. Ballard (1930–), and Thomas Pynchon (1937–). *Neuromancer*, in turn, influenced many science fiction authors, spawning an entire subgenre named *cyberpunk*. The widely read novel has exerted a great influence on popular images of the future potential—both for better and for worse—of the cyberspace age.

FURTHER READING

Gibson, William. *Neuromancer*. New York: Ace Books, 1984.

—*Jon Agar*

The New Hacker's Dictionary

Edited by Eric Raymond

The New Hacker's Dictionary is a compilation of **hacker** jargon that was collected over the course of several years by Eric Raymond (1957–), one of the most active evangelists of the **open source** movement. The *Hacker's Dictionary*, which began on the **Internet** as the Jargon File, is not merely a dictionary of arcane terminology, but also a funny guidebook and, as one reviewer put it, a "de facto ethnography of the early years of hacker culture."

Raymond prefers to think of himself as a *hacker*, one who likes to use computers and is good at it, not as a *cracker*, who breaks into others' computer systems. Ranked above the mere hacker is the *wizard*, defined by the *Hacker's Dictionary* as "a person who knows how a complex piece of software or hardware works....Someone is a hacker if he or she has general hacking ability, but is a wizard with respect to something only if he or she has specific detailed knowledge of that thing." However, even wizards must pass through the *larval stage*, "a period of monomaniacal concentration on coding apparently passed through by all fledgling hackers....A few so afflicted never resume a more 'normal' life, but the ordeal seems to be necessary to produce real wizardry."

It is well known that hackers survive on a diet of Coke and pizza, and it is therefore no surprise that the dictionary includes an entry for a pepperoni and mushroom pizza known as the *ANSI standard pizza* because hackers at Carnegie Mellon University used to order it. But even a well-fed hacker can experience *lobotomy* when "subjected to formal management training," for example, at **IBM**.

A hacker, when working, frequently goes into *hack mode*, "a Zen-like state of total focus on The Problem...[which] correlates strongly with wizardliness....The intensity of this experience is probably by itself sufficient explanation for the existence of hackers, and explains why many resist being promoted out of positions where they can code." When in hack mode, the hacker is working on The Problem, not on *one-banana problems*, those that a trained monkey could solve.

Of course, a hacker despises a *WIMP environment*, one with "Window, Icon, Menu, Pointing device (or Pull-down menu)." A real hacker prefers arcane command-line **interfaces** for their superior flexibility. The hacker is never a *wall follower*, that is, one who "compensates for lack of sophistication or native stupidity by efficiently following some simple procedure shown to have been effective in the past" as done by a robot that "successfully solved mazes by keeping a 'finger' on one wall and running till it came out the other end."

The New Hacker's Dictionary had sold almost a million copies by 1999 and many more have been copied on the Internet, illustrating the true hacker philosophy of sharing.

Further Reading

Raymond, Eric S., ed. *The New Hacker's Dictionary*. Cambridge, Mass: MIT Press, 1991; 3rd ed., 1996.
http://www.tuxedo.org/jargon

—*Raúl Rojas*

NeXT Computer

NeXT Computer Inc. was founded by **Steve Jobs** (1955–) in an effort to revolutionize the computing world. Steve Jobs cofounded **Apple Computer** with **Steve Wozniak** (1950–) in 1977 and served the company in various functions, but left Apple in 1985. His NeXT company was meant to deliver the machine he had envisioned in his time with Apple, but it was unable to compete in the marketplace.

In 1985, Apple was struggling financially and had hired John Sculley (1939–) from Pepsi as chief executive officer (CEO). Scully's role was to bring some traditional management concepts to Apple and reinvigorate their marketing efforts. However, the difference in management styles quickly created a rift between Jobs and Scully, culminating with Steve Jobs's removal from Apple's board of directors in 1986.

Jobs immediately began work on creating a new paradigm in computing built around many of the concepts first embodied in the **Macintosh**. The goal was to design a system that was both powerful for the end user and that made it extremely easy for developers to build applications.

In October 1988, Steve Jobs unveiled the first NeXT computer, at the Davies Symphony Hall in San Francisco. For U.S.$6500, it featured a 25-megahertz **Motorola** 68030 processor and a 68882 math coprocessor, 8-megabyte (MB) random access memory (**RAM**), a 17-inch monochrome monitor, a 256-MB read/write magneto-optical drive, and the **object-oriented** NeXTSTEP **operating system**. Analysts dubbed it the Cube because the main system box, which was all black, measured 1 foot on all sides.

The NeXT machine broke with many traditions prevalent in the computer industry at the time. Instead of a traditional 1-MB floppy drive, the unit included a 256-MB MO drive. The idea was to give users an improved ability to move large amounts of data easily between machines. However, the optical drive was too slow as a main storage medium, and the NeXT also included a conventional **hard disk**.

The distinguishing features of NeXTSTEP are the use of Display Postscript and the application frameworks. Many in the **desktop publishing** industry, who were already strong supporters of PostScript, welcomed the use of Display Postscript, which gave them the same high-quality resolution independent graphics of a typical laser printer on a standard monitor.

NeXT built the development environment around the programming language Objective-C and a tool called Interface Builder. The two tools combined to offer developers a completely object-oriented toolkit for building applications. It was common for early developers to boast of having built large applications in only a few days.

The NeXT workstation, although technologically advanced, was a commercial failure. Steve Jobs repeated some of the errors that he had made at Apple, by introducing a computer with a premium price tag that was incompatible with other machines. Equivalent offers, from **Sun Microsystems** and **Silicon Graphics**, were more attractive, cheaper, and could be used as servers or clients in computer networks. The company could not provide new versions of the hardware at the same pace as that of its larger competitors, so that eventually NeXT left the hardware business altogether in order to become a software company with a single product, the NextStep operating system.

In December 1996, Apple Computer bought NeXT for about U.S.$425 million in cash and Apple stock. The buyout brought Steve Jobs back to Apple, where he is now CEO. Jobs brought Apple back to profitability with a series of new Macintosh machines and allowed Apple to leverage the NeXT technology in the development of its new operating system, Macintosh OS X, scheduled for release in early 2001.

Further Reading

Freiberger, Paul. *Fire in the Valley: The Making of the Personal Computer.* Berkeley, Calif.: Osborn/McGraw-Hill; 2nd ed., New York: McGraw-Hill, 1999.

Stross, Randall. *Black Magic: Steve Jobs and the Next Big Thing.* New York: Atheneum; Toronto, Canada: Maxwell Macmillan, 1993.

—*Paul Shields*

Next Generation Internet Initiative

The Next Generation Internet Initiative (NGII) is a multiagency federal research and development program in the United States that is developing advanced networking technologies, introducing revolutionary applications that require advanced networking and demonstrating these capabilities on test beds that are 100 to 1000 times faster end to end than today's **Internet**. It was set up in October 1996 by the Clinton administration, endorsed by the Federal Networking Council Advisory Committee, and officially launched on 1 October 1997, with initial funds of U.S.$100 million for 1998.

The agencies participating in NGII are the Defense Advanced Research Projects Agency (DARPA), Department of Energy (DoE), National Aeronautics and Space Administration (NASA), National Institutes of Health (NIH), National Institute of Standards and Technology (NIST), and National Science Foundation (NSF). A test bed for NGII providing 100-fold improvement in Internet performance to end users is built on the following federal networks: NSF's very high performance Backbone Network Service (vBNS), NASA's Research and Education Network (NREN), the Defense Research and Education Network (DREN), and DoE's Energy Sciences network (ESnet).

The original goals of NGII were threefold. First, NGII works to connect universities and national laboratories with high-speed networks that are 100 to 1000 times faster than today's Internet; these networks will connect at least 100 universities and national labs 100 times faster than today's Internet, and a smaller number of institutions, 1000 times faster. Second, NGII promotes experimentation with the next generation of networking technologies; this initiative will address a variety of research challenges connected with a 100-fold increase in the number of Internet users. By serving as test beds, research networks are expected to help accelerate the introduction of new commercial services. Finally, NGII demonstrates new applications that meet important national goals and objectives; higher-speed, more advanced **networks** will promote a new generation of applications that provide support for scientific research, national security, distance education, environmental monitoring, and health care.

NGII currently focuses on applications and programs for fields such as health care, national security, distance education, energy research, biomedical research, environmental monitoring, and manufacturing engineering. Physicians at university medical centers will use large archives of radiology images to identify the patterns and features associated with particular diseases; with remote access to **supercomputers**, they will also be able to improve the accuracy of mammographies by detecting subtle changes in three-dimensional images. A top priority for the U.S. Department of Defense is *dominant battlefield awareness*, which will give the U.S. military a significant advantage in any armed conflict. This requires an ability to collect information from large numbers of high-resolution sensors, automatic processing of the data to support terrain and target recognition, and real-time distribution of these data to the warfighter (this will require much more **bandwidth** than is currently commercially available).

Universities are now experimenting with technologies such as two-way video to remote sites, VCR-like replay of past classes, modeling and simulation, collaborative environments, and online access to instructional software; distance education will improve the ability of universities to serve those who want new skills but who cannot attend class at a fixed time. Scientists and engineers working in different places will be able to work with each other and access remote scientific facilities as if they were in the same building; "Collaboratories" combining videoconferencing, shared virtual work spaces, networked scientific facilities, and databases will make research more efficient and more effective.

In the field of biomedicine, researchers will be able to solve problems in large-scale DNA sequencing and gene identification that were previously impossible to solve, thus opening the door to breakthroughs for curing human genetic diseases. As for environmental monitoring, researchers are constructing a virtual world to model the Chesapeake Bay ecosystem, which serves as a nursery area for many commercially important species. In manufacturing, **virtual reality** and modeling and simulation can dramatically reduce the time needed to develop new products.

NGII should not be confused with **Internet2**. The university-led Internet2 and the federally led NGII are parallel and complementary initiatives based in the United States. Internet2 and NGII are already working together in many areas. For example, through participation in an NSF NGII program, over 150 Internet2 universities have received competitively awarded grants to support connections to advanced **backbone** networks such as Abilene and the very high performance Backbone Network Service. Internet2 is also forming partnerships with similar advanced networking initiatives around the world. Working together will help ensure a cohesive and interoperable advanced networking infrastructure for research and education and the continued interoperability of the global Internet.

FURTHER READING

Fenton, Brian C. "Next-Generation Internet." *InfoWorld*, 1 Mar. 1997.

Grossman, Lev. "Building the Next Internet." *Time*, 25 Feb. 1999.

Mambretti, Joel, and Andrew Schmidt. *Next Generation Internet: Creating Advanced Networks and Services.* New York: Wiley, 1999.

Weil, Nancy. "Faster, Cheaper Internet on the Horizon." *InfoWorld*, 20 Sept. 1999.

—*Manuel Sanromà*

Novell Corporation

The Utah-based Novell Corporation was founded in 1983 by entrepreneur Ray Noorda (1924–). Novell provides networking services and software for both corporate and individual users. Novell serves 81 percent of the Fortune 500 companies and powers more than 3.8 million servers.

Noorda built Novell out of the ashes of the defunct Novell Data Systems PC company. At the outset, the company focused on the relatively new idea of providing a connection scheme, a **local area network** (LAN), permitting files and **printers** to be shared by multiple **personal computer** (PC) workstations. LANs were a new idea and it took four or five years before they became popular, but by the end of the 1980s, companies of nearly any size were buying LANs and Novell had established itself as the vendor of choice.

In the late 1980s, the company focused entirely on software and started to work on the problem of connecting not just PCs and their peripherals but all sorts of information technology systems, including **minicomputers** and **mainframes**. Eventually, nearly anything (including **Macintosh** and **Unix** systems) could be accessed across a Novell network. At the company's height, most of the largest companies (and many of the smaller ones) used Novell technology. But as **Windows** NT matured and the **Internet** began to beckon, Novell failed to keep up with its technological roots.

The company made a number of acquisitions in the early 1990s. Designed to diversify the company onto additional platforms (such as Unix) and into applications software (such as WordPerfect), they had the effect of defocusing the company. Robert Frankenberg became chief executive officer (CEO) in 1994 and sold off the acquisitions (e.g., WordPerfect was sold to Corel in 1996) and attempted to reorient the company, but with limited success.

The charismatic Eric Schmidt succeeded Frankenberg in 1997, sharply focusing the company around its network directory server and the Internet. In 1999, Novell managed a very successful upgrade release to NetWare 5.x, which was required for year 2000 compliance. Sales soared, but they dipped sharply in early 2000, perhaps as a result of excess inventory, perhaps because the emergency had passed and Novell customers were now looking at other solutions.

In 1999, Novell had more than U.S.$1.3 billion in revenue and $109 million in profits, down significantly from their heights. Novell is a small company when measured against industry software giants such as **Microsoft**, **Computer Associates**, or IBM's software division. Nevertheless, Novell's reliable products remain popular, its directory remains at the heart of a soaring Internet requirement for directory services, and its applications products, such as ZENworks (for network administration) and Groupwise (for **e-mail** and collaboration), have significant user bases.

FURTHER READING

Derfler, Frank J., Jr., and Les Freed. *How Networks Work.* Emeryville, Calif.: Ziff-Davis, 1993.

Kearns, David, and Brian Iverson. *The Complete Guide to Novell Directory Services.* Alameda, Calif.: Sybex, 1996; 2nd ed., San Francisco: 1998.

—*Amy D. Wohl*

Noyce, Robert

1927–90

U.S. Inventor and Business Leader

Robert Noyce invented the silicon **integrated circuit**, or *microchip*, the device that made it possible to build modern electronic equipment. He cofounded two major high-technology companies, **Fairchild Semiconductor** and **Intel**, and his management style at those companies made a vital contribution to today's corporate culture.

In 1949, as a university undergraduate, Noyce saw one of the first **transistors** ever built. He was fascinated. In a few years, transistors would replace the hot, bulky **vacuum tubes** that were the guts of early-twentieth-century radios and computers. But in the early 1950s, transistor technology was unfamiliar even to most scientists and engineers.

Noyce wanted to be at the forefront of transistor research. In 1956 he went to work for **William Shockley** (1910–89), one of the inventors of the transistor. Noyce became one of a dozen bright young engineers at Shockley Semiconductor Laboratory in Mountain View, California, the area that would soon become known as **Silicon Valley**.

The work was exciting, but Shockley was notoriously difficult to work with. There were technical disagreements, too: Shockley wanted to keep building germanium transistors, but Noyce and many of his colleagues believed that **silicon** would be a better material. So in 1957, eight of Shockley's engineers left to found Fairchild Semiconductor Corporation.

In terms of personality, Noyce was almost the opposite of Shockley. Noyce was demanding but good-natured. He was tapped as the research manager for the new company, and two years later became Fairchild's general manager and vice-president. At Fairchild, Noyce invented a fast silicon transistor. This was the device that would come to be known as the integrated circuit or microchip. Not only did Noyce's transistor operate fast; it was also much easier to manufacture than similar devices invented elsewhere, because it was chemically etched instead of painstakingly wired by hand. The integrated circuit would become the basis of every modern electronic device—from computers to coffeemakers—that we take for granted today.

In 1968, Noyce and colleague **Gordon Moore** (1929–) left Fairchild to start a new company, Integrated Electronics. Noyce was president. The company—its name soon shortened to Intel—focused on something new: computer memory. Noyce and Moore wanted to use silicon chips instead of magnetic systems to store computer information. In 1970, Intel introduced the first random access memory (**RAM**) chip to the market. A few years later, Intel engineer Marcian "Ted" Hoff (1937–) created the first **microprocessor**, or "computer-on-a-chip," the device that made it possible to build a computer small enough to fit on a desktop.

Noyce's contributions to the world of high technology were cultural as much as technical. He had no interest in the trappings of power, using a battered metal desk long after his employees had acquired bigger, better ones. Everyone at Fairchild and Intel worked in cubicles or open bays. There were no reserved parking spaces, no gourmet lunches for executives. Young, inexperienced engineers were encouraged to speak in meetings, even (perhaps especially) if they disagreed with the boss. Noyce expected—and got—hard work, initiative, and commitment from his recruits. Employees devoted themselves to getting the next hot product out on the market, often at the expense of their personal lives. This corporate culture still prevails in Silicon Valley in the year 2000.

Noyce resigned as Intel's president in 1975, staying on as chairman of the board until 1979. In 1977 he became chairman of the newly founded Semiconductor Industry Association (SIA), an organization created to address such industry issues as overseas competition.

In 1988, the SIA and the U.S. government jointly funded a research consortium, called Sematech, created to help the U.S. semiconductor manufacturing industry compete against Pacific Rim countries. Many in the semiconductor industry thought the organization would never get off the ground. Nevertheless, Noyce agreed to become its chief operating officer. He left California's Silicon Valley, where he had lived for 32 years, for Sematech's headquarters in Austin, Texas. Within a few years, Sematech was producing valuable research results. Noyce died of a heart attack in 1990 while still employed at Sematech.

Robert Noyce with a semiconductor wafer at Sematech in Austin, Texas, June 1989. (AP Photo/David Breslauer)

BIOGRAPHY

Robert M. Noyce. Born 12 December 1927 in Burlington, Iowa. B.S. in physics and mathematics from Grinnell College, 1949; Ph.D. in physical electronics from Massachusetts Institute of Technology (MIT), 1953. Cofounded Fairchild Semiconductor, 1957. Received patent for silicon integrated circuit ("Semiconductor Device-and-Lead Structure"), 1960. Vice-president and general manager, Fairchild Semiconductor, 1959–68. Cofounded Intel, 1968; president of Intel, 1968–75; chairman of board of Intel, 1975–79. CEO of Sematech, 1988–90. Recipient of numerous honors and awards, including the Ballantine Medal, Franklin Institute, 1966; Medal of Honor, IEEE, 1978; Faraday Medal, IEEE, 1979; National Medal of Science, 1979; IEEE Computer Society Pioneer Award, 1980; and National Medal of Technology, 1987. Died 3 June 1990 in Austin, Texas.

SELECTED WRITINGS

Noyce, Robert N., and Marcian E. Hoff, Jr. "A History of Microprocessor Development at Intel." *IEEE Micro,* Vol. 1, Feb. 1981.

FURTHER READING

Golden, Frederic. "Robert Noyce." *Time,* 29 Mar. 1999.

Hanson, Dirk. *The New Alchemists: Silicon Valley and the Microelectronics Revolution.* Boston: Little, Brown, 1982.

Riordan, Michael, and Lillian Hoddeson. *Crystal Fire: The Birth of the Information Age.* New York: Norton, 1998.

Wolfe, Tom. "The Tinkerings of Robert Noyce: How the Sun Rose on the Silicon Valley." *Esquire,* Dec. 1983.

—*Virginia Shea*

NSFnet

NSFnet was a computer **network** implemented by the U.S. National Science Foundation (NSF) in 1986. It was deployed initially to interconnect **super-**

computer centers funded by a NSF program. The program was coordinated by the Office of Advanced Scientific Computing (OASC), which was created in 1984 and first directed by John Connolly (1938–), to address the need for access to supercomputing power by U.S. academic researchers.

Even though it was conceived to address the particular needs of a specialized group of scientists, NSFnet was enormously significant for the development of the global **Internet** as we know it today. The shrewd leadership of a few academic scientists and program managers at NSF made NSFnet a critical link in the path toward a global information infrastructure. The first NSF director for networking, Dennis Jennings (1946–), made key decisions for implementing the network that would allow for its explosive expansion. First, he decided that it should be a general-purpose network, in keeping with the broad-based support for the program that the leading scientists such as Larry Smarr (1948–) and Kenneth Wilson (1936–) had cultivated. Second, he decided that the structure of the network would have three levels or tiers: the **backbone**, regional networks, and the local or institutional levels. NSF would oversee only the first level, while encouraging entrepreneurial participation at the other two under certain agreed upon rules. Third, the network protocol would be **TCP/IP**, developed in the **ARPANET** environment by **Vinton Cerf** (1943–) and **Robert Kahn** (1938–). TCP/IP was the main "rule" enforced upon would-be participants at the lower levels.

Jennings' successor as director of networking was Steve Wolff. Wolff led the actual implementation of the network from 1986, which included the coordinated inclusion of consortia and institutions that applied for connection to the network and later its privatization. The antecedent of CSnet, a network for academic computer scientists funded in its initial stages by NSF, was wisely built upon by NSFnet leaders in several ways. An agreement between Larry Landweber, one of the main CSnet proponents in the computer science community, and Robert Kahn to allow noncommercial outside traffic on ARPANET, was easily extended to the new NSFnet. Together with the outside contracting of network management and the design and provision of **routers** by private business, the critical mass of the global community of users in the scientific community made NSFnet a key stepping stone to the global Internet of the 1990s.

FURTHER READING

Cook, Gordon. "NSFnet Privatization: Policy Making in a Public Interest Vacuum." *Internet Research*, Vol. 3, No. 1, 1993, pp. 3–9.

Jennings, Dennis, Lawrence Landweber, Ira Fuchs, David Farber, and W. Richards Adrion. "Computer Networking for Scientists." *Science*, Vol. 231, 28 Feb. 1986, 943–950.

Mills, David, and Hans-Werner Braun. "The NSFNET Backbone Network." SIGCOMM 87, *Computer Communications Review*, Vol. 17, No. 5, 1987, pp. 191–196.

Rogers, Juan D. "Internetworking and the Politics of Science: NSFnet in Internet History." *The Information Society*, Vol. 14, No. 3, 1998, pp. 213–228.

—*Juan D. Rogers*

Oberon

The Oberon programming language grew out of experience with **Modula** and the desire to reduce the language to its essentials. Various constructs of Modula were discarded, such as the nestability of modules and coroutines. The essential addition is type extension, that is, the definition of new record types that feature additional attributes (record fields) but remain upward compatible with their base type. This is the essential ingredient of object-oriented programming, where extended types are called *subclasses*. It makes it possible to construct dynamic, inhomogeneous data structures, such as trees with different types of nodes, all of which are different extensions of the same base type.

Together with the possibility to associate procedures with records (in object-oriented terminology: methods with objects), type extension is the means to build data structures whose elements perform different, albeit similar actions when called by the same procedure name. A typical example is that of windows, where the same procedure (e.g., Draw) will have to perform different actions depending on the type of window present (text window, graphics window, etc.).

By reducing the language to the most essential but most powerful facilities, it was possible to keep the language small, the description concise (16 pages), the implementation compact, and the effort of learning commensurate. Oberon marks the departure from the notion of *batch processing*, executing one task after its predecessor, in favor of concurrent tasks, performed in steps and switching from one to another. It also marks the departure of distinguishing between **operating system** and user programs, instead considering the entire system as one hierarchy of modules loaded on demand, and also the departure of the notion of a program as the unit of execution, separating the module as the unit of compilation from the command as the unit of execution.

Oberon was inspired by the language and operating system Cedar, developed at the **Xerox Palo Alto Research Center** (PARC) in the mid-1980s. As with Modula, which had PARC's Mesa as its model, the complexity of Cedar motivated the search for a simpler, condensed language without embellishments of lesser value.

Oberon was implemented between 1986 and 1989 at the Swiss Federal Institute of Technology (ETH) in Zurich in a concentrated effort by **Niklaus Wirth** (1934–) and Jurg Gutknecht. Parallel with it went the design and construction of another workstation, called Ceres. The **software** project included not only the compiler, but also the entire Oberon System from scratch: storage management, file system, display system, text system, and device drivers. In the years 1989–93 various applications followed, such as graphics system, server system for centralized file storage via network (**Ethernet**), and laser printing. All software, without exception, was programmed in Oberon, proving the general-purpose capability of the language.

Subsequently, Oberon was implemented on several computers, including machines from **IBM**, **Sun Microsystems**, **Hewlett-Packard**, and **Apple Computer**, in such a way that programs could be ported from one platform to another without modification and adaptation. A version of the language called Oberon-2, designed by Hanspeter Moessenboeck, contains some additional constructs convenient for object-oriented programming, remaining fully upward compatible with Oberon.

FURTHER READING

Reiser, Martin, and Niklaus Wirth. *Programming in Oberon: Steps Beyond Pascal and Modula.* Reading, Mass.: Addison-Wesley, 1992.

Wirth, Niklaus. "The Programming Language Oberon." *Software: Practice and Experience,* Vol. 18, No. 7, July 1988, pp. 671–690.

Wirth, Niklaus, and Jurg Gutknecht. *Project Oberon: The Design of an Operating System and Compiler.* Reading, Mass.: Addison-Wesley, 1992.

— *Niklaus Wirth*

Object-Oriented Programming

Object-oriented programming is a technique for writing **software** based on *objects.* An object is a self-contained programming entity with well-defined characteristics and behavior. Objects are meant to better represent the real world, making it easier, in theory, to build, understand, reuse, and modify software. In a text processing program, for example, a window could be considered an object that can receive such messages as "clear," "change background color," and "change font." An object can be built using other objects as components. An object window in a text processing program, for example, consists of objects such as menus, scrollbars, and icons.

In theory, a programmer can write object-oriented programs in any language. However, there are a number of them that provide built-in support for this technique; these are known as object-oriented languages. In order for a language to be considered object-oriented, it must support encapsulation, inheritance, and polymorphism.

Encapsulation, also known as *information hiding,* means that data and the possible operations on them are stored in a single self-contained unit known as an *object.* Variables inside an object are called *instance variables*; the procedures within an object are known as *methods.* The methods may be visible outside the object or known and usable only within the object itself. The collective publicly available methods are also known as an object's *interface,* since it is the interface between the rest of the program and the object. In our example above, the contents of the text window in a text processing program are not accessible directly. If the programmer wants to manipulate the data (the text, fonts, formatting), he or she must resort to the object's methods. The program can interact with the data only by means of this object's interface. It is impossible to clear the text window other than by using the method "clear" defined and contained in the object.

Objects are instances of a *class,* which defines the general structure and behavior of an object. Multiple classes that share common behavior can be specified relative to one another through *inheritance,* generally used to express what is known as an "is-a" relationship. For example, a programmer writing a program might want to have a class of windows for text and a class of windows for drawings. The programmer might define the common behavior into a class called "window" and have the "drawing window" and the "text window" inherit methods and data from the class "window."

Multiple inheritance allows a class to inherit from several classes. Some aspects of supporting multiple inheritance in a programming language can be technically difficult. Because of these difficulties and because of the belief by some that the end effect of multiple inheritance can be achieved through other means, some object-oriented languages, most notably Java, do not support this feature.

Because of inheritance, it may be possible to assign objects of different types to each other. For example, if you have a variable of type "rectangle" and another variable of type "polygon," it should be possible to assign the value of the first to the second, because a rectangle is a polygon. Allowing variables to take on multiple forms, as in this example, is known as *polymorphism.* With polymorphism and inheritance, a programmer can manipulate an object without knowing in advance the exact form of the object.

Classes were first used in the **SIMULA** language, an object-oriented version of **ALGOL** 60 that was completed in 1967. As its name implies, SIMULA was designed to support programming discrete-event simulations, and hence required a data type that mapped well to real-world objects. Although SIMULA itself was object-oriented, the language predated the formal methodology now known as object-oriented programming. SIMULA even predates the notion of structured programming, a programming technique that emphasized top-down program design, first formalized in the late 1960s and embodied in languages such as **Pascal** and **C**.

Alan C. Kay (1940–) formalized the principles of object-oriented programming and coined much of the terminology when he began developing the **Smalltalk** language in 1971. Kay was inspired by his experiences with other computer languages, especially SIMULA and **LISP**, and by his academic background in biology. Objects communicate entirely by sending messages to each other, just as biological cells communicate with chemical messages. In addition to embodying many of the principles of object-oriented programming, Smalltalk was used for the development of a **graphical user interface** for the **Alto computer**, pioneering the concepts found in today's object-oriented frameworks for graphical user interfaces.

A number of programming languages today are object oriented, and many of the older programming languages have been extended to support object-oriented programming. Notable examples of the latter include **Ada**, LISP (CLOS, the Common Lisp Object System), and C (Objective-C and **C++**). Other object-oriented programming languages of note are **Java**, **Eiffel**, and Python.

The principles behind object-oriented programming have been further abstracted to address software design and analysis. This has led to further advances in the field of software engineering, from constructs for specifying object-oriented design, such as the Unified Modeling Language (UML), to the cataloging of recurring patterns in object-oriented software construction, known as *design patterns*.

FURTHER READING

Booch, Grady. *Object-Oriented Analysis and Design with Applications*. Redwood City, Calif.: Benjamin/Cummings, 1991; 2nd ed., 1994.

Meyer, Bertrand. *Object-Oriented Software Construction*. New York: Prentice Hall, 1988; 2nd ed., Upper Saddle River, N.J., 1997.

Wirfs-Brock, Rebecca, Brian Wilkerson, and Lauren Weiner. *Designing Object-Oriented Software*. Englewood Cliffs, N.J.: Prentice Hall, 1990.

—*Eugene Eric Kim*

OCR

See Optical Character Recognition.

OEM

The term OEM, an acronym for *original equipment manufacturer*, is a misnomer, since an OEM buys components from another company in bulk, assembles a device, and sells the product under its own company name and brand. **Siemens**, for example, sells **Fujitsu hardware** repackaged as Siemens equipment. The deal is convenient for both partners: The Japanese company gains access to a market dominated by German corporations and Siemens can save development costs. In this example, Siemens acts as the OEM.

OEMs are sometimes confused with VARs (value-added resellers). A VAR assembles a system with components from various manufacturers but usually includes extra **software** or functionality in the finished product. A company that assembles workstations for graphic designers and includes its own software in the package, is a VAR. If the only service provided by the company in this example is putting the components together, it is sometimes called a *systems integrator*.

—*Raúl Rojas*

Olivetti

Olivetti is an Italy-based company with more than 132,000 employees worldwide. Italy's largest telecommunications group, Olivetti introduced some of the first European commercial computers. Until 1997 Olivetti was also one of the main producers of **personal computers** (PCs) in Europe.

Olivetti was founded in 1908 by Camillo Olivetti (1868–1943) and was the first Italian typewriter company. Its history resembles somewhat **IBM**'s own shift from the office market to the computer industry. From being a typewriter business directed by Adriano Olivetti (1901–60), who was appointed director general in 1933, after World War II Olivetti moved swiftly into the electronic sector and in 1959 introduced Italy's first electronic computer, the Elea 9003 (Elaboratore Elettronico Automatico). The Elea was a transistorized machine with a ferrite core memory of up to 68 kilobytes. It offered multiprogramming (up to three programs could be started simultaneously) and **interrupts**.

In 1965, Olivetti introduced the P101 (Programma 101), a programmable desktop calculator similar to those produced by **Hewlett-Packard** a few years later. The P101 is regarded as an early form of the personal computer. The machine used magnetic stripes with places for 120 instructions. The P101 was designed by the engineer Mario Bellini, operated with **floating-point** numbers, and had a simple programming language. The patents registered by Olivetti for the P101 brought the corporation millions of dollars in royalties after other competitors introduced similar machines in the United States and Europe. In 1982, Olivetti made history again by introducing the first Italian personal computer, the M20, a machine based on the 16-bit processor Z8001 from Zilog. The M20 used **CP/M** as its operating system.

The full conversion of Olivetti into an electronics company took place after Carlo de Benedetti became its chief executive officer (CEO). In 1984, Olivetti started producing PC **clones** for the European market. The M24 was the first Italian clone, and although not fully IBM compatible, it was a remarkable success among Olivetti's traditional customer base. At the same time, Olivetti continued producing such electronic equipment as **printers**, fax, cash registers, and photocopiers.

Olivetti moved during the 1990s into telecommunications, founding the mobile telephone operator Omnitel and the fixed line operator Infostrada. However, it was felt that Olivetti had overextended its market reach, and a series of economic problems forced the corporation to reorganize, selling its personal computer business in 1997 and its office division to **Wang Laboratories** in 1998. Olivetti became a holding company focused on information management and telecommunications.

FURTHER READING

"50 Anni di Informatica in Italia e nel Mondo." *Computerworld Italia*, Millenium Edition, No. 45, 20 Dec. 1999.

Kicherer, Sybille. *Olivetti: A Study of the Corporate Management of Design*. New York: Rizzoli, 1990.

—*Margarita Esponda*

Olsen, Kenneth

1926–

U.S. Entrepreneur

Kenneth H. Olsen's main contribution to computing is the establishment of **minicomputers** ("minis") through his highly successful **Digital Equipment Corporation** (DEC). Minicomputers were small computers (by the standards of the day) that fit in a single cabinet. At its peak, DEC, under Olsen's long-term leadership, dominated this market with best-selling **PDP** series of minicomputers, such as the 12-bit PDP-8 (in the 1960s), the 16-bit PDP-11 (in the 1970s), and the 32-bit VAX-11 (in the 1980s).

Olsen's first experience with computing was at the Massachusetts Institute of Technology (MIT), where, having obtained two electrical engineering degrees, he took an active role in the Digital Computer Laboratory that developed the **Whirlwind** (the real-time flight simulation computer) and then the related **SAGE** computer used for air defense. Olsen led the construction of a smaller version of Whirlwind used to test the ceramic ferrite core memory for the full version of Whirlwind. This test computer was completed in only nine months; it worked well and the core memory was installed in Whirlwind during the summer of 1953. Olsen has described the Whirlwind as the first minicomputer, and he used the knowledge he acquired during his time at MIT to set up his own company to market this idea.

The subsequent SAGE computer was manufactured at **IBM**'s Poughkeepsie factory. Olsen, together with a few other engineers from the Digital Computer Laboratory, was sent by Norman Taylor to monitor progress. Olsen spent two and a half years at Poughkeepsie and learned much about computer production during this time. He noted inefficiencies at IBM and felt that he could do better. Back at MIT, he led a project to develop a transistorized research computer. As a manager, he built good team spirit, using his experience gained in observing IBM.

Olsen founded DEC with a colleague, Harlan E. Anderson, and his brother Stan Olsen in August 1957, initially producing electronic modules using **transistors**—still very novel at the time. Three years after the company was founded, DEC introduced the programmed data processor model 1 (PDP-1), one of the first to be based on transistors, which included a **cathode-ray tube** (CRT) monitor with a **keyboard** for very direct user interaction. The computer cost U.S.$120,000, which was cheap for the time.

The PDP-1 was the first incarnation of Olsen's unusual ideas about computers, assimilated from his experience at MIT. He realized that many computer users would be better off with a (comparatively) simple, cheap, and rugged computer that did not need a special room and operators for some applications, especially those that are real-time in nature. Other major existing manufacturers such as IBM stuck to more prestigious and expensive mainframes for a further decade or more. This gave Olsen a tremendous lead on the market, which started to take off in the mid-1960s with the first mass-produced minicomputer, DEC's PDP-8. During this period, Olsen received patents for the magnetic core memory and the line printer buffer, among others.

DEC developed into the leading minicomputer manufacturer. In 1970, DEC produced the PDP-11, which became the most popular minicomputer family ever. Olsen was an excellent manager of the company, serving as president until his retirement in October 1992. Under Olsen's leadership, DEC grew from an initial three employees working in 8500 square feet of leased space in an old woolen mill in Maynard, Massachusetts, a suburb of Boston, to one of the world's leading suppliers of computer systems, software, and services, with more than 120,000 employees and business transactions in more than 100 countries. The corporation pioneered and led the industry in interactive and distributed computing based on minicomputers.

Olsen will be remembered primarily for his foundation of the minicomputer industry through DEC, which maintained a leading position in this field for several decades. Olsen's insight was that smaller, cheaper computers would open up many more applications and result in increased sales. However, DEC never managed to capitalize on the subsequent microcomputer revolution. Indeed, Olsen rejected a suggestion in May 1974 by a young engineer at DEC, David Ahl, to produce a completely portable computer (based on a cut-down version of a PDP-8). DEC's management was not convinced that there was a market for such a personal device at the time. Ahl left the company, and the **personal computer** (PC) era of the late 1970s and 1980s was to be dominated by younger, more free-thinking pioneers. DEC was eventually taken over by **Compaq**, a PC manufacturer.

BIOGRAPHY

Kenneth H. Olsen. Born on 20 February 1926 in Stratford, Connecticut. Served in the U.S. Navy, 1944–46. B.S., 1950; master's degree in electrical engineering from Massachusetts Institute of Technology, 1952. Worked at MIT's Digital Computer Laboratory for seven years. Leader of the section of MIT Lincoln Laboratory that designed and built the MTC computer used in the SAGE Air Defense Computer design program. Supervised the building of the TX-0 and TX-2 high-performance transistorized digital computers. Founded the leading minicomputer manufacturer, Digital Equipment Corporation, 1957; served as its president until October 1992. Became chairman of Advanced Modular Solutions, Inc., Boxborough, Massachusetts, a provider of consultancy services and computers, including fail-safe systems and servers. Fellow of the Institute of Electrical and Electronics Engineers (IEEE) and the American Academy of Arts and Sciences, Boston; inducted into National Inventors Hall of Fame, 1990. Recipient of many awards, including the Founders Award from the National Academy of Engineering, 1982; Founders Medal from IEEE, 1993; and National Medal of Technology, 1993.

FURTHER READING

Eckhouse, Richard H., and L. Robert Morris. *Minicomputer Systems: Organization, Programming, and Applications (PDP-11).* Englewood Cliffs, N.J.: Prentice Hall, 1975; 2nd ed., 1979.

Rifkin, Glenn, and George Harrar. *The Ultimate Entrepreneur: The Story of Ken Olsen and Digital Equipment Corporation.* Chicago: Contemporary Books, 1988.

—Jonathan Bowen

"On Computable Numbers"

By A. M. Turing

"On Computable Numbers, with an Application to the Entscheidungsproblem" was the awkward title given by **Alan M. Turing** (1912–54) to his paper submitted in 1936 to the London Mathematical Society. It is now generally recognized as the foundation of modern **computer science**. When it was written, the word *computer* meant a person doing calculations—electronic computers were in the future.

In 1900, German mathematician David Hilbert (1862–1943) presented 23 open problems, which later came to be known as the *Hilbert problems*, at the International Congress of Mathematicians in Paris. The tenth problem was reformulated later in several guises, and it became known by the German name *Entscheidungsproblem*. It deals with the fundamental question of whether a machine (a mechanical procedure) can be used to prove or disprove arbitrary mathematical assertions. Turing could show that this is not possible because even the simple proposition "this mechanical procedure stops" (providing then a solution) is undecidable. This is the *halting problem* for **Turing machines**.

Turing had been introduced to Hilbert's Entscheidungsproblem by the lectures of the topologist M. H. A. Newman (1897–1984) at Cambridge University in 1935. By analyzing the idea of a method that could be applied mechanically by a person doing a computation, and defining the machine that could implement such a method, Turing gave a definitive answer (in the negative) to Hilbert's Entscheidungsproblem. There could not, even in principle, be a single method that would decide the truth of all mathematical assertions.

Turing started from first principles without reference to existing automatic calculators. He arrived at instruction tables to codify all possible methods and specified the *universal Turing machine* to read such tables and carry out the instructions. Turing's analysis depended on the universal machine reading instructions in the same way that any other form of data would be read. Thus the instruction tables can now be seen as comparable to computer programs, and the universal machine as embodying the essential idea of the stored-program computer.

Turing's paper did not leap to immediate fame. He made no effort to bring his work to the attention of those involved in calculating machinery, until 1945. His other prewar publications cited his paper only to extend its application in mathematical logic and to correct some technical details. Nevertheless, informal evidence shows that Turing was interested in practical machinery even then.

There is anecdotal evidence that mathematician **John von Neumann** (1903–57) knew of Turing's work when he offered Turing a post at Princeton in 1938, an offer Turing declined. (But it should be appreciated that von Neumann was working neither in logic nor in computation at that time.) The important 1943 paper on **cybernetics** by **Warren McCulloch** (1898–1969) and Walter Pitts (1923–69), "A Logical Calculus of the Ideas Immanent in Nervous Activity," was influenced by Turing's paper, and this was in turn cited by von Neumann in the ***First Draft of a Report on the EDVAC***, written in 1945. Further, J. R. Womersley, superintendent of the Mathematical Division at the National Physical Laboratory (NPL) in London, read the paper, which was a factor in Turing's appointment to the NPL in 1945 to pursue his design of an electronic computer. Thus the paper did have a direct influence on practical computing. It is also noteworthy that M. H. A. Newman, the first reader of Turing's paper, set in motion the Manchester computer project in 1945.

After the war Turing himself often cited "On Computable Numbers" as the basis of his ideas. He sketched a rigorous connection with practical computers in an unpublished 1948 work. Also in 1948, von Neumann referred in a lecture to this paper's fundamental importance. But Turing never published a clear account of the relationship between theory and practice and thus lost the chance to assert his claim to the essence of the modern computer. As the new engineering discipline of electronic computing established itself in the 1950s, Turing's theoretical work seemed remote. But in the 1960s its significance was reasserted, one signal being the establishment in 1966 of the **Turing Award** by the **Association for Computing Machinery**.

Further Reading

McCulloch, Warren S., and Walter Pitts. "A Logical Calculus of the Ideas Immanent in Nervous Activity." *Bulletin of Mathematical Biophysics*, Vol. 5, 1943, pp. 115–133. Reprinted in Rook McCulloch, ed., *The Collected Works of Warren S. McCulloch*, Vol. 1. Salinas, Calif.: Intersystems Publications, 1989, pp. 343–361.

Turing, Alan M. "On Computable Numbers, with an Application to the Entscheidungsproblem." *Proceedings of the London Mathematical Society*, Vol. 2, No. 42, 1936–37, pp. 230–265. Reprinted in Martin Davis, *The Undecidable.* Hewlett, N.Y.: Raven Press, 1965.

———. Correction. *Proceedings of the London Mathematical Society*, Vol. 2, No. 43, 1937, pp. 544–546. Reprinted in Martin Davis, *The Undecidable.* Hewlett, N.Y.: Raven Press, 1965.

———. "Intelligent Machinery." In D. C. Ince, ed., *The Collected Works of A. M. Turing.* New York: North-Holland, 1992.

von Neumann, John. First *Draft of a Report on the EDVAC.* Contract W-670-ORD-4926. Philadelphia: Moore School of Electrical Engineering, University of Pennsylvania, 30 June 1945. Reprinted in Nancy Stern, *From ENIAC to UNIVAC.* Woburn, Mass.: Digital Press, 1981.

———. "The General and Logical Theory of Automata, Followed by a Historical Discussion." In *The Collected Works of John von Neumann*, Vol. 5. New York: Pergamon Press, 1963.

—*Andrew Hodges*

On Distributed Communications

By Paul Baran

The collection of papers called *On Distributed Communications* was written by **Paul Baran** (1926–) and his colleagues at the RAND Corporation in the early 1960s. The papers describe a communications network that could continue functioning even after being partially damaged. Baran's design is very similar to that of the **ARPANET**, the precursor to today's global **Internet**. Baran's work was concerned with network survivability after a nuclear attack, and it is this connection that is probably the source of the apocryphal tale that today's Internet was originally built with that goal.

Like much of the work done at RAND at the height of the cold war with the Soviet Union, Baran's research was funded by the U.S. Air Force. Baran felt it was vital that the United States have a communications network that could survive a Soviet nuclear attack, especially since the network would probably be an important target. In a series of papers, he described the technology and layout required to build a network that would have no centralized command and control structures that could be destroyed. A completely distributed network had never been created before, and in the process of designing the system, Baran developed several groundbreaking ideas, including the idea of dividing messages into pieces that would each travel across the network independently.

This method of delivering data was very different from the way telephone systems worked and seemed haphazard to engineers at **AT&T**, who were convinced that the system would never work. Even after many discussions and papers answering their objections, Baran and his colleagues were unable to convince AT&T of the system's feasibility. In 1965, Baran halted work on the project.

Unknown to Paul Baran, two other men had independently made similar network designs. Just as Baran was halting work on his system in the United States, in Britain **Donald Davies** (1924–) was planning for and writing about his own vision of computer networking. Like Baran, his system had a distributed **architecture** and broke messages into many small pieces. He called the system **packet switching**, which is the term used to this day. Even earlier, Leonard Kleinrock (1934–) had published a 1961 paper on packet-switching theory. Kleinrock's work was picked up by **Lawrence Roberts** (1938–), who went on to do the high-level design of the ARPANET. Roberts later learned of Davies and Baran's work, and he consulted with them as he continued to develop the ARPANET.

FURTHER READING

Baran, Paul, et al. *On Distributed Communications,* Vols. I–XI. RAND Corporation Research Documents. Santa Monica, Calif.: RAND Corporation, Aug. 1964. *http://www.rand.org/publications/RM/baran.list.html*

Hafner, Katie, and Matthew Lyon. *Where Wizards Stay Up Late: The Origins of the Internet.* New York: Simon and Schuster, 1996.

Segaller, Stephen. *Nerds 2.0.1: A Brief History of the Internet.* New York: TV Books, 1999.

—*Anthony Anderberg*

Open Architecture

The term *open architecture* refers to electronic systems whose specifications have been made available to the public. Producers of components or entire systems are provided with the information they need to manufacture compatible machines and to interconnect all parts. Open architecture also describes the structure of the **Internet**, which is built on standard **interfaces**, **protocols**, a basic data format, and a uniform identifier or addressing mechanism. All the information needed regarding the interconnection aspects is publicly available. Some software also features open architecture, notable examples being **Unix** and **Linux**.

Traditionally, the word *architecture* refers to the framework guiding the construction of a structure or system. It describes vital elements of the whole and the rules for interconnection among components. In the case of computer **networks**, the challenge in designing an open architecture system is to provide local autonomy, the possibility of interconnecting heterogeneous systems, and communication across uniform interfaces. Providing a basic format for data and a common addressing mechanism makes possible data transmission across the boundaries of dissimilar networks. Similarly, in an open-architecture computer, the components may be designed or developed separately and each may have a unique way of interfacing with other components, but all will be able to connect using a public and common specification with the main system.

When the **Altair 8800**, one of the first **personal computers** (PCs), was introduced, the benefits of an open architecture were not totally clear. Altair avoided publishing details of its machine, but computer hobbyists in the San Francisco Bay area, organized in the legendary **Homebrew Computer Club**, dug into the Altair **bus**, figured out how it worked, and promoted the development of a bus that would be open to all who wanted to attach components. The **Apple I**, introduced a few years later by Homebrew veteran **Steve Wozniak** (1950–), had an open architecture: Each user received the complete hardware diagrams and the designers encouraged diverse add-ons built by hobbyists. These in turn increased the usefulness of the machine. **IBM** tried to copy this in its business model with the introduction of the IBM PC in 1981. The specification for the hardware was made available and the PC industry developed around a common architecture.

Until the PC appeared, computer designs were traditionally proprietary and specifications not publicly available. Users sometimes had to sign nondisclosure agreements in order to get information about their own machines. The PC changed all this because it led to a synergy between the companies developing **software** and **hardware** around a common platform.

The **Windows** operating system, in contrast, is an example of a *closed architecture*. Someone willing to build a Windows clone would have to reinvent many of the interfaces between programs and would not be allowed to copy the "look and feel" of Windows. The Unix and Linux programming environments, on the other hand, were created specifically as open architectures.

The dynamic development and spread of internetworking or computer systems are facilitated by an open architecture. It is also a business strategy used by companies that are latecomers to a market segment: Providing the specifications of the system can lure original equipment manufacturers and others to adopt the new machine or software.

FURTHER READING

Freiberger, Paul, and Michael Swaine. *Fire in the Valley*. Berkeley, Calif.: Osborne/McGraw-Hill, 1984.

Hauben, Michael, and Ronda Hauben. *Netizens: On the History and Impact of Usenet and the Internet*. Los Alamitos, Calif.: IEEE Computer Society Press, 1997.

Leiner, Barry, et al. "The Past and Future History of the Internet." *Communications of the ACM*, Vol. 40, No. 2, 1997, pp. 102–108.

Wayner, Peter. *Free for All: How Linux and the Free Software Movement Undercut the High-Tech Titans*. New York: Harper Business, 2000.

—*Ronda Hauben*

Open Source

The term *open source* refers to a development model for **software** where programs are written collaboratively by volunteers and the source code is freely available. Although open source's best-known example is **Linux**, the **Unix**-like **operating system** begun by **Linus Torvalds** (1969–) while a student at the University of Helsinki, it is by no means the only one. Open-source programs are found in practically every category of software, from operating systems—in addition to Linux, there are FreeBSD, OpenBSD, and other Unix variants—to databases, such as MySQL, to application software, **games**, and utilities.

Much of the **Internet**'s infrastructure runs on open-source software. The **Apache** server accounts for more than 60 percent of **World Wide Web** servers, while **Sendmail** is used by more than 75 percent of Internet **electronic mail** servers to deliver mail, and Bind is used by most domain name servers (DNSs) to link site names with **IP addresses**. A number of open-source scripting languages, such as **Perl**, Python, TcL, and PHP, are widely used in building Web sites.

Although the concept of an open-source movement is a relatively recent development, the philosophy that underpins open source is not new. In the early days of computing, sharing source code was commonplace. With commercial software, which began to become widely available in the 1980s, users typically get access only to an executable binary and are legally prohibited from making and distributing copies. Open-source programs, on the other hand, are created by a community of developers working together. The source code is freely available so that individuals or organizations can make improvements or customize a program to meet their needs. These changes are shared, so others benefit from them as well.

Prior to the rise of the Internet, these collaborative efforts often required mailing source code on tapes or **floppy disks**. The Internet has greatly facilitated the open-source development model, and it is now common for programmers around the world to collaborate in developing software that solves a common problem.

There are many varieties of open-source software licenses, leading to some confusion about exactly what the term means. The defining standard is generally recognized as the *GNU Public License*, better known as GPL. The GPL (also referred to as *copyleft*) was created by the **Free Software Foundation**, an organization started by programmer **Richard Stallman** (1953–), author of the open-source editor GNU Emacs. Stallman believes that open source is more properly called *free software*, where "free"

A novelty license plate expresses support for open-source software. (Courtesy of the Computer Museum History Center)

refers to freedom rather than price. Indeed, the definition published by the Free Software Foundation explicitly says that free software includes the freedom to redistribute copies, either gratis or for a fee. Many companies have sprung up around the open-source movement, making their income through distributing or supporting open-source software.

No one knows exactly how many open-source programmers there are. Linux distributor **Red Hat**, which wanted to share the wealth from its initial public offering by giving stock to members of the open-source community, identified 5000 key contributors to various open-source projects in 1999. Some estimates of the number of programmers contributing to Linux, however, range as high as 100,000. Many of these may be very small contributions, perhaps just isolating or fixing one bug.

What is certain is that the programmers are contributing to open-source projects largely for reasons other than monetary reward. Many improvements to open-source software come about because a particular programmer or organization has a specific need. A programmer might write a device driver for a video card that his or her particular computer uses, for example, or fix a bug that is causing it to crash. Or a department store that wants to use Linux might adapt it to work with the particular type of cash register it uses. These changes are then typically made available to others.

There is another motivation for working on open-source projects, which is public recognition. Status in the open-source world is based on excellence in coding. Among programmers there is enormous prestige associated with writing code that is accepted into high-profile open-source projects such as the Linux kernel.

As open-source companies become stronger financially, a growing number of programmers are being paid to develop open-source software. Linux distributors such as Red Hat, Caldera, and SuSe, together with services companies such as LinuxCare and Covalent, employ programmers who are actively involved in developing open-source products. In addition, as the open-source approach becomes more accepted by the mainstream information technology world, more traditional computer vendors have begun making contributions to the open-source code stream. Programmers at **IBM**, for example, have made significant contributions to the Apache Web server source code.

For many commercial users, one of the main advantages of open-source software is reliability. In the late 1990s, for example, Linux gained ground as a server operating system because it routinely ran nonstop for months or years, whereas one of its primary commercially produced competitors, Microsoft's **Windows NT**, frequently crashed or required rebooting. This high level of reliability is due to the extensive peer review that open-source software undergoes. As open-source advocate Eric S. Raymond (1957–) explained in his seminal essay "The Cathedral and the Bazaar," "Many eyes make all bugs shallow." In the centralized model of software development used by commercial software vendors, it may take a long period of time to fix a bug and distribute it to users, particularly if the problem is minor or affects only a few customers. In the distributed open-source approach, on the other hand, the large number of developers working on the system means that bugs frequently are fixed very quickly.

FURTHER READING

DiBona, Chris, Sam Ockman, and Mark Stone, eds. *Open Sources: Voices from the Open Source Revolution.* Beijing, and Sebastopol, Calif.: O'Reilly, 1999.

Raymond, Eric S. *The Cathedral and the Bazaar: Musings on Linux and Open Source by an Accidental Revolutionary.* Beijing, and Cambridge, Mass.: O'Reilly, 1999.

Wayner, Peter. *Free For All: How Linux and the Free Software Movement Undercut the High-Tech Titans.* New York: Harper Business, 2000.

—*Dan Orzech*

Open Systems Interconnection Reference Model

The Open Systems Interconnection (OSI) reference model was produced jointly by the **International Organization for Standardization** (ISO) and the Comité Consultatif International Téléphonique et Télégraphique (CCITT). It was a major attempt to provide a framework in which to discuss communications between computers. It laid the foundations for the standardization work on OSI, which was intended to be the de facto set of protocols for all computer communications.

The OSI protocols failed to become established, as the **TCP/IP** suite (the **Internet**) emerged in the late 1980s. Nonetheless, work on the OSI reference model made an important contribution to the concept of layered protocols and produced terminology and functions for the seven layers that outlasted the OSI protocols themselves. It continued to be taught as the basic framework for protocol discussions in many university courses for more than a decade after most of the OSI protocols themselves were considered dead.

The OSI reference model (often known as the OSI seven-layer model) arose from the standardization of HDLC (high-level data link control), the basis of all modern-day link protocols. The main question was defining the contents of a packet and standardizing the method. It was recognized that this was a complex task involving many pieces of very different functionality, and that an architecture was needed to structure and give direction to the work.

A new Sub-Committee (SC16) of what was then Technical Committee 97 of ISO was set up to work on both the architecture and the resulting protocol standardization. Responsibility for standardization in the network layer and below was placed with the existing SC6 (which had produced the HDLC standard originally).

The first meeting of SC16 was held in Washington, D.C. in 1978. The committee evaluated six fairly complete (and very different) drafts for "The Reference Model of OSI." These were submitted by the United Kingdom, France, Germany, the United States, Japan, and the European Computer Manufacturer's Association (ECMA). The submissions all contained only three or four layers, with the exception of the ECMA paper, which identified seven layers of standardization, much as we know them today. Most of these submissions were describing an implementation architecture concerned with functions to be performed within a single system, rather than concentrating (as the eventual OSI reference model did) on functions that required exchanges between systems, reflected as "bits on the line."

Work in CCITT on an OSI reference model proceeded in parallel and with relatively little cross-linkage and collaboration until 1984. At that time there were two OSI reference models in the world, one from ISO and one from CCITT. They both had seven layers, but they were different in some significant technical detail, and totally different as pieces of text. In 1984, CCITT proposed to ISO that they adopt the ISO draft as common text, provided that the ISO made certain changes. The end result was a common text that editorially was very close to the ISO text, but technically was almost identical to the CCITT draft.

Seven layers are defined in the draft: physical, data link, network, transport, session, presentation, and application. The *physical layer* is concerned with how to communicate 1's and 0's between two geographically separated points: for example, by sending gravitons, or modulating cepheid variables, or if you want to be more prosaic, by sending light down an optic fiber, or current or voltage in copper, or radio waves to a satellite.

The *data link layer* is concerned with how to frame the 1's and 0's into delimited and error-checked messages. It does this in such a way that errors on the line have minimum impact on framing and stand the maximum chance of being detected. Optionally, this layer may also provide recovery from lost (corrupted) messages using timers and retransmission, and flow control. The layer is concerned (as its name implies) with a single link between nodes.

The *network layer* is concerned with how to provide global addressing, and the associated routing to enable an end-to-end service between any computer system (anywhere) and any other computer system. The network service has two variants. It may provide no recovery options (any message corrupted on a link just gets lost), providing *connectionless network service* (IP is a good example of this) in which case recovery from lost (corrupted) messages has to be handled end to end. Or it may use link-level error recovery, and flow control on each connection, to provide a reliable "what goes in comes out" service called the *connection-oriented network service*—X.25 is a good example of this.

The *transport layer* contains specifications that are implemented only in host systems. It is concerned with improving the quality of service of the communication. Over a connection-oriented network service it is normal for this to be a null layer (no functionality), but over a connectionless network service it has to provide error recovery (by timers and retransmission of lost packets) and flow control. TCP provides this function in the TCP/IP stack and is generally seen as a transport layer protocol. (This issue of end-to-end versus link-by-link error recovery and flow control was one of the biggest controversies in the development of a worldwide network. TCP/IP won out with end-to-end recovery.)

The *session layer* is a toolbox of useful odds and ends that many applications might need. The tools are all broadly concerned with dialogue control, making provision for a strict two-way-alternating exchange using tokens, for dialogue separation to aid checkpointing and commitment protocols, and for orderly termination of communications. It has no equivalent in the TCP/IP suite.

The *presentation layer* is concerned with negotiating the encodings to be used for the elements of a protocol: very verbose, very compact, secure, insecure, human-readable, and so on. The *application layer* is concerned with the form and semantics of complete messages that are to be sent, defined at a level of abstraction about equivalent to data-type definition in a high-level programming language (no concern with bit-level representation of, for example, integers or lists or sequences of things).

FURTHER READINGS

I'Anson, Colin, and Adrian Pell. *Understanding OSI Applications.* Englewood Cliffs, N.J.: Prentice Hall, 1993.

Larmouth, John. "The Early Days of OSI: Report of Preliminary Work." In P. Radford, ed., *Open Systems and Interoperability.* Tewkesbury, Gloucestershire, England: Stanley Thornes, 1995.

———. *Understanding OSI.* Boston: International Thomson Computer Press, 1996.

—*John Larmouth*

Operating System

An operating system (OS), such as **Linux** or **Windows**, consists of a number of programs that run in a computer to make the user's job simpler. Most OS programs have access to more of the computer's **hardware** than is permitted to a normal user, and they may manipulate the user's programs. As computers became more powerful and operating systems more complex, they have became part of the computer rather than a privileged program that runs on it.

The first electronic computers of the 1950s contained the first elements of OSs: They had a means of getting a program *into* the computer before the computer was running a program. The **IAS machine** had a hardware function that would load one word of memory from paper tape, two instructions that, when executed, started a delicate dance of tape reading and self-modification that created a program-loading program in memory. This was called a *bootstrap.* A modern machine will have a small program in *read-only memory* (**ROM**) that is started at power-on. This is likely to do a minimum set of hardware checks, then read one block from a fixed location of a preassigned disk into memory. This *loader program* is then started and the computer is *booted.*

Also from the earliest days, probably from the **EDSAC**, it was realized that the best way to store a program was not exactly the same as it would appear in memory to be run. There were considerable advantages to loading a program starting at any location. It was also useful to be able to link separate programs together when they were loaded, such as a main program and a standard subroutine library. This meant that a stored program did not contain just instructions and data but also had instructions describing how it should be loaded into memory. These instructions might include "add the program's start address onto the address for this instruction" or "insert the address of subroutine XYZ into this instruction." This meant that the computer needed a *loader program* to transfer a user's program correctly into memory.

The majority of computer users do not want to know how to get each pixel of "Hello" to appear on their display any more than early users wanted to know how the letters were printed on their teletype. The operation of early magnetic tapes or line printers was very sensitive to timing, and the placement of data on drums and disks *had* to obey all the rules or the device would become unusable. These considerations clearly called for standard routines provided by people who understood the system well and who could be relied upon to adjust the routines whenever the hardware was changed. In time, users were prevented from using expensive hardware directly, and these *device drivers* became a privileged part of the operating system.

Many first-generation computers had no more than 1024 words of memory, but by the mid-1950s, Jay Forrester (1918–) had magnetic **core memory** working on **Whirlwind**, and large reliable memory was a possibility. By the end of the decade, small, fast transistors were becoming quite reliable, so that a complex logic design did not need to fill a room with hot vacuum tubes. **IBM**'s *Fortran Monitor System* (FMS) reduced input–output waiting time dramatically on their big IBM 7090 number cruncher by having punched card input read on a small IBM 1401 computer and *spooled* onto magnetic tape. This was transferred to the 7090, and a *batch* of jobs was run sequentially with the output *spooled* to another magnetic tape for printing on the 1401. This was followed in the early 1960s by projects such as the **LARC** from **UNIVAC**, **STRETCH** from IBM, and University of Manchester's **Atlas**, which developed much of the structure of the modern operating system.

For a further increase in efficiency there had to be more than one user's job available at a time. *Batch* processing was extended to *multiprogramming*, with multiple jobs in memory at the same time. Once the programs were in memory, one at a time had to be selected to run, and *job scheduling* was born. Input from paper tape or punched cards was spooled by overlapping reading with execution of other programs. Similarly, output was spooled, then printed while later programs ran. Even though memories grew, users wanted more. A solution was *virtual memory*, where each user was allocated all of a very large range of memory addresses. The processor hardware then had to map the running job onto locations in the much smaller physical memory. When a match failed, the job was delayed until the requested location was read from disk into an available part of physical memory, which was then mapped for the job. To make this approach manageable, *paging* was used to transfer fixed-size blocks between memory and disk, and these blocks were the unit of memory mapping.

New hardware ideas flowed from the cascade of requirements. Regions of memory could be *protected* so that user's programs did not damage each other. Slow devices could **interrupt** the processor whenever they finished doing something. Fast devices had *autonomous transfer units* or *channels* to transfer blocks of data without disturbing the main processor.

Some first-generation computer systems inspired a vision of the future. Whirlwind and **SAGE** had multiple, real-time graphical displays; IBM's *Airline Control Program* reservation system talked interactively to many booking stations and RAND's *JOHNNIAC Open Shop System* provided researchers with interactive teletype calculators.

The Massachusetts Institute of Technology (MIT) *Compatible Time-Sharing System* (CTSS, compatible with IBM's FMS) was developed by Fernando J. Corbató (1926–) to support *interactive access* through locally interfaced typewriters, or via dial-up modems. This was achieved by extending *multiprogramming* to *time-sharing*, where the job scheduler had to provide each user program with enough run time to respond usefully to typed commands. CTSS was first demonstrated in 1961 on an IBM 709 and subsequently ran on an IBM 7094 specially modified for two memory banks and extra instructions. CTSS ran in one bank and FMS ran in the other as a background job that could be *swapped* with up to 30 users saved as memory images on a drum. CTSS may have had the first **electronic mail** in 1965.

MIT's *Multiplexed Information and Computing Service* (**Multics**) aimed to extend CTSS with a *hierarchical disk structure* (i.e., directories), **virtual memory**, and **multiprocessor** support. This again extended the scheduler to the choice of which processor would run a task in the shared memory. Radically, this was all written in a new high-level language, **PL/1**. The virtual memory was composed of a large number of *segments*, each of which could be mapped to a disk file and *paged* into physical memory as required. A command could be the name of a program on disk, and Multics had search rules, working directories, a command shell, and redirectable input/output. To run a program its disk location was mapped to a free segment and entered. Similarly, program libraries were mapped to a segment and the *command executor* resolved subprogram calls. Another innovation was optimized disk performance using a nearest-seek-first algorithm to choose from a queue of requests. MIT started providing a time-sharing service on Multics to users in late 1969, and the system became a commercial product sold by **Honeywell**.

Dennis Ritchie (1941–) and **Ken Thompson** (1943–) worked on Multics until **Bell Labs** withdrew from the development effort in 1969. This interrupted Thompson's work on *Space Travel*, a solar system simulator. However, he located an unused DEC PDP-7 and wrote a simplified version of Multics. "MULTI" was converted to "UNI" as only one processor was supported and the "ICS" became "IX" (with a nod to a contemporary cartoon character, Asterix, who was both small and powerful), so the new operating system was christened **Unix**. It was soon moved to a PDP-11 and became the first *portable* operating system with support and development from a wide user community.

From the mid-1970s, inexpensive **integrated circuit**–based computers were developed and Unix inspired a simplified *control program/microprocessor* (**CP/M**), which was copied as QDOS, then reworked by **Microsoft** for IBM's **personal computer** as its *disk operating system* (**DOS**). DOS has been largely hidden from contemporary view by the **graphical user interface** called Windows.

From the late 1970s, **local area networks** (LANs) became more and more widely used, and *network operating systems* were specially tailored to support them. In addition, the OSs became *distributed* with *print servers* and *file servers* accessed over the LAN, and they even provided *multiprocessing* support.

The study of OSs is now formalized into resource management (time, memory, disk), queuing theory, and scheduling strategies. But the ghosts of Atlas and Multics are still hiding in the pastel boxes of modern systems.

FURTHER READING

Auslander, M. A., D. C. Larkin, and A. L. Scherr. "The Evolution of the MVS Operating System." *IBM Journal*, Vol. 25, No. 5, 1981.

Glaser, E. L., J. F. Couleur, and G. A. Oliver. "System Design of a Computer for Time Sharing Applications." *Proceedings of the Fall Joint Computer Conference*, 1965.

Goldstine, Herman Heine. *The Computer: From Pascal to von Neumann*. Princeton, N.J.: Princeton University Press, 1993.

Kilburn, T., et al. "The Manchester University Atlas Operating System, Part I: Internal Organization." *Computer Journal*, Vol. 4, Oct. 1961.

Lavington, Simon. *A History of Manchester Computers*. Manchester, Lancashire, England: NCC Publications, 1975.

Madnick, S. E., and J. J. Donovan. *Operating Systems*. New York, McGraw-Hill, 1974.

O'Neill, J. E. "'Prestige Luster' and 'Snow-Balling Effects': IBM's Development of Computer Time-Sharing." *IEEE Annals of the History of Computing*, Vol. 17, No. 2, Summer 1995.

Ritchie, D. M. "The Evolution of the Unix Time-Sharing System." *Lecture Notes in Computer Science*, Vol. 79, *Language Design and Programming Methodology*. New York: Springer-Verlag, 1980.

Ritchie, D. M., and K. Thompson. "The UNIX Time-Sharing System." *Communications of the ACM*, Vol. 17, No. 7, July 1974.

Shaw, J. C. "JOSS: A Designer's View of an Experimental On-Line Computing System." *Proceedings of the Fall Joint Computer Conference*, 1964.

Silberschatz, A., and P. B. Galvin. *Operating System Concepts*. Reading, Mass.: Addison Wesley Longman, 1983; 5th ed., 1998.

Tanenbaum, Andrew S. *Modern Operating Systems*. Englewood Cliffs, N.J.: Prentice Hall, 1992.

—*John Deane*

Optical Character Recognition

Optical character recognition (OCR) software analyzes scanned text, recognizes letters, or *characters*, and converts them to machine internal code. The utility of OCR lies in the ability to further process the converted characters with an editor. A secretary, for example, can scan a document and process it further, instead of having to type everything in—an enormous time saver.

In 1976, **Raymond Kurzweil**'s (1948–) Computer Products Inc. introduced the first general OCR system. Up until then, only a few special fonts, for example Courier, could be processed. Kurzweil's system, on the other hand, was an *omnifont* system—it could recognize any printed or typed character in any style or quality. In 1978, Kurzweil marketed a commercial version of his OCR program and two years later sold the company to **Xerox**. The Kurzweil OCR system is still enormously popular under its new name, Xerox TextBridge.

Before editable characters can be transferred, for example to a **word processing** program, the OCR software must segment the scanned material into passages, lines, and single characters. Even if the scanned document appears free of irregularities to the unaided eye, it is not necessarily free of pitfalls. Characters that narrowly border on one another, or slanted text, can be difficult to recognize. For example, "ri" could be misinterpreted as "n." A strong slant can lead to a problem in differentiating between characters, as well as text in which there is little space between the lines.

Two classical methods of identifying a character's pixel pattern are *pattern matching* and feature recognition. Pattern matching works efficiently for a clean text, such as the printed pages of a book. The pixels of a character are compared to bit patterns in a table until a best match is determined. The degree of accuracy depends on the programmed tolerance levels. Instead of having hundreds of different patterns for every character in the pattern-matching module, standardization methods are used to smooth the form of the characters. Irrelevant pixels are hereby ignored in the search for the best possible match. Generally speaking, the higher the tolerance level for error, the less it is actually recognized. The pattern-matching module can, however, be extended with a library of fonts and special characters to increase recognition capability.

Feature recognition, on the other hand, compares the geometric features of every character with data that describe the shape of a character. An "O," for example, can be described as a closed circle or an oval. With the feature recognition approach, bold text and different font sizes generally do not present an insurmountable problem. However, it is possible for an "F" to be interpreted as an "E" if the scanned image is noisy. This again means that the OCR accuracy rate is highly dependent on the quality of the document being scanned.

Feature extraction is the process of identifying all the information relevant to describe a letter: For example, an "O" has only one part and is categorized as such. An "A," on the other hand, is classified as a three-part letter. These categories, once determined, are then subcategorized: The number of cycles a character has is counted and then the number of openings it has. For example, a "P" belongs to the single-part characters with one cycle, an "8" has two cycles, and a "V" has one upward opening. Most of the processing time goes into the feature extraction process, while the comparison with stored features is rather straightforward and can be made with decision trees, neural networks, or classical statistical methods.

Topological analysis, another approach to OCR, breaks the characters down into lines and circles and compares them with stored descriptions of each character, searching for a match. This method can also handle lightly smudged copies and peculiarities in the text style.

Another approach to OCR consists in using **fuzzy logic** for the recognition process. Instead of categorizing the characters by assigning features absolute truth values (true, false), these are replaced with *linguistic variables* such as: Is the character rather straight? Rather curved? Rather strongly curved? Rather wide? An inference module then draws conclusions from the linguistic description of each character.

Many software and hardware companies now offer OCR products. The recognition rates for printed material are high enough for automatic unaided transcription. But the next frontier in this rather mature sector of the computer industry is the development of good OCR systems for handwriting, which currently are not as good as their printed text counterparts.

Further Reading

Mori, Shunji, Hirobumi Nishida, and Hiromitsu Yamada, eds. *Optical Character Recognition*. New York: Wiley, 1999.

O'Gorman, Larry, and Rangachar Kasturi, eds. *Document Image Analysis: An Executive Briefing* (IEEE Computer Society Executive Briefing). Los Alamitos, Calif.: IEEE Computer Society Press, 1997.

Sommer, Gerald, Kostas Daniilidis, and Josef Pauli, eds. "Computer Analysis of Images and Patterns." *7th International Conference, CAIP'97*, Kiel, Germany, 10–12 Sept. 1997. Berlin and New York: Springer-Verlag, 1997.

—*Jenna L. Brinning*

Optical Computing and Optics in Computing

It has been said that if lasers had been available at that time, optics would have been used in the first computers. As we all know, the first **digital computers** were electronic or electromechanical devices. Nevertheless, optical information processing found immediate applications, primarily military in nature, that were not feasible with electronics. Analog optical processing, for example, can fulfill tasks that require extremely high processing rates. Some examples are analog Fourier processing systems, correlation operators for pattern recognition, and optical coding of radar data.

The earliest considerations of optical technology in digital computing were put forward by **John von Neumann** (1903–57) in the 1940s. One of the first technical realizations of digital/optical computing were computer-generated holograms, introduced by Adolf W. Lohmann. In application areas such as holography and spatial filtering, optical analog processing can readily exploit its advantages over electronics—for instance, the inherent massive parallelism of optical components. A lens maps a two-dimensional pixel image at once, rather than single pixels sequentially. The light beams that transport data in free space can intersect without destroying the information. These apparent benefits could be exploited in a digital system, too. So a dream was born to build a digital optical computer in which data are transported at the speed of light and are transformed by ultrafast optical **logic gates**.

The step from analog to digital optics was taken with the invention of the laser in the 1960s. The idea in those years was to construct an all-optical logic gate by exploiting the laser quenching method, that is, switching off one laser with another one. But at the end of this first phase of digital optics, it was clear that optical logic gates were not competitive, mostly for thermal reasons.

During the second phase of digital optics, starting around 1970, conceptual work was done on appropriate **algorithms** and **architectures** for a future optical computer, whose time would come when electronics had reached its natural physical limits. Residue arithmetic became quite popular because it allows efficient processing with comparable simple hardware. However, the problem of building the optical logic devices remained. This situation changed during the third phase of digital optics, which began around 1980, with the discovery of strong optical nonlinear effects in semiconductors. Optical logic gates based on arrays of optically controlled modulators and microlasers, realized as multiple-quantum well devices in gallium arsenide technologies, were the result of this work. The performance data were comparable to that of electronic devices.

Concerning the number of integrated devices, **silicon** electronics was and is moving ahead into integration levels that are not yet reachable with gallium arsenide–based optoelectronic devices. Furthermore, the problem of building a reliable optical random access memory, which is crucial in an all-optical digital computer, has not been solved. As a result of all these difficulties, an all-optical digital computer still seems far-fetched. But at the same time, the immense advances in integrating tens of millions of **transistors** in a single chip brings about new problems in purely electronic systems. Modern **very large scale integration** (VLSI) chips are frequently restrained by data-throughput bottlenecks. The most apparent problem is the *pin limitation*: The pin number of a chip is not sufficient to provide high data input and output streams to use the enormous number of gates on a chip to capacity.

On the other hand, short-distance three-dimensional optical interconnects for VLSI systems can provide extremely high **bandwidth**. Sophisticated optoelectronic and micro-optic devices can be mounted directly on the surface of a silicon chip by flip-chip techniques. Two-dimensional laser and modulator arrays, originally invented as optical logic gates, and microlens arrays are examples of such devices. They allow us to realize thousands of optical pins using the entire chip area for communication instead of some 100 electrical pins, which are located at the chip's edges in current electronic chips.

This potential was recognized around 1990 and expresses new thinking. Optics will not replace electronics in digital computing; rather, it will support electronics in a synergetic way. The strength of optics in communication has to be combined with the strengths of electronics in processing. This new thinking is also expressed in a new terminology: One does not talk about optical computing but about optics in computing. This process has already started. Local area optical networks for computer clusters used in interboard and intraboard communication, such as a global optical clock distribution in Cray's supercomputer model T-3D, reflect a trend that is already state of the art in telecommunications: the increasing insertion of optical interconnects in computers.

In the future, analog optical computing will remain very useful. Some image processing tasks can only be solved in real time using analog optics. Still further into the future, optical quantum computing could allow computations impossible to perform with electronics.

Further Reading

Caulfield, H. John. "Perspectives in Optical Computing." *IEEE Computer*, Feb. 1998, pp. 22–25.

Li, Keqin, Yi Pan, and Si Qing Zheng. *Parallel Computing Using Optical Interconnections.* Boston: Kluwer Academic, 1998.

McAuley, Alistair D. *Optical Computer Architectures.* New York: Wiley, 1991.

—*Dietmar Fey*

Optical Fibers

Optical fibers allow high-speed communication at rates far exceeding those of other transmission media. They serve as the broadband pathways linking individuals, commercial enterprises, academia, government, cities, and nations. Less dramatically, fibers are replacing or augmenting electronic links within organizations and providing the backbone for digital cable television.

The possibility of transmitting information optically has been known for a long time. In the last 40 years, the development of light-guiding glass fibers and invention of the laser have allowed realization of this potential. Hallmarks of progress have been the development of **semiconductor** lasers that operate continuously at room temperature and the achievement of low-loss, low-dispersion optical fiber. Today it is possible to construct terabit fiber systems (10^{12} bits per second) that can carry more than 10 million telephone conversations or 100,000 television channels on a single fiber.

The history of the development of guided-wave optics goes back to the nineteenth century. In 1841, Daniel Colladon (1802–93) demonstrated the guiding of light in a water jet in Geneva, and in 1842 Jacques Babinet (1794–1872) showed the same effect using bent glass rods. Guided optics using total internal reflection progressed through the nineteenth century with the development of a number of applications to display and illumination. In the 1920s and 1930s, glass rods were used for television displays and fiber bundles were employed in imaging systems. The 1950s saw the development of clad fibers and the drawing of fibers sufficiently fine that only a single spatial mode of the radiation field could propagate in the fiber. After the invention of the ruby laser by Theodore Maiman (1927–) and the helium–neon laser by Ali Javan (1926–) in the early 1960s, several groups began to consider the use of optical fibers for information transmission.

The modes of a fiber are a set of confined solutions to the electromagnetic field equations for a given fiber structure. In single-mode fiber, only the simplest of these characteristic field distributions is allowed. While light-emitting diodes and multimode fibers could be used to transmit at low data rates and short distances, it was realized that single-mode fiber would not suffer from the dispersion that can cause optical pulses to spread as they propagate along a fiber. Since a properly designed laser can produce a single mode of the optical radiation field, it is ideally matched to single-mode fiber. The invention of the 0.84-μm GaAs semiconductor laser in 1962 gave further impetus to optical communications because of the high efficiency and compact size of these devices compared to other lasers. However, it was not until 1970 that Zhores Alferov (1930–) in Leningrad and Izuo Hayashi and Morton Panish (1929–) at **Bell Labs** achieved room temperature continuous operation of semiconductor lasers; long lifetimes were demonstrated in 1976. Also in 1976, J. Jim Hsieh at

Donald Keck with fiber-optic strands at Corning Inc. in Corning, New York, 31 October 1996. (AP Photo/Bill Sikes)

Massachusetts Institute of Technology's Lincoln Laboratory developed room-temperature, continuously operating InGaAsP lasers at 1.25 μm.

In the 1960s, advances were made in reducing fiber loss through developments in glass chemistry. Low transmission loss is important since received signals must be sufficiently powerful to overcome detection noise, while economic considerations as well as nonlinear processes limit transmitter powers. Progress in lowering attenuation was punctuated by the report in 1968 of a loss of 4 decibels per kilometer (dB/km) (four orders of magnitude per kilometer) in bulk glass by Charles Kao (1933–) and M. W. Jones at Standard Telecommunications Laboratories and the report in 1970 of a 17-dB/km loss in single-mode fiber by Robert Mauer's group at Corning. At this point all the ingredients were in place for the use of fiber in short-range communication. In 1976, NTT and Fujikura Cable reported a 0.5-dB/km loss at 1.2

μm and in 1978, NTT reported an 0.2-dB/km loss at 1.55 μm. This enabled intercity fiber transmission with tens of kilometers of repeater spacing. Since, in single-mode fibers, optical pulses spread due to wavelength dispersion, David Payne and Alex Gambling made another important discovery in 1975 when they found that there was a zero in material dispersion near 1.3 μm. This meant that extremely high data rates could be achieved over long distances. With the results on low loss and low dispersion in the 1.55- and 1.3-micrometer (μm) windows, respectively, and the development of long-lived InGaAsP semiconductor lasers operating in this wavelength region, a shift begins, albeit slowly at first, away from the use of 0.82-μm GaAlAs lasers. A similar shift from multimode to single-mode fiber also occurs.

The late 1970s and 1980s saw many tests of fiber-optical communications technology in long-distance communication. To overcome residual fiber loss, opto-electronic regenerative repeaters, consisting of a detector, detector electronics, pulse reshaping and retiming circuits, drive electronics, and a semiconductor laser, were spaced along the fiber. These experiments led to the operational deployment of a number of transmission links, including AT&T's Northeast Corridor system in 1983. This dual-wavelength system operated with a data rate of 90 megabits per second (Mbps) at 0.825 μm and 180 Mbps at 1.3 μm using multimode fiber. It was quickly superseded by high-bit-rate systems at 1.3 μm employing single-mode fiber. In 1988, the TAT-8 system began operation across the Atlantic at a rate of 280 Mbps. This was followed quickly by transpacific systems.

Further progress began with the development of fiber-optical amplifiers. Using rare earth dopants, the first fiber optical amplifiers were realized in 1964 by Charles Koester and Elias Snitzer (1925–). After a long hiatus, in 1987 Payne and his group at Southampton demonstrated optical amplification in the 1.55-μm low-loss wavelength region using erbium-doped fiber. Soon thereafter, pumping of these amplifiers was achieved with semiconductor diode lasers. Replacing optoelectronic regenerative repeaters with optical amplifiers improved reliability for both land-based and submarine systems.

Generally, the limits on laser modulation, higher-order dispersion, and optical nonlinearities constrained data rates to a few tens of gigabits per second on fiber systems operating at a single wavelength. The broad-band characteristics of gain-flattened erbium-doped fiber amplifiers enabled the use of multiple transmission wavelengths. This *wavelength division multiplexing* (WDM) allowed increases of 10 to 100 in the transmission capacity of a single fiber. Four-wave mixing, a potential drawback for WDM, was greatly reduced using dispersion segmentation and compensation. By 2000, communication service providers had installed a number of first-generation WDM systems. A single-fiber transmission capacity of 1.6 terabytes per second can be achieved using 160 channels each transmitting 10 gigabits per second (Gb/s) or 40 channels each transmitting 40 Gb/s. A further factor of 10 in capacity has been predicted using technologies such as stimulated Raman scattering and soliton propagation.

Fiber transmission systems are available for a wide range of transmission rate requirements, ranging from tens of Mb/s up to the Tb/s system just described. They are used not only for continental and intercontinental communication, but are also used at lower data rates within enterprises and campuses and at higher data rates for metropolitan networks. In cable television, much of the radio-frequency (RF) backbone has been replaced by fiber. The cable fiber network is terminated at groups of about 250 homes, with the final few hundred meters using RF transmission. This deployment has enabled bidirectional cable modem service, cable telephony, and digital cable television transmission.

Although fiber systems provide 1000-fold bandwidth increase at low cost, much work remains. The meshing of the optical (PHY) layer with higher layers is being studied. Control, interoperability, and transparency are features that need to be incorporated into optical networks. Protocol modifications that are suitable for optical systems are also under consideration. Finally, appropriate switching technologies must be developed in either the electronic or the optical domain.

FURTHER READING

Agrawal, Govind P. *Nonlinear Fiber Optics*. Boston: Academic Press, 1989; 2nd ed., San Diego, Calif., 1995.

———. *Fiber-Optic Communication Systems.* New York: Wiley, 1992; 2nd ed., 1997.

Desurvire, Emmanuel. *Erbium-Doped Fiber Amplifiers: Principles and Applications.* New York: Wiley, 1994.

Kaminow, Ivan P., and Thomas L. Koch. *Optical Fiber Telecommunications.* San Diego, Calif.: Academic Press, 1997.

Hecht, Jeff. *Understanding Fiber Optics.* Indianapolis, Ind.: Howard W. Sams, 1987; 3rd ed., Upper Saddle River, N.J.: Prentice Hall, 1999.

———. *City of Light: The Story of Fiber Optics.* New York: Oxford University Press, 1999.

—*Paul L. Kelley*

Optical Networks

Optical networks, which at present enjoy wide deployment, are those in which **optical fiber** has replaced copper and other materials as a transmission medium, providing higher **bandwidth**, lower error rates, immunity to noise, and overall lower-cost communication, while all network functions continue to be done electronically.

The initial large-scale introduction of optical technologies into telecommunications networks can be traced back to the mid-1980s. The resulting systems, also generally referred to as *first-generation optical networks*, are fast but are slowed down by the lower speeds and high cost of electronics. *Second-generation optical networks* will be fully optical and therefore faster.

While providing plentiful point-to-point bandwidth as compared to copper-based legacy transmission systems, the fundamental disparity between the rates of electronics and of optical transmission do not allow first-generation systems to scale to the increasing demands of emerging applications. While both optics and electronics switching speeds are growing exponentially, electronic processing speed is roughly doubling every 18 months; optical transmission speed doubles at least every nine months through increased bit rate and more wavelength channels per fiber.

Wavelength-division multiplexing (WDM) makes it possible to transmit multiple optical signals simultaneously over the same fiber, while dense WDM (DWDM) allows even a larger number of closer spaced wavelength channels. Both methods divide the huge per-fiber bandwidth into smaller portions of electronically manageable and individually accessible channels. Hence emerging WDM architectures require each node to handle data only at the rate of individual wavelength bandwidth, while allowing the global network to fully utilize the seemingly unlimited aggregate optical bandwidth without being held back by the upper limits of slower electronics. Thus WDM has become one of the fundamental enablers of the second-generation optical networks.

To understand the drivers of the evolution of the new-generation optical networks, it is important to understand the plethora of emerging applications and the requirements that their service places on the network. High-bandwidth applications, such as video telephony, videoconferencing, video distribution, and data transfer services, already exist on the **Internet** or the **World Wide Web**. Most of these applications can be characterized by their requirements in terms of bandwidth, latency, jitter, error tolerance, multicasting, and security. Real-time interactive applications, such as video telephony, will have strict jitter and latency requirements and will require bandwidth on the order of megabits per second in each direction, depending on the desired quality of the transmission.

Videoconferencing applications will have the same requirements as video telephony, but will require a greater amount of bandwidth, since the data must be transmitted to and from several destinations. Conferencing applications may also require some level of multicast support from the underlying network in order to provide more efficient use of the network bandwidth. Video distribution applications, such as video on demand or television broadcast distribution, will require bandwidth ranging from around 1.5 to 100 megabits per second (Mbps) for TV-quality video, to around 400 Mbps for the transmission of uncompressed high-definition TV streaming video. Video on demand and video broadcast applications may also require some level of multicasting support if a large number of users request the same video streams.

Finally, data applications, such as **software** distribution, or the transfer of audio or image files, are not as sensitive to latency as are video applications but may tend to be less tolerant of errors or data losses. As we can see, this wide range of traffic types demands a network design that can offer a variety of service types as well as different levels of service.

As mentioned above, WDM allows the efficient use of fiber bandwidth by dividing the optical spectrum into multiple, nonoverlapping wavelength (or frequency) bands, each of them supporting a single communication channel. Each channel can operate independently at any transmission rate that is compatible with electronic rates. Currently, WDM transmission systems consisting of up to 128 wavelengths, each supporting up to 10 gigabits per second (Gbps) are commercially available. In the future simultaneous transmission of optical signals over thousands of discrete wavelength channels are expected to reach 40 Gbps and higher transmission rates over each channel.

Optical transmission is "transparent": A wavelength channel does not care about the **bit** rate, modulation, format, or **protocol** of signals it carries. Paths of light, or light paths, are the fundamental way that all-optical communication is achieved between pairs of nodes. At the intermediate node, the cross-connects switch the light path through the node and obtain the desired optical (or wavelength) routing, so intermediate nodes do not have to be equipped to deal with a time-consuming and expensive reconversion to electronics.

Perhaps the most important advantage of introducing the optical layer into today's telecommunication systems is the resulting transmission and protocol transparency throughout the optical layer of the network. This transparency makes it possible to support a number of incompatible public and private services and applications by means of the same (optical in nature) network infrastructure and to support existing transport and switching solutions: SONET (Synchronous Optical Network), ATM (**asynchronous transfer mode**), or IP (Internet Protocol). Like WDM, the introduction of light paths, which can form a (dynamic) logical topology on top of an existing (fixed) physical topology, has been one of the key enablers for the introduction of second-generation optical networks.

Initially, the WDM layer will be transparent to the higher-layer protocols, providing basic optical transport services over light paths. As the network evolves, new applications and protocols may be developed that are aware of the optical layer and can take full advantage of additional services provided by it. These applications and protocols may be able to request light paths on demand, allowing for fully dynamic reconfiguration of logical network topologies as well as all-optical end-to-end connections for specialized classes of traffic. In the emerging wavelength-routed WDM optical layer, additional mechanisms are required for the control and management of light paths, providing optical reconfiguration, wavelength provisioning, and all-optical protection and restoration for light paths at the optical layer.

Emerging WDM systems must provide the appropriate services for higher-layer protocols, such as IP, ATM, SONET, and **Ethernet**. This vision of an all-optical, end-to-end WDM network is already driving many significant research and commercialization efforts in transport and optical networking companies. The concept of IP packets being transmitted directly over optics is a hot research topic, potentially leading to the exploration of an entirely new IP-routing layer. The Internet is growing rapidly, and in the next decade, IP traffic is expected to be dominant in the **backbone**. As such, it is especially important for the optical layer to be capable of supporting services for the IP layer, and for the IP layer to be capable of taking advantage of these services provided by the optical layer. The optical Internet network will have to be capable of providing not only huge aggregate bandwidth, but also guarantees with respect to quality of service, security, and fault tolerance. In the current generation of optical networks, these features are being provided electronically, primarily by SONET and ATM layers. Much research attention is currently focused on ways to implement IP directly over a WDM optical layer, with a minimal layer of electronics between these two layers, avoiding the cost and complexity of electronically driven layers. In these emerging solutions, IP routers will be interconnected via wavelengths or light paths, with the determination of a logical topology for the IP network, routing of light paths, and assigning wavelengths to them, all done at the light-path level.

Optical networking, once limited to core and backbone networks, has begun to spread into regional, metropolitan area, access, and local area networks. **Local**

area network (LAN) architectures of today have evolved rapidly in terms of the bandwidth offered to the end user, with current and emerging LAN standards such as gigabit Ethernet and 10-Gbps Ethernet utilizing high-speed optical fiber links. As the need for bandwidth in the local area increases with the emergence of high-speed applications, optical networks will become the indispensable communication solution.

FURTHER READING

Chlamtac, I. "Lightpath Communications: A Novel Approach to High Bandwidth Optical WANs." *IEEE Transactions on Communications*, Vol. 40, No. 7, July 1992.

———. "Optical Networking—Editorial." *SPIE/Kluwer Optical Networks Magazine*, Vol. 1, No. 1, 2000.

Chlamtac, I., et al. "Purely Optical Networks for Terabit Communication." *IEEE Infocom*, Apr. 1989.

Sivalingam, K. M., and S. Subramaniam, eds. *Optical WDM Networks: Principles and Practice*. Boston: Kluwer Academic, 2000.

—Imrich Chlamtac

Oracle Corporation

Oracle Corporation, headquartered in Redwood Shores, California, is best known for its **database management system** (DBMS), called Oracle. When it was introduced in 1979, Oracle was the first commercial DBMS based on the relational database model. Its cofounder and chief executive officer, Lawrence J. Ellison (1944–), is one of the wealthiest and most prominent figures in the computer industry and is well known for his extravagant lifestyle, his provocative speeches, and his harsh criticisms of competitors.

The Oracle DBMS is used primarily by large and medium-sized enterprises for implementing information systems. One of its most impressive features is its efficient handling of large numbers of concurrent transactions requiring sophisticated access synchronization and advanced parallel computing techniques. Its standard user interface for defining, populating, and modifying tables and for asking queries is the database manipulation language SQL. Together with SQL, the Oracle DBMS has evolved from a purely relational to an object-relational system. Triggered by the overwhelming success of the **World Wide Web**, Oracle added a number of new features to its DBMS to make it an **Internet**-enabled DBMS. The extensions include an Internet File System for storing multimedia contents and **HTML** (Hypertext Markup Language) documents in an Oracle database and for retrieving them via HTTP (Hypertext Transfer Protocol) and **FTP** (File Transfer Protocol), as well as the support of the programming language **Java** and the metalanguage **XML**.

Oracle Corporation (originally called Software Development Laboratories) was founded in 1977 by Ellison, Bob Miner, and Ed Oates. Their first project was a contract for the U.S. government with the code name Oracle, which would later become the name of their first product and of the company. Being the world's largest DBMS software company since 1987, Oracle's annual revenue rose from U.S.$12.7 million in 1984 to U.S.$8827 million in 1999, making it the world's second-largest independent software company today.

To increase its business opportunities and to change its image as a single-product vendor, Oracle has developed a suite of enterprise applications for manufacturing and supply chain management, financial accounting, human resources, and customer relationship management, which are being marketed under the name of *Oracle Applications*. Since DBMS software is in danger of becoming a commodity for which the prices and revenues may decline, this second major product line is considered important for the future growth of the company.

FURTHER READING

Wilson, Mike. *The Difference Between God and Larry Ellison: Inside Oracle Corporation*. New York: Morrow, 1997.

—Gerd Wagner

OS/2

OS/2 (Operating System Two) is an **operating system** for **personal computers** (PCs) distributed by **IBM**. Designed originally in collaboration with **Microsoft**, OS/2 is similar to **Windows**, but the **graphical user interface** (GUI) is somewhat different. Both operating systems differ in many other respects.

After the introduction of the **Macintosh** in the early 1980s, Microsoft and IBM started developing a successor to **DOS**, the original operating system delivered with each IBM PC and its **clones**. The new OS was to have a GUI and allow **multitasking**—that is, the simultaneous execution of several programs. At the same time, Microsoft was developing the first version of its Windows operating system.

OS/2 was delivered for the first time in 1987, still without the GUI. Although it was announced that legacy MS-DOS programs could run in the compatibility box of OS/2, this proved to be untrue for many important programs. The lack of third-party applications and the serious bugs contained in the first versions of OS/2 did not allow it to substitute DOS as was planned. Moreover, Microsoft soon pulled out of the project altogether and left IBM free to develop OS/2 on its own, while Microsoft concentrated on improved versions of Windows. For some time it was uncertain if OS/2 or Windows would become the successor to the venerable, text-oriented DOS. Eventually, IBM tried to position OS/2 mainly as an operating system for the corporate environment, which could link IBM mainframes and PCs in enterprise networks.

OS/2, now called the OS/2 Warp system, can execute DOS and Windows applications. The scripting language is called REXX. Full networking functionality has been added to OS/2 and the **software** bundled with the operating system allows the exchange of data with large IBM machines. IBM's vision has long been to transform OS/2 into the operating system of choice for its corporate users.

OS/2 is based in preemptive multitasking. This means that the OS allocates the running time for each process. This is different from cooperative multitasking in which if one process fails or refuses to yield the processor, all other processes stop running, that is, what happens when the screen of a Windows computer freezes because a program misbehaves. OS/2 also uses **multithreaded architecture**, which means that any program can start parallel processes that are serviced by the OS in the background.

Although IBM has steadily lowered the price of OS/2 and has introduced many new features in the Warp software (e.g., speech recognition technology), OS/2 has failed to reduce significantly the market share of Windows. The free operating system **Linux** has been more successful in this regard.

FURTHER READING

Stokes, Neil. *Getting to Know OS-2 Warp 4.* Upper Saddle River, N.J.: Prentice Hall, 1996.

—*Raúl Rojas*

P

Packard, David

See Hewlett, William and David Packard.

Packet Switching

Packet switching is a communications technology developed in the 1960s to interconnect networked computers. Packet switching and, more generally, packet communication, make possible the efficient and equitable sharing of networked resources on local computer networks and on the **Internet**.

Computers connected in networks send data back and forth. To accommodate such data equitably, packet-switching technology transmits data in small packets. Each message that constitutes the communication between computers is broken up into small data strings. Included with each string is address, control, and sequence information. The combination of control data and message data is called a *data packet*. It is sent onto the network toward the receiving computer. The data packets that make up one message are interspersed with other such data packets as they travel on the network. The original message gets reassembled at the destination computer. The great efficiency of packet switching comes from interspersing packets so that the communication channels are a highly shared resource.

Each computer on a network must have a unique number called its *network address*. The header contains the addresses of the source and destination computers. It can also contain a sequence number, a checksum, and other control information. With this information the packet can be transmitted from the source to the destination. At each node in the network, the header data can be examined to determine where to send the packet next. At the destination the sequence number allows the message to be reassembled in the correct order. The checksum is a number calculated at the source, treating the data as integers, that can be calculated again on the network or at the destination. If the new calculation does not match the first, the packet data are corrupted and must be resent. If the computer network has many nodes, the packets can be sent from node to node according to current conditions on the network. Such dynamic routing is called *connectionless* and the packets are called *datagrams*. Alternatively, the packets that constitute a single message can be given the same path. Then the routing would be called *connected* and would be closer to the older technology of circuit switching.

The first large-scale packet-switching experiment was the **ARPANET**, established in the United States to connect university and other Department of Defense contractors. Other well-known early packet-switching networks were the National Physical Laboratory (NPL) network in the United Kingdom and the Cyclades network in France.

Packet-switching technology sprang from a number of sources. In the 1950s, **Claude Shannon** (1916–2001) and others investigated the mathematics of networks. Leonard Kleinrock (1934–) built on this work in his Ph.D. thesis on communications nets. His combination of network and queueing theory suggested the efficiency of interspersing small demands on a communications network. **Paul Baran** (1926–), a researcher at the RAND Corporation, began around 1960 to investigate the construction of a communication network out of unreliable nodes. The unreliability could stem from military attack but could also be due to equipment failure. By 1962 his team suggested a "distributed adaptive message block network" with dynamic routing and reassembly of message blocks at the destination. Independently, **Donald Davies** (1924–) at the NPL had studied the **time-sharing** mode of computer operation and saw in that mode a clue to computer–computer communication. He introduced the name *packet* for the unit of data transmission containing header and message data. At about the same time, there was growing interest in improving computer use and communication. The U.S. Department of Defense developed a message-switching network, called AUTODIN, that sent and stored entire digital messages from node to node. Educom, an organization of educators, held a summer study on information networks that included **J. C. R. Licklider** (1915–90), who had envisioned an Intergalactic Network encompassing all computers and computer users.

Yet it remained for the ARPANET experiment to tackle and solve the difficult technical questions raised by a multinode packet-switching network. These include finding a mechanism to prevent any computer from flooding the network, called *flow control*; finding a way for crowded nodes to be relieved of the load on them, called *congestion control*; inventing routing update scheduling schemes that did not cause packets to circle back and forth, never leaving the network; figuring out the possible sources of network failure and how to prevent them; deciding on acknowledgment schemes and retransmission methods; and many other technical and conceptual challenges. The communications resource sharing made possible by packet-switching technology became the basis for the creation of the global Internet.

FURTHER READING

Comer, Douglas E. *The Internet Book: Everything You Need to Know About Computer Networking and How the Internet Works.* Englewood Cliffs, N.J.: Prentice Hall, 1995; 2nd ed., Upper Saddle River, N.J., 1997.

Hauben, Michael, and Ronda Hauben. *Netizens: On the History and Impact of Usenet and the Internet.* Los Alamitos, Calif.: IEEE Computer Society Press, 1997.

Kleinrock, Leonard. *Queueing Systems,* Vol. 2. New York: Wiley, 1976.

—*Jay Robert Hauben*

Papert, Seymour

1928–

South African–U.S. Mathematician, and Computer Scientist

Seymour Papert is recognized primarily for his contributions to the use of digital technologies in education, including the Logo programming environment and the LEGO Mindstorms system. He also conducted early research with **Marvin Lee Minsky** (1927–) on **artificial intelligence** (AI) and coauthored the influential book *Perceptrons.* He has spent many years researching and writing about the ways that children use computers and speaks widely in public about the potential of computers in education and the need for radical educational reform.

Born and raised in South Africa, Papert gained his degree in mathematics in 1952 from the University of Witwatersrand. He was also active in the antiapartheid movement. He continued his mathematics research at Cambridge University between 1954 and 1958, and then moved to the University of Geneva. Between 1958 and 1963 he worked with Jean Piaget (1896–1980), a Swiss philosopher and psychologist, a seminal thinker on the subject of the intellectual development of children. Papert's collaboration with Piaget sparked a lifelong interest in the ways in which children learn, especially mathematics. Piaget argued that children use their own forms of reasoning, which are appropriate to specific tasks, although by adult standards they may seem incorrect. Consequently, for Piaget it was important to allow children to learn through invention and experimentation, allowing them to make mistakes. It was this central insight that Papert later drew on so fruitfully with the Logo learning environment.

From the late 1950s Papert also worked in the new field of AI, collaborating with Minsky at the Massachusetts Institute of Technology (MIT). Papert was involved in founding the **MIT Artificial Intelligence Laboratory** in 1965. In 1969 Minsky and Papert published their groundbreaking book *Perceptrons.* This brought psychological theories of perception to bear on issues within AI, which as a field had been dominated by a data processing model of computer science. At the same time Papert had begun a small research effort in the AI Lab on using computers for learning. When microcomputers made possible the prospect of children gaining access to computers on a large scale, learning and education became the major focus of his work, with the ambitious goal of developing a long-term program of research on alternatives to the usual structures and understandings of school.

Specifically, Papert developed Logo, a programming language suitable for young children, and one aspect of the Logo learning environment. At this time Logo was unique in providing an instant visual response to commands entered from the keyboard. The visual display was both diagrammatic and textual, with the text display repeating the keyed commands. The diagrammatic display was the significant element, however. This consisted of an arrow that would draw on the screen in response to commands. Thus the command "FORWARD 2" would make the arrow move 2 units up the screen, leaving a trace. A combination of commands could thus be used to draw diagrams, so for instance "FORWARD 2; RIGHT 2; BACK 2; LEFT 2" would draw a square with a 2-unit side. This combination of commands could then be saved as a routine or procedure and used again: for example, as a subroutine within a larger procedure.

Papert also invented the small "turtle" robot, which could be instructed by Logo routines to make the same moves on the floor as the arrow on the screen, drawing as it went. This device, initially used mainly in schools, has now matured into the system of computerized construction kits marketed by LEGO as Mindstorms, named after Papert's influential book.

With more powerful computers modern forms of Logo allow young students to learn by carrying out complex projects in which they are free to experiment with powerful ideas from mathematics and science and to fail without admonition in what Papert called *microworlds*. His 1980 book *Mindstorms* was widely read, although controversial for some educationalists. It described his philosophy of education, together with numerous examples of successful application of the Logo learning environment, and additionally drew on the educational theories of Paolo Freire (1922–97) and Ivan Illych. Logo is now an established part of many school mathematics curricula, especially in combination with the turtle and the LEGO building brick system.

Papert has held appointments at MIT as professor of applied mathematics, professor of education, and held the LEGO Chair of Learning Research from 1992 until his retirement in 1998. He has recently been engaged in educational work with underprivileged children in many developing countries and in U.S. correctional institutions.

BIOGRAPHY

Seymour Papert. Born in Pretoria, South Africa, 1 March 1928. B.A., from the University of Witwatersrand, 1949; Ph.D. from the University of Witwatersrand, 1952; Ph.D., Cambridge University, 1959. Worked with Jean Piaget at the University of Geneva, 1958–63. Worked at MIT, 1963–80; founded Artificial Intelligence Lab, 1965; moved to Department of Mathematics, 1968. Went to the Centre Mondial d'Informatique, Paris, 1981–83. Returned to MIT Media Lab, 1985–present. Helped to establish MaMaMedia Inc., an Internet company that serves 6- to 12-year-old children, 1998. Currently Emeritus Professor, LEGO Chair of Learning Research, MIT. Recipient of numerous honors and awards, including Marconi International fellowship, 1981; J.S. Guggenheim fellowship, 1980; Software Publishers Association Lifetime Achievement award, 1994; and the Computerworld Smithsonian award, 1997.

SELECTED WRITINGS

Minsky, Marvin, and Seymour Papert. "Unrecognizable Sets of Numbers." *Journal of the ACM*, Vol. 13, No. 2, Apr. 1966, pp. 281–286.

———. *Perceptrons: An Introduction to Computational Geometry*. Cambridge, Mass.: MIT Press, 1969; expanded ed., 1988.

Papert, Seymour. *Mindstorms: Children, Computers and Powerful Ideas*. New York: Basic Books, 1980; 2nd ed., 1993.

———. *The Children's Machine: Rethinking School in the Age of the Computer*. New York: Basic Books, 1993.

———. *The Connected Family: Bridging the Digital Generation Gap*. Marietta, Ga.: Longstreet Press, 1996.

FURTHER READING

Abelson, Harold, and Andrea DiSessa. *Turtle Geometry: The Computer as a Medium for Exploring Mathematics*. Cambridge, Mass.: MIT Press, 1981.

Feurzeig, Wallace, G. Lukas, and J. Lukas. *The LOGO Language: Learning Mathematics Through Programming*. Gloucester, Mass.: Entelek, 1977.

Harvey, Brian. *Computer Science Logo Style*. Cambridge, Mass.: MIT Press, 1985; 2nd ed., 1997.

—Richard Hull

Parallel Processing

A natural way to reduce the execution time of a program is to perform independent calculations simultaneously, or in *parallel*, on different processing elements. For example, instead of using a single fast and expensive (super-)computer, many potentially less expensive computers could be used jointly to solve a computationally intensive problem (e.g., of weather forecasts). Because of the straightforwardness of the parallel computation concept and its potential performance gain, many of today's computers exploit parallelism in one way or another.

The concept of parallel computing is not new. In his 1842 description of **Charles Babbage**'s (1791–1871) **Analytical Engine**, Luigi Menabrea (1809–96) wrote: "When a long series of identical computations is to be performed, such as those required for the formation of numerical tables, the machine can be brought into play so as to give several results at the same time, which will greatly abridge the whole amount of the processes." For a long period of time, available technology was not capable of realizing these ideas.

It was not until the late 1960s, with the emergence of large-scale and **very large scale integration** (LSI and VLSI) technology, that parallel computing became reality. One of these first parallel computers was the **ILLIAC IV**, which contained an 8 by 8 array of processing elements. Although this machine was a technological breakthrough (it was the first machine with a large number of processing elements), it failed as a computer due to the fact that it was hard to program and performed poorly. Despite this, the ILLIAC IV was one of the important achievements that led to the start of the parallel computing era.

Parallelism can be exploited at various levels. That is, the tasks that are computed in parallel can have different grain (computational) sizes. Three types of parallelism can be distinguished: fine, medium, and coarse-grained. *Fine-grained parallelism* means that parallel computation is exploited at the level of instructions. An example is the instruction level parallelism (ILP) exploited by superscalar processors, which are capable of scheduling multiple (independent) instructions to be executed simultaneously. Basically, this process is hidden from the programmer, who is therefore not bothered by the tedious task of finding the parallelism. In *medium-grained parallelism*, small or medium-sized sequences of code, such as procedures, are executed on different processing elements. The use of threads, which are lightweight processes sharing a single address space, can be regarded as a form of medium-grained parallelism. An example of a thread-level parallel computer architecture is the MTA machine from Tera. Finally, there is *coarse-grained parallelism*, in which an application is divided in large subtasks (potentially containing thousands of instructions) that are executed in parallel. For example, parallel programs adhering to the SPMD (single-program, multiple-data) programming paradigm apply coarse-grained parallelism; every processing element executes a single common program and performs calculations on different parts of the data (i.e., operations are performed on multiple data in parallel).

For all three grain sizes, either *data parallelism* or *functional parallelism* can be exploited. In data-parallel programs, such as the ones adhering to the SPMD paradigm, each task performs the same series of calculations but applies them to different data. In functional parallelism, each task performs different calculations using either the same or different data.

The holy grail of parallel computing is to obtain a speedup of N when executing an application on N processing elements. We define speedup as the time needed for sequential execution divided by the parallel execution time. In other words, if the number of processing elements is doubled, we would like to get twice the performance. When this is true, the parallel application is described as *scalable*. However, the scalability of parallel applications is often limited by parts of the application that are inherently sequential (i.e., which cannot be performed in parallel). This means that for these applications there exists a maximal attainable speedup, an issue addressed by **Amdahl's law**.

In reality, the maximal speedup is often not obtained. Parallel execution typically requires synchronization to coordinate the information exchange between the parallel tasks. This synchronization process may introduce latencies when parallel tasks are waiting for each other to complete. The overhead of these synchronizations determines at which grain size parallelism can be exploited effectively. Fine-grained parallelism, for instance, requires frequent synchronization, usually after executing one or only a few instructions. Therefore, the synchronizations must be cheap. On the other hand, synchronizations in coarse-grained parallel applications are much less frequent. As a result, these applications can tolerate higher synchronization overheads.

FURTHER READING

Culler, D. E., J. P. Singh, and A. Gupta. *Parallel Computer Architecture, A Hardware/Software Approach.* San Francisco: Morgan Kaufmann, 1999.

Foster, Ian. *Designing and Building Parallel Programs: Concepts and Tools for Parallel Software Engineering.* Reading, Mass.: Addison-Wesley, 1995.

Fox, Geoffrey C., R. D. Williams, and P. C. Messina. *Parallel Computing Works.* San Francisco: Morgan Kaufmann, 1994.

Hwang, Kai, and Zhiwhei Xu. *Scalable Parallel Computing: Technology, Architecture, Programming.* Boston: WCB/McGraw-Hill, 1998.

Kumar, Vipin, et al. *Introduction to Parallel Computing: Design and Analysis of Algorithms.* Redwood City, Calif.: Benjamin-Cummings, 1994.

—*Andy Pimentel*

Parametron Computer 1

The Parametron Computer 1 (PC-1) was developed and built at Hidetosi Takahasi's Laboratory at the University of Tokyo in 1958. It was one of the first Japanese computers and is especially remembered because it used logic elements capable of computing majority logic, called *parametrons*. Parametrons are doughnut-shaped magnetic elements that work by combining the fields induced by cables coiled around the cores.

The initial impulse for the development of the PC-1 in Tokyo came from careful study of the architecture of the **EDSAC** computer built at Cambridge, but the Japanese then adopted a new approach regarding the logical structure of the machine. Conventional logic elements deal with one or two bits a time, and compute operations such as conjunction (AND), disjunction (OR), and negation (NOT). The Japanese adopted *threshold logic*, in which elements deal with several bits at a time, posing the question: Is the number of 1's in the input larger than a certain threshold? A threshold **logic gate** with five 1-bit inputs and the threshold 2 can then be used to ask if the majority of the five bits are 1s. The threshold *logic gate* produces a 1 if this is the case; otherwise, the result is 0.

It is easy to see that threshold gates include as a special case the conventional gates. The AND operation with two bits corresponds to a parametron with two 1-bit inputs and threshold 2. Only if both bits are a 1, the parametron "fires" a 1. The OR operation corresponds to the same arrangement but with a threshold of 1. If any of the two bits or both are 1, the parametron fires a 1, otherwise a 0. Negation was implemented in a special way in the parametrons, by using a cable coiled in reverse direction, which reduced the magnetic field induced by other inputs.

Threshold logic computers can be built using a much lower number of gates than for conventional machines and, in some cases, less than one-third for equivalent machines. Some parametron designs were built in Japan, but the cost of the individual gates is greater than that for standard gates. Therefore, no successful commercial threshold computers have ever been built.

The PC-1 was an interesting machine also in regard to the software that it used. The systems programmer, Eiiti Wada (1931–), achieved the feat of writing a start routine for the computer with the instructions arranged such that a conversion table was embedded in the code. The same memory area could thus be used for two different purposes, according to the execution context. The PC-1 is also notable for having been one of the first computers to implement **interrupts**.

The original development team still meets once every year in Japan to celebrate the "birth" of the PC-1, a unique machine in the history of computing.

FURTHER READING

Takahasi, Hirosi, ed. *Parametron Computers.* Tokyo: Iwanami Shoten, 1968 (in Japanese).

Wada, Eiiti. "The Parametron Computer PC-1 and Its Initial Input Routine." In Raúl Rojas and Ulf Hashagen, eds., *The First Computers: History and Architectures.* Cambridge, Mass.: MIT Press, 2000.

—*Raúl Rojas*

Pascal

Pascal is a programming language that became very popular in the 1970s and 1980s. It was developed in the late 1960s according to the concepts of **structured programming**, preserving the style of **ALGOL** 60. It features structured statements expressing conditional (IF) and repeated execution (WHILE, REPEAT, and FOR statements). Functions and procedures may be called recursively.

Pascal's principal innovation was to introduce structuring to data definitions, together with strict typing of all constants, variables, and functions. Its scalar data types are INTEGER, REAL, BOOLEAN, and CHAR. Further scalar types can be defined as enumerations of sets of constants. Composite types are defined as arrays (homogeneous), records (inhomogeneous), (small) sets, and files (sequences) of elements.

Pascal was designed by **Niklaus Wirth** (1934–) at the Swiss Federal Institute of Technology (ETH) in Zurich from 1968 to 1970, and first implemented on a large-scale CDC 6400 computer. It was subsequently ported to many other computers. Several such efforts were based on the P-code compiler, allowing Pascal to be made available by constructing an interpreter for P-code only. P-code was a kind of intermediate code that was executed by the run-time system.

Pascal has a relatively simple and consistent structure and therefore became a favorite language for teaching programming at schools and universities. The real success of Pascal came about eight years after its design, when microcomputers became available, providing access to computing for larger numbers of people, especially students. Pascal's small size enabled it to work with compilers using little storage and moderate computing power. Borland Inc. provided the first cheap compiler for a mass market, and at the University of California at San Diego a system was derived from the Pascal-P compiler and integrated with a program editor and a debugging facility into a compact system (UCSD-Pascal).

Pascal has exerted an influence on many later developments, including the language **Ada** and its successors, **Modula-2** and **Oberon**.

FURTHER READING

Jensen, Kathleen, and Niklaus Wirth. *PASCAL: User Manual and Report.* Berlin and New York: Springer-Verlag, 1974; 2nd ed., 1975.

Wirth, Niklaus. "The Programming Language Pascal." *Acta Informatica*, Vol. 1, June 1971, pp. 35–63.

———. "Recollections About the Development of the Programming Language Pascal." *Proceedings of the 2nd International Conference on the History of Programming Languages (HOPL II).* Reading, Mass.: Addison-Wesley, 1993.

—*Niklaus Wirth*

Pascal, Blaise

1623–62

French Mathematician

Blaise Pascal was a seventeenth-century mathematical prodigy who completed important work in projective geometry, conic sections, binomial coefficients, and hydrostatics. He also invented an early prototype of the modern-day digital calculator. Although his mathematical genius is undisputed, biographers believe that his true potential was never reached, due to an abrupt religious conversion after which his focus moved away from science and mathematics.

Blaise Pascal was the third child of four and the only son of Etienne Pascal (1588–1651), a minor French noble and government official. In 1632, Etienne moved his family from Clermont to Paris. Distrustful of the educational opportunities available, Etienne decided to direct Pascal's education personally based on the unorthodox pedagogy of Montaigne.

Etienne became determined that Blaise should not study mathematics before age 15 and removed all such texts from the house. The lure of "forbidden fruit" piqued Blaise's curiosity and he started to experiment with geometry at age 12. Soon after, Etienne noticed his son's exceptional skills and encouraged the budding mathematical genius.

In 1639, Etienne was appointed tax collector at Rouen. This new position kept Etienne busy, which inspired Pascal to find a less time consuming way for his father to compute taxes. Driven by a desire to spend more time with his father, in 1642 Pascal began work on an eight-dial mechanical machine that would complete arithmetic calculations. The result, called the *Pascaline*, is often considered one of the first digital calculators.

Pascal faced several technical problems during the three-year design of this early computing machine. Many of them were due to unusual relationships between the various denominations of French currency. Despite temporary setbacks, production of the Pascaline began in 1642 and continued off and on over the next 10 years. However, due to the high price and low demand, few were sold. Approximately 50 Pascalines have been preserved.

The next significant event in Pascal's life occurred in 1646 when his father's leg was severely injured. Etienne was nursed back to health by monks from a religious order just outside Rouen. These Jansenists were a puritanical sect of Dutch-influenced Catholics, which believed in charismatic Christian practices such as faith healing, clairvoyance, and other miracles. Following discussions regarding their faith, Pascal became deeply religious.

Around this same time, Pascal began what some biographers refer to as his physicist phase. Pascal became concerned with the pressures of liquids and gases. Through a series of experiments with fluid levels in tubes closed at the upper end, he showed that in a closed container, pressure is uniform in all directions on all surfaces. This finding came to be called *Pascal's principle*. He also showed how barometric pressure varies with altitude. Application of his discoveries led to the invention of the syringe and hydraulic press.

Pascal left Paris in 1648 and returned to Claremont. He stayed there for nearly two years, during which he wrote a treatise on conic sections. A year after his return to Paris, Pascal's father died.

In 1654, Pascal experienced a two-hour ecstatic vision, which moved focus of his life from the sciences to religious matters. The episode seemed to be related to a carriage accident during which he nearly lost his life. He wrote a detailed account of his vision and kept it in the lining of his coat for the rest of his life.

Pascal's writings and lectures became religious works, and in 1656, the first of the 18 Provincial Letters was published by the underground press. Over time, his writings reached more than a million people. Aside from the content, their style alone made them remarkable, causing some literary scholars to call Pascal the father of modern French prose.

During this same time period, Pascal's health declined; he was in constant pain due to a malignant stomach tumor. Other than a brief period of freedom from discomfort, during which he investigated properties of the cycloid, the curve traced by a point on the circumference of a rolling circle, Pascal spent little time in scientific pursuits and spent the majority of his time serving the poor and attending religious services throughout Paris.

In 1662, Pascal's malignancy spread to his brain and he died. It was not until eight years later that his *Pensées* ("Apology for the Christian Religion") was published. Many religious scholars consider this to be his finest literary work.

BIOGRAPHY

Blaise Pascal. Born 19 June 1623 in Claremont, France. Relocated to Paris, 1631, and to Rouen, 1640. Invented Pascaline digital calculator, 1642. Developed Pascal's principle, 1647. Converted to Jansenism, a form of Roman Catholicism, 1646. Near-death experience inspired second conversion, 1654. Published first of the Provincial Letters, 1656. Became ill, 1659. Died 17 August 1662. Publication of *Pensées*, 1670.

SELECTED WRITINGS

Pascal, Blaise. *Les lettres provinciales de Blaise Pascal*, H. F. Stewart, ed. Manchester, Lancashire, England: University Press; London, New York [etc.]: Longmans Green, 1920.

———. *Pensées de M. Pascal sur la religion, et sur quelques autres subjects*. Présentée par Georges Couton et Jean Jehasse L'édition de Port-Royal (1670) et ses complements (1678–1776). Saint-Étienne, France: l'Université de Saint-Étienne, 1971.

———. *Great Shorter Works of Pascal*. Translated with an introduction by Emile Cailliet and John C. Blankenagel. Westport, Conn.: Greenwood Press, 1974.

———. *Oeuvres complètes*. Édition présentée, établie et annotée par Michel Le Guern. Paris: Gallimard, 1998.

———. *Pensées and Other Writings*. Translated by Honor Levy. Oxford and New York: Oxford University Press, 1998.

FURTHER READING

Baudouin, Charles. *Blaise Pascal*. Paris: Éditions Universitaires, 1969.

Hazelton, Roger. *Blaise Pascal: The Genius of His Thought*. Philadelphia: Westminster, 1974.

—*Roger McHaney*

Pascal Calculator

The Pascal calculator, or *Pascaline*, designed by **Blaise Pascal** (1623–62), was one of the earliest adding machines. Pascal produced about 50 calculators during his lifetime. The Pascal calculators have a series of sprockets that are turned with a stylus to add numbers. Each sprocket rotates within a fixed ring. The ring has numbers corresponding to the number of sprocket holes from that position to a stop that extends over the sprocket. On decimal machines, the sprocket rings are marked from 0 to 9, with 0 just to the right of the stop and the numbers in increasing order counterclockwise around the ring. Each sprocket is coupled with gears to an indicator with numbers on its circumference.

Inserting a stylus into a sprocket hole and rotating the sprocket clockwise causes the corresponding indicator to advance by the number marked on the sprocket ring. When the indicator advances beyond 9 for a decimal digit, a carry increments the next-most-significant digit. The figure shows the design of the gears for a single digit. The sprocket (3) within ring (1) drives gear (5), which is coupled to gear (6). Rotating the sprocket causes gear (8) to rotate, which causes the indicator wheel (9) to turn. Gear (7) and detent (10) give the sprocket and the indicator discrete positions. Finally, there is a carry mechanism (parts [11]–[14]) that increments the more significant digit when a digit is advanced from 9 to 0. One number on each indicator is visible through the panel of the calculator. For a decimal calculator, all sprockets and indicators have 10 positions.

It is possible to build a simple calculator using a single-toothed gear to make the carry from one digit to the next, but the force required becomes excessive when there are several digits (e.g., when adding 1 to 9999 the carry must propagate five positions). Pascal designed a

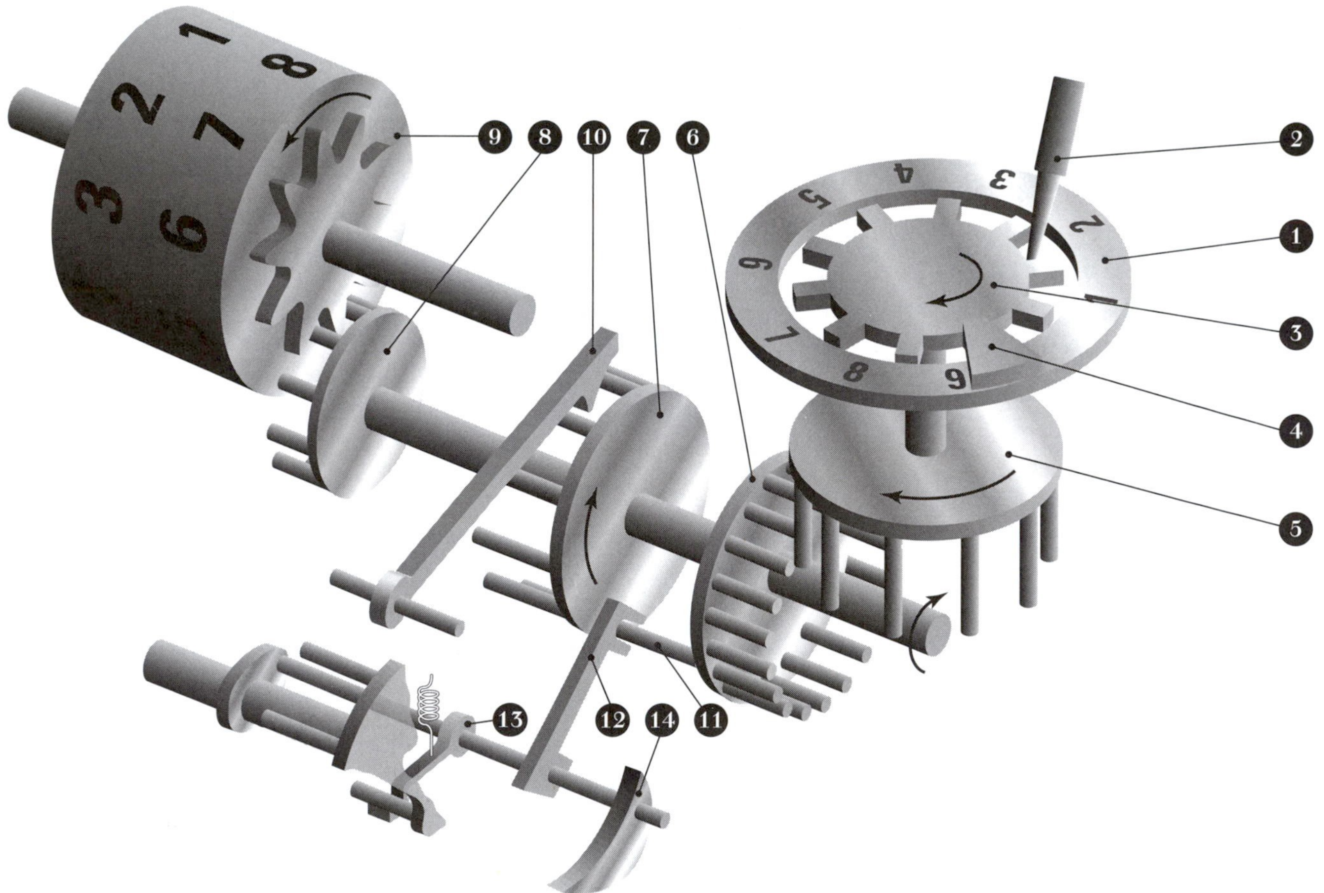

Internal mechanisms of the Pascal Calculator. (See entry for details on the numbered elements.)

Calculating machine designed by Pascal. Numbers are dialed on the rotors and results are shown in the windows on the top. (Courtesy of the National Museum of Photography, Film, and Television/Science and Society Picture Library)

complicated carry mechanism that uses a falling weight to reduce the force. The mechanism is acceptable for a desk calculator but would not be suitable for a pocket calculator, which can be operated in a wide variety of positions. Pascal's carry mechanism also has the drawback that the sprockets must be rotated only in a clockwise direction.

Addition is performed by rotating the appropriate sprockets. For example, to add 37 to 754, first all digits are cleared to indicate 0. Then the least significant sprocket is rotated four positions in a clockwise direction, the next sprocket is rotated five positions, and the third sprocket is rotated sprocket seven positions, by inserting a stylus into the sprocket and rotating . At this point the dials indicate 000 754. Then 37 is added by rotating the least significant sprocket seven positions. This causes a carry to the second digit position. At this point the dials indicate 000 761. Then the second sprocket is rotated three positions. At this point the dials indicate 000 791. To clear the machine for the next addition, each sprocket is rotated to indicate 0. This is performed from the least significant position to the most significant, as rotating a sprocket to 0 generates a carry into the next-more-significant digit. This example can be viewed as follows:

Action	Display
Clear	000 000
Add 754	000 754
Add 37	000 791

Thus: 754 + 37 = 791.

Subtraction may be performed by adding the diminished radix complement of the subtrahend and adding a 1 to the result if the result is positive. The sign of the result is indicated by the most significant digit: If it is 0, the result is positive; if it is the diminished radix, the result is negative. Since the most significant digit is used to indicate the sign of the result, operands may not be entered there during subtraction.

Pascal constructed variations of his calculator with fewer or more sprocket positions (and corresponding indicator wheels) at specific digits for monetary calculations. For example, the French monetary system during Pascal's time consisted of livre, sol, and deniers with 1 livre = 20 sols and 1 sol = 12 deniers. A calculator for this number system has a 12-tooth sprocket for the least significant (denier) position, a 20-tooth sprocket for the second (sol) position, and 10-tooth sprockets for the more significant (livre) positions. With monetary machines calculating the complements is a bit more difficult than for a pure decimal machine, as the diminished radix complement of x is $11 - x$ for the first (least significant) digit, $19 - x$ for the second digit, and $9 - x$ for the remaining digits. Some of the Pascal calculators have a small ring inside the sprockets with the diminished radix complements for each digit position. This feature was probably added to facilitate subtraction for the mixed radix (monetary) adding machines. Pascal made machines to accommodate the currency (livre, sol, and denier), where the two least significant digits have special sprockets with more teeth (20 for the sol digit and 12 for the denier digit). The book by Mourlevat includes photographs of several surviving Pascalines; about half of them are for currency calculations with the modified two least significant digits, and the other half have 10-tooth sprockets in all positions.

Pascal was not the first to design and construct an adding machine (that distinction goes to **Wilhelm Schickard** [1592–1635], who built a mechanical adding machine in 1621 that used a single gear tooth as the carry mechanism). Pascal was probably the first to build multiple copies of an adding machine, although each was handcrafted and the details of the design varied over time. The Pascal adding machines were not mass produced as we understand the term today.

In the twentieth century several adding machines that appear similar to Pascal's machine have been developed and mass produced. Early in the century the Calcumeter was developed and at least 60,000 were claimed to have been produced, although the serial numbers would indicate that over 100,000 were produced. The Calcumeter uses a spring-assisted carry mechanism. Later, the Lightning Calculator (a misnomer since it is in fact an adder) was produced initially in Grand Rapids, Michigan and later in Los Angeles, California. The Lightning Calculator used a simple gear-driven carry mechanism that requires significant force to effect a carry over several digits, but was apparently quite simple to manufacture.

FURTHER READING

De Brabandere, Luc. *Calculus: Non-electric Calculating Machines.* Liege, Belgium: Mardaga, 1994.

Kistermann, Friedrich W. "Blaise Pascal's Adding Machine: New Findings and Conclusions." *IEEE Annals of the History of Computing,* Vol. 20, No. 1, 1998, pp. 69–76.

Martin, Ernst. *The Calculating Machines (Die Rechenmaschinen): Their History and Development.* Translated and edited by Peggy Aldrich Kidwell and Michael R. Williams. Cambridge, Mass.: MIT Press, 1992.

Mourlevat, Guy. *Les Machines arithmétiques de Blaise Pascal.* Clermont-Ferrand, France: Académie des Sciences, Lettres, Arts, 1988.

Otnes, Robert. "The Calcumeter." *IEEE Annals of the History of Computing,* Vol. 20, No. 1, 1998, pp. 67–69.

Williams, Michael R. *A History of Computing Technology.* Englewood Cliffs, N.J.: Prentice Hall, 1985; rev. ed., Los Alamitos, Calif.: IEEE Computer Society Press, 1997.

—*Earl Swartzlander*

Patch

A patch is a quick-fix for some piece of **software** that is malfunctioning or whose security has been compromised. In the early days of computing, users reported software errors to the manufacturer, who programmed a "quick and dirty solution" before the problem could be solved definitively with the next software release. The patch was distributed in tapes to all customers. Usually, the patch was a binary file that substituted ("patched") some portion of the program binaries. The system administrator had to keep track of all patches, which in the case of complex operating systems, could run up to the hundreds. **IBM** reserved an unused portion of the binary file specifically for patches, called patch space.

In some cases the patch is distributed as source code, which has to be recompiled with the original program. This is done with **Unix** systems, which are usually delivered together with the source code.

One of the fastest patches in history was produced to stop the "Internet Worm" that infected computers connected to the **Internet** in 1988. The program used a **back door** in the software used to send **electronic mail** from one computer to another. It installed itself in the host computer, created a new process, and looked for new computers to infect. Programmers in Berkeley and at other places in the United States disassembled the binary code (i.e., recuperated the original source program), wrote a fix, and started distributing the patch for the mail system just a few hours after the worm had been detected.

Patches are still a common tool for programmers. The **Apache** server, used to deliver **World Wide Web** pages from a Web server, was originally a replacement for an older, public-domain Web server. Because it contained many patches, it was referred to as "a patch-y server, " which eventually became Apache.

Today, software companies distribute patches via the Internet. Users can search the company's Web site to see if a patch is available to fix the particular problem they are having.

—Raúl Rojas

PDP

PDPs (*programmed data processors*) comprise a remarkably successful line of small computers from **Digital Equipment Corporation**. The machines, built from 1960 to the present, had a major impact on the computer industry; they are often referred to as *minicomputers*.

Digital Equipment Corporation (DEC) was founded in 1957 in Maynard, Massachusetts by three former research engineers at the Massachusetts Institute of Technology (MIT): Harlan Anderson, Stan Olsen, and **Kenneth Olsen** (1926–). The company's first facilities were located in an old woolen mill (often referred to as simply "The Mill"), which became the scene for many new developments in computer technology. In the late 1950s, DEC produced transistor-based *system modules*, plug-in circuit boards with simple logic functions, which were used as building blocks for laboratory or demonstration systems.

The explicit goal of constructing a stand-alone computer system surfaced in 1959, when another former MIT engineer, Ben Gurley, was hired to design and build the PDP-1. The machine was small, elegant, and inexpensive compared to other computers of that era, which is why it was called a programmed data processor rather than a computer. The name was then used for various other small computers, until Digital changed its naming conventions.

The design of the first PDP was influenced by three earlier MIT machines: the Whirlwind (1951), constructed at the MIT Computer Laboratory, and the TX-0 and TX-2 (1956 and 1957), built at the MIT Lincoln Laboratory. These three computers were all considered small at that time, and had simpler input–output (I/O) structures than those of contemporary computers. The word length of the PDP-1 was 18 bits (shorter than that of other commercial computers), it had 4 to 64 kilowords of ferrite **core memory**, a 16-channel interrupt mechanism, and a high-speed communication channel (called **Direct Memory Access** [DMA]). Processor and memory occupied four 19-inch cabinets. The typical base price was U.S.$120,000. The success of the PDP-1 helped establish Digital as an important computer company.

Digital Equipment Corporation's PDP-8, 1965. (Courtesy of the Computer Museum History Center)

Since the PDP-1 was a remarkable success—one of the first commercial time-sharing systems and the first video game were written for it—the engineers at Digital started to work on several new designs, not all of which got to production: The PDP-2 name was reserved for a 24-bit machine, but it was never built, and PDP-3 was to be a 36-bit computer, but only one was manufactured. The PDP-4 was planned to be a small computer, with a word length of 12 bits, but it was decided in 1962 to go with 18 bits as the successor of the PDP-1. The PDP-4 was an even simpler system than its precursor but was only a limited success. One of its interesting features was the autoincrementing register, used for event-counting real-time applications such as pulse height analysis.

After introduction of the PDP-1, customers began to request a much smaller machine. The proposed new computer with a 12-bit word length, the DC-12 digital controller was inspired by the **Control Data Corporation** (CDC) 160, designed by **Seymour Cray** (1925–96), and the Laboratory Instrument Computer (LINC), designed by Wes Clark. The latter was a small stored-program computer designed for **real-time** applications, accepting both digital and analog inputs, processing them immediately, and providing control signals for experimental equipment. It is interesting to note that it was built using DEC system modules. The name DC-12 was later changed to PDP-5; Alan Kotok and **Gordon Bell** (1934–) laid down the basic instruction set, and Edson DeCastro (1938–) carried out the logic design. One of the most important features was a new I/O **bus**, which replaced the radial I/O concept of the 18-bit machines with preallocated space and wiring.

The PDP-6 was the foundation of DEC's 36-bit computer line. Development began in 1963, and the first machine was delivered one year later. The notion of using a 36-bit word length was intended to provide a time-sharing computational environment, which wasn't common at that time. Only three such systems were operational: one based on a PDP-1, the CTSS (Compatible Time-Sharing System) running on an IBM 7090, and an AN/FSQ-32V. With the wide word length of the PDP-6, DEC engineers were responding to the problems of some of these systems, which were felt not to have enough address bits. Not many PDP-6's were sold, but most of them went to universities, giving DEC a foothold in that arena.

Another machine with 18-bit word length, originally planned as a repackaged PDP-1, was the PDP-7, which used higher-density system modules. Later, PDP-4 compatibility was taken into account, as the latter architecture had a more extensive software library. Also, the PDP-7 marked the switch from Baudot (5-bit) characters to the 8-bit **ASCII** standard, and this was the first system made by DEC to incorporate wire-wrapping techniques at the packaging level.

The highly successful PDP-8 began life in 1965 as a PDP-5 built with more modern components, called *flip chips*. These new building blocks were not just faster and more reliable but also much smaller: The entire computer fit into a half-sized cabinet, making it the first "mini." The entire system could be placed on the desktop, and it could run off power from ordinary wall sockets; this was real progress at the time. It also kicked off the original equipment manufacturer (**OEM**) market, as PDP-8 systems could be integrated into total systems and sold by other corporations.

Similar to the PDP-5, the PDP-8 was a 12-bit computer, built for tasks that required minimal arithmetical computing. With its autoincrementing registers, the machine was perfectly suited for measurement and process control applications, but also for small-scale general-purpose multicomputing (TSS/8 time-sharing system). In the next 20 years, the PDP-8 had several incarnations, including: integrated circuits (PDP-8/i) and microprocessors (DECmate, PDP-8/A), taking advantage of various technology advances.

The next model, 1966's PDP-9, was in fact a PDP-7 with a redesigned memory system, permitting it to perform at almost twice the speed. A new daisy-chain bus was also incorporated.

The PDP-10 (also beginning in 1966) continued DEC's "classic" 36-bit computer line. The designation "PDP-10" refers to the KA10 processor, introduced in 1966, with logic implemented with discrete silicon transistors. The successor KI10 was shipped in 1972; this model used mixed discrete components and MSI TTL (transistor-to-transistor logic) integrated circuits.

The fast KL10/KL20 processor (1972–75) was built with ECL integrated circuits, while the KS10 was a cost-effective version of the instruction set, with the CPU occupying only a small cabinet. The PDP-10 name was dropped in the 1970s; the new designation was "DECsystem-10" and later "DECSYSTEM-20."

The PDP-10 series was a great success; many systems were installed at universities and companies using both real-time and time-sharing applications. The TOPS-10 and TOPS-20 **operating systems** are considered to be very solid programming environments; **Paul Allen** (1953–) and **Bill Gates** (1955–) wrote most of their early **Microsoft** software on this platform. In the year 2000 there are still companies that produce DECsystem-10/20-compatible computer systems, even though DEC abandoned development in the mid-1980s.

One of the most widespread computing platforms is the PDP-11. The first member of the PDP-11 family was introduced in 1970, and as of 2000, new models are still being designed and manufactured. DEC had first decided to design a 16-bit machine in 1967 code named "PDP-X," but the machine didn't meet the specifications, so the project was canceled. The new goal set for some of the engineers involved was an 8-bit machine, which got the nickname "desktop calculator." Later this project got canceled, too, when executives decided to give another chance to a 16-bit general-purpose computer, since it was perceived that there would be a market for it.

The first model, the PDP-11/20, was a very simple machine, with 32-kiloword maximal memory and a unified I/O interconnect called the *unibus*. An interesting feature was that the I/O devices were to be accessed through normal locations at the top of the memory range, which meant that there were no separate instructions for handling these devices. This kept the instruction set very clean, but customers demanded greater power and performance, so new models were introduced, ending with the PDP-11/70 (1975), which had a memory limit of 2 megawords and featured a set of extensions to the original architecture.

In 1975, Digital and Western Digital introduced the microprocessor-based LSI-11, which used a new microcomputer I/O system, the *Qbus*. Also in the mid-1970s, a new project was begun to produce a machine with some of the benefits of the PDP-11, but with a much wider addressing range and virtual memory management; this became the 32-bit Virtual Address eXtension, also known as the VAX family (1977). Meanwhile, DEC kept on designing new PDP-11 processors until 1990, when it sold the entire hardware/software division.

The PDP-12 (1969) was a modified PDP-8, which was combined with a LINC: It could execute both machines' instruction sets. The next designation was the PDP-14, as no PDP-13 was built or even designed. It wasn't a real computer: It was designed as a controller for electromechanical machinery, with 12-bit words but with only one one-bit register. One of the reasons not to use a normal PDP-8 in this area was the need for noise immunity.

The PDP-15 was another system family, with members in different performance ranges, all built with MSI TTL integrated circuits. To obtain better performance, the computers had separate main and I/O processors. The PDP-15/76 model had a small PDP-11 as the front-end I/O processor. More than 780 machines were shipped, making the PDP-15 the most successful member of DEC's 18-bit line.

The small computers that DEC marketed under this name had a considerable impact on today's computers, and not just in a technological sense: These inexpensive, easily maintainable (in terms of that time) systems brought computing out of the elite communities of the biggest universities and companies and closer to everyday life, whereas the bigger machines educated generations of well-trained computer specialists. The first video game (PDP-1), the early coinings of the word **hacker** (in the good sense), the **Unix** operating system, the **C** language (PDP-11), **BASIC** (PDP-8, PDP-10), and **Pascal** (PDP-8, PDP-11) all had something to do with PDP machines.

Further Reading

Bell, Gordon C., Craig J. Mudge, and John E. McNamara, eds. *Computer Engineering: A DEC View of Hardware Systems Design*. Upper Saddle River, N.J.: Prentice Hall, 1989.

—*Ákos Varga*

Pentium

Pentium is the name of the popular **microprocessor** produced by **Intel**, the largest **semiconductor** company in the world. The name Pentium was adopted when the 586 architecture was delivered (as a follow-up to the 286, 386, and 486 chips) because a name can be patented but a number could not. This prohibits the sale of chips named Pentium by other companies building functional copies of the microprocessor, as is the case for the Athlon chip, manufactured by **Advanced Micro Devices** (AMD).

Intel introduced the 8086 microprocessor in 1978. It was one of the first to provide 16-bit registers and a 16-bit memory **bus**. Although other options were available, the 8086 was adopted by **IBM** in 1981 as the core of its **personal computer** (PC) architecture. From then on, IBM PCs and compatibles remained tied to the Intel architecture, which has been evolving continually during the last 22 years.

The 80286 microprocessor was introduced by Intel in 1982; it was the basis of the PC/AT architecture. The new chip allowed addressing more than 1 megabyte (MB) of memory, one of the main design flaws in the original PCs. At the time, software applications were already being written that surpassed the available memory capacity of 1 MB in the first PCs.

The next chip generation was introduced in 1985. The 80386 microprocessor provided a 32-bit internal architecture with a 32-bit bus. The chip was much faster than the 8088 and the 80286 but was downwardly compatible with both of them. This was a very important component of Intel's strategy: Although every new processor introduced novel features, they were always compatible with older chips. **Software** written and compiled for the 8088 continued running on the 80386 in *native mode*. Of course, software developers could compile their programs for the new chip, but most of them opted for the lowest common denominator (the 8088), thus guaranteeing that the programs could run on any PC.

At this point a pattern can be identified: A new microprocessor generation is introduced roughly every three to four years (1978, 1982, 1985). Following this trend, the 80486 microprocessor was released in 1989. It included an internal **cache** to make execution faster and integrated the **floating-point** coprocessor with the integer unit in a single package. Until then, the **central processing unit** (CPU) and the floating-point coprocessor were two different chips that had to be placed side by side on the **motherboard**. Integrating the numeric coprocessor with the CPU meant that almost all of Intel's competitors in the floating-point field went out of business.

The next chip generation, the 80586, was released in 1993 and was renamed Pentium for the aforementioned patent reasons. Intel had fought a long series of battles with other semiconductor manufacturers, claiming that they had stolen parts of Intel's circuit design. It is not illegal to build a functional copy of a chip, but it is illegal to copy the chip layout of the original producer. Companies that design copies of a chip usually capture the entire design process on videotapes taken in a clean room, where the designers are isolated from the rest of the company. This separation is needed because the same company building the clone can also be a second source for Intel processors. In the semiconductor field, due to its cyclic nature, manufacturers usually produce chips for other companies in their own **silicon** foundries. This was the case with AMD, which was the manufacturer of Intel chips for Intel under a licensing agreement but was at the same time designing its own line of microprocessor clones. "Intel inside" stickers now make potential customers aware if an Intel chip or a clone from the competitors is used in a PC.

The Pentium has gone through two other major releases: the Pentium II was delivered in 1997 and the Pentium III in 1999. All Pentium chips have a 32-bit internal register architecture but a 64-bit external bus. This means that two 32-bit words can be loaded at the same time. This is important for the Pentium chips, because they use pipelining and have a *superscalar* design. Superscalar means that although the instruction stream is read sequentially from the memory, the instructions are executed in parallel. The Pentium also uses instruction reordering—that is, the internal execution order of the instructions is optimized for internal parallelism. This could mean, for example, that 10 instructions are executed in exactly the reverse order in which they are read, but this is not visible from the outside since the final results are provided as if the instructions had been executed in the original order. To keep its pipeline and functional units busy, the Pentium needs to access memory at the fastest possible rate. Therefore, several levels of caching are used to hold the data and the program. Whereas the 8088 chip had a clock rate of only 5 megahertz, the Pentium III can be clocked with up to 1 gigahertz, that is, 200 times faster.

The Pentium III includes many state-of-the-art features such as multiple branch prediction (to predict in advance if a program will branch), new instructions for data streaming (video and audio), and the MMX extensions. The MMX instructions work with the floating-point registers (which are 64 bits wide), handling them as a vector of eight 8-bit numbers. Each 8-bit number can represent, for example, the color of a pixel on the screen. The same operation can be applied at once to the eight components of the vector. This makes it possible to speed up many common multimedia operations. The MMX extensions are in fact a type of integrated small array processor of SIMD (single instruction multiple data) type.

Although Intel released the Itanium processor in 1999, a new 64-bit architecture developed together with **Hewlett-Packard**, the popularity of the Pentium line, and the sheer number of computers using this chip, mean that it will continue to be available well into the first decade of the twenty-first century.

FURTHER READING

Bistry, David, Carole DuLong, Mickey Gutman, and Mike Julier. *Complete Guide to MMX Technology*. New York: McGraw-Hill, 1997.

Brey, Barry. *Intel Microprocessors 8086/8088, 80186/80188, 80286, 80386, 80486, Pentium, Pentium Pro Processor and Pentium II: Architecture, Programming, and Interfacing*. Upper Saddle River, N.J.: Prentice Hall, 1999.

Jackson, Tim. *Inside Intel: Andy Grove and the Rise of the World's Most Powerful Chip Company*. Collingdale, Calif.: DIANE Publishing, 2000.

Triebel, Walter. *80386, 80486, and Pentium Microprocessor: The Hardware, Software, and Interfacing*. Upper Saddle River, N.J.: Prentice Hall, 1997.

—*Raúl Rojas*

Perl

Perl is a computing language, popularly referred to as a *scripting language* and most often compared to Python, Tcl, and Rexx. However, its inventor, Larry Wall, emphasizes that Perl is a general-purpose computing language suited to about the same range of tasks as such languages as **C**, **C++**, and **Java**.

Wall originally invented Perl in 1986 to generate reports common in system administration of **Unix** hosts. Early Perl did many of the same jobs as the common Unix utilities "sed" and "awk," but faster and with wider generality. Perl thus became popular among Unix administrators.

When the **World Wide Web** exploded during 1994 and 1995, Perl was widely adopted as the language of choice for scripting the common gateway interface (CGI) dynamic content. Perl's strong string manipulation capabilities and expressiveness are a good match for CGI tasks. Perl has been so successful in this role that many people mistakenly identify CGI and Perl, or believe that Perl is the only language that can be used to script Web content.

Perl has continued to mature in several dimensions that do not relate directly to either system administration or Web work. The most important advances of the second half of the 1990s included direct support of **object-oriented programming** styles; enhanced portability, especially to such operating systems as **Windows** and MacOS; **graphical user interface** (GUI) bindings; and mechanisms for support and maintenance of Perl that have made its adoption by commercial organizations more comfortable.

Perl's appeal, like that of any computing language, arises from the interplay of several dimensions. It is important to distinguish these aspects: the abstract language, particular implementations, the support library to the language, and the "social" practices and habits that surround the language.

The abstract Perl language superficially resembles other common languages, including awk, /bin/sh, and C. It is quite different from many other languages in that it does *not* aspire to such qualities as orthogonality and simplicity. Wall has a background in (human) linguistics and a strong sense that Perl should be an "evolved" language, like English. By this he means that it is full of abbreviations, alternative ways to achieve the same end, and context dependence. This is illustrated by the Schwartzian transform, a common idiom for an efficient and succinct sorting transform within Perl credited to independent consultant Randal Schwartz (1961–). A typical example of its use is

```
@sorted = map  { $_->[0] }
          sort { $a->[1] <=> $b->[1] }
          map  { [$_, -s] } @files;
```

This cryptic set of commands sorts entries stored as files, assigning the result to @sorted.

Perl implementations have always been of high technical quality. They have few errors, are widely available at no charge, and perform well. Perl's library is a particular strength. The comprehensive Perl archive network (CPAN) collects contributions from hundreds of volunteers who have authored useful add-ons to Perl. It is generally safe to assume that any new software technology will be accessible within Perl as soon as it is available to any language.

Finally, Perl's users have a strong tradition of collegiality and volunteerism that extends well beyond CPAN's riches. This and the many competent books devoted to Perl also make the language inviting to newcomers.

FURTHER READING

Wall, Larry, Tom Christiansen, and Randal L. Schwartz. *Programming Perl.* Sebastopol, Calif.: O'Reilly, 1991; 3rd ed., Cambridge, Mass., 2000.

Schwartz, Randal L., and Tom Christiansen. *Learning Perl.* Sebastopol, Calif.: O'Reilly, 1993; 2nd ed., 1997.

—*Cameron Laird*

Personal Computer

A personal computer (PC) is an entry-level computer system for individual use. The PC (or **microcomputer**) actually developed from the **semiconductor** industry. Instead of being a little **mainframe**, the PC more closely resembles an extremely large chip.

In 1968, **Robert Noyce** (1927–90) and **Gordon Moore** (1929–) started **Intel** and they developed a photolithography method to put three components on a single chip. The number kept increasing: today, the same area of **silicon** that once held a single **transistor** can be populated with more than a million components. Tracking this trend, Gordon Moore came up with **Moore's law**: The power of computing doubles every 18 months. Moore predicted that by the 1970s, chips would become available that contained logic circuits equivalent to those used in 1950s-era mainframes.

In November 1971, Intel publicly introduced the world's first single-chip **microprocessor**, the Intel 4004, invented by Intel engineers Federico Faggin (1941–), Marcian E. "Ted" Hoff (1937–), and Stan Mazor (1941–). This microprocessor was a fundamental shift in the approach to computer design. Here was a programmable device to which an engineer could add a few memory chips and a support chip or two and turn it into a real computer. Early buyers of these chips tended to use them in novel ways, such as digital watches, microwave ovens, and in electronic devices that could make sounds. Thus, the microprocessor began to operate transparently, as a hidden computer inside a variety of electric products, including power tools, appliances, telephones, and vending machines.

However, a more apparent use of the microprocessor chip was in video games. The first electronic video game, Pong, was developed in 1972 by **Nolan Bushnell** (1943–), an engineering major at the University of Utah. While attending college, Bushnell had a part-time job in an amusement park, where he acquired knowledge about coin-operated games. For his personal amusement, he was an avid player of Spacewar, a popular game played on university mainframe computers. But Spacewar was very complicated; Bushnell began to wonder if he could create a similar game for general use. So he invented the simple game Pong, based on the idea of a Ping-Pong table. Pong was easy to play and simple enough to fit on a microprocessor chip. In 1972, Bushnell started the Atari company to develop electronic video games. They also developed personal computers. Pong was astonishingly successful in both arcades and homes, and it was the starting point for the interactive home video game market.

A general-purpose computer based on a microprocessor first appeared in France in 1973. A Vietnamese immigrant named Thi T. Truong had his electronics company design and build a computer using the Intel 8008 microprocessor; he called it the MICRAL. Around 2000 were sold in the commercial marketplace.

In the United States, Ed Roberts wanted to sell computers to hobbyists: His machine, called the **Altair 8800**, is generally considered to be the first personal computer. To generate income for his floundering company named MITS (Model Instrumentation Telemetry Systems), Roberts decided to sell a kit to build "home computers" using the Intel 8008 chip. In July 1974, *Radio-Electronics* magazine had announced a kit based on the same chip for building a personal minicomputer. Jonathan Titus of Virginia Polytechnic University was selling a U.S.$5.00 booklet that described how to purchase the parts and assemble a computer called the Mark-8. In contrast, Roberts' kit included all the parts. Les Solomon, the editor of *Popular Electronics* magazine, was looking for someone who would design a computer kit for his readers. Solomon contacted Roberts, and MITS's Altair 8800 was featured on the cover of the January 1975 issue.

Computer kits ignited a grass-roots hobbyist movement through the formation of computer clubs. Members would gather to discuss how to build computers. One of the best known clubs was the **Homebrew Computer Club**, near San Francisco. Homebrew was started by Fred Moore (1940–1997) and Gordon French, two people appalled by the fact that the computer was being monopolized for power and profit by the same military–industrial complex that already controlled every other major technology in the United States. They were convinced that computers held the key to a vital participatory democracy and were anxious to get computers into the hands of individuals.

Discussions at Homebrew meetings focused on the Altair and its Intel 8080 microprocessor chip. Members would share electronic techniques and schematics, and demonstrate the latest microprocessor and electronics components. Group attendance grew rapidly and was soon filling an auditorium at nearby Stanford University. Meetings attracted a diverse group of computer enthusiasts from all parts of **Silicon Valley**. As a result of attending Homebrew meetings, the **Apple I** computer was built by **Steve Wozniak** (1950–). After Wozniak demonstrated his computer board at the Homebrew Club, his friend **Steve Jobs** (1955–) immediately saw the marketing potential for it. He contacted a retired Intel executive named Armas Clifford "Mike" Markkula (1942–) to help them start a company.

Wozniak, Jobs, and Markkula formed **Apple Computer** on 3 January 1977. Along with the Apple II, a number of other personal computers were also introduced that year. IMSAI built a clone of the Altair machine called IMSAI 8080. Radio Shack began selling its TRS-80 and Commodore introduced the Commodore PET, which came with a monitor, **keyboard**, and cassette player. Jobs and Markkula felt that the Apple II should be built for a market that went beyond hobbyists. Therefore, it was decided to put the computer inside a plastic case to make its appearance more appealing.

The preassembled Apple II came in a plastic case and was equipped with a video monitor, keyboard, a cassette interface to store data, and game paddles. It succeeded because it was the first microcomputer that looked like a consumer electronic product. People could buy the Apple II computer from a dealer who would fix it if it broke. Dealers would also give customers a little help in learning to operate the machine. **Software** written by others was available for the Apple II. For example, VisiCalc, a spreadsheet program written by Daniel Bricklin (1951–) and Robert Frankston, became available for the Apple II in 1979. The program freed businesspeople, accountants, and financial planners from the tyranny of pencil-and-paper spreadsheets, in which a single mistake could often create hours of tedious erasure and recalculations. Many business people purchased the Apple II simply because it ran VisiCalc; for this reason it became known as the **killer application** for the Apple II. It was through the efforts of enthusiastic employees that the machine became a business product.

After the success of the Apple II, **IBM** saw the importance of developing their own personal computer. Prior to 1980, IBM had started building smaller minicomputers and a number of desktop machines, including the SCAMP and the 5100 desktop computer.

Neither was particularly successful. In 1980, IBM's chairman Frank Carey believed that although IBM had no equals in the mainframe world, their greatest future growth would be in the lower PC market. To market an IBM personal computer rapidly, Bill Lowe, head of the IBM laboratory in Boca Raton, Florida, was asked to come up with an IBM product within one year.

Importantly, IBM used nonproprietary components to build the computer. The nonproprietary **open architecture** standards used to develop the IBM PC were in direct contrast with IBM's *proprietary architecture*, which was used to develop their earlier System/360 series. Open architecture follows the philosophy of open-system computer design. An *open system* is any system in which the components conform to nonproprietary standards rather than to the standards of a specific **hardware** or software supplier. IBM published the technical specifications for their personal computer to enable third-party companies to develop software and hardware add-ons.

The IBM PC was designed to use an Intel 8088 microprocessor; **Microsoft** was engaged to supply the basic software languages. Microsoft, a small software company at the time, had written a **BASIC** programming language for the original Altair and they had experience working with Intel's chip technology. **Gary Kildall** (1942–94), who had developed the first general-purpose **operating system** for personal computers, was approached by IBM to provide an operating system for the new machine. An operating system is software that directs the overall operations of the computer. Kildall's operating system software, called **CP/M** (Control Program for Micros), was designed to work with an Intel microprocessor. But IBM failed to come to an agreement with Kildall and turned instead to Microsoft.

At the time, Microsoft had specialized in creating programming languages, such as BASIC and **Fortran**. They did not have any experience developing operating systems. But **Paul Allen** (1953–) knew that a programmer named Tim Paterson (1956–) was working on a clone of CP/M that he called QDOS (Quick and Dirty Operating System). Microsoft made an agreement to acquire it from Seattle Computing, the company that employed Tim Paterson. After signing an agreement to license QDOS, Microsoft sublicensed it to IBM. By licensing the software instead of selling the operating system software to IBM, Microsoft could also license it to other computer manufacturers. QDOS later evolved into MS-DOS.

The official launch date for the IBM PC was set for 12 August 1981. The machine would cost anywhere from U.S.$1500 to U.S.$6000, depending on the complexity of the system purchased. The first IBM PC had one **floppy disk** drive and 64K (64 kilobytes [thousands of bytes]) of **RAM**, permanent random access memory. It came with a monochrome television-resolution screen, one much larger and easier to read than Apple's. IBM's entrance into the personal computer market took the market by storm and they soon outsold Apple's computers.

Prior to 1984, Microsoft began licensing their MS-DOS software to other companies, such as **Compaq**, to make IBM **clones**. Microsoft gave Compaq the source code to the generic version of MS-DOS along with the code to IBM's DOS. Compaq set out to make IBM-compatible computers that would be able to use IBM PC software right out of the box. Compaq was the first of the IBM-PC clone manufacturers. By early 1984, PC clones were flooding the market and the success of IBM's personal computer business was fading.

In 1984 Apple introduced their **Macintosh** computer with a **graphical user interface**. Both IBM and Microsoft began developing graphical interfaces for the IBM PC and its clones. IBM was developing **OS/2** and Microsoft was working on **Windows**. In May 1990, Windows 3.0 was introduced, and it was an immediate success. The mouse-driven Windows graphical user interface rapidly replaced command-line interaction. Within a few months, sales exceeded a million copies a month. In contrast, OS/2 failed to catch on as a product. After losing control of the personal computer market, IBM now also lost control of the PC operating system software market.

By 1991, personal computers using Intel-based microprocessors running Microsoft Windows software were dominating the personal computer marketplace, and their dominance continued into the next century. People now referred to personal computers as a *Wintel* standard, referring to the Windows operating system software running on an Intel chip. Although a revitalized Apple is making small gains in market share, the only emerging challenge to Microsoft's hegemony of personal computer operating systems is **Linux**, a non-commercial software program that has been developed by individual programmers. Similar to the grass-roots movement that fostered the development of the personal computer, Linux is a part of an open-system software movement that challenges corporate control of the operating system.

At last count, 370 million personal computers were being used around the world, and that number is expected to increase to 670 million in the year 2002.

Further Reading

Butcher, Lee. *Accidental Millionaire: The Rise and Fall of Steve Jobs at Apple.* New York: Paragon House, 1998.

Carroll, Paul. *Big Blues: The Unmaking of IBM.* New York: Crown, 1994.

Ceruzzi, Paul E. *A History of Modern Computing.* Cambridge, Mass.: MIT Press, 1998.

Ferguson, Charles H., and Charles R. Morris. *Computer Wars.* New York: St. Martin's Press, 1999.

International Telecommunications Union. *Key Indicators for the World Telecommunication Services Sector.* Geneva, Switzerland: ITU, 1999.

Manes, Stephen, and Paul Andrews. *Gates: How Microsoft's Mogul Reinvented an Industry—And Made Himself the Richest Man in America.* New York: Doubleday, 1993.

Sculley, John. *Odyssey: Pepsi to Apple—A Journey of Adventure, Ideas, and the Future.* New York: Harper and Row, 1987.

Stephenson, Neal. *In the Beginning . . . Was the Command Line.* New York: Avon Books, 1999.

—*Susan B. Barnes*

Personal Digital Assistant

As computers become smaller, lighter, and cheaper, users increasingly seek devices that can be used anywhere as a means of quick access to information. Although such pocket-sized computers have been dreamed of since the 1960s, it was not until the late 1990s that their use became widespread, thanks to improvements in battery capacity and wireless communication, as well as computing power. By 2000, many analysts were predicting that the *personal digital assistant* (PDA) would replace both the **personal computer** (PC) and the mobile phone.

Hand-held computers were first envisaged in 1968 by computing pioneer **Alan Kay** (1940–). He proposed a system simple enough for children to use, cheap enough for everyone to own, and weighing under 1 kilogram. Lacking the technology for a working prototype, he built a model from cardboard and lead: the *Dynabook*, so-called because it was intended to be the size and weight of a book, but adaptable to various applications.

A genuinely portable computer was built in 1980 by *GRiD*, a startup founded by Glenn Edens (1952–) and John Ellenby, two researchers who had worked alongside Kay at the **Xerox Palo Alto Research Center** (PARC). The GRiD could be carried in a shoulder bag and used the *clamshell design* found in many modern PDAs.

Over the following years, **laptops** were to incorporate many of the features Kay originally planned for the Dynabook; even the name was used by **Toshiba**, for the first PC powered by an internal battery. Laptops quickly got smaller and lighter, until in 1989 the games manufacturer Atari released the *Portfolio*, the first hand-held PC. It was designed to be IBM compatible, running MS **DOS** on an **Intel** 80C88 CPU, a configuration similar to the original IBM PC released eight years earlier. Hand-held PCs running **Windows** appeared in 1995, a class of machine known as *subnotebooks*. The first were Toshiba's *Libretto* and **Hewlett-Packard**'s *Omnibook*, but these lagged behind their desktop and laptop counterparts, because of the difficulty involved in miniaturizing components. They were targeted at business users who needed a full PC they could carry in their pocket, with a complexity and cost way beyond the children intended to be the Dynabook's users.

While PCs shrunk, portable machines became more complex. The earliest hand-held computing devices were pocket calculators, the first of which appeared in 1970. Called the *Pocketronic*, it was the result of a five-year project at **Texas Instruments** led by **Jack Kilby** (1923–), inventor of the **integrated circuit**. It could perform only the four basic mathematical operations—addition, subtraction, multiplication, and division—and was intended initially just to demonstrate the power of Kilby's invention. But the machine proved popular and soon faced competition from other companies eager for a slice of the growing market. Two years later, Hewlett-Packard released the *HP-35*: the first pocket-sized scientific calculator, so-called because it had 35 keys.

Revolutionary though early pocket calculators were, throughout the 1970s they still acted mainly as replacements for slide rules. The first with a permanent memory, enabling it to store a number when switched off, was Hewlett-Packard's *HP25C*, released in 1976. In 1979 its successor, the *HP41C*, became the first calculator able to display both letters and numbers.

In 1982, the South African company Psion began work on the first digital organizer: a calculator that could also store a list of names and telephone numbers. Psion was founded in 1980 by David Potter, and first became well known writing software for the Sinclair ZX series, compact home computers priced under U.S.$100. Sinclair's *ZX81* and *ZX Spectrum* were the United Kingdom's first mass-market computers, introducing a whole generation to programming during the early 1980s. The machines were no larger than some modern hand-helds, although couldn't be used as such because they required external display, storage, and power.

The original *Psion Organiser* shipped in 1984, with a one-line display and 36 keys. As well as advanced mathematical functions and an address book, it had two expansion slots for solid-state modules containing programs or user data. Psion supplied programs for scientific, financial, or database applications, and users could write their own using a variant of **BASIC** called *Psion Organiser Programming Language* (POPL). Two years later, the *Psion Organiser II* added a two-line display, a more sophisticated programming language, diary functions, and a serial port so that it could connect to other devices.

Following the Organiser II's success, other manufacturers raced to add similar features to their calculators. The most popular were Casio's *Business Online Scheduling System* (*Boss*) and Sharp's *Wizard*, both of which dispensed with Psion's complex programming language and concentrated on usability. They were marketed as high-tech replacements for the pocket-sized paper files popular at the time, but many potential users dismissed these early organizers as toys for "geeks." Their greatest problem was text input: All used tiny calculator-style buttons, usually arranged from A to Z and requiring awkward combinations of shift keys.

The first Organiser to achieve widespread success was Psion's *Series 3*, released in 1991. To the then-standard address book, time manager, and calculator, it added a simple word processor and spreadsheet, and could even synchronize data with a PC. Most important, its backlit display was large enough to implement a **graphical user interface**, unlike calculators hinged down over a *Qwerty* **keyboard** in the clamshell design pioneered by GriD.

Meanwhile, **Apple** was working on an alternative solution to the input problem: handwriting recognition. It launched the *MessagePad* in September 1993, surrounded by hype that first brought the expression PDA into common use. Often known as *Newton*, the name of its Mac-like operating system, the MessagePad was a hand-sized tablet with a touch-sensitive screen, designed to allow users to take notes in the same way that they would using an ordinary paper notebook. But the handwriting recognition software worked poorly, and the machine was expensive: around U.S.$1000, compared to no more than U.S.$400 for most other organizers. Although the software was improved in later models, MessagePads remained too expensive for most users, and the line was officially discontinued in February 1998.

The concept of a small pen-operated tablet didn't die with the MessagePad. In 1996, modem manufacturer US Robotics introduced the *Pilot*, a smaller and cheaper device measuring only 12 by 8 centimeters. Although it lacked handwriting recognition, requiring users to type on a *virtual keyboard*, it more than made up for this with a simple docking cradle for data transfer to a PC and a battery life of months. When US Robotics was bought by networking giant **3Com** a year later, the device was relaunched as the *PalmPilot*, with a new input system called *Grafitti*. Instead of teaching the machine human handwriting, users had to learn a series of simple strokes that the machine could easily interpret. It became an instant success, overtaking Psion in popularity. By 2000, when 3Com spun Palm Computing off as a separate company, it had more than 80 percent of the U.S. market share.

The popularity of hand-held computers didn't escape **Microsoft**, which by 1995 had a near monopoly on **operating systems** for desktop and laptop PCs. In late 1996 it released *Windows CE,* which looked just like the popular **Windows** operating system for PCs and even included cut-down versions of Microsoft's Office applications, designed to run on organizers of the Psion or Sharp variety. But despite the support of many manufacturers, some of whom added features such as color screens and music playback, CE initially failed to win a strong following. Users criticized its lack of compatibility with non-Microsoft applications and said that the Windows user interface was too cluttered.

Microsoft tried again in 1998, with a version of Windows CE for palm-sized devices that it optimistically dubbed the "Pilot killer." User reaction was again unfavorable: The Windows clutter made even less sense on an even more compact screen, and the Office applications were gone. But Windows CE continued to evolve, eventually finding its way into laptops, television sets, and thin clients.

By the late 1990s, two other developments were affecting PDAs: mobile phones and the Internet. Phones had begun to incorporate simple organizer-type features, at first just so that they could remember numbers, but then because customers wanted to access the Internet wirelessly. The phone manufacturers foresaw a future of *smartphones*, which would be more like computers than traditional handsets. Fearing domination by Microsoft or 3Com, the three leading cell phone vendors formed a joint venture with Psion in June 1998. Known as Symbian, it intended to build on Psion's *EPOC* operating system and license it for both phones and PDAs. A year later, mobile phones began to incorporate the *Wireless Application Protocol* (WAP), an open standard that scales down the World Wide Web for their small screens.

In 2000 many companies were claiming that the PDA's greatest days were still to come. A new short-range wireless technology called *Bluetooth* would enable one to act as a communications hub for a *personal area network* (PAN), which surrounded every user, encompassed every device, and beamed information automatically to PDAs carried by others. But no one could confidently predict whether this grandiose vision would be based on Microsoft, Palm, or Symbian, or indeed, whether it would occur at all.

Further Reading

Ehrenman, Gayle, and Michael Zulic. *Mastering Palm Organizers.* Alameda, Calf.: Sybex, 2000.

Kay, Alan. "Personal Dynamic Media." *IEEE Computer,* Mar. 1977.

Lazere, Cathy, and Dennis Sasha. *Out of Their Minds: The Lives and Discoveries of 15 Great Computer Scientists.* New York: Springer Verlag, 1997.

O'Hara, Robert. *Introducing Microsoft Windows CE: Your Guide to the New Version of Microsoft Windows for Your Handheld PC.* Seattle, Wash.: Microsoft Press, 1997.

Prochak, Michael. *On the Road: Pervasive Portable Computing with Powerbooks, PDAs, and Beyond.* Reading, Mass.: Addison-Wesley, 1995.

—*Andy Dornan*

Personal Robotics

The field of personal robotics is a relatively young area of research, which envisions that personal robotics will be analogous to personal computing in that one day, most individuals or households will have one or more robots of their own. These personal robots will coexist in homes, offices, stores, and so on, assisting humans, improving the quality of their lives, and even entertaining them. The types of tasks that personal robots will perform include house cleaning, serving food, security patrolling, walking the dog, tutoring children in science, mowing the yard, retrieving the mail, reminding about and delivering the proper medications, and so on.

A number of personal robots are currently available on the market or are soon to be commercially available. These personal robots range from intelligent pets and toys, to robots that perform specific tasks, to general-purpose service robots. The two main commercially developed robot pets are Sony's robotic dog, Aibo, and Omron's robotic cat, Tama. Aibo can respond to human actions, such as standing up after being patted on the head. It can wave hello with its paw, and play with certain objects. These functionalities are made possible by a number of moving joints, microphones, color cameras, and touch, heat, and infrared sensors. Tama, the

Toshimi Kudo, an Omron employee, and "Tama," Omron's robot pet cat, in Tokyo, 11 September 1998. (AP Photo/Kasumi Kasahara)

robotic cat, can develop a personality while interacting with her owner. Using microphones and pressure sensors, Tama can respond to sounds and touches, displaying the basic animal emotions. The Takara company of Japan has recently produced robotic fish for aquariums, including jellyfish, crab, and lobsters. A main attraction of robotic pets is their low maintenance requirement, while they provide entertainment and companionship. Another recent addition to the personal robot toys is My Real Baby, an intelligent baby doll manufactured jointly by iRobot Corporation and Hasbro, Inc. The doll is an interactive, animated doll capable of interacting with a child using emotionlike behavior, facial expressions, and other realistic reactions.

A number of personal robots have been designed and manufactured to perform a specific task. The majority of these robots perform repetitive tasks such as vacuuming floors or mowing lawns. The robotic vacuum cleaner DC06, by Dyson, is controlled autonomously by three on-board computers, enabling the robot to navigate obstacles and to avoid falling. DC06 uses multiple sensors to chart its position in the environment and plan its moves. The Eureka Company's Robot Vac is also an autonomous robot vacuum cleaner, with a round shape 15 inches in diameter. An onboard **microprocessor** controls the robot, using sonar sensors for obstacle avoidance. It is stated that Robot Vac can navigate around furniture legs and over electrical cords. Electrolux of Sweden has also introduced a robot vacuum cleaner, RVC, which is a round robot equipped with navigational radar for moving around a room. Using similar technology, Electrolux has also developed a prototype solar-powered robotic lawn mower for autonomous mowing of yards of different shapes and sizes. Robotic lawn mowers are available from a number of companies, capable of autonomously mowing lawns on charged batteries. Most robotic lawn mowers require a perimeter wire to be placed around the outer lawn edge to guide the robot.

Service robots are another major category of personal robots. They are autonomous, intelligent, mobile robots that can move around with people and for them, performing a variety of tasks and chores while providing companionship. One example of such robots is InteleCady, by the company of the same name, a service robot designed to function as a human golf caddie. InteleCady is controlled using onboard computers and is equipped with many technologies, including the global positioning satellite system (GPS), radio communication capabilities, and ultrasound navigational equipment. It can navigate independently using the detailed geography of a golf course. Sage, by Mobot, is an interactive robotic mobile guide, leading people through interactive journeys, such as museum tours. Sage can plug itself in for recharging and communicates with its service group using e-mail. Other functions of Sage include voice recognition, touch screen, token and coupon dispensing, and facial expressions. Available from Probotics, Cye is a service robot capable of vacuuming, serving as a mail delivery assistant, serving food, and providing security. Cye is 5 inches tall, weighs about 91 pounds, and has a variety of optional attachments. NEC offers R100, a small personal companion robot. R100 interacts with people using visual recognition, voice recognition, and Internet communication technologies. R100 can recognize faces, understand verbal commands, and move around rooms while accompanying people.

Health care is another important application area for personal robots. CareBot from Gecko Systems is one such example. CareBot is more than 4 feet tall, with a payload of over 150 pounds. It is categorized as a personal utility class robot, autonomously capable of house exploration, and obstacle avoidance. CareBot is designed such that users can add their own tasks by building on robot's behaviors. A variety of available optional attachments enable the robot to perform an assortment of chores. Another example of personal robots for health care applications is Flo, a prototype personal service robot (PSR), developed by researchers at Carnegie Mellon University and the University of Pittsburgh. Flo is designed and built to care for elderly people in a number of ways, including intelligent reminding, mobile manipulation, tele-presence, data collection, surveillance, and social interaction. Flo is also called a "Nursebot."

There are three major approaches to the design and fabrication of personal robots: hobbyists at home building robots, universities and research laboratories performing research on the theoretical and practical aspects of personal robotics, and companies working on personal robots to be manufactured and sold as consumer electronics products. The hobbyist approach to personal robotics is to use inexpensive components, at times taken from electronic equipment, and putting together working (or partially working) models of robots. Recently, the hobbyists have increased their interactions throughout a number of unofficial robotics clubs that have sprung up around the world.

Public and private research laboratories have been spending much greater amounts of money, trying to investigate the fundamental issues of personal robotics, and building working robotic systems in the process. For example, effort at the research labs at Honda Corporation to build a humanoid robot has required many engineers working over 10 years and with a budget of millions of dollars. Recently, companies have shown interest in the area of personal robotics, mainly by manufacturing and selling robotic toys.

Personal robots vary in a number of main characteristics, including physical appearance, intelligence, and application. A personal robot's physical appearance is dictated by the robot's tasks and the environment within which the robot has to operate. A robot used in a house should be able to navigate around obstacles and climb stairs if necessary. Such a robot can be equipped with legs, as walking robots are more capable of negotiating stairs. A robot that delivers objects must have a manipulator arm for grasping objects. A personal robot assisting the elderly must have a certain amount of power to be useful in daily chores. Three major shapes for personal robots include anthropomorphic designs (humanoids), animal-like robots, and appliance-shaped robots.

The intelligence of a personal robot is also dictated by what is expected of it. A robot that must clean the house should be able to distinguish between clothes to be washed and a cat. A robot expected to interact with people in an office may be required to distinguish among them. Three major classes of intelligence for personal robots include nonintelligent robots that simply perform predetermined tasks, regardless of the situation; semi-intelligent robots that can perform certain tasks on their own but require interactions with human users; and fully autonomous robots that are capable of planning their own tasks and require no human interaction to perform their tasks.

The applications of personal robots can be categorized into two classes: specific-task robots that are designed to do a few tasks, such as mowing the lawn; and general-purpose robots that can perform a variety of tasks, assisting their owners in their daily chores.

The future success of personal robotics depends on a number of factors: the achievements of researchers and hobbyists in improving the design of personal robots, ensuring their safe use while increasing their range of applications; a change in the attitude of consumers, accepting personal robots in their homes and offices as appliances and home electronics systems; a decline in the price of personal robots to make them more affordable for a large portion of the population; and the commercial success of companies in fabricating and selling the personal robots. Computers used to be specialized tools, affordable and utilized only by a few organizations, until the success of personal computers completely revolutionized computing. Analogously, personal robotics can revolutionize the field of robotics, bringing personal robots within reach for most people.

Personal robots will rely heavily on technologies developed for general robots, including path planning, navigation, sensing and image processing, motors and actuators, power sources, intelligence, and control. In addition, specific research in personal robotics has been taking place in a number of directions, including human–robot coexistence, artificial emotion, specialized robot body material, object delivery and handover, robot motion interpretation, and general attitudes toward personal robots. Human–robot coexistence deals with the issues involved in a robot occupying and behaving in the same space as humans. These issues involve, for example, personal robots navigating around humans and behaving in a manner comfortable to humans. Personal robots must avoid crossing into a person's personal space. Artificial emotions of personal robots are elements that can improve how robots and humans interact. A robot that displays emotional properties will be able to present a better idea of what its current state is to people around it. This can lead to a more pleasant personal robot that would behave in predictable ways.

Specialized materials for building personal robot bodies are essential, as these robots interact more often in peoples' lives, and therefore physical contact can occur. A personal robot should never harm people by coming in contact with them. The difficulty with this is that a robot must be powerful enough to perform heavy lifting jobs for its owner but also be well balanced enough not to hurt someone with that power. Object delivery and handover to people will be common tasks that must be performed by personal robots. These could involve a process as simple as approaching to a safe distance and then allowing the human to take the object, or as complicated as using a robotic arm to hand the object to the person. Safety is a high priority when the personal robot hands an object to a person.

The human interpretations of personal robots' movements play an important role in the robots' acceptance. The body movements of a personal robot are a way of communicating with humans around it, as people will often engage in the personification of animals, objects, and machines. A personal robot that can move in a manner similar to a person's movements may create a more pleasing environment. A few studies have been done to gauge human reaction to personal robots, but much more work remains to be done in this category. Positive attitudes toward personal robots will pave the way for their introduction into human societies.

FOR FURTHER RESEARCH

Arkin, Ronald C. *Behavior-Based Robotics.* Cambridge, Mass.: MIT Press, 1998.

Canny, John, and Arvin Agah. Special Issue on Personal Robotics. *Autonomous Robots Journal,* 2000.

Engelberger, Joseph F. *Robotics in Service.* Cambridge, Mass.: MIT Press, 1989.

IEEE Robotics and Automation Society. *Proceedings of the IEEE International Workshop on Robot and Human Communication (Ro-Man).* Piscataway, N.J.: IEEE Press, 1993.

Jones, Joseph L., Anita M. Flynn, and Bruce A. Seiger. *Mobile Robots: Inspiration to Implementation.* Wellesley, Mass.: Peters, 1993; 2nd ed., Natick, Mass.: Peters, 1998.

Raucci, Richard. *Personal Robotics: Real Robots to Construct, Program, and Explore the World.* Natick, Mass.: Peters, 1999.

—Arvin Agah

Piracy, Software

Software piracy is the act of making a copy of a computer program without the permission of the copyright owner. It is illegal because the owner has the exclusive right to determine when and how copies may be made.

The software industry estimates that 4 out of every 10 copies of software in use worldwide in 1998 were illegally reproduced, resulting in U.S.$11 billion in lost revenues to the industry. The Software and Information Industry Association in Washington, D.C. has identified a wide variety of types of software piracy. *Softlifting* refers to purchasing a single licensed copy of software and loading it on several computers, contrary to the license. This includes sharing software with friends, co-workers, and others. Often called "warez" trading, *internet piracy* is transmitting software unlawfully or providing infringing material that enables users to violate copyright protection mechanisms in software (such as serial numbers and cracker utilities) over the Internet. *Software counterfeiting* is the illegal duplication and sale of copyrighted software in a form designed to make it appear to be legitimate. *Hard disk loading* refers to computer dealers loading unauthorized copies of software onto the hard disks of **personal computers**, often as an incentive for the end user to buy the **hardware** from that dealer. Renting software for temporary use, as you would a video, is also considered piracy, as is *OEM/unbundling*, selling stand-alone software that was intended to be sold packaged with specific accompanying hardware.

Copyright has long been used as a means of providing protection for artists, musicians, and writers to ensure that they had legal recourse if someone tried to benefit from the results of their intellectual and creative efforts without their permission. The very earliest software developers were not concerned about the need to protect the intellectual work represented in the programs they created, because the community of people who understood computers was very small and programming was rather experimental. It was widely accepted among programmers that successful efforts would be distributed freely to others who were working on similar problems, in exchange for receiving the benefit of the work that others had done.

Most early software development was done by computer hardware companies, which had a vested interest in distributing the programs created by their software developers as widely as possible in order to increase the value of their computers to their customers. **IBM**, for example, actively supported the formation of SHARE, an organization of IBM customers that had as its explicit purpose the sharing of programming knowledge as it developed. IBM facilitated the sharing of programs developed by its own software developers and by its customers by maintaining a directory of programs that were available to be copied and used.

By the mid-1960s, however, there were a number of companies that were in business to sell software, and it became crucial to their success to be able to protect the investment they made in developing it. Since writing software is extremely expensive and making a copy of it very inexpensive, someone who does not have to recoup the development costs can sell a copy at a much lower price than the developer can, or even afford to give it away, creating an unfair competitive advantage. Companies that were investing large amounts of money to develop software wanted to be sure that they had legal recourse against anyone who used it without paying for it.

Because computer technology was so new, there were no provisions in the law to cover protection of computer programs from unauthorized use, but in 1964, the U.S. Copyright Office began to accept computer programs for registration under the *rule of doubt*, which says that when there is a question as to whether or not something can be copyrighted, it should be resolved in favor of registrability. It was not until 1980, though, that copyright law was actually

Spotting Pirated Software

Recognizing that many consumers are unaware that casual copying of software is illegal and don't know how to distinguish between legal and illegal software, the SIIA has published the following list of indications that a software copy may be unauthorized.

- Software is sold in a clear CD-ROM jewel case with no accompanying documentation, license, registration card, or certificate of authenticity.
- Software is marked as "academic" product.
- Software is marked as "OEM" or "For Distribution Only with New PC Hardware."
- Software CD-ROMs have handwritten labels.
- Backup disks received from a computer retailer contain handwritten labels.
- Graphics and coloring of accompanying materials, or the label on the inside of the jewel case, are poor.
- There are multiple programs from many different publishers on a single CD-ROM (commonly referred to as "compilation CDs").
- Manuals for software loaded on a PC by a computer retailer are photocopied or are not available and the retailer suggests buying a third-party book (such as *WordPerfect 2000 for Dummies*).

changed to provide specifically that computer programs could be copyrighted.

Although a number of software developers also explored patents as a means of protecting their programs, the patent process was too drawn out and expensive to be practical for most developers, and over time, the preferred method of providing protection against the unauthorized use of software became a combination of two practices. One of these is to place a copyright notice identifying the owner conspicuously on the software. The other is to enter into an agreement whereby the software is not sold, but licensed, to the customer. The customer receives a license to use the software under the terms specified in the agreement but does not own the software outright, and therefore, unlike owning a car or a compact disk player, has no right to dispose of it by giving or selling it to someone else.

With the proliferation of personal computers in the 1980s, software piracy became a major issue for the software industry. During the **mainframe** computer era, access to computers and the knowledge to make use of illegally copied software were fairly limited. However, personal computers have become ubiquitous, and making a copy of any kind of file, including a software program, is simple and fast. Software presents unique problems for copyright owners because not only is it easy to duplicate, but the copy is usually as good as the original. Unlike audio or video tapes, which tend to degrade with additional copies, digital wares can be copied and copies can be made from future copies almost endlessly with no impact on the way a program functions.

The majority of software developers today continue to use a combination of copyright protection and license agreements to try to prevent unauthorized use of their products. Although many software users don't realize it, they don't actually own the software they use. The text on the outside of a package of shrink-wrapped software or text that appears when software is installed or downloaded from the **Internet** is actually an agreement which states that the customer is receiving a license to use the software subject to restrictions such as not making additional copies, except that in most cases, one copy is to be saved as a backup version. Opening the shrink-wrapped package or clicking a button to indicate acceptance binds the customer legally to the terms of the agreement.

Enforcement is extremely difficult, however. Illegal copying can readily be done in one's home or office with little risk of detection. Two organizations, the Software and Information Industry Association (SIIA; formerly known as the Software Publishers Association) and the Business Software Alliance (BSA), have undertaken the task of attempting to identify and prosecute violators on behalf of the software industry. Relying heavily on anonymous reports of suspected violations, these organizations will contact organizations under investigation and request that they submit to a voluntary audit of their software. The majority of investigations are resolved by voluntary audits and cooperative compliance. However, when warranted, these organizations will file lawsuits and obtain permission from the federal courts to conduct searches of defendants' computers to ascertain whether illegal copies of software exist.

U.S. copyright law strongly supports the rights of software developers, and copyright violations can result in substantial fines. In some countries, however, copyright protection of software is not as clearly defined; nor are other governments as committed as the U.S. government to vigorous enforcement of intellectual property law. Both the BSA and the SIIA have therefore expanded their enforcement efforts internationally and jointly produce an annual report on software piracy rates throughout the world. The report for 1998 shows that 38 percent, or more than one out of every three copies, of the business software applications loaded onto **personal computers** (PCs) worldwide were pirated. Piracy rates are highest (well above 50 percent) in Eastern Europe, the Middle East, and Latin America. Although the percentage of pirated copies is lower in North America, Western Europe, and Asia/Pacific, the installed base of PCs in these regions is so much larger that they account for by far the largest dollar loss to software developers from illegal distribution of software.

The rapid proliferation of Internet use has greatly increased the means by which software can be distributed. **Bulletin board systems**, news groups, **electronic mail**, direct and remote links, Internet auction sites, and many other methods available only on the Internet have been used to distribute both legal and illegal copies of software. However, the Internet also creates an opportunity for a technological solution to the piracy problem. With the Internet, many kinds of businesses in addition to software companies have a need for a secure, nonreplicable way to transfer digital files, such as cash equivalent transactions or digital signatures.

In April 2000, **Xerox** and **Microsoft** announced that they were creating a company to develop software that would allow the electronic distribution of copyrighted material such as software, music, videos, or documents while protecting it against unauthorized copying. Several other companies, including IBM and **AT&T**, are also investing in research to develop a reliable means of encoding digital files so that they cannot readily be duplicated. Given the difficulty of enforcing the current law, an effective technological solution that would substantially reduce the dollars lost to piracy would be a great boon to the software industry.

FURTHER READING

1999 Global Software Piracy Report: A Study Conducted by International Planning and Research Corp. for the Business Software Alliance and the Software and Information Industry Association. West Chester, Penn.: International Planning and Research Corporation, May 1999.

Keet, Ernest E. *Preventing Piracy: A Business Guide to Software Protection.* Reading, Mass.: Addison-Wesley, 1985.

Software and Information Industry Association. *SPA Anti-piracy, a Division of SIIA.* Washington, D.C.: SIIA, 2000. *http://www.siia.net/piracy/default.asp*

Tetzlaff, David. "Yo-ho-ho and a Server of Warez: Internet Software Piracy and the New Global Information Economy." Talk delivered at the World Wide Web and Contemporary Cultural Theory Conference, Drake University, Des Moines, Iowa, 7 Nov. 1998. *http://www.drake.edu/swiss/webconference/tetzlaff.html*

—*Luanne Johnson*

PGP See Pretty Good Privacy.

Plankalkül

Plankalkül (*calculus of programs*) was the first high-level programming language ever conceived. It was designed by **Konrad Zuse** (1910–95), the German inventor, between 1943 and 1945, a time when the first computers were being built in the United States, United Kingdom, and Germany. It represents one of the major contributions to the history of ideas in the computer field, although it was never implemented for any kind of machine.

Plankalkül corresponds to Zuse's mature conception of how to build a computer and how to allocate the total computing work to the **hardware** and **software** of a machine. Zuse called the first computers he constructed (the Z1, Z2, Z3, and Z4) *algebraic machines*, in contrast to *logistic machines.* The first were specially built to handle scientific computations, the latter could deal not only with scientific but also with symbolic processing. Zuse's *logistic machine* was never built, but its design called for a one-bit word memory and a processor that could compute only the basic logic operations AND, OR, and NOT. It was a sort of minimal machine. Since the memory consisted of a long chain of bits, they could be grouped in any desired form to represent numbers, characters, arrays, and so on.

Plankalkül was to be the software counterpart of the logistic machine. Complex structures could be built from elementary ones, the simplest being a single bit. Sequences of instructions could be grouped into subroutines and functions, so that the user had only to deal with a very abstract instruction set that masked the complexity of the underlying hardware. Plankalkül exploited the concept of modularity, so important today in computer science, almost in an extremist way: Several layers of software would make the hardware transparent for the programmer. The hardware itself was able to execute only the absolutely minimal instruction set.

In Plankalkül, the programmer uses variables to perform computations. The notation is such that intermediate results are labeled Z1, Z2, Z3, and so on. Input variables are labeled V1, V2, V3, and so on, and results are labeled R1, R2, R3, and so on. To describe a variable and its type, Zuse used the *row notation*:

```
  | Z
V | 1
K | 2
S | 5.0
```

These four lines define the variable Z1 (note that the index is written in the next line, the V line), with *structure* 5.o, that is, five times structure "o," which represents a single bit. The K line tells us which component is being referred to. In this case we refer to the second bit of the five-bit field Z1. Therefore, the notation is two-dimensional, although it could be compressed on a single line. In a modern programming language, we would write Z1[2]. There are no separate variable declarations; any variable can be used in any part of the program and its type is written together with the name.

The type of a variable could be selected in a very flexible way. The only primitive type was "o" (a bit). A group of n bits was denoted as n.o, a group of m n-bit numbers as $m.n$.o, and so on. Any kind of primitive data type (characters, integers, reals), as well as vectors and matrices, could be defined in this way. A data type could be abbreviated using another letter, and this letter could be used as a building block for another composite type.

Variable assignment was to be done as in modern programming languages: The new value overwrites the old value of a variable. There are several operations that are also used in ways similar to other programming languages (addition, subtraction, etc.). The addition of two variables V1 and V2 (eight bits each) can be stored in an intermediate variable Z1 using the following piece of code:

```
  |  V      +   V      ⇒   Z
V |  1          2          1
K |  1          3          1
S    5.8.0      5.8.0      5.8.0
```

In Pascal, we would just write Z1[1]:=V1[1]+V2[3]. Note that the variables V1, V2, and Z1 have the same type: an array of five numbers of eight bits. The programmer has to see to it that the assignments refer to variables of the same type, since there is no type checking.

Arrays of objects can be indexed by using an auxiliary variable. The use of the index variables is shown using a line:

```
  |  V      ┌───  V      ⇒   Z
V |  1      │     2          1
K |  ───────┘     2          1
S    5.8.o        5.8.0      8.0
```

In this example, the second component of the array V2 contains the index for the array V1. The number is copied to the first component of Z1. In Pascal we would write Z1[1]:=V1[V2[2]].

Boolean operations produce results that are single bits. The zero is interpreted as FALSE and the 1 as TRUE. Boolean results can be used in conditional instructions. Plankalkül could work with conditional instructions of the If-Then-Else type, which would be written as guarded instructions of the form A → B. If the guard A is true, the command B is executed. Blocks of instructions could be written in Plankalkül by separating each instruction with a vertical line or by writing the instructions one under the other. A block is enclosed in parentheses. A block counts later as a single instruction and can be made part of another block.

There is also an iterative operator W, which repeats the execution of a sequence of instructions until all guards in the body of the loop fail:

```
W ┌ A   →   B ┐
  │ C   →   D │
  └ E   →   F ┘
```

Here, the scope of the W covers the three guarded instructions, which form a block. The loop is repeated if any of the guards are true. Execution of the loop is terminated when the three guards A, C, and E fail within the same iteration.

The elementary Boolean and arithmetic operations, guarded commands, and the W control structure formed the basis of Plankalkül. Other control structures and commands could be built using them. There was, for example, a W1 control structure that would correspond to the FOR command in a modern programming language–that is, an iteration that is performed a certain number of times. There were also other more specialized constructions that employ quantors (there exists an x such that, for all x, etc.) but they could be expressed also using the basic elements mentioned above. Zuse never built a compiler or interpreter for Plankalkül, but it seems that he was well aware that the more complex portions of Plankalkül could be written using the basic commands.

Subroutines and functions could be written in Plankalkül. A declaration was put in front of the code to make it clear which variables were the arguments and which the results. This declaration was the *boundary summary* (*Randauszug*) of the procedure. It was also possible to give operators as arguments. A subroutine could be written, for example, that received as argument the operator "+" or the operator "×," so that the same general code could be compiled with a different operator in the body of the routine. One complication of this scheme was the absence of a clear distinction between local and global variables. Most of Zuse's draft of 1945 deals only with global variables, but he also indicates that variables in different programs can have the same name but refer to different memory localities. However, subroutines could also be used as functions: Kla(x), in an example given by Zuse, was a function that checks if a character x is an opening parenthesis and returns a Boolean value.

Although Zuse published some small papers about the Plankalkül and tried to make it known in Germany, the language never was implemented. The main obstacles were its ambitious scope, the large variety of instructions that it contained, its modular architecture, which called for incremental compilation, and the availability of dynamical structures and functionals. Also, some aspects of the semantics are not quite clear and the absence of type checking would have made it extremely difficult to debug. A practical implementation of Plankalkül would certainly require a major revision of Zuse's draft of 1945. However, Plankalkül was way ahead of its time and many of the concepts on which it was based were only rediscovered much later. In the case of Plankalkül, Konrad Zuse suffered the same fate as **Charles Babbage** (1791–1871) and the **Analytical Engine**: Babbage had the right concepts but the wrong hardware. After 1945, many more years would be needed until programming languages could achieve the level of sophistication of Plankalkül.

FURTHER READING

Zuse, Konrad. *Der Plankalkül.* Technical Report 63. Bonn, Germany: Gesellschaft für Mathematik und Datenverarbeitung, 1972.

—*Raúl Rojas*

PL/1

Programming Language 1 (PL/1) was developed by **IBM** in the early 1960s. It was first released as an application development language for the System/360 operating system in 1964. IBM promoted PL/1 as a general-purpose language—a successor and replacement for **Fortran** and **COBOL**.

PL/1 was designed to be an ideal match for structured programming, a programming paradigm based on hierarchical decomposition that was to exert great influence on programming practices throughout the 1970s and early 1980s. Each of the control flow constructs used in structure code design are represented directly by PL/1 statements: loops, conditionals, and case selection. PL/1 also supports the GOTO statement, although use of GOTO was discouraged in many PL/1 programming texts.

Because it was intended for a wide variety of programming tasks, PL/1 is an extensive language. It is block structured and supports packages, procedures, and functions. It also supports many different data types and structures: numeric types, arrays, records, character strings, bit strings, and references. Most of the PL/1 concepts were drawn from other languages: block structure and recursive subroutines from **ALGOL**, common blocks and parameter transmission from Fortran, and formatted I/O and records from COBOL. The PL/1 features are more comprehensive and flexible than those in the original languages. For example, PL/1 supports a very extensive complement of record- and text-oriented input and output facilities, with provision for Fortran-style formats and COBOL-style picture specifications. Like **APL**, also developed at IBM, PL/1 supports applying arithmetic operations to entire arrays. In this case, however, the facilities in PL/1 fall far short of those in APL.

New concepts introduced in or substantially refined by PL/1 include type-parameterized (generic) procedures, multitasking with asynchronous events, macros, and exception handling. Unlike ALGOL, which was envisioned as a framework in which functionality could be built, PL/1 was packed with features for scientific, business, and academic computing. The complexity of the language helped to drive compiler research at IBM, leading eventually to separate debug and optimizing compilers as well as numerous subset compilers.

PL/1 was first standardized by **American National Standards Institute** (ANSI) in 1976; the standard omitted several of the more ambitious language features, including multitasking. Widely used for teaching programming in the 1970s, PL/1 eventually lost that niche to **Pascal** and in the 1980s, to **C**. IBM still supports PL/1 compilers for MVS, Windows NT, and other **operating systems**.

Further Reading

Pollack, Seymour V., and Theodor D. Sterling. *A Guide to PL/1*. New York: Holt, Rinehart, Winston, 1969; 3rd ed., 1980.

Pratt, Terrence W. *Programming Languages Design and Implementation*. Englewood Cliffs, N.J.: Prentice Hall, 1975; 3rd ed., Upper Saddle River, N.J., 1996.

Sammet, Jean E. *Programming Languages: History and Fundamentals*. Englewood Cliffs, N.J.: Prentice Hall, 1969.

—*Neal Ziring*

Plug and Play

Plug and play (PnP) is a feature of many computing devices that enables users to install expansion cards and connect new **hardware** to a system without having to update the machine's configuration manually. In theory, PnP devices are recognized by the computer automatically; the user does not have to reconfigure the system. The **Macintosh** computers had PnP capabilities long before they were common in the IBM **personal computer** (PC) world. It was not until **Windows** 1995 was introduced that PC systems could use PnP devices. The driving motivation was, of course, to make the PC as easy to use as a Macintosh. However, **Apple** evangelists sometimes ridicule PnP as "Plug and Pray" because Windows sometimes fails to recognize PnP hardware as it should.

Until PnP became ubiquitous, the installation of any adapters on an IBM-compatible machine—such as network or sound cards, **modems**, or **printers**—was a complicated and error-prone issue. The interrupt request lines (IRQs) and also the input–output (I/O) address of the device (i.e., the address used by the processor to communicate with the expansion board) had to be set by hand by removing or plugging metallic jumpers on the card. It was easy to make mistakes, and even when executed properly, two different expansion cards could have an IRQ or I/O-address collision, which could be removed only with the help of expert advice.

With PnP, on the other hand, adapters can just be inserted into the PC, and every time the PC boots, it scans for new hardware and checks for compatibility. *Legacy hardware* (i.e., non-PnP hardware) is detected while booting. If such a device is found, the system configures all PnP devices around the older hardware.

After all peripherals have been located, the **operating system** finds and loads the most recent extended systems configuration data (ESCD) file. If these data match the current configuration, the system will proceed with booting. If not, the system will redefine its ESCD, using the resource information obtained when scanning for legacy and PnP devices in the initial step. IRQ and I/O addresses are then allocated to the devices automatically, the configuration is saved, and the PC continues booting.

Hot plugging is a further development in the PnP direction. New hardware can be installed without having to stop the computer, and rebooting is not necessary. This feature is especially important in the case of removable hard disks or PCMCIA cards for **laptops**, which can contain anything from more memory to a modem, a frame grabber, or a **local area network** interface.

Further Reading

Bigelow, Stephen J. *The Plug & Play Book*. New York: McGraw-Hill, 1999.

Chase, Kate. *The IRQ Book*. New York: McGraw-Hill, 1999.

Shanley, Tom. *Plug and Play System Architecture*. Reading, Mass.: Addison-Wesley, 1995.

—*Jenna L. Brinning*

Portal

A portal is a single point of access in the **Internet** that, ideally, provides a user with all the information and entertainment that he or she likes. At the beginning, what we now call portals were referred to as *search engines*. Based on simple Boolean search technology applied to **HTML** (Hypertext Markup Language) documents, the initial value proposition was simple: No one could hope to find anything in the vastness of the **World Wide Web** through conventional means (e.g., volume and directory specifications and file names), so offering a full text index of document content provided a great leap forward and a chance to take advantage of the new hyperlinking capabilities built into the Web protocols.

In the next phase of their development, *navigation sites* became the term used to describe the functions provided by Excite, Infoseek, Lycos, and **Yahoo!** While in the first period, it was assumed that search engine users could navigate around through raw associative webs of links. The rapidly expanding Web made this an increasingly unwieldy process. To address user frustration and reduce the average seek time to locate relevant information, the navigation sites added the function of categorization—filtering popular sites and documents into preconfigured groups by the meaning of their content (sports, news, finance, etc.).

In the third phase of development the term changed once again to the now familiar *portal*. At the root of all this change is the proposition that a person should have a single point of access from which to make connections for all Web information needs: news, shopping, and serendipitous browsing of available content. Web consumers have been teaching the portal sites about this need. The needs of internal knowledge workers in the use of corporate or enterprise portals is no different.

In both consumer and corporate portals there is a basic progression: Search moves on to navigation (categorization), which moves on to personalization and expanded range of function into other areas of information and commerce. The key difference between consumer and corporate portals lies in the underlying mission of the portal itself: On the Internet, the portal sites' business model is built on attracting a portion of the advertising budgets of corporations that might otherwise advertise in other media. So the purpose of the public portals is to attract large numbers of repeat visitors, to build online audiences with the inclination to buy what the portal advertisers have to sell.

Inside the organization, on the other hand, the portal takes on an entirely different character. It takes its purpose from the overall mission of the organization: to add sufficient value for its customers to create a sustainable business model. It takes its features and functionality from the mandate to operate at world-class efficiency and effectiveness in order to remain competitive. That competitiveness requires a bidirectional model that can support knowledge workers' increasingly sensitive needs for interactive information management tools.

The key differentiator for the corporate or enterprise portal in relation to the Internet portals is the ability to organize information in the absence of a single, centralized, predetermined information ontology. In simple terms, individuals share the responsibility for defining the taxonomy of business-critical information, and through their publishing and other information-sharing activities generate a rich content environment at the corporate portal level, without the need for any single person to have a comprehensive overview of all taxonomies.

This new environment creates a single point of access for the increasingly knowledge-centric patterns of today's work world. Corporate portal developers focus on a user-centric information system that can provide access to working information within one interface—not a proprietary display for the deployment of segregated applications but a graphically rich, application-independent interface that will ultimately make the contemporary two-dimensional, window-based metaphors look as obsolete as the **IBM** 3270 terminal interface looks today.

Many in the industry credit the **Macintosh** window environment for contributing a major advance in the mid-1980s by allowing users to cut and paste text and data between applications for the first time. But having 20 windows open on a desktop clearly does not function to create obvious bonds (links) between the processes that underlie the information and the users' context of need. In fact, the early Macintosh windowing advance (copied and popularized in **Windows** by **Microsoft**) actually obscured the more fundamental advance in the early Macintosh—the hypermedia development environment Hypercard, which opened the promise of information integration that is currently being fulfilled on the Web.

Today, it is not outrageous to predict that all talk of applications will soon fade away. **Word processing**, **spreadsheets**, and databases will all become part of a single integrated business environment, in which corporate portals will play a central role in navigation and delivery of personalized information tools and content. The role of proprietary systems such as Microsoft's Windows will be seen as a relic of a former, highly restrictive, and from a user viewpoint, unacceptably unproductive era. Windows is the last technology from the age of information scarcity—portals are the first technology of the age of information abundance.

FURTHER READING

Bennion, Jackie. "Go Big or Stay Home." *Wired* 6.09, Sept. 1998. *http://www.wired.com/wired/archive/6.09/bell.html*

Filo, David, Jerry Yang, with Karen Heyman, et al. *Yahoo! Unplugged: Your Discovery Guide to the Web.* Foster City, Calif.: IDG Books Worldwide, 1995.

Spector, Robert. *Amazon.com: Get Big Fast.* New York: Harper Business, 2000.

Szuprowicz, Bohdan. *Implementing Enterprise Portals: Integration Strategies for Intranet, Extranet, and Internet Resources.* Computer Technology Research Corporation, Apr. 2000.

—*Thomas M. Koulopoulos*

Postel, Jonathan

1943–98

U.S. Internet Pioneer

Jonathan B. Postel was one of the central figures guiding the development of the **Internet** from its beginnings as the **ARPANET** to its present as the most ubiquitous computer **network** in the world. He had leading roles in some of the most important organizational bodies involved, including the Internet Assigned Numbers Authority (IANA), the **Internet Society**, and the Internet Architecture Board (IAB).

Postel was one of a small group of computer scientists who created the Advanced Research Projects Agency Network (ARPANET), a precursor of the Internet. At the University of California–Los Angeles (UCLA) he worked with **Vinton Cerf** (1943–), another Internet pioneer; they had also been at high school together. Postel worked on the software that connected hosts to the first ARPANET packet switch to route network traffic, and he helped to install that switch in October 1969. This event is sometimes thought of as the birth of the Internet.

The origin of the influential Internet Assigned Numbers Authority (IANA) can be traced back to the ARPANET's beginnings in 1969, when Postel first began keeping a list of network protocol numbers on a piece of notebook paper. He was involved with UCLA's Network Management Center, conducting performance tests and analysis on ARPANET's earliest nodes. He helped to develop many of the underlying Internet protocols, including the **domain name system** (DNS), File Transfer Protocol (**FTP**), Simple Mail Transfer Protocol (SMPT), telnet for remote interact with computers, and the basic Internet Protocol (IP) itself.

As the Internet grew, IANA's role in assigning unique numbers and names for the DNS became increasingly important and of commercial significance. Postel's careful management of this aspect of the Internet while it continued to expand exponentially was one of the critical factors in the success of the Internet as a global force in computer networking. By allocating blocks of addresses, it was possible to distribute the task hierarchically in a scalable manner. Postel oversaw the formation of **Internet Corporation for Assigned Names and Numbers** (ICANN), a successor organization to run IANA's responsibilities, after much discussion among those having an interest in the future of Internet.

For almost 30 years, Postel served as the RFC Editor for the request for comments (RFC) series of technical notes, which was originated by Stephen D. Crocker in the earliest days of the ARPANET. (RFC1 dates from 7 April 1969.) Some important RFCs laid the foundation for technical standards governing the Internet's operation, although many were designed merely to stimulate discussion. Most RFCs were issued and archived online in standard **ASCII** format, which made them highly portable between different computer systems.

Postel was also a trustee of the Internet Society, which was established as a nonprofit, nongovernmental, international, professional membership organization, focusing on standards, education, and policy issues concerning the Internet. This included the Internet Architecture Board (IAB), a technical advisory group overseeing Internet architecture, standards, the RFC series, IANA, and so on.

The influence of Postel on the running of the Internet was so profound that *The Economist* magazine once dubbed him "God" of the Internet. Certainly, he was extremely influential in the continued evolution of the Internet from its inception in 1969 until his death in 1998. He was a very private person who earned his authority quietly through his competence. He is missed by his colleagues, as the many online tributes show, but Postel's legacy in the Internet will live on for some time to come.

BIOGRAPHY

Jonathan Bruce Postel. Born 6 August 1943 in Altadena, California. B.S. and M.S. degrees in engineering from the University of California, Los Angeles (UCLA), 1966 and 1968; Ph.D. in computer science from UCLA, 1974. Worked at the University of Southern California's Information Sciences Institute (ISI) as the request for comments (RFC) document editor, on the Internet Assigned Numbers Authority (IANA), on the Internet Architecture Board (IAB), as director of the Computer Networks Division at ISI, and director of IANA, 1977–98. Recipient of numerous awards, including the SIGCOMM award, 1987, and the International Telecommunication Union's silver medal, 1998. Died 16 October 1998 in Los Angeles.

SELECTED WRITINGS

Postel, Jonathan B., ed. *Request for Comments (RFC).* RFC Editor, 1969–98. *http://www.rfc-editor.org*

———. "An Informal Comparison of Three Protocols." *Computer Networks,* Vol. 3, 1979, pp. 29–34.

———. "Computer Network Interconnection." In Gerhard Ritter, ed., *Information Processing 89, Proceedings of the IFIP 11th World Computer Congress,* San Francisco, 28 Aug.–1 Sept. 1989. Amsterdam: North-Holland/IFIP, 1989, pp. 659–660.

Postel, Jonathan B., Carl A. Sunshine, and Danny Cohen. "The ARPA Internet Protocol." *Computer Networks,* Vol. 5, 1981, pp. 261–271.

FURTHER READING

Cerf, Vinton G. "I Remember IANA (Tribute, Jonathan B. Postel 1943-1998)." *Communications of the ACM,* Vol. 41, No. 12, 1998, 27–28. Also RFC2468, 17 Oct. 1998. *http://www.rfc.net/rfc2468.html*

Hafner, Katie, and Matthew Lyon. *Where Wizards Stay Up Late: The Origins of the Internet.* New York: Simon and Schuster, 1996.

Leiner, Barry M., et al. "The Past and Future History of the Internet." *Communications of the ACM,* Vol. 40, No. 2, 1997, pp. 102–108.

Moschovitis, Christos, Hilary Poole, Tami Schuyler, and Theresa Senft. *History of the Internet: A Chronology, 1843 to Present.* New York: ABC–CLIO, 1999.

—*Jonathan Bowen*

Pretty Good Privacy

Pretty good privacy (PGP) is a cryptographic **software** suite, enabling the secure exchange of data. Its name is an understatement, since it has always used advanced technologies. PGP is the most popular **encryption** program in Europe, but it has earned the ire of various security agencies in the U.S. government.

PGP is based on a technology called **public key cryptography**, which ensures both privacy and strong authentication. Privacy means that only the intended recipient can read the data sent. For this to work, the recipient must provide his or her public key to a sender. This can be done via insecure lines of communication such as the Internet, because it permits only the sender to encrypt data, not to decrypt them. Only the receiver can decrypt the data using his or her corresponding private key. In the physical world, this is analogous to an armored mailbox: Anyone can deposit mail, but only the owner can read it. Authentication, or digital signatures, securely identify the sender of data. With PGP, the sender communicates his or her public key to the recipient along with the "signed" data. Again, this can be done via insecure lines of communication. The recipient then uses PGP to compare the authentication key calculated from the encrypted data with the public authentication key. If the two do not coincide, someone must have tampered with the information.

The history of public key encryption has been rocky and involves a wide variety of people. The cryptographer Whitfield Diffie (1944–) and the electrical engineer Martin Hellman (1945–) developed the technology in 1976. The DH **algorithm**, named after the last names of the two scientists, is still a commonly used key exchange protocol. A year later, Ron Rivest, Adi Shamir, and Len Adleman discovered a more general algorithm at the Massachusetts Institute of Technology (MIT). It became known as RSA, again after the last names of the three inventors.

The National Security Agency (NSA), asked MIT and the three scientists not to publish details of the algorithm, in the interest of national security. However, preliminary copies of a paper describing the algorithm had already been distributed, and in the July 1977 edition of *Scientific American*, an article entitled "New Directions in Cryptography" was published.

Due to the controversy, preparations for the paper were rushed and MIT did not apply for a patent. In the United States, it is possible to apply for patents up to one year after publication, and in 1983, MIT was granted the patent for the algorithm. In most countries outside the United States, however, it is necessary to apply for a patent *before* publication, so the algorithm became public property in much of the rest of the world. Since the research was worthless internationally, MIT later handed its U.S. patent over to a commercial company called Public Key Partners (PKP).

In 1991 the U.S. Senate introduced Bill 266, an anticrime bill that would have required all encryption software to include a "trap door," so that the government can read all encrypted messages. Legend has it that this bill, which later failed to pass into law, prompted Philip Zimmermann to write his program PGP 1.0 using RSA encryption. From here it soon found its way to numerous electronic bulletin boards and eventually leaked outside the United States via the **Internet**.

As the software became more popular, PKP complained to Zimmermann that his software violated their patent. The resulting media attention only helped increase the popularity of the software and by the time Zimmermann agreed to stop distributing PGP, the development and distribution had become a public cause among certain factions of the Internet community. Among them was MIT, which began offering PGP 2.5, with Zimmermann's approval. In an ironic twist, PKP now threatened MIT with legal action, even though it originally received the patent from the university. MIT did not retreat, claiming the right to use the algorithm. When PKP dropped its charges, MIT began acting as official U.S. distributor of PGP from their Web page.

The first releases of PGP were text-based, with a command line interface. Versions existed for numerous operating systems, including MS-DOS, Amiga, OS/2, Atari ST, and **Unix**. In 1997, the release of PGP 5.0 with graphical interfaces for **Windows** and the **Macintosh** computers boosted the acceptance of the application dramatically. Although it is still possible to encrypt files, the current version focuses on plug-ins for many popular e-mail applications. It transparently administrates public keys once they have been inserted.

To facilitate the distribution of public keys, PGP.NET recently introduced Web-based *key servers*. Although still in their infancy, these servers contain a database of about 500,000 registered public keys and are searchable by numerous criteria, including name and e-mail address. Once the public key is found, any user can send encrypted **electronic mails** or documents to the corresponding recipient. Similarly, any digitally signed document or e-mail can be verified if the public key is available on these databases or through direct communication.

The popularity of PGP continues, and at present it is the de facto standard encryption algorithm for Internet communication. Given an appropriate key, any encrypted data can be considered secure today. As processing speed increases it will become more and more feasible to break these codes, but analysts expect that this power will not be widely available for approximately another 10 years.

FURTHER READING

Diffie, Whitfield, and Susan Landau. *Privacy on the Line: The Politics of Wiretapping and Encryption.* Cambridge, Mass.: MIT Press, 1999.

Electronic Frontier Foundation. "EFF Legal Cases: PGP & Phil Zimmermann Archive." 12 Jan. 1997. *http://www.eff.org/pub/Legal/Cases/PGP_Zimmermann*

Garfinkel, Simson. *PGP: Pretty Good Privacy.* Sebastopol, Calif.: O'Reilly, 1995.

Newton, David E. *Encyclopedia of Cryptology.* Santa Barbara, Calif.: ABC-CLIO, 1997.
Zimmermann, Philip R. *The Official PGP User's Guide.* Collingdale, Penn.: Dinae Publishing Co., 1999.

—*Thomas Schwerk*

Printers

It was once fashionable to argue that computer technology would lead to the disappearance of paper, that digital records would replace paper archives, and that offices of the future would be "paperless." But inexpensive **personal computer** printers have changed not the overall volume of printed information but the way that information is printed out. Just as the 1980s **desktop publishing** (DTP) revolution shifted document design from professional typesetters to the personal desktop, so mass duplication of information is giving way to "print on demand."

All printers, from the crudest teletype to the most sophisticated laserjet, make an image (usually with ink) on paper. Different types of printers differ in the way they transfer the ink to paper (known as the *print engine*). Impact printers (such as dot-matrix and daisywheel) press the shapes of characters onto paper through an inked ribbon; nonimpact printers (such as inkjet or laser) transfer the ink by other methods or do away with ink completely (as in thermal printers that burn an image onto heat-sensitive paper). The method of ink transfer affects both the cost and speed of the printer and the cost and quality of the print.

Even the earliest computers had their printers. The nineteenth-century calculating engines of **Charles Babbage** (1791–1871) and George Scheutz were designed to produce printed output, and William Burroughs (1855–98; founder of the **Burroughs** corporation) had patented a printing calculator by 1888. Although the 1946 **ENIAC** produced its output on punched cards (the same method by which it took in its input), the 1948 BINAC computer could print its output using an electromagnetically controlled typewriter. The grandfather of the modern personal printer was more obviously typewriter than printing press. Developed early in the twentieth century by Charles

The first xerographic laser printer, from the Xerox Corporation, circa 1977. (Courtesy of Xerox Corporation)

and Howard Krum, the Teletypewriter (also known as a TTY or Teletype terminal) was a method of sending and receiving information by telegraph that later became famous as the chattering teleprinter and an input–output device for mainframes and minicomputers. Teletypes printed at around 30 to 50 words per minute (later models reached 300 words per minute) using a typewheel that pressed an inked ribbon onto a continuous roll of paper.

From the 1950s onward, mainframe computers used line printers that could print at speeds of around 600 lines per minute. Unlike typewriters, dot-matrix printers, and inkjet printers, which build up pages character by character and line by line with a printhead that moves back and forth (bidirectionally), line printers print an entire line at once. Multiple print hammers are lined up with each of the 80 or more columns in the current line. A rotating band of type (called a *chain* or *train*) circulates past the stationary hammers at speeds of around 7.5 feet (2.3 meters) per second. Each hammer is activated as the appropriate piece of metal type in the band lines up with it, so the line is printed not from left to right or right to left, but randomly as the chain spins around. To increase print speed, the chains of type may contain several repetitions of the basic character set arranged according to those letters that occur most frequently. Today's line printers can print several thousand lines per minute.

In the 1970s, the invention of the **microcomputer** and the explosive growth in the world's computer population prompted the development of inexpensive desktop printers. The first mainframe dot-matrix (or wire-matrix) printer was sold by **IBM** in 1957, but the low-cost personal dot-matrix printer was pioneered by the U.S. company Centronics and the Japanese company Seiko/Epson only in the 1970s. Seiko, which came to dominate the market, designed its first electronic printer (E.P.) as part of a race timer for the 1964 Tokyo Olympics. When it launched the printer commercially, it called the machine "son of E.P." or "E.P. son," and the Epson brand was born.

Using a matrix (array) of metal pins pushed against an inked ribbon in the shape of different characters, dot-matrix printers print one complete character at a time. More sophisticated models have more pins and can produce both better-quality print and high-resolution (finely detailed) graphic images. Line-matrix printers work in a slightly different way, printing an entire line of characters at once with multiple passes of the printhead. In other words, a line-matrix printer builds up a page line by line, whereas a dot-matrix printer builds up a page character by character.

Dot-matrix printers were cheap, versatile, and fast (the industry-standard Epson MX-80, launched in 1980, could print around 80 characters per second), but they were also noisy and produced poor-quality output. In the late 1970s and early 1980s, better-quality print meant using a daisywheel printer in which the characters were formed by pressing metal or plastic keys, radiating out from a wheel like the petals of a daisy, against an inked ribbon. The time taken to rotate the daisywheel makes this type of printer exceptionally slow (10 characters per second or slower) and although print quality is far superior to that produced by dot-matrix printers, daisywheels cannot reproduce graphics.

Inexpensive laser printers were born of the need to combine the speed of dot-matrix printers with the quality of electric typewriters and daisywheels. Perhaps surprisingly, they predate the personal computer by more than a decade. **Xerox** first began developing laser printers in 1969, when engineer Gary Starkweather (1938–) modified the xerography technique the company had exploited so successfully in its photocopying machines. In a laser printer, a laser beam writes an image of a page line by line onto a rotating drum using a rapidly rotating mirror. The drum becomes electrostatically charged in a way that corresponds to the pattern of light and dark in the image. As the drum rotates, the charged areas of its surface pick up powdered ink called toner and deposit it on a sheet of paper moving underneath. Finally, heat and pressure seal the toner onto the paper.

Capable of printing at a resolution of 500 dots per inch (dpi; comparable with today's average resolution of 600 dpi) and fast enough to produce one or two pages per second (compared to today's average of one page every few seconds), the original Xerox laser printer, the Dover, was revolutionary. By 1977, Xerox was selling a 120-page-per-minute laser printer for around U.S.$350,000. IBM's launch of its 3800 range of laser printers in 1976 had convinced Xerox that "Big Blue" represented its major commercial threat. But the real threat came in 1979 when the Japanese company Canon launched a desktop printer called the LBP-10, based on a compact semiconductor laser. By 1984, using Canon's technology, **Hewlett-Packard** had launched its first LaserJet printer for U.S.$3495—less than 1 percent the cost of Xerox's 1977 machine—and went on to sell 10 million LaserJets in less than a decade. In 1985, **Apple Computer** launched a U.S.$7000 machine called the LaserWriter to partner its new **Macintosh** computer. Featuring PostScript, a kind of programming language that revolutionized the way that computers could "describe" pages precisely to their printers, it brought about the desktop publishing revolution.

Through much of the 1980s and 1990s, laser printers remained beyond the reach of home computer users. Business users could justify their purchase by sharing one laser printer between many users, but home users needed a more affordable technology: inkjet. The basic principle of inkjet printing is generally credited to Canon. In 1977, one of its researchers reputedly left a soldering iron near a syringe full of ink, then watched as an air bubble formed in the syringe, making ink shoot out in a jet. In an inkjet printer, a moving printhead sprays a pattern of ink onto the paper using either heat (thermal inkjets), pressure-sensitive crystals (piezoelectric inkjets), or the formation of bubbles inside the ink nozzles (BubbleJets—Canon's proprietary name for its technology). Inkjets combine the affordability of dot-matrix printers with quality approaching that of a laser printer, but they are typically much slower than laser printers, may need special glossy paper to produce good-quality printouts, and are more costly per page to run.

Dot-matrix, laser, and inkjet printers differ substantially in their basic method of printing, yet even very different kinds of printers have much in common. Most printers, for example, have different print modes. Some dot-matrix printers have a fast "Draft" mode and a much slower "Near letter quality (NLQ)" mode; inkjets have similar options to save ink and increase speed. Printers also have a feed mechanism for transferring paper through the machine. Once, virtually all computer printers used tractor feed, a method of pulling paper through a printer using sprocket holes punched down each side. Some printers could switch between tractor feed and friction feed, a less precise method that fed the paper through the machine by pressing it between rubber rollers, as in a typewriter. The most sophisticated printers can print on both sides of the paper, a technique known as *duplex*.

One of the latest developments in printing technology is the invention by MIT and IBM researchers of *electronic ink* (e-ink), billions of microscopic ink capsules embedded in ordinary paper that can turn white or black with an applied voltage. Electronic ink pages combine the sharpness of a printed page with the rapid refreshing of a computer monitor and can switch instantly from displaying a full-page newspaper to a double-page spread from a book. Although systems such as this may render certain types of printing obsolete in future, industry analysts see no immediate decline in traditional printing. In the medium term, Internet distribution of information is forecast to increase personal computer printing and reduce large-volume printing and photocopying.

FURTHER READING

Cost, Frank. *Pocket Guide to Digital Printing.* Albany, N.Y.: Delmar, 1996.

Cringely, Robert X. *Accidental Empires: How the Boys of Silicon Valley Make Their Millions, Battle Foreign Competition, and Still Can't Get a Date.* New York: Harper Business, 1996.

Durbeck, Robert C., and Sol Sherr, eds. *Output Hardcopy Devices.* Boston: Academic Press, 1988.

Vizard, Frank. "Electric Tales." *Popular Science*, June 1997, pp. 97.

Zable, J. L., and H. C. Lee. "An Overview of Impact Printing." *IBM Journal of Research and Development*, Vol. 41, No. 6, 1997, pp. 651.

—*Chris Woodford*

Privacy, Online

Online privacy is concerned with preventing the exposure of a person's (or organization's) online activities without the person's permission. Privacy is properly specified relative to one or more "adversaries" from whom the person wishes this information to be hidden, and who may passively observe or actively manipulate a system to obtain information about the person's activities. Protecting online privacy requires hiding either the activities being performed or the identity of the person performing them. When a system protects privacy by hiding the identity of the person performing the actions, it is said to provide *anonymity*.

It is useful to contrast privacy with *confidentiality*, which usually refers to preventing disclosure of content (e.g., files or messages) to an adversary; access controls and **encryption** can be useful for this purpose. These technologies tend to be less applicable to protecting online privacy, where exposure of activities (as opposed to content) is to be prevented. For example, encrypting an **electronic mail** message can effectively hide the content of that message from a network eavesdropper, but it does not hide the fact that the sender is communicating with the receiver. In particular, the recipient address cannot be sent encrypted, since then the network would not know to whom to deliver the message.

Numerous technical means have been proposed for protecting online privacy in a variety of situations. Examples include location privacy, which involves hiding the location and movements of a user from other users or certain network elements in networks supporting mobile communication; sender (or receiver) anonymity, which entails hiding the identity of the intended sender or recipient of a message from a network eavesdropper; purchase anonymity, which prevents online merchants or banks from identifying the customer associated with an online purchase, or from linking multiple payments to the same (unknown) customer; and private information retrieval, which enables a client to retrieve data from a server without revealing what it retrieved.

Historically, online privacy was primarily a military concern, since exposure of online activities—especially communication patterns between military headquarters and outposts—could suggest future troop movements or attack plans. More recently, online privacy has received increasing attention as more persons perform daily activities on the **Internet** and **World Wide Web**. Although few Internet technologies whose primary purpose is privacy protection have been deployed at the time of this writing, some do exist. One is the Anonymizer (*http://www.anonymizer.com*), a Web server that enables persons to access other Web servers anonymously.

FURTHER READING

Cranor, L. F., ed. "Internet Privacy." Special section in *Communications of the ACM*, Vol. 42, No. 2, Feb. 1999, pp. 29–67.

Kahn, D. *The Codebreakers.* New York: Simon and Schuster, 1996.

—*Michael Reiter*

Probabilistic Algorithms

A probabilistic algorithm is an **algorithm** whose result and/or the way the result is obtained depends on chance. These algorithms are also sometimes called *randomized* or *stochastic algorithms.* Methods applying chance to find a solution to a problem were originally named Monte Carlo techniques. This name was first used for numerical computations of the atomic bomb during World War II.

In some applications the use of probabilistic algorithms is natural—for example, simulating the behavior of some existing or planned system over time. In this case the result is stochastic by nature. *Stochastic* means that the outcome in the simplest case is not always a specific number but can be any number in some interval; the time it takes to drive from point *A* to point *B* is stochastic because it varies from one attempt to another. To apply a probabilistic algorithm to simulate driving we must describe driving in detail, including waiting times at crossings. In such a description, chance is implemented by using *random numbers*, numbers that are sampled from some given distribution over a given interval. By applying the algorithm (simulating) many times it is possible to estimate, for instance, the average driving time. The longer we simulate, the better this estimate will be.

In other applications the solution to the problem is deterministic, but the problem can be transformed so that it can be solved by applying a probabilistic algorithm (e.g., numerical integration, optimization). For these numerical applications the result obtained is always an approximation, but its expected precision improves with the number of experiments N. The error decreases typically as the inverse of the square root of N, but by using sophisticated variance reducing techniques, much faster convergence is sometimes achievable. Contrary to deterministic algorithms, the error decrease of probabilistic algorithms is independent of the dimensionality of the problem.

Probably the earliest probabilistic procedure used to estimate a fixed number was described by Georges Buffon (1707–88) in 1777. This old and famous experiment for estimating the number pi = 3.141592... is known as *Buffon's needle experiment*. Buffon described his experiment in this way: "I assume that in a room, the floor of which is merely divided by parallel lines, a stick is thrown upwards and one of the players bets that the stick will not intersect any of the parallel lines on the floor, whereas on the contrary the other one bets that the stick will intersect some one of these lines; it is required to find the chances of the two players. It is possible to play this game with a sewing needle or a hairpin."

Given the length L of the stick and the distance d between the parallel lines, it can be shown that the probability P that the stick hits one of the parallel lines is $2L/\pi$. Solving for π, we find $\pi = 2L/P$. Throwing the stick N times and recording n hits, P can be estimated as n/N, so that an estimate of π is $2LN/n$. The table below gives the results for some values of N in one simulation experiment on a computer:

N	Estimate of π
10	4.0
100	3.2
1,000	3.16
10,000	3.142

There are also applications where only an exact result is acceptable (e.g., sorting and searching) and where the introduction of randomness influences only the ease and efficiency of finding the solution. In some cases it is possible to transform a deterministic algorithm into a probabilistic one by replacing a deterministic choice by a random one. By this the performance of the algorithm will be independent of the data so that worst-case performance is avoided.

Some decision problems (problems for which the answer to an instance is *yes* or *no*, e.g., primality testing, string equality testing) could easily be solved by exhaustive search. However, exhaustive search is often not feasible, and then probabilistic algorithms can be applied, giving a result that is correct with some probability just less than 1. The idea behind the probabilistic algorithms used here is the following: If one wants to assess that "x is A" (e.g., "x is a prime number"), the problem is posed in a form that defines a set W containing a rather large proportion p of witnesses that in the case "x is not A" will say *No*. If we choose n elements at random from W without finding a witness, the probability q of "x is not A" is the number $(1 - p)$ to the nth power. This probability can be made arbitrarily small by increasing the number of experiments. This algorithm, that is always correct if the answer is NO but may err if answering YES, is said to have one-sided error.

One incentive for using probabilistic algorithms is that their application does not normally require sophisticated mathematical knowledge. Further, programming is often rather trivial, which means that an acceptable approximation can be obtained quickly. One can say that the use of probabilistic algorithms sometimes allows us to compensate for theoretical knowledge and analytical work by making extensive simple machine computations. In other cases, existing probabilistic algorithms are the simplest and even the most efficient available.

FURTHER READING

Brassard, Gilles, and Paul Bratley. *Algorithmics: Theory and Practice*. Englewood Cliffs, N.J.: Prentice Hall, 1988.

Halton, John H. "A Retrospective and Prospective Survey of the Monte Carlo Method." *SIAM Review*, 12 Jan. 1970, pp. 1–63.

Harel, David. *Algorithmics: The Spirit of Computing*. Reading, Mass.: Addison-Wesley, 1987; 2nd ed., 1992.

Motwani, Rajeev, and Prabhakar Raghavan. *Randomized Algorithms*. Cambridge and New York: Cambridge University Press, 1995.

—*Aimo Törn*

Prodigy

Prodigy was one of the first online services in the United States. Started in 1984, it introduced consumers to **electronic mail** and online advertising long before the **Internet** became a household name. The company was one of the top three online services, together with **America Online** (AOL) and **CompuServe** but was in continual decline until 1996, when it was down to 193,000 subscribers. After being acquired by a telecommunications group, Prodigy diversified into the bilingual market, became an aggressive Internet service provider, and by 1999 boasted 1.2 million subscribers in the United States.

The story of Prodigy illustrates the way that the Internet (specifically, the **World Wide Web**) changed the online services market. The company was founded by **IBM** and Sears. The intention was that IBM would take care of the network and Sears would look after the commercial aspects of the venture. Prodigy offered services to their subscribers in a proprietary environment. Users dialed server computers and needed a different program for each provider; Prodigy users could not interact with CompuServe users, for example. Prodigy's browser was even incompatible with the **Windows** operating system at first. In the online services market there were high barriers to entry for newcomers, since a national online service based on local telephone calls required offices and equipment in hundreds of major cities across the United States.

When the Internet became accessible for the home user and the first Web browsers became available, this "closed world" philosophy came into conflict with user needs. Small startups, called **Internet service providers** (ISPs), could supply more information than Prodigy and AOL simply by giving access to the Web. Moreover, these ISPs could start a national service immediately without having to install branches in many cities. Traditional online services were slow to react to all these changes, and a continuous drain of qualified personnel increased Prodigy's woes.

The turnaround came in the late 1990s, when Prodigy fully embraced the Web and started strategic alliances with companies such as Baby Bell SBC Communications, which added 650,000 customers to Prodigy's own base. Since its main shareholders are the Mexican telecommunications holding company Carso Global and Teléfonos de México, Prodigy started a bilingual online service that is popular in the United States and Latin America. The company was back in good shape in 1997, when it went public on **Nasdaq**, raising U.S.$1.68 billion. In March 2000 Prodigy reached an agreement with **Microsoft** to make the Microsoft Network the default page for its 6 million Mexican subscribers.

Prodigy had revenues of U.S.$65 million and net losses of U.S.$35 million in the first quarter of 2000. The losses were due mainly to a string of acquisitions of online service providers during 1999.

FURTHER READING

Peterson, Thane. "Prodigy: A Bath for IBM and Sears." *Business Week*, 20 May 1996.

Swisher, Kara. *AOL.COM: How Steve Case Beat Bill Gates, Nailed the Netheads, and Made Millions in the War for the Web.* New York: Times Business, 1999.

—*Frank Darius*

Productivity Paradox

The 1950s and 1960s were a golden era for the world's developed economies, particularly that of the United States. Productivity increased year by year at 3 percent and higher, and inflation remained low. Then something happened. From the early 1970s right through to the mid-1990s, U.S. productivity fell dramatically to around 1 percent per annum. Similar descents have been seen in Europe and Japan. The dramatic decrease in productivity coincided with substantial investments in computer technology, something that should theoretically improve productivity. This is the phenomenon called the productivity paradox.

Productivity is an economic concept. Put simply, it is the amount of output produced per unit of input. The definition and measurement of inputs and outputs, however, is not straightforward. Although there are often obvious outputs such as the number of products produced, a good measure of productivity should also try to measure more intangible aspects, such as quality, service, adaptability, and so on. The number of employee hours and equipment needed are simple, measurable inputs used by a business. However, to really measure productivity, factors such as worker training and goodwill between the organization and its customers and between its suppliers also need to be considered.

Business needs to be productive to succeed, and much management thought is put into how the value of an organization's outputs can be increased without using more resources. Technology has always been a tool that businesses have turned to in an attempt to enhance their productivity. Author Thomas Landauer (1958–) uses the example of the extraordinary gains seen in the Industrial Revolution. Prior to the introduction of cotton processing technology, it could take a skilled worker 50,000 hours to produce 100 pounds of thread. Cotton processing inventions between 1868 and 1879 reduced this lifetime of work to a mere 300 hours.

In contrast, many economists, including Robert Solow (1924–) and Steven Roach, argue that computer technology has had minimal positive economic impact. A distinction is usually made between phase 1 and phase 2 applications. Phase 1 computerization is the application of computing to low-level processes such as chemical and manufacturing processes. Phase 2 computerization is the use of computers to aid information workers. Typical phase 2 systems are management information systems, spreadsheets, and other office automations. Some impressive productivity gains could be seen in phase 1 applications, such as the use of computing to automate production completely. However, Roach carried out a study which suggested that despite the widespread introduction of phase 2 computing tools, their impact was very disappointing, particularly in service industries (banking, insurance, health care, etc.).

An intense debate has been going on since the late-1980s in an attempt to understand why computers seem to be so ineffective economically. Several economists have argued that the analyses of productivity have been so flawed as to bias the case against computers. For example, some have pointed to the lack of sophistication in the measurement of inputs and outputs. They argue that to get a true picture, factors such as customer service and product quality need to be considered, instead of simply counting the products. Other arguments include the need for radical organizational changes to accompany computerization: Businesses need to organize so they can work smarter, not just harder.

In his 1993 book *The Trouble with Computers,* Landauer argued that the real problem is that computer systems are difficult to use. Instead of helping users to be more efficient and effective, they frustrate, delay, irritate, and confuse. Similar arguments and evidence have been put forward by many researchers in the computing science field of **human–computer interaction**. Systems ranging from the common videocassette recorder through to airplane cockpit controls have been shown to have serious "human factor" problems. Landauer and many others argue that for computing technology to have a more positive economic impact, the users must be central to the design process; their capabilities, limitations, and preferences must be taken into account.

At the beginning of the third millennium, most analysts have agreed that computers do have great potential to benefit businesses and economies in significant ways. A 1999 paper by Daniel E. Sichel of the U.S. Federal Reserve argued that significant productivity gains had been made in the previous three years. The revolution in communications and relationships ushered in by the **Internet** and the **World Wide Web** is seen by many to be the key transforming economic agent of the future. The productivity paradox is expected to pass into history.

FURTHER READING

Brynjolfsson, Erik, and Lorin M. Hitt. "Beyond the Productivity Paradox." *Communications of the ACM*, Vol. 41, No. 8, Aug. 1998, pp. 49–55.

Landauer, Thomas K. *The Trouble with Computers.* Cambridge, Mass.: MIT Press, 1993.

Lucas, Henry C. *Information Technology and the Productivity Paradox.* New York: Oxford University Press, 1999.

Roach, Steven. "America's Technology Dilemma: A Profile of the Information Economy." Memorandum. New York: Morgan Stanley, 1987.

Sichel, Daniel E. "Computers and Aggregate Economic Growth: An Update." *Business Economics,* Vol. 34, No. 2, Apr. 1999, pp. 18–24.

Willcocks, Leslie P. *Beyond the Productivity Paradox.* New York: Wiley, 1999.

—*Matt Jones*

Program

A program is a list of instructions for a computer written in a special language, called a *programming language*. Programs constitute the **software** that runs on the hardware of a concrete system. Usually, an **operating system** (OS) coordinates execution of the user's programs and the user **interface**.

With the invention of the computer during World War II, a new occupation was created: the professional programmer, whose exclusive assignment is to write software for computers. The first programmers were the computer developers themselves, but soon other persons were specializing in this activity. *Systems programmers* code operating systems and utilities; they are located in the higher levels of the hierarchy. *Application programmers* code individual applications. In 1998, there were 650,000 persons in the United States whose job description fitted the definition of programmer. Almost 60 percent of them had a graduate degree of some kind, and their median annual earnings were U.S.$50,000. It is expected that the number of programmers will continue growing faster than the average for other professions until at least 2008.

Programs have become increasingly complex. In the past, computers were limited in resources, and programmers had to use all their skills to make the software fit into the available memory. One memorable example is the system code written by Eiiti Wada (1931–), one of the first Japanese programmers, for the **Parametron Computer 1** (PC-1). The program consisted of instructions, some of which were also data for a conversion table used by the program itself. Wada managed to fit two things—the code and a table—into the same memory area. The reputation of early programmers was enhanced by such feats.

Modern programs are not as small and lean as they once were. When **Netscape** decided to publish the code for the Netscape **browser** in 1998, the final packet, named Mozilla, consisted of 1.5 million code lines. The code for the **Windows** operating system, now well above 10 million lines, doubles every 866 days, which corresponds to an annual growth rate of 33.9 percent. Nathan Myhrvold (1969–), chief technology officer at **Microsoft**, calls this Nathan's first law, which states that, like a gas, software expands until it fills its container (i.e., the computer's memory). But Windows growth is small compared to the explosion of Internet browser code, which doubles every 212 days. The most complex machines built by humans today are not physical but virtual machines—that is, programs.

A program is normally broken into statements that are executed sequentially, but this depends on the kind of programming language. Imperative programming languages operate with the notion of variables and variable states. The state of a variable is what we store into it (i.e., a number, a character, a reference). Variables can be overwritten and the programmer needs to keep track mentally of the program state. An alternative, much favored later by **John Backus** (1924–), the creator of **Fortran**, is functional programming in which variables cannot be overwritten. They behave like mathematical variables and all computations are done by calling functions. Functional programs have a definite mathematical flavor. They are called *declarative* because the program itself looks like a high-level specification of the task at hand. Logical programs such as those written in **Prolog** are also declarative, but the strategy is another one. Here the programmer does not specify the exact sequence of function applications but leaves the computer to work out the details. The entire program is like a logical puzzle that is solved by applying logical inference steps. Finally, programs can be also written in **object-oriented** languages. Object orientation tries to encapsulate the definition of objects and procedures, called *methods*, into *classes*, which can grow and become specialized. This makes possible the reuse of software modules without as many problems as in the case of unstructured languages.

How can the productivity of programmers be measured? Their output depends to a great extent on the kind of programming language used. Functional programs are typically smaller but more expressive and can substitute hundreds of lines of code written in imperative languages. Some surveys try to track the productivity of programmers in terms of thousands of lines of code, per one person in one year (KLOCS/person-year). According to the Meta Group, which surveyed 1100 companies, programmers averaged 10.9

KLOCS/person-year in 1997. The number of bugs found per 1000 lines of code was 1.69 in the United States. Taken at face value, this number would imply that there are thousands of still undiscovered bugs in the latest release of your favorite operating system, be it Windows or **Macintosh**. How productivity and even the size of software should be measured effectively has developed into the field of software metrics, still in its infancy and halfway between an art and a science. (See **Software, Cost of** for more.)

Programmers were not long ago the high priests of the computer world. Many of them developed a special programmer ethos of sharing code that preceded the commercialization of software. The **open-source** movement, spurred by programmer activists such as **Richard Stallman** (1953–) at the Massachusetts Institute of Technology, has at its root this tradition of sharing. Code was passed from one generation of programmers to another, which debugged the code and developed it still further. Many of the traditions and folklore of this period were collected through the **ARPANET** and later through the Internet and have been collected in the **New Hacker's Dictionary**. Real programmers, as the dictionary proclaims, think that "if it was hard to write, it should be hard to understand." According to the dictionary, programs are "a magic spell cast over a computer, allowing it to turn one's input into error messages."

Is programming a science or an art? The discussion on this point has been long and is still unresolved. Tellingly, in 1968, **Donald Knuth** (1938–) titled his magnum opus ***The Art of Computer Programming*** rather than *The Science of Programming*. On the other hand, **Edsger Dijkstra** (1930–) called his 1976 book *A Discipline of Programming*, and **Niklaus Wirth** (1934–) had been more blatant one year earlier with his book *Algorithms + Data Structures = Programs*. Apart from the fact that this is one of the few books to include a formula in the title, the text is very explicit that every program must define abstract structures as containers for the data and deal with the algorithms or methods to transform them. Whereas finding the appropriate data structures is a real art, analyzing the algorithms is hard science. The discipline of programming moves between these two extremes: the mathematical formalism embodied in algorithms, and the craftmanship that goes into finding the best data structure for a given task.

What does the future hold for the programming discipline? Some researchers think that visual programming is easier to grasp and could increase the productivity of programmers. In visual programming, operations and data structures are defined by clicking on objects displayed on the screen, moving them around or connecting them with arrows. Although more intuitive, this approach is unfeasible for large software projects, and so far it seems that trained programmers can deal more easily with a verbal representation of instructions than with a visual one.

A radically different approach is genetic (or evolutionary) programming, in which a computer lets an entire population of programs evolve and recombine. These programs compete for survival: Only the fittest—the better ones—survive in the next generation. Traditional, sequential programs cannot be recombined (intermixed); therefore, this technique requires a special coding strategy to let programs propagate their superior substructures to daughter programs. Some good random-number generators have been produced in this way, but apart from toy problems that have been cracked in this fashion, so far no realistic tasks have been solved.

However, genetic programming makes us realize that the first programs were not written by humans. The genetic code, embodied in our DNA, has all the characteristics of a machine code. The four letters A, G, T, C, one for each nucleotide, constitute the alphabet in which our body plan is written. A set of three letters represents an amino acid. The DNA double helix is read sequentially by a biological machinery that reads the code and assembles complete proteins, which in turn help to read other parts of the code. Biologists already talk about the *genetic program* contained in genes and the similarity is authentic. The cell and its gene activation machinery resemble small computers executing a program.

Up to now, nature has proven to be a better programmer than humans. It is still a long way until programs will be written in a form that is simple and error free. For a long time, programs will still be "bloody instructions which, being taught, return to plague their inventor" (*Macbeth*, Act 1, Scene 7).

FURTHER READING

Dijkstra, Edsger. *A Discipline of Programming*. Englewood Cliffs, N.J.: Prentice Hall, 1976.

Hayes, Brian. "The Invention of the Genetic Code." *American Scientist*, Vol. 86, No. 1, 1998.

Knuth, Donald E. *The Art of Computer Programming*. Reading, Mass.: Addison-Wesley, 1968; 3rd ed., 1997.

Wirth, Niklaus. *Algorithms + Data Structures = Programs*. Englewood Cliffs, N.J.: Prentice Hall, 1975.

—*Margarita Esponda*

Project MAC

Project MAC was the first of a number of Centers of Excellence supported by the Advanced Research Projects Agency (**ARPA**) under the leadership of **J. C. R. Licklider** (1915–90). Under the direction of Robert Fano (1917–), the goal of Project MAC was to explore the development of a new form of computing: interactive computing and online collaboration.

When Licklider joined ARPA in November 1962, he planned to support the creation of Centers of Excellence at selected U.S. universities. Licklider's seminal paper, "Man–Computer Symbiosis," published in 1960, outlined the need to explore the relationship between the human and the computer and proposed a technical program to create new forms of human–computer interaction.

Robert Fano (1917–), a senior professor at the Massachusetts Institute of Technology (MIT), and a colleague of Licklider's, formulated the proposal for the first such Center of Excellence. Project MAC was to promote "machine-aided cognition" through the use of "multiple-access computers." The project started with a six-week summer study with 57 participants from university, government, and industry. This established a community of researchers with a common interest in the development of **time-sharing** and online interactive computing. The goal of developing an online research community was achieved within the first six months of the project. The MAC system soon included graphical input–output capability. Access was gained through telex and TWX telegraph networks, making possible tests and demonstrations of the online community not only in the Boston area but also on the west coast and at a few European locations.

The interdisciplinary Project MAC program allowed users from a number of different fields to explore the system and to discover how it could be helpful in their research. The system also encouraged users to contribute to the developing online community the programs they wrote and the techniques they discovered. Many applications, including e-mail, text processing, editing, and the conception of creating tools for users, were pioneered by the Project MAC community. The concept of a computer time-sharing system as a public utility also became apparent. Users came to rely on the system and its proper functioning and were accordingly upset when it was not available.

By the summer of 1964, Project MAC researchers began to work on **Multics**, a new computer and operating system to replace the compatible time-sharing system (CTSS) in use at the time. Multics soon became a joint collaboration between MIT, **Bell Labs**, and General Electric. By October 1969, the operation of Multics was turned over to the MIT computing center. Because the original goal of Project MAC had been reached—time-sharing and interactive computing were developed successfully and spread around the world—the project was no longer a priority research project.

By the 1970s the character of Project MAC changed from a multidisciplinary research effort to a computer science–oriented laboratory. The name was then also changed, first to MAC Laboratory and then in 1975 to Laboratory for Computer Science.

PROJECT MAC DIRECTORS

Robert Fano	1963–1968
J. C. R. Licklider	1968–1971
Edward Fredkin	1971–1974
Michael L. Dertouzos	1974–1975*

** Michael L. Dertouzos has continued as the director of the Laboratory for Computer Science.*

FURTHER READING

Fano, Robert. "Project MAC." In Jack Belzer, Albert G. Holzman, and Allen Kent, eds., *Encyclopedia of Computer Science and Technology*, Vol. 12. New York: Dekker, 1975, pp. 339–360.

Hauben, Michael, and Ronda Hauben. *Netizens: On the History and Impact of Usenet and the Internet.* Los Alamitos, Calif.: IEEE Computer Society Press, 1997.

Licklider, J. C. R. "Man-Computer Symbiosis." *IRE Transactions on Human Factors in Electronics*, Vol. HFE-1, Mar. 1960, pp. 4–11.

—*Ronda Hauben*

Prolog

Prolog is a programming language that arose from research done by Alain Colmerauer (1941–) in France and Robert Kowalski (1941–) at Edinburgh University in the early 1970s. The name *Prolog* (*programmation en logique*) was coined in 1972 by Phillipe Roussel at the University of Marseilles.

Whereas languages such as **Fortran** and **Pascal** are very well suited for numeric processing, they are cumbersome for programs that deal with symbols, such as those used in natural language processing. The language LISP, designed by **John McCarthy** (1927–) in 1959, was one of the first symbol-oriented languages and remains widely used today. Prolog represents another computational paradigm that has its roots in formal logic.

In Prolog the user does not tell the program directly how to solve a task, but gives it a formal declarative description. The user defines a set of facts that are taken to be true, as if they were axioms. Then he or she can define a set of rules that describe how the facts can be used to answer queries. For example, the fact that Adam is the father of Abel would be coded in Prolog simply as: "father(adam,abel)"; note that lowercase letters are used, because words beginning with uppercase letters are considered variables in Prolog. A rule such as "X is the grandfather of Y, if X is the father of Z and Z is parent of Y" can be written in Prolog as "grandfather(X,Y) :- father(X,Z), parent(Z,Y)". After having given this rule to the system, the user can ask queries about the persons in the set of facts and Prolog will give the correct answer. Prolog implements logical inference using the set of rules and facts defined by the user.

Prolog employs two principal mechanisms: unification and resolution. *Unification* means that every time a query is given to the system, Prolog looks for a matching rule or fact in its database. Only rules or facts that match the input (that can include variables) are considered for further processing. *Resolution* is a mechanism for logical inference that is more powerful than inference rules such as modus ponens. (*Modus ponens* means that if we know that A is true, and that the rule "A implies B" is also true, we can immediately deduce that B is true.) Resolution is more general and includes modus ponens as a special case as well as other inference rules used by human beings. Resolution is easier for the computer to use since it is a single inference rule and can be applied mechanically. If a rule does not match, the system backtracks and looks for another matching rule and another way to prove the query.

Prolog was the main language adopted by the Japanese scientists in the framework of the 10-year Fifth Generation Computer Program started in the early 1980s. The stated objective of the program was building machines capable of executing millions of logical inferences per second. Some Prolog machines were actually built in Japan, the United States, and Europe, but they were never an alternative to conventional computer technology. Prolog lost some ground after the end of the Fifth Generation initiative, but it is still a popular language for artificial intelligence applications.

FURTHER READING

Clocksin, W. F., and C. S. Mellish. *Programming in Prolog*, Berlin and New York: Springer-Verlag, 1981; 4th ed., 1994.

Feigenbaum, Edward A., and Pamela McCorduck. *The Fifth Generation: Artificial Intelligence and Japan's Computer Challenge to the World.* Reading, Mass.: Addison-Wesley, 1983.

Kowalski, Robert. *Logic for Problem Solving.* New York: Elsevier North Holland, 1979.

Sterling, Leon, and Ehud Shapiro. *Art of Prolog.* Cambridge, Mass.: MIT Press, 1994.

—*Raúl Rojas*

Protocol

A protocol is an agreement between two parties that allows messages to be exchanged following a standard procedure. In a computer network the agreement specifies how messages, or *protocol data units* (PDUs), are formatted and defines the procedures required to deliver these PDUs. For example, an **Ethernet** PDU consists of five bitfields: destination address, source address, control fields, payload, and frame check. The *addresses*, *control fields*, and *frame check* are necessary protocol overhead that allow the *payload* (the actual data) to be delivered correctly. Continuing the example, the procedure to transmit a protocol data unit is, in outline:

1. If the Ethernet medium is busy, wait a random time, then try again.
2. If the medium is quiet, start sending and check for a collision.
3. If there is a collision, stop sending, wait a random time, then try again.

The associated procedure to receive an Ethernet PDU is, also in outline:

1. If the medium becomes busy, receive the message (up to a maximum length).
2. If the message is too short, discard it (there was probably a collision).
3. If the *frame check* indicates a corrupted PDU, discard it.
4. If the *destination address* matches the receiver's medium access control (MAC) address list, accept the PDU; otherwise, discard it.

Practical networks use a *protocol stack* (i.e., several protocols linked together), which may be described by the ***Open Systems Interconnect*** (OSI) model. Here the payload at one level holds the PDU for the next level, which has its own format, conventions, and overhead. Possibly the most visible protocol today is the *Hypertext Transfer Protocol* (**HTTP**), which is the principal protocol used by the **World Wide Web**. Typically, this would be carried in a stack consisting of **TCP/IP**—the *Transmission Control Protocol* (TCP) within the *Internet Protocol* (IP).

Other common top-level protocols are *File Transfer Protocol* (FTP), *Simple Mail Transfer Protocol* (SMTP) and **Telnet**, which provides terminal access to a remote computer.

Many protocols have been developed to interconnect computers, or whole ***local area networks*** (LANs) over considerable distances. The simplest might be *Point-to-Point Protocol* (PPP), which connects two computers with **modems** over a phone line. Where there is more than one possible destination, **packet switching**, connection-oriented protocols such as X-25 and *Integrated Services Digital Network* (**ISDN**) have been used to transfer low traffic loads, while *Frame Relay* or *Synchronous Digital Hierarchy* (SDH), and the similar *Synchronous Optical Network* (SONET) have been used for high-volume links. Recently, the connection-oriented **Asynchronous Transfer Mode** (ATM) protocols have supplanted many older protocols in this class.

Further Reading

Black, Ulysses D. *Computer Networks: Protocols, Standards and Interfaces.* Englewood Cliffs, N.J.: Prentice Hall, 1987; 2nd ed., 1993.

Braden, R., ed. *Requirements for Internet Hosts: Communication Layers.* Internet Engineering Task Force Request for Comments, 1122 (rfc1122), Oct. 1989.

IEEE. *802.3-1998 Part 3: Carrier Sense Multiple Access with Collision Detection (CSMA/CD) Access Method and Physical Layer Specifications.* IEEE Local and Metropolitan Area Networks. New York: IEEE Press, 1998.

ITU-T Recommendations on CD-ROM. International Telecommunication Union Electronic Publishing Service.

Stallings, William. *Computer Communications: Architectures, Protocols, and Standards.* Silver Spring, Md.: IEEE Computer Society Press, 1985; 3rd ed., Los Alamitos, Calif.: IEEE Computer Society Press, 1992.

—*John Deane*

"A Protocol for Packet Network Intercommunication"

By Vinton Cerf and Robert Kahn

The article "A Protocol for Packet Network Intercommunication," published in May 1974, describes the philosophy and design for a protocol to interconnect diverse packet communication networks. Written by **Vinton Cerf** (1943–) of Stanford University and **Robert Kahn** (1938–) of the Advanced Research Projects Agency's Information Processing Techniques

Office (**ARPA/IPTO**), this protocol has come to be known as the Transmission Control Protocol/Internet Protocol or **TCP/IP**. It is the protocol that has made a global **Internet** possible.

In their article, Kahn and Cerf identified a significant technical problem and proposed a protocol design and philosophy for its solution. The problem, which became evident in the early 1970s, is: How is it possible to interconnect diverse packet networks and to make resource sharing possible across the boundaries of dissimilar networks?

The **ARPANET** had solved the problem of creating a **packet-switching** network to connect diverse computers and diverse **operating systems**. To interconnect diverse packet networks, however, introduced new problems and complexities, including variations in packet format and size, in addressing mechanisms, and other conventions. A design for a protocol for internetwork packet communication would need to be able to accommodate such differences.

In early 1973, shortly after he joined ARPA/IPTO, Kahn began considering the problem of providing an architecture to accommodate heterogeneous packet networks. He identified these ground rules:

1. No changes would be required in the internal operations of participating networks.
2. Gateways would provide the means to reformat packets to meet the requirements of different networks and to route packets.
3. Communication would be on a best-effort basis, using transmission and retransmission of packets to get them to their final destination.
4. There would be no global control at the operations level.

These rules form the basis for an open networking architecture. Kahn recognized the need for a protocol to embody these ground rules and invited Cerf to collaborate with him on the design. They presented a draft article describing the design and philosophy for such a protocol in September 1973 at a meeting of networking researchers in Sussex, England. The published version of the article appeared in *IEEE Transactions on Communications* in May 1974.

The protocol design provides the means to create a metalevel architecture by designing software for host computers on the diverse networks and for gateways to interface between them. This makes it possible to set up an "association" between hosts on diverse networks without regard to determining any particular path for data transmission. It identifies the need for a means of addressing that will be understood by the gateways and the hosts on the diverse networks. The gateways make it possible to reformat packets to accommodate the different packet sizes among different networks and to route packets. The flow control and windowing mechanism make it possible to transmit and retransmit packets until they are received and reassembled at the destination host. The article includes a number of other concepts to implement an internetworking protocol in diverse networks.

Rarely has a technical article had such an impact. It provides the design for the infrastructure for the global Internet. To understand the nature of the Internet, it is important to read, study, and understand the philosophy and design of the internetworking protocol described in this seminal article.

FURTHER READING

Abbate, Janet. *Inventing the Internet.* Cambridge, Mass.: MIT Press, 1999.

Cerf, Vinton G., and Robert E. Kahn. "A Protocol for Packet Network Intercommunication." *IEEE Transactions on Communications,* Vol. 22, No. 5, May 1974, pp. 637–648.

—*Ronda Hauben*

Public Key Cryptography

The term *cryptography* refers to the encoding of information in such a way as to make it incomprehensible for a third party. In public key cryptography, a public key is used to encode the information and a secret key is used to decode it. The *public key* is made known to the general public in a "telephone book," while the *secret key*, as the name implies, is known only to its owner. The advantage of this split-key method is that anybody can encrypt information for anybody else without having to arrange a previous exchange of secret keys. However, the encrypted information can be decrypted only by the intended recipient of the information.

The principle behind public key cryptography and the most common **algorithms** can best be explained by example. Assume that a sender, Alice, and a receiver, Bob, want to communicate. Alice's message, which is a long series of bits in the computer, can be considered to be just a number. For example, all letters in this sentence could be encoded using the **ASCII** 8-bit code and its concatenation would produce a binary number with around 1000 bits. This is the message M that Alice wants to transmit.

Since the message M is a number, we could use another number, which we call the public key P, to transform the message into something very difficult to interpret. We could raise the number M to the power P, yielding an enormous number in which the original information has been scrambled. Alice sends M^P to Bob, and the message is decrypted by extracting the Pth root of this number, getting the original message M.

In this case the public key is P and the secret key is the inverse of P (i.e., $1/P$). Extracting the Pth root of a number corresponds mathematically to raising that number to the $(1/P)$th power. In this simple example, the method is not yet secure because from the knowledge of the public key P, the inverse $1/P$ can readily be obtained and anybody can decrypt the "secret" message.

However, this simple approach can be made secure by employing another type of arithmetic, called *modulo arithmetic*. Modulo arithmetic is done with a finite set of numbers: for example all numbers between 0 and 15 (i.e., 16 numbers). Addition is done in the normal way, but when the result is greater than 15, it "wraps around" and starts again from zero. In modulo-16 arithmetic, 2 plus 2 is 4, but 15 plus 1 is 0, 15 plus 2 is one, and so on. The result of the addition of two numbers in this arithmetic is the rest of the normal addition result when divided by 16.

Modulo arithmetic has many interesting properties. The addition operation can be defined as explained above. Every number has an inverse: for example, $4 + 12 = 0$. This means that the additive inverse of 4 is the number 12. The additive inverse of 8 is 8 itself. Additive inverses are like negative numbers in the usual arithmetic. Subtraction can then be defined as addition with the additive inverse of the second argument.

The important point, though, is that if addition can de defined, the multiplication operation can be defined too. To multiply 4 by 5 we add five times 4 to itself, yielding 20 in the normal arithmetic but 4 in the modulo-16 arithmetic. Having multiplication, it is also possible to raise a number to any power P, because this corresponds to P multiplications of the number with itself.

The nice property of modulo arithmetic is, first, that all results are bounded by the maximum representable number. In modulo-16 arithmetic, for example, no result can be larger than 15, no matter how many multiplications we perform or how large the exponent P of a number is. Second, although raising numbers to a known power is easy, finding the inverse of the power, in order to extract the Pth root, can be made extremely difficult by carefully choosing the modular arithmetic range that we want to use and the number P. Using modulo arithmetic, Alice still sends to Bob the number M^P (now computed in a modular setting), but extracting the Pth root of this number becomes almost impossible. In other words, although P is known, its multiplicative inverse $1/P$ is now not so easy to compute.

The most famous public key algorithm is the RSA method, named after its inventors, Ron Rivest, Adi Shamir, and Len Adleman. The public key is actually a pair of numbers (e,n), where e is the power to which the message will be raised and n the modular arithmetic range. For real applications these numbers are very large, usually in the range of several thousand bits. That is, Alice's message is actually the number M raised to the eth power, modulo n. The secret key is another pair (d,n), where d is just the number needed to invert the previous exponentiation operation. As said before, from the knowledge of (e,n) it is very difficult to compute d. The public and secret key are chosen in such a way that computing d requires the factorization of a very large number. Prime number factorization is a problem for which no efficient algorithm is known. RSA keys can in principle be computed and the method can be compromised, but in practice the keys are so large and the needed computational effort so large that the algorithm is considered secure.

Public key cryptography was first proposed by Whitfield Diffie (1944–) and Martin Hellman (1945–) in 1976, but their method had some shortcomings that were solved with the RSA approach, introduced in 1977. U.S. Patent 4,405,829 was awarded to the inventors and is known as the *RSA Patent*.

Further Reading

Rivest, Ronald L., Adi Shamir, and Len Adelman. "On Digital Signatures and Public Key Cryptosystems." *MIT Laboratory for Computer Science Technical Memorandum* 82, Apr. 1977.

Schneier, Bruce. *Applied Cryptography: Protocols, Algorithms Source Code*. New York: Wiley, 1995.

Stallings, William. *Data and Computer Communications*. Upper Saddle River, N.J.: Prentice Hall, 1996.

—*Raúl Rojas*

Punched Card Systems

Punched card systems stored data as combinations of holes in paper cards, to be processed by machines such as sorters and tabulators; cards were first punched and verified, and then sorted for tabulation. The first punched card systems were built during the 1890s to process counting statistics. During the next half century, they were used for summation statistics, bookkeeping, and for managing records. The machines evolved to enable quicker processing and to enable more complex operations.

The engineer **Herman Hollerith** (1860–1929) invented the first punched card system in the 1880s to process the 1890 census of the United States. Since 1850, U.S. censuses encountered problems due to a growing population, increasing exactness requirements, and the absence of a permanent institution to manage census processing. Hollerith's Electric Tabulating System was created to bring greater speed and accuracy to the 1890 census, the most extensive information processing effort yet attempted. The system was also used for census statistics in four European countries with limited success—of the four countries, only Norway used the system to process a second census.

A punched card tabulating machine. (© Bettmann/CORBIS)

Population statistics were comparatively simple, requiring only counting and some sorting of records. The first punched card system utilized punched cards of 6⅝ by 3¼ inches (in.) (c. 16.8 by 8.3 centimeters [cm]) divided into 24 columns each of 12 punching positions, and it was comprised of two simple constructs with manual card feed: a key punch and a non-printing tabulator with a sorting box. The results were read from counters.

The standardized general statistics punched card system was developed by Hollerith from 1892 to 1907. It featured standard punched cards of 7⅜ by 3¼ in. (c. 17.7 by 8.3 cm) with 45 columns each of 12 punching positions, round holes, and a numeric punching code; an adding nonprinting tabulator with mechanical feed; and a sorting machine with mechanical feed. Later, this system was improved through the use of automatic group control, the first method of record-controlled processing. Automatic group control enabled the tabulator to stop for manual reading or later automatic printing of a subtotal—for example, when all successive cards in one income group ended and the next started.

Hollerith founded the Tabulating Machine Company in 1896; his punched card system came into widespread use in the United States and in Europe, especially during World War I. As the market for punched card systems grew, two major competitors emerged: James Powers (1871–1927) in the United States (1913) and Fredrik Rosing Bull (1882–1925) in Norway (1921). In 1911, Hollerith sold his company to a trust, which in 1924 was renamed **IBM**.

Punched card–based bookkeeping required the ability to print a numeric list of records in successive punched cards and to make totals on a group of cards. The idea of punched card bookkeeping was conceived in 1906 in the United States by the engineer John Royden Peirce (1877–1933), who was inspired by the large potential for machine-based bookkeeping, which at the same time was the basis for the development of **keyboard** adders into keyboard bookkeeping machines. Peirce pursued this track together with Powers. Peirce was a clever conceptualist, but he produced few functioning machines. In 1922, IBM bought his company, and he became an IBM employee. In 1913, Powers launched a numeric tabulator, which could print lists and totals. IBM obtained a numeric printing tabulator only in 1921.

The breakthrough of punched card–based bookkeeping in the United States and in Europe during the 1920s contributed to the evolution of punched card systems. Machine capability and speed were improved. During the 1920s, subtracting tabulators were constructed, and during the 1930s, multiplication was included, either through additional tabulator improvements (DEHOMAG in Germany) or separate nonprinting punched card multipliers, which punched the results onto punched cards (IBM and Remington Rand in the United States, Bull in France).

Meanwhile, various proprietary punched card formats were introduced. Several smaller cards were introduced successfully by the British Powers company (Powers-SAMAS) to attract small and medium-sized customers. In 1928, IBM introduced a patented 80-column card with rectangular holes on the former 45-column card (7⅜ by 3¼ in. [c. 17.7 by 8.3 cm]) to enable records larger than 45 characters. In 1929, the American Powers company (by then a part of Remington Rand) introduced a competing 90-column card of the same size. Third, letter printing was developed. The first commercial alphabetic punched card representation was introduced by the British Powers company in 1921 to enable letter specifications. Also, this was the object of IBM's first letter representation system in 1931.

Managing personal records such as names and addresses with punched cards was a part of Peirce's 1906 concept of punched card–based bookkeeping. His idea required an alphanumeric system. It was not implemented for a quarter of a century for two reasons: first, billing companies and insurance companies had well-functioning systems based on typewriters or Addressographs. Second, it proved difficult to construct a representation of the full alphabet of 26 letters—in addition to 10 digits—on a punched card and a tabulator to read and print the information. Peirce constructed the first alphanumeric system on contracts with three major U.S. insurance companies in 1916-22, and built a few tabulators, but the system never became commercially available.

The first fully alphanumerical system was introduced in 1931 by the Bull company of France, followed by IBM (1933), and Remington Rand (1939). All alphanumeric systems were proprietary, and conversion between two systems required the punched cards to be manually repunched. Bull and IBM aimed their development work at insurance companies, but alphanumeric systems became generally used by that field only after World War II. In the United States, punched cards were adapted for use by the Social Security Administration in 1937.

Punched cards were used in France after 1934 as a basis for a mechanized recruitment and mobilization system to boost the French Army against the growing German threat, but no mechanized mobilization system was implemented by the outbreak of World War II. After the French defeat of 1940, Vichy France implemented a punched card-based mobilization register over the next two years. Punched card–based registers were used during the war, for example to keep track of active service personnel. After the war, large punched card–based registers were used in many countries for public assignments such as income tax and civil registration. They were also used by private firms—for example, insurance companies mailing charge forms to policyholders. This made the 1950s the heyday of punched card systems. Managing personal records revealed mayor limitations: the cumbersome physical handling of punched cards, and the problems of merging big punched card files.

The key difference between the Bull, IBM, and Powers systems was their basic technology. The Bull and IBM systems were based on electromechanical technology, whereas Powers used purely mechanical components; the only electrical part in the machine was an electric motor. In the mechanically based Powers machines, the cards were read by thin iron bars, which either went through a hole or were stopped by the card. The information was transferred to the computing units in the same manner. Programming a Powers tabulator was performed by wiring a connection box, which contained a set of thin iron bars, one for each punching position. When there was a hole in a punching position, the iron bar in the connection box affected the calculating or printing units. In the electromechanical IBM and Bull machines, the card reading was achieved by closing a current through the holes, and programming was done by wiring a plugboard. The current that passed through a hole was transmitted to the calculating units via jackplugs and wires, like the manual telephone switchboards of the era.

Punched card–based systems were first used for scientific and technical calculations in the 1920s. In the 1950s they were used extensively for this purpose; their limited calculation capability was a major reason for the development of programmable and electronic calculators, culminating in the first computers. From the late 1940s, the producers adopted electronic technology to improve the capability and speed of punched card machines, which provided the producers with their first experience in producing and running programmable electronic machines, later utilized in computer production.

Between 1950 and 1970, computers gradually replaced punched card machines. IBM earned more on their punched card systems than on computers until 1962, the British ICL company until 1965. The transition to computers reduced punched cards to an input medium, used until around 1980.

FURTHER READING

Austrian, Geoffrey. *Herman Hollerith: Forgotten Giant of Information Processing*. New York: Columbia University Press, 1984.

Bashe, Charles, L. R. Johnson, J. H. Palmer, and Emerson W. Pugh. *IBM's Early Computers*. Cambridge, Mass.: MIT Press, 1988.

Campbell-Kelly, Martin. *ICL: A Business and Technical History*. Oxford: Oxford University Press, 1990.

—Lars Heide

Quantum Computer

A quantum computer is one with which massively **parallel processing** can be performed, with quantum effects playing a decisive role. All computers are physical objects, and computation is a physical process that has to obey the laws of physics. On the atomic scale, matter obeys the rules of quantum mechanics, which are quite different from the classical rules that determine the properties of conventional **logic gates**. Today's advanced lithographic techniques can etch logic gates and wires less than 1 micrometer across onto the surfaces of **silicon** chips. Soon they will yield even smaller parts and inevitably reach a point where logic gates are so small that they are made out of only a handful of atoms. So if computers are to become smaller in the future, new quantum technology must replace or supplement what we have now. But quantum technology can offer much more than just packing more and more bits to silicon and multiplying the clock speed of **microprocessors**. It can support an entirely new type of computation, known as *quantum computation*, with qualitatively new **algorithms** based on quantum principles.

The story of quantum computation goes back to 1981 when the physicist Richard Feynman (1918–88) observed that simulations of some quantum experiments on classical computers appear to involve an exponential slowdown in time as compared to the natural run of the experiment. Instead of viewing this fact as an obstacle, Feynman regarded it as an opportunity. If it requires so much computation to work out what will happen in a complicated quantum experiment, then, he argued, the very act of setting up an experiment and measuring the outcome is tantamount to performing a complex computation. After all, any real computation is a physical process, be it classical or quantum. Thus any computation can be viewed in terms of physical experiments that produce outputs that depend on initial preparations called *inputs*.

Despite Feynman's work, the unusual power of quantum computers was not really anticipated until 1985, when David Deutsch of the University of Oxford published a crucial theoretical paper in which he laid down the foundations of the quantum theory of computation by describing a universal quantum computer and the first quantum algorithm. After the Deutsch paper, the hunt was on for something interesting for quantum computers to do. At the time all that could be found were a few rather contrived mathematical problems, and the entire issue of quantum computation seemed little more than an academic curiosity.

It all changed rather suddenly in 1994 when Peter Shor (1959–) from **Bell Labs** in New Jersey devised the first quantum algorithm, which, in principle, can perform efficient factorization of large integers. This became a potential **killer application** for quantum computers. Difficulty of factorization underpins security of many common methods of encryption—for example, RSA, the most popular **public key** encryption, gets its security from the inherent difficulty of factoring large numbers.

To explain what makes quantum computers so different from their classical counterparts, we have to look into the physics of storing and processing of information. Let us start with a basic unit of information—namely, a **bit**. From a physical point of view a bit is a physical system that can be prepared in one of the two different states representing two logical values—no or yes, false or true, or simply 0 or 1. For example, the voltage between the plates in a capacitor represents a bit of information: A charged capacitor denotes bit value 1, and an uncharged capacitor, bit value 0. One bit of information can also be encoded using two different polarizations of light or two different electronic states of an atom.

However, if we choose an atom as a physical bit, quantum mechanics tells us that apart from the two distinct electronic states, the atom can also be prepared in a *superposition* of the two states, meaning that the atom is in both state 0 and state 1. Thus whereas conventional, nonquantum computers perform calculations on fundamental pieces of information called *bits*, which can take the values 0 or 1, quantum computers use objects called *quantum bits*, or *qubits* (pronounced "queue-bits"), which can represent both 0 and 1 at the same time. There is no equivalent of this superposition in the classical world; it is a purely quantum mechanical phenomenon. Since we are used to seeing classical physics at work in the everyday world, such quantum phenomena often seem counterintuitive.

To push the idea of superposition of numbers further, consider a register composed of three physical bits. Any classical register of that type can store in a given moment of time only one of eight different numbers (i.e., the register can be in only one of eight possible configurations, such as 000, 001, 010, ..., 111). A quantum register composed of 3 qubits can store in a given moment of time all eight numbers in a quantum superposition. Adding qubits to the register increases its storage capacity exponentially (i.e., 3 qubits can store eight different numbers at once, 4 qubits can store 16 different numbers at once, and so on). In general, L qubits can store 2^L numbers at once. Once the register is prepared in a superposition of different numbers, one can perform operations on all of them.

For example, if qubits are atoms, suitably tuned laser pulses affect atomic electronic states and evolve initial superpositions of encoded numbers into different superpositions. During such evolution each number in the superposition is affected, and as a result we generate a massive parallel computation, albeit in one component of *quantum hardware*. When we measure the atoms one by one at the end of such computation, we will see them in their binary states (either 0 or 1), which will give us only one number at the output. But this output depends on the entire evolution proceeding the measurement—on the computations on all the numbers in the superpositions prior to the final measurement.

To accomplish the same task, any classical computer has to repeat the same computation several times or use several discrete processors working in parallel. For classical computers the amount of parallelism increases in direct proportion to its size, whereas for quantum computers it increases exponentially with size. This affects the execution time and memory required in the process of computation and determines the efficiency of algorithms.

For an algorithm to be efficient, the time it takes to execute the algorithm must increase no faster than a polynomial function of the size of the input. Think about the input size as the total number of bits needed to specify the input to the problem—for example, the number of bits needed to encode the number we want to factorize. If the best algorithm for a particular problem has the execution time (viewed as a function of the size of the input) bounded by a polynomial, we say that the problem belongs to class P.

Problems outside class P are known as *hard problems*. Thus we say, for example, that multiplication is in P whereas factorization is not in P. "Hard" in this case does not mean "impossible to solve" or "noncomputable." It means that the physical resources needed to factor a large number scale up such that for all practical purposes, it can be regarded as intractable. However, some of quantum algorithms can turn hard mathematical problems into easy ones, factoring being the most striking example so far. Potential use of quantum factoring for code-breaking purposes has raised the obvious suggestion of building a quantum computer.

In principle we know how to build a quantum computer: We can start with simple quantum logic gates and try to integrate them together into quantum networks. A quantum logic gate, like a classical gate, is a very simple computing device that performs one elementary quantum operation, usually on 2 qubits, in a given period of time. Of course, quantum logic gates are different from their classical counterparts because they can create and perform operations on quantum superpositions. However, if we keep on putting quantum gates together into networks, we quickly run into serious practical problems. Apart from the technical difficulties of working at single-atom and single-photon scales, one of the most important problems is that of preventing the surrounding environment from being affected by the interactions that generate quantum superpositions. The more components, the more likely it is that quantum computation will spread outside the computational unit and will irreversibly dissipate useful information to the environment. This process is called *decoherence*. Thus the challenge is to engineer atomic systems in which qubits interact only with themselves, not with the environment.

Some physicists are pessimistic about the prospects of substantial experimental advances in the field. They believe that decoherence will in practice never be reduced to the point where more than a few consecutive quantum computational steps can be performed. More optimistic researchers believe that practical quantum computers will appear in a not too distant future, pointing out that quantum decoherence can be, up to a certain point, controlled by the use of quantum **error-correcting codes**. Experimental and theoretical research in quantum computation is now attracting increasing attention from both academic researchers and industry worldwide. New technologies for realizing quantum computers are being proposed, and new types of quantum computation with various advantages over classical computation are continually being discovered.

Further Reading

Brooks, Michael, ed. *Quantum Computing and Communications.* New York: Springer-Verlag, 1999.

Brown, Julian. *Minds, Machines and the Multiverse: The Quest for the Quantum Computer.* New York: Simon and Schuster, 2000.

Deutsch, David. *The Fabric of Reality.* New York: Allen Lane, 1997.

Deutsch, David, and Artur Ekert. "Quantum Communication Moves into the Unknown." *Physics World,* June 1993.

Vedral, V., A. Barenco, and A. Ekert. "Quantum Networks for Elementary Arithmetic Operations." *Physical Review A,* Vol. 54, 1996, pp. 147–153.

—*Artur Ekert*

QuickTime

QuickTime is a multiplatform, industry-standard **multimedia** technology that was developed by **Apple Computer** in 1991. It enables the development, playback, and storage of real-time movies, sound, **virtual reality**, three-dimensional media, animation, **graphics**, and high-quality images. It can work together with more media formats than any other available technology. QuickTime constitutes the heart of the *QuickTime media layer*, which also includes QuickTime Virtual Reality (QTVR) and QuickDraw 3D (QD3D).

QuickTime is no mere **software** system extension, but rather, a complete modular architecture with more than 200 software components. Each is loaded by the system only when actually needed. Different modules are used, because multimedia presentations can combine text, sound, video, and so on. Instead of having several files, which have to be synchronized externally, a QuickTime file holds all these different streams in a single file. The QuickTime Player, part of the QuickTime package, makes it possible to play the video and sound stream; with PictureViewer, images can be viewed and exported to standard publishing formats. Using the **browser** plug-in, over 60 types of media can be recognized and viewed while surfing the **Internet**.

QuickTime deals with the different **bandwidth** of each computer system by using a variety of different compression technologies designed for the various bit rates. Media files can be created, in which tone and image look and sound good at the various bit rates. QuickTime supports every relevant file format for images and video, such as **MPEG**, **JPEG**, GIF, TIFF, PICT, AVI, BMP, WAV, Targa, DV Stream, and so on. **MIDI** standards are also supported, and the audio component of QuickTime offers different qualities, differentiating, for example, between speech and music.

When media files are created, exported, or imported, they can be compressed before publishing using compressors such as Cinepak, Sorenson, and Intel Indeo. With this versatility, media produced with QuickTime is compatible and thus can be geared for nearly any audience. QuickTime also supports over 35 formats for Web content production. All key standards for real-time Web streaming are supported in the latest version of QuickTime.

Thousands of Web sites offer QuickTime content. Many computer games are based on the QuickTime technology, and it has become popular in the pop music industry to include a QuickTime video clip of the band on audio compact disks.

Further Reading

Sydow, Dan Parks. *QuickTime Macintosh Multimedia.* New York: MIS Press, 1994.

Towner, George, and Apple Computer. *Discovering Quicktime: An Introduction for Windows and MacIntosh Programmers.* San Francisco: Morgan Kaufmann, 1999.

—*Jenna L. Brinning*

RAID

RAID (redundant array of independent disks) is an industry-standardized scheme for multiple-disk database design. The RAID scheme consists of seven levels, 0 through 6. These levels do not imply a hierarchical relationship; instead, they designate different design architectures.

Regardless of architecture, RAID schemes share three characteristics. First, they are a set of physical disk drives viewed by the **operating system** as a single logical drive. Second, data are distributed across the physical drives of an array. Finally, redundant disk capacity is used to store parity (redundancy) information, which guarantees data recoverability in case of a disk failure. The details of the second and third characteristics differ for the different RAID levels. RAID 0 does not support the third characteristic. Of the seven levels, levels 2 and 4 are not offered commercially and are not likely to achieve industry acceptance.

For RAID 0, data are distributed across all the disks in the array. If two different input–output (I/O) requests are pending for two different blocks of data, there is a good chance that the requested blocks are on different disks. Thus the two requests can be issued in parallel, reducing the I/O queuing time.

Data are viewed as being stored on a logical disk. The disk is divided into strips. The strips are mapped round robin to consecutive array members. A set of logically consecutive strips that maps exactly one strip to each array member is referred to as a *stripe*. In an *N*-disk array, the first *N* logical strips are physically stored as the first strip on each of the *N* disks, forming the first stripe; the second *N* strips are distributed as the second strips on each disk; and so on. The advantage of this layout is that if a single I/O request consists of multiple logically contiguous strips, up to *N* strips for that request can be handled in parallel, greatly reducing the I/O transfer time.

RAID 1 achieves redundancy by duplicating all the data. Data striping is used, as in RAID 0. But in this case, each logical strip is mapped to two separate physical disks so that every disk in the array has a mirror disk that contains the same data.

With RAID 1, a read request can be serviced by either of the two disks that contain the requested data. A write request requires that both corresponding strips be updated, but this can be done in parallel. Recovery from a failure is simple. When a drive fails, the data may still be accessed from the second drive.

RAID 3 make use of a parallel access technique, in which all member disks participate in the execution of every I/O request, with data distributed in small strips. RAID 3 requires only a single redundant disk, no matter how large the disk array. A simple parity **bit** is computed for the set of individual bits in the same position on all the data disks. In the event of a drive failure, the parity drive is accessed and data are reconstructed from the remaining devices. Once the failed drive is replaced, the missing data can be restored on the new drive and operation resumed.

RAID 3 can achieve very high data transfer rates. Any I/O request will involve the parallel transfer of data from all the data disks. For large transfers, the performance improvement is especially noticeable. On the other hand, only one I/O request can be executed at a time. Thus, in a transaction-oriented environment, performance suffers.

RAID levels 5 and 6 make use of an independent access technique in which each member disk operates independently, so that separate I/O requests can be satisfied in parallel. Independent access arrays are more suitable for applications that require high I/O request rates and are relatively less suited for applications that require high data transfer rates. In the case of RAID 5 and 6, the strips are relatively large. With RAID 5, a bit-by-bit parity strip is calculated across corresponding strips on each data disk, and the parity strips are distributed across all disks. A typical allocation is a round-robin scheme. For an *N*-disk array, the parity strip is on a different disk for the first *N* stripes, and the pattern then repeats. For RAID 6, two different parity calculations are carried out and stored in separate blocks on different disks. Thus a RAID 6 array whose user data require *N* disks consists of $N + 2$ disks. The advantage of RAID 6 is that it provides extremely high data availability. Three disks would have to fail to cause data to become unavailable. On the other hand, RAID 6 incurs a substantial write penalty, because each write affects two parity blocks.

FURTHER READING

Chen, P., E. Lee, G. Gibson, R. Katz, and D. Patterson. "RAID: High-Performance, Reliable Secondary Storage." *ACM Computing Surveys*, June 1994.

Friedman, M. "RAID Keeps Going and Going and...." *IEEE Spectrum*, Apr. 1996.

Katz, R., G. Gibson, and D. Patterson. "A Case for Redundant Arrays of Inexpensive Disks (RAID)." *ACM SIGMOD Conference of Management of Data*, June 1988.

———. "Disk System Architecture for High Performance Computing." *Proceedings of the IEEE*, Dec. 1989.

RAID Advisory Board Staff. *The RAID Book: A Handbook of Storage Systems Technology*. Edited by Paul Massiglia. Poway, Calif.: Annabooks, 1997.

—William Stallings

RAMAC

Developed from 1952 to 1956, the **IBM** RAMAC (random access method of accounting and control) machine was the first to operate using a **hard disk**. The RAMAC was created at IBM's laboratory in San Jose, California, by a group led by Reynold B. Johnson (1906–98). The successful project led to the establishment of IBM's hard disk division in San Jose.

The 305 RAMAC unit was the size of a refrigerator and consisted of 50 platters 24 inches in diameter, stacked on a rotating spindle with a total capacity of 5 megabytes (MB). There were also three access mechanisms: that is, up to three different records could be read at once. The disks used 50 tracks per inch, and each track stored data at a density of 100 bits per inch.

The problem that led to the invention of the hard disk was the increasing number of punched cards that were necessary to store programs and data. In the early 1950s around 95 percent of stored data was kept on punched cards, and IBM was manufacturing millions of them in San Jose. IBM first tried to solve the problem by using magnetic tapes. However, tapes have an inherent problem: Information can only be looked up in sequential order. If the desired information is at the end of the tape, the entire tape has to go under the read-write head. So when a request came from the U.S. Air Force to build a special computer to track down its inventory, the engineers at IBM decided to experiment with disk files. The Air Force required 50,000 inventory items with 100 characters each (i.e., 5 MB).

The RAMAC was conceived as a *transaction processing* machine, different from a *batch processing* computer. In a batch system, a pile of punched cards was processed and the result was another pile of cards. Processing was a kind of linear operation, accessing the entire batch of data in one run and producing a new data file. With a transaction-processing machine, single records are accessed and updated in one step. A tape or punched cards are unsuitable for this purpose, as they cannot be accessed randomly.

Previous to the work done on RAMAC, other companies had experimented with disks that were not spinning continuously. They were started once the read-write head was in place and stopped after having read the desired information. The read-write head could be in contact with the disk, since the angular velocity was so small. The RAMAC, on the other hand, had disks spinning all the time. To keep a disk spinning, a way had to be found to keep the read-write head from coming into contact with the magnetic surface.

The first approach tried by IBM's engineers was to deliver pressurized air to the heads, but this was too expensive because it required a bank of compressors. Eventually, they found out that the head could fly barely above the surface of the disk if it was built to glide above the airflow produced by the spinning disk. The airhead could fly directly to the correct track, and since the disks were spinning constantly, the access time was dramatically lower than for a stop-and-go unit.

In order to get a flat surface, the disks were coated with a magnetic paint poured on the disk when it was spinning. The paint was an iron oxide suspension (the same as that used to paint the Golden Gate Bridge in San Francisco) with good magnetic properties. The final unit was expensive by current standards: The 305 RAMAC cost U.S.$35,000 a year to lease, or U.S.$7000 per megabyte per year.

Many other storage technology breakthroughs were also invented later at IBM's San Jose plant. These include the removable disk pack (1961), **floppy disk** drive (1971), and Winchester hard disk (1973). An entire industry was spawned by RAMAC: The hard disk sector today is a U.S.$50 billion business served by more than 100 companies.

FURTHER READING

Ceruzzi, Paul. *A History of Modern Computing.* Cambridge, Mass.: MIT Press, 1998.

Christensen, Clayton. *The Innovators Dilemma: When New Technologies Cause Great Firms to Fail.* Cambridge, Mass.: Harvard Business School Press, 1997.

—*Frank Darius*

RAM and ROM

The acronyms RAM and ROM stand for *random access memory* and *read-only memory*, respectively. RAM is used to store the programs being executed, the user data, the **operating system**, and any other software needed by the computer when running. RAM chips are volatile—that is, they lose the information stored in them when the power is turned off. ROM chips store those parts of the **software** used to bootstrap the computer and low-level routines accessed at power-up. Software can be stored permanently in ROM chips and does not get lost when the computer is turned off. Fonts for a **printer** can also be stored in ROM chips, since they will not be modified during the lifetime of the device.

RAM chips received this name because the information stored in them can be accessed directly. The capacity of RAM chips is measured in bits, and a 4-kilobit RAM chip is one capable of holding 4096 single bits. The bits are numbered from 0 to 4095, and when an address is set at the address pins of the chip, the corresponding bit can immediately be read or overwritten. Therefore, to read a bit at address 100, for example, it is not necessary to read the previous 99 bits, as in the case of a magnetic tape in which all information is stored sequentially and the reading head has to pass through all the data. Thus we speak of "random access" to the bits stored in a RAM chip.

There are several types of RAM: *dynamic* and *static memory* chips. The first kind of memory elements is built out of **flip-flops**, circuits in which each stored bit is being recirculated permanently in order to keep it in store. Static memory chips operate using small capacitors in which a small charge can be deposited. The absence of charge represents a 0; a charge represents a 1. Since the charge tends to leak, static memory chips have to be refreshed periodically by reading all the bits stored in them and recharging those capacitors in which a 1 has been found. The refreshing is done by the processor or by special on-chip refreshing hardware.

Information can be stored in a ROM chip by melting fuses arranged in an array. A melted fuse represents a 0 and an intact fuse a 1, because it allows a small current to be transported to the chip's output line. A ROM chip is written only once, to be read many times. The **BIOS** (Basic Input/Output System) routines of an IBM **personal computer** (PC) or compatible machine are stored in ROM chips. PROMs (programmable ROMs) are special chips that can be loaded with information, but which can also be reloaded several times using a special procedure.

CD-ROMs are just another technology for the permanent storage of information. In the case of CD-ROMs, the information is burned on a plastic material by using a laser that modifies its chemical properties at a small spot. These modification can be measured later using another laser.

FURTHER READING

Prince, Betty. *Semiconductor Memories: A Handbook of Design, Manufacture, and Application.* Chichester, West Sussex, England, and New York: Wiley, 1983; 2nd ed., 1991.

———. *High Performance Memories: New Architecture DRAMs and SRAMs—Evolution and Function.* Chichester, West Sussex, England, and New York: Wiley, 1996; rev. ed., 1999.

—*Raúl Rojas*

RealAudio

RealAudio was the first successful streaming audio format for use on the **World Wide Web**, originally developed by Progressive Networks (later to become Real Networks) in 1995. As such, RealAudio is one of the oldest multimedia facilities on the Web. The major innovation of streaming audio is that it can start playing before the entire audio file has been received. This contrasts with audio formats such as WAV, AIF, and Sun AU format, where the entire file must be downloaded before the audio is played on the user's computer.

In addition to the advantage of streaming, the RealAudio format provided a significant improvement in the compression of audio data compared to previous formats. The RealAudio format allowed a file to be a tenth the size of the equivalent WAV format audio file. Thus digital audio could be downloaded over a telephone modem and played in real time at reasonable quality. RealAudio allowed AM radio quality to be achieved at approximately 1 kilobyte per second, as available on a 14.4 kilobaud (bits per second) modem. Subsequent improvements in modem speeds, computer speeds, and data compression techniques have allowed even better results to be attained. For example, **RealVideo**, also from Real Networks, allowed low-quality video to be transmitted on a telephone line.

Data compression techniques have improved as faster computers have allowed decoding of better compression in real time. In addition, Real Networks has studied how people hear sounds. Psychoacoustical research has demonstrated that some frequencies of sound can be eliminated without greatly affecting understanding. Thus, Real Networks has different methods for encoding voice alone, voice with music, and music only. Frequencies important for voice understanding can be preserved while the rest are highly compressed or eliminated.

The RealAudio format has had a number of competitors. Apple's **QuickTime** format includes streaming audio as well as allowing video and **virtual reality**. Macromedia has also made use of the wide distribution of their Shockwave Web **browser** "plug-in" to introduce streaming audio. Neither of these formats requires a special server, whereas RealAudio has traditionally done so. RealAudio (and RealVideo) can be encoded so that they can be streamed from a normal Web server without requiring a separate Real server. Microsoft introduced Active Streaming Format (ASF), which runs from **Windows NT** servers. The **MP3** format has proved very popular for digital music encoding on the **Internet**, and many portable MP3 players are available.

As well as Real server software, Real Networks has produced various pieces of software for handling RealAudio on personal computers; RealPlayer plays audio and video, RealJukebox stores, organizes, and plays digital music, and RealDownload aids in downloading files.

RealAudio, together with RealVideo, is part of the Synchronized Multimedia Integration Language (SMIL), a World Wide Web standard for multimedia presentations, which helps to promote its continued use. RealAudio has been an important milestone in the use of audio for multimedia on the World Wide Web, although the use of streaming and dramatically improved compression, both of which made continuous digital audio via the Internet over a telephone a practical reality.

FURTHER READING

RealAudio newsgroup.
news:alt.binaries.sound.realaudio

Real.com.
http://www.realaudio.com

Reid, Robert H. "Real Revolution." *Wired*, 5.10, Oct. 1997.
http://www.wired.com/wired/archive/5.10/progressive_pr.html

—*Jonathan Bowen*

Real-Time Systems

Real-time systems are usually **fault-tolerant**, often **embedded**, computer systems that are controlling some device, be it a **network**, an airplane, an automobile, or a robot. The benchmark by which real-time systems are judged is response time, which has to match the course of events being controlled.

David Parnas (1941–) has remarked that all systems are real-time systems—it's simply that some are faster than others. Airplane controllers have response times measured in milliseconds. **Automatic teller machines** can be much slower, since the state of a person using the machine changes more slowly than aerodynamic forces at 500 knots. Some people, who have not come to the same realization as Parnas, do not even consider automatic tellers as real time since they are so slow. Note that response time is relatively independent of processor time: A 0.5 machine that handles 0.5 million instructions per second can control an airplane. Processor speeds are so fast that real-time systems can easily have sufficient response time to be embedded in many products.

As an example of the spread of real-time systems, digital controllers are used in the Space Shuttle's main engines, on newer turbofan engines, and in standard automobile powertrains. All of these engine types depend on the combustion of volatile fuels to generate energy. The Shuttle engines have the most powerful fuels and the least margin for failure. While a poor air–fuel mixture in an internal combustion engine may cause it to stop running (and thus result in pulling the car to the roadside), a similar error in the Shuttle could instigate a catastrophic failure. Therefore, the response time and the data sampling period of the Shuttle is perhaps more life-critical than an automobile. However, they both have requirements for appropriate sampling rates, response time, and fault tolerance.

Sampling rate is an important consideration for real-time programmers. In an analog device, all data are captured. In a digital system, due to the need to use chunks of data converted from analog sensors, data are lost between samples. For a ground-based radar tracking a relatively slow airliner at 500 knots, a few seconds between data samples is not critical. Tracking an incoming missile requires a much higher sampling rate. In applications where the processors are limited by reliability concerns to older and slower types, directly placing data in memory is a frequent solution. It usually takes some prototyping to discover the most effective sampling rate for a new mix of computer and task. It takes a significant amount of fine tuning to get the correct sampling rate and response-time.

Another consideration in making a real-time system is the structure of the **operating system**. Some variations of **Unix**, for example, have been coded to provide a response time guarantee, which is needed in real-time systems. Some authors believe that a cyclic operating system is best because it executes each process for a fixed interval in turn, ensuring that all have at least some time to run in each cycle. In this manner they avoid process starvation and make adjusting the sample rate a function of how many processes are running and the length of a cycle. Others believe in an asynchronous priority-interrupt executive, in which the process with the highest-priority runs until it has completed its preset chunk, then the one with the next-highest priority runs, and so on. If a process is running and one with a higher priority needs some time, then the current process is interrupted, following which the executive runs the higher-priority process and returns to the interrupted process if it still has the highest priority of those pending. Supporters of this method claim that essential processes are never starved, while critics point out that there is a high probability of starving low-priority processes.

Clearly, obtaining and retaining much-needed data while completing processing tasks in time requires a balancing act. Application programmers ensuring that their software completes processing within a specified interval must take into account the structure of the executive and its scheduling algorithms. They must also know how much data loss is tolerable. Real-time programming is one of the biggest challenges in the field of software engineering.

FURTHER READING

Klein, Mark H., et al. *A Practitioner's Handbook for Real-Time Analysis: Guide to Rate Monotonic Analysis for Real-Time Systems*. Norwell, Mass.: Kluwer Academic Publishers, 1993.

Laplante, Phillip *A Real Time Systems Design and Analysis.* Piscataway, N.J.: IEEE Press, 1996.

—*James Tomayko*

RealVideo

RealVideo is a software system to broadcast video content via the **Internet**. It was released by RealNetworks, Inc in 1995. RealVideo uses its own proprietary **streaming** format to compress the input signal for different transmission **bandwidths**. The **algorithms** used, called *perceptual coders*, are lossy, which means that the encoding–decoding process leads to a loss of information but one that is hardly noticeable for the user. The system consists of three main components: the player, the encoder, and the server.

The RealPlayer is the client program that enables users to see and listen to RealVideo clips. The client works as a plug-in or as a helper application in a standard browser such as **Netscape** Navigator or Internet Explorer. This means that after having installed the client, it will pop up automatically when you click on a link that leads to a RealVideo clip. The client software is available for a wide range of computer and operating systems. The RealVideo Encoder creates the clips for RealVideo. The input to this program can be a predigitized audio or video clip, a live video or audio signal, a predigitized video clip, or a live video signal. Finally, the RealServer is the sender program that delivers RealVideo clips over a network. One server can deliver clips to many players at the same time. A user wanting to broadcast video via the **Internet** also needs a Web server, since RealVideo clips are typically accessed through Web pages.

The overall problem with video and audio streaming applications is that each user needs his or her own copy of the data. Serving the number of viewers as, for instance, a national television station is currently impossible because the Internet does not provide the neccessary bandwidth. The first attempt to solve this problem was the **MBONE**, a virtual network of linked servers that could broadcast video and audio over different portions of the Internet, eliminating redundancies. The MBONE was started in 1992, but after its initial success fell in disuse.

According to RealNetworks, 130 million different users have registered to use the RealPlayer since it was released in 1995. For the year 1999, the company reported net revenues of U.S.$131.2 million. Other companies offer alternative software for streaming video over the Internet, such as NetShow sold by **Microsoft** and the **QuickTime** Streaming Server by **Apple Computer**.

Further Reading

Ozer, Jan. "Streaming Video: A Welcome Reception." *PC Magazine*, 7 Oct. 1997.

—*Gerald Friedland*

Recursion

A mathematical function that is used to write its own definition is called *recursive*. Similarly, any computer procedure that calls itself at run time is called a *recursive procedure*. Recursion is a fundamental concept in computer programming; almost all modern programming languages are recursive.

A simple example of the recursion concept is computation of the factorial function. The factorial of a positive integer, for example 5, is defined as the product of all positive integers smaller or equal to that number. For example:

$$\text{factorial}(5) = 5 \times 4 \times 3 \times 2 \times 1 = 120$$

The same definition can be written using recursion by stating that the factorial of a positive integer N is equal to the product of N by the factorial of $N - 1$. In symbolic form;

$$\text{factorial}(N) = N \times \text{factorial}(N - 1)$$

Additionally, a stop condition is needed to prevent the infinite application of this rule. The stop condition in our example would be

$$\text{factorial}(1) = 1$$

Both definitions of the factorial function produce identical results when applied to the same number. However, the recursive definition is often simpler and easier to grasp.

For example, if we want to sort a list of numbers in ascending order, a recursive procedure for this task might read as follows:

To SORT a list of N numbers in ascending order:

- *If the list consists of a single element, we are done.*
- *If not, then SORT the first half of the list, SORT the second half, and MERGE both halves.*

The MERGE procedure combines two sorted lists into one by working down the lists, always taking out the smaller of the two values on top of the lists. It is the same method that we would apply when combining two hands of playing cards that have been sorted previously. Notice that this verbal definition of the sorting method applies sorting twice, once to the first half of the list and then again to the second half. But at every step the length of the lists is half as large as before, so that we will eventually finish. The stop condition is reached every time one of the halves consists of a single item.

Implementing recursion in a programming language requires a method to save the present state of the recursive procedure, start again the procedure with new arguments, and return to the previous state. It is as if we notice, in the middle of a task, that we have to solve a subtask using the same tools that we are holding right now. We concentrate on the subtask, but afterward we come back to the main task, which can now be finished. Usually, recursive procedures use a *stack* to store the state of the computer and retrieve it later.

The first commercial programming languages, including **Fortran** or **COBOL**, were nonrecursive. Neither was **Plankalkül**, a programming language conceived by **Konrad Zuse** (1910–95) in 1945. However, LISP, designed by **John McCarthy** (1927–) in 1959, makes extensive use of recursive definitions. Recursion entered the mainstream of computing when the concept was adopted by programming languages such as **ALGOL**, **Pascal**, and **C**. Even Fortran now allows recursive definitions.

It is interesting to point out that the study of recursive functions and classification of the several possible forms of recursive definitions were much discussed topics among mathematicians in the 1930s. The analysis of recursive functions led **Alonzo Church** (1903–95) at Princeton to the same conclusions regarding computability that **Alan M. Turing** (1912–54) had reached at Cambridge, England, while studying a more mechanical computational model, the Turing machine.

Further Reading

Cormen, Thomas H., Charles E. Leiserson, and Ronald Rivest. *Introduction to Algorithms.* Cambridge, Mass.: MIT Press, 1990.

Roberts, Eric. *Thinking Recursively.* New York: Wiley, 1986.

—*Tania Rojas-Esponda*

Red Hat

Red Hat, Inc., founded in 1994 and based in Durham, North Carolina, has rapidly become a market leader in **open-source** software, services, and information. Specifically, it has been very well known for the Red Hat **Linux operating system**. This is based on Linux, a revised version of **Unix** developed by **Linus Torvalds** (1969–) in 1991.

In 1995, two entrepreneurs, Robert Young and Mark Ewing, decided to use their marketing and technical expertise to promote a new venture to be called Red Hat Linux. By the following year, Red Hat Linux version 4.0 was named desktop operating system of the year by InfoWorld. This award was repeated in 1997 for Red Hat Linux 5.0. In 1998, Sybase, **Oracle**, and Informix announced that their databases would be compatible with Red Hat Linux. In May, Corel also announced Red Hat Linux compatibility for its WordPerfect Office Suite. Red Hat Linux 5.2 was released in November 1998. The Red Hat Linux OS was becoming so successful that even **Microsoft** used it in refuting U.S. Justice Department charges, in an attempt to demonstrate that they did not have an operating system monopoly.

In April 1999, Red Hat launched Red Hat Linux 6.0, an operating system that helped in the needs of enterprise-wide servers with symmetric multiprocessing (SMP) support. It included a choice of two **graphical user interfaces** (GNOME and KDE) and the Red Hat Package Manager to simplify the installation of individual pieces of software. In June 1999, Red Hat, Inc. announced that it would go public with a U.S.$96.6 million stock offering.

Red Hat's policy has been to share all the **software** innovations that it has developed freely with the open-source community under the GNU General Public License (GPL). Using this approach, it has attained a leading position as a distributor of the Unix-based Linux operating system in the late 1990s and beyond.

FURTHER READING

Young, Robert, and Wendy G. Rohm. *Under the Radar: How Red Hat Changed the Software Business and Took Microsoft by Surprise.* Scottsdale, Ariz.: Coriolis, 1999.

—*Jonathan Bowen*

Reduced Instruction Set Computer

Reduced instruction set computers (RISC) use an approach to **computer architecture** that began in the mid-1980s and soon revolutionized the computer industry. The philosophy behind RISC design can be summarized as: Make it simple, therefore faster.

The motivation for RISC processors arose from technological developments that altered the architectural parameters traditionally used in the computer industry. The general trend until the mid-1970s was the design of ever-richer instruction sets, which could take some of the burden of interpreting high-level computer languages from the **compiler** to the **hardware**. The idea was to reduce the gap between the programming languages and the underlying hardware, by introducing many special instructions. Theoretically, this would make compilers simpler.

The RISC pioneers recognized that the performance of computer systems depended on three factors: the number of instructions in the program, the cycle time of the machine, and the number of instructions executed in each cycle. Bringing the hardware closer to the **software** meant that the number of instructions needed for a program was reduced, but at the cost of increasing the number of instructions per cycle. Dave Patterson (1947–) of the University of California at Berkeley and John Hennessy (1952–) of Stanford University took another route: By simplifying the instruction set and by getting rid of special instructions used only a small fraction of the time, the streamlined machine could use a faster clock and could execute more instructions per cycle.

The RISC movement got started when quantitative measurements of program performance showed that complex instruction set computing (CISC) used fewer than 10 to 20 instructions more than 90 percent of the time. Concentrating the design efforts on these instructions means that the frequently used instructions are made faster. RISC computers eliminated, for example, many addressing modes typical of computers such as the **VAX** but made much faster the few addressing modes that *were* kept. RISC processors also try to optimize the use of a large register file, avoiding frequent accesses to the slower memory. And last but not least, the streamlined instruction set allows the computer architect to pipeline instructions—that is, the processor works on several instructions at the same time, using its several pipeline stages. RISC processors are inherently parallel.

The first processor that would eventually lead to the RISC concept was the **IBM** 801, a machine developed in the 1970s but which remained a laboratory curiosity. The RISC I, built at Berkeley in 1981, and the MIPS processor, built at Stanford a few years later, showed that the approach was feasible and that the necessary technology was available. In the mid-1980s almost all major computer companies started developing RISC processors, and even CISC machines, like the **Intel** 86xx series, were built later using a "RISC kernel."

FURTHER READING

Patterson, Dave, and John Hennessy. *Computer Architecture: A Quantitative Approach.* San Francisco: Morgan Kaufmann, 1992.

—*Raúl Rojas*

Register

A register is a "container" used by the processor of a **digital computer** to store a number that will soon be needed again. Therefore, registers are memory cells, but usually faster that those provided by the main memory. Registers are often implemented with dynamic **RAM** (random access memory) chips, which offer a smaller cycle time than the static chips used for main storage. Registers are the first level in the memory hierarchy.

Computers built according to the canonical **von Neumann architecture** have a clear separation of the processor from the main memory. The first transforms and operates on numbers provided by the latter. However, whereas the processor can be very fast, executing instructions at the rate of one every 2 nanoseconds (ns) at a 500-megahertz clock rate, the memory chips are usually slower, needing from 20 to 50 ns to deliver a number. This mismatch can be alleviated by placing a **cache** memory between main memory and the processor, but the easiest strategy is to place fast registers in the processor itself. Once a number has been loaded into the registers, it is kept there for as long as possible, to be used as an argument for arithmetical and logical operations. Programs usually exhibit *locality of reference*; that is, information referenced at a certain time will be referenced a few steps later. Keeping results in the registers helps to speed up execution.

Registers are almost as old as computing machines. Even punched card Hollerith tabulators made abundant use of them, to accumulate numbers read from the cards. The first computer designed by the German engineer **Konrad Zuse** (1910–95) in 1936, the **Z1**, included two registers in its floating-point **central processing unit**.

Earlier microprocessors were limited in the number of registers they used. The increasing number of transistors available on a single chip made it possible later to design processors with 32 registers or even more. Having more registers is usually better, but the compiler has to know how to use them efficiently. This is known as the *register allocation problem*.

There are several types of register architectures. In *register–memory architectures*, operations can be started (e.g., an addition) with one argument stored in a register and the second stored in memory. This makes instructions more powerful, since they can refer to both registers and memory cells. In *register–register architectures*, on the contrary, all arguments have to be loaded to registers first. These are also called *load–store architectures*, since there is an instruction (load) to bring numbers from the memory to the registers and one (store) to copy registers to memory. RISC (**reduced instruction set computers**) machines are built around a register–register architecture, because the processor instructions should be as simple as possible.

Many processors distinguish between address and general-purpose registers. *Address registers* are used to hold addresses for memory references. The arithmetic performed on them is simpler since there can only be positive addresses. Processors such as those in the **Intel** family (8086 and upward) use *segment registers* to address memory. A segment register stores the address at the beginning of a segment (which can be a code segment or a data segment) and provides a reference point to address the rest of the segment using a second register.

Some machines operate using a register stack. In a stack of registers, numbers are stored on top of the stack and a new storage operation puts a new number on top (the same way that we can stack books on top of each other). The numbers can be read in the inverse order that they were put into the stack (last in, first out).

The SPARC processor, developed by **Sun** in the 1990s, employs a *register ring*. That is, up to 512 registers can be used, but at every single time the program or procedure running sees only 32 of them. This is called a *register window*. When a new procedure is called, the contents of the registers do not have to be saved to main memory: The register window is just advanced to a fresh set of registers. When the procedure is finished, control returns to the calling program and the old register window is used again.

Most modern processors make a distinction between *integer registers*, used to store integer numbers, and *floating-point registers*, used to store binary fractions with an exponent. Floating-point registers have a different layout according to the conventions used in the processor. Some **bits** are used to store the binary exponent of the number, others to store the mantissa and the sign. Copying a number from an integer register to a floating-point register is not a trivial operation and involves some calculations.

A state-of-the-art processor such as the Itanium, unveiled by Intel in 1999, uses a large set of internal registers: 128 integer registers, 128 floating-point registers, 8 branch registers, and 64 one-bit predicate registers. The predicate registers are used for speculative execution—that is, program branches are executed before it is known whether or not they will be taken. Later, only one branch is followed and unnecessary operations are canceled.

FURTHER READING
Blaauw, Gerrit A., and Frederick P. Brooks. *Computer Architecture: Concepts and Evolution*. Reading, Mass.: Addison-Wesley, 1997.
Patterson, David A., and John L. Hennessy. *Computer Architecture: A Quantitative Approach*. San Mateo, Calif.: Morgan Kaufmann, 1990; 2nd ed., 1996.

—*Margarita Esponda*

Register Renaming

Computers move data from the memory to the **central processing unit** (CPU) in order to process it. Since memory chips are usually slower than the processor, the data transferred to the processor are stored in internal cells, or **registers**, which are reused as often as possible. For example, if the processor has to operate repeatedly using five numbers stored in memory, it is convenient to load them first into five registers and reuse them in the CPU. A computer that minimizes the number of accesses to memory is avoiding the processor-memory bottleneck, (often called the *von Neumann bottleneck*), and works much faster.

Register renaming is a technique that allows the processor to allocate registers to a program dynamically. Only the documented registers are visible to the programmer, but auxiliary registers in the machine are used to hold data temporarily, expanding the effective number of available registers. Register renaming works invisibly—the processor does dynamic assignment of registers "on the fly."

Register renaming is useful for dynamic *loop unrolling*. Sometimes pieces of code are used repeatedly, for example, in a loop. Loops are hard to process because at the end of the loop a branch to the beginning of the loop is executed. Since modern **microprocessors** are optimized for forward processing (i.e., they execute a linear sequence of instructions as fast as possible, perhaps also in parallel), a branch makes them lose time. The programmer saves his fingers by writing a small loop that will be repeated 100 times in the machine, but the processor loses time.

Loop unrolling consists of expanding the loop. In the example above, the compiler writes the body of the code 100 times. If the body of the loop consists of five instructions (without counting the branch at the end), loop unrolling will transform these five instructions into 500. Loop unrolling can be done at compile time, in which case the big problem is the number of registers available in the processor. The compiler has to use different register names for the various iterations, to avoid data collisions in case execution of the instructions is overlapped.

Loop unrolling can be done dynamically if the processor implements register renaming. The instructions are loaded sequentially by the processor. Any time an instruction is fetched, the processor starts using its auxiliary registers instead of the registers used by the programmer. Even if the same instruction is fetched repetitively, the processor disentangles use of the registers, allowing the parallel execution and overlapping of the different sections of a loop. This technique, combined with branch prediction, is now used almost universally in fast processors.

Register renaming is also called the *Tomasulo Algorithmus* for the name of the inventor of this technique. It was first used in the **IBM** 360/91 computer in the mid-1960s. This machine pioneered many new concepts in computer architecture.

FURTHER READING
Hennessy, John, and David Patterson. *Computer Architecture : A Quantitative Approach*. San Francisco: Morgan Kaufmann, 1992.
Tomasulo, R. M. "An Efficient Algorithm for Exploiting Multiple Arithmetic Units." *IBM Journal of Research and Development*, Vol. 11, No. 1, 1967, pp. 25–33.

—*Raúl Rojas*

Report Program Generator

The Report Programmer Generator (RPG) programming language was developed by **IBM** in 1964, initially for use on the System/360 **mainframe** and the System/3 small data processing system. Designed specifically for generating business reports, RPG offers extensive features for record handling, data selection, collating, and tabular-output formatting. Its computation features are modest, and it provides only rudimentary flow-control structures.

All RPG programs have the same basic processing cycle—read, process, and print—based on the operation cycle of the electric accounting machines common in the days before computers. RPG's cycle is only slightly more sophisticated: Read one or more input records, perform some calculations, print one or more output records. The program logic is simply to repeat this cycle until an error occurs or until all input is processed. RPG supports multiple input sources and output destinations. The source code of an RPG program normally consists of four sets of specifications: file description, input, calculation, and output. File description and input specifications define the sources, fields, and data types that comprise the report program input. Calculation specifications define simple arithmetic and string operations to be performed on the input; RPG and RPG-II supported only the four basic arithmetic operations, and only one operation could be performed in each calculation specification. Output specifications define the report content and format, based on the input and calculation results, plus any desired headers and page layout. RPG is typically used with a control language or control framework; the control language used with RPG-II was named Operator Control Language (OCL).

There have been many dialects of RPG, beginning with RPG-II for the System/3 in 1965. The most recent version, RPG-IV, was released by IBM in 1994. RPG-IV added subroutines, exception handling, graphical user interfaces, and many other facilities to RPG, while preserving the basic language structure.

RPG was one of the earliest task-specific languages, and the first for business data processing. It proved that computer users could program their machines to perform vital work without understanding **algorithms** and without worrying about architectural details (e.g., word size, internal number representation).

Partly because it was so simple, RPG was used as a training language in data processing from the late 1960s through the 1970s and early 1980s. RPG systems still enjoy significant use in corporate data processing and management information systems environments. IBM and Lattice offer RPG compilers, development systems, and add-ons. The newest versions of RPG support data exchange with relational databases, graphical user interfaces, localization, and interaction with other programming languages.

Further Reading

Clark, Frank J., and Joseph M. Whalen. *RPG I and RPG II.* Reading, Mass.: Addison-Wesley, 1974.

IBM. *ILE RPG/400 Programmer's Guide.* White Plains, N.Y.: IBM Corporation, 1994.

Little, Joyce C. *RPG: Report Program Generator.* Englewood Cliffs, N.J.: Prentice Hall, 1971.

—*Neal Ziring*

Reverse Engineering

Reverse engineering is the process of analyzing an existing **software** system in order to recover the system's original design, to identify its various elements and their relationships, and to determine how it was developed from the component level on up. The process does not change the system but produces a representation of it in a more intelligible, usually graphical, form. Reverse engineering can also be applied to complete computer systems—understanding and redesigning hardware to create a new version of the system that is compatible with the original and yet different enough to be sold independently. Reverse engineering must take place in a **clean room** in order to avoid copyright violations.

Reverse engineering of software is an indispensable part of software maintenance, since maintenance—be it simple bug fixing or major enhancement—can not be performed without complete understanding of the problem or the existing system. Reverse engineering tools and techniques are used extensively when huge legacy systems are migrated to new machines that employ new programming paradigms and technology.

The scope of reverse engineering includes program comprehension, redocumentation, recovering design approach and design details at any level of abstraction, identifying reusable components, identifying components that need restructuring, recovering business rules, and understanding high-level system description. Processes attempting to redesign, restructure, or enhance the functionality of a system are not within the scope of reverse engineering, but they usually follow reverse engineering processes.

The reverse engineering of software is becoming increasingly important because the software world is experiencing paradigm changes more frequently than ever before. The time it took for the transition from the flat monolithic to the structured programming paradigm was much longer than when going from the structured to the object-oriented paradigm. Also, new methodologies, such as component-based programming, are emerging. Reverse engineering tools and techniques are of immense importance in making the transition over paradigm shifts quicker, easier, and cheaper.

FURTHER READING

Ingle, Katheryn. *Reverse Engineering*. New York: McGraw-Hill, 1994.

Lano, Kevin, and H. Haughton. *Reverse Engineering and Software Maintenance: A Practical Approach*. New York: McGraw-Hill, 1994.

Müller, Hausi, et al. "Reverse Engineering: A Roadmap." In Anthony Finkelstein, ed., *The Future of Software Engineering*. Limerick, Ireland: IEEE Computer Society Press, 2000.

—*Mohammad Ashrafuzzaman*

RISC Ses Reduced Instruction Set Computer.

Ritchie, Dennis and Ken Thompson

1941– and 1943–

U.S. Computer Scientists

The greatest contribution of Dennis M. Ritchie and Ken Thompson to computing has been the design and implementation of the **Unix** operating system and its associated **C** programming language at **Bell Labs** in the early 1970s. Both are highly portable, providing the **software** basis of many computers, especially workstations. The influence of their legacy lives on, largely in the updated forms of **Linus Torvalds**'s (1969–) **Linux** operating system for **personal computers**, and **Bjarne Stroustrup**'s (1950–) C++, an **object-oriented** extension of the C language.

Dennis Ritchie joined Bell Labs in 1967. Previously, his father, Alistair E. Ritchie, had a long career there, having coauthored *The Design of Switching Circuits* with W. Keister (1907–) and S. Washburn. This book on switching theory and logic design was produced just before the **transistor** era, another innovation of Bell Labs. Soon after joining, Ritchie contributed to the **Multics** project, then a joint effort of Bell Labs, Massachusetts Institute of Technology (MIT), and General Electric. Ritchie helped with a compiler for the BCPL language on the Multics machine (GE 645) and on the GE 635 under the GECOS system. He also wrote the compiler for ALTRAN, a language and system for symbolic calculation.

Ken Thompson was also hired by Bell Labs to work on the Multics project, which was a huge operation with many people involved. Multics was supposed to support hundreds of online users but in reality could handle only a small number. In 1969, Bell Labs withdrew from the project, and Thompson decided to develop his own operating system. Ritchie, also fresh from the Multics project, assisted Thompson in this task. Many people developed Multics, so Brian Kernighan later coined the term *Unix* for Thompson and Ritchie's more personal system.

The original Unix operating system was implemented using PDP-7 **assembler** language. Once it was essentially working, it was felt that a high-level language was needed. Initially, Doug McIlroy (1938–) implemented a language called TMG, but Thompson felt that a real computing service required **Fortran**. However, in the matter of a week or so, the definition for a new language, B, was produced instead. This had a very spartan syntax, due partially to the programmers' taste and partially to space restrictions on the compiler.

In 1970, a PDP-11 arrived to replace the PDP-7 at Bell Labs, and Unix began to be moved to it, but still in assembler. The B language was soon implemented on the PDP-11. Experience with B proved that it was not completely satisfactory, due to its cut-down nature. For example, there was only one type, the machine word. Hence Ritchie started to develop C from it. For a brief transition period, an intermediate language NB (New B) existed. Once C was available, most of Unix was reimplemented in this new language.

Many of Ritchie's C language principles and ideas were derived from Thompson's earlier language B, which in turn owned much to the languages BCPL and CPL. CPL (Combined Programming Language) was developed at Cambridge University in England during the 1960s. An important idea behind this language was that it was capable of high-level machine-independent programming while allowing the programmer to manipulate data at the bit level. A major drawback of CPL was that it was too large for practical use in many applications with the **hardware** technology of the time.

In 1967, a smaller version of CPL was produced by Martin Richards while working away from Cambridge University, at MIT. This was known as BCPL (Basic CPL). It retained the important features of the language, but with limitations to make a working compiler feasible. BCPL came to the attention of Ken Thompson, and in 1970, working at Bell Labs, he took this scaling-down process further to form the B language. This was designed specifically for use in systems programming, such as for writing operating systems. Finally, in 1972, Ritchie added such of the features of BCPL back into the language to make it more general purpose, producing the C programming language.

In the early days of Unix, Thompson used to produce Unix distribution tapes himself, often with a note that read "Love, ken." Early Unix users still use his first name only (sometimes uncapitalized, because it is also his login account name and part of his **electronic mail** address) in discussions, especially in **Usenet** newsgroups. Similarly, "Dennis" without a last name refers to Ritchie (and he is also often known as his login name, "dmr").

In 1979, Thompson visited the University of California–Berkeley on sabbatical leave. There he worked with **Bill Joy** (1955–) and Özalp Babaoglu (1955–) on adding paging and other enhancements to Unix. This led to the widely distributed Berkeley version of Unix for **VAX** computers, used for much of the 1980s. When Joy joined **Sun Microsystems**, Sun workstations used SunOS, a derived version of Unix. Hence Unix entered the commercial world and it continues to be used widely, especially as a reliable platform for servers.

Ritchie and Thompson's creation of the Unix operating system was their major joint achievement. After Unix had become well established in Bell Labs and a number of other educational, government, and commercial organizations, Steve Johnson, Ritchie, and Thompson ported the operating system to the Interdata 8/32 computer. This demonstrated the portability of Unix and helped in its subsequent widespread growth. The last important technical contribution Ritchie made to Unix was the Streams mechanism for interconnecting devices, protocols, and applications.

Ritchie and Thompson still work at Bell Labs. Ritchie is head of the System Software Research department in the Computing Sciences Research Center of Bell Labs/Lucent Technologies in Murray Hill, New Jersey. He manages a small group of researchers exploring distributed operating systems, languages, and routing/switching hardware. Accomplishments of the group include the Plan 9 (1995) and the Inferno operating systems (1996).

BIOGRAPHY

Dennis M. Ritchie. Born 9 September 1941 in Bronxville, New York. B.S. in physics, M.S. in applied mathematics from Harvard University. Doctoral thesis on subrecursive hierarchies of functions, 1968. Worked for Bell Labs, 1967–present. Worked on Multics, 1967–69; developed the C programming language, 1972; and Unix, 1970–79. Later appointed head of System Software Research Department, 1990.

Ken Thompson. Born 4 February 1943 in New Orleans, Louisiana. B.S. and M.S. in electrical engineering from University of California–Berkeley, 1965 and 1966. Worked at Bell Labs, 1966–present. Worked on Multics, 1967–69; developed the B programming language, 1969; and Unix, 1970–79.

Ritchie and Thompson are recipients of many (mainly joint) awards, including the Association for Computing Machinery (ACM) award for the outstanding paper in systems and languages, 1974; IEEE Emmanuel Piore Award, 1982; Bell Laboratories Fellow, 1983; ACM Turing Award, 1983; ACM Software Systems Award, 1983; U.S. National Academy of Engineering, 1988; C&C Foundation award of NEC, 1989; IEEE

Hamming Medal, 1990; Tsutomu Kanai Award, 1999; U.S. National Medal of Technology, 1999.

SELECTED WRITINGS

Kernighan, B. W., and Dennis M. Ritchie. *The C Programming Language*. Upper Saddle River, N.J.: Prentice Hall, 1978; 2nd ed., 1989.

Morris, R., and Ken Thompson. "UNIX Password Security." *Communications of the ACM*, Vol. 22, No. 11, 1979, pp. 594–597.

Ritchie, Dennis M. "The Evolution of the Unix Time-sharing System." In *Language Design and Programming Methodology*. Lecture Notes in Computer Science, Vol. 79. Berlin: Springer-Verlag, 1980. Reprinted in *AT&T Bell Laboratories Technical Journal*, Vol. 63, No. 6, Pt. 2, 1984, pp. 1577–1593.

———. "Reflections on Software Research." *Communications of the ACM*, Vol. 27, No. 8, 1984, pp. 758–760.

———. "The Development of the C Language." *HOPL II*, 1993, pp. 201–208.

Ritchie, Dennis M., and Ken Thompson. "The Unix Time-Sharing System." *Communications of the ACM*, Vol. 17, No. 7, 1974, pp. 365–375. Updated version in *Bell System Technical Journal*, Vol. 57, No. 6, Pt. 2, July–Aug. 1978, pp. 1931–1946. Reprinted in *Communications of the ACM*, Vol. 26, No. 1, 1983, pp. 84–89.

Ritchie, Dennis M., S. C. Johnson, and M. E. Lesk. "The C Programming Language." *Bell System Technical Journal*, Vol. 57, No. 6, 1978, pp. 1991–2019.

Thompson, Ken. "Regular Expression Search Algorithm." *Communications of the ACM*, Vol. 11, No. 6, 1968, pp. 419–422.

———. "The Unix Time-Sharing System: Unix Implementation." *Bell System Technical Journal*, Vol. 57, No. 6, 1978, pp. 1931–1946.

———. "Reflections on Trusting Trust: Half of the 1983 Turing Award Lecture." *Communications of the ACM*, Vol. 27, 1984, pp. 761–764.

Thompson, Ken, and Dennis M. Ritchie. *Unix Programmer's Manual*, 6th ed. Santa Barbara, Calif.: Computer Center, University of California, 1979.

FURTHER READING

Bergin, Thomas J., Jr., and Richard G. Gibson, Jr., eds. *History of Programming Languages II*. New York: Association for Computing Machinery; Reading, Mass.: Addison-Wesley, 1996.

AT&T Bell Laboratories Technical Journal, Vol. 63, No. 8, Pt. 2, 1984.

Slater, Robert. *Portraits in Silicon*. Cambridge, Mass.: MIT Press, 1987.

—*Jonathan Bowen*

Roberts, Lawrence G.

1937–

U.S. Engineer and Inventor

In the late 1960s and early 1970s, Lawrence Roberts combined computer science genius with strong management skills to help create the **ARPANET**, forerunner of the **Internet**. As a result, Roberts is widely referred to as one of the "fathers" of the Internet.

After earning B.S., M.S., and Ph.D. degrees in computer science from the Massachusetts Institute of Technology (MIT), Roberts joined the MIT affiliated Lincoln Laboratory. At Lincoln, he worked on the first transistorized TX-0 and TX-2 computers and wrote the entire operating system for the TX-2. In 1965, he teamed with Thomas Merrill to conduct the first experiment in networking two computers. Using a low-speed dial-up telephone line, Roberts connected his TX-2 computer in Massachusetts to Merril's Q-32 machine in California. The computers exchanged messages and proved that networking was indeed possible. In 1966, Merril and Roberts presented the results of their experiment in a paper titled "Toward a Cooperative Network of Time-Shared Computers."

In the same year and at the age of 29, Roberts was hired by Bob Taylor (1931–) to head up **ARPA**'s effort to develop a resource-sharing computer network. Roberts was tasked with designing the network, and at a 1967 conference in Ann Arbor, Michigan, he presented his ideas to a less than enthusiastic audience. His initial proposal called for directly connecting host computers to one another, thus requiring each host to handle networking functions. In a 1994 interview, Roberts recalled the poor reception that his idea received as follows: "Most places acted like this is my computer, and I don't want anyone else using it."

Following the Ann Arbor conference, Roberts integrated Wesley Clark's idea of having a system of intermediate computers, or nodes, that would sit between the host computers and handle all networking functions, such as sending, routing, and receiving messages, error correction, and assuring that messages reached their destinations. He termed these intermediate machines interface message processors (IMPs), the predecessor of what we now call **routers**.

At an October 1967 **Association of Computing Machinery** conference in Gatlinburg, Tennessee, Roberts presented a paper outlining his new network, which for the first time he called the ARPANET. The inclusion of the IMPs along with persistent lobbying helped convince participating ARPA research centers that the proposed network was a good idea. At the Gatlinburg conference, Roberts was also exposed to the packet-switching ideas of **Donald Davies** (1924–) and **Paul Baran** (1926–).

Roberts combined all of these elements into a 1968 request for quotation, which was sent out to 140 companies interested in building the first IMPs. In December 1968, the contract was awarded to **Bolt, Beranek and Newman** (BBN), which was given a 1 September 1969 deadline for delivery of the first IMP to UCLA. Roberts helped oversee the creation of the IMPs as well as software development at the four sites—UCLA, the Stanford Research Institute, the University of California at Santa Barbara, and the University of Utah—which would make up the initial ARPANET. The IMPs were built successfully, and in December 1969, Roberts' packet-switched network successfully connected all four host computers, thus giving birth to the ARPANET and laying the foundations for its eventual development into today's Internet.

Following the successful foundation of ARPANET, Roberts wanted commercial communications companies to realize the potential of a packet-switched network. As a result, he tasked **Robert Kahn** (1938–) with putting together a public demonstration of ARPANET at the first International Conference on Computer Communication (ICCC) in October 1972. Hundreds of people participated in the two and a half-day demonstration, which proved the feasibility and usefulness of packet-switched networks.

Roberts continued to foster the growth of the network he helped create when in 1973 he wrote the first **electronic mail** management program, RD, which allowed users to list, selectively read, file, forward, and respond to messages. His program helped make e-mail the **killer application** of ARPANET.

Later in 1973, Roberts left ARPA to head up a BBN spin-off called TELENET (not to be confused with the remote log-in program Telnet), which was the first commercial provider of a private packet-switching service, and eventually became Sprint. From 1983 to 1993, Roberts served as chief executive officer (CEO) of NetExpress, a packet-switched facsimile and ATM equipment company. Between 1993 and 1998 he was president of ATM systems. Today, Roberts is president and CEO of Palo Alto, California–based Packetcom, which is developing next–generation Internet infrastructure.

Larry Roberts long and impressive list of accomplishments in computer networking truly qualify him as one of the "fathers" of the Internet.

BIOGRAPHY

Lawrence G. Roberts. Born 21 December 1937. B.S., MS., and Ph.D. in computer science from Massachusetts Institute of Technology (MIT), 1959, 1960, and 1963. Successfully connected and sent messages between two computers on opposite sides of the country, 1965. Joined ARPA to help develop a resource-sharing computer network, 1966. Proposed the design of the ARPANET, 1967. Issued request for quotation to build the first IMPs, 1968. Oversaw the development and successful implementation of the initial four-node ARPANET packet-switched network, 1969. Wrote RD, the first e-mail management program and joined first commercial packet-switching service, TELENET, 1973. Developed several successful packet-switched network companies, 1983–98. Currently president of Packetcom.

SELECTED WRITINGS

Merril, T., and L. G. Roberts. "Toward a Cooperative Network of Time-Shared Computers." *Proceedings of the AFIPS Fall Joint Computer Conference,* Oct. 1966, pp. 425–431.

FURTHER READING

Abbate, Janet. *Inventing the Internet.* Cambridge, Mass.: MIT Press, 1999.

Crawley, James W. "A Net Gain." *The San Diego Union-Tribune,* 4 Sept. 1994, p. I1.

Hafner, Katie, and Matthew Lyon. *Where Wizards Stay Up Late: The Origins of the Internet.* New York: Simon and Schuster, 1996.

Moschovitis, Christos J. P., Hilary Poole, Tami Schuyler, and Theresa M. Senft. *History of the Internet: A Chronology, 1843 to the Present.* Santa Barbara, Calif.: ABC-CLIO, 1999.

Segaller, Stephen. *Nerds 2.0.1: A Brief History of the Internet.* New York: TV Books, 1999.

—*Christopher D. Hunter*

Robotics

The word *robot* conjures a variety of images. Some might remember the televised picture of the small wheeled vehicle named *Sojourner* that moved on the surface of the planet Mars in 1998. For some people the word refers to characters from the movies, such as R2-D2 and C-3PO. For others, the word conjures up visions of dangerous mechanical beasts they have seen in comic strips or in science fiction movies. For others they are machines of superhuman intelligence. For still others, the word carries images of numerous mechanical arms assembling automobiles. Robots are also believed to be machines that eventually will relieve us from everyday tasks, such as mowing the lawn, vacuuming the carpet, or cleaning toilets. The field of robotics encompasses all these areas and more, involving the science, development, and applications of intelligent machines, machines that receive information from the world using sensors and then perform some actions in the world. In fact, a robot is sometimes defined as a machine that provides an intelligent connection between perception and action. Furthermore, the word is used to denote machines under remote human control (also known as *teleoperated* robots) as well as those capable of partial or completely autonomous behaviors.

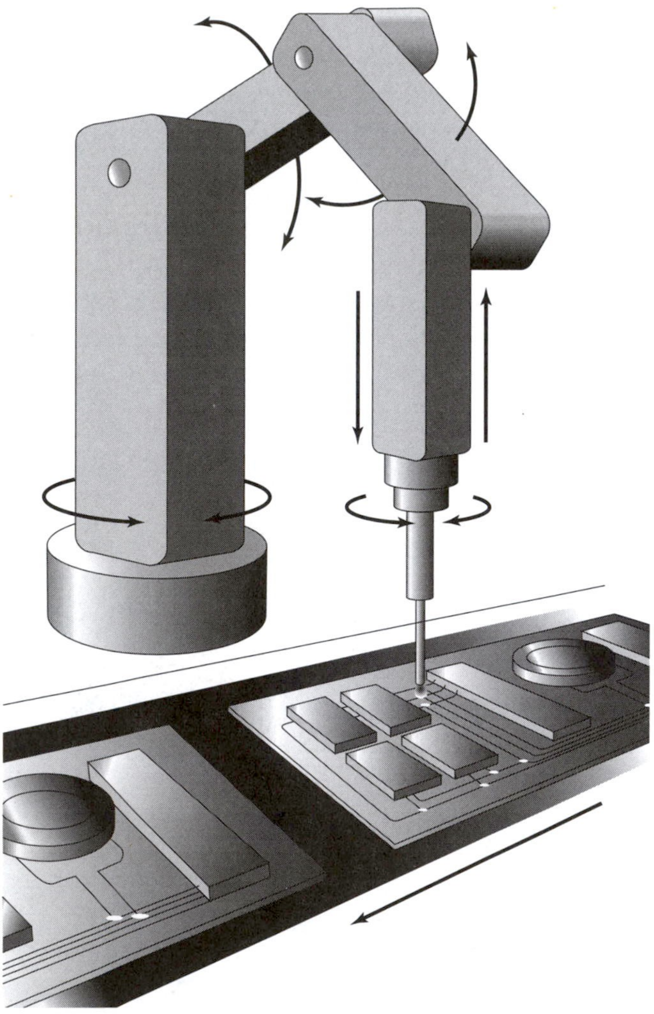

Figure 1. *Typical industrial robot, used for mechanical assembly. (Illustration based on an image courtesy of Adept Technologies)*

The word *robot* is derived from the Czech word *robota* meaning "work," which appears in a play entitled *R.U.R.* (*Rossum's Universal Robots*), written in 1921 by Karel Capek (1890–1938). The play concerns the creation and fabrication of human-appearing artificial workers known as robots. The robots are manufactured in factories by other robots. They perform all manual labor formerly performed by humans, and when they wear out, they are recycled for raw materials. Eventually, they rebel against their masters and kill most humans. Thus use of the word *robot* to refer to a machine that performs work which humans find undesirable is now some 80 years old.

Manufacturing robots are computer-controlled mechanical manipulators that are used for such functions as material transport, welding, painting, or assembly in a factory environment. The may be large and powerful enough to handle an entire automobile engine or small and precise enough to place computer chips in their proper locations in electronic fabrication.

It is evident that robots such as these are basically mechanical arms, equipped with a "hand" or *end effector* for grasping tools or materials, sensors such as vision or touch, and a computer for control. The inspiration for the design of robot manipulators is the structure of the human arm. Whereas human arms move by contraction of muscles, robot manipulators use electric, hydraulic, or pneumatic motors to obtain motion. Figure 1 shows an industrial robot used for assembly purposes.

The structure of robot manipulators may differ significantly from that of a human arm. For example, a robot arm can be extended by telescoping. Such a

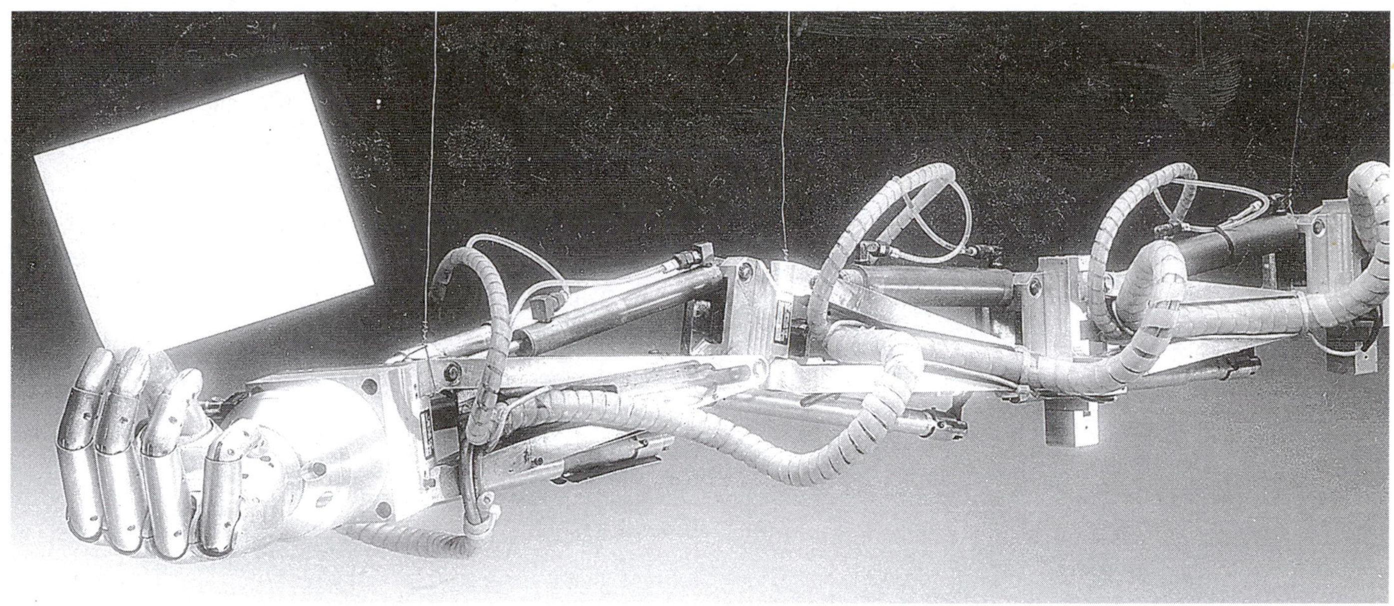

Figure 2. *The Tentacle Arm, developed by Marvin Minsky in 1968. (Courtesy of the Computer History Museum)*

prismatic degree of freedom does not exist in nature. The robot shown in Figure 1 moves about a central vertical axis, which may be considered a "shoulder," with additional joints for an "elbow" and "wrist". Again, a shoulder capable of rotating 360° does not exist in nature. Robot arms may also have many articulated segments, so that they can move like an elephant's trunk or a snake.

Robot end effectors can be designed to mimic the function and even the structure of the human hand, such as the five-fingered hand shown in Figure 2. However, many robots make use of special-purpose end effectors that are specifically designed to grasp particular objects, such as a wrench, a screw, or an electronic chip. Evolution tends to favor general-purpose devices, while engineering design can provide outstanding special-purpose devices.

In the past most industrial robots were only preprogrammed devices, with no real-time input from the environment. A computer program to describe the desired robot motion was usually written in a special robot programming language. Alternatively, the endpoint of the robot could be moved manually through the desired trajectory (such as the desired path of a paint sprayer); the motion was stored and then used to command the robot. At the present time, nearly all industrial robots use some sensory inputs and computers that enable them to respond to changes in the environment and act accordingly.

The earliest *mobile robots* were automatic guided vehicles (AGVs) used to transport materials and supplies on the factory floor. These devices often followed a wire embedded in the floor. Both walking and wheeled mobile robots began to appear in university laboratories in the 1960s and 1970s. A biped walking robot constructed at Waseda University in Japan walked many kilometers during a World's Fair in Tokyo. During the 1980s, researchers in Germany and in the United States began developing autonomous (robot) automobiles, capable of using on-board computer vision and other sensors to travel along highways at normal highway speeds. During the past 20 years a number of robotic vehicles were developed for the military, including robot tanks, trucks, and helicopters. Mobility under the water has also become possible with the development of small robot submarines.

At present there is increasing interest in the field of **personal robotics**, which has spurred the development of mobile robots capable of assisting people in a variety of ways. A robot known as HelpMate travels along hallways in some 70 hospitals, delivering meals to patients. It is capable of calling the elevator and moving to a different floor of the hospital, where it uses prestored maps to locate a desired destination. Prototype robot vacuum cleaners and lawn mowers have been built, as well as robots capable of crawling up and cleaning an all-glass skyscraper using feet equipped with suction cups. There are also mobile robots that can travel the perimeter of a building and perform sentry duties.

Yet, despite the remarkable advances in robotics made possible by improved sensors and low-cost computer chips, service robots are not yet widely available. There are several reasons for this state of affairs. First, if robots are used as assistants to people or work in close proximity to people, they must be nearly 100 percent reliable. A robot vacuum cleaner that breaks down frequently will not be acceptable. Further, the cost of service robots must be sufficiently low to encourage their use. Clearly, low cost and high reliability will be possible only with mass production. To date, large companies have not been willing to invest the capital needed to produce and distribute such robots. We anticipate that this situation will change during the next 20 or 25 years.

The toy industry, entertainment centers, and the mass media (motion pictures and television) are major users and developers of robots, both autonomous and teleoperated. Many robots are built primarily for science fiction movies, such as the *Star Wars* series. Of course, what appear to be autonomous, intelligent robots could simply be special effects, involving a blend of teleoperated manikins and **virtual reality**, as with some of the dinosaurs shown in recent films.

On the other hand, toys provide an outstanding market for robots. An example of such a device is the robot "dog" AIBO developed by Sony Corporation in Japan. This device is a true four-legged robot, equipped with vision, touch sensors, and acoustic sensors (microphones) to provide perceptual inputs from the environment. It is capable of a number of independent behaviors, such as chasing a ball, sitting and waving with a front paw, lying down, and standing up. A team of AIBOs has been programmed to play soccer. A special-purpose electronic card can be inserted into the device to provide new behaviors. Experts believe that AIBO is only the first of an increasing number of autonomous robotic toys that will reach the market.

There are currently some 250,000 manufacturing robots in the world, performing endless repetitive tasks in factories throughout the industrialized world. In addition, the use of robots with mobility and "intelligence" in its various aspects is growing rapidly. It is clear that future robots will be equipped with more and more powerful computers, thus increasing their ability to work autonomously. In other words, future robots will be increasingly intelligent and in certain applications their intelligence will approach (and may surpass) that of their human co-workers. There will be more applications of groups of mobile robots, for such tasks as planetary exploration, construction tasks in hazardous environments, and environmental monitoring and cleanup. Robots will also become smaller and smaller. We anticipate the development of both micro- and nanoscale robots. Such tiny systems could be injected into the bloodstream and remove cholesterol deposits from arterial walls, or deposit chemotherapeutic agents directly into a malignant tumor. Yet another trend points toward the development of humanoid robots, which not only look like, but also behave like, human beings. There will also be increasing development of robotic toys with more and more intelligence and ability.

Clearly, these trends are both fascinating and alarming. They offer the potential of providing us with automated assistants not only in the factory, but also in household tasks, the care of the infirm and the elderly, and the drudgery or routine of maintenance. However, as these machines acquire the ability to learn, plan, solve problems, and organize work in ways that may supplant human abilities, can we be sure that they will always obey their creators? As systems become more complex, they may behave in new and unexpected ways; such phenomena are known as *emergent behaviors*. The humanoid robots of the play *R.U.R.* rebelled against their human masters; ensuring that future robots will always be benevolent and obedient will require human intelligence, creativity, vigilance, and sensitivity.

FURTHER READING

Arkin, Ronald C. *Behavior-Based Robotics*. Cambridge, Mass.: MIT Press, 1998.

Jefferis, David. *Artificial Intelligence: Robotics and Machine Evolution*. New York: Crabtree, 1999.

Kortenkamp, David, R. Peter Bonasso, and Robin Murphy, eds. *Artificial Intelligence and Mobile Robots: Case Studies of*

Successful Robot Systems. Menlo Park, Calif.: AAAI Press with MIT Press, 1998.

Nof, Shimon Y. *Handbook of Industrial Robotics*. New York: Wiley, 1985; 2nd ed., 1999.

—*George A. Bekey*

Router

A router (or gateway) is a component of a **local area network** (LAN) or **wide area network** (WAN). It is connected to two or more networks from which it receives packets. It uses each packet's *network layer destination address* (e.g., its **IP** [Internet Protocol] **address**) and its *routing table* to determine whether the packet is to be dropped or forwarded to one of the connected networks. A *routing table* consists of many entries, containing, among others, the destination address, the gateway address, and network **interface**. The destination address contains a *network address* and a *host address*.

For each packet received, the router will do a series of checks trying to find out if the packet can be immediately delivered to one of the networks connected to the router, or if it should be forwarded to another router which can continue with the search of the final destination network. If all these fail, the packet is discarded and a "destination unreachable" error message is returned to the sender. If the decision is to forward the packet, a header called *time to live* is reduced by one; at zero the packet is discarded. If all seems well, the received packet is sent unaltered to a device on a network the router is connected to—this may be just one step in many required for the packet to reach its destination.

Different router types are used solely within an *autonomous region*, or to interconnect them. A small network might use a *static router configuration* which explicitly identifies each network address and gateway address, including a *default* gateway to reach the outside world. In larger networks this task is better carried out automatically by an *interior gateway protocol*. One of the most popular is the *Routing Information Protocol* (RIP), which initially broadcasts a *request* on each network to which it is connected. Other routers send back a *routing response* with their list of network addresses and distances measured in router hops (16 means *infinity*). The router then combines these lists into its routing table which it broadcasts every 30 seconds or whenever it detects a change.

For a design that seems fairly simple, the RIP has demonstrated some perverse difficulties. One problem can occur when a network link fails—broadcast route updates get out of synchronization and routing loops are created, which send packets back and forth until their time-to-live expires. Similarly, route updates bounce back and forth, adjusting the distance to the lost network until *infinity* is reached. This process can take many minutes to stabilize, and it is accompanied by packet storms and network degradation. A series of updates to the RIP attempt to correct these features.

A successor to RIP is *open shortest path first* (OSPF), which exchanges *hello* messages to confirm network connectivity and list known neighbors. Listed routers become targets for *link status requests* answered by *database descriptions*, which list the remote router's immediate connections. The included *link metric* is not a simple hop count but an indication of the cost of using the link. When the router has a collection of these, it will calculate a *shortest path tree* to all destinations and form its routing table.

OSPF converges faster than RIP after a failure, it does not regularly send its entire routing table, it permits smart routing, and messages may be authenticated (unlike the RIP) to avoid denial-of-service attacks. The connection of LANs to the rest of the Internet is a serious responsibility. Although some exterior routers will be able to fall back on regional gateways to provide a default route, the Internet backbone routers need enough memory to record *all* destination networks.

The *Exterior Gateway Protocol* (EGP) has the administrative constraint that it must be told to what routers it is allowed to send packets. It starts finding routes with an *acquisition request* and checks the link with regular exchanges of *hello* and *I heard you* messages. The *routing table* is built from the responses to a poll request, which contain complex tree descriptions in a *routing update*. The EGP shares some of RIP's problems, including the inability to support load sharing and slow recovery from network failures. A number of enhanced versions of the EGP have been proposed, including the *Border Gateway Protocol* (BGP), which has worked well for domains that carry transit packets. Router manufacturers have also provided proprietary protocols. The term gateway is now used more for a protocol translation function than for a router.

Further Reading

Comer, Douglas. *Internetworking with TCP/IP*. Upper Saddle River, N.J.: Prentice Hall, 2000.

Perlman, Radia. *Interconnections: Bridges and Routers*. Reading, Mass.: Addison-Wesley, 1992.

Stallings, William. *Handbook of Computer-Communications Standards*. Carmel, Ind.: Howard W. Sams, 1990.

Stevens, W. Richard. *TCP/IP Illustrated*. Reading, Mass.: Addison-Wesley, 1994.

Tanenbaum, Andrew S. *Computer Networks*. Upper Saddle River, N.J.: Prentice Hall, 1996.

—*John Deane*

RPG See Report Program Generator.

Ryad Series

In the mid-1960s, the Soviet Union and other member countries of the Council for Mutual Economic Assistance (CMEA) designed, developed, and put into production a family of third-generation computers, known as the Unified System or, in Russian, Ryad. The Unified System was intended to be upwardly compatible in the sense that programs that ran on one of its models would run without change on any larger model. By 1980 the Unified System may have been second only to the **IBM** 360/370 series in the number of **mainframes** installed. By 1992, after the dissolution of the USSR, CMEA, and the Warsaw Pact, this extensive, integrated program had for the most part broken up and withered away. However, as many as 4000 of these machines may still have been in operation in Russia and Belarus in 1998.

The overall undertaking and the machines it produced were officially designated as the *Edinaya Sistema*, Russian for "Unified System," and abbreviated by the Cyrillic *EC* (transliterated as either ES or YeS). Language differences among the participating countries produced other variants. For example, the Polish abbreviation was JS, and the German Democratic Republic (GDR) used ESER. *Ryad* (alternative transliteration: *Riad*), meaning *row* or *series* in Russian, was the term used in the first public announcement in December 1967, and remained the popular name for the program.

By the mid-1960s, the serious inadequacies of computer **hardware** and **software** in the USSR and Eastern Europe were apparent to many. Shortly after the success of the IBM 360 series became apparent—and after two failures to produce indigenous upwardly compatible groups of machines—the Soviets decided to start work on a new family of general-purpose data processing computers. The original December 1967 official statement implied that it was a Soviet project. However, by 1968 the USSR was working to persuade its allies to join the effort. Hungary, Bulgaria, and the GDR were the most amenable. Poland wanted to continue its ODRA program, and Czechoslovakia also had a program of its own and proved to be less than fully committed to the ES. Romania participated in name only, preferring to look to the United States and France for help. Cuba was added later with a marginal role.

The decision on the basic architecture of the new system was made after extensive discussion both within the USSR and among the CMEA participants. Pride was an important factor in the argument favoring the use of an indigenous design. The GDR wanted to use the IBM system/360 architecture and to make the *Ryads* compatible with the IBM machines; it had been pursuing this approach on its own, probably aided by either direct or indirect access to IBM and other U.S. technology in Western Europe. Ultimately the Soviets chose to use the well-established IBM architecture, with the expectation that this would minimize development risk, produce a feasible result as expeditiously as possible, and provide access to a large inventory of working software developed for the IBM machines.

The first *Ryad* computers, prototypes of the small ES-1020 model, were put on display in Bulgaria and Poland in 1971. Within two months the small initial batch was back at the Minsk Ordzhonikidze Plant for "redesign." It was not until May 1973 that six of the seven models originally specified in 1970 could be put on display in Moscow. Of the six exhibited, only the smallest three, one Hungarian and two Soviet, were said to be in serial production. By early 1974, the Czech and East German models had gone into production. Neither the Hungarian nor the Czech model had much compatibility with the other *Ryads*. Four additional models appeared between 1975 and 1977.

Input/output devices and auxiliary storage were the weakest part of the Unified System. In 1973, orders were being accepted for only about half of the announced peripherals. Many of those not available were devices for auxiliary storage and servicing of remote users via telecommunications channels. Hungary was most successful in meeting its goals for peripherals; the Soviet Union was perhaps least successful. Most of the equipment was at IBM's mid-1960s levels. However, in some ways the peripherals were a major achievement: Despite performance, reliability, and availability problems, for the first time CMEA computer systems in widespread use came equipped with something approaching a complete set of peripherals, most notably disk storage.

With an enormous effort, the CEMA countries did moderately well in adapting the IBM 360 **operating systems** to the ES hardware. They thereby placed themselves in a position to "borrow" huge quantities of systems and applications software that had taken IBM and its customers billions of dollars and thousands of person-years to produce.

The models of the Unified System were not a reverse engineering of the IBM 360 and subsequent IBM machines—that would imply duplication down to the level of circuit components and, if truly successful, interchangeability of parts between the original and the copy. The ES attempt to copy IBM products was an effective functional duplication. The architecture, instruction set, and data channel interfaces were the same, permitting the use of IBM software and interchange at the CPU or major subsystem level with relatively little difficulty. Although there was no detailed copying of electronic components or manufacturing techniques, the CMEA countries achieved limited compatibility of media, permitting the exchange of cards, magnetic tapes, and disk packs. ES peripherals were also widely used with non-ES machines.

There were good technical and economic reasons for adopting this strategy. The project had very high-level backing, and the commitments of personnel and facilities were comparable to that of IBM itself. The acquisition of extensive functional capability was the most important goal for the socialist economies, which did not have to compete directly on world markets. This strategy would be continued.

By the mid-1970s, the CMEA participants were sufficiently satisfied with the first two groups of computers, subsequently called the ES-I machines (with model numbers ending in 0, 1, 2, or 3), to initiate an ES-II undertaking patterned after the IBM 370 series that went into production in the early 1970s. By 1979, most of the ES-II models existed as at least prototypes and were displayed at the official *Ryad* tenth anniversary exhibit in Moscow. By 1982, at least a half dozen ES-II computers (with model numbers ending in 5 or 6) and an assortment of new peripherals were in at least initial batch production.

An ES-III effort was announced in 1977, although by the mid-1980s this looked more like a marginal extension of the ES-II program than an effort to keep up with the newest IBM mainframes. By the late 1980s, the ES-III machines (with model numbers usually ending in 6, 7, or 8) were probably not being built at much more than the replacement rates for machines being retired. The CMEA countries, and the USSR in particular, were having great difficulties with volume production, especially of high-performance semiconductor memory and large-capacity disk stores.

About 15,000 ES mainframes had been produced by 1989, with the great majority operating in the Soviet Union, many of those at large state enterprises. By 1992, after the dissolution of CMEA and the breakup of the USSR, the geographically scattered production facilities were cut off from each other, the design bureaus, and ES management facilities. At that time few customers in the former Soviet republics were still getting the centrally planned allocations specifically for the purchase of ES machines, and they turned to other sources of computing, often in the form of imported or domestically assembled **personal computers** (PCs) or small secondhand mainframes. Retirement of some ES machines occasionally included extraction of the gold content from their circuits to buy Western PCs.

Efforts to continue the program quickly became mostly limited to Russia and Belarus, where perhaps 4000 ES computers remained operating in the mid-1990s. At the largest of all the ES manufacturing plants, the Minsk Ordzhonikidze plant, attempts to work out various forms of arrangements with IBM for components, coproduction, or maintenance of installed ES or IBM mainframes came to little. Attempts to develop new machines, including an ES-IV series, also largely foundered as it became clear that the factories could not master new technologies without huge investments, and that such investments would not be forthcoming. Production of new ES computers probably ended by 1995.

For about a quarter of a century, the Unified System provided the most visible and extensive forms of computing in the USSR and most other CMEA countries, although it never absorbed the entire computer industries of these countries. The focus was on Ryad because it is by far the largest program and intended to provide general-purpose computing to significant parts of the economies, and many of the other computer development programs in the USSR were classified. During the history of CMEA the Unified System was one of the most important attempts to provide integrated multinational technological solutions to serious needs.

FURTHER READING

Davis, N. C., and Goodman, S. E. "The Soviet Bloc's Unified System of Computers." *ACM Computing Surveys*, Vol. 10, No. 2, June 1978, pp. 93–122.

Goodman, S. E. "Socialist Technological Integration: The Case of the East European Computer Industries." *The Information Society*, Vol. 3, No. 1, 1984, pp. 39–90.

Goodman, Seymour E., et al. *Global Trends in Computer Technology and Their Impact on Export Control.* Washington, D.C.: National Academy, 1988.

McHenry, William K. *The Year 2000 Problem in Russia: Evidence and Analysis.* Report for the Mitre Corp., 2 Mar. 1999.

—*Seymour Goodman*

S

SABRE

SABRE was the first real-time airline reservations system. Completed in 1964, SABRE not only revolutionized the airline business but also demonstrated the superiority of real-time systems for some computing tasks.

The development of automated systems for processing airline reservations began in the mid-1940s when Teleregister Corporation built the Reservisor system for American Airlines. Installed in Boston, it handled flights for that city only and employed a matrix of relays into which plugs were inserted manually to indicate whether a flight was open or closed. The success of this system led to the development, starting in 1949, of the Magnetronic Reservisor, which utilized magnetic relay and vacuum-tube circuits. It was later installed at LaGuardia airport in New York. In August 1956 a larger and faster model was installed in the American Airlines ticket office in New York City; it could process one to two requests per second. Several other U.S. airlines also purchased Reservisor systems.

The first reservation system based on a fully electronic computer was developed in 1957–58 by Eastern Airlines and Sperry Rand Corporation, utilizing a **UNIVAC** File Computer. The File was a **vacuum-tube** computer that used **magnetic drums** for mass storage. Similar systems were installed for Northwest Airlines in 1959 and Capitol Airlines in 1960. They were capable of processing up to 2.7 requests per second. Eastern and Northwest later moved their systems to transistor UNIVAC 490 computers. Trans-Canada Airlines developed its ReserVec system, which used a pair of transistor computers built by Ferranti Corporation between 1959 and 1963. It could handle 10 requests per second.

All the systems mentioned so far were seat inventory programs that only kept track of how many seats were sold and how many were available. Airlines needed more sophisticated programs to record passenger names and issue tickets. In 1957, American Airlines and **IBM** began developing such a system, which they called SABRE, reportedly inspired by an advertisement for the Buick LeSabre automobile. An acronym was later concocted—Semi-Automatic Business Research Environment. An initial system was installed in 1960; the nationwide network was completed in 1964. It was implemented on dual IBM 7090 computers connected to six high-speed magnetic drums and 16 disk storage units. The drums and many components of the SABRE communications network were adapted from items developed by IBM for the SAGE air defense project. The initial SABRE system processed 26,000 transactions per day with a response time of less than 3 seconds.

Passenger-name reservation systems were developed at other airlines. IBM used its experience from SABRE to develop lower-volume systems for Delta Airlines (Deltamatic) and Pan Amerivan (Panamac) in 1963. Beginning in 1965, Air Canada used a **Burroughs** D82 computer to handle flights for Montreal and Toronto and in 1970 switched to the ReserVec II system, based on a UNIVAC 1108, for all flights. Air France wrote its own system for the UNIVAC 1108, which went into service in 1969. After the introduction of the System/360, IBM implemented the PARS system in 1968 for Eastern Airlines and sold it to United and TWA in 1970. SABRE was rewritten for the 360 in 1970. The descendants of these IBM and UNIVAC systems are still being used by airlines.

FURTHER READING

Copeland, Duncan G., Richard O. Mason, and James L. McKenney. "Sabre: The Development of Information-Based Competence and Execution of Information-Based Competition." *IEEE Annals of the History of Computing*, Vol. 17, Fall 1995, pp. 30–57.

Dornian, Alan. "ReserVec: Trans-Canada Airlines' Computerized Reservation System." *IEEE Annals of the History of Computing*, Vol. 16, Summer 1994, pp. 31–42.

—*George Gray*

SAGE

The Semi-Automatic Ground Environment (SAGE) was the world's first computer-based air defense **real-time system**. Work on its design began in 1958, and when it was fully operational, it linked hundreds of radar stations in a large-scale network. SAGE was, in fact, an early example of a distributed network and distributed computing.

SAGE was intended to protect the United States from long-range bombers and missiles, which were a major concern after the Soviet Union demonstrated their technical skills with the 1957 launch of *Sputnik*, the first artificial satellite. The radar stations were linked by telephone lines, and the information was collected at several central locations to be processed by new computers specially designed for the task.

The coordination and the software for the project was in the hands of MITRE, a nonprofit organization founded from the Computer Systems Division at Massachusetts Institute of Technology (MIT). In 1963, SAGE was fully deployed, linking the radar to 22 command centers and three combat centers. The machines used at the centers evolved from the work done by Jay Forrester (1918–) on the Whirlwind system. After the **Whirlwind** had been developed at MIT, a contract was awarded to **IBM** to build the new Whirlwind II. The computer, later renamed AN/FSQ-7, weighed 250 tons. One was built for each of the 22 command centers.

The new computers required groundbreaking research from their builders to accommodate simultaneous users in the same system. New forms of displaying information visually also had to be invented, to fully exploit the data processing capabilities of the operators themselves. The integration of the entire system required the development of **software engineering** techniques for developing, assessing, evaluating, and completing large projects, as is done today in the software industry. Programming, a mere handicraft until then, became part of industrial engineering.

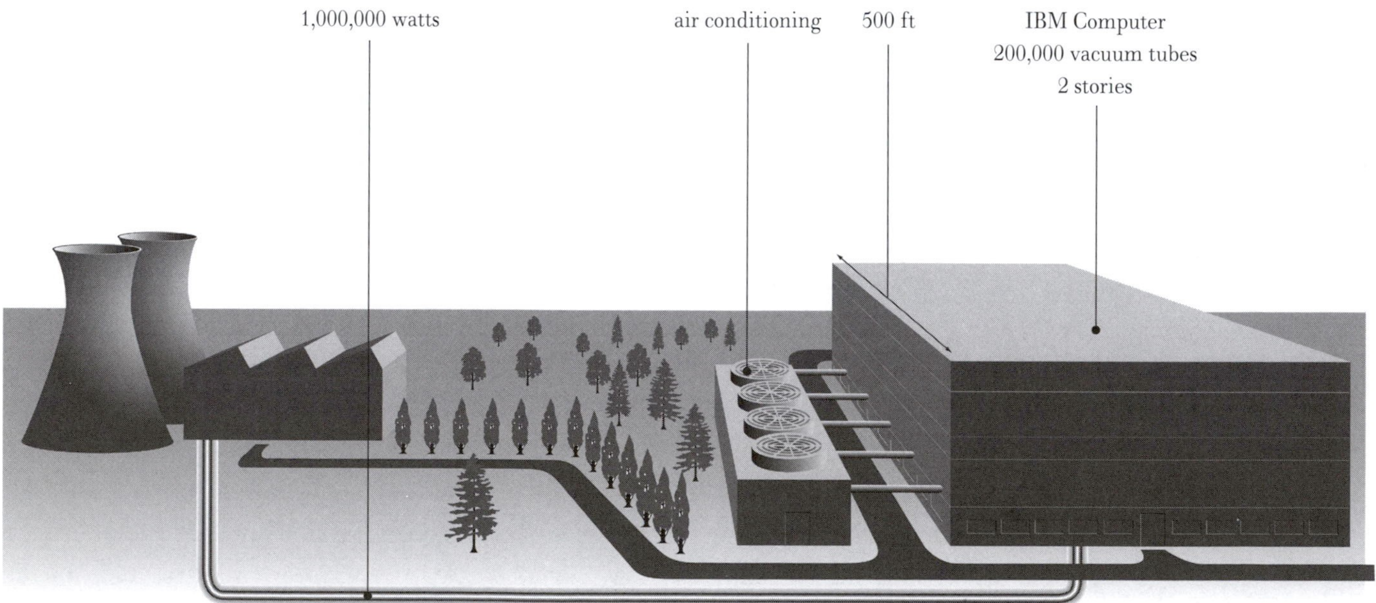

Semi-Automatic Ground Environment (SAGE) computer.

The SAGE computers processed information in real time, presenting the result to operators on circular screens. The user could ask for more details about a specific object by touching the screen with a light gun and could also enter commands in the same way. Each computer was enormous, needing a full megawatt of power to drive its 55,000 vacuum tubes, making SAGE the largest vacuum-tube system ever built. SAGE was operational until 1983.

The SAGE system was designed to be triggered by an alarm from early warning radar installed at the U.S. borders, in Canada, or even on top of offshore oil platforms (the shortest route for Soviet missiles was over the North Pole). The warning was sent through telephone lines to a direction center, which notified interceptors and headquarters. SAGE then tracked the bomber or missile and calculated the interception parameters, which were sent to ground-to-air missiles and other interceptors.

Although the work done for SAGE was classified, much of the technology eventually became available and was used in civilian air traffic control systems. **Joseph Licklider** (1915–90), who worked on the development of SAGE, later became the director of IPTO (Information Processing Techniques Office) at **ARPA**, and started research that culminated in creation of the **ARPANET**.

FURTHER READING

Annals of the History of Computing, Special Issue on SAGE, Vol. 5, No. 4, 1983.

Hughes, Thomas P. *Rescuing Prometheus*. New York: Pantheon Books, 1998.

Jacobs, John F. *The SAGE Air Defense Systems: A Personal History*. Bedford, Mass.: MITRE Corporation, 1986.

—*Frank Darius*

SAP

SAP is one of the largest **software** companies in the world, and one of the few European global players in the software industry. The name is an acronym for *Systeme, Anwendungen, Produkte in der Datenverarbeitung*, or in English, *Systems, Applications, and Products*. SAP was founded in Germany in 1972 by five former **IBM** employees who later became multimillionaires. The original name of the company was *Systemanalyse und Programmentwicklung* (*System Analysis and Program Development*).

In the 1970s, most business data processing was done off-line, using punched cards to hold the data, processing the programs overnight in special computer centers. The founders of SAP, who did consulting for IBM clients, noticed that many companies were developing the same types of programs for their business needs and immediately saw a business opportunity. Their idea was to provide those companies with a generic solution, which could be customized and would allow interactive online data processing using time-shared computers.

During the last 25 years, SAP has marketed two main products, R/2 and R/3. Both systems are packets of program modules that provide all the functionality required for business computing. R/3 provides a user interface that separates the user from the **operating system** (OS) so that it seems to be the OS from the user's perspective. R/2, introduced in 1979, was targeted for mainframes with a time-sharing operating system, whereas R/3, introduced in 1992, is based in the server–client model so effective in local area networks. The server is the main computer where the data are kept; the clients are the individual workstations or personal computers that allow retrieval or modification of the data.

SAP software became popular in the first half of the 1990s, and the company opened distribution offices in all major industrial countries in the world. At one point, SAP was the second- or third-largest software company in the world. However, the success of R/3, a closed proprietary system, led the company to ignore the **Internet** and the emerging **electronic commerce** business. While startups were introducing new products for networks, SAP was locked with its proprietary strategy. After having enjoyed 60 percent yearly growth rates, the company reached a sales plateau in the late 1990s and SAP shares fell in the stock market.

SAP countered by embracing the Internet and starting specific **portals** for the business community, such as "mySAP.com". Companies get information and support through the portal and can even make use of the *application hosting service*—companies provide the data, which is processed in external computers. The SAP software makes the process transparent for the user.

At the end of 1999, SAP had worldwide revenues of more than U.S.$5 billion. It employs more than 20,000 persons in 50 countries. The main competitor of SAP in the enterprise computing marketplace is **Oracle**, which has a more diversified product range.

FURTHER READING

Dietz, Lisa Ramsay, Robert Lyfareff, and Gareth M. deBruyn. *What Every Business Needs to Know About SAP.* Roseville, Calif.: Prima Publishing, 1999.

Plattner, Hasso. *Anticipating Change: Secrets Behind the SAP* Empire. Roseville, Calif.: Prima Publishing, 2000.

—*Raúl Rojas*

Satellite Networks

Satellite networks were first proposed by British science-fiction writer Arthur C. Clarke (1917–) while serving as a lieutenant in the Royal Air Force during World War II. In just 50 years, communications satellites have evolved from science fiction to a key component of global networks.

Clarke set out his ideas in a short article called "Extra-Terrestrial Relays," which appeared in the October 1945 issue of the magazine *Wireless World.* In four pages, Clarke outlined most of the principles of modern satellite communications, including the microwave radio frequencies that could be used, the rocket technology required to reach orbit, and the need for a parabolic reflecting dish to receive signals. He also calculated the power necessary to transmit signals through Earth's atmosphere, explaining that this could be acquired through solar energy.

Clarke's most useful insight was his discovery of what is now called the *geostationary orbit,* a precisely circular trajectory that exactly matches Earth's rotation. It had been known for more than 200 years that the orbital period of a satellite depends on its distance from Earth, and the period increases as it gets higher. For example, the Space Shuttle uses a relatively low orbit of no more than 400 kilometers (km), circling Earth in around 90 minutes; the moon is 1000 times more distant and takes nearly a month. Clarke calculated that at 35,784 km the orbital period would be exactly 24 hours. This means that if a satellite is placed at this altitude above Earth's axis of rotation—the equator—it will not move at all relative to the ground, appearing to hang in the sky. Users could simply point an antenna up toward a fixed spot without having to track orbits or worry about satellites disappearing over the horizon.

Although Clarke feared that many readers would find his ideas "too far-fetched to be taken very seriously," satellite development actually progressed even faster than he predicted. The relays envisaged by Clarke required continuous maintenance and so had to be mounted on space stations with a permanent human crew. This was rendered unnecessary by miniaturization, in particular the invention of the **transistor** in 1948.

One scientist who did take Clarke's ideas seriously was John R. Pierce (1910–), an electronics researcher at **Bell Labs.** He began more detailed research into satellite communications in 1954, but his work was largely ignored until the Soviet Union launched their *Sputnik* satellite in October 1957. As well as showing that a rocket could blast an object into low orbit, *Sputnik* also carried two battery-powered radio transmitters that bleeped for 21 days, proving that communication from space to Earth was possible.

The first satellite intended solely for communication was launched by the United States in December 1958. Known as the *Signal Communication by Orbital Relay Experiment* (SCORE), it grew out of a U.S. Navy project that had originally tried to bounce radio signals off the moon, using it as a natural communications satellite. SCORE managed to transmit prerecorded Christmas greetings from President Eisenhower for 21 days, but it could not be used for the type of immediate communication envisaged by Clarke and Pierce.

Two years later, Pierce saw an opportunity to test a real-time satellite system. The newly formed National Aeronautics and Space Administration (NASA) planned to launch an inflatable sphere 30 meters across, intended for atmospheric study. Pierce persuaded the agency to coat the balloon in reflective

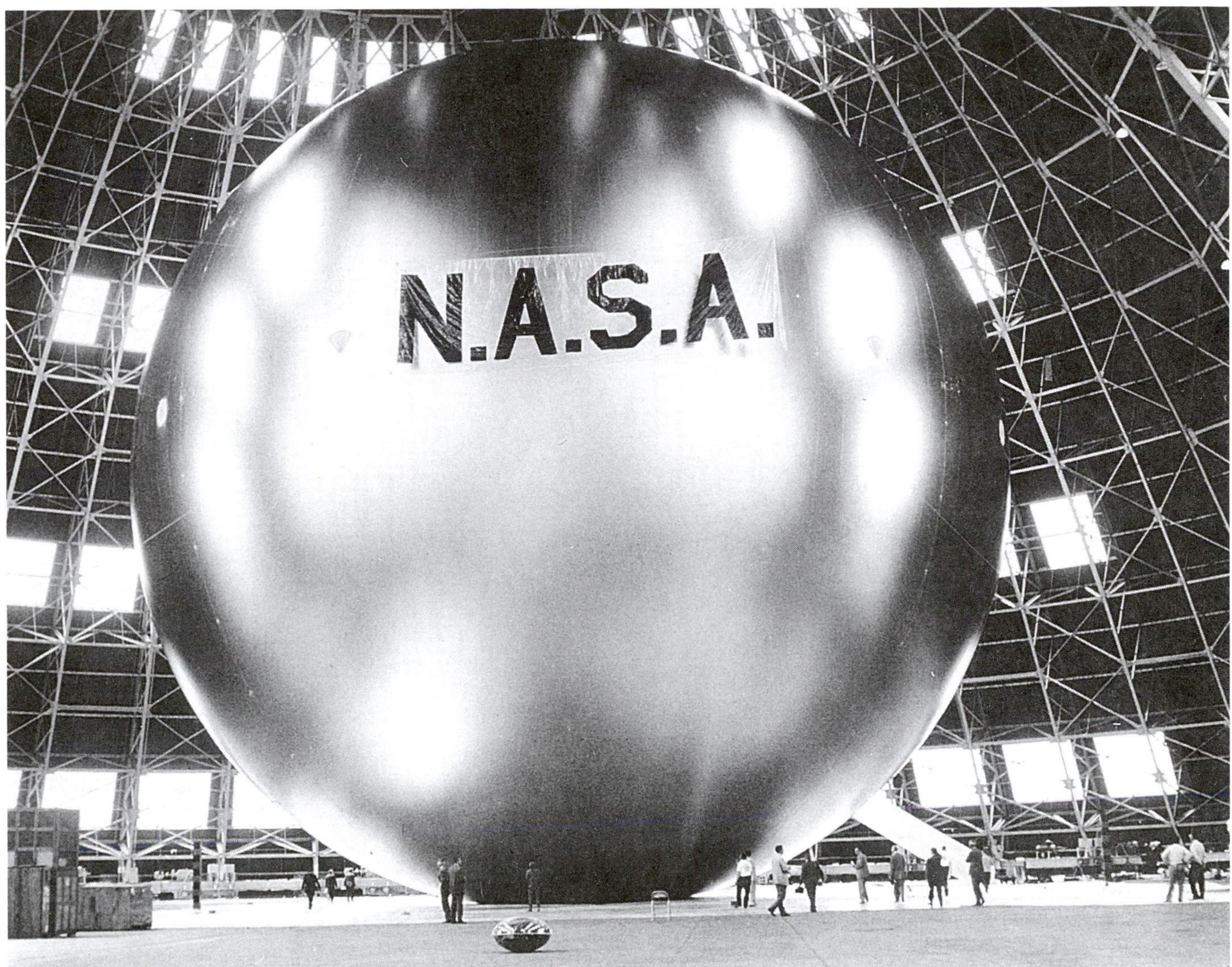

Echo 1 satellite. (Courtesy of NASA)

material, which would allow it to act as a giant mirror for radio waves transmitted from Earth. Named *Echo 1*, the first such satellite was lost to a rocket failure, but the second attempt proved successful. *Echo 1A* was launched in August 1960 and was used for five years in experimental transmissions of data, fax, and voice across America. In February 1962, it enabled the first satellite broadcast of a television program, from California to Massachusetts.

Echo was a passive satellite, because it only reflected waves bounced off it. Passive satellites were simple to build and could handle a wide range of frequencies, but their signals were so faint after a return trip into space that an intelligible signal was difficult to pick up. Two **AT&T** engineers working on the project, Arno Penzias (1933–) and Robert Wilson (1936–), used an antenna so sensitive that they picked up radiation from the Big Bang instead, accidentally earning themselves a Nobel Prize for Physics.

In July 1962, NASA launched AT&T's *Telstar*: the first active satellite and the first of any type to be designed and run by a private company. A sphere coated in solar cells, it contained thousands of transistors and a *transponder*, a device designed by Pierce that could amplify signals more than 10,000-fold. *Telstar* beamed the first transatlantic television signals from the United States to Britain and France only hours after launch. It was later used for experimental telephone, data, and fax transmissions. The satellite failed after less than a year, probably because of nuclear explosions in the upper atmosphere, but was replaced with the larger and more powerful *Telstar 2* within months.

The next step in the evolution of satellite networks moved the technology toward Clarke's sought-after geostationary orbit. This was much more difficult to achieve than the low orbits of earlier satellites, due to both the higher altitude and the precise positioning needed. The satellites themselves were also harder to build, because the greater height meant that they had to be lighter, yet transmit with greater power. Known as the *Syncom* series, they were constructed by Hughes, then still an aircraft company but set to become one of the largest satellite builders and operators.

The first attempt failed: *Syncom 1* was launched successfully by NASA in February 1993, but lost power before it could be maneuvered into the intended position. *Syncom 2* reached a geosynchronous orbit over Brazil in July 1963, which means that it matched the rotation speed of Earth but still drifted slightly, as its orbit was not perfectly circular or aligned with Earth's plane of rotation. From the ground, geosynchronous satellites appear to follow a figure of eight, centered on the equator and crossing it twice a day. The following year, *Syncom 3* became the first true geostationary satellite. Positioned above the Pacific, it carried television pictures of the Tokyo Olympic Games to U.S. viewers before being commandeered by the U.S. military for use in the Vietnam War.

With a working prototype in orbit, telecommunications companies at last began to recognize the potential of satellites. The first commercial operator was the Communications Satellite Corp. (Comsat), an enterprise set up by the U.S. government in 1962 but privatized the following year. In 1964 it joined similar agencies in 17 other countries to form the International Telecommunications Satellite Organization (Intelsat). Together, they launched a satellite called *Early Bird* in April 1965, the first to be run commercially. Stationed over the Atlantic, its transponders could carry 240 phone calls between Europe and the United States.

Satellite capacity quickly grew: In 1965, Intelsat added satellites above the Indian and Pacific oceans, enabling its network to reach all populated areas of the planet. Improvements in computer technology during the 1970s multiplied the number of calls that could be carried by successive generations of satellites. The most important advance was the directional antenna, which enabled satellites to focus their transmissions on a particular portion of Earth's surface. The first to implement this was *Satcom*, placed above Ecuador in 1975. Its greatest achievement was not the antenna itself but a system called *three-axis stabilization*, which stopped the satellite from spinning and kept it pointed toward the right spot.

By 1980, geostationary communications satellites were the favorite method of completing intercontinental phone calls. Intelsat alone had launched 27, the most advanced of which could each carry 6000 simultaneous conversations, and its original 18 countries had grown to 142. There were also many other private and government networks in orbit, with new applications emerging. The *Comstar* series, run jointly by AT&T and Comsat, introduced satellite TV in 1976. For the first time, customers could buy their own receiver dish and watch programs directly from the satellite.

Data transfer was not originally a priority for satellite systems, although it had been actively researched. In 1972, the U.S. Department of Defense's Advanced Research Projects Agency (**ARPA**) even created an experimental satellite-based network called SATnet. It used a system called *Host Access Protocol* (HAP) for sending short data packets over satellites, which was eventually abandoned in favor of the modern **TCP/IP** protocols. SATnet too was largely abandoned, as most early **Internet** nodes could be connected physically to the backbone.

The concept of transmitting data via satellite was resurrected in the 1980 by the invention of the *very small aperture terminal* (VSAT), a relatively inexpensive transmitter that could be mounted on any office building. This coincided with the arrival of the personal computer and the near-collapse of satellite telephony. New sub sea fiber optic cables could carry phone calls faster and more cheaply than the satellites, removing their lucrative intercontinental trunk traffic. Instead of connecting large dishes on either side of an ocean, satellites moved into the *last mile* or *local loop* market, aiming to reach customers directly.

VSATs were typically aimed at large corporate entities that required a high-speed data connection, usually in remote areas where terrestrial networks were not available. They became particularly popular in Africa and Central America, in part because a dish can be smaller and cheaper the closer it is to the equator. After the fall of the Iron Curtain, VSATs were also used extensively to bypass the local telecommunications monopolies in many Eastern European countries.

The Internet boom of the 1990s created a demand for high-speed data services among small businesses and personal users, most of whom could not afford a full VSAT system. Instead, satellite operators took advantage of the **World Wide Web**'s asymmetry: That is, most data flow from a Web server to a user, with only a small amount going the other way. This meant that surfers needed only a television-style dish to receive pages and graphics, as their mouse clicks could travel back over a regular phone line. The first such system was DirecPC, released by Hughes in 1996.

Up until the 1990s, almost all communications satellites used high geostationary orbits in the crowded Clarke Belt. These are perfectly suited for fixed satellite antennas but do have some disadvantages. Equatorial orbits are impractical for the far north or south, where atmospheric interference means that large dishes are needed and the satellites lie so low on the horizon that they can easily be blocked by buildings or the natural landscape. The Clarke Belt is so high that radio signals take about a fourth of a second to get there and back, adding a noticeable delay. This distance also weakens the signal, meaning that the antenna has to be pointed at exactly the right point in the sky.

Low earth orbit (LEO) systems were intended to overcome all these problems, by using constellations of many satellites at an altitude of about 800 km. This is higher than most exploration by astronauts but lower than the Van Allen radiation belts, which ring Earth and can interfere with communications. Because each satellite covers a small area and is relatively close to the user, antennas can be nondirectional and not surrounded by a dish: In theory, customers can replace the dish with a device similar to a mobile phone.

The first such system was *Orbcomm*, which provide limited paging and telemetry applications from 1997, using 24 satellites launched cheaply from high-flying aircraft. Its system is known as a *Little LEO* constellation, because it does not try to cover all of Earth at one time. Instead, user terminals wait until a satellite comes into view before sending data, which can result in a latency of several minutes.

Big LEO schemes, aiming to cover the entire Earth in real-time, were initially less successful. The first was *Iridium*, a voice-only system that went bankrupt because of competition from terrestrial cellular networks. Its terminals were larger and more expensive than conventional mobile phones and didn't work indoors, and most potential customers were in poorer countries, which couldn't afford the high call charges. In 2000, it was announced that all 89 of the Iridium satellites would be *deorbited*, or deliberately burned up in Earth's atmosphere. But this didn't stop other operators from planning broadband data systems. The most elaborate was *Teledesic*, which like Iridium uses *intersatellite links* (ISL) to avoid the need for any equipment on the ground for connections between two of its users.

The satellite communications industry continues to grow, and it is the scene for some very ambitious plans. **Vinton Cerf** (1943–), one of the pioneers of the Internet, is already developing an *interplanetary network* (IPN). Beginning with a series of satellites around the planet Mars, he hopes ultimately to extend the Internet throughout the solar system, so that it can be used to control future space probes.

FURTHER READING

Clarke, Arthur C. "Extra-Terrestrial Relays." *Wireless World*, Oct. 1945, pp. 305–308.

———. *The Exploration of Space*. New York: Harper, 1951; rev. ed., New York: Pocket Books, 1979.

Gordon, Gary D., and Walter L. Morgan. *Principles of Communications Satellites*. New York: Wiley Interscience, 1993.

Morgan, Walter L. *Communications Satellite Handbook*. New York: Wiley, 1989.

Pierce, J. R. *The Beginnings of Satellite Communication*. Berkeley, Calif.: San Francisco Press, 1968.

Roddy, Denis. *Satellite Communications*. Englewood Cliffs, N.J.: Prentice Hall, 1989; 2nd ed., New York: McGraw-Hill, 1996.

—*Andy Dornan*

Scanner

A scanner is a device that enables a computer to interpret a printed page. It uses a charge-coupled-device (CCD) chip to digitize pictures dot for dot. Usually, a moving halogen light is used to illuminate the original—thus the word *scanning*. There are different types of scanners for various purposes, including flatbed scanners, paper ports, slide scanners, drum scanners, hand scanners, and three-dimensional scanners. Scanners are also used in **optical character recognition** systems, in which digitized images of printed pages are transformed into text files for processing by computers.

The historical development of the scanner can be traced all the way back to 1843, when the first facsimile machine was patented by the Scotsman Alexander Bain (1818–1903). In 1856, the Italian Giovanni Caselli (1815–91) designed the first machine that could transmit text and images, calling it *pantelegraph*. A commercial facsimile service was started in Paris in 1865, after Napoleon III (1808–73) had expressed great enthusiasm for Caselli's device. Pictures were sent between the main French cities using pendulums that oscillated over a rotating drum. A message or an image printed on electrically conductive material was wrapped around it. A needle scanned the roll, receiving and transmitting signals only in those spots covered with ink. News agencies were regularly sending and receiving images from major European cities in 1910. In 1948 the fax machine from **AT&T** could send a 15 by 20 centimeter photo in seven minutes.

A breakthrough in scan technology came in 1981 when **Sony** developed and manufactured the first digital camera, the Mavica, which used a CCD chip. The CCD chip, which is used not only in scanners, but also in digital and video cameras, has tiny plates which hold anywhere between hundreds of thousands to millions of pixel sensors. Each sensor consists of a light-sensitive condenser and some transistors. Scanners scan images by projecting light onto the hard copy—the light is reflected and registered by the CCD chip(s). The scan software reads the incoming data and reconstructs the image as a computer graphic. The more pixels a device has, the more bits are coded, resulting in better-quality images.

Scanners with 24, 30, and 36 bits per pixel are common today, even in private households, (the number of bits refers to that scanner's color depth). In the example of a 24-bit scanner, eight bits are allocated to each primary color (red, green, blue), and each color has 256 variations (2^8), resulting in 16.7 million colors (256^3). A 30-bit scanner allocates 10 bits to each of the three primary colors, resulting in 1 billion displayable colors (1024^3), and a 36-bit scanner allocates 12 bits to each color, with 68.7 billion possible tone variations (4096^3). The data depth defines how many luminance levels can be relayed from the scanner to the computer. Eight bits allow 256 luminance levels; 10 bits 1024; and 12 bits, 4096 luminance levels.

The market for scanners was very competitive at the end of the twentieth century. Fierce price wars among vendors in 1998 caused scanner prices to fall drastically, resulting in some 13.9 million scanners shipped that year. The International Data Corporation (IDC) subsequently predicted worldwide shipments of more than 38 million color flatbed scanners for the year 2003. Some of the top vendors for flatbed scanners are Mustek Systems Inc., Microtek, Agfa, and Umax.

FURTHER READING

Gonzalez, Rafael C., and Richard E. Woods. *Digital Image Processing*. Reading, Mass: Addison-Wesley, 1993.

Marz, Helen C., and Robert L. Nielsen, eds. "Cameras, Scanners, and Image Acquisition Systems." *SPIE Proceedings*, 3–4 Feb. 1993, San Jose, Calif., Vol. 1901, 1993.

Pratt, William K. *Digital Image Processing*. New York: Wiley, 1978; 2nd ed., 1991.

—*Jenna L. Brinning*

Schickard, Wilhelm

1592–1635

German Inventor

Wilhelm Schickard was a polymath with interests ranging from languages to astronomy and from painting to mathematics; he is best known for the *Schickard calculator*, the first known mechanical calculator.

Schickard became a friend of the astronomer Johannes Kepler (1571–1630), who, in 1623, had just carried out enormous chains of calculations explaining planetary motion when Schickard wrote to him: "What you have done in a logistical way, I have just tried to do by mechanics. I have constructed a machine consisting of eleven complete and six mutilated sprocket wheels which can calculate. You would burst out laughing if you were present to see how it carries by itself from one column of tens to the next or borrows from them during subtraction." In subsequent letters he described his "calculating clock" in detail, with drawings. It contained two devices: a six-digit adding machine with a single-toothed carry gear between digits and an overflow indicator, plus a compact set of multiplication tables (probably inspired by Napier's rods) arranged on six vertical cylinders which were rotated to set the multiplicand. Horizontal bars labeled "2" to "9" could be slid to expose "partial products" on the cylinders which had to be added to finish the multiply. Schickard had a copy made for Kepler, but it was destroyed in a fire.

Schickard's letters were found in a Russian observatory in 1935 but then lost during World War II. They were rediscovered in 1956 and described the following year at a conference attended by Baron Bruno von Freytag-Löringhoff (1912–96) from Tübingen University. He constructed a working copy in 1960, which is in the Tübingen local history museum.

Knowledge of Schickard's calculator was lost for 300 years, and thus it played no part in the development of calculating machines. However, it is the first known mechanical calculator to add and subtract automatically.

BIOGRAPHY

Wilhelm Schickard. Born 22 April 1592 in Herrenberg, Germany. Attended a monastery school. B.A. in theology and oriental languages and M.A. from University of Tübingen, 1609 and 1611. Became a Lutheran deacon, then pastor. Met Johannes Kepler, 1617. Professor of Hebrew, University of Tübingen, 1619. Invented the first calculating machine, 1623. Professor of astronomy, University of Tübingen, 1631. Became school inspector and prepared first surveyed map of Württemberg. Died 24 October 1635 in Tübingen, Germany of the black plague.

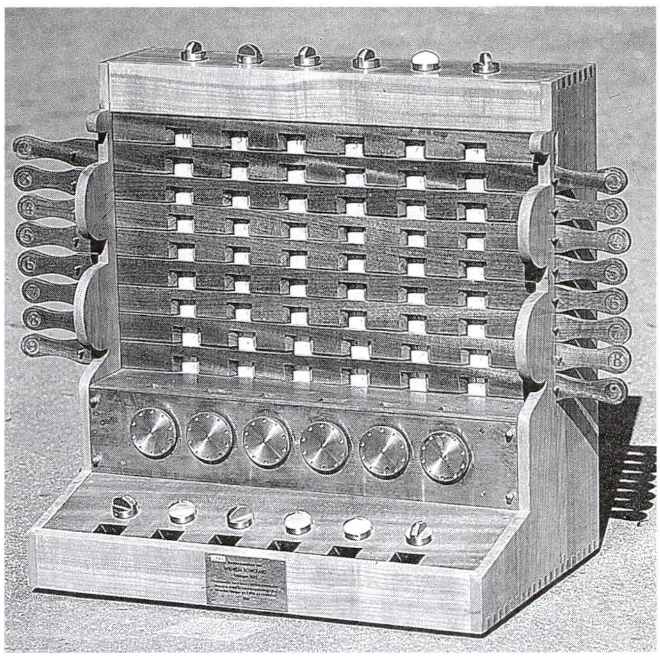

Schickard Clock. (Courtesy of the National Museum of Photography, Film and Television/Science and Society Picture Library)

SELECTED WRITINGS

Wilhelm Schickard's letters to Kepler. Translated from Latin to German by Benjamin Nill. Wilhelm-Schickard-Institut für Informatik Graphisch-Interaktive Systeme (GRIS), Universität Tübingen, Sept. 1999. *http://www.gris.uni-tuebingen.de/projects/studproj/schickard/index.html*

FURTHER READING

Augarten, Stan. *Bit by Bit: An Illustrated History of Computers.* New York: Ticknor and Fields, 1984.

Freytag Löringhoff, Baron von. *Wilhelm Schickard und seine Rechenmaschine von 1623.* Tübingen, Germany: Attempto, 1987.

Seck, Friedrich. *Wilhelm Schickard 1592–1635: Astronom, Geograph, Orientalist, Erfinder der Rechenmaschine.* Tübingen, Germany: JCB Mohr, 1978.

Westfall, Richard S. "Wilhelm Schickard." Galileo Project, Catalog of the Scientific Community, Dec. 1996. *http://es.rice.edu/ES/humsoc/Galileo/Catalog/Files/schickrd.html*

"Wilhelm Schickard." History of Mathematics Archive, Mathematical Institute of the Technical University of Budapest. *http://www.vma.bme.hu/mathhist/Mathematicians/Schickard.html*

—*John Deane*

Search Engine

The most significant limitation on the power of computers to store information effectively is not the capacity of their memories or storage devices but the ease with which users can retrieve the stored information at a later date. A search engine is a piece of **software** designed to maximize the chance that users will find the information they need. Search engines are most familiar as easy-to-use "front ends" to the **World Wide Web**. Indeed, the ultimate success of the Web as a distributed library of all human knowledge will depend critically on the development of improved search engines.

In the early days of the Web, in the mid-1990s, finding information was more a matter of luck than science. Web-viewing programs called **browsers** were specifically designed to follow hypertext-linked information from one Web page to another in the hope that users might eventually stumble across something that interested them. But the explosive growth of the Web meant that better strategies for finding information were required. One approach, pioneered by Stanford University Ph.D. students Jerry Yang (1969–) and David Filo (1966–), involved laboriously constructing a directory of Web sites categorized according to their broad subject matter. The result, **Yahoo!**, continues to be one of the world's most visited Web sites.

The other approach involved using computer programs called *crawlers*, *spiders*, or *robots* to visit Web sites and construct a database of their content that users could query to find information they needed. This method is the essence of search engines such as AltaVista, Lycos, HotBot, Webcrawler, and Infoseek. The method was introduced before the Web existed by a program called **Archie**, which compiled an index of **FTP** (File Transfer Protocol) sites and the available files.

The Web pages referred to as search engines are, in fact, only one part of a search engine's structure. Apart from a search engine program, the main components are a database of all the Web pages the search engine has visited, a query server that allows users to search the database using keywords, and one or more agent programs to build the database.

The search engine program is the most important of these components, because it manages the process of constructing and maintaining the database. It decides which **URLs** (Web page addresses) need to be indexed using suggestions submitted by Web users (typically through a Web page called "Add URL" or "Submit a site" linked to the search engine's home page) and unexplored links in pages it has already visited. Some search engines build up a graphical map of the Web's dense interconnections and deduce from this which pages link to which other pages and thus which sites they should visit first.

Given the size of the Web and its rate of growth, search engines typically use many agent programs working in parallel to retrieve information from Web pages. Better known as spiders or crawlers, the agent programs are designed to visit URLs much like a Web browser, retrieve the content, and pass it back to the search engine for incorporation into the database. Programs known as *deep crawlers* or *deep spiders* explore each page recursively: They visit not just one page, but each page linked by that page, and so on through to the lowest level of the structure until every link has been explored. An alternative method of building up a database is used by a system called Harvest, in which Web sites compile their own indexing information and send it periodically to the search engine.

A search engine's database may be split into two parts. The map of the Web that directs the explorations of the agent programs is one part. The other part is a collection of information about the Web page URLs (Web pages and sites the search engine has visited). Different search engines store different information about the Web pages they know, but typically they record some or all of the page's text content (including the frequency with which certain words are mentioned), a list of other Web sites that link to those pages (the popularity of the page among other Web sites), the number of times the page has been accessed through the search engine's front page (the popularity of the page among users), and information specifically supplied to the search engine by Web page designers.

This last type of information is collected from information concealed inside Web pages using what are known as **HTML** (Hypertext Markup Language) *meta* tags.

Unlike the HTML tags that describe the content and control the presentation of Web pages, meta tags are effectively invisible comments from a Web page author to a search engine that describe the page's content with a single sentence description and a set of carefully chosen keywords. The trouble with meta tags, however, is that Web page authors frequently add or repeat keywords to increase the traffic to their sites. This reduces the overall effectiveness of meta tags from the search engine's point of view.

All of a search engine's components are hidden from users, with the exception of the Web page through which users submit their searches to the query server. Typically, the Web page contains a data entry field into which keywords are typed according to the information the user wants to find. Some query servers accept keywords and **Boolean algebra** operators such as AND, OR, and NOT, so a typical search engine query might be "Apple AND computer NOT fruit." Other query servers allow users to increase or decrease the importance of certain search terms with plus and minus signs. Most query servers also use a list of stop words, commonly used words such as *the*, *and*, or *website* that are ignored during a search. Beyond a basic keyword search, it is increasingly common for search engine Web pages to offer access to other services, such as news or stock reports—such pages are called **portals**.

The difference between browsing for information and searching with a search engine is rather like the difference between fishing and shooting. Yet even using a search engine does not guarantee finding the information that users need. Each search engine indexes only a fraction of all possible Web pages, and with pages constantly being added, removed, or moved around from server to server, a search engine's internal model of the Web is necessarily incomplete and out of date. Metasearch engines, that is, Web pages that call several search engines at once, improve the chances of finding information by offering users a simple way to query a number of different search engines at the same time.

Another problem is the very ambiguity of language and the chance that Web page authors and search engine users will use different words or concepts to mean essentially the same thing. Many words have multiple meanings—"apple," for example, might refer to fruit, computers, or the Beatles' record company. Searching for information about one type of apple will produce unwanted information about all the others. Equally, single concepts may be represented by many different words—chairs, for example, are described by words such as *sofa*, *settee*, *chaise lounge*, *armchair*, or *recliner*. Searching for any of these words will not yield potentially relevant information about any of the others. In other words, effective searching assumes that users already understand something about the concepts and the areas of knowledge they want to find out about.

With the biggest search engines now categorizing over 100 million Web pages each, even a carefully thought out collection of search words can produce hundreds or even thousands of potentially relevant "hits." Search engine designers are relying on increasingly sophisticated techniques to deduce which of these is most likely to provide the information users actually want. Two of the newest search engines, Google developed at Stanford University, and Clever developed at **IBM**, build up a model of the way Web pages refer to one another and deduce from this which pages provide the most authoritative information on different subjects. This information is used to rank page hits in order of probable importance.

The idea of building text-based indexes dates from the Web's origins as a text-only, content-rich network of information. But increasingly, Web pages are constructed not like the pages of newspapers—as blocks of HTML-formatted text with images inserted between them—but like the pages of magazines, with both images and text contained inside binary image files. This reduces the effectiveness of traditional search engines in two ways. First, any text contained in image files is not detected by spider programs and is not therefore indexed in the search engine's database. Second, there is still no truly effective way of searching the Web for anything other than text information. Some search engines, notably AltaVista, can search the Web for multimedia graphic, sound, or video files, but the hits they return are based only on the names of those files or the text information surrounding them, not on the content of the files themselves. This may change in time. At the Massachusetts

Institute of Technology's Artificial Intelligence Laboratory, researchers are currently developing methods of searching for images that *look like* an image that the user wants to find by matching common features or finding other visual similarities.

Ironically, most of these problems are invisible to Web users. Search engines usually find and return some useful information; the information they do not return—and therefore the overall effectiveness of the search—is never apparent. The drive for more effective search engines has come partly from the architects of digital libraries (archives of computer-based information). Although they recognize the potential of the Web as a global repository of all human knowledge, digital librarians despair at the haphazard manner with which one of humankind's most important inventions is being thrown together. Even with the best search and metasearch engines, finding information on the Internet can still be a hit-and-miss affair. For this reason, developing more effective search engines may prove to be one of the most important technical challenges of the twenty-first century.

FURTHER READING

Alper, Joseph. "Assembling the World's Biggest Library on Your Desktop." *Science,* 18 Sept. 1998, p. 1784.

Bloom, Floyd. "Refining the On-Line Scholar's Tools." *Science,* 26 Jan. 1996, p. 429.

"Digital Libraries." Special Issue Digital Libraries. *IEEE Computer,* Feb. 1999, p. 45.

Graubard, Stephen R., and Paul O. LeClerc, eds. *Books, Bricks, and Bytes: Libraries in the Twenty-First Century.* Piscataway, N.J.: Transaction, 1997.

Keller, Michael. "Libraries in the Digital Future." *Science,* 4 Sept. 1998, p. 1461.

Lesk, Michael. *Practical Digital Libraries: Books, Bytes, and Bucks.* San Francisco: Morgan Kaufmann, 1997.

Lynch, Clifford. "Searching the Internet." *Scientific American,* Mar. 1997, p. 44.

—*Chris Woodford*

Searching and Sorting

Two fundamental operations in computing are searching and sorting. Every time we query a bill on the telephone or make a transaction via an **automatic teller machine**, a number that is a unique identifier for the customer is used to retrieve the relevant record. This may involve a search among anything from thousands to tens of millions of records.

Any business must have a complete set of customer records and at any time must have accurate information relating to each customer. The fundamental requirement is to be able to update customer details, insert new records, delete old ones, and perhaps reorganize the data periodically for audit or for specific tasks such as billing: these tasks require that a given record can be found easily. A customer making a query should not need to know anything of the internal workings of the system and expects the information to be at hand more or less immediately. Hence, from the outset, the quest for efficient searching **algorithms** has been important in business systems.

A *record* is a collection of items sufficient to identify the thing that is important for the application. So, for example, a record in a vehicle registration center might contain name, address, date of birth, date passed test, vehicle registration, and driver number. This last item is unique to each driver, and every record must be assigned an exclusive reference, in order that it may be identified uniquely. This makes the task of finding a given record simpler: if we can find the required reference, the record can be retrieved immediately.

So, how do we discover whether a given number is present in a set of numbers? For example, to find the number 31 in the list:

4, 17, 12, 84, 99, 31, 103, 2, 86

the only thing we can do is to look along the list until we find it or reach the end of the list, in which case we can say that it is not there. This approach is often called a *sequential search*, or a simple *linear search*, and the method can be summarized as follows. Given an array $a[\max]$, where max is the number of items to be considered, and x, a value to find in the array, do the following: While the end of the array has not been reached, check to see whether the first value ($a[1]$) is equal to x. If it is, return to that position; otherwise, consider the next position value; and so on.

If the end of the array is reached (a[max]), the value was not present, so return a "not present" message.

This simple procedure checks each position repeatedly to see whether the value is the one sought. If so, it returns that array position value; if the end of the array is reached without the item being found, an "error" is returned. The problem with this approach is that in a real application there could be millions of files, and the item we want might be the final one. More important, whenever the item we require is not in the list, we will always search all the way to the end.

The simplest way to improve the searching process is to order the items first. If the list under consideration in this example is sorted into ascending order, it reads:

2, 4, 12, 17, 31, 84, 86, 99, 103.

Now the process is improved because searching can stop as soon as any value is greater than the one we are looking for: This implies that on average we should only ever have to inspect half the items in the list.

Better still, we can use an intuitive method to speed up the time of search. This takes advantage of the fact that when data are ordered, we know roughly where any given item is: For example, when looking up a name in a telephone directory, we do not begin at "A" and examine one entry at a time until we find the name we are looking for. If the name begins with "M," we immediately go to about the middle of the book, and if it begins with "S," we look about two-thirds of the way in. However, this insight cannot be communicated directly to computers: They can only follow a specific sequence of instructions, an *algorithm.*

Such an algorithm is designed so that the middle value of a sorted list is always selected first, and then, based on whether or not that is greater than the required item, just one-half of the list—either the lower or upper half—is searched again, starting with the middle value of that half. This is called *binary search*, and in a list of 1 million values, it will not take more than 21 guesses to find any given value. Algorithms such as this are of considerable practical value, as long as the overhead associated with having to sort the list prior to searching is acceptable. When a list is updated frequently, it may not be acceptable, but for one that does not change often and so does not have to be re-sorted frequently, it is usually the search algorithm of choice.

Another method that is relatively efficient in practice is *insertion sort.* The basis of the technique is similar to the way in which many people sort things naturally, especially playing cards. When a hand of cards is picked up after dealing, the cards are in no particular order: If we are sorting in ascending order, a common method is to scan along from left to right, ordering the "smallest so far" at each stage. For example, given an unsorted hand and ignoring suits (i.e. sorting on the basis of value only) the hand may change as it is sorted, as shown.

10♣ 5♥ 7♥ 9♦ 6♠
Hand as dealt

→ 5♥ 10♣ 7♥ 9♦ 6♠
→ 5♥ 7♥ 10♣ 9♦ 6♠
→ 5♥ 7♥ 9♦ 10♣ 6♠
→ 5♥ 6♠ 7♥ 9♦ 10♣
Hand sorted

This method, although intuitive, must, of course, be specified algorithmically. The first step in the example was to consider the ten of clubs and the five of hearts: since the five is smaller, these were exchanged. The next card to consider was the seven of hearts, which is smaller than the ten but not the five; so the seven went into the second position and the ten had to "shuffle up" to make room. This process continues until the hand is sorted. That is what is happening in natural language, so the next step is to write an algorithm that specifies the process unambiguously and precisely, in a step-by-step way.

Assume that n integers are under consideration. The process may be considered as an iteration up to n: Beginning with the second, compare each item with its neighbor to the left, and if the value to the left is larger, move that item one place right. Continue until a value is reached that is smaller or we reach the start. Then put the card under consideration into the "vacant" slot—that is, its proper place. Consider an array of five items, $a[1\ldots5]$:

10	5	7	9	6

Beginning with the second item, both the value (five) and position (two) are saved; the saved value is then compared with the value in the position that is one less than that in the position counter (i.e., position one). Since the saved value of five is less than the ten, and we are not at the start, the ten is moved into the five's place, overwriting it, and the position counter is decremented, giving:

10	10	7	9	6

In this case, as the position counter equals one, we are at the start; hence there are no more items to consider, so the five is written into the current position (position one), giving:

5	10	7	9	6

We then move right one position, and compare the value in position three, which is the seven, with the value that is one less than that in the position counter (i.e., ten). Since the seven is less than the ten, the ten overwrites the seven, giving:

5	10	10	9	6

and the position counter is decremented to two. The saved value of seven is now compared to the item in position one (one less than that in the position counter), which is five. This is not greater than seven, so the saved value is written into the current position (two) and no other action takes place on this iteration, giving:

5	7	10	9	6

The process continues, with the final two iterations resulting in:

5	7	9	10	6
5	6	7	9	10

FURTHER READING

Brassard, Gilles, and Paul Bratley. *Fundamentals of Algorithmics.* Englewood Cliffs, N.J.: Prentice Hall, 1996.

Knuth, Donald. *The Art of Computer Programming.* Blue Ridge Summit, Pa.: TAB Books, 1983; 3rd ed., Reading, Mass.: Addison-Wesley, 1997.

Sedgewick, Robert. *Algorithms.* Reading, Mass.: Addison-Wesley, 1983; 2nd ed., 1988.

Standish, Thomas. *Data Structures, Algorithms and Software Principles.* Reading, Mass.: Addison-Wesley, 1995.

—*David Brunskill*

Selective Sequence Electronic Calculator

The Selective Sequence Electronic Calculator (SSEC) was constructed by **IBM** in the late 1940s to serve as a showpiece for Big Blue's cutting-edge technology. After opening ceremonies were held in January 1948, it was set up in the IBM office building in New York, where pedestrians could watch it through large picture windows. The passing office workers soon nicknamed it "Poppa."

Just after World War II, IBM became more and more interested in large-scale calculating machines. After their experience with the **Harvard Mark I**, and particularly when it became obvious that cordial relations between Harvard and IBM had broken down, IBM decided that the Mark I could no longer be considered as the machine that showcased IBM technology. At this point the **ENIAC** had been shown to work and the Harvard Mark I was simply too slow to be state of the art. IBM had great expertise in mechanical and relay-based calculating machines but had also done some research into the newer **vacuum-tube** digital circuits. Thus the decision as to which technology to use for a new machine was not obvious.

They eventually settled on a hybrid in which vacuum tubes would be used for the high-speed portions of the device and sections not needing electronic speed would be built from relays. About 13,000 vacuum tubes were used to build the arithmetic unit and eight high-speed registers; 23,000 relays were used for the circuits controlling the machine and for 150 slow storage **registers**. It was controlled via punched paper tapes containing the instructions to be executed, but unlike the earlier Harvard Mark I, it had 66 different paper tape readers for instructions and could transfer control from one to another as required. This allowed much more flexibility for program control and even allowed various standard "subroutines" to be kept available at all times. While the arithmetic unit could actually perform about 250 additions per second, the total machine was limited by the speed at which the paper tape readers could access the next instruction. This meant that the throughput of the device averaged about 50 instructions per second.

The machine was difficult to program, so it tended to be used for jobs which, once the instruction tapes were set up, could be run over and over again with different data. It was, however, very reliable. For example, it was used to calculate tables of the positions of the five outer planets every 40 days for all years between 1653 and 2060. This job required about 5,000,000 additions and 7,000,000 multiplications, a task it performed perfectly. Not many machines of this era could boast such reliability. IBM actually leased time on the machine, perhaps the first large calculating machine to be so used. During the latter part of its life it was in almost continuous use by various government agencies, particularly the Atomic Energy Commission, which used it in nuclear power plant and weapons development.

A portion of the IBM SSEC. Some of the controlling paper tape readers, with loops of tape, can be seen at the far left. (Courtesy of IBM)

When, in 1951, IBM produced their first electronic stored program computer (the IBM 701), the SSEC had outlived its usefulness as a technological showpiece. It was dismantled and replaced with the first of the IBM 701s in August 1952.

Further Reading

Campbell-Kelly, Martin, and William Aspray. *Computer: A History of the Information Machine.* New York: Basic Books, 1996.

Williams, Michael. *A History of Computing Technology.* Los Altimos, Calif.: IEEE Computer Society Press, 1997.

—*Michael R. Williams*

Semiconductor

Semiconductors transformed computers from the room-sized monsters of the 1940s into the single-chip **microprocessor** invented in 1971. A semiconductor is a crystalline solid, such as **silicon** or germanium, used to manufacture miniature electronic components. The continued evolution of the computer industry depends on the development of increasingly advanced semiconductors that can be exploited in increasingly powerful chips.

Basic physics explains how semiconductors can be transformed into useful electronic components. Atoms of any material consist of a positive central nucleus surrounded by outer electrons. In a crystal of a conductor such as gold, the outer electrons move easily if a voltage is applied; the moving electrons form an electric current, and this makes gold conduct electricity well. In an insulator such as rubber or plastic, the outer electrons are involved in bonding the material together. The lack of free electrons prevents an insulator from conducting electricity.

Although semiconductors normally conduct electricity very poorly, their most important property is being able to conduct well under circumstances that can be precisely controlled. Silicon has four outer electrons, which means that one silicon atom can bond with four others in a crystal, leaving no free electrons to carry a current. However, if atoms of other substances are introduced into a silicon crystal, in a process called *doping*, the conductivity of the crystal can be changed. Atoms of arsenic, phosphorus, and antimony have five outer electrons. Replacing a silicon atom with one of these atoms produces one more electron than is needed for bonding to the surrounding silicon atoms. This extra electron can be used to carry a negative electrical current (so this type of doping is called negative type, or *n-type*). The conductivity of silicon can also be changed by another kind of doping. Atoms of aluminum, gallium, and boron have only three outer electrons. Exchanging a silicon atom for one of these atoms thus produces a *hole* where an electron is missing. The hole—the lack of an electron—can be used to carry a positive electrical current (so this type of doping is called positive type or *p-type*). Holes conduct electricity in the opposite way to electrons.

Electronic components such as diodes (which pass a current only one way) and **transistors** (which amplify currents or switch them on and off) can be made by joining n and p-types. Thus a diode can be made by putting a piece of n-type silicon next to a piece of p-type silicon. A transistor can be made by sandwiching a layer of p-type silicon between two layers of n-type silicon (to make what is called an *npn junction transistor*) or by joining a piece of n-type silicon between two pieces of p-type (to make a *pnp junction transistor*). A number of these transistors can be connected together into families to form **logic gates**, electronic devices capable of applying the logical operations of **Boolean algebra** to tiny electrical currents. The families include transistor-transistor logic (TTL), metal-oxide semiconductor (MOS), complementary-metal-oxide semiconductor (CMOS), and a very high-speed system known as emitter-coupled logic (ECL). The instructions used to program microprocessors are derived essentially from Boolean algebra, and the commands in higher-level programming languages are converted into this machine language by compilers and interpreters. In short, it is not so hard to appreciate how high-level programs in languages such as C or **COBOL** work by causing electrons to move through crystals of semiconductors at the atomic level.

If the science of semiconductors seems deceptively simple, the technology by which they are turned into useful electronic components is perhaps the most intricate and complex manufacturing process every devised by humankind. The transistor invented by **John Bardeen** (1908–91) and **Walter Brattain** (1902–87) in 1947 consisted of two tiny wires called whiskers pressed firmly onto the surface of a piece of n-type germanium. Junction transistors, invented by their colleague **William Shockley** (1910–89), were produced using a technique called *seed pulling* (also called the *Czochralski technique*). Using this method, pure germanium was heated to a molten state in a crucible, doped with an n-type impurity, and frozen onto the surface of a seed crystal slowly lowered into and then pulled out of the crucible. But the semiconductor crystal still had to be wired by hand into a relatively large package that could be soldered into a traditional electronic circuit. Transistors were an improvement on the vacuum tubes that had preceded them, but they were still large, expensive, and unreliable by today's standards.

The microelectronic revolution was spurred by the invention of the **integrated circuit** by **Jack Kilby** (1923–) of **Texas Instruments** and **Robert Noyce** (1927–90) of **Fairchild Semiconductor** in the late 1950s. An integrated circuit consists of thousands or millions of separate components and the connections between them, formed on chips of semiconducting material no bigger than a fingernail. It was Noyce's team at Fairchild that devised the *planar process* by which integrated circuits could be produced commercially. First, a large photographic template of the circuit is made using **computer-aided design** (CAD). Next, a thin circular wafer of silicon cut from a large crystal with a diamond saw is covered with a light-sensitive coating called *photoresist*. Using a process called *optical lithography*, a powerful light is shone through the photographic template to leave a pattern in the photoresist corresponding to the original circuit diagram. This is repeated hundreds or thousands of times to form as many individual chip designs on the wafer. The photoresist is then removed chemically to leave the final circuit pattern. Gases are then used to etch (mark) only those areas where doping is required and ions (charged atoms) are showered onto the wafer doping these areas to create either n or p-type material. Metal links and insulating layers are then added between the tiny components. Finally, a computer system tests each chip electrically before the wafer is sawed into separate chips. Those chips that work correctly are wired into a plastic or ceramic package.

Engineering and manufacturing advances have constantly increased the number of components that can be squeezed onto a chip, which is referred to as the *scale of integration.* Thus, engineers refer to SSI (small-scale integration—tens of components per chip), MSI (medium-scale integration—hundreds of components per chip), LSI (large-scale integration—thousands of components per chip), and VLSI (**very large scale integration**—hundreds of thousands or even millions of components per chip).

But it is not just in the number of components that semiconductor devices have evolved. Engineers have explored methods of increasing the speed of chips using other semiconductors, such as gallium arsenide (which switches roughly 1000 times faster than silicon), mixtures of silicon and germanium (sometimes mixed with carbon, which also gives a 1000-fold speed increase), and silicon carbide (intended for high-temperature, high-power applications). Some researchers have attempted to replace semiconductors with superconductors of almost infinitely small resistance that use superfast electronic switching devices called *Josephson junctions.* Another technique involves replacing the aluminum interconnections with copper wires to increase the speed at which information flows through a chip. (However, the copper has to be coated with a special insulating gel to prevent electrons from leaking into the semiconducting silicon.) Another technique uses x-ray lithography, instead of optical lithography, to imprint the pattern of chips on the semiconductor; as x-rays have a wavelength around 100 times smaller than visible light, they can draw finer circuits containing even more components. A conceptually similar process called *molecular beam epitaxy* (MBE) is used to create semiconductors on a much smaller (quantum) scale, suggesting that it may ultimately be possible to store information by manipulating a single electron in a single quantum "well" and so vastly increasing the amount of information that can be stored in a given area. Another new process developed by Ball Semiconductor Inc. suggests that it is possible to develop silicon semiconductors in spherical "ball crystals" in days rather than the weeks it takes to produce traditional silicon wafers and at a fraction of the cost. These and other techniques are continuing to ensure that semiconductors keep pace with the predictions of **Moore's law** (a prediction by **Gordon Moore** [1923–] that the number of transistors that can be squeezed onto a chip doubles roughly every 18 months) and that chips can continue to grow smaller, faster, and more powerful.

Semiconductors are valuable not just in microprocessor and memory chips. The miniature lasers used in **CD-ROM** drives (and audio CD players) are made from tiny semiconductors that emit light at a precisely controlled frequency. Current research aims to produce blue lasers, whose shorter wavelength allows them to read information from much smaller areas and produces a fourfold increase in the capacity of optical storage devices. Semiconductors also make up the arrays of light-sensitive detectors called *charge-coupled displays* (CCDs) used in digital cameras, fax machines, and scanners. When photons (wavelike particles) of light strike the doped crystalline silicon lattice in a CCD, electrons are freed in a pattern that corresponds to the incoming light. The CCD thus converts an analog pattern of light into a digital pattern of electrical impulses that can be processed by a microprocessor or a computer. Precisely the reverse process is used in flat-panel displays. For example, TFT (thin-film transistor) **liquid crystal displays** (LCD's) consist of an array of silicon transistors deposited on a large piece of glass. These switch liquid crystals on and off in a pattern of tiny red, green, and blue pixels (individual dots or squares) corresponding to the image desired. An improved type of display called *continuous grain silicon* (CGS) can switch pixels on and off much more quickly, resulting in much smoother-moving images. Semiconductor lasers and light detectors are also used to transmit and receive information at either end of the fiber optic cables used in the long-distance telecommunications networks that connect the **Internet**.

Semiconductors thus form the basis of most of the key technologies that have underpinned the microelectronic and **personal computer** revolutions. But scientists have constantly speculated over whether semiconductor technology can continue to develop at the same pace in future. The massively increasing cost of developing new microprocessor and memory devices (a new chip plant may cost as much as U.S.$2 billion) has led some commentators to suggest that technical barriers are now being approached that will make it uneconomical for Moore's law to continue. Others have argued that leaps of innovation will continue to clear technical obstacles and that, like the automobile industry before it, the semiconductor industry will develop not by producing more powerful products at lower cost, but by producing a more diverse range of chips for a wider range of products.

Another question is whether the semiconductor industry that grew up in California's **Silicon Valley** can continue to maintain a technical lead over (indeed, perhaps even survive) foreign competition. Some fear that the battle is already lost. U.S. producers saw their market share of general-purpose memory chips decline from 100 percent in 1975 to just 5 percent a decade later and alleged that unfair trade practices by the Japanese were responsible. But other important factors also played a role, such as the economic trend toward globalization; increasing environmental regulations, driving producers from Western countries to less-regulated nations (chip manufacture is a notoriously environmentally unfriendly process); and the increasing competitiveness of Pacific nations. Also, as some commentators have pointed out, what has been bad for U.S. producers has been very good indeed for U.S. consumers, continually driving down the cost of personal computers and peripherals.

Semiconductors are the most ordinary and, at the same time, the most extraordinary of materials. Silicon semiconductors, derived from sand, have made possible an industry estimated to be worth at least U.S.$120 billion in annual sales that employs hundreds of thousands of people worldwide. More important, they have given the world microprocessors, personal computers, fiber optic telecommunications, and the Internet. They are undoubtedly one of humankind's most significant inventions.

FURTHER READING

Gunshor, Robert, and Arto Nurmikko. "Blue-Laser CD Technology." *Scientific American*, July 1996, p. 34.

Gwennap, Linley. "Birth of a Chip." *BYTE*, Dec. 1996, p. 77.

Hutcheson, G. Dan, and Jerry D. Hutcheson. "Technology and Economics in the Semiconductor Industry." *Scientific American*, Jan. 1996, p. 40.

Mazurek, Jan, and Nicholas Ashford. *Making Microchips: Policy, Globalization, and Economic Restructuring in the Semiconductor Industry*. Cambridge, Mass.: MIT Press, 1999.

Randazzese, Lucien. "Semiconductor Subsidies." *Scientific American*, June 1996, p. 32.

Schrope, Mark. "The Dope on Silicon." *New Scientist*, 11 Sept. 1999, p. 42.

Seife, Charles. "Gel Makes Go-Faster Chips." *New Scientist*, 20–27 Dec. 1997, p. 19.

Van Zant, Peter. *Microchip Fabrication: A Practical Guide to Semiconductor Processing*. San Jose, Calif.: Semiconductor Services, 1986.

Volokh, Eugene. *The Semiconductor Industry and Foreign Competition*. CATO Institute Policy Analysis 99. Washington, D.C.: CATO Institute, 1988.

Wagner, Peter. "How Microchips Shook the World." *BYTE*, Dec. 1996, p. 69.

Ward, Mark. "The End of the Chip?" *New Scientist*, 25 July 1998, p. 7.

—*Chris Woodford*

Sendmail

Sendmail is a mail transfer agent and a de facto standard for the **Internet**; it was running in around 76 percent of the mail servers in 1999. Sendmail receives incoming **electronic mail** from external or local machines and delivers it to the intended recipient. By interpreting the address in the e-mail header, Sendmail can decide how to route the messages.

Sendmail was written at the University of California Berkeley by Eric Allman (1956–) as part of the BSD **Unix** release. Sendmail was first distributed as *delivermail* in 1979 with 4.0 and 4.1 BSD Unix. Commercial versions of Sendmail have been spun off the original public domain version. The Sendmail Consortium oversees the development of the new open source variants. Over the years, other programmers as well as companies like **Sun Microsystems** and **Hewlett-Packard** have contributed to the sendmail code.

In 1980, the addressing conventions of the Internet were undergoing changes. The new addressing scheme is the one used today, in which domain names are attached to the computer name. This greatly increased the number of possible addresses, but made delivery of e-mail very difficult, since old and new addresses coexisted for some time and different versions of mailing programs were available. Sendmail was designed to be compatible with **AT&T**'s Unix mail programs, the **ARPANET** mail system, and others in use at the time.

When the user wants to send an e-mail, the e-mail interface program calls sendmail, which temporarily stores the message. Sendmail then starts an SMTP (Simple Mail Transfer Protocol) transfer with the appropriate network computer. The Simple Mail Transfer Protocol was defined for use in the ARPANET and plays the same role for e-mail that File Transfer Protocol (**FTP**) plays for file transfer, or **Telnet** for remote log-in. If any errors are detected during transmission with the SMTP protocol, a message is returned to the user describing the problem encountered.

The evolution of Sendmail into a commercial product provides an instructive example of the general approach followed by Internet software pioneers. A commercial version of the program offers some important enhancements that are attractive for small or medium-sized businesses. However, the program is fully downward compatible with older, public domain versions of the program, which are available at no charge. After some time, the public domain version either catches up with the commercial version or the commercial version is put into the public domain. Either way, a new commercial version becomes immediately available and again offers increased functionality. A de facto standard can be maintained in this way, since only the larger businesses pay for the product and many programmers contribute to the public domain version.

FURTHER READING

Avolio, Frederick M., and Paul Vixie. *Sendmail: Theory and Practice.* Woburn, Mass.: Digital Press, Boston, 1995.

Costales, Bryan, Eric Allan, and Neil Rickert. *Sendmail.* Cambridge, Mass.: Butterworth-Heinemann, 1994.

—*Raúl Rojas*

Shannon, Claude

1916–2001

U.S. Mathematician and Scientist

Claude Shannon is best remembered for his work on information and communications theory, which led to a scientific approach to communications engineering problems. He also was among the first to discover the connection between Boolean logic and circuits, setting the basis for the creation of the **digital computer**.

After finishing his B.S. degree at the University of Michigan in Ann Arbor, Shannon won a research assistantship at the Massachusetts Institute of Technology (MIT) running **Vannevar Bush**'s (1890–1974) pioneering **analog computer**, the Differential Analyzer. Shannon's job at MIT was to figure out how to put on the machine differential equations to be solved, and after the solution, to set the Analyzer up for the next problem. An important part of his responsibility was to return the machine to working order when it broke down.

The analog computer was mechanical and had spinning disks and integrators. There was also a complicated control circuit with relays. Shannon became interested in understanding the nature of the relay. Having studied **Boolean algebra** while at the University of Michigan, he soon realized that there was an isomorphic relationship between AND and OR logical expressions, and series and parallel relay circuits. Shannon sought to interleave the topology of the switching circuits—the way the contacts are connected up—with the Boolean algebra expressions. He recognized that a series circuit can be described by AND in logic, and a parallel circuit can be described by OR. Building on these relationships, Shannon set up a number of postulates and reached important conclusions.

Shannon wrote his M.S. thesis, "A Symbolic Analysis of Relay and Switching Circuits," describing his research. His paper was published in 1938 and won him the Alfred Nobel prize given by the combined engineering societies. Others who worked with relay circuits were aware of how the circuits worked, but they didn't have the Boolean algebra system to describe the circuitry. Shannon's work made it possible to use mathematics to design circuits using the smallest number of contacts.

With a recommendation from Bush, Shannon moved to the mathematics department at MIT to work on his Ph.D. This was a pattern to be continued throughout Shannon's life, the interweaving of the fields of mathematics and electrical engineering.

Shannon began to explore the properties underlying communications systems. In a letter to Bush in February 1939, Shannon explained that he was trying to identify the fundamental properties of a general system for the transmission of information. He was seeking a general model for the transmission of information from a sender to a receiver. He was searching to represent this process in a general way that would include the diverse means of communicating information, such as telephony, radio, television, or telegraph.

In popular speech, the word *information* is understood to include the meaning that is being conveyed. In the field of communications engineering, the word *information* is used to convey the message or sequences of messages to be communicated, without regard to what the meaning is. The task of the communications engineer is to transmit the information reliably, regardless of and without concern for the meaning.

In considering this problem, Shannon created a model for communication and described its general properties. The model includes several parts: an information source, a transmitter, a channel, a receiver, and an information destination. By isolating the different components, it becomes possible to work separately on encoding the information into a signal to be transmitted or to decode the signal that is received. This process helps to solve the problem of accurately transmitting a replica of a message from a source to a destination.

Shannon's ***A Mathematical Theory of Communication*** was published in 1948 in two parts, in the July and October issues of *The Bell System Technical Journal.* In this important paper he established a set of principles or laws governing the process of transmission of information and provided a scientific way to determine how much channel capacity is needed to communicate a given amount of information. Shannon also identified a measurement for information, which John Tukey (1915–) of **Bell Labs** called the *binary digit* (or ***bit***).

Bell Labs provided Shannon with the support to be able to explore the research problems that interested him. One of the areas of research that caught his fancy had to do with how machines could learn. Thinking through the problem, Shannon became interested in teaching a machine to play a game like chess. He spent hours playing chess at Bell Labs, trying to understand how to teach a computer to play the game. An article he wrote on computer chess was published in *Scientific American* in 1950. This article became an inspiration for others interested in the area of computer chess, including Tom Truscott, the co-creator of **Usenet**.

Shannon's interest in machine learning led him to explore a number of other concepts. He created machines to study these, and one of the best known is the maze-solving mouse Theseus. Built in 1950, this was a life-size magnetic mouse controlled by relay circuits. The mouse moved through a maze of 25 squares. Shannon created a strategy for Thesesus to learn to get through the maze using trial and error to set relays in the position that provided the mouse with a path through the maze. Once the mechanical mouse succeeded in learning how to get through the maze, once the relays were set, the mouse could be put anywhere and it would quickly reach its goal. The mouse was equipped with a "brain," which was a circuit of around 75 relays. The "muscles" were a pair of motors driving an electromagnet using magnetic action to move the mouse through the maze. If the maze changed, the mouse would need to explore the new areas, but once it learned how to get through them, it would again be able to move quickly to its goal.

Shannon's fascination with machine intelligence led him to work with **John McCarthy** (1927–) to put out a volume of papers on "Automata Studies." Published in 1956 by Princeton University Press, this contained articles by John McCarthy, **Marvin Minsky** (1927–), and Shannon, among others. **John von Neumann**'s (1903–57) contribution was an examination of the problem of how to make a reliable system using unreliable components, a conceptual problem, the solving of which is important both for creating computers and for creating the **Internet**. Shannon, drawing inspiration from von Neumann's work, took a different approach to the problem, exploring how to create a reliable circuit using unreliable relays.

Returning to MIT first as a visiting professor in 1956, and then as the Donner Professor of Science in 1958, Shannon gave model lectures as he continued his research into areas that interested him, including juggling. He was also the mentor to Ph.D. students, including **Ivan Sutherland** (1938–), who created **Sketchpad**, the first interactive graphics program, as his thesis.

Shannon pioneered communication theory and the concept of information. He recognized that these concepts would have important implications for research about the human nervous system as well, but that such work would require serious and concrete studies in biology. However, he warned against the bandwagon effect of taking a concept such as information from the field of communications engineering and applying it indiscriminately to other fields of study.

Shannon was not only intrigued with the question of intelligence in machines, he was also interested in the subject with regard to humans. In a talk titled "Creative Thinking" that he gave at Bell Labs in March 1952, he shared his observations and experience about how a researcher approaches difficult problems. Among the various methods he discussed were getting to the essentials of the problem, exploring different aspects of the problem, or looking at the solution and then working backward to the nature of the problem. Describing his design work creating various sorts of computing machines, he focused on a problem he encountered in trying to do a certain calculation with a machine that played the game of Nim. Eventually, he found that if he started with the required result and ran the problem backwards until the input value reached the number he desired, he could solve his problem. In this way the feedback from the machine suggested a simpler design than he had not considered previously.

How to explore the capability of the computer to think and to learn is part of the legacy of Shannon's pioneering work. Along with this legacy, however, comes a social challenge, and Shannon's work also contributes to an understanding of how to meet it. In a lecture presented at MIT in 1962, titled "Computers and Automation: Progress and Promise in the Twentieth Century," Shannon referred to the problems of unemployment and economic relocation brought about by the first industrial revolution. He described how the second industrial revolution can present similar difficulties. These new technologies, however, also bring into the world a larger gross national product for the same total person-hours of work. According to Shannon, automation can lead in the direction of a higher standard of living and more leisure. It is a difficult challenge, but Shannon argues that just as with other research problems, an intelligent scientific attack on the problem of achieving an equitable distribution of the larger work product made possible by automation should be able to bring about a satisfactory solution.

BIOGRAPHY

Claude Elwood Shannon. Born 30 April 1916 in Gaylord, Michigan. B.S. in electrical engineering and mathematics from the University of Michigan, 1936; MS, in electrical engineering from Masachusetts Institute of Technology (MIT), 1938; Ph.D. in mathematics from MIT, 1940. Worked at the Institute of Advanced Studies at Princeton, 1940–41. Research mathematician at Bell Labs, 1941–56; consultant at Bell Labs until 1978. Fellow at the Center for the Study of Behavioral Sciences in Palo Alto, California, 1957–58; Donner Professor of Science at MIT, 1958–78. Recipient of numerous honors and awards, including AIEE award, 1940; Rice University medal of honor, 1962; IEEE Medal of Honor, 1966; and the National Medal of Science, 1966. Died 26 February 2001, in Murray Hill, New Jersey.

SELECTED WORKS

Shannon, Claude Elwood. "A Chess-Playing Machine." *Scientific American*, Feb. 1950, pp. 48–51.

———. *Claude Elwood Shannon: Collected Papers.* Edited by N. J. A. Sloane and Aaron D. Wyner. New York: IEEE Press, 1993.

Shannon, Claude Elwood, with Warren Weaver. *A Mathematical Theory of Communication.* Urbana, Ill.: University of Illinois Press, 1949.

FURTHER READING

Horgan, John. "Claude E. Shannon." *IEEE Spectrum*, Apr. 1992, pp. 72–75.

Pierce, J. R. *Symbols, Signals and Noise: The Nature and Process of Communication.* New York: Harper, 1961.

—*Ronda Hauben*

Shareware

Shareware is **software** that customers are allowed to try before purchasing. Unlike public domain software, shareware is commercial, proprietary software, with the authors or their representing interests retaining copyright privileges. Typically, a functional copy of the software is distributed at zero or low cost. After obtaining and evaluating the software, the user must register the software with the controlling party and pay whatever fee is specified.

The terms of evaluation vary in stringency. Some shareware authors rely on the honor system, asking that users register, but not attempting to enforce it. Other authors encourage purchases by either restricting the functionality of the unregistered software or by offering perks for registration. For example, most shareware packages use some form of a "nag screen," reminding users that they must register the software if they decide they want it. Users who register these packages usually get a version of the software without the nag screen. Other common restrictions include disabling parts of a software's functionality, or disabling it altogether after a certain amount of time has passed. Common perks include support and notices of future versions.

The concept of shareware was first formalized by Andrew Fluegelman, who, in 1982, wrote a communications program for the **personal computers** (PCs) called PC-Talk. Inspired by public radio, Fluegelman distributed the program freely over various bulletin board sites and asked users to pay U.S.$25 if they liked the program. Fluegelman dubbed this marketing model *freeware* and trademarked the term. Around the same time, other programmers, notably Jim Knopf, author of PC-File, and Bob Wallace, author of PC-Write, started distributing their own software under similar terms. To avoid the hassles of using the trademarked Freeware, many authors decided to adopt the term *shareware*, which Wallace had been using for his own software.

While the term *freeware* eventually became the de facto term for software that cost nothing to use, the requirements of shareware became more specific. Whereas Fluegelman merely encouraged his users to pay, the definition of shareware evolved so that users were required to pay. In April 1987, several shareware authors formed the Association of Shareware Professionals (ASP) to help its members create and market shareware. Although **encryption** and the **Internet** have made other distribution schemes feasible, shareware continues to be a popular way to market software.

FURTHER READING

Biondo, Jay. *A Walk on the Shareware Side: A Complete Reference About Shareware on the Internet.* Irving-Cloud Publishing Company, 1997.

—*Eugene Eric Kim*

Shell

Traditionally, the command line **interface** to the **operating system** (OS) of a computer is called its shell. It is the module of the OS that prompts the user and executes user commands. Some authors also talk of menu-driven shells, but this connotation of the term is not very common.

Operating systems of the past did not clearly separate the user interface from the rest of the system. The **Unix** operating system adopted such a clear-cut distinction that the user can even select between different types of shells for the same system. The most popular shells for Unix are the Bourne shell, the C-shell, and the Korn shell. The commands that the user types in each shell are transformed into system calls to the *kernel*, or central part, of the operating system. One attractive feature of Unix shells is that they are programmable—that is, a sequence of commands can be written in a file that is executed later. The file is called a *shell script*. In this way, the user can extend the set of commands of the operating system without much effort.

In Unix, a new shell can be started on top of another. The *Bourne shell*, the oldest of all, is started with the command "sh," for example. It prompts the user with a dollar symbol. The *C-shell*, written at the University of California–Berkeley, has a different prompt and more features. A shell can be used to define environment variables that alter the way that programs run, or to define the directory paths. The kind of terminal being used, for example, can be encoded in an environment variable so that the OS knows how to display information on the screen or teletype.

With the advent of the **Internet**, in which commands and password travel through public channels, a way of protecting information is needed. The *secure shell* (ssh) for short is a shell augmented with cryptographic options that allows a user to log into another computer through a network. In secure mode, ssh encodes the traffic using IDEA (International Data Encryption Algorithm), an **algorithm** developed in Zurich at the ETH (Eidgenossiche Technische Hochschule; Swiss Federal Institute of Technology). After having opened a session with a remote host, ssh sends traffic via an encrypted session. An attacker who has managed to take over a network can only force ssh to disconnect, but cannot alter the traffic.

Some authors argue that the concept of a shell goes back to the operating system **Multics**, operational in 1965 at the Massachusetts Institute of Technology. Multics later influenced the designers of Unix. In Multics, the command interpreter launched programs not by starting a new process (as in Unix) but by linking the code of the program to the running code of the OS. The shell became a way to communicate with the new program and encapsulate it.

FURTHER READING

Anderson, Gail. *The Unix C Shell Field Guide.* Upper Saddle River, N.J.: Prentice Hall, 1986.

Carasik, Anne. *Unix Secure Shell.* New York: McGraw-Hill, 1999.

Kernighan, Brian W., and Robert Pike. *The Unix Programming Environment.* Upper Saddle River, N.J.: Prentice Hall, 1983.

—*Raúl Rojas*

Shockley, William

See Bardeen, John, Walter Brattain, and William Shockley.

Siemens

Siemens is a major manufacturer of **personal computers** (PCs) and is Germany's largest electronics supplier. It is named after the Siemens family, who controlled its predecessor companies from their beginnings in 1847 to the incorporation of the modern Siemens AG in 1966.

The founding father of the business is generally regarded to be Ernest Werner von Siemens (1816–92), an electrical engineer who in 1847 founded a telegraph construction firm called Telegraphen-Bau-Anstalt von Siemens & Halske. His partner, Johann George Halske (1840–90), withdrew 20 years later, leaving full control of the company to Werner and his three younger brothers: Karl Wilhelm (1823–83), Carl, and August Friedrich. Karl Wilhelm later emigrated to England, where he became Sir Charles William Siemens, head of the company's British subsidiary. The unit of conductance, the *mho*, is often called the *siemens* in honor of the brothers' contributions to electrical energy.

Siemens & Halske began to construct telegraph cables across Germany and then internationally, establishing offices in St. Petersburg in 1855 and London in 1857. The latter built long-distance cables throughout the British Empire and in 1875 opened the first direct cable connecting Britain to the United States. The company also expanded into other types of electrical engineering in Germany and elsewhere, including power generation and railways.

By the early twentieth century, the Siemens & Halske conglomerate was spinning off many of its operations into new companies. In 1903, *Siemens-Schuckertwerke GmbH* was born from the merger of Siemens's power-engineering interests with another firm, *Shuckert and Co.* In 1932, the medical equipment arm combined with the company *Reiniger Gebbert & Schall* to form *Siemens-Reiniger-Werke AG.* The three companies and their foreign subsidiaries were collectively known as the *House of Siemens.*

Siemens has been widely criticized for its activities during the Nazi era (1933–45), when it used slave labor and was involved in construction of the Auschwitz death camp. Its head, Hermann von Siemens (1885–1986), was interned on war crimes charges from 1946 through 1948. Siemens has paid out more compensation to former slaves than have most other equally culpable German corporations, although survivors still say that it has never formally apologized or admitted responsibility.

Siemens played an important role in reconstructing West Germany after the war, finally merging all its constituents to form Siemens AG in 1966. In the 1980s, Siemens entered the **minicomputer** and PC market with the acquisition of the German company Nixdorf, which became Siemens-Nixdorf. Siemens later sold the division, which is now the Wincor company. Over the years, Siemens became the only European computer maker to have success outside its own country, but the important U.S. market has eluded it. In 1999, it set up a new U.S. company, Unisphere Solutions, which intends to concentrate on high-speed data networking equipment and operate independent of the German parent. Back in Europe, Siemens had become the fifth-largest supplier of mobile phones, making it well positioned to take advantage of the **wireless networks** market.

FURTHER READING

Feldenkirchen, Wilfried. *Werner Von Siemens: Inventor and International Entrepreneur.* Historical Perspectives on Business Enterprise Series. Columbus, Ohio: Ohio State University Press, 1994.

———. *Siemens: 1918–1945.* Historical Perspectives on Business Enterprise Series. Columbus, Ohio: Ohio State University Press, 1999.

Reardon, Marguerite. "Siemens' Haunted History." *Data Communications*, Aug. 1999, p. 53.

—Andy Dornan

Silicon

Silicon is semiconducting material, and it has also become an icon of the computer era. The word is used in conjunction with many others—almost as a synonym of computer chips. **Silicon Valley**, Silicon Alley, silicon foundry, and Silicon Glen are just some of the neologisms of our time.

Computer chips are built using **semiconductor** materials and metallic interconnections. Semiconductors do not conduct electricity as easily as metals, and neither are they good insulators. When they are combined with other elements in a process called *doping*, they can be made to conduct electricity in a controlled manner. **Transistors**, which are simple logic switches, can then be built.

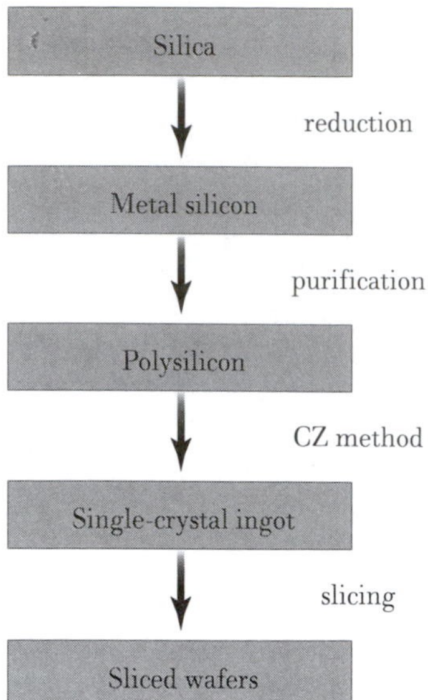

Process of making silicon.

Silicon is the most abundant element in nature and also in computer chips. In fact, it is used as the substrate for the entire chip. First, it is extracted from silica using a metal that reacts with silicon; then the metallic silicon is purified using a chemical process. The next step is growing silicon ingots (large rods of silicon) from a single crystal. A silicon ingot is, in principle, a single giant crystal with few imperfections and great purity. It is grown using the *Czochralski* (CZ) or *float zone technique*. The first method consists in molting the silicon in a closed furnace containing an inert atmosphere. A single crystal is used to pull out the material slowly. As the silicon solidifies, it adopts the same orientation as the seed crystal.

When the ingot is complete, thin slices are cut and are used as *wafers* for the chips. The diameter of the ingots used was 20 centimeters (cm) until 1999, then the semiconductor industry started the transition towards 30-cm wafers, which will be the standard for several years until 45-cm wafers arrive. The larger the wafer, the more chips that can be built on them, and the cheaper they become. The figure summarizes the steps of the production process from silica to the wafers. Computer chips are sculpted on the silicon wafer using several layers of materials which are deposited using chemical etching and photolithography. The process demands a high degree of purity and exactitude, and it requires extremely expensive equipment, and therefore chip factories have become unaffordable for small companies. In the last years, the cost of a semiconductor facility has been duplicating every two years. Since chip production is becoming increasingly expensive, it makes sense to separate production from design, at least in the case of low-volume chips. *Silicon foundries* are companies specialized in manufacturing all kinds of chips for clients who do their own design but cannot own a fabric.

The term *silicon cycle*, refers to the periodic ups and downs of the semiconductor industry. Since this sector produces the raw material for the rest of the electronic industry, it is the first affected in the production chain. The silicon cycle goes from growth to recession in four years. It has been empirically "observed" that the peak usually coincides with an Olympic year.

FURTHER READING

O'Mara, William C., Robert B. Herring, and Lee P. Hunt, eds. *Handbook of Semiconductor Silicon Technology*. Park Ridge, N.J.: Noyes Publications, 1990.

Singh, Jasprit. *Semiconductor Devices: An Introduction*. New York: McGraw-Hill, 1994.

—*Raúl Rojas*

Silicon Graphics, Inc.

Based in Mountain View, California, in the heart of **Silicon Valley**, for two decades Silicon Graphics, Inc. (SGI) has been a world leader in high-performance computing technology, especially for three-dimensional **graphics** applications. It has also been instrumental in the development of the **Virtual Reality Modeling Language** (VRML). The company's systems have ranged from desktop workstations and servers to **supercomputers** in the world, delivering computing and three-dimensional visualization facilities for scientific, engineering, and entertainment applications. In particular, Pixar has used the platform for computer animation in the film industry. Disney films and other blockbuster films such as *Jurassic Park*, have benefited from SGI technology.

SGI was founded by James H. Clark (1944–) in 1982 with seven cofounders. They were Kurt Akeley, David J. Brown, Tom David, Mark Grossman, Marc Hannah, Charles "Herb" Kuta, and Charles "Rocky" Rhodes. All of them were members of Jim Clark's research group in the Computer Systems Laboratory at Stanford University.

The company was born from Clark's Geometry Engine, a special-purpose **very large scale integration** (VLSI) computer graphics processor, especially good for fast transformations necessary in real-time three-dimensional graphics. Marc Hannah undertook the original VLSI design. The U.S. Department of Defense Advanced Research Projects Agency (DARPA) supported the foundational research. **Hewlett-Packard** fabricated the first copy of the initial data path design, and **Xerox Palo Alto Research Center** (PARC) fabricated the first fully functioning version of the entire Geometry Engine chip.

The original full system was an adapted version of the Stanford University Network (SUN) terminal, designed and licensed by **Andreas Bechtolsheim** (1955–), a Ph.D. student at Stanford. Bechtolsheim later used this technology to cofound **Sun Microsystems**, a rival workstation manufacturer. The Silicon Graphics version replaced the SUN frame buffer board (one of three in the SUN terminal) with three new boards. These included frame buffer controller and bit plane boards, and also a Geometry Engine and pipe adapter board to enable fast three-dimensional graphics.

Like the original SUN system, the first Silicon Graphics IRIS system was a terminal (available in 1983). Later versions, such as Sun, became **Unix** workstations (available from 1984), but they used the AT&T System V version of Unix rather than the Berkeley Unix of **Bill Joy** (1955–), also cofounder of Sun. This was largely due to the employment by Silicon Graphics of a number of **Bell Labs** engineers, including Steve Bourne, who wrote the original Bourne **shell** for user interaction with Unix.

The early SGI technology was based on the **Motorola** 68000 series of **microprocessors**. The first Geometry System used the original 68000 16-bit processor with 256 kilobytes of random access memory (**RAM**; expandable up to 2 megabytes) running at a clock speed of 8 megahertz. The geometry subsystem included from 10 to 12 copies of the Geometry Engine itself. The color raster subsystem provided 1024 x 1024 pixels each of up to 256 colors, including **hardware** support for polygon filling, vector drawing, and arbitrary characters. Firmware aided colored or textured lines and polygon, character clipping, color mapping, and selectable single or double buffering.

The company's initial public offering (IPO) took place in 1986. Like Sun, Silicon Graphics moved to **reduced instruction set computing** (RISC) technology from 1987. The company merged with MIPS Computer Systems in 1992. In 1993 the company made an agreement with the computer games company Nintendo to create the low-cost Nintendo64 video-game console, including three-dimensional graphics technology that cost many times more only a few years previously. In the same year, SGI reported its first billion-dollar sales year. The SGI Reality Center provided the world's most advanced immersive visualization facility for group **virtual reality** (VR), first made available in 1994.

On 6 January 1994, SGI's chief executive officer, Ed McCracken, on good terms with President Bill Clinton (1946–) and Vice President Al Gore (1948–), was named as co-chair of President Clinton's National Information Infrastructure Advisory Council. Just a few weeks later, on 27 January, Jim Clark left SGI to start another billion-dollar company, Mosaic Communications, later renamed **Netscape**, with **Marc Andreessen** (1972–). Further company mergers occurred in 1995, and especially significantly, with the supercomputer company **Cray Research**, Inc. in 1996, resulted in the company producing multiprocessor supercomputers.

After a highly successful period, the company's fortune foundered somewhat in the late 1990s. In 1999 the company started to produce desktop systems based on **Intel** processors and the Microsoft **Windows NT** operating system, in line with many other **personal computer** manufacturers, as well as the **Linux** operating system.

Further Reading

Clark, James H. "A VLSI Geometry Processor for Graphics." *IEEE Computer*, Vol. 13, No. 7, July 1980, pp. 59–68.

———. "The Geometry Engine: A VLSI Geometry System for Graphics." *Computer Graphics*, Vol. 16, No. 3, July 1982, 127–133.

Kaplan, David A. *The Silicon Valley Boys*. New York: HarperCollins, 2000.

Silicon Graphics, Inc. *Silicon Graphics Home Page*. *http://www.sgi.com*

———. *SGI Company Fact Sheet*. *http://www.sgi.com/newsroom/factsheet.html*

—*Jonathan Bowen*

Silicon Valley

Silicon Valley is the name given to an area of western California centered around the town of Palo Alto, where many of the world's most inventive and most profitable computer companies have been based since the 1950s.

Stretching from the San Francisco Bay area in the north to San Jose in the south, and from the Santa Cruz mountains in the west to the Coast Range in the east, it occupies a total area of around 300 square miles. But Silicon Valley is as much an entrepreneurial style of doing business and an attitude of mind as a real geographical place. As the home to companies such as **Hewlett-Packard**, **Intel Corporation**, **Sun Microsystems**, **Adobe Systems**, and **Netscape Communications**, the influence of this comparatively tiny region of the United States is felt around the world.

Although Silicon Valley's dramatic growth has occurred mostly in the last 50 years, its origins can be traced back to 1906, when Lee de Forest (1873–1961; the "father of radio") invented a small current amplifier, which he named the Audion valve. This revolutionary device, which became a part of most radios and other electronic appliances developed before the invention of the **transistor** in 1947, owed part of its development to U.S.$500 research funding provided by Stanford University. It was the beginning of a long, close, and mutually profitable relationship between Stanford University and the electronics industry.

Much of Silicon Valley's early development is due to a single man: Frederick Terman (1900–82). Terman was professor of electronic engineering at Stanford and encouraged his students to start their own businesses to develop good ideas. Two students who followed that advice were **William Hewlett** (1913–) and **David Packard** (1912–), who started the Hewlett-Packard company in the 1930s, initially developing electronic equipment for Disney's movie *Fantasia.* Other students profiting from a close association with Stanford included the brothers Sigurd (1901–61) and Russell Varian (1898–1959), who in 1937 invented a microwave-generating device known as the klystron (the central component in radar and medical scanning equipment).

Before the arrival of the electronics and computer industry that would make it famous, the Santa Clara Valley was better known as a fertile fruit-growing region—the "Valley of Heart's Delight." That began to change in 1887 when Pacific Railroad baron Leland Stanford (1824–93) bequeathed nearly 9000 acres of land and U.S.$20 million to found a university in honor of his son, who had died shortly before taking up a university place. Stanford rapidly became a breeding ground for important electronic research, but by 1951 found itself running short of money. Frederick Terman, who had been working to forge closer links between the university and the electronics industry, saw an opportunity to solve the financial crisis by developing a Stanford research park. He envisaged an industrial estate, built on Stanford's vast acreage of land, occupied by high-tech companies that could cooperate closely with the university. The Stanford Industrial Park opened in 1951, when Varian Associates signed a lease on the first unit, and Varian become the Park's first occupant in 1953.

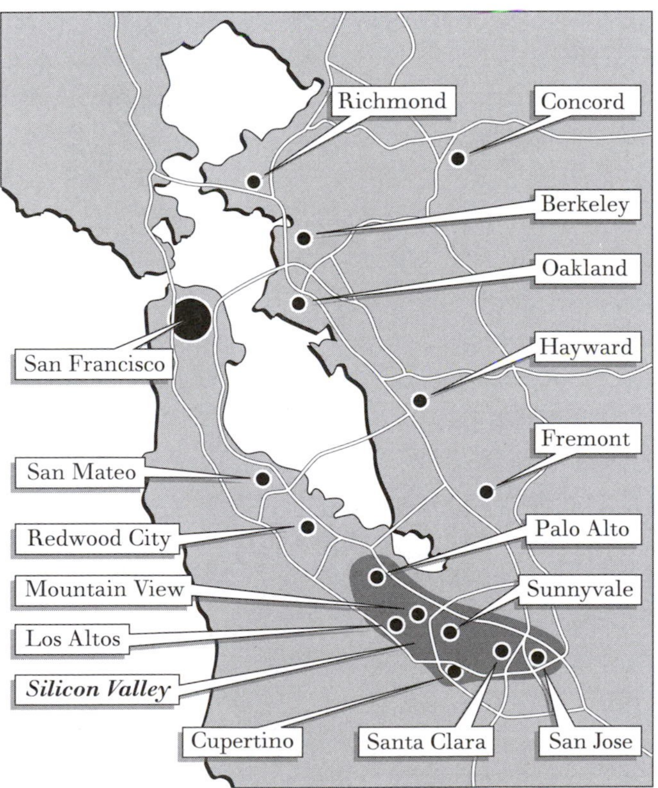

Area of California known as Silicon Valley.

Later, the Park gained a number of other important tenants. Most significant of these was a tiny company known as Shockley Transistor, run by **William Shockley** (1910–89), one of the three-man team responsible for developing the transistor at **Bell Labs** in the late 1940s. Shockley's company was probably the first example of what is now known as a Silicon Valley start-up: It was formed by a group of highly talented people with an idea and some venture capital. But it also helped to set the precedent for what ultimately happens to most Silicon Valley startups. Only two years after its formation, the eight talented engineers who Shockley had recruited decided that they could no longer tolerate his idiosyncratic management style and left to found a startup of their own.

This new enterprise, **Fairchild Semiconductor**, rapidly became one of the most influential companies in Silicon Valley. It developed the planar process, a technique for compressing hundreds, thousands, and ultimately even millions of miniature electronic components into a neat package on a single slice of silicon known as an **integrated circuit**. But within a decade, the founders of Fairchild had left to found new startups. Most famously, **Gordon Moore** (1929–) and **Robert Noyce** (1927–90), who were the last of the original eight founders to leave, founded Intel Corporation in 1968. Intel has been one of Silicon Valley's greatest success stories. In 30 years, the company has grown from a tiny startup employing just seven people to a multinational employing around 65,000. In 1998, Intel's revenue topped U.S.$26 billion and the company spent over U.S.$2.6 billion on research and development. Apart from Intel, Fairchild employees have started around 40 other Silicon Valley companies, including **Advanced Micro Devices** (AMD) and National Semiconductor.

Silicon Valley has had close links with the U.S. military since the Varian brothers produced their radar-generating klystron just before World War II. But the importance of state-of-the-art electronics in ensuring a military advantage over hostile nations meant that other defense contractors soon moved to California. In 1956, Lockheed decided to open a research and development laboratory on the Stanford Industrial Park, attracting massive defense investment to the area, and ultimately becoming Silicon Valley's biggest employer. Initially one of the largest purchasers of semiconductor products, the U.S. Defense Department has remained a key source of funding, contributing substantially to the development of supercomputers and of the Internet.

For all the important developments in the 1950s and 1960s, the 1970s were certainly Silicon Valley's most important decade. The term *Silicon Valley* was first used in 1971, when journalist Don Hoeffler (1923–86) renamed the Santa Clara Valley to sum up the phenomenal growth in the electronics business. That year also marked the arrival of Silicon Valley's most important invention since the transistor, the **microprocessor** (single-chip computer) developed at Intel. Within just a few years, Silicon Valley companies such as **Apple Computer**, whose founders **Steve Wozniak** (1950–) and **Steve Jobs** (1955–) had seen demonstrations of early microcomputers at the Bay Area Amateur Computer Users Group (better known as the **Homebrew Computer Club**), were building and selling their own computers based on these tiny chips. The **Apple I and Apple II** were two such early machines and they led directly to the personal computer revolution when they spurred **IBM** to launch its own microcomputer in 1981. In 1970, Silicon Valley also saw the establishment of possibly its most creative and most influential research laboratory, **Xerox Palo Alto Research Center** (PARC), where engineers would develop the first high-speed computer network (**Ethernet**), the first laser **printer**, the original **graphical user interface** (the "look and feel" of modern computers from which the Apple **Macintosh** and **Windows** interfaces would be developed), and numerous other important innovations.

Silicon Valley continued to set the pace of development in the computer industry throughout the 1980s. One of the most important contributions was the development of desktop publishing, which grew out of PARC research. This eventually led to the easy-to-use Apple Macintosh, announced in 1984, and Adobe Systems' PostScript, a graphical programming language that simplifies the production of high-resolution printed and displayed information. The 1980s also witnessed a dramatic transformation of the PC hardware business as Silicon Valley manufacturers, notably **Compaq**, used a technique known as reverse engineering to produce ***clone*** machines that were entirely compatible with the industry-standard IBM PC, but retailed at a much lower price. Back at Stanford in the mid-1980s, Sun (originally Stanford University Networks) Microsystems developed the first high-performance, **reduced instruction set computer**–based, **Unix** workstations.

Silicon Valley has also made a major contribution to the rise of the **Internet** (and particularly the **World Wide Web**) during the 1990s. Today's Silicon Valley startups are much more likely to be Web-related businesses than traditional hardware manufacturers or software houses. The best known of these is Netscape Communications Corporation, founded in the Silicon Valley town of Mountain View in 1995, which manufactures Web browser and server software. The San Francisco Bay area continues to be the heartland of the Web development community, and counts ***Wired*** magazine, the Internet search service **Yahoo!**, and Internet broadcaster CNET among its many influential members.

Some industry commentators have speculated whether Silicon Valley will continue to play such a key role in the computer industry of the twenty-first century. With the rise of the Internet, there is no particular reason why computer developers need locate physically near one another or inside California. Indeed, following the success of Silicon Valley, other areas around the world have developed into smaller-scale technological hot-spots, including Silicon Alley in New York City, Silicon Glen in Scotland, and the Cambridge University Science Park in England. Industry commentators such as Robert X. Cringely (1953–) have demonstrated that Silicon Valley is as much an attitude of mind (and a relatively amateurish way of doing business) as a 300-square-mile slice of California. Cringely argues that technical brilliance, sheer determination, and mountains of junk food count for more in Silicon Valley than anything as simple as financial reward. There is no reason, in theory, why these conditions could not be replicated elsewhere.

Yet there is something unique about Silicon Valley. The Silicon Valley style—sneakers, junk food, cubicles instead of offices, and staff who own millions or billions of dollars of equity but still work 100-hour weeks—is a world away from the dark-suited sobriety on which the success of traditional computer companies, such as IBM, were built. Silicon Valley is not only a milestone in computer history, but also a milestone in American history: one definition of what the "American dream" means at the end of the twentieth century.

The world of computing has changed drastically in Silicon Valley's first 50 years. However that world develops in the next 50 years, it is likely to be based on advanced semiconductors for the foreseeable future. The dense concentration of computer and electronics businesses in this tiny part of California, the continued influence and excellence of Stanford University, and the sheer dynamic excitement of an area that has produced many of the computer world's most important recent innovations mean that Silicon Valley is likely to be the capital city of computing for some years to come.

FURTHER READING

Cringely, Robert X. *Accidental Empires: How the Boys of Silicon Valley Make Their Millions, Battle Foreign Competition, and Still Can't Get a Date.* New York: Harper Business, 1996.

Kaplan, David A. *The Silicon Boys and Their Valley of Dreams.* New York: William Morrow, 1999.

Reid, Robert H. *Architects of the Web: 1000 Days That Built the Future of Business.* New York: Wiley, 1997.

—*Chris Woodford*

SIMULA

SIMULA (Simulation Language) is a computer programming language that was conceptualized, designed, and created at the Norwegian Computing Centre in Oslo by Ole-Johan Dahl (1931–) and Kristen Nygaard (1926–). SIMULA's primary use is to develop computer models of systems such as ticket counters, production lines, manufacturing systems, and concurrent processing of computer programs.

Originally, SIMULA was intended to facilitate the development of simulation models for complex real-world systems. It contained elements of both a standardized system description and a programming language. With system concepts based on Nygaard's experience working with operations research projects in the early 1950s, SIMULA was implemented as a discrete-event computer simulation language. Initial constructs were influenced by symbolic notation used in the 1950s to construct flow diagrams representing system operation and rules governing system behaviors.

The first concepts for SIMULA were developed in 1961. Nygaard had a framework of ideas to represent random variation in the occurrence of delays experienced by customers passing through a network of processes. These processes consisted of a queue portion and a service portion. The service portions were constructed with a series of statements governing the action of passive entities or customers that used these stations. Customers were created at a given station and after completing service would be transferred to the queue of another station. After obtaining and completing service there, the process would be repeated. These transfers would continue until the customer had traversed the network and left the system. The timing and sequence of these stations would determine the number of customers that could be served over a period of time.

Although Nygaard had experience with computers, he did not have sufficient knowledge to develop his own programming language. He recruited software expert Ole-Johan Dahl to help him move SIMULA from theory to implementation. In the spring of 1962, Nygaard and Dahl released the first formal proposal for SIMULA. They decided that the best way to make it a real programming language was to link it to an existing language. **ALGOL** 60, popular in Europe at the time, was selected and SIMULA was developed as an extension that allowed discrete-event simulation construction. Later, SIMULA was expanded and reimplemented as a full-scale general-purpose programming language.

Although SIMULA has never achieved wide usage, the concepts developed within the language have been highly influential on modern computer programming. SIMULA has been credited with introducing **object-oriented programming** concepts such as classes, objects, inheritance, and dynamic binding. Today, a wide variety of discrete-event computer simulation software packages, such as GPSS/H, SIMAN, and ProModel, are used to create similar applications.

Further Reading

Holmevik, Jan Rune. "The History of SIMULA." *Annals of the History of Computing*, Vol. 16, No. 4, 1994, pp. 25–37.

—*Roger McHaney*

"Sketch of the Analytical Engine"

By Luigi Menabrea

The "Sketch of the Analytical Engine" was a description of **Charles Babbage**'s (1791–1871) **Analytical Engine**, written by Luigi Menabrea (1809–96) and translated by **Lady Ada Augusta Lovelace** (1815–52). The account, combined with Lovelace's extensive notes, constitutes the earliest complete description of a programmable computer.

Charles Babbage visited Turin, Italy, in 1840 to promote his still-theoretical Analytical Engine, a programmable successor to the **Difference Engine**. He visited the King of Italy, gave talks, and spent extended time with Luigi Menabrea of the Royal Engineers. Menabrea promised to publish a detailed description of the engine for European audiences. After much impatience on Babbage's part, his "Sketch of the Analytical Engine" appeared in the *Bibliothèque Universelle de Genève* in October 1842. Unfortunately, it was written in French, which limited its readership at home.

Babbage had developed a correspondence and personal relationship with Lady Ada Augusta Lovelace, daughter of poet Lord Byron (1788–1824) and an aspiring mathematician. Babbage convinced her to translate Menabrea's article. The fact that female mathematicians were quite rare at that time may have increased the curiosity value of her work. Lovelace produced more than a translation; her notes were at least twice the length of the original article. Ada included a detailed description of how to program the engine to calculate Bernoulli numbers, using both operation and variable cards to program this trigonometric series. Due to this program, she has been touted as the world's first programmer, and the U.S. Department of Defense named its computer language Ada in her honor. Some historians have questioned whether she received too much credit, as there is evidence that Babbage helped her during her translation and note writing. Nonetheless, the ideas outlined in "Sketch" will influence the engineering of the first programmable computers more than a century later.

Further Reading

Hyman, Anthony. *Charles Babbage*, Prinction, N.J.: Princeton University Press, 1982.

Menabrea, L.F. "Sketch of the Analytical Engine. " *Bibliothèque Universelle de Genève*, No. 82, Oct. 1842. Translated by Ada Augusta Lovelace in Henry Prevost Babbage, *Babbage's Calculating Engines*. London: Spon and Co., 1889, pp. 6–51.

Stein, Dorothy. *Ada: A Life and a Legacy*. Cambridge, Mass.: MIT Press, 1985.

—*James Tomayko*

Sketchpad

Sketchpad has been called the most important computer program ever written. Completed in 1962, Sketchpad was the first system built for interactive **computer graphics**. It was a technological milestone because it demonstrated that computers could be used for something other than numerical data processing.

Sketchpad was created by **Ivan Sutherland** (1938–), a graduate student of **Claude Shannon** (1916–2001) and **J. C. R. Licklider** (1915–90), as his Ph.D. thesis project at the Massachusetts Institute of Technology (MIT). The project utilized a graphical style of interaction that enabled a computer to respond quickly to users' actions by updating immediately drawings displayed on a screen. This sophisticated drawing program was developed on the TX-2, the first computer built using **transistors** rather than **vacuum tubes** as switching elements to process information. Sutherland was working specifically on the problem of getting information from the computer to be displayed on various kinds of display screens. During this process, he developed a direct relationship between bits of information stored in a computer's magnetic memory and pixels or dots of light displayed on the screen.

In addition to creating visual displays, Sketchpad was a type of simulation language that allowed computers to translate abstract information into visual forms. Using a lightpen, **keyboard**, and display screen, Sketchpad introduced the idea of master drawings and instance drawings. It enabled programmers to define a variety of different constraints on the parts of a master drawing. Constraints could be both simple and complex. For example, the end of line *A* should be two inches from point *B*, or the truss of mass *M* should bend according to Newton's law of gravitational force. Drawings (an instance) were created with a lightpen, checked against the requested constraints, and adjusted to conform to the constraints.

Sketchpad is considered to be a starting point for computer graphics, **computer-aided design** (CAD), and the development of **virtual reality** systems. The program also influenced the work of **Alan Kay** (1940–), who created the first **graphical user interface** and the **object-oriented** program **SmallTalk**. Additionally, Sketchpad influenced Ted Nelson (1940–), who invented **hypertext** and also authored important commentaries on the future of computing.

After developing Sketchpad, Sutherland became the director of **ARPA**'s Information Processing Techniques Office. He left ARPA in the mid-1960s to work on three-dimensional head-mounted displays and graphics systems. Finally, he teamed up with David Evans to form a pioneering computerized flight simulation and image generation company, the Evans and Sutherland Computer Company.

Further Reading

Nelson, Theodor H. *Computer Lib: Dream Machines*. Chicago: Nelson, 1974; rev. ed., Redmond, Wash.: Microsoft Press, 1987.

Rheingold, Howard. *Virtual Reality*. New York: Summit Books, 1991.

—*Susan B. Barnes*

Slide Rule

The slide rule is an analog computing device that computes products, quotients, squares, and square roots by the use of logarithms.

Logarithms were invented by the Scottish mathematician John Napier (1550–1617). Napier published two books on logarithms: *Description of the Marvelous Canon of Logarithms* (1614), which is a tabulation of logarithms, and *Construction of the Marvelous Canon of Logarithms* (published posthumously in 1619), which explains the theoretical basis for construction of the tables.

In 1620, Edmund Gunter (1581–1626) designed a scale with numbers from 1 to 10 arranged from one end to the other such that the distance from 1 to any other number is proportional to the logarithm of the number. Multiplication can be done with a Gunter's scale and a pair of dividers. To multiply *A* times *B*, the dividers are set equal to the distance from 1 to *A*. Then the dividers are moved so that the lower point is at *B* and the product is read at the location of the higher point. A similar process is used for division. Multiplication is reduced to addition when using logarithms because the logarithm of the product of two numbers is the sum of the logarithm of each number.

William Oughtred (1574–1660) suggested making two Gunter's scales so that one could slide against the other. Now multiplication of *A* times *B* is accomplished by sliding the starting point of one scale so that 1 on that scale is opposite to *A* on the second scale. *B* is found on the first scale and the product is on the second scale opposite point *B*. Oughtred also developed a circular slide rule with logarithmic scales marked around the edges of two disks (one slightly smaller than the other) which are pinned at their centers so that one can rotate relative to the other.

By the mid-seventeenth century slide rules consisting of a sliding stick between two fixed sticks had been developed. Amedee Mannheim (1831–1906) added a movable cursor, producing the final design of the slide rule of the twentieth century. Mannheim slide rules have scales on one side and a cursor on only one side of the scales. Duplex designs put scales on

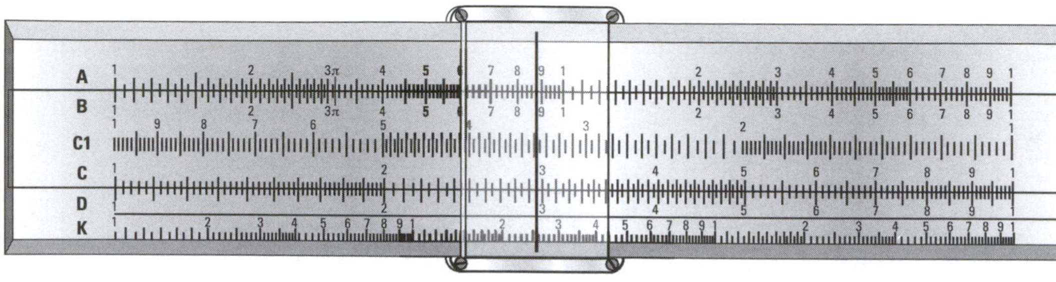

Figure 1. *A basic slide rule.*

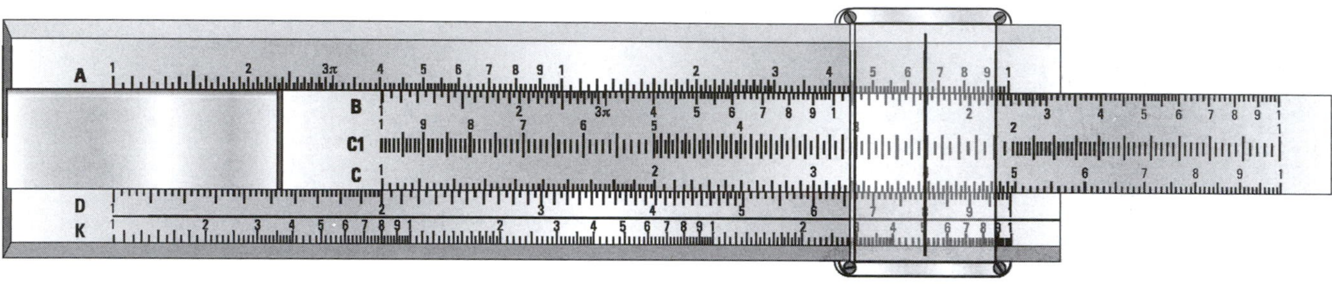

Figure 2. *Multiplication of 2 times 4 on a slide rule.*

both sides and use a double-sided cursor so that more scales can be placed on the rules.

The C and D scales are used for multiplication as shown in figure 2. The 1 on the C scale is placed opposite the first factor (2) on the D scale. Then the product (8) is read on the D scale opposite the second factor (4) on the C scale. Division is performed similarly. In this case the divisor (4) on the C scale is placed opposite the dividend (8) on the D scale. The quotient (2) is read on the D scale opposite to 1 on the C scale.

In the United States, Keuffel and Esser (starting in the late 1890s) and Pickett (starting in the 1940s) were major slide rule designers and manufacturers. Keuffel and Esser (and most other firms worldwide, such as Dennert & Pape and A. W. Faber Castell in Germany, and Thornton in Britain) used a wood core with celluloid facings that were engraved with the various scales. Sun Hemmi in Japan used bamboo. Pickett in the United States used metal (a magnesium alloy from 1945 to 1950 and aluminum from 1950 to 1975) for their rules with enameled scales printed on them. Dennert & Pape's ARISTO slide rules were made from polyvinyl chloride plastic.

Most slide rules are about 12 inches long with scales that are about 10 inches long. These rules generally provide about three-digit accuracy. Pocket slide rules are about half as long with about two-digit accuracy. A relatively smaller number of double-length slide rules were made that would achieve up to four-digit accuracy.

The slide rule greatly facilitates multiplication, division, and forming powers and roots, but in the 1970s they were replaced rapidly by hand-held electronic calculators. The **Hewlett-Packard** HP-35 introduced in 1972 could perform all the functions of an advanced slide rule but with much better accuracy (typically, electronic calculators provide about 10-digit accuracy, while as noted above, most slide rules were limited to about three digits).

FURTHER READING

Ayoub, Raymond. "Napier and the Invention of Logarithms." *Journal of the Oughtred Society* Vol. 3, No. 2, 1994, pp. 7–13.

Cajori, Florian. *A History of the Logarithmic Slide Rule and Allied Instruments.* New York: Engineering News Publishing Company, 1909.

———. *On the History of Gunter's Scale and the Slide Rule During the Seventeenth Century.* Berkeley, Calif.: University of California Press, 1920.

Williams, Michael R. *A History of Computing Technology.* Englewood Cliffs, N.J.: Prentice Hall, 1985; 2nd ed., Los Alamitos, Calif.: IEEE Computer Society Press, 1997.

—*Earl Swartzlander*

Smalltalk

Smalltalk is a programming language designed in the early 1970s by **Alan Kay** (1940–) at the **Xerox Palo Alto Research Center**. Kay borrowed ideas from other languages, such as **SIMULA** and Logo, to develop Smalltalk, the **software** for a planned computerized notebook called the *Dynabook*.

Kay's experiments with children and the way they interact with computers fostered Smalltalk's interactive environment, where the user is encouraged to "learn by doing." In this environment, messages can be sent to programming objects by typing code into a *workspace* window. The resulting object is opened in a new window called an *inspector*, where its state can be examined and additional messages can be sent. Integrated *project browsers, transcript windows,* and an advanced *debugger*, along with incremental compilation, all contribute to the ability to create, test, and modify programs quickly, even while they are running.

Kay designed Smalltalk from the ground up to be simple, consistent, and intuitive. The language has only five reserved words: *true, false, nil, self,* and *super*. It is based on the concept that everything is an object and that objects respond to messages. Ninety-nine percent of the Smalltalk language and its environment are written in Smalltalk itself, on this premise. *Primitive* types such as characters, integers, and floats are objects to which you can send messages. *Language constructs* such as classes and methods are also objects. Smalltalk utilizes these powerful reflective abilities to fully automate *refactoring* of user-created class hierarchies.

Variables are used to give a name to an object. Unlike statically typed languages, in which variables and method arguments must declare and conform to a particular type, Smalltalk variables specify no type and can point to any object. This symmetry allows Smalltalk to provide its heterogeneous object structures with good performance. Memory consumed by objects no longer referenced is automatically reclaimed by a garbage collector.

Since Alan Kay didn't know what computing platform would be available for the next version of Smalltalk, the language runs on a **virtual machine**, an abstract computer that can be emulated by real computers. Porting Smalltalk from one computer to another implies that only the virtual machine code has to be rewritten. This is much simpler than rewriting the entire Smalltalk system.

Nearly 30 years after its conception, Smalltalk continues to be the language of choice for high-complexity applications where time to market is essential. Applications such as **Texas Instruments** semiconductor manufacturing system, the U.S. Department of Defense's joint-warfare simulation system, and Disney's **multimedia** applications are characteristic of the types of applications for which Smalltalk is being well utilized.

FURTHER READING

Bergin, Thomas J., and Richard G. Gibson, eds. *History of Programming Languages.* New York: ACM Press, 1996.

Lewis, Simon. *The Art and Science of Smalltalk.* Upper Saddle River, N.J.: Prentice Hall, 1995.

Liu, Chamond. *Smalltalk: Objects and Design.* Greenwich, Conn.: Manning, 1996.

—*Chris Muller*

Software

A computer is of little use without instructions that tell it what to do and how to do it. In contrast to the machine itself, which is solid and inflexible, those instructions or programs are abstract and malleable. Beginning in the 1950s, this distinction came to be thought of as **hardware** (the computer) versus software (the instructions).

The idea of controlling machinery through changeable instructions can be traced back to the early nineteenth century and the Jacquard loom, which used belts of perforated cards to weave different patterns automatically. Later in the century, Jacquard's work inspired **Charles Babbage** (1791–1871) to consider using punched cards to control his **Analytical Engine**, a general-purpose mechanical calculator which he meticulously planned but never completed. Between World Wars I and II **Konrad Zuse** (1910–95) in Germany, used punched tape to convey instructions to the control unit of a calculating machine he designed and built. Postwar computers, beginning with the **Manchester**

Mark I in England and the **EDVAC** (electronic discrete variable automatic computer) in the United States, were designed to store and manipulate instructions electronically inside the machine.

Initially, general-purpose electronic **digital computers** were programmed in machine language, the binary code with which a computer actually works. But strings of ones and zeros are very difficult for human beings to understand, so in the 1950s more comprehensible symbolic languages were developed. At first, programs were converted manually from symbolic to machine language after they had been written, but the computer itself was quickly put to work performing this task. New languages were developed that included more abstract operations, which no longer directly corresponded to machine operations. These soon took the form of highly structured but nevertheless English-like languages such as **Fortran** (Formula Translation) and **COBOL** (Common Business Oriented Language). Rapidly multiplying in number, such high-level languages promised (but never fully delivered) the ability to run a single program on many different computers, assuming that the appropriate translator was installed.

Software was soon separated into two fundamental categories that persist to this day: *system software* (including the **operating system** and programming language translators), which supports the operation of the computer, and *application software*, which actually performs the work the computer is intended to accomplish.

In the early days of commercial computers, software typically came *bundled* with the hardware. As both system and application software grew increasingly complex, software became a substantial part of total system cost. In the late 1960s computer manufacturers, beginning with **IBM**, which was also under government antitrust pressure, unbundled hardware and software and began to charge for them separately. This opened a large window of opportunity for third-party software developers, who aimed to provide not only *customized software* but also *packaged software* which spread development costs across a population of users. Packaged software has been essential to the proliferation of personal computers. At a meeting in Germany in the 1990s, Konrad Zuse told **Bill Gates** (1955–), chief executive officer of **Microsoft**, that at the time he developed his computers, it never occurred to him that someone could make money out of selling what we now know as software.

FURTHER READING

Campbell-Kelly, Martin, and William Aspray. *Computer: A History of the Information Machine.* New York: Basic Books, 1996.

Ceruzzi, Paul E. *A History of Modern Computing.* Cambridge, Mass.: MIT Press, 1998.

Goldstine, Herman H. *The Computer from Pascal to Von Neumann.* Princeton, N.J.: Princeton University Press, 1993.

—Stuart Shapiro

Software, Cost of

Estimating the cost of producing software **programs**, either on a custom or a package basis, has been a headache for developers since the first software programs were produced in the 1950s. Despite much progress toward better structuring and speedup of the software development process, producing accurate estimates of both time and cost continues to be a serious problem.

Since the 1960s, major investments have been made at universities and research labs and by **hardware** manufacturers and software producers to turn program development into an engineeringlike process with the same type of discipline and predictability as expected by manufacturing and construction organizations in producing physical products and facilities.

Great advances have certainly been made in reducing the cost of producing both systems and applications programs through the creation of advanced programming languages and much better tools for design and testing. **Fortran** (Formula Translator), developed in the late 1950s, was the first scientific application programming language. **COBOL** (Common Business Oriented Language), developed in the early 1960s, was the first broadly used commercial application development language. Since then there have been third- and fourth-generation languages to reduce the need for reprogramming common, repetitive functions and to simplify transaction specifications, database references, and report preparation. Most recently, the introduction of component-based development appears to be another step forward to reusing common functional elements and to avoid rewriting code.

All of these program development languages and tools are intended to enable a programmer to write fewer statements (or simpler statements) which will compile (or be interpreted) into more lines of object code. Nevertheless, many organizations still have great difficulty in estimating how much effort will be needed to produce a particular system or application program. This continues to plague both custom and product software development projects.

What makes the estimating process so difficult? Whenever a development team tackles a new problem, it is extremely hard to determine, in advance, all the factors and elements that will eventually need to be considered and programmed in constructing the solution. There are always a large number of surprises that add to the work effort and calendar time required, and these add-ons and changes increase the cost disproportionately. This is a case where 2 + 2 may equal 8, not 4.

Historically, the principal measurement used to estimate the programming effort required was lines of code (LOCs). This was usually described as thousands of LOC, or KLOC. But it was obvious that there was a large discrepancy in the effort needed to write 10 KLOC for a straightforward accounting application and KLOC of systems management code. The choice of language also made a major difference. Writing in COBOL produced three to five lines of object code for each COBOL source statement, whereas writing in **assembler** produced only one line of object code for each assembler source statement.

Another factor was the need to manage the fields and databases required. The larger and more complex the files, the more difficult was the programming required. These problems were reduced substantially in the 1970s and 1980s with the introduction of hierarchical and flat-file **database management systems**. The number and complexity of reports, as well as the range and variability of transactions, added to the amount of work needed. Again, the introduction of new tools and techniques has simplified the task of designing reports and specifying transactions.

SOFTWARE DEVELOPMENT: THE WATERFALL APPROACH

- Determine requirements.
- Formulate system or application specifications.
- Create general design.
- Test design against specifications (often called *Alpha test*).
- Construct detailed design documents.
- Write programs.
- Unit test and correct each program.
- Perform system and integration tests and make corrections.
- Prepare user documentation, training, and installation guides.
- Set up and train customer support personnel.
- Package program and related materials needed for delivery (internal use or to be marketed).
- Conduct actual use tests by customers (often called *Beta test*).
- Correct programs, documentation, and so on, to correct problems found in Beta test.
- Release program for general use.
- Provide customer or user support as problems occur.
- Correct any bugs identified and distribute fixes on a planned basis.
- Obtain feedback on needed additions and improvements.
- Set up enhancement release cycle.
- Use the same process for each subsequent release (minor changes) or version (major changes).

There are two basic issues to be understood in providing reliable cost estimates for software programs: the costs to be estimated, and the program metrics that will assist in the accurate estimation of the costs. One of the problems that companies have in estimating and measuring the cost of producing custom and package software is that they must take into consideration all the costs involved in producing, distributing, maintaining, supporting, and enhancing the programs. The principal cost elements to be estimated and measured are overhead costs (salaries and benefits for people involved in all stages of development, plus direct overhead and administrative costs); equipment (computers, communications, and other hardware and services necessary to build, test, and deliver the programs); and software (programs used in the designing, developing, testing, supporting, and maintenance of the new software).

Starting in the 1960s, various development methodologies have been formulated to plan and manage the entire program development process, from determining market and use requirements to delivery and installation and then through the full use cycle. The principal methodologies for significant systems and application products all have similar primary tasks, which are outlined in the box. This methodology is called the *waterfall approach* because there is a cascading series of steps required.

In the last 10 years, particularly as a result of interactive personal computer applications, another approach, sometimes called the *whirlpool* or *iterative concept* has been used. In effect, the designers build a limited or prototype system, try it out, and then modify and add to it on a sequential basis. There may be as many as three to five iterations before the company feels that a marketable or usable program has been created. Nevertheless, the same tools are involved and the same cost elements must be considered.

As mentioned above, the second issue to be considered is the process of defining a planned program and estimating the costs involved in its production and support. There are a variety of metrics that can be used to define a program in terms of its number and type of functions, complexity of interrelationships, frequency, and nature of database references and transaction processes. Among the best known is a system called *function point analysis*.

Developed in the 1970s, function point analysis looked at five characteristics of a program: number of user inputs, number of user outputs, number of user inquiries, number of files, and number of external interfaces. For each of these factors, a numeric weight was assigned depending on whether the characteristic was simple, average, or complex. The numbers in each category were multiplied by the weighting factor and then processed through a formula that included a further factor to account for the significance and complexity of the system as a whole.

Function point analysis was originally directed toward commercial application programs but was later extended to *feature point analysis*, which incorporated consideration of calculation **algorithms** so that the technique could be applied to real-time, process control, embedded, and scientific applications.

Although many studies have been performed to try to come up with a standard number of KLOC per thousand function points and then a standard effort level per KLOC, these studies have failed to produce replicable results across different companies or even for different departments or project teams within a company. The best approach seems to be to build up data for each project team related to KLOC, choice of language and function, or feature point measures, and use this as a basis for making future projections.

As a final note, recognize that modern **personal computer** or server-oriented programs using advanced development techniques can produce large amounts of code for relatively little effort (e.g., a high number of KLOC per work year) because of the ability to reuse components. With modern techniques, it is often hard even to measure the KLOC per program, so that this historic metric may have to be replaced in the next few years.

Further Reading

Calvert, David. *Software Metrics.* 15 July 1996. *http://hebb.cis.uoguelph.ca/~deb/27320/metrics1.html*

Fenton, Norman E., and Shari Lawrence Pfleeger. *Software Metrics: A Rigorous and Practical Approach.* London and New York: Chapman and Hall, 1991; 2nd ed., London and Boston: PWS Publishing, 1997.

Kan, Stephen H. *Metrics and Models in Software Quality Engineering.* Reading, Mass.: Addison-Wesley, 1995.

—*Burt Grad*

Software Engineering

In the early years of electronic **digital computers**, programming was very much an art. Computer memory was precious and efficiency vital. Arranging instructions so as to minimize the use of the former while maximizing the latter depended to a great extent on individual cleverness. As programs grew in size and complexity, however, this seat-of-the-pants programming style appeared increasingly inadequate as a means of producing reliable software on budget and on schedule. Beginning in the late 1960s, advocates of a more systematic and disciplined approach seized upon the term *software engineering* to refer to their goal.

The term first came into widespread use at an international conference of the same name sponsored by the North Atlantic Treaty Organization (NATO) Science Committee in 1968. Participants from government, industry, and academia gathered to discuss what should be done in response to a perceived "software crisis" marked by budget and schedule overruns, as well as by seemingly endemic defects, or **bugs**. Although most of the participants agreed that there were problems, there was considerable disagreement as to whether *crisis* was an appropriate label for those problems and whether *engineering* was an appropriate label for the solution. Although the conference organizers had used the term *software engineering* to be provocative, they couldn't have anticipated the long-running and often vociferous debate it would initiate. There was even less agreement at a follow-up conference the next year.

Over the next 20 years, attempts to define software engineering—either in theory or in practice—ran into numerous difficulties. First and foremost, there was substantial disagreement on whether engineering was even the most appropriate objective. Some individuals felt strongly that software development was an art or a craft, and that attempts to make it look more like engineering were misguided. Others felt that given the opportunities that software afforded for mathematical rigor, the concept of engineering wasn't sufficiently ambitious, and they called for the establishment of software science. Still others perceived software development as a unique type of activity in its own right.

Not only were there disagreements over the appropriateness of the engineering label, there were disagreements over just what that label meant. Due to the relative youth of the computer science field, many computing professionals had educational and even professional backgrounds in fields other than computing; those backgrounds sometimes colored their views of both the appropriateness and the meaning of *engineering*. Many who were grounded in mathematics and the sciences argued that if software engineering were truly to be engineering, it had to be based on formal mathematics. Many who came to this issue from an engineering or commercial data processing background, on the other hand, saw such arguments as excessively dogmatic; their view of engineering revolved around practicality and efficacy.

Nowhere were these tensions more evident than in the debates over formal verification of programs. Formal verification attempts to prove that a program is correct (i.e., meets its functional specifications) in the same way that one proves a theorem through propositional logic, since any program can be reduced to such statements. In theory, this would provide a degree of certainty unavailable through program testing, which by definition could never prove a program was without flaws.

However, accomplishing this is not so easy in practice. Because programs are typically very long and complex, actually carrying out a logical proof of correctness can be extraordinarily time and labor intensive, even when using a computer program (which itself must be proven correct) to assist in the process. Moreover, human error can easily corrupt the proof process and the entire exercise assumes that the program's specifications were correct to begin with. The issue of formal verification produced numerous passionate debates, at least in part because nowhere did differing conceptions of the nature of software development clash in such clearly fundamental ways.

However, quality assurance was only the area of most heated dispute. Virtually every aspect of software engineering has been characterized by the development of diametrically opposed approaches. Such was the case with programming languages, which pitted advocates of a single universal language that would be used to write just about all software, against those who argued in favor of highly specialized languages well suited to particular types of problems.

Such was also the case with the software development process itself. The software life cycle is generally thought to consist of requirements definition, functional specification, design, testing/verification (to ensure specifications are met), validation (to ensure requirements are met), and maintenance (corrections and enhancements). Some viewed the process as essentially linear in the same way that a waterfall always flows down, perhaps over intermediate steps, but always in one direction. This was the *waterfall life-cycle model*. Others believed the process should be fundamentally iterative, proceeding through each phase, then beginning the cycle again. This became known as *rapid prototyping* or more generically, as the *iterative* or *cyclical life-cycle model*.

Competing philosophies also existed regarding CASE, computer-aided/assisted software engineering. CASE attempted to apply the power of computers to the problem of software development, expanding on that first and most important application, the use of assemblers and **compilers** to convert, respectively, symbolic programming languages and high-level programming languages into executable machine language. These sorts of tools became known as *lower CASE* because they are employed downstream or toward the end of the development process. Beginning in the 1970s, efforts were made to develop *upper CASE* tools that would assist in earlier, upstream phases of the process, such as design work and/or the determination of functional requirements. At one extreme were tool kits, collections of CASE tools with little in the way of coordinated interconnection, while at the other extreme were tightly integrated development environments oriented around a specific programming language, methodology, or problem type.

Nevertheless, a degree of consensus regarding approaches to software development did exist. The idea that large programs should be broken down into component modules, for example, generated little controversy, especially after David Parnas (1941–) argued in 1972 that module design should focus on *information hiding*. Under this concept, modules communicate with each other only through formal interfaces rather than by interacting directly with each other's internal operations, thus reducing complexity. In other words, each module would be treated as a functional abstraction by any other module. Such concepts, however, were essentially sophisticated versions of some rather basic tenets of problem solving, in this case the classic strategy of divide and conquer. Although these provided a vital common ground for the software community, they struck many as glaringly insufficient for an engineering discipline.

Many thought of *structured programming* in similar terms. Proclaimed a revolution by some in the early 1970s, structured programming at its core was a collection of programming practices, including more orderly logical control flow, which made for more understandable programs. At a basic level, pretty much everyone could agree with most of these practices; it was often remarked that no one favored unstructured programs. However, the fanfare with which structured programming was introduced and the implication that it constituted a cure-all for software difficulties ended up generating a hostile reaction of equal fervor.

Indeed, over the decades software engineering has been characterized by the search for the single best way of approaching every facet of software development from defining program requirements to design to quality assurance. Virtually every major concept or trend has had something to recommend it but typically has suffered from a version of what Frederick Brooks (1931–) dubbed the "silver bullet syndrome." In 1987, Brooks argued that software engineering had fallen victim to a desire to find a single technique or approach that would magically solve all the difficulties endemic to software development—one silver bullet that would slay the software monster.

However, the history of software engineering, while replete with manifestations of the silver bullet syndrome, also offers examples of a more pluralistic alternative. At the height of the debates over formal verification and testing, for example, some voices called for a hybrid approach that combined verification with testing. Similarly, a spiral software life cycle was proposed to capture the benefits of both linear and cyclical models. The most popular programming languages have generally been those that strike a balance between general purpose and special purpose, typically targeting a broad application area such as science or business. As software engineering matures, its advocates are displaying an increased interest in this type of synthesis.

FURTHER READING

Brooks, Frederick P., Jr. *The Mythical Man-Month: Essays on Software Engineering*. Reading, Mass.: Addison-Wesley, 1995.

Myers, Colin, Tracy Hall, and Dave Pitt, eds. *The Responsible Software Engineer: Selected Readings in IT Professionalism.* London: Springer, 1997.

Pfleeger, Shari L. *Software Engineering: Theory and Practice.* Upper Saddle River, N.J.: Prentice Hall, 1998.

Shapiro, Stuart. "Splitting the Difference: The Historical Necessity of Synthesis in Software Engineering." *IEEE Annals of the History of Computing,* Vol. 19, No. 1, 1997, pp. 20–54.

—*Stuart Shapiro*

Software Piracy See Piracy, Software.

Sony Corporation

Sony Corporation is a post–World War II Japanese technology giant, known as a cutting-edge developer of consumer electronics products that have become commonplace throughout the world.

Sony's history can be traced back to September 1945, when electronics engineer Masaru Ibuka (1908–97) returned to Tokyo following World War II. He set up shop on the third floor of the bombed-out Shirokiya Department Store in Nihombashi. By October, Ibuka had established Tokyo Tsushin Kenkyujo (Totsuken). Ibuka called on Akio Morita (1921–99), an acquaintance from the Japanese Wartime Research Committee. Together, they began to produce replacement parts for phonographs. On 7 May 1946, they incorporated their company and secured a contract to supply equipment to the Occupation forces at the Japan Broadcasting Company. While working in this capacity, Ibuka saw an American-made tape recorder. He decided that this should be the next product their company manufactured. Months were spent in development, and in 1950, Japan's first tape recorder, the *G-Type*, was available.

In 1952, Ibuka traveled to the United States. Shortly after, he and Morita paid U.S.$25,000 to become the first foreign licensees of **Bell Labs**' new **transistor** technology. In 1955, Totsuken released Japan's first transistor radio. In 1957, they introduced a pocket-sized, battery-operated version, which was sold worldwide. The exposure helped Morita realize that the rest of the world needed a recognizable corporate name. The Latin word *sonus*, for "sound," was modified to give it a Japanese feel. The result was *Sony*.

Sony continued to create or improve numerous electronic devices. Technological advances prompted new products, such as the first transistorized television, the Walkman portable stereo, the Watchman hand-held television, the Betamax video-cassette player, the Trinitron TV color system, and computer components such as the 3.5-inch **floppy disk**, flat-screen plasma monitors, and "memory sticks" for digital storage of audio files.

Sony's technology leadership role has also had downsides. For example, a considerable investment in Betamax VCR technology failed, due to a lack of crucial alliances with major movie and television producers. Sony's purchase of Columbia and Tri-Star film studios in the 1990s for U.S.$3.4 billion and costly mistakes by studio executives resulted in losses of U.S.$3.2 billion. Also, investment in a new DVD format fell short of **Toshiba**'s offering.

In 1993, Sony created Sony Computer Entertainment (SCE) to develop video-game **software** and **hardware**. The resulting product, the 32-bit PlayStation, has become one of Sony's all-time best-selling products. An updated machine, PlayStation 2, was released in 2000 after much anticipation throughout the world.

In 1995, Nobuyuki Idei (1937–) took over the job as president of Sony. After restructuring the organization and rolling out the innovative Vaio notebook personal computer, he announced that Sony's future would embrace the Internet. Despite advances, the corporation's 1999 sales remained flat at U.S.$62.5 billion and were viewed as dismal by analysts. In the year 2000, investors remained skeptical and were reserving judgment until a new eSony emerges.

FURTHER READING

Scally, Robert. "Game Consoles Thrust into Next Generation of Technology." *DSN Retailing Today,* Vol. 39, No. 10, 22 May 2000, p. 27.

Schlender, Brent. "Sony on the Brink." *Fortune,* 12 June 1995.

"Sony Slides into a Slump." *Business Week,* 5 June 2000, p. 66.

—*Roger McHaney*

Sorting See Searching and Sorting.

Spam

Spam is a nickname for unsolicited **electronic mail**, usually advertising a product or service, and mass postings on bulletin board services.

The term was derived from the canned product Spam (special assorted meat), which recycles low-quality leftovers and by-products into an edible block. Credit is also due to a comedy sketch by the British group Monty Python about a restaurant that serves "spam, spam, spam, spam, spam, spam, baked beans, spam, and spam"—in other words, great quantities of nothing you want, which is how most **Internet** users feel about online spam.

In the past, mass mailings of paper pamphlets were a common tool used by companies to raise their profile in a particular neighborhood. However, due to the extremely low success rate, many of these marketing measures were not cost-effective.

The Internet has extended the concept to a virtual neighborhood of e-mail addresses. In the early 1990s advertisers started sending out electronic messages in the form of e-mails to a large audience of Internet users. Much like its paper equivalent, a list of addresses is all that is necessary. But unlike paper junk mail, the process is considerably less expensive: e-mail addresses can be "harvested" from chat forums, messaging systems, or by intercepting Internet traffic and analyzing it electronically for strings of characters that resemble an e-mail address. With this list in hand, a computer on the Internet can distribute thousands of messages an hour at virtually no cost to the advertiser.

Since many private users connect to the Internet at relatively low speeds using a dial-up connection via a modem, these unwanted e-mails block their lines, thereby increasing on-line costs. Additionally, the Internet as a whole is slowed down by the additional traffic. This has led to a heated debate on the legal means to control use of the Internet for commercial direct mailings. The U.S. Federal Trade Commission (FTC) is currently preparing the judicial basis that would make the sending of e-mails with fictitious return addresses illegal. Since this would prevent from spamming only advertisers that are not interested in an e-mail response, the Coalition Against Unsolicited Commercial E-Mail (CAUCE) has demanded a law that would make all marketing through unsolicited e-mail illegal. Some experts do not consider this law politically feasible, but expect the emergence of a list to which consumers can submit their e-mail address with the request to be spared the unwanted messages. Spammers will then have the responsibility to ensure that they do not include addresses on this *Robinson list.*

Many popular e-mail **software** packages include *spam detectors*, which search any incoming e-mail for specified phrases such as "Free!" or "Get rich." If it finds a corresponding e-mail, it either deletes it or places it in a special spam folder. Since these kinds of filters use a simple algorithm, their effectiveness is limited to the simpler attacks and is liable to fail, placing wanted messages in the spam folder. Also, the filtering has to be done after the message has been downloaded, so the damage—the wasted bandwidth—has already occurred to a large extent. Although more sophisticated approaches are being developed, most users continue to check all incoming e-mails manually.

FURTHER READING

Moschovitis, Christos J. P., Hilary Poole, Tami Schuyler, and Theresa Senft. *History of the Internet: A Chronology, 1843 to the Present.* Santa Barbara, Calif.: ABC-CLIO, 1999.

Schwartz, Allan, and Simson Garfinkel. *Stopping SPAM.* Sebastopol, Calif.: O'Reilly, 1998.

—*Thomas Schwerk*

Speech Recognition System

The job of a speech recognition system is to take some spoken language and produce a list of words. A speech recognition system will not *understand* what is said—it will just be able to list the words spoken. To understand spoken language we need a *speech understanding* system, which integrates speech recognition and natural language understanding technologies.

Even the simpler task of speech recognition has proved extremely difficult to do well. It is only in the last few years that useful recognition systems have become widely available, and these systems are still not highly accurate. Recognizing speech is complicated by several factors. First, spoken language is continuous; we don't pause between words, so it is very difficult for a system to determine where one word ends and another begins. Consider the sentence "It is hard to recognize speech." If spoken quite quickly, this might be (mis)recognized as "It is hard to wreck a nice beach." Also, different speakers pronounce words quite differently; accent, gender, and other factors influence pronunciation. One speaker may even pronounce a word differently on different occasions. We say things differently depending on emotions (e.g., anger), health (e.g., a bad cold), and on what we are trying to emphasize. Words also are pronounced differently depending on where they occur in a sentence and on the words that precede and follow them. Words may also be spoken quickly or more slowly.

Furthermore, in many practical applications, spoken language is accompanied by background noise. A speech recognition system will have to be able to determine what part of the signal corresponds to your speech and what part corresponds to your car engine noise or the clock ticking in your office.

Given all these factors, it is not surprising that development of high-quality recognition technology has been slow. Early research in the 1940s, sponsored by the U.S. Department of Defense, was motivated by the ambitious aim of automatically monitoring foreign language broadcasts. This would now be regarded as a very difficult problem, challenging even the technology of the twenty-first century, so not surprisingly, little progress was made. Attention then shifted to simpler tasks, such as recognizing digits or basic instructions. An early system developed by **Bell Labs**, for example, could recognize any of 10 digits from a single speaker. The speech signal was compared with 10 stored patterns, and the one that matched best was chosen.

This simple system achieved good (97 to 99 percent) accuracy, but only for this very simple task. More useful systems of the future would have to deal with a number of complicating factors, such as larger dictionaries. Matching signals to 10 prestored words is manageable; if you want to be able to deal with speech that may contain any of, say, 10,000 words, this word-matching approach becomes intractable. To be more useful, systems would also have to recognize sequences of words—entire sentences, or at the least, multiword instructions. This requires, in turn, guessing where breaks between words occur. Last but not least, multiple speakers need to be recognized. Having prestored patterns for one speaker is useful only for that speaker; for another speaker to use the system it would have to be configured ("trained") for them. Ideally, we want systems that can handle different speakers without training, or at least with minimal training.

To handle larger dictionaries, we must look to sound units smaller than the word—it does not work simply to match to a dictionary that contains the speech signal for each word. Words are made up of a number of smaller sound units called *phonemes* (e.g., "th," "e"). There are a fairly small number of such basic sound units (about 40 for English), and recognizing phonemes can be viewed as a more tractable first step to recognizing words. If we store in our dictionary the phoneme sequence for each word, we can look up possible matching words once we have determined a phoneme sequence from the speech signal.

We still cannot get accurate word recognition if words are considered in isolation. There is too much variation in how words (and phonemes) sound. We need more information. People use a lot of common sense when recognizing speech. Some word sequences make sense, and others don't. When listening to a speaker, we assume that he or she is speaking correct English (or other natural language), saying something that fits the context. If we mishear a word, or a word is unclear, we will usually be able to work out what was intended. Speech recognition must therefore use some of this contextual information to choose among the various possible word sequences.

In the 1970s there were some attempts to develop systems that combined and integrated many of the sorts of cues that human beings use to choose a sensible interpretation, using **artificial intelligence** techniques (e.g., the Hearsay II system). However, it was soon realized that the most successful systems were those that used fairly simple kinds of contextual cues, but which combined the available information using sophisticated statistical models (hidden Markov models [HMMs]). These systems might work just on prestored probabilities of one word following another rather than attempting to check that the whole sentence made sense, but by combining the different probabilities that arise through the entire recognition process, the result is good overall performance.

Modern speech recognition systems therefore use a variety of different statistical models: A language model will tell us how likely it is that a given word follows another; a pronunciation model will tell us the likelihoods of different possible pronunciations of a word; and a phoneme model will tell us the likelihood that a given signal corresponds to a given phoneme sequence, taking into account the different ways in which phonemes can be articulated. By combining all these models we can determine, given a speech signal, which word sequence is most likely.

Speech recognition systems today have gone a long way beyond the Bell Labs digit recognition system. are Cheaply available dictation systems can now create a typed version of the user's speech with a fairly high degree of accuracy. Such systems clearly allow a large vocabulary but may assume quiet conditions and are not "speaker independent." Telephone-based services now use speech recognition systems. These are designed to recognize short responses and instructions from a very small set (i.e., have a small vocabulary) but do work reliably for any speaker and can cope with a noisy telephone channel. Speech-controlled devices have also started to appear, allowing users to give simple instructions to a **personal computer** (PC) or videocassette recorder, and many mobile phones incorporate simple speech recognition systems, allowing users to access services more easily.

To have two-way interaction through speech, we need to be able to *synthesize* as well as recognize speech. Speech synthesis systems do the reverse job of recognition—they create spoken output from a sequence of words. Synthesis technology has been advancing along with recognition, and now a (relatively) natural and understandable output is possible.

Speech recognition technology has therefore moved from the research labs onto your personal computer, available cheaply with current hardware. Yet *speech understanding* is still a long way off. You can talk to your PC, but don't expect it to understand you or say anything sensible back, unless the instructions and replies you give it are from a previously specified predictable set.

Further Reading

Gold, Bernard, and Nelson Morgan. *Speech and Audio Signal Processing.* New York: Wiley, 2000.

Jelinek, Frederick. *Statistical Methods for Speech Recognition.* Cambridge, Mass.: MIT Press, 1997.

Jurafsky, Dan, and James H. Martin. *Speech and Language Processing: An Introduction to Natural Language Processing, Computational Linguistics, and Speech Recognition.* Upper Saddle River, N.J.: Prentice Hall, 2000.

Levinson, S. E. "Structural Methods in Automatic Speech Recognition." In *Proceedings of the IEEE,* Vol. 73, No. 11, 1995, pp. 1625–1650.

Newman, D., and J. Baker. *The Dragon Naturally Speaking Guide: Speech Recognition Made Fast and Simple.* Berkeley, Calif.: Waveside, 1999; 3rd ed., 2000.

Rabiner, Lawrence R., and Biing-Hwang Juang. *Fundamentals of Speech Recognition,* Englewood Cliffs, N.J.: Prentice Hall, 1993.

—*Alison Cawsey*

Speech Synthesizer

A speech synthesizer is any electronic or mechanical device capable of converting short commands into sounds that resemble human speech. The first speech synthesizers were hydraulic–mechanical systems; modern speech synthesizers use conventional sound cards and generate the appropriate sound frequencies with special **hardware** or purely by using **software**.

The building blocks of speech are called *phonemes.* This is the smallest sound segment whose substitution would change the meaning of a word, as in "cat" and "rat." These two words begin with different phonemes. There are around 40 different phonemes in English, and the art of building a speech synthesizer consists, first, in producing phonemes and concatenating them in a natural way to form words. The main problem is the prosody (the speech rhythm) and timing of the phonemes.

Simple speech synthesizers can be built using *copy synthesis.* Words are recorded digitally from human speech and stored individually. The words can then be arranged together to form sentences. The method can also be used with phonemes, but the resulting speech sounds dull and artificial.

The main types of current hardware speech synthesizers are vocal tract analogs (VTA) and terminal syn-

From left, Gene Frantz, Richard Wiggins, Paul Breedlove, and George Brantingham: the team that created Speak n' Spell, a toy that captures the human voice on a chip. (Courtesy of the Computer Museum History Center)

thesizers (TA). The human vocal tract can be modeled as a sequence of tubes with varying diameters. Each tube reinforces certain frequencies and suppresses others; this is called *resonance*. Special electronic circuits can imitate the resonance process, and the driving frequency used is similar to the one produced in the vocal chords. A terminal synthesizer is designed to simulate the final output of the human vocal tract in terms of the frequencies present in speech. These frequencies are arranged into bands called *formants*, whose shape is imitated by the synthesizers.

One of the first commercial speech synthesis systems was developed by **Raymond Kurzweil** (1948–) as a reading aid for the vision impaired. In the early 1970s the KRM-1 (Kurzweil Reading Machine 1) was developed at the Massachusetts Institute of Technology and Kurzweil's startup company. The first public demonstration was made in 1976. Many other versions followed later, and in the late 1970s portable speech synthesizers for personal computers were available that cost a few hundred dollars.

Another early use for speech synthesizers was explored by **Texas Instruments**, which released the Speak & Spell game in 1978. Team members Gene Frantz, Richard Wiggins, Paul Breedlove, and George Brantingham were able to replicate the human voice on a single chip. In 1988 Kurzweil introduced the Personal Reader, which was the first reading machine for the blind with an integrated **scanner**.

The main challenge for building high-quality speech synthesizers is the number of linguistic rules that have to be integrated into the system. The human ear is very demanding and can immediately distinguish artificially generated speech. Some researchers are therefore trying to build systems that learn from speech samples, rather than being programmed from scratch. Such adaptive learning speech synthesizers should produce higher-quality output.

FURTHER READING

Dutoit, Thierry. *An Introduction to Text-to-Speech Synthesis.* Boston, Mass.: Kluwer Academic, 1997.

Flanagan, J. L. *Speech Analysis, Synthesis and Perception.* Berlin: Springer-Verlag, 1972.

Kurzweil, R. "The Kurzweil Reading Machine: A Technical Overview." In M.R. Redden and W. Schwandt, eds., *Science, Technology and the Handicapped.* Report 76-R-11. Washington, D.C.: American Association for the Advancement of Science, 1976, pp. 3–11.

Linggard, Robert. *Electronic Synthesis of Speech.* Cambridge: Cambridge University Press, 1985.

—*Frank Darius*

Spreadsheets

The electronic spreadsheet is often given credit for inspiring the **microcomputer** revolution. Until the release of VisiCalc in May 1979, most business people viewed the **personal computer** (PC) more as a novelty or curiosity than an indispensable work resource. Spreadsheets convinced many people that computers could be a vital part of a business environment; for this reason they are often referred to as the **killer application** for microcomputers. Today, various spreadsheet applications (e.g., Excel from **Microsoft**, Quattro Pro from Corel) form the centerpieces of personal productivity **software** suites.

Some controversy exists regarding the originator of the concepts used in spreadsheets. In 1952, the term *spread sheet* was used in Eric L. Kohler's (1892–1976) *Dictionary for Accountants* to refer to a noncomputerized worksheet providing a matrix-type, two-way analysis of accounting data. In the early 1960s, Richard Mattessich (1922–) at the University of California at Berkeley pioneered computerized spreadsheets for business accounting. His concepts were made operational using the **FORTRAN** IV programming language in a mainframe environment and later influenced other mainframe spreadsheet software development.

By the late 1970s, new computing options had begun to emerge. Handheld calculators and microcomputers started to change expectations for information technology use. In 1978, Daniel Bricklin (1951–), an MBA student at the Harvard Business School, grew dissatisfied with only being able to view the results of complex calculations on his calculator. He envisioned a scrolling screen where intermediate values could be viewed and changed to affect problem solutions. He borrowed an **Apple II** computer from Dan Fylstra of Personal Software and wrote a prototype spreadsheet program in Apple BASIC. Bricklin's interactive visible calculator let users work in a matrix of five columns and 20 rows.

Sensing the commercial potential of his software, Bricklin enlisted Bob Frankston—who added functionality and efficiency to the program, making it small enough to run in microcomputer environments—and Dan Fylstra, for marketing. In January 1979, Bricklin and Frankston formed Software Arts Corporation. In May of the same year, Fylstra and his company, Personal Software, which would later become VisiCorp, placed an ad for the "visible calculator," VisiCalc, in *Byte* magazine. Nearly a million copies of the program were sold during its lifetime.

The demand for this new software, which was now called a *spreadsheet*, continued to increase throughout the early 1980s. The introduction of the **IBM** PC and its **Intel** microchip opened new markets for business software. Distracted by legal conflicts between their Software Arts Corporation and VisiCorp, Bricklin and Frankston failed to position their software aggressively in the expanding microcomputer marketplace. Instead, it was **Mitchell Kapor** (1950–) and his spreadsheet program, Lotus 1-2-3, that quickly gained acceptance as the new standard.

Prior to developing Lotus 1-2-3, Mitch Kapor had a close association with VisiCorp. For about six months in 1980, he worked there as a product manager. He also developed Visiplot/Visitrend for VisiCorp, for which he received U.S.$1 million. Using that money and additional money from venture capitalist Ben Rosen, he and Jonathan Sachs started **Lotus Development Corporation** in 1982. Their primary product, Lotus 1-2-3, was a user-friendly spreadsheet that incorporated charting, data presentation features, and database capabilities. Lotus introduced the concept of naming cells, cell ranges, and macros. Lotus 1-2-3 became a bestseller, allowing Lotus Development Corporation to acquire Software Arts and VisiCalc, which it discontinued shortly thereafter.

Microsoft was the next big player to enter the spreadsheet market, with its product Excel. Originally developed in 1985 for the **Macintosh**, Excel used a graphical interface with a point-and-click capability. When implemented on DOS-based machines in the mid-1980s, it offered users an interface that was easier to use than the old command line standard of MS-DOS. Microsoft released the **Windows** operating system in 1987 and Excel was one of the first products available for it. By 1989, Excel was Microsoft's flagship application program.

By the end of the 1980s, most vendors in the spreadsheet arena were in court. Lotus Development filed a lawsuit against Mosaic Software and Paperback Software claiming they had infringed on Lotus 1-2-3. Software Arts, the original developer of VisiCalc, took Lotus to court saying that Lotus 1-2-3 was an infringement of VisiCalc. Lotus won the legal battles, but while these were going on, Microsoft won the market-share war, pushing Lotus 1-2-3 from its market-leading position. In 1995, IBM acquired Lotus Development, and Microsoft Excel was the clear spreadsheet market leader.

Today, spreadsheets are used for a wide variety of applications, particularly situations where 'what-if' analysis must be performed. A major feature of spreadsheet programs is that formulas can be embedded in cells (intersections of rows and columns). These formulas refer to values based on location. If a user changes a value, the implication on related values can be observed immediately. This makes the spreadsheet ideal for building a model.

FURTHER READING

Bricklin, Dan, and Bob Frankston. "VisiCalc '79." *Creative Computing*, Vol. 10, Nov. 1984, pp. 122, 124.

Mattessich, Richard. "Budgeting Models and System Simulation." *Accounting Review*, July 1961, pp. 384–397.

Mattessich, Richard, and Giuseppe Galassi. "History of the Spreadsheet: From Matrix Accounting to Budget Simulation and Computerization." *Accounting and History: A Selection of Papers Presented at the 8th World Congress of Accounting Historians*. Madrid: Asociación Española de Contabilidad y Administración de Empresas, 2000.

"VisiCalc Production Ends." *PC Magazine*, Vol. 4, 6 Aug. 1985, pp. 33.

—*Roger McHaney*

Spread Spectrum

Spread spectrum is a communication technique used in cellular telephones and radio systems. It is very resilient to noise and interference as well as to multiple-path reception of the same signal. Using spread spectrum, several users can access the same communication frequency without interfering with each other.

There are several spread spectrum techniques, but one of the easiest to implement and more commonly used is the *direct-sequence method*. Assume that we want to transmit a message coded as a sequence of signed **bits** (i.e., the sequence consists of the digits 1 and −1). The message to be sent could look like the following sequence of five signed bits: 1, 1, 1, −1, 1. However, there could be interference from another user transmitting the sequence −1, 1, 1, 1, 1, for example. The receiver gets the sum of these two signals, and since all results are positive or zero, the receiver assumes, incorrectly, that the transmitted data were 1, 1, 1, 1, 1.

In the direct-sequence spread spectrum method, each signed bit is coded using many shorter signals. The coding for a 1 could consists of 10 signed bits, which are selected randomly (e.g., the sequence 1, −1, 1, 1, −1, 1, −1, 1, −1, −1). Each time a 1 has to be transmitted, this sequence is sent; if a −1 has to be transmitted, the negative sequence is sent. At the reception end, the user multiplies the bits obtained with the known random sequence and obtains a total sum of 10 when a 1 is transmitted, and a sum of −10 when a −1 is transmitted. The purpose of the random sequence is to pull the two signals apart and add fault tolerance to the system.

Assume that there is interference in the channel. If a sequence consisting only of 1's is being sent at the same time as our signal, multiplying these 1's with the random sequence and adding the result gives zero (because there are as many 1's as −1's in the random sequence). This means that the method attenuates any signal that does not conform to the random patterns of 1's and −1's that we selected for transmission. Since the sequence is random and is known only to server and receiver, it is unlikely that noise would exhibit the same variation pattern. Also, if several users want to use the same frequency, they just get assigned different random sequences, with zero correlation. To each user, the signals of the other users look like random noise that is canceled by the system.

There are alternative spread spectrum techniques, such as *frequency hopping* (changing the frequency of transmission according to a random sequence, known only to sender and receiver), and others. These techniques are called spread spectrum because the original data are spread over different signal or transmission frequencies.

In cellular telephony the company Qualcomm pioneered spread spectrum techniques and a special technology called CDMA (code-division multiple access). *Code division* refers to the process of assigning different users different random code sequences for their data.

Further Reading

Peterson, Roger L., Rodger E. Ziemer, and David E. Borth. *Introduction to Spread Spectrum Communications.* Englewood Cliffs, N.J.: Prentice Hall, 1995.

Viterbi, Andrew. *CDMA: Principles of Spread Spectrum Communication.* Reading, Mass.: Addison-Wesley, 1995.

—*Raúl Rojas*

Stallman, Richard

1953–

U.S. Computer Scientist

Richard M. Stallman's major contribution to computing is as founder of and major contributor to the **GNU Project**, which was launched in 1984 to develop the free **Unix**-compatible **operating system** GNU (a self-referential acronym standing for "GNU's Not Unix"). Although Unix had been distributed freely to academic institutions before the GNU, this was the first project to emphasize the open source approach for **software** distribution as its major mission. Stallman's aim was for GNU to be completely free software. The copyright notice ensured that anyone was free to modify and redistribute the software provided that the original copyright notice remained intact. Stallman coined the term *copyleft* to describe the GNU copyright terms. Copylefted software is free software whose distribution terms do not let distributors add any additional restrictions when they redistribute or modify the software. The result is that every copy of the software, even if it has been modified, is free software.

Throughout his working life, Stallman has been based at the Massachusetts Institute of Technology (MIT), in the highly respected Artificial Intelligence Laboratory. In the 1970s he developed Emacs, an extensible editor, which can be extended using a **LISP**-like language. Xemacs, a version to work with the **X-Windows system** developed by MIT and widely adopted as the basis for windows systems on Unix-based workstations, is also available. Emacs became part of the GNU system that Stallman developed largely in the 1980s.

The **Free Software Foundation** (FSF), based in Boston, was founded by Stallman with the aim of eliminating restrictions on copying, redistribution, understanding, and modification of computer programs. Its activities include promoting the development and use of free software for all types of computing and especially in helping to develop the GNU operating system.

Stallman was the principal author of GNU C, a portable optimizing compiler that was designed to support diverse architectures and multiple languages. The compiler supports over 30 different architectures and seven programming languages. Stallman also wrote the GNU symbolic debugger (GDB), GNU Emacs extensible editor, and various other GNU programs.

The subsequent **Linux** effort, another free Unix-based operating system, initiated by **Linus Torvalds** (1969–), owes much to the GNU project. Linux-based variants of the GNU system, built on top of the kernel Linux developed by Torvalds, are in widespread use. There are probably over 10 million users of GNU/Linux systems around the world.

Stallman's approach to software development is the antithesis of that of commercial companies such as Microsoft. Under the umbrella of the Free Software Foundation and the GNU Project, he has written and promulgated during his career much free software that has been widely used by computer scientists and programmers. Without Stallman's efforts, it is likely that the open source movement would be nowhere near as advanced as it is today.

BIOGRAPHY

Richarch Matthew Stallman. Born 16 March 1953 in New York. B.A. in physics from Harvard, 1974. Joined Massachusetts Institute of Technology Artificial Intelligence Laboratory, while a student at Harvard, 1971. Since 1984, his work has centered around the GNU (GNU's Not Unix) Project, an open source collection of software, including the Emacs editor. Recipient of numerous awards, including the ACM Grace Hopper Award, 1990; MacArthur Foundation fellowship, 1990; Electronic Frontier Foundation's Pioneer award, 1998; and Yuri Rubinski Award, 1999.

SELECTED WRITINGS

Stallman, Richard M. "Surveyor's Forum: Structured Editing with a LISP." *ACM Computing Surveys*, Vol. 10, No. 4, Dec. 1978, pp. 505–507.

———. "The Right to Read." *Communications of the ACM*, Vol. 40, No. 2, Feb. 1997, pp. 85–87.

———. *Gnu Emacs Manual.* Lincoln, Neb.: iUniverse.com, 2000.

———. *Using and Porting GNU CC: For Version 2.95.* Boston: Free Software Foundation, 2000.

Stallman, Richard M., and Robert Chassell. *Texinfo: The GNU Documentation Format for Texinfo Version 3.11.* Boston: Free Software Foundation, 1997.

Stallman, Richard M., and Charles Donnelly. *The Bison Manual: Using the YACC-Compatible Parser Gernerator for Version 1.29.* Boston: Free Software Foundation, 1999.

Stallman, Richard M., and Roland McGrath. *GNU Make A Program for Directing Recompilation, Make Version 3.77.* Boston: Free Software Foundation, 1998.

Stallman, Richard M., and Gerald J. Sussman. "Forward Reasoning and Dependency-Directed Backtracking in a System for Computer-Aided Circuit Analysis." *Artificial Intelligence*, Vol. 9, No. 2, Oct. 1977, pp. 135–196.

FOR FURTHER READING

DiBona, Chris, Sam Ockman, and Mark Stone, eds. *Open Sources: Voices from the Open Source Revolution.* Sebastopol, Calif.: O'Reilly, 1999.

Free Software Foundation.
http://www.fsf.org/fsf

GNU Project.
http://www.gnu.org

Richard Stallman Home Page.
http://www.stallman.org

Wayner, Peter. *Free For All: How Linux and the Free Software Movement Undercut the High-Tech Titans.* New York: Harper Business, 2000.

—Jonathan Bowen

Steele, Guy L., Jr.

1954–

U.S. Computer Scientist

Guy L. Steele, Jr. has been a leading contributor to programming language design. Steele has been involved in the list processing language **LISP**, the **C** programming language, **Fortran** (especially for parallel **supercomputer** applications), and **Java**. He has had a special interest in parallel **algorithms** and techniques.

Early in his career, Steele worked on the LISP language and LISP implementation, especially the Scheme dialect of LISP with Gerald Jay Sussman (1947–). He also designed the original Emacs editor command set (further developed by **Richard Stallman** [1953–]) and was the first person to port the **TeX** document processing system.

Steele was involved with the newly formed **Thinking Machines Corporation** in the late 1980s and early 1990s. This company offered novel and highly parallel supercomputers called the **Connection Machine**. Steele led the systems **software** group, developing a microcoded **instruction set**, compilers for high-level parallel programming languages, and communications architecture for the CM-1, CM-2, and CM-5 Connection Machine computer systems. He worked on a version of LISP that included fine-grained parallel symbolic processing and on Fortran for high- performance applications. Around 1990, Steele led the team that achieved the fastest speed until then for a production application of 14.182 gigaflops, for which they received a 1990 **Gordon Bell Prize** honorable mention.

Working at **Sun Microsystems** from 1994 onward, Steele was responsible for the specification of the Java programming language with **Bill Joy** (1955–) and James Gosling (1955–). He also continued his interest in parallel algorithm research and collaborated with Eric Raymond (1957–) as a coeditor of the **New Hacker's Dictionary**. Steele's wide experience in programming language design over a quarter of a century have led him to believe that such activity must now be more of an organic process where both a user community and development community are involved.

BIOGRAPHY

Guy L. Steele, Jr. Born 2 October 1954 in Cape Girardeau, Missouri. A.B. in applied mathematics from Harvard College, 1975; S.M. and Ph.D. in computer science and artificial intelligence from the Massachusetts Institute of Technology, 1977 and 1980. Assistant professor of computer science at Carnegie Mellon University, 1980–84. Senior scientist at Thinking Machines Corporation, 1985–94. Distinguished Engineer, Sun Microsystems, 1994 to present. Served on numerous American National Standards Institute (ANSI) standards committees, including X3J3 (Fortran), X3J11 (C language), and X3J13 (Common LISP). Led team that received a 1990 Gordon Bell Prize Honorable Mention, 1990. Named a Fellow of the American Association for Artificial Intelligence, 1990; named Association for Computing Machinery (ACM) Fellow, 1994. Recipient of numerous awards, including the ACM Grace Murray Hopper Award, 1988, and the ACM SIGPLAN Programming Languages Achievement Award, 1996.

SELECTED WRITINGS

Gosling, James, Bill Joy, and Guy L. Steele, Jr. *The Java Language Specification*. Reading, Mass.: Addison-Wesley, 1996; 2nd ed., 2000.

Harbison, Samuel P., and Guy L. Steele, Jr. *C: A Reference Manual*. Englewood Cliffs, N.J.: Prentice Hall, 1984; 4th ed., 1995.

Hillis, W. Daniel, and Guy L. Steele, Jr. "Data Parallel Algorithms." *Communications of the ACM*, Vol. 29, No. 12, 1986.

Koelbel, Charles H., et al. *The High Performance Fortran Handbook*. Cambridge, Mass.: MIT Press, 1994.

Raymond, Eric, ed., and Guy L. Steele, Jr. *The New Hacker's Dictionary*. Cambridge, Mass.: MIT Press, 1991; 3rd ed., 1996.

Steele, Guy L., Jr. "Multiprocessing Compactifying Garbage Collection." *Communications of the ACM*, Vol. 18, No. 9, 1975.

———. *Common Lisp: The Language*. Burlington, Mass.: Digital Press, 1984; 2nd ed., Bedford, Mass.; Digital Press, 1990.

Steele, Guy L., Jr., et al. *The Hacker's Dictionary*. New York: Harper and Row, 1983.

Steele, Guy L., Jr., and Richard P. Gabriel. "The Evolution of Lisp." *History of Programming Languages Conference (HOPL-II)*, Preprints, Cambridge, Mass., 20–23 April, 1993. *ACM SIGPLAN Notices*, Vol. 28, No. 3, 1993.

Steele, Guy L., Jr., and Gerald J. Sussman. "Design of a LISP-based Microprocessor." *Communications of the ACM*, Vol. 23, No. 11, 1980.

—*Jonathan Bowen*

Stibitz, George

1904–95

U.S. Engineer

George R. Stibitz is considered by some to be the "father" of the modern **digital computer**. He was an important early pioneer of relay-based binary digital calculating devices and gave the first demonstration of remote job entry (RJE), a farsighted portent of things to come. He considered himself a "mathematical engineer," a rather apt title given the logical basis of digital computing.

Stibitz's initial work in the late 1930s was undertaken about 80 years after **George Boole** (1815–64) had codified logic mathematically. He demonstrated that Boole's logical algebra could be implemented using electrical circuits with "on" representing "true" and "off" representing "false." **Claude Shannon** (1916–2001), a master's degree student working independently at the Massachusetts Institute of Technology (MIT), had similar ideas around the same time.

Stibitz's interest in computers was initiated by an assignment to study the magnetomechanics of telephone relays in the late fall of 1937 at **Bell Labs**. At the time he was not knowledgeable about relays but was interested in assessing their properties and capabilities. Relays were the main component in telephone switching systems, but Stibitz found the logic functions that relays were able to perform especially fascinating. Thus he started to consider the binary circuits controlled by the relays and the expression of arithmetic operations in binary form.

In November 1937 he constructed the first two-digit binary adder. This consisted of a piece of board, metal strips from a tobacco tin, two relays, two flashlight bulbs and a pair of dry battery cells, assembled on his kitchen table at home. This was dubbed Model K after the location where it was built. (A replica can be found in the Smithsonian Institution in Washington, D.C.) After demonstrating this device at Bell Labs, he designed a multidigit binary adder. He also realized that a relay-based machine could perform the functions of a desk calculator.

The problem of interfacing decimal numbers (as used by people) to binary devices became of interest to Stibitz. He considered it unlikely that people would be willing to use binary notation directly but was equally convinced that computers should be based on binary circuits. He developed *excess-3 notation* to help in this interfacing. By adding three to each binary number in an addition, the sum would be increased by six. Thus decimal nine would become 15 (1111 in binary) and larger sums would produce an overflow (i.e., a decimal carry). An additional advantage is that the binary complement of a sum in excess-3 format is the binary form of the decimal complement. His investigation into the excess-3 system took place early in 1938.

Developments in the theory of filters and transmission lines at Bell Labs, useful in the design of telecommunications systems, led to an increased requirement for computations involving complex numbers. At the time, desk calculators were laboriously employed for this work. A complex multiplication (typically undertaken to 8 to 10 decimal places) involved four separate multiplications and the use of two intermediate numbers. An initially proposed solution was the mechanical combination of existing calculators, but T. C. Fry, head of the mathematical engineering group, asked Stibitz if his relay-based devices could handle complex numbers in mid-1938.

Stibitz produced schematic diagrams of a complex number calculator with relay storage for eight-digit numbers in excess-3 format and switching using rotary switches. The output was to be sent to a Teletype printer. S. B. Williams evaluated this design and decided it was feasible but suggested using the newly available crossbar switches for storage and replacing the rotary switches with relays for the transfer of numbers. The system was debugged during 1938 to 1939. Initially, only multiplication and division were handled, but it was quickly realized that addition and subtraction were important, too, and the circuitry was revised to include these as well. The Model 1, as it was to become known, was operational toward the end of 1939. It consisted of 450 telephone relays in combination with 10 crossbar switches, and it could calculate the quotient of two eight-place complex numbers in around 30 seconds. Three Teletypes were used to input data to the machine.

In September 1940, after a number of month's routine use at Bell Labs, the Model 1 was demonstrated at a meeting of the American Mathematical Society held at Dartmouth College, Hanover, New Hampshire. Williams had designed an interface that allowed the signals for the numbers to be transmitted in a serial manner using a standard telegraph line. The Model 1 was still in New York, and after a presentation by Stibitz, attendees at the meeting were invited to submit problems via a Teletype. Answers were returned using the same telegraph line and printed on the Teletype. This was the world's first demonstration of remote computing. The computer pioneers **John Mauchly** (1907–80) and **Norbert Wiener** (1894–1964) both attended this lecture, which must have been an impressive example for them at the time.

Although the Model 1 was a success, its high cost (U.S.$20,000 for design and construction) was enough to deter the administration at Bell Labs from repeating the exercise for several years. In fact, the Model 1 remained in operation until 1949. Stibitz had ideas for extending the capability to polynomials and other rational functions, but these had to remain dormant for reasons of cost. However, World War II meant that there was a requirement for some specific large computations. Stibitz's Model 2 subtabulated data for testing antiaircraft directors. It incorporated changeable taped programs and self-checking or error detection code. He used an alternative *biquinary code* instead of the previous excess-3 code to allow checking using fewer relays.

In 1940, Stibitz suggest using floating-decimal scientific notation to avoid the problem of having to investigate the probable magnitude of values in a long calculation. The scheme was not actually used until about 1945 in the Model 5 design. The Model 2 and 3 were constructed under the supervision of E. G. Andrews. The Model 5 was produced by both Williams and Andrews. Stibitz suggested that some elements be combined. As well as using the floating-decimal scheme suggested by Stibitz, the Model 5 could also punch intermediate data onto a reel of tape and read some of these back for later use in a problem. A jump instruction allowed control to be transferred from one tape to another, and back later if required. Two units were built and one managed a record 167 hours of up-time in a week (168 hours). Preventive maintenance involved only part of the Model 5 at any given time, so it could continue in operation.

Stibitz's relay computers included many novel features. In 1937, he designed and built the world's first electrical binary adder. Developing on this, in 1939, Stibitz and S. B. Williams built the Complex Number Calculator (CNC), the world's first electrical digital computing device designed specifically for complex arithmetic, using excess-3 code. A demonstration of this computer was also the first example of remote job entry using telegraph lines for communication to a distant location. The Model 2 of 1943 used interchangeable punched tape codes, error-detecting code, and independent computer components cooperating on single problems. The floating-decimal notation and a simple jump instruction were included in the Model 5 of 1945.

The pioneering work of Stibitz was undertaken largely in parallel with **Konrad Zuse**'s (1910–95) efforts to produce relay-based computers in Germany, but Stibitz worked independently. Indeed, Zuse and Stibitz jointly won the 1965 Harry Goode Award for their early contributions to computer engineering. They will both be remembered for their important progenitorial roles in the establishment of computing.

BIOGRAPHY

George Robert Stibitz. Born 30 April 1904 in York, Pennsylvania. A.B. in applied mathematics from Denison University, 1926; M.S. in physics from Union College, 1927; Ph.D. in mathematical physics from Cornell University, 1930. Mathematical consultant, Bell Labs, 1930–41. Worked at the U.S. Office of Scientific Research and Development, 1940–45; served on the U.S. National Defense Research Committee, 1941. Independent consultant in applied mathematics for various government and industrial agencies, based in Burlington, Vermont, 1945–64. Joined the Department of Physiology at Dartmouth Medical School, as a research associate, 1964; professor, 1966; professor emeritus of physiology, 1970. Recipient of numerous awards, including the Harry Goode Award for lifetime achievement in engineering from the American Federation of Information Processing Societies, 1965; and the IEEE Computer Pioneer Award, 1982. Died 31 January 1995 in Hanover, New Hampshire.

SELECTED WRITINGS

Stibitz, George R. *The Dartmouth Computer and Medicine* Hanover, N.H.: Dartmouth College, 1966. Reprinted from *Dartmouth Medical Quarterly*, Vol. 2, No. 3.

———. "Early Computers." In Nicholas Metropolis, ed., *A History of Computing in the Twentieth Century*. New York: Academic Press, 1980.

———. *The Zeroth Generation: A Scientist's Recollections (1937–1955) from the Early Binary Relay Digital Computers at Bell Telephone Laboratory and OSRD to a Fledgling Minicomputer at the Barber-Colman Company*. Privately printed. Hanover, N.H.: Dartmouth College, 1993.

Stibitz, George R., and Jules A. Larrivee. *Mathematics and Computers*. New York: McGraw-Hill, 1957.

FURTHER READING

Dartmouth College Library. *An Inventory of the Papers of George Robert Stibitz Concerning the Invention and Development of the Digital Computer*. Compiled by Ingrid Vignos. Hanover, N.H.: Dartmouth College, 1973.

Ritchie, David. *The Computer Pioneers: The Making of the Modern Computer*. New York: Simon and Schuster, 1986.

—*Jonathan Bowen*

Stored Program

The concept of the *modifiable stored program* embodies the principle that programs and data can be stored and manipulated alike, there being no essential distinction between them as symbolic entities. Modern computing exploits this principle for managing, translating, and communicating programs; dynamical addressing, languages, and operating systems require it. This idea, foreign to **Charles Babbage** (1791–1871) and pre-1945 calculators, emerged in the 1945 plan for **EDVAC** and in **Alan M. Turing**'s (1912–54) 1946 ACE proposal.

Controversy has raged over the stored program's origin. Its theoretical base can be found in Turing's universal machine concept of 1936–37. Turing thought of instructions as data to be processed by another set of instructions, drawing on Kurt Gödel's (1906–78) representation of statements *about* numbers, *as* numbers. The Universal Turing machine has the description of other **Turing machines** (i.e., **algorithms**) placed in its tape, the same storage as is used for all kinds of data. It is crucial to Turing's logical theory that a Turing machine may read its own description. **John von Neumann** (1903–57) learned of Turing's work while Turing was at Princeton in 1936–38. The logician Martin Davis (1928–) has gone as far as to say that that von Neumann came to his formulation of the EDVAC principle through his knowledge of Turing's ideas.

On the other hand, the engineering-based tradition sees the concept as one that naturally arises in making instructions available. The engineer **John Presper Eckert** (1919–) held that he had anticipated the idea before von Neumann was involved. There are many confusing factors. Von Neumann, although generally credited with the stored-program principle, apparently saw no interest in exploiting it for the logic of programming. Turing's ACE design exploited the principle strongly, and he consistently described post-1945 computers as practical forms of his universal machine. Turing's statement that the machine itself could take over any routine programming work holds the seed of all modern computing, but he never made a clear claim to the stored program as a concept. His colleague Max H. A. Newman (1897–1984) also made a clear statement in 1948 of the principle of storing data and instructions alike as words, a formulation that appears in the earliest descriptions of the Manchester computer, which first demonstrated the stored-program principle in June 1948. But Newman never laid down how those ideas derived from Turing's logical work.

More confusingly, Turing himself referred to Babbage's **Analytical Engine** as a form of universal Turing machine. But Babbage probably never had a picture of a program in its modern sense, and still less of the flexibility given by seeing instructions as a form of data.

FURTHER READING

Davis, Martin. *The Universal Computer.* New York: Norton, 2000.

Goldstine, H. H. *The Computer from Pascal to von Neumann.* Princeton, N.J.: Princeton University Press, 1993.

Hodges, Andrew. *Alan Turing: The Enigma.* London: Burnett Books, and New York: Simon and Schuster, 1983.

Metropolis, N., J. Howlett, and G.-C. Rota, eds. *A History of Computing in the Twentieth Century.* New York: Academic Press, 1980; rev. ed., 1985.

Turing, Alan. "Proposed Electronic Calculator." *National Physical Laboratory Report,* 1946; first published in B. E. Carpenter and R. W. Doran, ed., *A. M. Turing's ACE Report of 1946 and Other Papers* Vol. 10, in the Charles Babbage Institute Reprint Series for the History of Computing. Cambridge, Mass.: MIT Press, 1986.

Von Neumann, John. "First Draft of a Report on the EDVAC." Reprinted (in part) in Brian Randall, ed., *Origins of Digital Computers: Selected Papers.* Berlin and New York: Springer-Verlag, 1982; reprinted with corrections in *IEEE Annals of the History of Computing* Vol. 15, No. 4, 1993.

—Andrew Hodges

Streaming Audio and Video

Streaming refers to the process of transmitting a data file that can be played right after its first portion has been received without waiting for the complete file. Broadcasting audio or video content via computer networks is difficult since digitizing an analog audio or video signal results in huge amounts of data, several times larger than the network can handle. This is especially a problem for live transmissions where the data must be sent in real time to the consumer. For this reason the data have to be compressed.

Standard *lossless compression algorithms* that are normally used to decrease the size of text or program files (such as ZIP) cannot be applied for two reasons: first, the compression ratio is too small; and second, in order to decompress the data you need the entire compressed data file. This would mean downloading the entire video or piece of music before being able to enjoy it, and, in case of a live transmission, waiting until the event is finished.

Streaming is the solution to this problem. The input is divided into short units, called *packets,* which are then compressed. One packet is the smallest amount of data that can be decompressed and shown to the user. Another advantage is that if one packet gets lost, the receiver might drop it and wait for the next packet or ask the sender to resend it. This is especially important for cellular phones, where streaming is also used. For video, a packet would contain one or several pictures, whereas for music this would be several seconds of audio data, depending on the algorithm and network capabilities.

Lossy compression algorithms are applied in order to get a sufficiently high compression ratio. These algorithms eliminate perceptual redundancies, in other words, the characteristic properties of human vision and hearing are exploited in order to suppress details of a picture or sound that cannot be seen or heard because our perception is too inaccurate. After decompression the original data have been changed slightly, but our eyes and ears will hardly notice.

In 1991 the **International Organization for Standardization** (ISO), together with other organizations, begin standardizing several methods for compressing and synchronizing audio and video data using perceptual coding for streaming in different quality levels. The popular but formally incorrect names for these standards are **MPEG** I and II, **MP3**, and MPEG 4. MPEG 4 and also a new version, MPEG 7, are currently under development.

There are several commercial **software** products currently available—such as **RealAudio** and **RealVideo** by RealNetworks, Inc. and NetShow by **Microsoft**—that implement audio and video streaming over the **Internet**.

FURTHER READING

Tanenbaum, Andrew. *Computer Networks*. Englewood Cliffs, N.J.: Prentice Hall, 1981; 3rd ed., Upper Saddle River, N.J., 1996.

—*Gerald Friedland*

STRETCH and LARC

The STRETCH (or Stretch) and the LARC were two high-performance computers built by **IBM** and Sperry Rand for the U.S. Atomic Energy Commission (AEC) laboratories in the late 1950s. Both machines stretched the boundaries of computer technology (hence the name of IBM's computer) and introduced concepts that would be used in many machines of the 1960s and 1970s.

In 1954 the University of California Livermore Radiation Laboratory requested proposals for a scientific computer that would be significantly faster than any machine then in production. Livermore selected the proposal of Remington Rand (later Sperry Rand) over one from IBM. Work on the Livermore Automatic Research Computer (LARC) began in 1955, with a scheduled completion date of September 1957. The design, a joint effort by Livermore and Remington Rand's **UNIVAC** group, involved having a separate computing unit (CU) and input–output processor (IOP) with the (never realized) possibility of adding a second CU. The LARC used decimal arithmetic: Its 60-bit word providing eleven 5-bit digits plus a sign for single-precision fixed point and 22 digits for double precision. There were also **floating-point** formats. To gain speed, the design provided for overlapped execution of up to four instructions. The LARC had 20,000 words of memory (later expanded to 30,000), with a 4-microseconds, read-write time, and used 12 **magnetic drums** for secondary storage.

Development of the LARC took much longer than expected and cost far more than the contract price. To help with the expense, the U.S. Navy agreed to buy a second LARC. The LARC for Livermore was finished in May 1960, 27 months behind schedule; it was in use until December 1968. The Navy LARC went into service in February 1961 and was retired in 1969.

In 1956, another AEC laboratory, at Los Alamos, New Mexico, awarded a contract to **IBM** to develop a high-speed computer. IBM's Project Stretch resulted

IBM 7030, or STRETCH computer. (Courtesy of the Computer Museum History Center)

in the development of new circuit packaging techniques and a 131,072-byte core memory with a read-write time of 2.2 microseconds. The STRETCH computer (designated the IBM 7030) had a 64-bit word (holding eight 8-bit bytes) and was designed to have up to six overlapped instructions. It was delivered to Los Alamos in April 1961, one year behind schedule, and was in use until 1971.

During the development, IBM had agreed to sell the 7030 to seven other customers, but the price (U.S.$7.8 million) caused the company to lose money, so it was not sold to anyone else. Many of the components developed by Project Stretch were incorporated into the somewhat smaller IBM 7090 computer, which was introduced in November 1959, and other concepts (such as the 8-bit byte) found their way into the IBM System/360 design.

FURTHER READING

Lukoff, Herman. *From Dits to Bits: A Personal History of the Electronic Computer.* Beaverton, Oreg.: Robotics Press, 1979.

Pugh, Emerson W. *Building IBM: Shaping an Industry and Its Technology.* Cambridge, Mass.: MIT Press, 1995.

—*George Gray*

Stroustrup, Bjarne

1950–

Danish Computer Scientist

Bjarne Stroustrup is best known as the designer and implementer of the **C++** programming language, an **object-oriented** extension of C. C++ has become one of the most widely used languages supporting object-oriented programming. Through C++, Stroustrup has pioneered the use of object-oriented and generic programming techniques in application areas where efficiency is important.

Stroustrup designed C++ to combine the early object-oriented programming organization of **SIMULA**, a language based on **ALGOL** 60 developed by Ole-Johan Dahl (1931–) and others in the 1960s, with the efficiency and flexibility of C for systems programming. Stroustrup first encountered SIMULA on the Cambridge University computer center's **IBM** 360/165 mainframe, and he was impressed by its class concepts. He was much less enamored by the BCPL programming language, a precursor of C, due to coding and debugging difficulties. His experience at Cambridge laid the foundations for his initial ideas in designing C++. **Bell Labs**, where he moved after Cambridge, was the birthplace of C, which helped to foster his ideas for an object-oriented extension.

The most important book by Stroustrup is *The C++ Programming Language;* it is one of the most widely read books of its type and has been translated into at least nine languages. A later book in 1995, *The Design and Evolution of C++,* was innovative in describing the way that C++ was shaped by Stroustrup's ideas and ideals, as well as the problems and practical constraints he encountered.

Stroustrup's greatest contribution to computer science has been the laying of the foundations for the object-oriented C++ programming language. Due in no small part to his continuing efforts, C++ has become one of the most influential programming languages in the history of computing.

BIOGRAPHY

Bjarne Stroustrup. Born 30 December 1950 in Aarhus, Denmark. Received computer science Cand. Scient. degree, the Danish equivalent of a master's degree, from the University of Aarhus, 1975; Ph.D. for design of distributed systems at the Cambridge University Computing Laboratory, 1979. Moved to the Computer Science Research Center of Bell Telephone Laboratories in New Jersey, 1979. Remained at Bell Labs throughout his career. Designer and original implementer of the programming language C++ and actively involved in its standardization by ANSI and ISO. Recipient of the Association for Computing Machines Grace Murray Hopper Award, 1993.

SELECTED WRITINGS

Ellis, Margaret A., and Bjarne Stroustrup. *The Annotated C++ Reference Manual.* Reading, Mass.: Addison-Wesley, 1990.

Stroustrup, Bjarne. "On Unifying Module Interfaces." *Operating Systems Review,* Vol. 12, No. 1, 1978, pp. 90–98.

———. "Adding Classes to the C Language: An Exercise in Language Evolution." *Software—Practice and Experience,* Vol. 13, No. 2, 1983, pp. 139–161.

———. *The C++ Programming Language.* Reading, Mass.: Addison-Wesley, 1986; 3rd ed., 2000.

———. *The Design and Evolution of C++.* Reading, Mass.: Addison-Wesley, 1995.

———. "A History of C++." In Peter Salus, ed., *The Handbook of Programming Languages*. Indianapolis, Ind.: Macmillan Technical, 1998.

FURTHER READING

Hamilton, Scott, and Bjarne Stroustrup. "The Real Stroustrup Interview." *IEEE Computer*, Vol. 31, No. 6, 1998, pp. 110–114.

Stevens, Al. "Interview with Bjarne Stroustrup." *Dr. Dobbs Journal*, Vol. 159, Winter 1989, pp. 14–17.

—*Jonathan Bowen*

Structured Programming

Structured programming is a methodology that, if followed, should produce programs that are both elegant and correct. The term was coined by computer scientist **Edsger W. Dijkstra** (1930–) in the late 1960s.

In 1962, Dijkstra observed that a computer program was a series of essentially mathematical statements. Thus, he thought it should be possible to prove a program mathematically correct with respect to a specification. Although sound in theory, Dijkstra found this process to be difficult in practice. By 1965, he (and others) had realized that one of the major difficulties was the "go to" statement available in many programming languages, which allowed an arbitrary jump in the flow of control. By 1968, Dijkstra had become so convinced that this was a major problem that he published his now infamous article **"GO TO Statement Considered Harmful."** However, Dijkstra's concerns were not just limited to such statements. Later in 1968, he published the results of his (successful) efforts at developing an **operating system** using a layers of abstraction approach that is used commonly to this day.

In 1969, Dijkstra coined the term *structured programming* as the title of a contribution for a report on a conference. He emphasized the importance of error avoidance as opposed to error correction (i.e., errors should not be introduced in the first place, rather than being introduced to be removed later). Then in 1971, **Niklaus Wirth** (1934–) introduced program development by stepwise refinement, systematizing the earlier work of Dijkstra. The following year, David L. Parnas (1941–) published his well-known article on *information hiding*. The 1972 landmark book, *Structured Programing*, edited and written by Dijkstra, Ole-Johan Dahl (1931–), and **C. Antony R. Hoare** (1934–), formed the cornerstone of the field.

During the late 1960s some software engineers began to realize that structured programming (largely involving structured coding) was not sufficient. For example, Harlan D. Mills (1919–) of **IBM** focused more on the design process for large projects, an early version of structured design. Larry Constantine, at IBM during the 1960s and 1970s, with others developed *composite design*, later to be renamed *structured design*.

A fundamental principle of the structured programming approach was that the programmer must keep the program within the limits of his or her intellectual understanding; methods for achieving this aim include top-down design and construction, limited control structures, and limited scope of data structures. The term *structured programming* has come to mean any software development technique that includes structured design and results in the development of a structured program. Structured design may be effected by any one of a number of systematic top-down design techniques used in software engineering, usually after structured analysis. In top-down design (sometimes called *stepwise refinement*), the aim is first to describe functionality at a very high level, then to partition it repeatedly into more detailed levels, one level at a time, until the detail is sufficient to allow coding. This approach to software design was prevalent at IBM and grew out of structured programming practices. Structured analysis may be undertaken by one of a number of requirements analysis methods used in software engineering.

A structured program is one constructed from a basic set of control structures, each having a single entry and exit. Typically, these included sequential composition of statements, conditional selection of statements (e.g., an "if . . . then . . . else . . ." construct) and repetition, sometimes called *iteration*, of statements (e.g., a "while" loop). Newer programming languages may also include parallel composition.

Early languages such as **ALGOL** and **Pascal** allowed the convenient construction of structured programs, whereas **Fortran** (highly dependent on the "GO TO" statement) did not, unless considerable restraint of programming style was exercised by the programmer. This was possible but often not exercised, resulting in large programs that were difficult to understand and maintain. Even Fortran (originally issued in 1956) has extended its syntax (especially in Fortran 77) to make structured programming more natural.

A number of structured design techniques were produced and promulgated by leading scientists in the 1970s and early 1980s. These include Michael Jackson's JSP (Jackson Structured Programming), a data-driven approach for use especially with the programming languages **COBOL** and **PL/1**. and the related JSD (Jackson System Development). Ed Yourdon's (1944–) eponymous Yourdon software design method was one of the first to allow structured systems analysis. Other approaches were proposed by De Marco, Ward–Mellor (for real time), Warnier–Orr, and so on.

The ideas of structured programming were very important in the development of software engineering practice, and many have become well accepted by professional programmers. Since its heyday, additional concepts, such as object orientation (popular since the 1980s), and techniques such as UML (Unified Modeling Language, popular since the 1990s) have developed the initial ideas of structured programming in the goal of reducing errors.

FURTHER READING

Dahl, Ole-Johan, Edsger W. Dijkstra, and C. A.R. Hoare, eds. *Structured Programming.* London and New York: Academic Press, 1972.

DeMarco, T. *Structured Analysis and System Specification.* New York: Yourdon Press, 1979.

Dijkstra, Edsger W. "GO TO Statement Considered Harmful." *Communications of the ACM,* Vol. 11, No. 3, 1968, pp. 147–148.

———. *A Discipline of Programming.* Englewood Cliffs, N. J.: Prentice Hall, 1976.

Jackson, Michael A. *Principles of Program Design.* London and New York: Academic Press, 1975.

Meyer, Bertrand. "From Structured Programming to Object-Oriented Design: The Road to Eiffel." *Structured Programming,* Vol. 10, No. 1, 1989, pp. 19–39.

Orr, Kenneth T. *Structured Systems Development.* New York: Yourdon Press, 1977.

Parnas, David L. "On the Criteria to Be Used in Decomposing Systems into Modules." *Communications of the ACM* Vol. 15, No. 12, 1972, pp. 1053–1058.

Shapiro, Stuart. "Splitting the Difference: The Historical Necessity of Synthesis in Software Engineering." *IEEE Annals of the History of Computing,* Vol. 19, No. 1, 1997, pp. 20–54.

Ward, P. T., and S. J. Mellor. *Structured Development for Real-Time Systems.* New York: Yourdon Press, 1986.

Warnier, Jean Dominique. *Procédures de traitement leurs données.* Translated by B. M. Flanagan (Logical Construction of Programs). New York: Van Nostrand Reinhold, 1974.

Wirth, Niklaus. *Systematic Programming: An Introduction.* Englewood Cliffs, N.J.: Prentice Hall, 1973.

———. "On the Composition of Well-Structured Programs." *Computing Surveys,* Vol. 6, No. 4, 1974, pp. 221–227.

—*Jonathan Bowen*

Structured Query Language

Structured Query Language (SQL) was designed in the early 1970s to interact with the relational database System R from **IBM**. It is now the query language (i.e., the language used to retrieve information) for most commercial **database management systems** (DBMSs) although many dialects exist. In 1986, the first standard version, SQL1, was adopted by the **American National Standards Institute** and **International Organization for Standardization**. A second standard version of SQL, called SQL2 or SQL-92, was specified in 1992. There is now an emerging standard called SQL3 which encompasses many notions from programming languages in order to overcome some limitations of SQL2.

Before describing SQL, it is useful to review how relational databases are structured. A *database* is a large collection of related data stored in files. Banking, libraries, and travel reservations are examples of traditional database applications. The *relational model* for database systems was proposed in 1970 as an alternative to the network and the hierarchical model used in the 1960s. The relational model is now widely used mostly because of its simplicity and sound theoretical foundations. Leading DBMS such as **Oracle**, Sybase, IBM's

DB2, **Microsoft**'s ACCESS and the SQL server or Paradox are based on the relational paradigm.

In the relational model, data are stored in one or many *relations*, also called *tables*. Consider, for example, a library application where we want to manage entities such as books, readers, and loans. The description of all books that belong to the library and of all users who may borrow books from the library may be stored in the tables BOOK and USER, respectively. The properties of each entity, such as a book, are called *attributes*. For example, 'last-name' and 'address' are attributes of the relation USER. A particular instance of an entity (e.g., the person 'Juliet Audiffred') has a value for each of its attributes.

A table or relation is a set of rows, also called *tuples*. For instance, 'Juliet Audiffred, 1000 Hyde St. San Francisco CA 94109' is a tuple. In such a tuple, an attribute such as 'first-name' obeys a certain type (e.g., value 'Juliet' is of type 'string'). These types are standard types such as real or string but also more elaborate predefined types such as 'date' (with format MM/DD/YY).

The description of all tables stored in a particular database is given by a *schema*. Working with the entities considered in the library application, we may consider the following three-table schema:

BOOK (reference, title, author, year)
USER (personID, first-name, last-name, status, address)
BORROWS (personID, reference, check-in-date, check-out-date),

where reference, personID, check-in-date, and so on, are attributes. The attributes 'reference' and 'personID' are used by the library to reference a unique book and a unique person, respectively. This is the concept of a key, crucial in a DBMS environment. In addition to the relations BOOK and USER mentioned previously, the fact that a person borrows a certain book is stored in the relation BORROWS. Notice that for the sake of simplicity we omitted the attribute types in the schema above.

The first step when defining a database is to design an appropriate schema. Many schemas may be possible for an application. For instance, in the library example, one could define a schema with only one table that gathers all information. However, such a database design leads to anomalies, in this case redundancy. The information regarding 'Juliet Audiffred' will have to be repeated 10 times if this person currently has 10 loans. Good database design is guaranteed by the conformance to 'normal forms', which forces schemas to verify certain rules.

Two levels of expertise are distinguished when interacting with a database. First, database designers have to be able (1) to define the type of data that need to be stored for a given application (i.e., an application schema) and (2) to store or update these data. This is done using a *data definition language* (DDL). Second, database end users have to be able to query data, which means to express specific data they want to be retrieved from a database (e.g, all database books that exist in the library). A *data manipulation language* (DML) serves this purpose. Two formal languages are associated with the relational model: the relational algebra and the relational calculus. The most popular commercial relational language is SQL. It borrows elements from both algebra and calculus. In all its versions, SQL allows one to write statements for data definition, query, and update. It is thus both a data definition language DDL and a DML.

A schema such as the one given above is defined using the DDL part of SQL, through the CREATE SCHEMA and the CREATE TABLE statements. The global schema and then relation BOOK are defined the following way (to make it more legible, attribute types are kept simple):

```
CREATE SCHEMA LIBRARY AUTHORIZATION
Brian Smith
CREATE TABLE LIBRARY.BOOK
(reference: string,
title: string,
author: string,
year: integer,)
```

In the schema above, 'Brian Smith' is the administrator of the database. Other information related to the key as well as constraints on the data n—known as integrity constraints in the database jargon—were omitted.

Conversely, the DROP TABLE and DROP SCHEMA commands are used to remove a table and a whole schema, respectively (once all tables have been removed). Populating the database is done through the INSERT instruction. The command:

INSERT INTO BOOK
VALUES (A23451,'Fundamentals of Database Systems', Elmasri/Navathe, 1994)

has the effect of filling out a row of the table. There is also a DELETE operation to clear parts of the table. Updating the database (changing values) is done through an UPDATE statement.

We now present the main features of SQL as a data manipulation language. SQL is a declarative or nonprocedural language, which means that one specifies what data have to be retrieved rather than how to retrieve the data. SQL is based on both the (nonprocedural) *relational calculus*, which allows one to describe specific data using logical formulas, and the (procedural) *relational algebra*, which is a set of operators defined on the relation domain (basically, a relational operators takes one or many relations as arguments and returns a relation).

An instruction of the SQL language is the SELECT-FROM-WHERE statement, which can best be described by using some sample queries to the database. We often make reference to the corresponding operation of the relational algebra. For example, the query:

Query 1: List all book titles of the library database

corresponds to the projection operation of the relational algebra. The idea is to project out all unwanted attributes. In this particular case, all attributes from the BOOK relation except the title of a book are eliminated. To process this query, all information is to be retrieved from the BOOK table only. The FROM keyword is thus followed by BOOK. The SELECT clause gives the list of attributes that will be part of the result, here 'title'. The query is then expressed as:

SELECT title
FROM BOOK

If some titles appear many times in the database, they will appear many times in the query result as well. This query:

Query 2: List all references to books borrowed by Juliet Audiffred

necessitates consideration of both relations BORROWS and USER. This operation is called a *join* in the relational algebra. For the tuple that corresponds to Juliet Audiffred in the USER relation (with a certain personID value), we want to match all tuples from the BORROWS relation, and finally return the references to the books borrowed. In this join operation, the join attribute is personID. We finally want to keep the reference attribute of relation BORROWS. The query can be expressed as follows:

SELECT BORROWS.reference
FROM USER, BORROWS
WHERE USER.first-name = 'Juliet'
AND USER.last-name = 'Audiffred'
AND USER.personID = BORROWS.personID

The first two WHERE conditions are no more than relational selections. The last condition is the join condition, which forces tuples to match. Because the attribute names are the same in both relations, prefixing is necessary.

It is also possible to group some tuples according to user-defined criteria and to realize some basic computations. Functions known as *aggregate functions* can be applied on sets of tuples. They include computing the minimum, the maximum, or the average of a set of values.

Even though SQL has been widely used in the past 20 years, it has some limits as far as the computation of functions is concerned. SQL is not computationally complete, which means not every computation can be expressed in this language. To circumvent this, SQL may be used in conjunction with a programming language such as **C++** or **Java**. It is then referred to as *embedded SQL*.

Another limitation concerns the use of richer types than basic predefined types such as integer, string, or even date. Suppose that users need to define and manipulate their own types (e.g., a spatial type such as a polygon). This was not possible in the first versions of SQL. However, this is now possible with the last version of SQL, used by most vendors, who offer a richer data model. This model is referred to as *relational extended to abstract data types* (or user-defined types with associated operations).

SQL has been evolving since its first version in 1970. It has also been officially accepted by the object-oriented database community in 1994, through the introduction of OQL (object query language, a SQL extension) by the Object Database Management Group (ODMG; part of the Object Management Group). Because of the existence of classes with methods (or types and functions) inherent to the object-oriented paradigm, the two problems mentioned above are alleviated in OQL. The SQL2 and SQL 3 standards are available online through the site of the National Institute of Science and Technology (NIST).

FURTHER READING

Chamberlin, Don, et al. "SEQUEL 2: A Unified Approach to Data Definition, Manipulation and Control." *IBM Journal of Research and Development*, Vol. 20, No. 6, 1976, pp. 560–575.

Date, Chris, and H. Darwen. *A Guide to the SQL Standard.* Reading, Mass.: Addison-Wesley, 1987; 4th ed., 1997.

Elmasri, R., and S. Navathe. *Fundamentals of Database Systems.* Redwood City, Calif.: Benjamin-Cummings, 1989; 3rd ed., Reading, Mass.: Addison-Wesley, 2000.

Melton, J., and A. Simon. *Understanding the New SQL: A Complete Guide.* San Mateo, Calif.: Morgan Kaufmann, 1993.

Ramakrishnan, Raghu. *Database Management Systems.* Boston: McGraw-Hill, 1998; 2nd ed., 2000.

Ullman, Jeffrey, and Jennifer Widom. *A First Course in Database Systems.* Upper Saddle River, N.J.: Prentice Hall, 1997.

—*Agnes Voisard*

Sun Microsystems

Based in California, Sun Microsystems is an international corporation specializing in network computing. Sun was founded in 1982 by **Andreas Bechtolsheim** (1955–), **Bill Joy** (1955–), Vinod Khosla (1955–), and Scott McNealy (1954–), and has expanded to over 150 countries, with revenues in 1999 of approximately U.S.$11 billion. During the 1990s, Sun was the number one distributor of **Unix** multiuser systems.

During his studies at Stanford University, Bechtolsheim built a workstation out of standard off-the-shelf components. He met Khosla, McNealy, and later Joy, and together, the four started Sun, an acronym for Stanford University Network. Scott McNealy, chief executive officer and president of Sun since 1982, is today the person probably most readily associated with the company.

Sun's vision and slogan is "the network is the computer"; accordingly, its first machines included networking capabilities. Sun also introduced the first workstation based on **TCP/IP** communication. Today, Sun offers many products indispensable for the **Internet**, corporate **intranets** and firm-to-firm **extranets**, such as high-powered workstations, enterprise servers, network storage, network **software**, and desktop systems.

Sun was able to establish itself on the computer marketplace with new technologies, such as NFS (network file sharing) in 1984; PC-NFS, which brought networking to personal computer users in 1986, the SPARCstation 1 in 1989; the Solaris OS, which offered symmetric multiprocessing in 1991; and the first **multiprocessor** desktop computer, the SPARCstation 10, introduced in 1992. By 1993, Sun had shipped over 1 million Unix-based systems. Solaris software eventually offered a 64-bit operating environment with the ability to support thousands of users and multiterabyte data warehouses and globally functional e-mail. All of these features made Solaris servers a popular choice for corporate networks.

Sun Microsystems' most popular technology of the late twentieth century was probably the platform-independent **Java** programming language. With Java, introduced in 1995, software developers can write applications that run under any operating system. At the end of the 1990s, Sun had made many new advances, such as the development of the Jini technology, which lets all sorts of appliances be instantly connected to a network. In 1998, a three-year alliance with America Online was started with the intention of developing next-generation Internet appliances and supporting e-commerce. Sun acquired the

Sun founders Bill Joy, Andreas Bechtolsheim, and Scott McNealy, pose in the Sun parking lot. (©Ed Kashi/CORBIS)

German software company Star Division in August 1999, which offered a free downloadable software suite called Star Office. Sun continued to offer the office software package free for downloading from its Web site in the year 2000. The acquisition of Star Division is congruent with McNealy's prediction that the personal computer (PC) as we know it today will one day become obsolete, and the user will attain access to data through the net.

After the successful spread of Java, McNealy concentrated on his vision of a **network computer**. Such machines should be inexpensive and "hollow": instead of having a complete PC at home or work, a user would have a machine called a *thin client*, capable only of downloading and running programs from a network (from Sun's perspective, preferably Java programs). The network would be independent of the client's operating system. Although large sales of network computers did not materialize in the 1990s, it is expected that this sector will grow in conjunction with falling communication costs.

FURTHER READING

Moschovitis, Christos J. P., Hilary Poole, Tami Schuyler, and Theresa Senft. *History of the Internet: A Chronology, 1843 to the Present.* Santa Barbara, Calif. and Oxford, England: ABC-CLIO, 1999.

Southwick, Karen, and Eric Schmidt. *High Noon; The Inside Story of Scott McNealy and the Rise of Sun Microsystems.* New York: Wiley, 1999.

—*Jenna L. Brinning*

Sun Microsystems v. Microsoft

In this lawsuit **Sun Microsystems** alleges that **Microsoft** engaged in acts of trademark and copyright infringement as well as acts of unfair competition, designed to undercut Sun's **Java** technology. As of

July 2000, the case is still pending in San Jose, California, in the U.S. District Court for the Northern District of California. Each side has won important victories in the early stages of this lawsuit.

Java is an attempt by Sun to create a technology that allows **software** developers to create **programs** that can run on any **operating system**, such as **Windows** from Microsoft, **Unix**, or **Macintosh**, without having to rewrite the software program for each specific operating system. This goal is sometimes referred to as "write once, run everywhere."

Microsoft licensed Java from Sun and then took steps to make its version of the Java technology dependent on and especially useful with Microsoft's operating system, Windows. The key underlying issue of the lawsuit is whether Microsoft's actions violate Sun's rights to any other legal prohibitions. Some of the same issues have also been raised in the government's antitrust case against Microsoft; see ***Microsoft, U.S. v.***

Sun obtained two different orders from Judge Ronald Whyte (1942–) against Microsoft. The first was a court order, a preliminary injunction, that prohibited Microsoft from using Sun's "100% pure Java" trademark. The judge accepted Sun's argument that Microsoft was developing Java-related technology that was meant to work only with Windows, ignoring provisions in the Sun license of Java technology to Microsoft that required Microsoft to remain true to the "write once, run everywhere" goal.

Sun then obtained a second preliminary injunction against Microsoft based on some of the same Microsoft actions, primarily on a theory of copyright infringement. Microsoft appealed the second preliminary injunction to the U.S. Court of Appeal for the Ninth Circuit. That court issued a ruling questioning Judge Whyte's reasoning. Whyte reconsidered his ruling based on the Ninth Circuit opinion and agreed with Microsoft that he was wrong to base his ruling on a claim of copyright infringement. He reissued a very similar preliminary injunction, however, this time relying more heavily on the claims of unfair competition against Microsoft. Whyte later dismissed the copyright claim from the lawsuit completely. The factually and legally complex issues in this case are still unsettled and will be finally decided only if and when this case goes to trial.

Further Reading

Schlender, Brent. "The Adventures of Scott McNealy: Today's Episode His Fight to Save the World Wide Web from the Evil Empire." *Fortune*, Vol. 13, Oct. 1997, p. 70.

Southwick, Karen. *High Noon: The Inside Story of Scott McNealy and the Rise of Sun Microsytems.* New York: Wiley, 1999.

—*Rich Gray*

SUN-1

The Stanford University Network (SUN) workstation, or SUN-1, was developed by **Andreas Bechtolsheim** (1955–) at Stanford University in Palo Alto, California, in the heart of **Silicon Valley**. It was based on three boards connected via the Multibus, a flexible **bus** structure developed by **Intel Corporation** and used by many commercial **microprocessor** systems. One board included the **Motorola** 68000 16-bit microprocessor; another provided 3-megabyte-per-second **Ethernet** access, a widely used **local area network** standard; a third board provided a 1-megapixel 1-bit-deep frame buffer.

The SUN story begins at the Stanford Artificial Intelligence Laboratory (SAIL). SAIL's Digital Equipment DEC10 computer, which had been used by such people as **John McCarthy** (1927–) and **Don Knuth** (1938–), had an **operating system** and associated artificial intelligence programming language developed at Stanford. The system included a videodisk frame buffer, normally 1 bit deep for monochrome displays. Ralph Gorin (1948–) at the computer facility spotted Bechtolsheim's development work, recognized that this could provide a next-generation computer terminal, and supported his efforts.

Bechtolsheim licensed his design for U.S.$10,000 to local companies while doing his Ph.D on the metastability of **flip-flops**. He saw this as a fairly lucrative sideline. One user was James Clark (1944–), an associate professor at Stanford, who augmented the design with high-speed computer graphics support in **hardware** and went on to found the company **Silicon Graphics** using this technology in 1982.

Meanwhile, Vinod Khosla (1955–) had come to the United States from New Delhi, after founding a failed startup company in India. He earned a master's degree in biomedical engineering from Carnegie Mellon University in Pittsburgh and then joined the Stanford M.B.A. program in the late 1970s. Khosla graduated from Stanford in 1980 and helped start Daisy Systems, a company specializing in **computer-aided design** (CAD). At the time, few people thought it feasible to produce a dedicated computer for each engineer in CAD or CAM (**computer-aided manufacturing**) applications. However, Khosla thought the new concept of workstations connected via the Ethernet network in operation at Stanford would allow engineers to collaborate electronically in a convenient manner—a revolutionary idea at the time. A chance telephone call in 1981 brought Khosla in contact with Bechtolsheim, and it seemed to Khosla that the SUN project could be the answer to his search.

Bechtolsheim and Khosla wrote a six-page business plan for building and selling the SUN workstation, dated 21 February 1982. They raised venture capital of U.S.$284,000, largely on trust. **Sun Microsystems** was originally to be called SUN Workstation, but this was rejected as being too narrow in scope.

The third on board was Scott McNealy (1954–), who had attended Harvard and Stanford, where he and Khosla met. He had joined the **Unix** start-up company Onyx Systems in San Jose, south of Silicon Valley. Khosla was keen to work with McNealy and recruited him soon after raising the initial venture capital. Bechtolsheim, Khosla, and McNealy worked hard for about three months to produce a prototype SUN-1 workstation. It ran the Unix operating system, but the variant they were using was not completely satisfactory.

Bill Joy (1955–), a graduate student at the University of California, Berkeley, across the San Francisco Bay from Stanford, had developed Berkeley Unix, a new variant with virtual memory and networking facilities running on Digital Equipment **VAX** minicomputers. Bechtolsheim, Khosla, and McNealy visited Berkeley to convince Joy to join their fledgling company. Bechtolsheim was as expert with hardware as Joy was with **software** and the two immediately developed a rapport, discussing technical issues. Joy was becoming disenchanted with the lack of resources and space available at Berkeley, so he did not need much convincing to sign up as a cofounder of SUN.

The SUN-1 was essentially a prototype. The SUN-2, produced in late 1982 using the Motorola 68010 microprocessor, included virtual memory support and ran Bill Joy's Berkeley Unix. This workstation had some significant reliability problems, but the subsequent SUN-3 and SPARC workstations were highly successful. SUN's well-known slogan "the network is the computer" can be traced to its origins as a Stanford University Network terminal.

FURTHER READING

Segaller, Stephen. *Nerds 2.0.1: A Brief History of the Internet.* New York: TV Books, 1999.

Southwick, Karen. *High Noon: The Inside Story of Scott McNealy and the Rise of Sun Microsystems.* New York: Wiley, 1999.

—*Jonathan Bowen*

Supercomputer

The term *supercomputer* has traditionally been used to describe the fastest computers available at any given time. Such computers have typically been used for "number crunching" problems containing many calculations (often involving **floating-point** arithmetic), including scientific simulations, structural analysis, computational fluid dynamics, physics, chemistry, electronic design, nuclear energy research, the analysis of geological data (e.g., petrochemical prospecting), meteorology and animated graphics (e.g., for the film industry). They have normally been very expensive and small in number as a result. The best known supercomputer manufacturer has been **Cray Research**, founded by the legendary **Seymour Cray** (1925–96).

Cray worked for a number of startup companies after originally joining Engineering Research Associates (ERA) in 1946. He immediately made an impact as an engineer with great expertise and confidence that belied his years. With William Norris (1911–) and others, he formed **Control Data Corporation** (CDC) in 1957. In 1962, Cray established a Control Data Corporation laboratory near Chippewa Falls, Minnesota, 80 miles from the headquarters in Minneapolis/St. Paul, where he led the design of the

CDC 6600 computer. This remoteness meant that he was less bothered by CDC management.

The CDC 6600 machine was announced in 1964 and about 100 were sold for around U.S.$8 million each. The design took advantage of the newer and faster silicon **transistor** technology instead of germanium transistors. It was probably the first computer to be popularly described as a supercomputer. The CDC 6600 achieved the fastest clock speed at the time (100 nanoseconds [ns] or 10 megahertz [MHz]) and it was one of the first computers to use Freon for refrigerant cooling. It was also the first commercial computer to use a CRT (**cathode-ray tube**) console. Probably the first computer **games** using a monitor (including Baseball, Lunar Lander, and Space Wars) were produced for the CDC 6600, which acted as an incentive in getting it operational. Software was typically developed using **Fortran** or **assembler** for the ultimate in speed. The CDC 6600 was a useful computing workhorse well into the 1970s and was an important landmark in the foundation of the field of supercomputing.

The subsequent CDC 7600 had a typical core memory of 65,536 sixty-bit words (equivalent to about 0.5 megabytes) and a clock speed of 27 ns (37MHz). It ran around five times the speed of the CDC 6600, a very significant step change in speed considering that both were single-processor machines. However, the CDC 7600 could be unreliable. Its low mean-time-to-failure meant that good job and file recovery procedures were required. The company later produced the CDC Star but by this time, Seymour Cray had left CDC to form his own company, which offered rivals that were more successful.

As computer architect at the newly established Cray Research, Cray provided the technical vision of the **Cray-1** computer, which was twice as fast as the CDC 7600 as well as exhibiting balanced scalar and vector performance. The computer was also innovative in its use of reciprocal approximation for division. The design reflected a simplicity not found in competing computers. In addition, the Cray-1, launched in 1976, was more reliable than the CDC 7600. The technology used was based on well-established early small-scale **integrated circuits**, housed in a distinctive and iconic circular case that even included seating. Like all good designs, the circular layout was dictated by engineering need, in this case of reducing the length of wires between modules to increase the speed.

Subsequent generations were less successful. Steve Chen developed a multiprocessor architecture version, the Cray X-MP, based on the Cray-1 design, but this was not Cray's style. He preferred to begin with a clean sheet of paper for a new design, using the most appropriate technology available at the time. The Cray X-MP/48, popular in the late 1980s, for example, housed four processors in one cabinet. This allowed parallel execution of problems, allowing them to be partitioned into a number of asynchronously executable subproblems. This **multitasking** mode of use was the beginning of parallel computing for supercomputers. Each X-MP processor could execute an instruction in 8.5 ns and had a main memory of 8 million 64-bit words. The processors were significantly faster than those in the Cray-1 and included very efficient interprocessor communication.

The Cray Y-MP followed the Cray X-MP. For example, the Cray Y-MP8/864, popular in the early 1990s, provided eight processors that could be run independently or in parallel. More than a gigaflop (1 billion floating-point operations per second) was possible. The machine included 64 megawords of directly addressable central memory, together with a solid-state storage device (SSD) of 256 million words that acted like a dedicated high-speed disk drive. The clock speed was 6 ns (167 MHz).

At Cray Computer Corporation (CCC) in Colorado, Cray worked on the Cray-3, which was never marketed successfully, due to inordinate delays until funding finally ran out. A major difficulty was the dissipation of heat, especially in designs using three-dimensional configurations of components, where the problem was often insurmountable. The Cray-3 included modules containing about 1000 chips in the space of 4 cubic inches. A typical configuration included four processors, 128 megawords of memory, 20 gigabytes of disk space, and a clock speed of 2.08 ns (480 MHz). This was the fastest clock speed of any supercomputer then available. The Cray-3 used gallium arsenide integrated circuits instead of silicon technology for all its logic circuits. This circuitry was contained in the top 8 inches of the computer in a system cabinet with a bronzed acrylic lid. A larger cabinet beneath, called the *control pod*, contained controls and monitoring devices for the cooling system and power supplies. The machine was very power hungry, requiring 90,000 watts of power and emitting 310,000 British thermal units of heat per hour.

In early 1996, Cray founded his last company, SRC Computers (short for Seymour Roger Cray). A parallel computer consisting of 512 **microprocessors** capable of 1 trillion floating-point operations per second (12,000 times the speed of a Cray-1) was planned. Unfortunately, Cray suffered a fatal car accident on 22 September 1996, bringing to an end an era of supercomputer design.

The original Cray Research, Inc. merged with **Silicon Graphics, Inc.** (SGI), the graphics workstation manufacturer, in 1996, thus moving SGI into the supercomputer arena. SGI was already interested in high-performance graphics processing, for film animation and for their Reality Center, which provided an advanced immersive visualization facility for group **virtual reality** (VR), first available in 1994. SGI supercomputer models in the late 1990s, employing a high degree of parallelism, included the PowerChallenge XL and Origin2000.

Although Seymour Cray's various companies and their successors dominated the supercomputer market for several decades, other dedicated and existing well-established companies have also offered supercomputer products. The independent company **Thinking Machines Corporation** offered its novel and highly parallel **Connection Machine** in various versions during the late 1980s and early 1990s. **IBM**, although best known for producing **mainframe** computers, also ventured into the realm of parallel supercomputing with the RS/6000 Scalable POWERparallel (SP) cluster system, available in the 1990s. **Hewlett-Packard** has offered the Exemplar scalable **parallel processing** system with up to 512 processors and 512 gigabytes of memory in the late 1990s.

By their very nature, supercomputers have been limited in number. Success has normally resulted from uses of well-tried technology (often a decade old) being used to its limits rather than the utilization of very novel and untried technology, for which difficulty of design or unreliability has often caused its ultimate downfall. Users without unlimited budgets but with computationally intensive problems to solve have normally gone for the much larger mainframe market (traditionally dominated by IBM).

The history of supercomputers—the fastest computers in the world at any particular time—has been a bumpy journey for those involved; and failure has been all to easy even with brilliant engineers involved. Customers for supercomputers have often regarded them somewhat as status symbols. In many cases, money was not the issue if the product was available and reliable enough. Applications such as modeling nuclear explosions and weather forecasting have always been able to consume more processing power to increase the accuracy of their predictions.

Supercomputing has lost some of its glamor since computing has become generally and dramatically cheaper as hardware design progresses with larger numbers of transistors on each microchip using smaller internal dimensions for individual transistors and wiring. In addition, parallel processing means that absolute speed of a single processor has increasingly become less of a limiting factor than in the past. In the longer term, new paradigms, such as the use of quantum computers, offer the theoretical possibility of dramatic speedup of algorithms, perhaps even at the supercomputer level. By their very definition, there will always be a place for supercomputers, whatever direction the design of computers takes. The immediate future of supercomputing has to involve increasing parallelization, due to the physical limitations of sequential machines.

FURTHER READING

Hillis, W. Daniel. *The Connection Machine*. Cambridge, Mass.: MIT Press, 1985.

Karin, Sidney, and Norris Parker Smith. *The Supercomputer Era*. Boston: Harcourt Brace Jovanovich, 1987.

Metropolis, N., ed. *Frontiers of Supercomputing*. Berkeley, Calif.: University of California Press, 1986.

Murray, Charles J. *The Supermen: The Story of Seymour Cray and the Technical Wizards Behind the Supercomputer*. New York: Wiley, 1997.

Thorton, James E. "The CDC 6600 Project." *Annals of the History of Computing*, Vol 2, No. 4, 1980.

—*Jonathan Bowen*

Sutherland, Ivan

1938–

U.S. Inventor and Computer Scientist

Ivan Sutherland pioneered the field of interactive **graphics** with his invention of **Sketchpad** in 1963. Many of his innovations continue to be important and visionary decades after their conception.

When he was 12 years old, Ivan Sutherland learned about computers from computer pioneer Edmund Berkeley (1909–88), who had built a small computer that he called Simon. Simon could add numbers up to 15, but could not divide. Sutherland wrote a program for Simon to divide numbers up to 15 by 1, 2, or 3. He had to rewire Simon to be able to run the program.

Berkeley introduced Sutherland to **Claude Shannon** (1916–2001), known as the father of information theory. Years later Shannon became Sutherland's Ph.D. supervisor when Sutherland attended graduate school at the Massachusetts Institute of Technology (MIT). At MIT, Sutherland was able to use the TX-2, one of the largest and most advanced computers of its time. The TX-2 made possible interactive input, through a display, light pen, and bank of switches. He made use of these devices to create Sketchpad, the first interactive graphics program, which became the subject of his Ph.D. thesis.

Sketchpad laid the foundations for the field of interactive graphics. Among the computing concepts introduced by Sketchpad were memory structures to store objects, the ability to zoom in and out on the display, the ability to make perfect lines, corners and joints, and the rubber-banding of lines. Sketchpad made it possible for a human being and a computer to "converse" using line drawings.

In 1964, shortly after completing his Ph.D., Sutherland became the second director of the Information Processing Techniques Office (IPTO) of the Advanced Research Projects Agency (**ARPA**). Continuing the traditions established by its first director, **J.C.R. Licklider** (1915–90), researchers were to be funded on the basis of their capability in fields of interest to IPTO, not for specific projects. Sutherland managed a U.S.$15 million budget. The areas of time sharing and online use of computers were the main thrust of the programs that Sutherland directed at ARPA/IPTO.

In 1968, Sutherland joined the graphics research group being assembled by David Evans. He and Evans worked together to build an IPTO center of excellence program in graphics at the University of Utah. They also started Evans and Sutherland, a company pioneering computer graphics applications. Their work helped establish Salt Lake City as an important center for computer graphics research.

Now a vice-president at Sun Microsystems, Sutherland's research interest continues to be problems in advanced hardware technology. His experience has taught him that developing new technology takes courage and that the best results are achieved when the problem is one that interests the researcher.

BIOGRAPHY

Ivan Edward Sutherland. Born 16 May 1938 in Hastings, Nebraska. Received B.S. in electrical engineering from Carnegie Mellon University, 1959; M.A. from California Institute of Technology, 1960; Ph.D. from Massachusetts Institute of Technology, 1963. Consultant, Lincoln Laboratory, 1961–64. Director of IPTO, 1964–66; associate professor, Harvard University, 1966–68; cofounded Evans and Sutherland, 1968; associate professor and then professor, University of Utah, 1968-1976; Fletcher Jones Professor and Computer Science Department head, California Institute of Technology, 1976–80; founded Sutherland, Sproull, and Associates, and Advanced Technology Ventures, 1980–90; vice–president and fellow, Sun Microsystems, Inc. 1990–present. Recipient of many awards, including the 1988 Turing Award.

SELECTED WORKS

Raibert, M. H., and I. E. Sutherland. "Machines That Walk." *Scientific American*, Jan. 1983, pp. 44–53.

Sutherland, I.E. "Sketchpad:—A Man–Machine Graphical Communication System." *Proceedings of the Spring Joint Computer Conference*, Detroit, Mich., May 1963, and MIT Lincoln Laboratory Technical Report 296, Jan. 1963.

———. "Computer Displays." *Scientific American*, Vol. 222, No. 6, June 1970, pp. 56–81.

———. "Micropipelines." *Communications of the ACM*, June 1989.

———. "Technology and Courage" In R. F. Rashid, ed., *CMU Computer Science: A 25th Anniversary Commemorative.* New York: ACM Press, 1991.

Sutherland, I. E., and C. A. Mead. "Microelectronics and Computer Science." *Scientific American*, Sept. 1977, pp .210–228.

FURTHER READING

Frenkel, Karen A. "An Interview with Ivan Sutherland." *Communications of the ACM*, Vol. 32, No. 6, June 1989, pp. 712–718.

Interview with Ivan Sutherland, conducted by William Aspray, 1 May 1989, Charles Babbage Institute.

—*Ronda Hauben*

SWIFT

The Society for Worldwide Financial International Communication (SWIFT) is a cooperative founded in 1973 by 239 banks from 15 countries. Its purpose is to develop and manage a private communication **network** that provides electronic financial settlement services. SWIFT has grown steadily over the years and now boasts a membership of 6700 financial institutions in 189 countries. The network transmitted over 1 billion financial messages in 1999. Daily payments over the SWIFT network now exceed U.S.$5 billion.

The development of international trade after World War II led to an increasing number of banking settlements and currency-exchange operations, especially in Europe. In the early 1970s the need was felt for an electronic communication channel that would speed such transactions. Sixty American and European banks commissioned a feasibility study for a scheme that was called the Message Switching Project. After only three years, the founding countries (13 European nations, Canada, and the United States) decided to start the network; they were completely linked at the end of 1975. The headquarters and command center were installed in Belgium. Other command centers were installed a few years later in the United States and the Netherlands. Although the network was founded by banks, SWIFT was later opened to other financial institutions. Now, only 2214 of the 6700 members are in fact banks; the others are brokers, investment managers, stock exchanges, and so on.

Together with SWIFT, an international network, there are many other national or regional banking settlement systems in operation. In the United States, banks connect to the CHIPS, BANKWIRE, and FEDWIRE (owned by the U.S. Federal Reserve Bank) networks. In the United Kingdom, banks own the CHAPS network, and French banks are supported by the SAGITTAIRE network.

The SWIFT network was conceived as a hierarchical system: Banks first connect to regional processing centers (RPCs) in each country. The RPCs concentrate messages and validate the transactions, delivering them to one of SWIFT's three operating centers (OPCs). The OPCs use the store-and-forward method, in which each message is stored securely and then delivered to the final destination. System control centers monitor the performance of the network 24 hours a day.

The increasing volume of transactions led to a more modular approach, called the SWIFT II system, introduced in 1988. For increased security, connection to the SWIFT network requires dedicated SWIFT terminals. All stages of a transaction are controlled: input, approval, and verification of messages. All transactions are acknowledged by the receiver, and an audit trail is stored that makes it possible to retrace any transaction to its origin. SWIFT assumes all financial liability for transactions accepted into the network.

Maintaining trust in the network has been one of the key technological issues faced by the SWIFT consortium from the beginning. After the European Community threatened to start an antitrust process in 1997, SWIFT was opened to nonshareholders—the increasing number of members itself created a security problem. In the 1990s the SWIFT consortium started using encryption **software** based on **public key cryptography**.

SWIFT was established as a private network and is not connected directly to the **Internet**. Its standards are not widely available, as for the Internet, since a high level of security has to be maintained. However, software and components for Internet Protocol (IP) networks have become much cheaper than software and **hardware** for proprietary protocols. Therefore, SWIFT decided to switch to an IP-based network, with enhanced security, which is to be completely in place in 2001.

The SWIFT network has also been updated continually to offer new services. Starting in October 2000, *continuous linked settlement* (CLS) transactions have been supported. Previously, in foreign currency transactions, one party paid before the other. If the second payment did not arrive (as in the case of the failed

Herstatt bank in 1975), this could led to massive disruptions of the financial system. In CLS transactions, payments have to be made simultaneously or the transaction fails. The SWIFT consortium would also like to offer some kind of support for electronic commerce, but it still unclear what the relation could be between the trusted private SWIFT network and the comparatively insecure Internet.

FURTHER READING

Etzkorn, Jörg. *Rechtsfragen des International Elektronischen Zahlungsverkehrs mit SWIFT*. Berlin: Walter de Gruyter, 1991.

SWIFT Annual Report, 1998. Brussels: Society for Worldwide Financial International Communication, 1998.

—*Margarita Esponda*

System/360 See IBM Mainframes.

T

TCP/IP

All communications networks require *protocols*, sets of agreed standards used for signaling and data transfer. The *TCP/IP suite*, which contains the protocols used by the **Internet**, has become one of the computing community's most important standards. It is named after its two most important constituents, *Transmission Control Protocol* (TCP) and *Internet Protocol* (IP).

Communication protocols are layered, meaning that each takes on a particular, tightly defined function and runs over another. At the top of the stack are the actual applications run by users, and at the bottom are rules governing the electrical, light, or radio signals within a cable or interface. TCP/IP is media independent and so does not concern itself with the very lowest levels: It can use any type of physical networking technology, including satellite, wireless, and telephone links as well as **local area networks** (LANs). According to the **Open Systems Interconnection** (OSI) model, an idealized framework that divides protocols into seven categories, TCP/IP spans the top five, from the *application layer* down to the *network layer*.

TCP/IP was developed in 1973 by **Vinton Cerf** (1943–) of Stanford University, **Jonathan Postel** (1943–98) of California University, and **Robert Kahn** (1938–) of the Advanced Research Projects Agency (**ARPA**), the U.S. Department of Defense (DoD) program that spearheaded Internet development. It was intended to simplify connection between computers made by different companies, all of which at that time used their own proprietary protocols. The government eventually specified that all computers sold to the DoD had to support TCP/IP, a major reason for its initial success. By 1983, it had spread throughout **ARPANET**; by 1995 it was ubiquitous, built in to most computer systems.

The suite's most fundamental component is IP itself, responsible for the path taken by data through the network. IP was one of the first *packet-switched* protocols, meaning that it split data into small chunks (packets) and let each find its own way across a network. Previous technologies, such as the phone system, were *circuit switched*: They had to set up a link between any two devices that needed to communicate, then tear it down after the communication had finished. Packet switching is theoretically more efficient, because it uses capacity only as needed. It is also more robust, as packets can be sent via alternative routes if part of a network fails.

IP requires that every packet sent across a network be encoded with an *IP address*, a unique number that identifies its destination. The present version of IP is known as v4, because these addresses use four bytes: there were no versions 1 to 3. Throughout the network, special computers called **routers** read the address and send the packet there via the most efficient path. Even sequential packets bearing the same destination address may follow different paths, as routers continuously update each other based on factors such as network congestion. Modern routers are sometimes called *layer 3 switches*, because IP corresponds to layer 3 of the OSI model.

Unlike other packet-based technologies, such as **asynchronous transfer mode** (ATM), IP has a flexible packet size. All hosts and routers must accept packets containing up to 576 bytes, of which the first 24 form the *header*, a control field that includes IP addresses and other routing information. Larger packets would reduce the *protocol overhead*, as they would mean that fewer 24-bit headers have to cross the network, but they could slow down routers, which have to store each packet in memory while finding the best route to its destination. For this reason, 576 bytes is usually considered the maximum on the public Internet, although the protocol allows packets of up to 65,535 bytes, larger than most files.

IP rapidly overtook proprietary protocols, but it was not designed to be the foundation of a global communications network. It has been particularly criticized for its lack of *quality-of-service* features: There is no guarantee that even high-priority packets will actually arrive at their intended destination. IP networks can easily be overrun by excess traffic, either by accident or by a deliberate *denial of service* attack, during which a malicious user floods a router with packets.

Another drawback of routing is that it increases *latency*, the time taken for a packet to cross a network. Each router can take many microseconds to forward a packet, which adds up to a noticeable delay if the packet has to pass through many routers. Large networks also suffer from *jitter*, the variation in latency caused by packets being routed via different paths. In extreme cases, this can mean packets arriving at their destination in the wrong order.

IP's final problem is its addressing scheme, which allows only about 4 billion possible addresses. This seemed plenty when the protocol was limited to one government department but is not sufficient for an Internet aiming to encompass everyone on Earth as well as consumer devices such as television sets and mobile telephones. A newer IP standard, known as v6, will solve this problem by using a 16-byte address field. It was defined in 1997 but has not yet passed into common use.

IP itself provides no facilities to check whether packets have actually arrived intact. This is the main task of TCP, which corresponds to *layer 4* of the OSI stack, known as the *transport layer*. If data have not been received correctly, TCP will resend it; and if a single network link is inadequate or unreliable, it will try to arrange for multiple links.

TCP is a *connection-oriented* protocol, which means that it sets up a virtual connection across a network: before sending any data, the source and destination hosts perform a *handshake*, telling each other that they are ready to transmit and receive. The sending node will then transmit only a fixed quantity of data and wait until it receives an acknowledgment that this has been received before sending another. The amount of data sent at once, called the *window*, depends on a network's capacity and latency. Most TCP/IP **software** starts with a small window, then gradually enlarges it until the maximum capacity of the link is reached; this is why data transfer rates across the Internet often increase as a file is downloaded.

TCP/IP was originally intended to be a single protocol, an evolution of the ARPANET's early *Network Control Protocol* (NCP). Together, they provide a very reliable way to guarantee data transfer across a packet-switched network. But they do so at a price: The time taken waiting for TCP acknowledgments can add significant delay to a signal, while TCP's system of enlarging the window size doesn't work on networks that suffer from high jitter, such as cellphone systems. For this reason, its designers decided in 1974 to separate the two protocols, allowing IP to be used for applications that do not demand TCP's reliability.

The other transport protocol in the TCP/IP suite is *User Datagram Protocol* (UDP). Unlike TCP, UDP is *connectionless* and does not require acknowledgments. It is simpler than TCP, but less reliable, so is used for applications where speed matters more than accuracy. UDP became increasingly common during the late 1990s, thanks to the growth of packet video, voice-over IP, and mobile Internet access.

Both TCP and UDP can carry data from several applications at once, a process known as *multiplexing*. The protocols keep track of which data belong to which applications by assigning each window or datagram a 16-bit identifier, known as a *port* or *socket*. Every application accesses TCP or UDP through its own specific port, the most common being port 80, used by Web browsers. In 1988, routers began to incorporate *layer 4 switching*, which meant that they could read the port number and prioritize or block traffic based on its application.

The TCP/IP suite also contains many higher-level applications, corresponding to the top three layers of the OSI model. Many of these are visible to users, but some vital protocols are often hidden to all but network administrators. The most important are *Simple Network Management Protocol* (SNMP) and the **domain name system** (DNS). SNMP enables technicians to keep the Internet running, while DNS translates numerical IP addresses into the ".com" and ".org" names familiar to users.

The first TCP/IP applications to gain widespread acceptance were *File Transfer Protocol* (**FTP**) and *Simple Mail Transfer Protocol* (SMTP), both developed in 1980 by Jon Postel. The former allowed files to be accessed from anywhere, and the latter is the foundation of Internet e-mail. But the application that really drove the protocol to dominance was *Hypertext Transfer Protocol* (HTTP). This was developed by **Tim Berners-Lee** (1955–) in 1989 and is used on the **World Wide Web**.

In 1990, more than 200 companies were selling or licensing implementations of TCP/IP, known as *stacks*. The market disappeared a few years later when TCP/IP networking began to be included in operating systems. But new TCP/IP applications continue to be developed, such as systems for broadcasting audio and video over the Internet.

Although TCP is increasingly giving way to UDP, IP itself has become the most important protocol for data networking. By 1998, many analysts were predicting that it would soon take over other kinds of networks, too, eventually even replacing the telephone system.

FURTHER READING

Abbate, Janet. *Inventing the Internet.* Cambridge, Mass.: MIT Press, 1999.

Beauchamp, K. G., and Gee-Swee Poo. *Computer Communications.* Wokingham and Berkshire, England: Van Nostrand Reinhold, 1987; 3rd ed., Boston: Thomson Computer Press, 1995.

Ben-Arie, Moty. *A World of Protocols.* Tel Aviv, Israel: Radcom, 1998.

Hein, Mathias, and David Griffiths. *SNMP: Simple Network Management Protocol 2: Theory and Practice.* New York: Wiley, 1995.

Siyan, Karenjit. *NetWare Training Guide: NetWare TCP/IP and NetWare NFS.* Indianapolis, Ind.: New Riders, 1994.

—*Andy Dornan*

Telecommunications Act of 1996

On 8 February 1996, President William Clinton (1946–) signed the first major overhaul of U.S. telecommunications law in nearly 62 years. This legislation, the 280-page Telecommunications Act of 1996, updated laws that had been written when the radio, telephone, and telegraph were the primary means of electronic communication. In addition to sweeping changes in a variety of industries, the act is often viewed as the federal mandate that established a national *information superhighway* and guaranteed universal access in a variety of ways.

Prior to signing this act into law, U.S. national policy regarding new telecommunications technology had largely been set through court decisions and amendments to the original 1934 act. Several significant milestones led up to the development of a new national policy. Among these were Judge Harold Greene's (1923–2000) Modified Final Judgment in 1982 that led to the **AT&T breakup** two years later. In 1984, an amendment to the 1934 Communication Act, the Cable Communications Policy Act, set U.S. national policy regarding the cable television industry. In 1992, the Cable Act of 1984 was altered with the Cable Television Consumer Protection and Competition Act. Controversy regarding many areas of telecommunications made it apparent that more than policy "patches" were needed to modernize legislation. In 1994, the U.S. Congress made its first attempt to create sweeping telecommunications law. Subsequent versions of the legislation continued to work its way through Congress in 1995, but it was not until 1996 that both the Senate and House of Representatives were satisfied.

The final version of the 1996 act affected a wide range of industries and technologies, each related to telecommunications. Areas that were previously closed to competition were now opened—among those most affected were cable television, broadcast television, telephone, radio, and electric utilities. Some analysts estimated that the industries affected generated close to one-sixth of the U.S. revenue. Despite the changes, the managers of affected industries supported the regulations, promising lower consumer prices, wider ranges of services, and quicker responses to consumer needs.

One of the major impacts of the Telecommunications Act of 1996 was the deregulation of cable television. Small systems were immediately deregulated, but large cable companies had to wait until 1999 before their extended basic service packages were deregulated. One exception was those cable companies that competed with direct broadcast satellite; the act did not consider them competition for cable systems. In addition, cable television companies were prohibited from acquiring more than 10 percent of most telephone companies. However, they were allowed to enter the local phone market. Other rules dealing with interconnectivity, obscenity, and programming suitable for children were also spelled out.

Broadcast television was affected in three major ways. First, ownership restrictions were loosened to allow wider coverage areas and a lifting of the 12-station cap. Second, broadcasters were required to provide a rating system for program content. Along with that idea was the mandate for a violence **microprocessor** or V-chip that reads the rating signal and blocks undesirable programming. The third major change lengthened and altered the method for license renewals.

Telephone companies saw a wide set of changes. They were given permission to provide video programming in the service areas and choose to be regulated as cable television, common carrier, or open video systems. If they retained classification as a telephone company, they were prohibited from buying more than 10 percent of most cable television companies. Under the act, local phone companies were permitted to offer long-distance service and the long-distance providers were permitted to offer local service.

Electric utility companies were also mentioned in the Telecommunications Act. They were required to provide access to their "right-of-way," meaning that they could now partner with companies seeking access to "final mile" connections. Since nearly every U.S. home is connected to electric utilities, the new information superhighway could find its way into many homes through this route.

In addition to the goals of deregulating competition and assuring universal access, Senator James Exon (1921–) of Nebraska and Senator Slade Gorton (1928–) of Washington successfully attached an amendment called the **Communications Decency Act** (CDA) to the Telecommunications Act. The CDA amendment caused a great deal of controversy since it would have regulated **Internet** content. Further, Web site owners would have been held responsible for ensuring that their content was not accessed by inappropriate groups (e.g., children). This amendment was challenged by more than 20 groups immediately upon passage. On 26 June 1997, the U.S. Supreme Court ruled that the Communications Decency Act violated constitutional free speech guarantees.

Although the Telecommunication Act of 1996 has been in effect for several years, its full consequences are still unknown. Under this new umbrella of regulation, a variety of companies have been empowered to participate in the development of a new information infrastructure, and as a result, telecommunications firms in the United States have an opportunity for change and growth that has not been experienced since the 1930s.

FURTHER READING

Aufderheide, Patricia. *Communications Policy and the Public Interest: The Telecommunications Act of 1996*. New York: Guilford Press, 1999.

Cimatoribus, M. A. De Tommaso, and P. Neri. "Impacts of the 1996 Telecommunications Act on the U.S. Model of Telecommunications Policy." *Telecommunications Policy*, Vol. 22, No. 6, 1998.

Ferris, Charles D., et al. *Guidebook to the Telecommunications Act of 1996*. New York: Matthew Bender, 1996.

Telecommunications Act of 1996. Govt. Doc.: AE2.110. Washington, D.C.: U.S. Government Printing Office, 1996.

Whitman, Michael E. "A Look at the Telecommunications Act of 1996." *Information Systems Management*, Vol. 14, No. 3, 1997.

—*Roger McHaney*

Telnet

From the computer user's point of view, telnet is a command or program for connecting to remote computers. From the technical point of view, telnet is a terminal emulation protocol that allows the user's computer to serve as a terminal for a remote computer, so that an interactive session can be started.

The user types "telnet" at the prompt or calls "telnet://" from a browser and then telnet starts. A telnet request to log into the computer "foo" at Stanford may look like:

```
telnet foo.stanford.edu
```

The computer will respond with something similar to:

```
Trying 157.36.123.10
Connected to foo.stanford.edu
...
```

and then the remote computer will ask for a user ID and password.

Telnet is based on **TCP/IP** (Transmission Control Protocol/Internet Protocol), a protocol that allows a stream of packets to be delivered from one machine on the **Internet** to another. The network application layer sits on top of TCP/IP, and protocols such as telnet (remote login), **FTP** (remote file transfer), and SMTP (electronic mail) are some of its constituents.

Remote login was one of the most valuable features of the original **ARPANET** (created in 1969), the predecessor of the Internet. For the first time, users could log in to mainframes from remote locations using packet communication. At the beginning, communication programs had different names in the machines connected. Users of the TOPS-10 **operating system**, for example, used the program named IMPCOM. As early as 1970, one year after the ARPANET was on place at just a handful of sites, there were already discussions about a remote "logger" protocol. The first reference in the Request for Comments (RFC) archives to "telnet" is RFC 097 from 1971.

In 1980, **Jonathan Postel** (1943–98) authored RFC 764 in which the Telnet protocol was refined; it was later revised in RFC 854. Postel wrote: "The TELNET Protocol is built upon three main ideas: first, the concept of a 'Network Virtual Terminal'; second, the principle of negotiated options; and third, a symmetric view of terminals and processes." Each side in a remote login session maps its communication to a virtual network terminal, which is the same for all participants and consists of a keyboard and a printer. *Negotiated options* means that one party can request the other to use an option, which can be accepted or denied. This allows terminals and computers with different characteristics to agree on the lowest common denominator. Option requests go back and forth when communication is first established. All telnet commands consist of at least a two-byte sequence: the Interpret As Command (IAC) character (225) and a number that specifies the command. For example, the Are You There (AYT) command, useful to check if communication has not broken down, consists of the sequence of numbers 255–246 interspersed with the TCP/IP packets.

Further Reading

Melvin, J. T., and R. W. Watson. "First Cut at a Proposed Telnet Protocol." *RFC* 097, Feb. 1971.

Postel, Jonathan. "Telnet Protocol Specification." *RFC* 764, June 1980.

Postel, Jonathan, and J. Reynolds. "Telnet Protocol Specification." *RFC* 854, May 1983.

Stevens, W. Richard. *TCP/IP Illustrated.* Reading, Mass.: Addison-Wesley, 1994–96.

—Raúl Rojas

Ternary Computers

Modern computers use the **binary system**: All arithmetical operations are performed internally using 2 as the numerical base. An alternative are ternary computers, which compute using base 3. An example of such a machine is the SETUN computer built by Nikolay Brusentsov (1925–) in 1958 at Moscow University.

In base 3, each digit in a number is multiplied by a power of 3 (1, 3, 9, 27, and so on). The three digits 1̶, 0 and 1 can be used at each position, where 1̶ means −1. For example, the ternary number 101 is equal to the decimal number 10, since $1 \times 9 + 0 \times 3 + 1 \times 1 = 10$. The ternary number 11̶0 is equal to the decimal number 6, since $1 \times 9 + (-1) \times 3 + 0 \times 1 = 6$. This was the type of coding used in the SETUN computer. Positive and negative numbers can be represented in this way without having to write a sign in front of the number.

It is not difficult to prove that the ternary system is more compact than the decimal or binary system.

Assume, for example, that we are given 30 sheets on which we can write decimal, binary, or ternary digits. Using the decimal system we can only represent numbers with up to three decimal places (since we need 10 sheets, numbered 0 to 9 for each decimal position). Using the binary system, we could write numbers with up to 15 bits; with the ternary system we could represent numbers with up to 10 ternary digits. In the decimal case we can represent the numbers from 0 to 999, (i.e., 1000 numbers). In the binary case we can represent 2^{15} numbers (i.e., 32,768 numbers). In the ternary case we can represent 3^{10} numbers (i.e., 59,049 numbers). The ternary system is therefore almost twice as comprehensive as the binary system, using the same number of sheets or *states*, and almost 60 times better than the decimal system.

The ternary system also allows one to use ternary logic, in which the truth values are "true," "false," and "unknown." Logical operations can be defined that are more general that the binary logical operations. However, although the ternary system is more compact and more general logical operations are possible, the cost of ternary electronic components is much higher than the cost of binary elements. Binary computers are therefore more cost-effective.

The SETUN computer, one of the few ternary logic systems ever built, was manufactured in a small series of 50 machines in the USSR. Thirty of the computers were used at Soviet universities. The machine was eventually discontinued.

FURTHER READING

Blaauw, Gerrit A., and Frederick P. Brooks, Jr. *Computer Architecture: Concepts and Evolution*. Reading, Mass.: Addison-Wesley, 1997.

Knuth, Donald. *The Art of Computer Programming*. Reading, Mass.: Addison-Wesley, 1997.

—*Raúl Rojas*

TeX

TeX is a typesetting language for high-quality composition of technical material. Normal text, complex mathematical formulas, and in general, any kind of document can be typeset using this system. TeX annotates documents using special commands that tell the computer how to format a page or what font to use. New commands can be built out of old commands, and it is possible to write programs for general-purpose calculations, making TeX one of the most versatile typesetting systems in use today. TeX is free **software**; it can be downloaded from a large number of **Internet** sites.

TeX was developed by **Donald Knuth** (1938–) at Stanford University in the early 1980s. Knuth, a famed mathematician and computer scientist, decided to write his own typesetting system during work on his well-known series of books ***The Art of Computer Programming***. He got so involved with the correct typesetting of these books, that he decided to write his own program. He picked the name TeX in allusion to the Greek word with the same spelling that means "art" but also "technology." TeX differs in many details from Knuth's first typesetting system, which he later called TeX-78.

Although plain TeX is versatile and powerful, it is rather difficult to use. Therefore, some easier-to-use *macropackages* have been developed that contain most of the predefined functions that the normal user will ever need. The most widely used is LaTeX (Lamport TeX), written by Leslie Lamport (1941–) at Stanford Research International in the 1980s. The current version, LaTeX 2e, is maintained by a group of volunteers who have added some new features, such as interchangeable fonts. The output of TeX processing is written to DVI (device independent) files that can be converted to PostScript or Adobe PDF files for output by a laser **printer**.

A text is formatted in LaTeX by using some simple annotations. A text to be typeset in italics, for example, is enclosed in braces and the escape sequence "\it" is put at the beginning, as in: {\it this text in italics}. Mathematical formulas are enclosed in dollar signs: $x + y = z$. A subindex 1 can be added to the x in this formula by writing $x_1 + y = z$. This simple example shows the main advantage of LaTeX or TeX over word processing programs such as MS-Word or WordPerfect: that complex formatting, even formulas, can be entered using only the keyboard. This might sound more difficult to do than using menus, but for technical writers writing long pieces, it is faster and very easy to learn.

There are several TeX macrocollections, such as the one distributed by the American Mathematical Society, AMS-TeX, and a number of commercial ones. But in general, TeX has remained stable over a period of many years and old TeX files can still be processed. There are many TeX user organizations and a very active TeX Internet community.

FURTHER READING

Knuth, Donald. *The Art of Computer Programming*, Vols. 1–3. Reading, Mass.: Addison-Wesley, 1968; 3rd ed., 1997.

—*Raúl Rojas*

Texas Instruments

Dallas-based Texas Instruments (TI) is a **semiconductor** company with more than 40,000 employees worldwide. In 1999, revenues were more than U.S.$9 billion.

The company was founded in 1930 as Geophysical Service (GS), an independent contractor in Texas servicing the oil industry with seismic exploration tools and expertise. In 1941 the firm used that expertise to receive their first Navy contract for submarine-detection equipment. As World War II raged, the company moved into the electronics field, performing work for the U.S. Army Signal Corps and the U.S. Navy. After the war ended, GS refocused on the growing field of electronics. By 1948, they received a major airborne radar system contract with the U.S. government. Revenues totaled U.S.$7.6 million in 1950; employees numbered 1128.

The company changed its name to Texas Instruments Incorporated in 1951. In 1952, TI entered the semiconductor business by purchasing a license from Western Electric Company to manufacture **transistors**. In 1954, TI produced its first commercial **silicon** transistor and created the first mass-produced high-frequency germanium transistor. That year TI also designed the first consumer transistor radio, the Regency, to help promote transistor products.

While continuing to look at the commercial potential for its business, TI stayed very involved with government contracts. The company continued to be a leader in military radar systems, and its transistor products were increasingly built into many other leading-edge electronic systems including space satellites and computer systems.

In 1958, TI engineer **Jack Kilby** (1923–) demonstrated an early **integrated circuit** (IC). These new devices were soon embraced by military designers seeking to miniaturize the electronic circuits being used in computer, missile, and radar systems. However, manufacturers of nonmilitary electronic products were more cautious. The high production cost and unknown reliability of ICs initially limited their use in commercial products. In 1967, seeing this reluctance as a great impediment to the company's growth, Kilby and his engineering team developed a prototype electronic calculator to promote the use of ICs for everyday uses and to demonstrate their reliability.

Semiconductor products began to be accepted more and more in the late 1960s and early 1970s as reliability grew and prices dropped. As a leader in the field, TI expanded its sales and manufacturing operations to a variety of overseas locations, including the Netherlands, France, Italy, Australia, and Argentina, to meet the growing need.

While TI was prospering with semiconductor products in the areas of **microprocessor**, memory, and industrial control technology, its attempts to forge into the new world of consumer and business computers were not so successful. Its innovative TI-99 series of home computers during the 1980s (using their own microprocessor technology) was eventually discontinued as **IBM**-compatible and **Intel** component-based systems became the standard in the world market. An effort in the 1990s to return to the computer market with the TravelMate notebook series was phased out due to competitive pressures.

Today, the company's business focuses primarily on the semiconductor market but also includes digital signal processing technology, materials and controls, and educational and productivity devices. Its success over the years appears to be due to its continuing efforts to innovate in design, manufacturing, and marketing.

FURTHER READING

Greenia, Mark W. *History of Computing: An Encyclopedia of the People and Machines That Made Computer History.* (CD-ROM). Antelope, Calif.: Lexikon Services, 2000.

"Special 15th Anniversary Issue." *Electronic Engineering Times*, 16 Nov. 1987.

Veit, Stan. *Stan Veit's History of the Personal Computer.* Alexander, N.C.: WorldCom Press, 1993.

—*Guy D. Ball*

Thinking Machines Corporation

The Thinking Machines Corporation, founded in 1983 by **Daniel W. Hillis** (1958–), developed groundbreaking solutions to **parallel processing** problems. Although not financially successful, Thinking Machines revolutionized high-performance computing.

While a computer science student at MIT, Danny Hillis came to the conclusion that the future of supercomputing rested in exploiting massive parallelism. His idea was simple to state, yet difficult to implement: Instead of using a single powerful processor, why not use hundreds or even thousands of small lightweight processors in a computer? The concept was outrageous at the time, when even **microprocessors** were still expensive. Furthermore, Hillis planned to build a machine of the single instruction multiple data (SIMD) type. A SIMD machine consists of many processors with local memories (multiple data), all of which execute the same instruction at every step (thus "single instruction"). Conventional parallel machines work with many processors executing different instructions at each step (multiple instruction multiple data [MIMD]). It was not easy to program a SIMD machine to do useful work.

The Connection Machine. (Courtesy of the Computer History Museum)

The **Connection Machine** was Hillis's answer to the problem. He described the machine in his Ph.D. dissertation, which he wrote in seven days. The machine could be expanded to include 65,536 bit-serial processors. This means that information was moved between them using a single communication line in which the individual bits were pushed one after the other into the line. Traditional microprocessors transfer several bits in parallel, but this makes them more expensive. Serial-bit processors were not unknown in the history of computing—they had been used in the 1950s when electronic components were still expensive. The serial processors were connected using a **hypercube architecture**: The processors were the vertices and the communication lines the edges of a 12-dimensional cube. Hillis started the Thinking Machines Corporation to sell and develop the new computers. The CM-1 was delivered in 1985, the CM-2, an improved model in the same packaging, in 1987.

The Connection Machine was an immediate scientific success, but few were sold outside the academic world. Elegant **algorithms** were developed for the Connection Machine, for example, for sorting numbers or for processing lists, but the processors slowed down **floating-point** calculations.

Eventually, a floating-point coprocessor was added and with the introduction of the Connection Machine 5 (CM-5) in the 1990s, Thinking Machines abandoned the purist path it had followed. Off-the-shelf SPARC microprocessors were used and were connected using a fat-tree architecture (a kind of redundant tree connection pattern). A few years later Thinking Machines applied for protection from creditors and stopped delivering computers, although it continued selling software and some services.

Perhaps Hillis's greatest achievement was showing what a fertile imagination can produce when it is free to subvert old truths. His book on the Connection Machine is one of the few Ph.D. dissertations that have become a best seller, widely read beyond the typical audience of hard-core computer scientists.

FURTHER READING

Hillis, Daniel W. *The Connection Machine.* Cambridge, Mass.: MIT Press, 1985.

—*Raúl Rojas*

Thompson, Ken See Ritchie, Dennis, and Ken Thompson.

Threads

Threads are fragments of code in a program that can be executed concurrently or in parallel. The use of threads is intended to simplify the design of complex programs, to improve program performance in a **multiprocessor** system, or both.

Threads can be traced back to the first multiprogramming **operating systems** of the mid-1960s. The University of California–Berkeley Timesharing System (BTS) supported multiple simultaneous users, each of whom could be running multiple programs. While users were prevented from interfering with each other, BTS allowed processes being run by the *same* user to modify their memory locations to share access to data. The BTS kernel kept only minimal information for each of these lightweight processes (LWPs), and it could switch between them much faster than between users.

Edsger Dijkstra's (1930–) study of the interactions between LWPs led to his seminal work on semaphores, which provided the basis for all subsequent threads work. The basic difficulty with threads is that variables being accessed concurrently can become inconsistent. For example, if two threads share a variable, one incrementing the variable and the other decrementing the variable, the result may be no change of value, *or* an increment, *or* a decrement—depending on the type of hardware and the exact timing of the threads.

Dijkstra proposed a special variable he called a *semaphore* and two functions to manipulate it. One (which he called "V") signals the semaphore, while the other (which he called "P") waits until the semaphore is signaled, then removes the signal. Most importantly, these functions are not sensitive to thread timing.

A semaphore can provide a mutual exclusion mechanism (*mutex*) to control access to any group of variables. The threads involved must share a convention about what is protected and use a *lock* function to get exclusive access to the protected group of variables. A matching *unlock* function frees the group for another thread to modify them. Of course, a program can have more than one mutex to control access to different groups of variables, and it becomes possible immediately for threads to lock mutexes in different sequences and enter a *deadly embrace* with each thread waiting for a mutex already locked by another thread. This can be avoided by defining a sequence for locking mutexes.

The other basic use of semaphores is to signal between threads. Typically, this requires a mutex for protection of variables to be used in the signal plus a semaphore acting as a blocking *condition*, which can be released when new values should be examined. Naturally, using conditions with mutexes provides additional opportunities for deadly embraces.

Threads gained practical significance as operating systems came to support interactive use. A program could be split into a user-interface thread and one or more other threads to do the actual work. Through the late 1970s a number of experimental operating systems were developed and one stream led to Richard Rashid's **MACH** about 1985. Initially, this was **Unix** compatible and large, but over some five years it became the streamlined MACH microkernel. Its basic characteristics were that it supported multiple operating systems, provided a large address space, supported transparent network access, included threads, and could run on multiple processors. It was made available on multiple architectures and was supported by **IBM**, **Digital Equipment Corporation**, **Sun Microsystems**, and **Hewlett-Packard** through the Open Software Foundation (OSF). This activity produced a library of routines called *C-threads*, which has been standardized by the **Institute of Electrical and Electronics Engineers** as part of the Portable Operating System Interface (POSIX) and adopted by most computer vendors as *P-threads*.

Threads are now used within operating systems to control slow devices and by multiprocessor network servers to maintain communication with multiple clients. Threads can be experienced directly with a **World Wide Web browser**, which will respond to button clicks and menu requests while a requested page is loading and while loading different information "simultaneously" into multiple windows. The Web-related language **Java** supports threads directly.

As improvements in processor technology approach physical limits, the only way to increase computer performance will be to use multiple processors running in a cooperative, shared environment inspired by threads.

FURTHER READING

Beveridge, Jim, and Robert Wiener. *Multithreading Applications in Win32: The Complete Guide to Threads.* Reading, Mass.: Addison-Wesley, 1997.

Butenhof, D. R. *Programming with POSIX Threads.* Reading, Mass.: Addison-Wesley, 1997.

Dijkstra, E. W. "Cooperating Sequential Processes." In F. Genuys, ed., *Programming Languages.* London and New York: Academic Press, 1968.

Institute of Electrical and Electronics Engineers. *IEEE ISO/IEC 9945-1:1996 (IEEE/ANSI Std 1003.1, 1996 Edition) Portable Operating System Interface (POSIX),* Part 1: *System Application: Program Interface (API).* New York: IEEE, 1996.

Lampson, Lichtenberger, and Pirtle. "A User Machine in a Time Sharing System." *Proceedings of the IEEE,* Vol. 54, No. 12, 1966, pp. 1766–1774.

Morrison, M., et al. *Java Unleashed.* Indianapolis, Ind: Sams.net, 1997.

Tanenbaum, Andrew S. *Modern Operating Systems.* Englewood Cliffs, N.J.: Prentice Hall, 1992.

—*John Deane*

3Com Corporation

The Santa Clara, California-based 3Com specializes in networking **interfaces**, **Internet** telephony, and wireless computing products. Founded by **Robert Metcalfe** (1946–) in 1979, 3Com has evolved into a Fortune 500 company with more than 11,000 employees and offices in almost 50 countries.

After completing his graduate work in computer science at Harvard in 1972, Metcalfe accepted a research job at the **Xerox Palo Alto Research Center** (Xerox PARC). His doctoral thesis was rejected by Harvard on the grounds it was "insufficiently theoretical," so Metcalfe worked on a revised thesis while at Xerox PARC. The result was **Ethernet**, a **packet-switching** technology for connecting **local area networks** (LANs) that was inspired by Metcalfe's previous experiences with the **ARPANET** and **AlohaNet**. But unlike those Internet prototypes, Metcalfe and colleague David Boggs (1950–) connected PARC's newly minted **Alto computers** to coaxial cable rather than telephone lines or radio.

Like much of the innovative work done at Xerox PARC in the 1970s, the potential of Ethernet went unexploited by Xerox. In 1977, Metcalfe received the patent for Ethernet, and on 4 June 1979, Metcalfe founded his own company—3Com (Computer Communication Compatibility). Over the next 11 years, 3Com grew from a one-man operation to a U.S.$400 million company. Ethernet became the industry standard for LANs, and 3Com expanded its business into network servers and related products.

In August 1990, Metcalfe lost a boardroom showdown and Eric Benhamou (1955–) was installed as chief executive officer, a job he continues to hold as of this writing. Under Benhamou the company has grown exponentially, abetted by key acquisitions such as the 1992 purchase of hub manufacturer BICC Data Networks, which opened 3Com's doors to the European market. In August of the following year, 3Com demonstrated the first 100 megabit per second (Mbps) *Fast Ethernet*, a tenfold increase in speed over the original, 10 Mbps Ethernet specification. By 1997, 3Com would be the leading provider of Fast Ethernet cards.

The acquisition of U.S. Robotics in 1997 brought 3Com into the **modem** and remote network access businesses, and perhaps most important, it brought the hand-held computing leader Palm, Inc. into the 3Com fold. Just two years later, the wildly successful Palm controlled about 68 percent of the hand-held computing device market. 3Com announced plans to spin off the company as an independent subsidiary. The PalmPilot had been 3Com's most successful product in some time, and now that Palm is an independent company, industry analysts have expressed concern about where 3Com will be headed in the future. The answer, according to 3Com, lies in high-speed network access (such as cable and digital subscribe line modems) and wireless networking of all shapes and sizes, LAN telephony, and Internet appliances.

In 1995 3Com branched out into a new area entirely—professional sports. 3Com is the official sponsor of 3Com Park, formerly known as Candlestick Park, the home of the San Francisco 49ers and Giants sports teams.

FURTHER READING

Hiltzik, Michael A. *Dealers of Lightning: Xerox PARC and the Dawn of the Computer Age*. New York: Harper Business, 1999.

Kirsner, Scott. "The Legend of Bob Metcalfe." *Wired*, 6.11, 1988.

Segaller, Stephen. *Nerds 2.0.1: A Brief History of the Internet*. New York: TV Books, 1998.

—*Hilary W. Poole*

Time-Sharing

Among the string of major advances in computing, time-sharing is among the most important. By parceling out use of a computer in small time quanta, time-sharing made computer power available to a large community of users.

The late 1940s saw the introduction of electronic computers such as the ISA and **EDSAC**, with internal control via **stored programs**. These computers were operated by programmers who sat at terminals setting switches and monitoring output. Users took turns having use of the entire computer. Much of the time a user would be thinking and the computer would be idle. The 1950s saw new programming languages developed that dramatically increased the use of computers—so much so that it was considered wasteful to allow one user full use of a machine. Users were required to submit their jobs on punched cards that could be batched together and fed first onto a tape and then to the computer, so that its use could be continuous. But the greater machine efficiency was achieved at the expense of human inefficiency and frustration. A user might have to wait hours or days to see an answer that it took the computer seconds or less to compute. This made computer use very difficult.

This unsatisfactory situation was addressed in 1959 by both Christopher Strachey (1916–75) and **John McCarthy** (1927–). At a UNESCO conference, Strachey called for a way to share a computer on a time basis. Batch jobs would still run but programmers could work on their programs and interact with the computer simultaneously. Separately, McCarthy proposed to the Massachusetts Institute of Technology (MIT) that it adopt a time-sharing operation mode for the transistorized computer it expected in 1960. He foresaw that such computer use would be the basis of a computer utility serving the entire community, with access on demand for whatever need a user might have.

McCarthy was the chair of the computer use subcommittee of the long-range computational needs committee discussing the future of computing at MIT. He was also part of a community, including **J. C. R. Licklider** (1915–90) and **Marvin Minsky** (1927–), trying to understand the potential of computer use. Licklider's insight was that computers and human beings could form a symbiosis whereby each would help the other to improve continually in what it does best. McCarthy saw time-sharing as the way to make computer use available to every member of society.

Fernando Corbató (1926–) in the MIT Computation Center took up the challenge to create on an existing computer a working prototype of the time-sharing system that McCarthy and Strachey were proposing. His aim was to modify the **hardware** and develop the **software** necessary so that many users could use a large computer simultaneously without interfering with each other. Such sharing could not be random. A supervisory program would be responsible for sharing the computer's time and services equitably among users, coordinating the operation of the various units of the computer and controlling access of users to the system. To achieve this supervisory function, some modification would be needed to the hardware of the IBM 709 **vacuum-tube** computer that was available to Corbató.

Together with Majorie Merwin-Daggett and Robert Daley, Corbató demonstrated a rudimentary working system with four teletypewriters in November 1961. Modifications continued with the transistorized computer using two large core memories when they became available. The supervisory program was put on one core memory. Users programs would be given space on the other so they could quickly be swapped in and out of use by the supervisor program. An interval timer served as an alarm clock. The supervisor program would interrupt a user's program when that user's quantum of time was finished. The state of the processor (i.e., the program line number and the contents of the registers) would be saved. In a way it was something like a snapshot. The next user's program would then be given full use of the processor for its quantum of time. Later, when it was the first user's turn again, the contents of the registers would be restored to that user's values and the program would pick up just where it left off. Users' programs were prevented from interfering with each other by reserving two registers to indicate memory ranges available to the current user. The supervisor program filtered each use to ensure that it remained within its proper range. All user input–output (I/O) requests went to the supervisor, which could interrupt the current user's program at the end of the current step to allow the computer to service the I/O request. A user could, however, press a "stop output" button if it seemed that the output requested was too much and therefore a disservice to other users.

The basic round-robin allocation of time gave each user an equal quantum in turn. Corbató's team wanted to facilitate and encourage interactive use of the computer, so Corbató devised a scheduling **algorithm** that gave small jobs priority over bigger jobs. In this way the delays experienced by interactive users were kept tolerably short and each had the illusion of being the sole user of a large computer. To make a smooth transition possible, and not force batch users to rewrite their programs, the system allowed interactive computing in the foreground, interspersed with batch jobs in the background. For this reason Corbató's system was called the Compatible Time Sharing System (CTSS). At the beginning of **Project MAC** in 1963, CTSS was adopted as the **operating system** upon which project MAC would be based. From then on, development of CTSS was a part of the project.

An important service provided by the CTSS supervisory program was a file system that allowed users to store and retrieve their own files and programs. No matter where in the system the supervisor physically stored their files, each user was given an apparent storage area called a *directory* for storage of user-named program and data files. Users could assign permission levels for others allowed access to files they had created. Files could be put in a public directory for access by other users. A library of subroutines and the available programming languages were in the public directory. For the system to be fully general, users were offered the use of as many programming languages as could be squeezed into the system.

Users of CTSS could give instructions to the system supervisor for scheduling. These were called *commands*. By 1966, more than 100 were available, of which more than half of these were created and contributed by users. Commands were six characters long but could be followed by parameters that allowed them to be customized for particular uses. Commands and programs could be scheduled by typing in their name and needed parameters. A program was created by which one user could create a file intended for another user. The second user was then alerted at log-on that a message was waiting. Another program in the public directory allowed two logged-on users to type to each other's terminals and "chat."

Students were encouraged to create programs for the system. Jerry Saltzer (1939–), a graduate student, created a document-formatting program. Combined with text editors that were available, users had the means to create and print out high-quality documents. The reference manual for CTSS was available as files in the public directory. Any user could refer to it when needed. Updates were entered in reverse chronological order so that a user could quickly see any updates. In these and other ways, an environment was created that made use of the system attractive and productive. To make it reliable and trustable, all data were copied to a tape twice a day. If there was any failure or loss, users knew they could get back most of their work from these tapes.

Project MAC began with a summer study in 1963. More than 100 researchers revolved through that study. Based on their use of the system, many were persuaded to add their research efforts to develop time-sharing. **Maurice Wilkes** (1913–) from England and Louis Pouzin from France, among others, spent time at MIT and took back with them enthusiasm for time-sharing. When Licklider became director of the Information Processing Techniques Office of the Advanced Research Projects Association (**ARPA**/IPTO), he viewed it as his mission to spread time-sharing as a means to interactive computing and human–computer symbiosis. In addition to CTSS, other time-sharing projects were started. Some, notably the Dartmouth Time Sharing System (DTSS) and the Johnniac Time Sharing System (JOSS) were designed to offer one programming language to all users.

Time-sharing enhanced interactivity and was a stimulus to the development of video display and graphical input devices. It was not long after time-sharing systems began to appear that it seemed obvious that the community of users and shared resources could be expanded if two or more such systems were networked together. The **ARPANET** packet-switched network experimentation was undertaken to interconnect time-sharing host computers.

After CTSS, Corbató and others attempted to design and build the prototype public computer utility that they were sure was on the horizon. They called it MULTICS. They wanted to design the hardware and software from the beginning with the goal of having all the features and robustness necessary to serve the entire society. The effort was a grand one. **Ken Thompson** (1943–) at **Bell Labs**, who had worked on MULTICS and valued the programming environment at which it aimed, started to build a time-sharing operating system with the opposite basic principle: His system, soon known as **Unix**, was based on putting the minimum necessary aspects for time-sharing structure in its kernel. Everything else a user needed could be built by the user and others on top of the kernel. Thompson and his coinventor **Dennis Ritchie** (1941–) created a compact kernel and coded it in a language that could be implemented on many platforms. Working at Bell Labs, their creation could not be commercialized. It spread rapidly around the world and further ensured the fulfillment of John McCarthy's prediction that all future computing would be on time-sharing computers.

Time-sharing succeeded in spreading computing power and interactivity between humans and computers just as it pioneers had foreseen. Even the personal computer revolution was fueled by the **BASIC** language, which was created for DTSS and modeled on the commands of CTSS. The multiaccess and multisharing nature of the **Internet** provides a means to spread the advantages of time-sharing. The challenge for Internet development is to bring these advantages to all Internet users.

Further Reading

Fano, R. M., and F. J. Corbató. "Time-sharing on Computers." In *Information* (A Scientific American Book). San Francisco: Freeman, 1966.

Hauben, Ronda. "Cybernetics, Time-sharing, Human-Computer Symbiosis and Online Communities." In Michael Hauben and Ronda Hauben, eds., *Netizens: On the History and Impact of Usenet and the Internet.* Los Alamitos, Calif.: IEEE Computer Society Press, 1997.

McCarthy, John. "Time-Sharing Computer Systems." In Martin Greenberger, ed., *Computers and the World of the Future,* (originally published as *Management and the Computer of the Future*). Cambridge, Mass.: MIT Press, 1986.

"Time-Sharing and Interactive Computing At MIT, Part I: CTSS." *IEEE Annals of the History of Computing,* Vol. 14, No. 1, 1992, pp. 10–54.

Wilkes, Maurice V. *Time-Sharing Computer System.* New York: Elsevier Science, 1975.

—*Jay Robert Hauben*

Token Ring

A token ring is a type of **local area network** (LAN) in which all computers are connected in ring or star **topology**. Token ring is the second most popular LAN technology after **Ethernet**. A *token-passing scheme* is used to prevent the collision of data between two computers that want to send information at the same time.

In a token ring network, packets containing no information (empty frames) are continuously circulating on the ring. When a computer wants to send some information, it inserts a token (this may mean just switching a single bit from 0 to 1) into an empty frame and inserts the data and a destination identifier into the frame. Each frame is examined by each successive computer. If a computer recognizes that it is the destination for the data, it copies the data from the frame and removes the token. When the frame gets back to the source computer, it sees that the token has been removed and knows that the data have been received. It removes the data and the destination identifier from the frame. Now the frame continues to circulate as an empty frame, ready to be taken by any computer in the ring when it has data to send.

One advantage of token-passing networks over other technologies, such as Ethernet, is that they are deterministic, meaning that it is possible to calculate the maximum and minimum amount of time it will take before any end computer will be able to transmit. This, as well as other reliability-increasing features such as fault managment mechanisms, makes token ring networks a good choice for real-time applications such as factory automation.

Token ring was developed around 1980 at an **IBM** research facility in Zurich, Switzerland. There is also an **Institute of Electrical and Electronics Engineers** (IEEE) specification (IEEE 802.5) that is very similar to and completely compatible with IBM's token ring network. One difference is that IBM token ring networks are specified using a star topology: All end computers are attached to a device called a *media access unit* (MAU). The IEEE 802.5 standard does not depend on a particular network topology. The term *token ring* is generally used to refer to both IBM's token ring network and IEEE 802.5 networks.

IBM introduced the first token ring product, a network adapter for the IBM **personal computer** (PC), in October 1985. The first token ring adapters operated at 4 megabits per second (Mbps); the speed of token ring networks was improved in 1989 when IBM introduced the first 16 Mbps token ring hardware. After this the 802.5 standard was also extended to support operation at the new speed. In 1994, the leading token ring vendor companies formed the Alliance for Strategic Token Ring Advancement and Leadership (ASTRAL) to promote token ring technology in the face of increasing popularity of (and competition from) the Ethernet standard.

In 1997 the draft for the IEEE 802.5r standard became available which defined the dedicated token-ring (DTR) operation. This doubled the transfer rate by allowing full duplex transmissions (this means that each computer is able to transmit and receive separate data streams concurently).

In the same year the High Speed Token Ring Alliance (HSTRA) was formed "to rapidly develop the technologies, standards and products necessary to deliver 100 Mbit/s token ring to the still very sizeable token ring customer base." One year later the draft IEEE 802.5t standard became available defining a 100 Mbps operation speed for token ring. The first 100 Mbps token ring adapters were introduced in the same year.

IEEE 802.5v, which standardizes the gigabit token ring, is currently under development.

FURTHER READING

Bird, David. *Token Ring Network Design.* Wokingham, Berkshire, England, and Reading, Mass.: Addison-Wesley, 1994.

Carlo, James T., et al. *Understanding Token Ring Protocols and Standards.* Boston: Artech House, 1998.

Dell'Acqua, Alexa A., and John F. Mazzaferro. *IBM's Token-Ring Network.* Charleston, S.C.: Computer Technology Research Corporation, 1992.

Held, Gilbert. *Token-Ring Networks: Operation, Construction, and Management.* Chichester, West Sussex, England, and New York: Wiley, 1994.

—*Gerald Friedland*

Topology, Network

When computers are interconnected in a **network**, there are different ways of setting up the communication paths between them. The specific arrangement of the computers in relation to the communication medium is the network topology, the shape of the network at hand.

The purpose of computer networks is to allow sharing of information across different machines. Two main issues are the type of communication protocol and the layout of the communication lines between the machines in the network. For example, point-to-point communication between all computers is possible if each machine has a private line to any other. This is too expensive, and therefore a cheaper alternative is *broadcasting networks*, in which any message from a computer can be received by any other. **AlohaNet**, one of the first packet networks, used a radio link with the same frequency for all computers connected. This is a classic example of a broadcasting topology. The principal commercial network topologies are bus, ring, star, and general graph arrangements.

In a *bus topology*, all computers are connected to a single cable that is used for all the data traffic between the machines. The arrangement is similar to that of the AlohaNet, but using an electrical medium. To avoid transmission collisions, the use of the bus has to be managed in some way. This can be done by assigning time slots to the computers, which can only transmit in round-robin fashion. The first computer can transmit in the first time slot, the second in the second time slot, and so on. Of course, the time slots are short enough to avoid long delays when a machine wants to transmit. Although this scheme is very simple, it is also very inefficient, because a machine with much data to be transmitted is allocated only a small portion of the total bandwidth, even if the other machines are idle.

A usual alternative to time slots is to use collision detection in bus networks. Since all machines tap the transmission line, before attempting to send a message, each of them first "hears" if the bus is available. If not, it waits. When the bus becomes available, the transmission is started. It is possible that two machines start transmitting almost at the same time, and a collision occurs. In that case, both machines detect that the data on the bus is being scrambled, stop transmitting, and back off for a short, random amount of time. After waiting, they try to transmit again. The idea of the random waiting time is to avoid consecutive collisions that would block the bus.

Ethernet is a bus network invented in the early 1970s by **Robert Metcalfe** (1946–) and David Boggs (1950–). Ethernet uses CSMA/CD (carrier-sense multiple access with collision detection), a transmission protocol roughly similar to the technique described above. Ethernet also uses *exponential back-off*, which means that after consecutive collisions the interval of time from which the random waiting time is chosen is doubled. In this way, if many computers collide in the bus, the period doubling takes them apart and allows orderly access of the bus.

Ethernet networks have been successful because the bus topology is very simple and it can be used with inexpensive cabling, such as **twisted-pair cable** telephone lines. Ethernet also runs on a number of different media such as coaxial cable and optical lines. Ethernet cards have steadily been improved, going from transmission speeds of 10 megabits per second (Mbps) to the current gigabit speeds.

In a *ring topology*, all computers are connected to a common bus, which is then closed to form a loop. **Token ring** networks work using this arrangement. Collisions are avoided by using a different approach as in Ethernet networks. In a token ring, a special packet, the *token*, is always circulating in the network. Each computer receives and passes it along the ring. If a computer wants to transmit, it absorbs the token, starts transmitting packets, and releases the token when it is done. The token-holding time is limited, so that every computer in the ring has a chance to send information.

Although collisions are avoided with this approach, *starvation* can happen if the token is absorbed by a machine that does not release it again because of failure. In this case, after waiting for some period of time, a machine generates a new token randomly and sends it to the other computers. The token ring protocol then makes sure that not more than one token has been generated. When two or more tokens are in the ring, the extra tokens are absorbed and transmission resumes in the normal way.

Another problem that can affect a token ring is the failure of one segment of the communication ring. If this happens, the ring is broken and the token cannot circulate. To provide fault tolerance, a token ring can be built as a double ring. If one segment in one ring fails, the second ring is used in a special way. One notable example of a token ring network with high transmission speed is the FDDI (**fiber distributed data interface**) standard, which is used over optical data lines providing 100 Mbps speed. FDDI networks are typically used as backbones for wide-area networks. Token ring network research was pursued primarily by **IBM**, who published a specification in 1981.

A *token bus network* is a type of hybrid between a bus network and a token ring. The computers communicate through a bus, but use a token, such as in a token ring, to avoid contention for the bus. Token bus networks are covered by the IEEE 802.4 standard.

A *star topology* is used when a central machine or hub is connected through private lines to many other machines. This is the typical topology of mainframes and their terminals. The **mainframe** is the center of the star and the terminals are situated at the tips of the rays. The main advantage of a star topology is that every computer or terminal can use the full speed of the communication channel.

Star networks have made a comeback in the realm of **local area networks**. A hub is placed at the center of the star and receives the data from many computers. Each computer has a private line of, for example, 10 Mbps to the hub. The hub can route messages from one computer to the other and can also connect the star to a very fast communication channel, with a speed of, for example, 1000 Mbps. In this way, each workstation needs only cheap twisted-pair cabling, while the communication out of the star is made using a more powerful network (e.g., gigabit Ethernet running over optical links). This would be an example of a hybrid topology, in which different segments of the network use different standards and transmission speeds as well as topology.

The most all-purpose type of network topology is a *general graph*, in which any node can be connected to any other node using private lines. This is the architecture of the **Internet**, in which local area networks are connected together in a general graph without any special structure. When a packet is to be sent over the network, it has to be routed by the computers at the nodes, which collaborate at this task. One approach that can be used to route packets over general graphs is to superimpose a *virtual topology* on the real network. A protocol is started at the nodes, and through the exchange of some messages, a *spanning tree* is found. This is a structure in which one node (the root) communicates with some children nodes, which in turn have other children nodes, and so on. In a tree, there is only one communication path from each node to any other (the packet from one node goes up to a common parent and then down to the destination node). The tree is spanning, because it covers all nodes in the network. Using this approach, once the spanning tree has been built, it is very easy to route messages. If one communication link fails, the spanning tree has to be rebuilt.

In the case of clusters of processors used for parallel computing, there are many other types of network topologies such as *mesh*, *torus*, and **hypercube**. Computers connected in a mesh are arranged in a quadratic grid, with the machines sitting at the crossings of the communication lines. If the upper and lower boundary, as well as the left and right boundary, are glued together, we obtain a torus, a doughnut-shaped structure. In a hypercube, the computers sit at the corners of three-dimensional cubes and the edges are the communication lines. Cubes in higher dimensions (hypercubes) provide more communication paths and place for more machines.

FURTHER READING

Metcalfe, Robert, and David Boggs. "Ethernet: Distributed Packet Switching for Local Computer Networks." *Communications of the ACM*, Vol. 19, 1976, pp. 395–404.

Sharma, Roshan Lal. *Network Topology Optimization: The Art and Science of Network Design*. New York: Van Nostrand Reinhold, 1990.

Stallings, William. *Data and Computer Communications*. New York: Macmillan; London: Collier Macmillan, 1985; 6th ed., Upper Saddle River, N.J.: Prentice Hall, 2000.

Tannenbaum, Andrew. *Computer Networks*. Englewood Cliffs, N.J.: Prentice-Hall, 1981; 2nd ed., Upper Saddle River, N.J., 1996.

—*Raúl Rojas*

Torres Quevedo, Leonardo

1852–1936

Spanish Engineer

Leonardo Torres Quevedo is the most renowned Spanish engineer of the twentieth century. He made important contributions to **cybernetics** and to the emerging field of computing; he is especially remembered for his **analog computers** and for his written description of a plausible **digital computer**.

Torres Quevedo published his first scientific paper in 1891 and began a 30-year period of intense activity in which he worked on many different projects. He conceived a new type of Zeppelin and, in 1905, built the first Spanish prototype. He experimented with radio control of boats and machines, a technique he called *Telekino*. Torres Quevedo also built several analog computing devices. One of them was his *algebraic machine*, an analog device that could find the roots, real or complex, of algebraic equations of up to eight terms. Moving parts were used to represent numbers in scales that could be linear or logarithmic.

The automatic chess player built by Torres Quevedo in 1912 aroused great interest across Europe. It could play an endgame scenario against a human opponent: The **automaton** played with the black king and rook, the human with a white king. The chess player used a mechanical arm to move the chess pieces and sensors in the board to identify their positions.

Perhaps Torres Quevedo's greatest invention was one he left unfinished. In his 1913 memoir *Ensayos sobre Automática* (Essays on Automatics), he described a digital computer that would be capable of storing decimal numbers and performing binary operations. The machine would be controlled by a program, which could include conditional branches, that would be stored in a drum. The memoir also contains the first published description of **floating-point** arithmetic. Torres Quevedo did not build this machine, but his *electromechanical arithmometer*, exhibited in Paris in 1920, could perform the basic arithmetic operations on numbers typed at a **keyboard**, and print the result. The electromechanical components were similar to those described in the memoir and were many years ahead of their time.

BIOGRAPHY

Leonardo Torres Quevedo. Born 28 December 1852 in Santa Cruz de Iguña, Spain. Degree in civil engineering, 1876. Published his first scientific paper, 1891. Appointed as head of the Laboratory of Applied Mechanics, Madrid, 1901. Medal of the Spanish Science Academy, 1916. Exhibited his electromechanical arithmometer in Paris, 1920. Elected member of the French Academy of Sciences, 1927. President of the Spanish Academy of Sciences, 1928. Died 18 December 1936 during the Spanish Civil War.

SELECTED WRITINGS

Torres Quevedo, L. "Electromechanical Calculating Machine." In Brian Randell, ed., *Origins of Digital Computers: Selected Papers*, 3rd ed. Berlin: Springer-Verlag, 1982.

———. "Essays on Automatics—Its Definition—Theoretical Extent of Its Applications." In Brian Randell, ed., *Origins of Digital Computers: Selected Papers*, 3rd ed. Berlin: Springer-Verlag, 1982.

FURTHER READING

Chase, George C. "History of Mechanical Computing Machinery." *Annals of the History of Computing*, Vol. 2, No. 3, 1980, pp. 198–226.

"Leonardo Torres y Quevedo." In J. A. N. Lee, ed., *International Biographical Dictionary of Computer Pioneers*. Chicago and London: Fitzroy Dearborn, 1995, pp. 663–666.

Randell, Brian. "From Analytical Engine to Electronic Digital Computer: The Contributions of Ludgate, Torres and Bush." *Annals of the History of Computing*, Vol. 4, No. 4, 1982, pp. 327–341.

Rodriguez, Alcalde, L. *Torres Quevedo y la Cibernetica*. Madrid: Ediciónes Cid, 1966.

———. *Biografia de D. Leonardo Torres Quevedo*. Madrid: Institución Cultural de Cantabria, Consejo Superior de Investigaciónes Científicas, Diputación Provincial de Santander, 1974.

—*Raúl Rojas*

Torvalds, Linus

1969–

Finnish–U.S. Software Developer

Linus Torvalds is best known as the creator of the **Linux** operating system **software** and a major figure in the **open source** software movement. Born in Helsinki, Finland, Torvalds cites his country's public education as a major factor in his decision to create high quality freely distributed software.

Linus Torvalds's story began in 1991 when he was a computer science student at the University of Helsinki. Many of the programming assignments for his university classes required using the **Unix** operating system. Frustrated with having to rely on university computing facilities, he investigated the possibility of running Unix on his home computer. Cost made this prohibitive, with Unix software selling for U.S.$5000 and the workstation needed to run it selling for almost U.S.$10,000. Torvalds saw this as a challenge and set about to create a Unix clone that would run on his desktop computer.

Early in 1991, Torvalds created an operating system kernel he called Freax, short for "free Unix," that worked on desktop **personal computers**. He decided to post his creation on the **World Wide Web** and make it freely available to other users wishing to experiment with Unix. The Web site's **FTP** manager didn't like the name *Freax* because it reminded him of "freaks," which is sometimes a synonym for "computer hacker." He named the FTP site Linux, which was the label Torvalds had used during development. In October 1991, Torvalds released Linux .02, the first functional

Linus Torvalds at the Comdex Computer Conference in Las Vegas, Nevada, 15 November 1999. (©Reuters Newmedia Inc./CORBIS)

version of the operating system. At the same time, he patented Linux under the **Free Software Foundation**'s General Public License, which prevents distribution that does not include the source code.

Shortly after his initial posting, Torvalds received five e-mails from other people using his software. Soon the number swelled past 100. Many university users, with the same problems that prompted Torvalds' development, started using it enthusiastically. Word of its potential quickly spread across the **Internet**. What happened next was completely unexpected by Torvalds: Programmers from all over the world began collaborating and adding features to the system. Universities adopted Linux in their programming courses. Businesses began using Linux as a server. All the while, Torvalds remained close to the software and acted as a moderator, deciding which portions of code needed to be added to new releases.

By the mid-1990s, Torvalds had become a cult figure in computing circles. He was in high demand as a speaker at computing conferences and had been offered large amounts of money to commercialize his product. Fundamentally opposed to profiting personally from Linux software, Torvalds instead opted to move to Santa Clara California in 1997 and take a job as a software engineer with Transmeta, a **Silicon Valley** company focusing on mobile Internet computing.

Biography

Linus Benedict Torvalds. Born 28 December 1969, in Helsinki, Finland. M.S in computer science from the University of Helsinki. Developed Linux Software and released source code to public domain, October 1991. Software engineer, Transmeta, 1997. Continues to maintain and release new versions of Linux; speaks at numerous computer conferences.

Selected Writings

Sobell, Mark G. *A Practical Guide to Linux.* Foreword by Linus Torvalds. Reading, Mass.: Addison-Wesley, 1997.

Further Reading

Diana, Alison Calderbank. "Linus Torvalds." *Computer Reseller News*, No. 815, 9 Nov. 1998, p. 129.

Dibona, Chris, Mark Stone, and Sam Ockman, eds. *Open Sources: Voices from the Open Source Revolution.* Beijing, and Sebastopol, Calif.: O'Reilly, 1999.

Glascock, Stuart. "Faithful Converge to See Linux Creator Linus Torvalds." *Computer Reseller News*, No. 792, 8 June 1998, p. 26.

Moody, Glyn. "The Greatest OS That (N)ever Was." *Wired*, 5.08, Aug. 1997. *http://www.wired.com/wired/archive//5.08/linux_pr.html*

Scoville, Thomas. "Martin Luther, Meet Linus Torvalds." *Salon*, 12 Nov. 1998. *http://www.salonmagazine.com/21st/feature/1998/11/12feature.html*

Wayner, Peter. *Free For All: How Linux and the Free Software Movement Undercut the High-Tech Titans.* New York: Harper Business, 2000.

—Roger McHaney

Toshiba Corporation

The Tokyo-based Toshiba Corporation has a long history as one of Japan's premier electronics firms. Its primary focus is on the design and production of information technology support components such as semiconductors, liquid-crystal devices, high-definition displays, and optical disk drives. Toshiba ended fiscal year 1999 (31 March 2000) with consolidated sales of over U.S.$54 billion, making it the world's eighth-largest integrated manufacturer of electric and electronic equipment.

Toshiba's history can be traced along two branches. The first was originated in 1875 by Hisashige Tanaka (1799–1881), a well-respected inventor of various mechanical dolls and the perpetual clock. His company, Tanaka Seizo-sho (Tanaka Engineering Works), was Japan's first manufacturer of telegraphic equipment. Renamed Shibaura Seisaku-sho (Shibaura Engineering Works), this company became one of Japan's largest manufacturers of electrical power system components. The second branch originated in 1890, when Ichisuke Fujioka and Shoichi Miyoshi established Hakunetsu-sha & Co., Ltd., Japan's first plant for electric incandescent lamps. Hakunetsu-sha moved into the consumer product arena and in 1899 was renamed Tokyo Denki (Tokyo Electric Co.).

In 1939, Shibaura Seisaku-sho and Tokyo Denki merged to form an integrated electric equipment manufacturer, Tokyo Shibaura Denki (Tokyo Shibaura Electric Co., Ltd.). In 1954, the company produced TAC, Japan's first digital computer for the University of Tokyo, marking its serious entry into the computing marketplace. Along the way the company acquired the nickname Toshiba. The name stuck, and in 1978, Tokyo Shibaura Denki officially renamed itself Toshiba.

Important advances contributed by Toshiba include the first Japanese word processor (1978), 4- and 16-megabit dynamic **RAM** (1986–88), the world's first **laptop** computer (1986), 4- and 16-megabit NAND-type electrically erasable programmable **ROM** (1991–92), and the high-density optical disk (DVD) (1995). In 1997, Toshiba was the world's leading producer of laptops. In April 1999, it decentralized management of its major businesses and introduced eight in-house companies. Each has the authority and autonomy to operate independently within its area of specialty. Top management of the Toshiba Group focuses on developing strategy for Toshiba as a whole and on the supervision of financial performance.

FURTHER READING

Guth, Rob. "Toshiba Corp.: From Toasters to DRAMs, This Global System Fits All." *ComputerWorld*, 10 Mar. 1997.

"Toshiba Moving Full-Steam Ahead." *Computer Reseller News*, Vol. 852, 26 July 1999, p. 7, 14.

—*Roger McHaney*

Transistor

A transistor is a miniature electronic component manufactured from semiconducting material that can be used to amplify (increase the strength of) an electric current or switch it on and off. Although transistors are packaged as single components, they are now perhaps more familiar in the form of **integrated circuits**, single-chip packages containing millions of transistors and associated components. In this form, transistors make up larger devices such as memory chips and **microprocessors**.

The transistor was invented at **Bell Labs** in 1947 by **John Bardeen** (1908–91) and **Walter Brattain** (1902–87), who developed a somewhat cumbersome, hand-wired device known as a *point-contact transistor*. Their colleague **William Shockley** (1910–89) subsequently devised the much improved junction transistor, which was more compact and easier to manufacture. Transistors were packaged as integrated circuits from 1958 onward through the work of **Jack Kilby** (1923–) of **Texas Instruments** and **Robert Noyce** (1927–90) of **Fairchild Semiconductor**.

Transistors replaced **vacuum tubes**, which were bulky, unreliable, and wasted a great deal of power through heat. Transistors did not fundamentally change the **architecture** of computers; they worked as switches just as vacuum tubes had done. But they did make computers cheaper, more reliable, and more compact, and therefore more affordable and more powerful, and it was this that proved the key to the microelectronic and computer revolutions.

There are numerous different kinds of transistors, but they all work in broadly the same way. Semiconducting materials such as **silicon** or germanium, which are normally very poor conductors of electricity, are *doped* (have small amounts of impurities introduced into them) to improve their electrical conductivity. Different impurities cause a semiconductor to have either a majority of negative electrical charge carriers (electrons), in which case the semiconductor is called *n-type*, or a majority of positive charge carriers ("holes" or spaces where electrons should be), in which case the semiconductor is called *p-type*. Joining n and p-type semiconductors so they are fractions of a millimeter apart produces a transistor, a device in which a small electrical current can be used to switch on or off a much larger electrical current. In the words of the Bell Labs' press spokesman on the day the device was announced to the public in 1948: "We have called it the transistor because it is a resistor or semiconductor device which can amplify electrical signals as they are transferred through it." *Transistor* was thus short for *transfer resistor*.

A simple junction transistor consists of a thin region of p-type semiconductor (called the *base*) sandwiched between two regions of n-type semiconductor (called the *emitter* and the *collector*); this is known as an *npn junction transistor*. (An alternative arrangement sandwiches an n-type region between two p-type regions and is known as a *pnp junction transistor*.) When no voltage is applied to the base, the lack of free electrons in the p-type region between the emitter and the collector means there is a high resistance between them, so no current can flow. But if a small voltage is applied to the base, electrons flow into it from the emitter, helping other electrons to flow from the emitter to the collector. In practice, an input voltage is connected between the base and the emitter and the output voltage is collected between the collector and the emitter. No input voltage produces no output voltage; small changes in the input voltage produce much larger changes in the output voltage. This explains how a transistor acts as either a switch or an amplifier. Because both electrons and holes (charges with two different poles) are involved in the operation of a junction transistor, the device is often called a *bipolar transistor*.

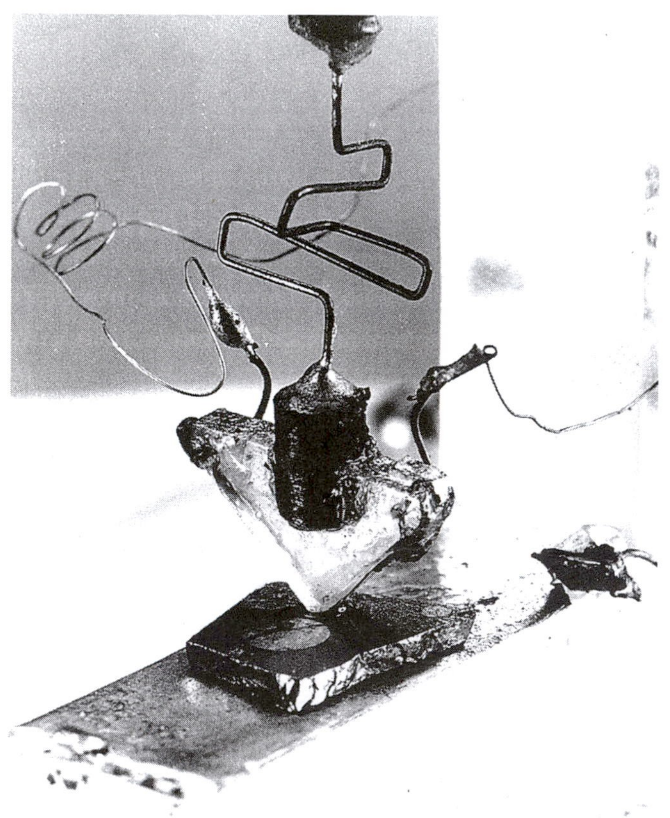

Point-contact transistor, 1947. (Courtesy of the Computer Museum History Center)

A different kind of transistor, the *field-effect transistor* (FET), controls the flow of current between a terminal called the *source* (analogous to the emitter) and another terminal called the *drain* (analogous to the collector) using a third terminal called the *gate* (analogous to the base) that sits between the source and the drain. An n-type FET is similar to an npn junction transistor. Normally, electrons trying to flow from the source to the drain cannot pass through the p-type region between them. No current flows and the FET is effectively off. However, applying a small positive voltage to the gate produces a positive electrical field that helps electrons flow in a thin channel from the source to the drain, turning the FET on. Because only one type of charge carrier is involved in the operation of the device, a FET is a *unipolar transistor*. Unlike an ordinary junction transistor, a FET is made by forming two n-type regions on a p-type layer called the *substrate* or two p-type regions on an n-type substrate. FETs are usually produced by fabricating a metal electrode (the gate) onto a layer of semiconductor (the n and p-type material), with a layer of insulating silicon dioxide (called the *oxide*) between them. This technique produces a *metal-oxide semiconductor* (**MOS**), after the names for the three layers, and transistors produced this way are referred to as MOSFETs.

Large arrays of transistors make up two of the essential components of a computer: logic gates and memory. **Logic gates** use **Boolean algebra** to compare electrical signals and make simple decisions. A single, simple logic gate can be built from a few discrete (individually packaged) transistors, resistors, and diodes, but multiple logic gates are also packaged into single-chip integrated circuits. The two most popular types of packages are the complementary metal-oxide semiconductor (**CMOS**) and transistor–transistor logic (TTL).

Logic gates can be combined to make devices that add or compare binary numbers, but they can also be used to store information. Normally, a transistor is a transient device: It switches on only when an input signal is present and reverts back to its original state when that input is removed. But if the output from a transistor is fed back into its own input using a logic gate, the transistor maintains itself in either an on or an off state. Successive inputs toggle it between the on and off states and the transistor stays in that state until the next input arrives. In other words, this type of circuit (called a **flip-flop**) is a simple memory device.

A type of memory known as *static random access memory* (SRAM) stores individual bits (binary digits) of information using a transistor flip-flop of this kind. *Dynamic random access memory* (DRAM), used in **personal computers** and workstations, stores each bit using a combination of one transistor and one capacitor (a device that stores electrical charge). Flip-flops also make up the basic architectural components of microprocessors. The registers, program counter, and arithmetic/logic unit (ALU) in a microprocessor are all based on components made from flip-flops. Computers may seem enormously complex, but in reality they are little more than vast and intricately interconnected arrays of flip-flop transistors acting as logic gates and memory.

Different types of transistors are suited to different applications. Because MOSFETs can be packed more densely, manufactured more reliably, and use much less power than junction transistors, they have long been favored in computer chips. Various semiconductor materials also have advantages and disadvantages. Bardeen, Brattain, and Shockley's early transistors were made using germanium. Silicon could operate at higher temperatures, was more stable, and used less power and soon became the semiconductor of choice, but germanium is still widely used for high-frequency applications (such as wireless communication). In the early 1990s, researchers at **IBM** perfected a technique of combining silicon and germanium to make low-power, high-speed transistors that switched many times faster than traditional circuits. Combined silicon and carbon (silicon carbide) devices are expected to offer better performance under extreme conditions, such as high temperature and high radiation or while operating at high power. They have attracted a great deal of attention for possible use in space. Transistors made using organic materials (plastics) have attracted interest for use in such devices as cheap, lightweight smart cards.

Scientists have long believed that physical limitations inherent in the manufacture of semiconductor devices will one day defeat the axiom of ever-increasing chip capacity known as **Moore's law**. Bardeen and Brattain's 1947 transistor was just a few millimeters (thousandths of an inch) across. Today, transistors in microprocessors are typically only 180 nanometers (180 billionths of a meter) across. In November 1999, researchers at Bell Laboratories announced a new type of "vertical" MOSFET that could be manufactured as small as 50 nanometers, 2000 times smaller than a human hair. Unlike in a conventional MOSFET, where the source, drain, and gate are arranged side by side, the components in this *vertical replacement-gate* (VRG) *MOSFET* are stacked on top of one another—in a kind of semiconducting skyscraper—to save space. The new device also features a gate on either side, which means that it can switch twice as quickly as a conventional transistor. An even smaller device called a *single-electron transistor* (SET) relies on single electrons "tunneling" through it to switch it on or off and may be produced in sizes as small as 10 nanometers. Devices such as this may enable chips to meet the predictions of Moore's law for some years to come.

FURTHER READING

Brattain, Walter H., and F. A. D'Altroy. "Transistor." In *Collier's Encyclopedia*, Vol. 22. New York: Macmillan, 1992.

Guo, Lingjie, Effendi Leobandung, and Stephen Y. Chou. "A Silicon Single-Electron Transistor Memory Operating at Room Temperature." *Science*, Vol. 275, No. 5300, 31 Jan. 1997, p. 649.

Hergenrother, J. M., D. Monroe, F. P. Klemens, et al. *The Vertical Replacement-Gate (VRG) MOSFET: A 50-nm Vertical MOSFET with Lithography-Independent Gate Length.* Bell Laboratories research report. Murray Hill, N.J.: Bell Laboratories, 1999.

Kastner, Marc A. "The Single-Electron Transistor." *Review of Modern Physics*, Vol. 64, 1992, p. 849.

Meyerson, Bernard S. "High Speed Silicon-Germanium Electronics." *Scientific American*, Mar. 1994, p. 62.

Riordan, Michael, and Lillian Hoddeson. *Crystal Fire: The Invention of the Transistor and the Birth of the Information Age.* New York: Norton, 1997.

Schrope, Mark. "The Dope on Silicon." *New Scientist*, 11 Sept. 1990, p. 42.

Service, Robert. "Plastic Transistors Gain Speed on Silicon." *Science*, Vol. 273, No. 5277, 16 Aug. 1996, p. 879.

Stix, Gary. "Material Advantage: IBM Pushes Silicon-Germanium Chips into the Marketplace." *Scientific American*, Jan. 1994, 129.

"The Middle Age of the Transistor." *The Economist*, 3 Jan. 1998, p. 77.

"The Solid-State Century." *Scientific American Online*, Special Issue, Oct. 1997.

—*Chris Woodford*

Transputer

The transputer is a **microprocessor** developed by Inmos Corporation (later acquired by SGS-Thomson and renamed STMicroelectronics). It was the first microprocessor designed specifically for **parallel processing**.

The main differences between transputers and conventional microprocessors are **hardware** support for context switching among processes in a single transputer processor, stack-based general-purpose **registers**, and point-to-point communication links to connect two transputers. The transputer is based around a RISC core with a very small instruction set. The word *transputer* is derived from "transistor and computer," not because it is made of transistors, but because it is a computer that can be used as a component for building larger systems, in the same way that transistors can.

Unlike traditional microprocessors, the transputer has support for **multitasking** via an on-chip scheduler; the scheduler supports any number of processes running concurrently, sharing the processor time. Transputers support two levels of priorities, high and low. Low-priority processes are executed whenever there are no active high-priority processes. The stack pointer (Wptr) of each process is kept in one of two queues in memory, depending on the process's priority. High-priority processes are assumed to be executed for a short period of time. If one or more high-priority processes are able to proceed, then one is selected from the high-priority process queue and runs until it has completed or waits for I/O (input/output). If no high-priority process is able to proceed, one or more low-priority processes is selected from the low-priority queue for execution. The process selection criterion for both queues is based on a simple round-robin **algorithm** of all active processes in the queue.

The communication links are the most important feature of the transputer. Every member of the transputer family has one or more communication links, each of which can be connected to a link of some other transputer. This allows transputer networks of arbitrary size and topology to be constructed. The links operate concurrently with the transputer processor, transferring data directly from the one transputer to another.

Transputer systems can be programmed in a wide range of programming languages, but the preferred language is Occam. Introduced by Inmos in 1984, Occam is considered the assembly programming language of the transputer. Every transputer implements the Occam concepts of concurrency and process communication. The concurrent processing and message-passing concepts of Occam are based on **C. Antony R. Hoare**'s communicating sequential processes (CSP) model. The transputer and Occam were designed together—in fact, the transputer contains several instructions and hardware support to provide maximum performance and optimal implementation of Occam.

Since 1984, several generations of transputer processors were introduced. The transputer processor family consists of the special-purpose M212, the 16-bit T212, T222 and T225, and the 32-bit T400, T414, T425, T800, T801, T805, and T900.

The T2 and T4 family of transputer supported either 2 kilobytes (KB) (T212, T222, T414) or 4 kB (T225, T400, T425) of fast on-chip memory. Other than the low-cost T400, which supported only two com-

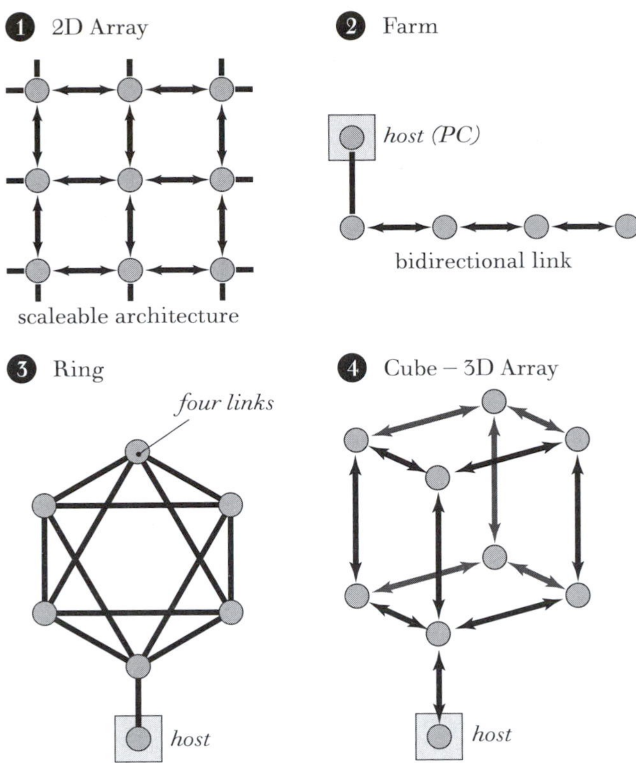

Figure 1. *Types of transputer networks.*

munication links, all T2- and T4-based transputers contained four standard Inmos communication links.

The 16-bit M212 transputer was a disk processor. It contained 1kB of on-chip memory, two communication links, and disk interface hardware to provide support for a floppy disk or Winchester disk interface. It also included 4kB of preprogrammed **ROM**, which contained a set of procedures to perform some basic disk accessing.

The ubiquitous 32-bit T8 family of microprocessors were the first transputers to contain a **floating-point** processor. Providing the computing power equivalent to a DEC VAX 8600 or a 20 megahertz (MHz) **Intel** 386 processor with a math co-processor, the T8-based transputers were extremely fast for its time. With 4kB of fast on-chip memory, four communication links, and a 64-bit floating-point unit that could operate concurrently with the main processor, this class of transputers was used in many CPU intensive tasks such as image and signal processing, weather forecasting, and system simulations.

Introduced in 1991, the 32-bit T9000 transputer was a pipelined superscalar architecture, which allowed multiple instructions to be executed every processor cycle. It had 16 kB cache, which could be programmed as 16 kB on-chip memory or 8 kB of on-chip memory and 8 kB of cache. Four communication links were provided which supported virtual channels in hardware and dynamic message switching. Virtual channels and dynamic message switching provided the ability to route messages between nonneighboring transputers faster. It provided the required abstraction level for programmers so that software-based **routers** were not necessary.

On 31 December 1999, STMicroelectronics halted the production on all transputer microprocessors and its related components, thus ending a 15-year legacy. However, the technology introduced by the transputer has survived in several conventional microprocessors, such as Analog-Devices SHARC processors, which contains six communication links. Currently, *Beowulf clusters* and *networks of workstations* (NOW) are used as virtual transputer systems to solve many computationally intensive applications. The high-speed communication

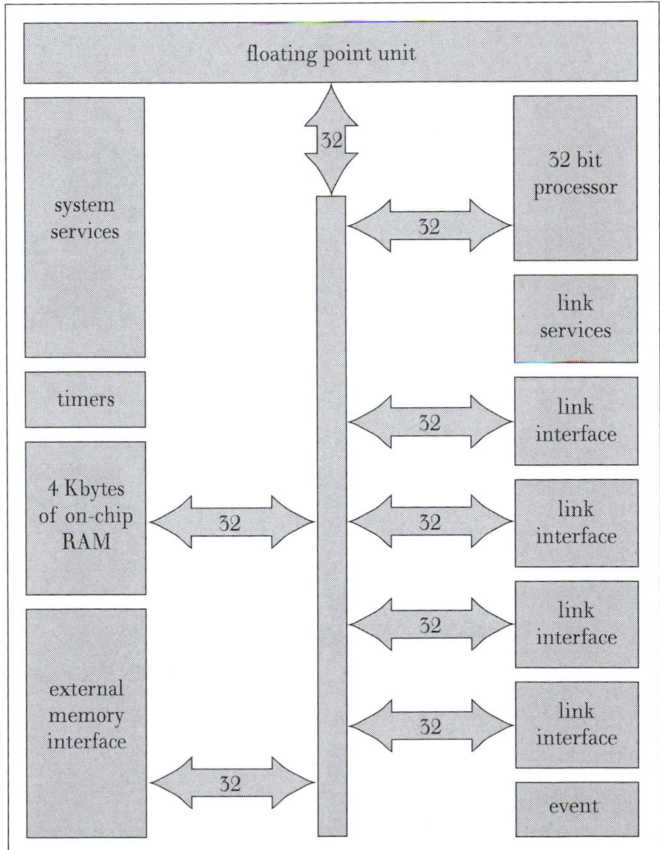

Figure 2. *The T805 transputer.*

links that were introduced in the T9000 transputer are now an IEEE standard (IEEE-1355). With the ease of building massively parallel supercomputers, the transputers will always be regarded as the LEGO block of parallel processing in microprocessor history.

FURTHER READING

Cok, Ronald S. *Parallel Programs for the Transputer.* Englewood Cliffs, N.J.: Prentice Hall, 1991.

Inmos Limited. *Communicating Process Architecture.* New York: Prentice Hall, 1988.

———. *Transputer Reference Manual.* New York: Prentice Hall, 1988.

Meenakshisundaram, Ramachandran. *The Unofficial Transputer Homepage.* *http://members.xoom.com/transputer*

Perihelion Software Ltd. *The Helios Parallel Operating System.* New York: Prentice Hall, 1991.

Roberts, John. *Transputer Assembly Language Programming.* New York: Van Nostrand Reinhold, 1992.

—*Ramachandran Meenakshisundaram*

Trojan Horse

A Trojan horse is a **program** that appears to do one thing while it is also performing other hidden—usually undesired—activities. Computer **viruses** are a type of Trojan horse. However, by convention, experts normally call programs Trojans only if they are deliberately misleading programs that do not self-replicate.

The expression *Trojan horse* comes from the legendary horse statue that Greek warriors presented to the walled city of Troy. The Trojans brought the horse inside their city, and under the cover of darkness Greek soldiers emerged from inside the horse to open the city's gates to their invading comrades. Similarly, a common Trojan program lurks on a computer waiting for the victim to log into an account. It mimics the log-in screen, thereby stealing the victim's user name and password. Such Trojans are common at university computer centers, where many students share computers.

Although viruses normally attack **Windows** computers, Trojans are common among most **operating systems**. Among **Unix**-type operating systems, perhaps the most common class of Trojan is the *root kit.* This is a collection of Trojan programs that mimic common systems administration tools, while hiding files and processes belonging to someone who has illegally broken into a computer.

Microsoft's operating systems are also vulnerable to Trojans. There are many legitimate *remote administration tools* that allow a user to access a Windows computer over the **Internet** or by dialing a modem directly. Many hackers have written similar, malicious programs that hide in other programs. Once the victim has installed such a Trojan, it typically waits for the victim to get on the Internet. Then the Trojan will e-mail the attacker or broadcast a message to an Internet relay chat group that calls an entire group of malicious hackers to enter the victim computer.

Two notorious Windows Trojans were Back Orifice 2000 and NetBus. The latter allows the hidden attacker to turn on any camera and microphone attached to the victim computer. This makes it a powerful espionage tool. DIRT, written by "Spy King" Frank Jones (1937–), is a Windows Trojan used by law enforcement to gather evidence in criminal investigations.

Windows users can avoid infection with most Trojans by installing commercial antivirus software. Unix-type operating systems rely on programs such as Tripwire and Internet Security Scanner to identify the telltale tracks of Trojans. In general, it is harder to clean Trojans out of Unix systems than it is to clean Windows computers.

FURTHER READING

Slade, Robert. *Robert Slade's Guide to Computer Viruses: How to Avoid Them, How to Get Rid of Them, and How to Get Help.* New York: Springer-Verlag, 1994; 2nd ed., 1996.

—*Carolyn Meinel*

Turing, Alan M.

1912–54

British Mathematician and Computer Scientist

Alan Turing is famous as a theorist of **computer science**; for his 1936–37 work introducing the **Turing machine** to define computability, and for his 1950 paper (introducing the **Turing test**) as the foundation of the philosophy of **artificial intelligence**. He is less known for his work relating the theoretical to the practical, although his 1945–46 plans describing an electronic stored-program computer in the modern sense, with detailed circuit diagrams, were highly advanced. Turing's background in logic prepared him to envision a number of things ahead of others: the implications of common storage for programs and data; the computer as a general processor rather than as an arithmetical machine; and the prospect of artificial intelligence.

Turing longed to turn his ideas into practice, and it was to his disappointment that he was personally unable to achieve this. There was one sphere in which he did achieve a synthesis of logical and practical with enormous success, but it was to remain completely unknown to the public during his lifetime. His leading role in breaking the Germans' Enigma cipher systems from 1939 onward remained an Anglo-American secret for 20 years after his death. As a result, Alan Turing has often been omitted from the history of computers when this is seen as a history of computing *objects*. But he has always been granted a leading place in the history of computing *ideas*.

Turing's earliest roots were in natural science. but he turned to mathematics for his degree at Cambridge University. His first research interests were in probability theory and logic. It was a course in mathematical logic offered by the topologist M. H. A. (Max) Newman (1897–1984)—rather than numerical work—that led him to think about computation. The resulting 1936 *Turing machine* definition of an **algorithm** bridged abstract logic and questions of practical calculation. Turing's definition of the *universal machine* rested upon a theory in which programs acting on numbers are themselves equivalent to numbers. These logical concepts, more advanced than Babbage's, were to become the basis of the stored-program computer, in which programs and data are stored alike. The Turing machine has become a crucial part of the foundation of modern computer science.

Although it is right to stress that Turing's construction was theoretical, his work differed from that of other logicians, in that his concept of a machine-scanning paper tape suggested something that could be implemented. Turing did, in fact, immediately interest himself in implementing logical operations in electromagnetic relay switching, with a specific application to cryptography. During his two years at Princeton from 1936 to 1938, extending his work in mathematical logic, Turing also met **John von Neumann** (1903–57), and von Neumann learned of Turing machines, but it should be noted that neither figure had an interest in numerical computation at that stage.

On return to England, Turing was recruited by the British government to work on breaking the German Enigma-ciphered communications from September 1938. He became the chief scientific figure at Bletchley Park, the center of British work. Turing was able to apply logic and probability theory to the Enigma, but equally important were his versatility and willingness to embody his ideas in advanced engineering. The design of the *Bombes*, for a probable word attack on Enigma, was essentially his. These machines embodied in relays an extremely ingenious algorithm for testing a certain logical condition. Turing developed further

Alan Turing. (Courtesy of the National Portrait Gallery, London)

statistical methods, based on quantifying weight of evidence, which paralleled **Claude Shannon**'s (1916–2001) information measure. He had the benefit of brilliant Polish mathematical work on the Enigma, and the collaboration of other British mathematicians and engineers. Nevertheless Turing was notable for his autonomy, particularly for taking on alone what was generally regarded as impossible— breaking into the U-boat Enigma system.

After 1941, Turing's work was influenced by the entry of the United States into the war, and by the possibilities of electronic technology. Turing was sent on a top-level mission to the United States in 1942 to inspect the American-built Bombes and an electronic speech encipherment system. He returned determined to build a more elegant speech encipherment system of his own. In 1943, Turing witnessed the success of large-scale electronic switching in the **Colossus** at Bletchley Park. This, it should be noted, assisted in breaking not the Enigma but another type of German cipher. Nor was it Turing's project; in fact, it was organized by the same Newman whose lectures had introduced him to logic. But Turing's statistical methods had played an important part in formulating the process.

Parallel with these developments, Turing informally discussed his ideas for the future of machines in mechanizing mental processes: not only chess playing but also the possibility of machines capable of learning. By 1944 the concept of the universal machine, the practical experience of applying many algorithms, the speed of electronics, and the ambition of artificial intelligence came together in Turing's ambition to build what he called a practical version of the universal machine; or informally, building a brain. In modern terms, he envisioned a stored-program computer. As autonomous as ever, he intended to design the electronics himself, on the basis of his (successful) experience with the speech system. This was probably a mistake, but it did not prevent a promising start to his plans. Turing was appointed in October 1945 to the National Physical Laboratory, the chief British civilian scientific establishment, with the brief of designing a computer.

Turing's plan for the ACE (Automatic Computing Engine) was approved in March 1946. This document cited the **EDVAC** report but offered an original and independent architecture with registers. Its main force, however, was in programming ideas. Turing stressed that the machine would require no reengineering—only new programming—for a wide range of activities, of which nonnumerical examples including chess playing were given. Turing further exploited the universal machine concept by expounding a preference for programming rather than complex electronics. His proposal even implemented conditional branching as programmed with operations on the addresses, thus exploiting the common storage of data and instructions. He outlined the programming of the stack principle for subroutine calling, and the idea of languages convenient for the user which the machine could translate. His guiding principle was that anything that became routine could be programmed for the machine to do itself. Unfortunately the engineering of storage dominated every other consideration, and the delay line storage mechanism, which Turing had favoured as being readily available, entailed considerable delay. Turing resigned from the NPL in 1948, when nothing had actually been built. The Pilot ACE was in fact completed in 1950, and was in the vanguard of computing, but Turing never derived fame from it.

Instead, Turing's progress lay in advancing computing ideas rather than practice; in 1948 he pursued the idea of program modification, and he developed neural network ideas giving a concrete picture of how a mechanical system could "learn" through changes induced by experience. Informally, he took part in the lively cybernetic discussions of the postwar period. Much remained unpublished, but his underlying goals for computation, in which program modification played a vital part, appeared in his philosophical paper of 1950. This, including the imitation game operational definition of intelligence now known as the *Turing test*, comprised his most public work and indeed, is still regarded as the foundation of the philosophy of artificial intelligence.

Turing had meanwhile been attracted to a post at Manchester University. It was again Max Newman who played the critical role, by offering Turing the post of deputy director of the computing laboratory. Newman was the director on paper, but in practice the direction lay with the engineers, led by Frederic

Williams (1911–77) and **Tom Kilburn** (1921–2001), after their success in June 1948 with the world's first working stored-program computer. It was largely forgotten that Newman had farsightedly initiated the project in 1945, having derived the basic principle from Turing. Placed in a somewhat stressful role, Turing did not exploit his chance to promulgate an advanced approach to programming, nor did he write the treatise on the theory and practice of computation that would have made his reputation secure.

Turing found it frustrating for his ideas not to be appreciated, but he did not pursue the standard academic means of securing attention. Modest in publication, he also only rarely attended conferences or nurtured alliances. He was strongest in starting off big ideas rather than with crowning his success with the complete development of detail. His awkward manners inspired both exasperation and affection in others. He was agreed by all to be a very informal, original, youthful, and truthful figure, but these qualities did not always ensure acceptance.

In 1951 he turned to new work, becoming a pioneer in the use of a computer for pure research. He had used the prototype Manchester machine for work in number theory; he used the fully engineered version for his new theory of biological growth, which required the simulation of nonlinear processes. This too remained incomplete and largely unpublished at his death in 1954, which came two years after his criminal trial and loss of security clearance as a homosexual.

BIOGRAPHY

Alan Mathison Turing. Born 23 June 1912 in Paddington, London, England. Educated at Sherborne School, 1926–31. Undergraduate at King's College, Cambridge University 1931–34. Fellow of King's College, 1935. Defined computability through Turing machine concept, 1936. Ph.D. from Princeton University, 1938. Worked at the (British) Government Code and Cypher School 1938–45; chief scientific consultant, 1941–45. Bombe design and essential break into the naval Enigma systems 1939–40. National Physical Laboratory, 1945-48. Electronic computer design (the ACE), 1946. 1948 onward: deputy director of the computing laboratory and reader in the theory of computation, University of Manchester. Elected Fellow of Royal Society 1951. Arrest, trial, and loss of security clearance as a homosexual in 1952. Death by cyanide poisoning on 7 June 1954.

SELECTED WORKS

Turing, Alan M. "On Computable Numbers, with an Application to the Entscheidungsproblem." *Proceedings of the London Mathematical Society*, Vol. 2, No. 42, 1936–1937, pp. 230–265; correction, No. 43, 1937, pp. 544–546.

———. "Computability and Lambda-Definability." *Journal of Symbolic Logic*, No. 2, 1937, pp. 153–163.

———. "Systems of Logic Based on Ordinals." *Proceedings of the London Mathematical Society*, Vol. 2, No. 45, 1939, pp. 161–228.

———. "A Method for the Calculation of the Zeta-Function." *Proceedings of the London Mathematical Society*, Vol. 2, 1943, pp. 180–197 (submitted 1939).

———. "Proposed Electronic Calculator." National Physical Laboratory report, 1946. Published first in B. E. Carpenter and R. W. Doran, eds., *A. M. Turing's ACE Report of 1946 and Other Papers*, Vol. 10 in the Charles Babbage Institute Reprint Series for the History of Computing. Cambridge, Mass.: MIT Press, 1986.

———. "Lecture to the London Mathematical Society." Feb. 1947. Published first in B. E. Carpenter and R. W. Doran, eds., *A. M. Turing's ACE Report of 1946 and Other Papers*, Vol. 10 in the Charles Babbage Institute Reprint Series for the History of Computing. Cambridge, Mass.: MIT Press, 1986.

———. "Intelligent Machinery." National Physical Laboratory Report, 1948. Published in C. R. Evans and A. D. J. Robertson, eds., *Cybernetics: Key Papers*. Baltimore: University Park Press, 1968. Also in *Machine Intelligence*, Vol. 5, 1969, pp. 3–23.

———. "Rounding-off Errors in Matrix Processes." *Quarterly Journal of Mechanics and Applied Mathematics*, Vol. 1, 1948, pp. 287–308.

———. "Computing Machinery and Intelligence." *Mind*, Vol. 49, 1950, pp. 433–460.

———. "The Word Problem in Semi-Groups with Cancellation." *Annals of Mathematics*, Vol. 52, No. 2, 1950, pp. 491–505.

———. *Programmers Handbook*. Manchester, England: Manchester University Computing Laboratory, 1951.

———. "The Chemical Basis of Morphogenesis." *Philosophical Transactions of the Royal Society of London*, Series B, Vol. 237, 1952, pp. 37–72.

———. "Chess." A subsection of chapter 25, "Digital Computers Applied to Games." In B. V. Bowden, ed., *Faster than Thought*. London: Pitman, 1953.

———. "Some Calculations of the Riemann Zeta-function." *Proceedings of the London Mathematical Society*, Vol. 3, 1953, pp. 99–117.

———. "Solvable and Unsolvable Problems." *Science News*, Vol. 31, 1954, pp. 7–23.

FURTHER READING

Britton, J. L., R. O. Gandy, C. E. M. Yates, D. C. Ince, and P. T. Saunders, eds. *The Collected Works of A. M. Turing.* New York: Elsevier, 1992. These volumes include most of Turing's unpublished work.

Carpenter, B. E., and R. W. Doran, eds. *A. M. Turing's ACE Report of 1946 and Other Papers.* Cambridge, Mass.: MIT Press, 1986.

Herken, R., ed. *The Universal Turing Machine.* London: Oxford University Press, 1988; 2nd ed., New York: Springer-Verlag, 1994.

Hodges, Andrew. *Turing: A Natural Philosopher.* No. 3 of the Great Philosophers Series. London: Phoenix, 1997; New York: Routledge, 1997.

———. *Alan Turing: The Enigma.* New York: Walker Books, 2000.

Andrew Hodges maintains a Turing website at: *http://www.turing.org.uk/turing/*

—Andrew Hodges

Turing Award

The A. M. Turing Award is the most prestigious technical recognition in the **computer science** field; it is sometimes referred to as the "Nobel Prize" of computer science. The **Association for Computing Machinery** started bestowing this honor in 1966 to persons selected for their contributions to computing. The prize was named for **Alan M. Turing** (1912–54), who first described a universal computing device in 1936.

Some early pioneers of computing have received the award, as is the case of **Maurice V. Wilkes** (1913–), who was the chief designer of the first stored program computer, the **EDSAC**, built at Cambridge University in 1949. Others have made contributions to the development of programming languages; examples include **John McCarthy** (1927–) for **LISP**, **John Backus** (1924–) for **Fortran**, Kenneth E. Iverson (1920–) for **APL**, **Dennis Ritchie** (1941–) and **Ken Thompson** (1943–) for **C**, and **Niklaus Wirth** (1934–) for **Pascal** and **Modula**. Richard Karp (1944–), Stephen A. Cook (1939–), Michael O. Rabin (1931–), and Manuel Blum (1938–) were honored by their contributions to theoretical computer science, while **Marvin Minsky** (1927–), Allen Newell (1927–92) and Herbert Simon (1916–), and **Edward Feigenbaum** (1936–) received the prize for their work in the area of **artificial intelligence**.

TURING AWARD RECIPIENTS

1966 A.J. Perlis	1984 Niklaus Wirth
1967 Maurice V. Wilkes	1985 Richard M. Karp
1968 Richard Hamming	1986 John Hopcroft
1969 Marvin Minsky	1986 Robert Tarjan
1970 J.H. Wilkinson	1987 John Cocke
1971 John McCarthy	1988 Ivan Sutherland
1972 Edsger W. Dijkstra	1989 William Kahan
1973 Charles W. Bachman	1990 Fernando Corbató
1974 Donald E. Knuth	1991 Robin Milner
1975 Allen Newell	1992 Butler W. Lampson
1975 Herbert A. Simon	1993 Juris Hartmanis
1976 Michael O. Rabin	1993 Richard E. Stearns
1976 Dana S. Scott	1994 Edward Feigenbaum
1977 John Backus	1994 Raj Reddy
1978 Robert W. Floyd	1995 Manuel Blum
1979 Kenneth E. Iverson	1996 Amir Pnueli
1980 C. Antony R. Hoare	1997 Douglas Engelbart
1981 Edgar F. Codd	1998 James Gray
1982 Stephen A. Cook	1999 Frederick Brooks
1983 Ken Thompson	2000 Andrew Chi-Chih Yao
1983 Dennis M. Ritchie	

The accompanying table shows the recipients of the Turing Award by year. Altough the award is an international prize, only Wilkes, J. H. Wilkinson, **Edsger Dijkstra**, **C. Antony R. Hoare**, Wirth, Robin Milner, and Amir Pnueli did most of their work outside the United States or Canada.

FURTHER READING

ACM Turing Award Lectures: The First Twenty Years, 1966 to 1985. New York: ACM Press; Reading, Mass.: Addison-Wesley, 1987.

—Raúl Rojas

Turing Machine

The Turing machine is a mathematical construct, devised by the British mathematician **Alan M. Turing** (1912–54) to specify precisely what should be understood by a *mechanical process*, what would nowadays generally be called an **algorithm**. The

Turing machine arose in his attack on the *Entscheidungsproblem* (decision problem) as posed by David Hilbert (1862–1943): Is there a method that can in principle be applied to all mathematical assertions which will decide their truth or falsity? Mathematician Kurt Gödel's (1906–78) 1931 work showing the incompleteness of axiomatic systems had made this seem unlikely, but rigorous settlement of the question depended upon finding a precise definition of *method* that would be sufficiently general to be compelling. This Turing supplied in 1936, by seizing on the idea of a method that could be applied *mechanically* by a person doing a computation.

Rather than being an analysis of computing machines, Turing's paper gave an analysis of what could be done by people acting mechanically. Nevertheless, he represented the mechanically working human being using the imagery of a machine rather like a teleprinter, reading but also writing on a paper tape. Turing formalized his picture by specifying a tape marked in squares, with one symbol (from a finite alphabet) in each square. He then specified a small number of atomic operations to be performed on this tape—each of them primitive, indubitably mechanical in nature, and performed only one at a time—but sufficient to encompass everything that could be called a *method.* These operations are those of scanning one square, moving one position to left or to right according to what is read, and writing a new symbol according to what is read. Only a finite number of symbols may be on the tape at any time, but an unlimited amount of tape is available. The key idea is that a machine may have finitely many configurations or states. A table of behavior then lays down precisely, for each configuration, what the machine is to do in response to what it has read. Although we speak of *the* Turing machine, there are infinitely many Turing machines, a different Turing machine for each different table of behavior. Given the general formalism, any particular Turing machine simply is the table of behavior.

Turing argued convincingly that this repertoire sufficed for everything that would count as a method; and he defined the term *computable numbers* for those numbers (real numbers written out as infinite decimals) that can be computed by a Turing machine. *Computable* is not equivalent to *definable.* One can define explicit uncomputable numbers and explicit problems that cannot be solved by a Turing machine. Turing's analysis picked out what is now known as the *halting problem*, which refers to predicting what an arbitrary Turing machine will do. It is easily shown that there is no Turing machine that can perform the required prediction (a proof by contradiction follows from using such a machine to predict its own behavior). From this observation Turing was able to answer Hilbert's *Entscheidungsproblem* in the negative.

The American logician **Alonzo Church** (1903–95) had arrived at the same conclusion. But Church required that a method—in his words the *effectively calculable*—could be identified with operations of the logical lambda calculus. This assumption became known as *Church's thesis.* Turing's definition of computability was soon shown to be equivalent to Church's, but it rested on a compelling basis. Turing's definition has retained general acceptance.

Turing observed in his analysis that reading a table of behavior and interpreting the entries is itself a mechanical operation. This gave rise to his idea of the *universal Turing machine.* This is a particular kind of Turing machine which has a table of instructions such that it will read the table of instructions of any other Turing machine (when placed in a suitably encoded form on its tape) and do what that Turing machine would have done. In modern terms, this is the function of a **digital computer**, which reads and implements the instructions placed in its memory as a program. Turing may possibly have known of **Charles Babbage**'s (1791–1871) ideas, but there is no evidence of this. Further, his universal machine embodies an important conceptual advance. To Babbage, instructions and data were qualitatively distinct. Turing's construction requires that instructions (i.e., a table of behavior) can be stored and read like any other symbolic data. It is this principle that distinguishes the modern stored modifiable program computer from Babbage's **Analytical Engine**.

It is always remarked that Turing's 1936 paper concerned a theoretical machine, but Turing immediately thereafter developed an interest in implementing logical operations, and when electronics became available in 1945 he showed great enthusiasm for constructing a universal practical computing machine. A further hint of future work lay in Turing's original paper: He made a bold argument for why his definition of computability would include every conceivable method, by presenting the configurations of a Turing machine as corresponding to a human calculator's states of mind. Turing himself later extended this idea into the discussion of the possible mechanization of all mental processes. The Turing machine is now an important concept in the cognitive sciences.

The Turing machine has generated a huge literature in **computer science**, and in particular is the foundation of complexity theory. A recent development is that of quantum computation, in which configurations become quantum states.

FURTHER READING

Herken, R., ed. *The Universal Turing Machine.* New York: Oxford University Press, 1988; 2nd ed., New York: Springer-Verlag, 1994. The historical context is discussed fully in articles by R. O. Gandy, S. C. Kleene, and others.

Hodges, Andrew. *Turing: A Natural Philosopher.* London: Phoenix, 1997.

Minsky, M. *Computation: Finite and Infinite Machines.* Englewood Cliffs, N.J.: Prentice Hall, 1967.

Turing, A. M. "On Computable Numbers, with an Application to the Entscheidungsproblem." *Proceedings of the London Mathematical Society* 2, Vol. 42, 1937, pp. 230–265. Reprinted in Martin Davis, *The Undecidable: Basic Papers on Undecidable Propositions, Unsoluable Problems and Computable Functions*, Hewlett, N.Y.: Raven Press, 1965.

—*Andrew Hodges*

Turing Test

The Turing test is an operational criterion for intelligence introduced by the British mathematician **Alan M. Turing** (1912–54) in the paper "Computing Machinery and Intelligence" (1950), which is generally regarded as a founding contribution to the philosophy of artificial intelligence. The test, which Turing called the *imitation game*, is its most famous aspect (see figure).

Turing's test presents the question "Can a machine think?" in a form amenable to experiment. It is intended to circumvent philosophical problems about the nature of mind by introducing an operational definition based on a materialist view in which minds are identified with the functioning of the brain. It depends on two claims: (1) that intelligence can be distinguished from other faculties by an experiment where communication is permitted only through written messages, and (2) that if a machine can send messages indistinguishable from human communications, it should be held to possess intelligence.

Unfortunately, Turing introduced his imitation principle through a misleading analogy with a different game in which a man and a woman compete to convince a judge that they are the woman. Some commentators hold that the test has to do with a computer imitating a man imitating a woman, or assert that questions of gender are significant in Turing's thought. This is mistaken, as Turing's illustrations of his test show.

Turing's test is based entirely on observable output, avoiding the discussion of consciousness. However, many philosophers have continued to hold that human beings have an intrinsic quality that cannot be possessed even by a machine that successfully imitates human behavior. Other critics wonder whether digital information can be a satisfactory guide to intelligence. Turing's own wide-ranging discussion reveals concerns about emotion, experience, and other questions at the

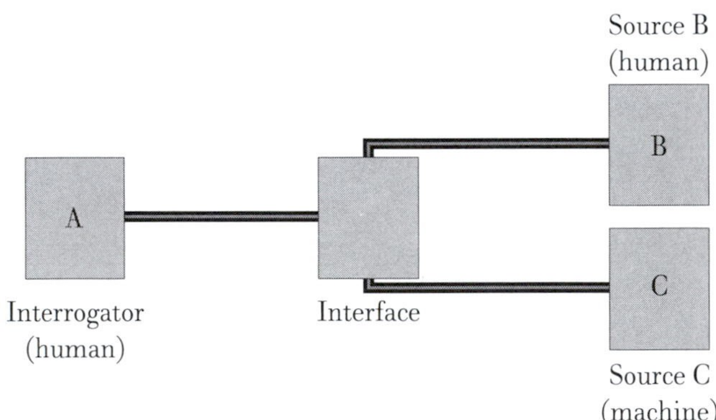

1. The human interrogator (**A**) can communicate with sources **B** and **C**.
2. One source (**B**) is human and has never met **A**. The other source (**C**) is a machine.
3. **A** must determine which of the two sources is human.

Turing Test. The interrogator, a human, can communicate with two sources, one human and one machine. The interrogator must decide which is which.

interface between thought and action, but shows that he nevertheless considered his criterion to be the appropriate one for the discussion of intelligence.

Turing himself predicted that within 50 years computers would maintain a conversation for five minutes and pass the test with 70 percent success. Turing's scenario has stimulated many competitions for conversation-making programs, leading to criticisms that the test is a distraction from more systematic artificial intelligence research. But Turing's game does have the merit of taking seriously the word *intelligence*.

The imitation game is only one aspect of Turing's paper, which has more constructive elements that put the ancient mind–matter problem in the scientific arena of the digital machine. Turing holds that computability is fundamental, argues that the action of the brain is computable, and that a computer (as a universal machine) can do anything computable. He describes approaches to artificial intelligence through explicit programming and through implicit methods of teaching. Turing vividly illustrates the potential scope of machines as going beyond the mechanical in the everyday sense.

FURTHER READING

Hodges, Andrew. *Turing: A Natural Philosopher.* London: Phoenix, 1997.

Hofstadter, Douglas R., and Daniel C. Dennett. *The Mind's I: Fantasies and Reflections on Self and Soul.* New York: Basic Books, 1981.

Penrose, Roger. *Shadows of the Mind: A Search for the Missing Science of Consciousness.* New York: Oxford University Press, 1994.

Turing, A. M. "Computing Machinery and Intelligence." *Mind*, Vol. 59, 1950, pp. 433–460. This paper has been reprinted in several collections, in particular in Margaret Boden, ed., *The Philosophy of Artificial Intelligence.* New York: Oxford University Press, 1990. It is reprinted together with Turing's 1947 and 1948 papers in D. C. Ince, ed., *The Collected Works of A. M. Turing: Mechanical Intelligence*, Vol. 3. New York: Elsevier, 1992.

Twisted-Pair Cable

Twisted-pair cable is the standard connection medium for many telephone and networking applications. It consists of regular copper wires surrounded by an insulator. To reduce electromagnetic induction, two insulated copper wires are twisted around each other: One wire carries the signal and the other is grounded and absorbs signal interference.

There are two types of twisted-pair cables: unshielded twisted pair (UTP), which is the most commonly used type, and shielded twisted pair (STP), which provides better protection against crosstalk and electrical interference, providing higher transmission speeds.

The different applications of twisted-pair cables have been standardized by the ANSI/EIA (**American National Standards Institute**/Electronic Industries Association) Standard 568, which was released in 1991. This standard is also known as *CAT standard*, because it *categorizes* twisted-pair cabling systems (wires, junctions, and connectors) in terms of the transmission rates that they can sustain. Five categories currently exist:

- CAT 1 specifies twisted-pair cables for applications that require transmission rates of less than 1 megabit per second (Mbps), such as plain analog telephones services, and doorbell wiring.
- CAT 2 specifies twisted-pair cabling systems for transmission rates up to 4 Mbps. This was mainly used for **IBM** token ring networks.
- CAT 3 cables must pass tests up to 16 Mbps. These cables are very commonly used for 10-Mbps **Ethernet** networks.
- CAT 4 cables can bear up to 20 Mbps and are not used only for IBM's 16-Mbps **token ring** networks.
- CAT 5 twisted-pair cables can be used for transmission rates up to 100 Mbps and is the most popular cable used in new installations today.

CAT 6 and 7, which standardize cable technology for gigabit Ethernet and networks beyond 100 Mbps, are currently under development. Currently, for higher transmission rates (such as long-distance gigabit Ethernet), **optical fiber** must be used.

Starting in the early 1980s, Ethernet's 10-Mbps **bandwidth** appeared inexhaustible. Many computers, running mostly stand-alone applications, could be served by using a single Ethernet network. At that time, coaxial cable, the primary type of cable used by the cable television industry, was typically used: Every computer in the network was part of a daisy chain of devices connected directly to a single shared coaxial cable. As computer systems became faster, application software emerged that used networks more frequently and therefore required higher bandwidth. **Local area networks** (LANs) also became more popular and had to be more reliable and easier to maintain.

In the past 10 years, more and more local area networks have been realized with twisted-pair cables. The primary advantages of twisted-pair cable compared with other wiring technologies are the low price and the wide availability. Using twisted pair, computers are no longer connected to a shared cable, but rather, to an Ethernet hub. There are several types of hubs: passive hubs, intelligent hubs, and switching hubs. Passive hubs serve simply as a conduit for the data, enabling it to flow from one computer to the other. Intelligent hubs contain additional hardware for monitoring the network traffic going through, helping the administrator to find errors inside the network more quickly. Switching hubs actually read the destination address of a network packet and forward them directly to the correct target. Twisted pair is becoming more and more popular and is, together with optical fiber, likely to become the main wiring technology to be used in LANs.

Further Reading

Computer Society. *System Considerations for Multisegment 10 Mb/s Baseband Networks*, Sec. 13: *Twisted-Pair Medium Attachment Unit*. New York: IEEE, 1990.

Gilster, Ron, and Diane McMichael Gilster. *Build Your Own Home Network*. Berkeley, Calif.: Osborne McGraw-Hill, 2000.

Speaker, Mark, and Mark Thompson. *The Complete Idiot's Guide to Networking Your Home*. Indianapolis, Ind.: Que, 1999.

Spurgeon, Charles E. *Ethernet: The Definitive Guide*. Cambridge, Mass.: O'Reilly, 2000.

—*Gerald Friedland*

Two's Complement

Numbers are represented in the **binary system** using strings of binary digits (**bits**). Digital computers operating with binary numbers can perform all necessary arithmetical operations. However, the question arises of how best to represent signed numbers in computers. One method would be to use two extra symbols (+ or −) to mark the positive and negative numbers. This would, however, require a bit of storage in memory. Computer architects realized early that there is a more efficient way of dealing with binary signed numbers: the two's-complement representation.

There are two ways of thinking about the two's-complement representation. When using it, a maximum number of bits for the numbers is defined in advance. Since computer memories work with, for example, 16-, 32-, and 64-bit words, this is a straightforward requirement. Assume for example that numbers will be processed using only eight bits. A two's-complement representation can be thought of as assigning weights 1, 2, 4, 8,16, 32, 64, and −128 to the eight successive bits from right to left. Notice that the last weight is negative. Using these weights, any decimal number between −128 and +127 can be represented. The number −128, for example, is just the binary string 10000000. The number −1 corresponds to the string 11111111 (eight ones). The reader can check that the weights of the bits, multiplied by the corresponding bit, lead to these numbers. Notice also that since the weight −128 is larger than the sum of all other positive weights, any number with a one in the most significant bit is negative, whereas any number with a zero is positive. We know immediately that the number 11110000 is negative, without having to perform any calculations.

The second way of thinking about two's-complement numbers is related to the way in which a positive binary number is transformed into the corresponding negative number. To transform the number 00000011 (a decimal 3) into −3, we do the following: Complement all eight bits of the original number and add a 1 to the result. In our case, the complement of the binary number 00000011 is 11111100 (every 1 is transformed into 0, and vice versa) . Adding a 1 yields 11111101, which is the two's-complement representation of −3, as the reader can check using the weights mentioned above.

When the binary representation uses more than 8 bits, the same approach is used, but only the most significant bit gets assigned a negative weight. All other weights, which are potencies of 2, are positive.

The main benefit of using the two's-complement representation is that subtraction of binary numbers can be reduced to addition. To subtract the number A from the number B, just complement A, add a 1, and add the result to B. The result is then B+(−A), that is, B−A, as desired. The arithmetical logical units of today's computers work in this way.

FURTHER READING

Knuth, Donald. *The Art of Computer Programming*, Vol. 2, *Seminumerical Algorithms*. Reading, Mass.: Addison-Wesley, 1981.

Koren, Israel. *Computer Arithmetic Algorithms*. Englewood Cliffs, N.J.: Prentice Hall, 1993.

—*Raúl Rojas*

Unisys

Unisys Corporation was formed in 1986 by the merger of Sperry Rand Corporation and **Burroughs** Corporation. The two companies had been moderately successful in the large- and medium-scale computer market during the 1960s and 1970s but found it increasingly difficult to compete with **IBM**. W. Michael Blumenthal (1926–), chairman of Burroughs, believed that a merged company could achieve economies of scale by combining its administrative and sales forces. The name for the new company was chosen from suggestions submitted by employees; it is not regarded as an acronym.

The merged company found itself with four major product lines (Sperry 1100/2200 and 80 series and Burroughs A and V series) as well as a group of Sperry Unix servers and the Burroughs clustered Convergent Technologies Operating System (CTOS) servers. To allay the fears of nervous customers who thought that some of the lines would be discontinued, Blumenthal stated that the four major ones would be supported "in perpetuity." The merger had encumbered Unisys with a significant debt load, so the company sold off several nonessential divisions and embarked on a drastic program of staff reductions.

Unisys was hit hard by the recession of 1990–91, and many industry observers predicted that it would become bankrupt. James Unruh (1941–), Blumenthal's successor as chairman, guided the company through an austerity program that, among other things, involved the eventual termination of support for the 80 and V series. Fortunately, Unisys engineering had developed powerful new computer models in the 2200 and A series. Strong sales of these models brought Unisys out of the recession somewhat earlier than many other computer manufacturers.

The difficulties of trying to compete against **Windows** and **Unix** environments running on **Intel** processors led Unisys to develop its heterogeneous multiprocessing (HMP) architecture. This involved a close connection between one of the traditional (2200 or A series) environments and an Intel environment running either Unix or **Microsoft**'s Windows NT. Unisys provided a suite of systems software that enabled applications to be developed to utilize both parts of the HMP machines, which were introduced in 1996 under the name ClearPath.

Unruh was succeeded as Unisys chairman in 1997 by Larry Weinbach (1940–). He took advantage of prosperous business conditions to pay off much of the company's debt and relax the austerity program. The company also put emphasis on producing large multiprocessor computers that would run Microsoft's Windows NT operating system. The cellular multiprocessing (CMP) architecture, announced in 1999, involves computers of up to 32 processors. These can be all Intel or, using HMP, a mixture of Intel and a maximum of sixteen 2200 or A processors.

FURTHER READING

Hoffman, Thomas. "Unisys: Back from the Brink." *Information Week*, 13 Jan. 1992.

Tarsala, Michael. "How Unisys, and Larry, Got Their Groove Back." *Investor's Business Daily*, 27 Aug. 1998.

—*George Gray*

UNIVAC

Throughout the 1950s the name *UNIVAC* was synonymous with the word *computer*. Use of a

UNIVAC (universal automatic computer) by the American CBS television network to accurately predict the winner of the 1952 presidential election shortly after the polls closed indelibly fixed the machine in the public's mind.

The UNIVAC was designed by **J. Presper Eckert** (1919–95) and **John W. Mauchly** (1907–80), who had previously led the creation of the **ENIAC**, arguably the first large-scale fully electronic computer. They had left the University of Pennsylvania in 1946 in a dispute over invention rights and formed the Eckert–Mauchly Computer Corporation to commercialize computing machines. While building the pioneering BINAC, a highly reliable computer intended for airborne use, they were awarded a contract by the National Bureau of Standards for a machine to help process data from the 1950 census. UNIVAC was the result.

It was a direct descendent of the ENIAC in the sense that it was a decimal machine when the world was moving to the simpler binary number system inside computers. There were 11 digits per word plus a sign for numbers, or 12 digits for alphanumerics. It had a practical memory of about 1000 words that used mercury delay line technology, then prevalent in the first stored program machines. To handle the masses of census data, the UNIVAC had the first magnetic tape storage devices, and as they were the most prominent moving parts, for many years magnetic tape drives would serve as the icon of a giant computer. Each tape was 1500 feet long and contained 1,440,000 digits, or 120,000 words. When delivered in 1951, late and over budget, the machine had a slow typewriter device for basic output. In 1953 this deficiency was removed by the introduction of a 600-character-per-minute line printer. Later a card punch with printing capability was added. A dozen or so UNIVAC I's were sold.

The UNIVAC computer is used to predict a winning horse. (Courtesy of the Library of Congress)

Due to funding pressures brought on by wildly underestimating costs and the death of their venture capitalist, Eckert and Mauchly sold the company to Remington Rand, long-time supplier of office machines, in 1950. Rand formed a UNIVAC Division, and successors to the first model were steadily produced under that brand name even after the 1955 merger with Sperry.

Further Reading

Berkeley, Edmund C. *Giant Brains; or, Machines That Think.* New York: Wiley, 1949.

Schmitt, William F. "The UNIVAC Short Code." *Annals of the History of Computing,* Vol. 10, 1986, pp. 7–18.

Shurkin, Joel. *Engines of the Mind: A History of the Computer.* New York: Norton, 1984.

Stern, Nancy. *From ENIAC to UNIVAC: An Appraisal of the Eckert–Mauchly Computers.* Bedford, Mass.: Digital Press, 1981.

—*James Tomayko*

Unix

Unix is an **operating system**, a program that controls the resources of a computer on behalf of its users, by running programs, managing secondary storage, and communicating with peripheral devices and other systems. Since its birth on a single machine in 1969, Unix has spread worldwide, running on all types of general-purpose computers and serving a very large user community.

The first Unix system was created at **Bell Labs** in 1969 by **Ken Thompson** (1943–) on a discarded **PDP-7**. Thompson was joined soon thereafter by **Dennis Ritchie** (1941–), and they developed a version of Unix that ran on the PDP-11/20, a newer, although still quite limited machine. In 1973, the system was rewritten from the original assembly language into the **C** programming language, which was being developed by Ritchie simultaneously.

Beginning in 1975, Unix was licensed to universities at no cost and to commercial enterprises for a modest fee; this included the source code for the operating system itself and for all the tools and applications it supported. Because the source code was included as part of the license, users were able to adapt, refine, and extend the system to meet their own needs; this flexibility contributed to its early success. Also, because almost all the code was written in C, Unix was relatively independent of the PDP-11 architecture, and during the late 1970s, several groups ported it to other machines. This high degree of portability has continued to the present, and Unix is available for essentially all modern machines.

Some of these modern implementations are based on lineal descendants of the original code from Bell Labs or the major contributions made at the University of California at Berkeley ("Berkeley Unix"); others are *ab initio* implementations from the external specifications. The most notable example of the latter is **Linux**, a ground-up version created originally by **Linus Torvalds** (1969–) and now carried on by a large number of volunteers spread across the world and connected by the **Internet**.

There are at least three basic notions that distinguished Unix from other systems in the early days, although these have been adapted by other systems in the intervening years: a uniform hierarchical file system, a programmable command interpreter or shell, and mechanisms for redirecting input and output to files and pipes.

Unix provides a hierarchical file system in which all information in secondary storage is stored as a tree. The root of the tree contains files and directories; directories contain further files and directories. The purpose of the file system is to put a logical structure on information and to hide details of how the information is stored physically: for example, by concealing the size and other parameters of disks.

Unix has from the beginning presented the characteristics of other resources as file systems, most notably by the idea that peripheral devices such as disks, tapes, and so on, are files and thus accessed and controlled by the same operating system interfaces as regular files. This unifying notion has been extended to include processes and files stored on other machines via network file systems.

The standard Unix interface seen by most users is a program called the *shell*, which accepts commands from the user and causes the operating system to run them. The shell is not part of the operating system; thus it may be replaced by another shell at will, and in fact there are a variety of shells in common use, reflecting different features and user preferences. All shells share certain common features, however. They all provide wildcard expansion of file names that match patterns of file names in the file system. For instance, the "*" character matches any sequence of characters in a name, so the pattern *.txt matches all names in the current directory that end with ".txt".

Shells also provide input/output redirection and pipes. The notation "> filename" causes redirection of program output that would normally have appeared in a user's command window to be directed instead to a file; similarly, "< filename" takes input from the file instead of from the keyboard. These operators make it easy to capture the output of one program and send it to the input of another. One canonical example is:

```
who >f1   # collect list of logged-in users in file f1
wc <f1    # count lines to give count of users
```

The notation "program1 | program2"—that is, two command invocations separated by "|"—causes the output of program1 to be sent directly to the input of program2 without an intervening file; the system manages the flow of information and synchronization of the two programs. Thus the previous example can be rendered in a pipeline as:

```
who | wc # count logged-in users
```

Finally, the shell can be directed to take its input from a file instead of from the user's keyboard. With this feature, and some of the trappings of a programming language (variables, conditional statements, and loops), the shell becomes a true programming language.

The ability to connect programs in pipelines and encapsulate the result in shell scripts is perhaps the most characteristic aspect of Unix use. It caused a significant change in the way that programs were developed, as programmers came to realize that it was often much easier to create a new program by combining two or more existing programs that appear to work as if they were a single program. It also led to a style of designing programs to work in pipelines, to be used as components in larger processes. In this way, complicated tasks could often be factored into simpler, more focused pieces that were easier first to create and subsequently to maintain.

Since file name expansion and redirection mechanisms are implemented by the shell, not by individual programs, they apply to all programs and work the same way in all; this is an important contrast to systems in which individual programs manage these operations themselves, often in different ways.

Thompson and Ritchie's original goal was to create a system that provided a comfortable and convenient environment for programmers like themselves who were creating new programs. Because the original **hardware** that Unix ran on was limited in size and capabilities, they were selective in what was included in the system and sought to find general mechanisms that would serve many needs without much code. As a result, Unix was in its original form simple and spare, yet powerful, and ran efficiently on the limited machines of the time.

Current machines are, of course, far bigger and more powerful, and Unix has grown in size and to some extent in power as well. It continues to be a program-development environment, but it is also much used as a system on which to run programs. Notable examples include Web servers; the majority of Web servers today run on Unix, although this is changing. Unix supports modern multiprocessor architectures well, so it is often used for large **time-sharing** systems. There are also numerous large-scale database systems that run on Unix.

At the same time, there are some areas in which Unix does not compete, whether by design or circumstance. The standard versions of the system are not guaranteed to meet specific response time requirements, so Unix is not generally used in such real-time settings. Unix also does not provide any significant number of commercial application packages such as word processors, spreadsheets, presentation systems, and the like that are so much a part of systems like **Windows** or the **Macintosh**; thus its use in home computing and office environments is much more limited. Finally, its market share is affected by the growth of **Microsoft**'s NT system, which is aimed at much the same market and which does include the standard complement of major applications. Unix suffers here not only from the lack of application **software**, but also from a surfeit of variants—each manufacturer adds features and embellishments that make their offering more attractive, at the price of incompatibility. This is a serious issue for the long-term survival of Unix.

Unix was the first system to demonstrate compellingly the advantage of implementation in a high-level language. Portability made it easy to move the system to each new machine, and in fact encouraged the founding of new companies by reducing one major barrier to entry. A new hardware company could simply provide Unix, rather than having to develop an entirely operating system; a new software company could simply make its products work on Unix rather than having to make them work on a variety of systems. Unix also pioneered the tools approach to developing software, particularly a rich set of small tools, often based on specialized languages (such as the shell itself). The role of tools and languages is somewhat diminished today, but behind many of the more visible **graphical user interfaces** a text-based language is often hidden.

FURTHER READING

Banahan, Mark, and Andy Rutter. *The UNIX Book.* New York: Wiley, 1983.

Bergin, Thomas J., and Richard G. Gibson, eds. *A History of Programming Languages II.* New York: ACM Press; Reading, Mass.: Addison-Wesley, 1996.

Lions, John. *Lions' Commentary on Unix.* San Jose, Calif.: Peer-to-Peer Communications, 1996.

Wilson, James. Berkeley *Unix: A Simple and Comprehensive Guide.* New York: Wiley, 1991.

—Brian W. Kernighan

URL

A uniform resource locator (URL) provides a unique name for resources on the **World Wide Web**. This is extremely important for defining Web hyperlinks. **Tim Berners-Lee** (1955–), who invented the Web in the early 1990s, originally introduced the URL concept, although it was originally called a universal resource identifier (URI). Together with **HTML** (Hypertext Markup Language) and HTTP (Hypertext Transfer Protocol), it forms a central constituent that has contributed to the success of the Web.

During 1990 and 1991, Berners-Lee developed the important components of the Web system. One of these was an address scheme for pointing to a particular location within the Web information space. He initially termed this a universal document identifier (UDI), although there is an obvious conflict with "unilateral declaration of independence," which would have limited the popularity of this abbreviation. In any case, the name space grew to include many types of entity, including programs as well as static documents. Berners-Lee renamed UDI to universal *resource* identifier. Others felt that "universal" was too all encompassing and preferred the term *uniform. Locator* also replaced the term *identifier*, although Berners-Lee continued to prefer and use the abbreviation URI.

A URL includes information on the protocol to be used (e.g., "http"), the **Internet** host where the desired resource resides (e.g., "www.w3.org") and optionally, a port number to be used (e.g., "80" is the default for HTTP). In addition, directory and file name information, and even an "anchor" location within an HTML file or a query string for a program, may be appended (e.g., "Addressing/index.html#anchor"). One of the powers of the URL addressing scheme has been that existing protocols, such as the File Transfer Protocol (**FTP**), were subsumed in the name space (e.g., using "ftp" instead of "http"). In addition, future protocols could easily be incorporated.

Whatever the nomenclature (URL or URI), Berners-Lee has considered the uniform resource locator to be the most important concept of the Web. URLs contain all the essential information in a compact format for locating resources uniquely and in a global manner on the Internet. They have rapidly become part of everyday life, as Web addresses become almost as common as telephone numbers in the developed world.

FURTHER READING

Berners-Lee, Tim. *Weaving the Web: The Past, Present and Future of the World Wide Web by its Inventor.* London: Orion Business Books, 1999.

———. "Universal Resource Identifiers in WWW: A Unifying Syntax for the Expression of Names and Addresses of Objects on the Network as used in the World-Wide Web." *RFC* 1630, June 1994. *http://www.faqs.org/rfcs/rfc1630.html*

Berners-Lee, Tim, L. Masinter, and M. McCahill. "Uniform Resource Locators (URL)." *RFC* 738, Proposed Standard, Dec. 1994; updated by *RFC* 1808 and *RFC* 2368. *http://www.faqs.org/rfcs/rfc1738.html*

Berners-Lee, Tim, R. Fielding, and L. Masinter. "Uniform Resource Identifiers (URI): Generic Syntax." *RFC* 2394, Draft Standard, Aug. 1998. *http://www.faqs.org/rfcs/rfc2396.html*

World Wide Web Consortium. *Naming and Addressing: URIs, URLs, ... http://www.w3.org/Addressing*

—Jonathan Bowen

Usenet

Usenet is often described as a distributed bulletin board of newsgroups. It is also called an online conferencing system or a global online community of users. These descriptions are all true, but they do not capture the essential nature of Usenet. Usenet is, above all, a users' network.

Usenet consists of thousands of newsgroups on a wide range of topics, enabling users to discuss these topics publicly with other users in an online conversation that spans the globe. Users contribute articles, which are referred to as *posts.* Posts can be just a few lines in length or far longer. They can be questions, responses to other posts, descriptions of some problem a user has identified and wants help to solve, and they can even be **ASCII art** or **software**. Using an automated process and programs, these posts are sent to other users worldwide via the **Internet** or other transport means, such as UUCP (Unix-to-Unix CoPy), over telephone lines. It is not uncommon to post to Usenet and receive responses from users in diverse parts of the globe a few hours or even minutes later.

An important design principle that has helped Usenet to grow and spread is that control over communication resides in the receiving side, not in the sender or any central organization. The design principle of Usenet is that the receiver controls what is received. This is in contrast to mailing lists where there is a central point of control for what is sent to those on the list. On Usenet, a user contributes a post. The posts are then sent out by the participating computing systems and become part of what is called a *Usenet feed.* The programs and standards that make it possible for the sites participating in Usenet to exchange posts are called *netnews.*

The birth of Usenet demonstrates its close connection with the **Unix** community. Tom Truscott (1953–), a graduate student at Duke University, spent the summer of 1979 working at **Bell Labs** with many of the pioneers who created Unix. Returning to Duke in the fall, he wanted to have a way to continue the kind of cooperative relationships he had while at Bell Labs. After discussing the situation with Jim Ellis, the two conceived of Usenet as a way to create a network to support online collaboration. They planned to explore how to use some little known features for remote software operation and communication that were being distributed with the most recent version of the Unix operating system. They met and began to work with other students to create Usenet.

Originally, Usenet was transported using UUCP, auto-dial-up modems and telephone lines. In 1986, the Network News Transfer Protocol (NNTP) was created. NNTP made it possible to send Usenet over the Internet. Others continue to use UUCP as a transport mechanism, either over telephone lines or over the Internet.

Usenet posts are stored on a "News" server to which the user has access, rather than kept in the user's mailbox. A user decides which newsgroups to subscribe to and which posts to read. Posts are expired by the participating computing systems according to their desires.

Since its beginning in 1979, Usenet has continued to grow, both in numbers of newsgroups and gigabytes of articles. Similarly, it continues to spread to an ever-increasing number of users in an ever-wider geographic area. As of March 2000, a full Usenet feed could include over 60,000 newsgroups and over 100 gigabytes daily of data. Newsgroup topics are diverse, providing for discussion of the subjects of interest to this global online community. Among those who contribute to Usenet and rely on it are a technical community for whom public up-to-date communication is a vital necessity to keep up with the development of computer and communications technology. Newsgroups exist to discuss such topics as economics (*sci.econ*), the Internet protocols TCP/IP (*comp.protocols.tcp-ip*), matters related to the administration of Usenet (*news.admin.misc*), the problems of being a writer (*misc.writing*), or the experience of living in Japan (*fj.life.in-japan*).

Topics on Usenet are grouped by hierarchies such as *comp* for computer-related subject (e.g., *comp.unix.misc*) and *rec* for topics related to hobbies and the arts (e.g., *rec.arts.theatre.plays*, *rec.aviation*). There are also hierarchies that are related to diverse countries and languages. For example, the *at* hierarchy is for Austrian newsgroups, with most of the posts in German (e.g., *at.internet.breitband*).

The process for creating newsgroups and for contributing articles to them encourages and thrives on user input. The vitality of Usenet stems from the participation of the users in both the content and form of the developing network.

FURTHER READING

Brown, Janelle. "A Kinder, Gentler USENET." *Salon*, 15 Sept. 1998. *http://www.salonmagazine.com/21st/feature/1998/09/15feature.html*

Hauben, Michael, and Ronda Hauben. *Netizens: On the History and Impact of Usenet and the Internet.* Los Alamitos, Calif.: IEEE Computer Society Press, 1997. *http://www.columbia.edu/~hauben/netbook*

Pfaffenberger, Bryan. "'If I Want It, It's OK': Usenet and the (Outer) Limits of Free Speech." *Information Society*, Vol. 12, No. 4, Oct./Dec. 1996.

Spencer, Henry, and David Lawrence. *Managing Usenet.* Sebastopol, Calif.: O'Reilly, 1998.

Woodbury, Gregory G. "Net Cultural Assumptions." *Amateur Computerist*, Vol. 6, No. 2/3, Fall/Winter 1995. *http://studentweb.tulane.edu/~rwoods/internet/amcomp62.html*

—*Ronda Hauben*

UUNET Technologies

UUNET (Unix-to-Unix Network) is one of the world's largest **Internet service providers** (ISPs) with more than 2000 points of presence (PoPs) around the world. The company, based in Ashburn, Virginia, was formed in 1987 by Rick Adams, one of the original developers of **ARPANET** (U.S. Defense Advanced Research Project Agency), the precursor to the public Internet.

UUNET was born out of Adams' pioneering efforts to expand use of the Internet beyond military and academic use to connect private businesses. The company sold its first commercial connection to the Internet in 1988. Now, as a tier 1 ISP, UUNET Technologies Inc. forms part of the national **backbone** of the public Internet. The UUNET carries more than 50 percent of the world's Internet traffic and serves over 70,000 business customers in 114 countries.

In 1996, UUNET was acquired by MFS Communications Company Inc. In the same year, MFS was acquired by WorldCom Inc., which remains the company's parent company. In addition to Adams, who no longer works at UUNET, there have been two other leading figures at the company. John Sidgmore (1951–), currently chairman of UUNET and vice-chairman of WorldCom, joined the ISP in 1994 with the title of chief executive officer. Sidgmore has been credited with providing the direction that spurred the company's massive growth in the late 1990s. Michael D. O'Dell, UUNET's senior vice-president and chief scientist, is a visionary who has mapped out the overall network architecture. The network has been designed to be *scalable*, meaning that it can handle high volumes of traffic, and *reliable*, meaning that users experience minimum downtime .

But the Internet backbone is just one portion of the business. As an ISP, the company also offers business services. In 1996 the company formed a Web hosting–colocation business unit which has largely defined the company. As a Web hosting business partner, UUNET will manage a company's Web site from a data center that is set up with multiplatform server farms that have built-in security and redundancy. Or a company could chose to colocate their own server equipment within UUNET's data center, retaining control of the management of the site but accessing UUNET's secure high-speed Internet connections on the premises. Other value-added services that UUNET offers to customers include virtual private networking (VPN), in which the public network provides capabilities similar to private lines, remote access, and managed security. UUNET was the first ISP to come out with a service level agreement (SLA) for customers as a way to measure the reliability of its VPN, hosting, and high-speed Internet access services.

The UUNET backbone has increased progressively in speed over the years. By the end of the year 2000 the company will have completed its network upgrade in the United States from OC-48 (optical carrier level 48) to OC-192 (optical carrier level 192) SONET (synchronous optical network) rates, which quadruples the speed of the network from 2.4 gigabits per second to 10 gigabits per second (a gigabit is equal to 1 billion bits). This will make UUNET an ISP with one of the fastest networks on the Internet.

FURTHER READING

Dodge, John and John Rendlemen. "MCI's Sidgmore Forges Ahead in Shifting Net Landscape." *eWEEK*, 24 Jan. 2000.

—*Stephanie Neil*

Vacuum Tube

A vacuum tube (called a *valve* in the United Kingdom) is an electronic device contained in an evacuated glass container that is sometimes used to amplify signals or for other purposes. Vacuum tube memories were used in many early computers, although they are very expensive and power consuming.

A metallic cathode is heated to enable electrons to leave its surface and move inside the tube. A metallic plate has positive voltage with respect to the cathode and attracts the electrons, in this way closing an electric circuit. The tube has to be evacuated, since a gas such as oxygen and nitrogen would prevent the electrons emitted by the cathode from reaching the plate. A cathode and a plate form a *diode*, useful because it lets the electrons flow in only one direction, from cathode to plate.

Of the several forms of vacuum tubes used in early computers, the *triode* was the most prevalent, because two triodes could be contained in the same evacuated glass bulb. In a triode, an additional component is used that controls the number of electrons per second, or current, that reaches the plate. This third electrode is called a *grid*. The grid is interposed between the cathode and the plate. The more positive the grid is with respect to the cathode, the more electrons that reach the plate. A triode provides power gain to the circuits in which it is used.

A single triode, connected as an amplifier, works as an inverter. For example, a positive signal of 0.1 volt (V) applied to its grid will cause its plate voltage to drop from +150 V to +140 V, a change of −10 V. It is clear that the polarity of the original signal (0.1 V) was inverted and the magnitude of the signal was amplified by 100. These numbers are representative of a typical triode inverter used as an amplifier.

Two triodes, in one glass envelope, became a much needed computer component for early computers. An important computer circuit is the **flip-flop**. It consists of two triodes connected such that the output of one is the input of the other. In use, the plate of each triode is connected, through a resistor, to a positive power source of about +150 V. The cathode of each triode is connected to the negative power source, which is called *ground*. The grid of each triode is connected, through a first resistor, to about -15 V, and, through a second resistor, to the plate of the other triode.

The flip-flop switch has only two stable states, "on" and "off." If, for example, the left inverter is on, and thus conducting current, this can represent a 1. If the left inverter is off, the right inverter must be on; this represents a 0. It therefore can store one bit of information. A flip-flop can now be described as the output of a first inverter, which is connected to the input of a second inverter, whose output is connected to the input of the first inverter. There is a simple thought experiment that will assist in understanding how the flip-flop works. Think of two people in a double bed with an electric blanket with two heating elements and two temperature controllers. For this thought experiment assume that the temperature controllers are reversed. The person on the left side of the bed has the temperature controller that controls the heating element for the person on the right side of the bed, and vice versa.

The **Selective Sequence Electronic Calculator** (SSEC) from **IBM** was dedicated in January 1948. It contained 21,400 relays and 12,500 vacuum tubes. It was used to solve problems involving atomic fields, hydrodynamics, optics, fluid flow, and planetary orbits.

Another forerunner of the computer was IBM's 604 Electronic Calculating Punch, delivered in the fall of 1948. In a 10-year period about 6000 of these machines were built. The 604 contained 1250 vacuum tubes. In comparison, by October 7, 1954, an experimental transistorized 604 contained 2200 junction transistors. It occupied less than half the volume and consumed about 5 percent of the power. The last of IBM's vacuum tube machines was announced in January 1957 as the Type 709 Electronic Data Processing System.

In the late 1940s and early 1950s, vacuum tubes were being produced by CBS Hytron, General Electric, RCA, Sylvania, Tungsol, and several others. These tube manufacturers each produced many millions of vacuum tubes each year. By the early 1980s many of these vacuum tube manufacturers were either out of business or engaged in other activities.

FURTHER READING

Bashe, Charles J., Lyle R. Johnson, John H. Palmer, and Emerson W. Pugh. *IBM's Early Computers.* Cambridge, Mass.: MIT Press, 1986.

—*Joseph Logue*

Digital Equipment Corporation's VAX 11/780. (Courtesy of the Computer Museum History Center)

VAX

The Virtual Address eXtension PDP-11 (VAX-11) from **Digital Equipment Corporation** provided a sophisticated multiuser computer service to millions of users through the last two decades of the twentieth century.

In 1974, Digital decided that its **PDP** series should be extended to support much larger programs. Designs using a 16-bit architecture proved unsatisfactory and Digital decided to develop a 32-bit machine that would be "culturally compatible" with the PDP-11s, under the direction of William Strecker. The VAX's 32-bit memory address gave a 4-gigabyte *virtual memory* space mapped in 512-byte pages. A program reference to a memory address that was not in physical memory generated a *page fault* and suspended the program while the operating system read the required page from disk. Data types included 8-, 16-, 32-, and 64-bit integers, 32- and 64-bit **floating-point** numbers, bit fields, character strings, and packed decimal strings. The VAX also featured a set of 16 registers, plus very consistent addressing with many modes and a complex set of 244 instructions, tailored to support high-level language compilers. The machine used the same peripheral, file, and disk formats as were used on PDP-11s, and it had a PDP-11 compatibility mode to run existing programs developed for PDP-11s under the RSX-11M operating system. (This mode was dropped in some later VAX implementations.) The user commands for its virtual memory operating system (VMS) were based on RSX-11M.

The VAX-11/780 was produced in 1977 with a performance of around 1 million instructions per second (MIPS). It was particularly notable for having a small PDP-11 attached as the bootstrap and console controller. Subsequent machines were smaller and faster, with additional capabilities such as vector processing, multiple processors, and fault tolerance. At its peak in the early 1990s, over 500,000 systems were in use. The last VAXes (or, to enthusiasts, *VAXen*), a compact server and a desktop model, will stop production in 2000.

The VAX range provided relatively low cost computing to a huge number of businesses and institutions in many countries. Although they were often seen as scientific machines, supporting **Fortran** and **C** compilers, they were equally successful in commercial environments, with **COBOL** and database products. They had enthusiastic user support through the DEC Users' Society (DECUS), which held enormous annual meetings around the world. The VAX introduced many to the arcane world of systems management and allowed the development of large *software* projects that could not have been contemplated on earlier systems. The VAX was the main computer platform sold by Digital Equipment until the company was acquired by **Compaq** in 1997.

FURTHER READING

"After More Than 20 Years, VAX Production Ceases, Service and Support Continue." *http://www.compaq.com/emea/inform/q399/openvms/vax.html*

Bell, C. Gordon, J. Craig Mudge, and John E. McNamara, eds. *Computer Engineering: A DEC View of Hardware Systems Design*. Bedford, Mass.: Digital Press, 1978.

"System Performance Data." *http://www.digital.com/seg/appb.htm*

Digital Equipment Corporation. *VAX 11/780 Architecture Handbook*. Maynard, Mass: Digital Press, 1977.

———. *VAX 11 Architecture Handbook*. Bedford, Mass.: Digital Press, 1979.

Goldenberg, Ruth E., Lawrence J. Kenah, and Denise E. Dumas. *VAX/VMS Internals and Data Structures: Version 5.2*. Woburn, Mass.: Butterworth-Heineman, 1991.

Levy, Henry M., and Richard H. Eckhouse, Jr. *Computer Programming and Architecture: The VAX*. Bedford, Mass.: Digital Press, 1988.

Lipcon, Jesse. "Open VMS: 20 Years of Renewal—OpenVMS Installed Base Growth." *http://www.openvms.digital.com/openvms/20th/vms20/sld036.htm*

—*John Deane*

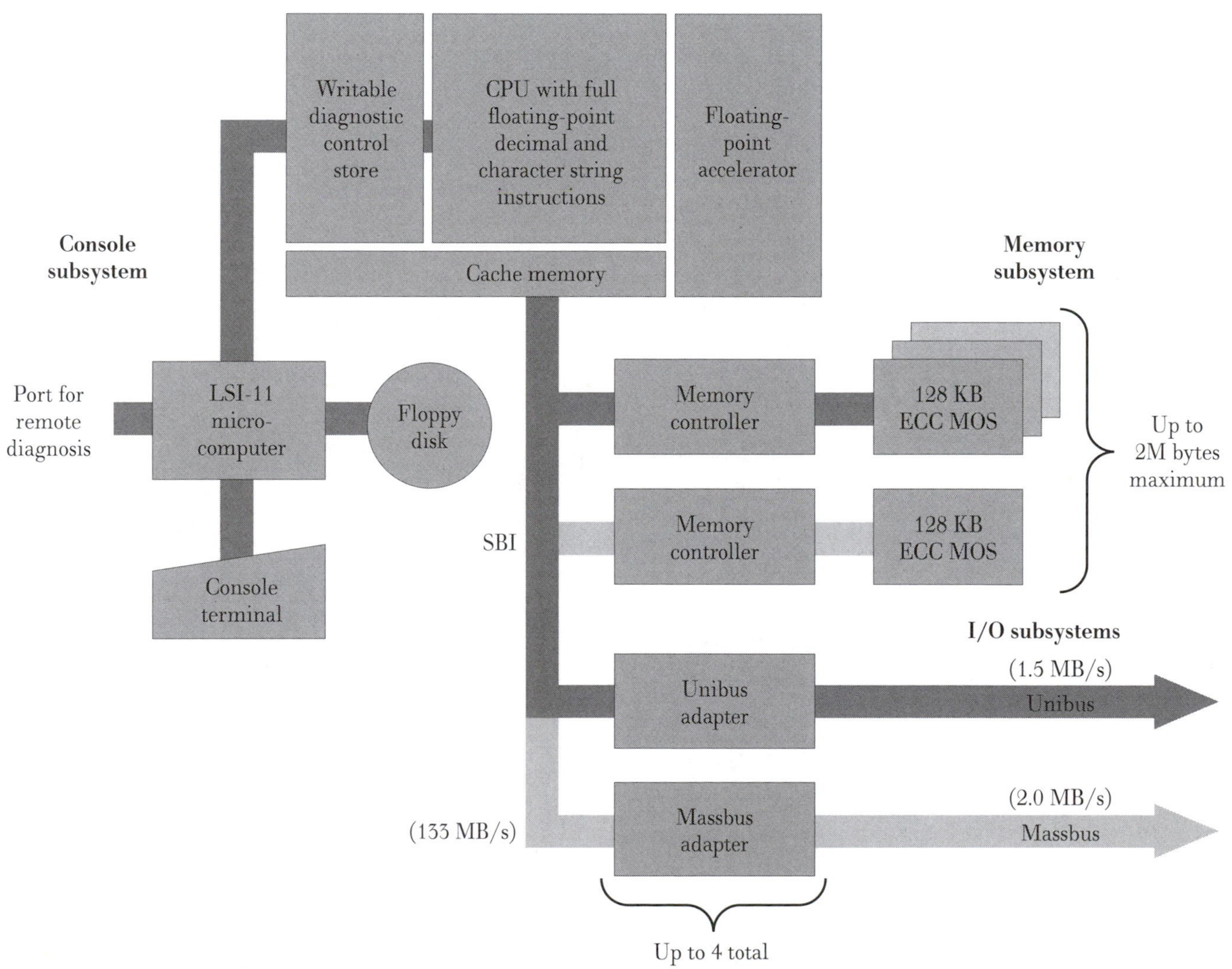

Diagram of a VAX-11/780 system.

Very Large Scale Integration

Very large scale integration (VLSI) is a **semiconductor** technology for designing and fabricating complex patterns on **silicon**. It focuses on the development of methodologies, architectures, and **computer-aided design** and processes to design, fabricate, and test systems with a million or more gates on a chip.

In 1971, **Intel** produced the 4004 chip. It was an arrangement of microscopic **transistors** that were packed into a space the size of a matchbook cover, yet contained the computer power of a mainframe computer of the late 1940s. A year later, Intel produced the 8008 chip, with double the processing power, and two years later, in 1974, a chip that again doubled the computing power previously available.

By the mid-1970s there were significant developments in submicron device technology but it was not clear how to harness the new untapped design power. Who would be able to manufacture custom elements with millions of gates?

The ability to start with a blank piece of silicon and place wires, **logic gates**, and other components wherever one wishes raises a number of questions. How are choices to be made? What choices will lead to what computation capability? In what time? How is it possible to determine how to make sensible choices of what computing structures should be built?

As early as 1971, **Carver Mead** (1934–) had developed a series of courses in **integrated circuit** (IC) design at the California Institute of Technology (Cal Tech). As a consultant to corporations such as Intel, Mead knew of the level of industrial research and development in metal-oxide semiconductor (MOS) large-scale (LS) integrated circuit design technology. Mead introduced students to the basic practices being used in industry. His contacts also gave him access to industrial fabrication facilities. His students were able to create impressive IC devices as a result of his courses.

Mead's research was supported by the Information Processing Techniques Office (IPTO) of the Advanced Research Projects Agency (**ARPA**), headed at that time by **Ivan Sutherland** (1938–). Like Mead, Sutherland wanted to extend the boundaries of computer hardware capability. Sutherland left the University of Utah and joined Mead at Cal Tech.

Mead and Sutherland asked how minuscule a transistor could be and still be functional. They also wondered how complex a system could be while still being manageable. With transistors becoming smaller and more densely packed on the silicon surface of an integrated circuit, such questions were of increasing importance. Mead and Sutherland called the potential change in integrated circuit miniaturization, *VLSI.*

Where components were slow and expensive and the wires connecting them were cheap, a sequential design was appropriate. Sequential processing, however, involved the bottleneck of one operation being performed at a time. With the development of MOS technology, new architectures and new design methods and tools were needed. What should be the geometric arrangement of the logic components on a flake of silicon and of the pathways linking them? Instead of linear sequences, an architecture more like that of densely packed city streets became the objective.

In 1975, after having followed semiconductor technology developments since 1972, **Robert Kahn** (1938–) at the IPTO saw the potential improvements in computer capability that were becoming possible. The time was ripe for supporting university research to begin to develop VLSI technology.

In mid-1977, Kahn prepared an internal position paper proposing a VLSI research program. As he conceived it, the VLSI program would emphasize three major objectives: (1) submicron design, (2) semiconductor fabrication, and (3) computer **architecture** and design.

In July 1977, DARPA (ARPA had been renamed the Defense Advanced Research Projects Agency) commissioned the RAND Corporation to evaluate the scope of research that DARPA might support. A report entitled "Basic Limitations in Micro Circuit Fabrication" was prepared by Sutherland, Mead, and Thomas Everhardt, and issued in November 1977. The report proposed that important advances in integrated circuit technology could be made, with a potential for an eightfold improvement.

The authors also commented on the fact that the industry would be unlikely to do the needed research and development to make such advances, because of the lack of commercial demand for higher-power IC designs. But even though this would not be an area of industrial research and development, research and defense systems would need these order-of-magnitude improvements.

Kahn wanted researchers to break the 1-micrometer barrier to permit the design of chips with 1 million or more gates. Kahn recognized the potential of chips to have greater speeds and capacities. Although there was the potential for such new capability, university researchers, those who might be able to develop the potential, were having difficulty gaining access to the fabrication facilities needed to produce and test new chip designs. Often, such access depended on personal connections with fabrication facilities. The more complex chip designs became, the longer it would take for university researchers to get access to a fabrication facility.

Alarmed about this decreasing access just when the potential to exploit the new technology was growing, DARPA began to consider the creation of a VLSI program. The program would have two goals: the improvement of the materials aspects of semiconductor technology, and the development of new architectures and design tools and methods.

For the university research community to be able to develop this new technology, access to an IC fabrication system with fast turnaround times would be needed. IPTO was interested in research on new and simpler IC design techniques and on procedures to provide fast turnaround time for production of new university IC designs.

In 1976, Bert Sutherland, head of the Systems Science Laboratory at the **Xerox Palo Alto Research Center** (PARC), invited Mead to give a talk on the design of silicon-based integrated circuits. Mead was proposing a new way of thinking about computer design. He was concerned with the problems of shrinking transistor size and greatly increasing density. Design principles used traditionally were no longer appropriate.

Listening to Mead's talk were PARC researchers Lynn Conway (1938–) and Douglas Fairbairn. Conway had experience designing a **supercomputer** at IBM's research laboratory in Yorktown Heights and had designed **minicomputers** at Memorex. Fairbairn had a research background at Stanford University. During the next year, Mead collaborated with Conway and Fairbairn, teaching them his theories of microelectronics and computer science. Conway and Fairbairn created design methods and tools that would make it possible for engineers to design complex new architectures using the types of workstations that had been created at PARC.

Computer systems that had previously required racks of components and wires could now be created by designs etched into silicon flakes and formed into tiny chips. Modules could be created that could be combined to build the types of systems desired. Conway and Mead were able to design these chips and turn them over to **Hewlett-Packard** for fabrication. Conway recognized that there was not only a need to develop the new scientific methods and technology but also to affect a cultural change in the methods used if this new technology was to be adopted.

The schematics for VLSI used novel and new design techniques that were different from previous generations of integrated circuits. Since the new technology was as yet unproven, a body of chips would need to be manufactured to demonstrate its feasibility. There was also a need to develop a body of experience with the new technical and design processes. Conway felt that this experience would best be developed interactively, and in a way that encouraged communication among the research community. She also planned to create a text using interactive collaboration in a way similar to that which the development of time sharing had pioneered. The **ARPANET** and the interactive research culture it fostered would provide a platform for her work developing a course for teaching VLSI design methodology.

The DARPA VLSI program began in January 1978. One of the major thrusts was to arrange for fabrication and testing of experimental device designs. In fall 1978, Conway was to teach a course on VLSI as a guest instructor at the Massachusetts Institute of Technology. She made arrangements to communicate what she was doing with other researchers on the ARPANET, and she asked Kahn at IPTO if designs being done by students could be sent via the ARPANET to PARC for fabrication and testing. Kahn allowed the use of the ARPANET for the VLSI design transfers to PARC, where chip layout was done. Then masks were ordered from Micro-Mask, Inc., and Hewlett-Packard handled the details of chip fabrication.

Conway next began to extend access to her design methods to other institutions. She organized a remote-entry multiproject chip (MPC) fabrication that would be available to these institutions via electronic mail. By 1980 DARPA arranged with the Information Sciences Institute (ISI) at the University of Southern California to take over the silicon broker service from PARC. ISI-USC established MOSIS (the MOS Implementation System) and developed a multiple-step process.

The VLSI design and fabrication process developed through these experiences led to a body of knowledge in the creation of both design tools and methods and fabrication processes. The geometry engine and the RISC chips, among a number of successes by VLSI university researchers, became the basis for companies such as **Silicon Graphics, Inc.** and **Sun Microsystems**. VLSI research has led to the ability to create and fabricate increasingly complex chip architectures, and VLSI design courses have become a recognized part of the curriculum at universities around the world.

Further Reading

Conway, Lynn A. "The MPC Adventures." *Proceedings of the 2nd Cal Tech Conference on Very Large Scale Integration*, Jan. 1981, pp. 5–27.

Mead, Carver, and Lynn Conway. *Introduction to VLSI Systems*. New York: Addison-Wesley, 1980.

Sutherland, Ivan E., and Carver Mead. "Microelectronics and Computer Science." *Scientific American*, Vol. 237, No. 3, 1977, pp. 210–228.

—*Ronda Hauben*

Videotex

Videotex deserves to be remembered as an early version of the **World Wide Web**. Indeed, although the Web has turned out to be the winner, it is still lacking features of some Videotex systems.

Sam Fedida, an engineer with British Telecom, was not the first to propose an information and communication network but was first to implement such a system on a large scale. Begun in the early 1970s and called Prestel, it was based on a simple observation: Most families have a television set and a telephone, so why not use the telephone to access services in a network of computers and use the TV set as display? The only additional components one would need would be a decoder (built in or sitting on the TV set as a set-top box) to display the information transmitted, a modem to send the analog telephone signals in digital form from the telephone to the decoder, and the remote control keypad of the TV set as a minimalistic **keyboard**.

Prestel provided 24 lines of 40 characters on the TV screen. Using 16 colors and a large set of special "mosaic" characters consisting of little colored rectangles, Prestel allowed the display of surprisingly appealing textual and graphical information. Although primitive compared with today's high-resolution graphics, it was infinitely better than what we see now, some 20 years later, on *WAP* (**wireless application protocol**) *handys* (cellular telephones) for Web browsing. Prestel did have limitations, yet it also had features that are still missing in today's Web. Quality of service was guaranteed: With the original asymmetric 1200/75-baud modems, a Prestel page would appear line by line in a total of 6 seconds, with faster modems later reducing this to 0.75 second. Micro payments through page charges (collected with the phone bill) were part of the system from the start. Information was structured according to a general classification scheme. The visions associated with Prestel are in fact the visions of today's Web.

Prestel was adopted in many countries, most notably in Europe. Comparable systems were introduced in Japan, Canada (with its Telidon system in the lead as far as graphics are concerned), and the United States (with the North American Presentation-Level-Protocol Syntax).

The graphic limitations of Prestel led to the proposal of a new European standard, CEPT Videotex, with features unusual for the early 1980s, such as

4096 colors, redefinable character sets, and (optional) geometric graphics, as we now have in all advanced graphic systems. Some of the elements in the CEPT standard that sound odd, such as 32 flashing frequencies of different intensity, were introduced as an attempt to make sure that popular non-European computers such as the **Commodore 64** or the **Apple II** would *not* be able to handle Videotex, allowing the European information technology industry to catch up behind the "shield" of the standard. This attempt failed: A number of countries kept sticking to the original Prestel standard, and in 1982 the French introduced their own version, called Minitel. Germany was quite successful with its version, Bildschirmtext (BTX), but eventually had to merge it with the Web.

Two evolutions of Videotex are particularly worth mentioning. The French Minitel was pushed very aggressively. Many Minitel terminals (usually black and white but with a full keyboard) were distributed free to millions of households instead of printed telephone directories. This was partially successful, and in the 1990s Minitel had millions of devoted users, but even Minitel could not withstand the pressure from **personal computers** (PCs) and the Web.

The Austrian telecommunication authority followed the advice of a research study which recommended that Videotex should not be seen as mainly an information system, but as a network for CEPT-compatible computers. Since no such computers existed, a Z80-based color graphics computer, MUPID, was developed: It handled all the features of CEPT, including geometric graphics. It was even usable as full-fledged personal computer since it made it possible to download what was then called *telesoftware*, which we now would call **applets**. Telesoftware was written in a **BASIC** dialect, and the BASIC engine was integrated in MUPID. Together with the then-popular **CP/M** operating system, MUPID was a genuine networked personal computer with word processing and the like, at a time before the first (IBM) PC. Some 50.000 MUPIDs were produced in the 1980s (a sensation for the then-low-tech country Austria), but acceptance was not sufficient to withstand the onslaught of the now-omnipresent PC connected to the Web.

FURTHER READING

Gecsei, J. *The Architecture of Videotex Systems.* Englewood Cliffs, N.J.: Prentice Hall, 1983.

Maurer, H., and I. Sebestyen. "Unorthodox Videotex Applications." *Information Services and Use* 2, 1982, pp. 19–34.

———. "Report on Videotex Development in Austria." *Electronic Publishing Review*, Vol. 4, No. 1, 1984, pp. 45–57.

—*Hermann Maurer*

Virtual Community

Virtual communities exist in what science fiction writer William Gibson (1948–) called the *nonspaces* created by computer systems, or **cyberspace**. Cyberspace is theoretical; it lacks physical presence. Participants construct an illusionary social reality through written exchanges. For example, groups of people exchange ideas and information through the posting of messages on **bulletin board systems** (BBSs), by sending **electronic mail** messages to a common list of recipients, and by exchanging private e-mail.

Howard Rheingold (1947–) coined the term *virtual community* in 1993 to describe the interpersonal relationships he developed with other people through a computer network called the *Whole Earth 'Lectronic Link* (WELL). After 10 years of active online participation, Rheingold observed that whenever computer-mediated communication (CMC) technology becomes available to people, they build virtual communities in ways similar to those in which microorganisms create colonies. Rheingold defined virtual communities as social aggregations that materialize from the network when a group of people engage in discussion long enough and with sufficient human feeling to form webs of interpersonal relationships.

These relationships do not depend on physical closeness. Members of these communities interact with each other through their virtual presence, often called *telepresence*, in cyberspace. The word *presence* refers to the actual, natural perception of an environment, in contrast, telepresence refers to the mediated understanding of an environment. Telepresence is the experience of presence that is created when using a communication medium, such as a telephone, computer network, or teleconferencing system.

A variety of forms of both synchronous and asynchronous CMC contexts foster the formation of virtual communities. For example, there are **MUD** communities, as well as communities formed through bulletin boards, newsgroups, and discussion lists. In contrast to traditional communities that are based on geographic proximity, electronic communities are generally established because of shared recreational, personal, and professional interests. Topics include role-playing games, providing mutual support for addiction or medical problems, discussing a hobby, exchanging computer information, and talking about popular television programs. New media scholar Nancy Baym researched an online fan group called *rec.arts.tv.soaps* (r.a.t.s.), a recreational discussion list of daytime soap operas. She contends that after a decade of online communication, the thousands of people who have participated in r.a.t.s. have created a dynamic community that is filled with social nuance and emotion.

Early researchers intrigued by CMC focused on its use in organizational contexts because it was first introduced into these settings. In organizational settings, the dominant theories about CMC throughout the 1980s suggested that it was impersonal and sometimes more hostile than face-to-face communication. This view became known as the *cues-filtered-out perspective*, and it describes research that argues which computers have low social presence and, as a result, they deprive participants of prominent social cues. With the removal of social cues, the discourse is left in a social vacuum and it is quite different from face-to-face interaction.

However, the expectations of cues-filtered-out researchers were not realized when experienced computer users were studied. In contrast, experienced users would mix work correspondence with informal social messages. Research conducted on the communication behavior of CMC users by Ronald E. Rice and Gail Love revealed that a percentage of the correspondence between CMC users contains socioemotional content, which they defined as interactions that displayed solidarity, agreement, tension relief, antagonism, tension, and disagreement. As a result, studies began to focus on the social and interpersonal uses of CMC. According to researchers, the interactive characteristic of new media can satisfy interpersonal needs because these media are flexible enough to personalize information. As a result, computer networks can help foster a sense of social presence. Social presence is reflected in how participants in a communication exchange would evaluate the medium being used based on the criteria of unsociable/sociable, insensitive/sensitive, cold/warm, and impersonal/personal. For example, people generally expect a business letter to have less social presence than a face-to-face meeting.

Two factors that relate to social presence are interactivity and the public versus private aspect of the interaction. *Interactivity* refers to the two-way communication between senders and receivers of messages: for example, face-to-face and CMC correspondence. However, the lack of visual information in CMC tends to foster increased self-disclosure. People tend to find it extremely comfortable to disclose personal information when they are interacting with a computer. For this reason, many organizations have supported the development of computer-administered interviews, such as electronic surveys for doing medical diagnosis, employment, and personnel evaluations. Similarly, when people sit at home alone typing their inner thoughts into the computer, they have a tendency to perceive the experience as being a private rather than a public one. This tendency toward self-disclosure is an important factor in the formation of virtual communities, and many of these groups perceive themselves to exist in "private" areas of cyberspace.

Sometimes the private world of virtual communities is shared with the general public. For example, in December 1993, journalist Julian Dibbell (1963–) wrote an article about a virtual rape for New York City's weekly newspaper the *Village Voice*. In the article he described a virtual rape on LambdaMOO, a MUD community started in October 1990 by Pavel Curtis (1960–). Dibbell's description of a rape in a role-playing game illustrated how the fantasy world of cybersex could stir up passions in the physical flesh existing in the real world. The young women who created the female characters involved in the "virtual" rape suffered actual posttraumatic distress. The story revealed that what happens inside a MUD-made world is neither exactly real nor exactly make-believe; instead, online relationships can be emotionally meaningful to the people involved.

Inside LambdaMOO, the negative behavior of one individual character created a situation in which members had to deal with issues that parallel the social concerns of traditional communities. As a result, the group began to experiment with the development of a "virtual" legal system. In some ways, social behavior on MUDs is a direct mirror of behavior in real life. For example, the Lambda legal system borrows from the American legal system and players tend to assume that freedom of speech and right to privacy in the real world apply to their online counterparts.

Although legal issues in MUDs parallel real life, online environments create a situation in which participants can engage in debate, experiment with creating laws, and critique behavior on both an individual and a social level. As a result, virtual communities have the potential to become a utopian space for critiquing and rethinking the institutional structures that exit in actual communities. Online role-playing games and the virtual communities that they create offer an opportunity for people to reshape their understanding of self, politics, and social structures.

Computer networks are now changing our concept of community. Although members of virtual communities meet in imaginary space, they tend to behave as if the group met in a physical place. Traditionally, communities were viewed as groups of people who live in the same geographic area and follow the same set of behavioral rules. In virtual communities, people share similar interests by "talking" to each other through the written word. In addition to interests, group members share birth announcements, deaths, and personal triumphs or sorrows. Members of virtual communities that stay together for long periods of time tend to want to meet in-person and it is common for these groups to arrange face-to-face gatherings.

FURTHER READING

Barnes, S. B. *Online Connections: Internet Interpersonal Relationships.* Cresskill, N.J.: Hampton Press, 2000.

Baym, N. K. "The Emergence of Community in Computer-Mediated-Communication." In S. G. Jones, ed., *Cybersociety: Computer-Mediated Communication and Community.* Newbury Park, Calif.: Sage, 1995, pp. 138–163.

Dibbell, J. "Rape in Cyberspace: How an Evil Clown, a Haitian Trickster Spirit, Two Wizards, and a Cast of Dozens Turned a Database Into a Society." *The Village Voice,* 21 Dec. 1993, p. 39.

———. *My Tiny Life: Crime and Passion in a Virtual World.* New York: Henry Holt, 1998.

Rheingold, Howard. *The Virtual Community: Homesteading on the Electronic Frontier.* Reading, Mass.: Addison-Wesley, 1993.

Rice, R. E., and G. Love. "Electronic Emotion: Socioemotional Content in a Computer-Mediated Communication Network." *Communiation Research,* Vol. 14, No. 1, Feb. 1987, pp. 85–108.

Williams, R., and R. E. Rice. "Communication Research and New Media Technologies." In R. Bostrom, ed., *Communication Yearbook,* Vol. 7, Newbury Park, Calif.: Sage, 1983, pp. 200–224.

—*Susan B. Barnes*

Virtual Machine

The term *virtual machine* (VM) refers to an abstract machine that is not built in **hardware** but is emulated in **software** by a host computer. There are several reasons to have a VM; one of them is portability. If a system is defined on top of a VM, using the commands it provides, it is later easier to port the system to another host computer. Only the VM has to be reprogrammed, not the entire system.

Usually, a high-level programming language is compiled (transformed) into a sequence of assembler instructions for a target computer. However, each computer requires its own compiler because every machine usually provides a different instruction set. If the compiler is large and complex, rewriting it can be very difficult. For the implementation of the **Java** programming language, which is supposed to run on any machine connected to the **Internet**, a different strategy had to be adopted. An abstract (virtual) machine was defined together with its instruction set. This is the *Java virtual machine* (JVM). All Java **compilers and interpreters** produce code for the JVM and the browser has only to simulate this machine in software. Writing a new version of the JVM for another computer has the complexity of a student project, writing the compiler for Java is much more difficult. Recently, **Sun Microsystems** introduced the *K virtual machine,* a very small virtual machine for Java specially designed for portable consumer devices such as cellular phones or personal organizers.

The programming language **Pascal** became popular after a virtual machine developed at the University of California–San Diego led to many compatible versions. Pascal was compiled into P-code, the instruction set of the virtual machine. Another notable example is the *Warren abstract machine* (WAM), developed by David Warren at the University of Edinburgh, which became the instrument of choice for implementing the programming language **Prolog**.

Another reason to have a virtual machine is to offer the programmer the illusion of having a single system when in reality many computers are working in parallel. This makes programming easier but the actual networking harder. The Parallel Virtual Machine (PVM) is a software package that connects many **Unix** or **Windows NT** machines as a single system. The package provides abstract instructions that hide the complexity of networking all machines together.

FURTHER READING

Geist, Al. *PVM: Parallel Virtual Machine.* Cambridge, Mass.: MIT Press, 1994.

Lindholm, Tim, and Frank Yellin. *The Java Virtual Machine Specification.* Reading, Mass.: Addison-Wesley, 1997; 2nd ed., 1999.

—Margarita Esponda

Virtual Memory

Every computer has a physical memory to store data and programs. This actual memory can be made to appear larger using virtual memory techniques; by means of virtual memory we can load a program of, for example, 5 megabytes in a physical memory that is just 1 megabyte large. The extra megabytes are simulated by shuffling data from physical memory to the **hard disk**, and vice versa.

Physical memory can never be too large: As Nathan Myhrvold (1969–), chief technology officer at **Microsoft** has observed, **software** always grows to fill all available space. Especially in time-shared **multitasking** systems, with many programs running at the same time, memory is a scarce resource. However, when a program is loaded into memory, only a small fraction of its code is being accessed every second. Most of the data and code lays idle, waiting to be used. This presents the opportunity to displace such not-yet-referenced data from the memory chips to the hard disk, which is slower. Later, when the displaced data need to be accessed, they can be brought back to physical memory.

To make the exchange of information from physical memory to the hard disk more efficient, the addressing space is divided into small *pages* of a few kilobytes (kB). For example, if the page size is 4 kB, a program that needs 20 kB can be loaded in five consecutive virtual memory pages. At the beginning, only the first page is loaded to physical memory and the rest is kept in the hard disk. Once the second page has to be accessed, it is loaded from the hard disk to the memory. In this way, only small chunks of data are moved each time from the slower device to the faster device. The **hardware** and **operating system** of the computer take care of doing all the housekeeping needed to load and clear pages in physical memory, and they also keep track of which pages belong to which programs. Moving pages from physical memory to the hard disk and back is called *swapping*. Operating systems reserve a portion of the hard disk exclusively for swapping. When swapping is done through a computer network (i.e., when the local system has no hard disk), it can slow down the system significantly.

To deal with virtual memory a difference is made between virtual and *physical addresses*. Physical addresses run from zero to the highest address in the memory chips installed. *Virtual addresses* run from zero to the maximum possible address that the processor can generate. For example, if the processor chip has 32 pins for addresses, a theoretical maximum of 4 gigabytes can be referenced. In a system with such virtual memory, huge programs can be loaded in the virtual addressing space available.

Since the available addressing space is divided into pages, there is no simple correspondence between virtual and physical addresses. For example, a page starting at virtual address 1 million could be loaded starting at physical address zero. A table is needed to keep track of the starting address of each virtual page: Called the *translation look-aside buffer* (TLB), this is stored in main memory. Part of the buffer, the last referenced entries in the table, is kept inside the processor to speed up the translation of virtual addresses into physical ones. When a virtual address is not found in physical memory, swapping has to be started. This is called a *page fault*. When the virtual page is found in the table, we have a *page hit*. A page fault is very expensive in terms of computing cycles, because it can take as much as 100,000 cycles to swap the missing page.

Some computers use a specialized memory management unit (MMU) to do the mapping of virtual into physical addresses. The MMU can be programmed to provide special services to the operating system, such as protection of pages belonging to the operating system from unauthorized access by user programs. In most **microprocessors** the MMU has been integrated with the microprocessor in the same package.

Once all physical memory has been filled with pages and a page fault is detected, the operating system has to decide which page should be displaced from physical memory to the hard disk in order to make space for a new page. One technique often used for this purpose is the LRU (least recently used) method. The page that has not been accessed for the longest time is sent to the hard disk and its space in physical memory is used for the new page that must be loaded. Special hardware or software keeps track of the references to pages in order to provide the information needed for the LRU **algorithm**.

The first virtual memory system was implemented in the **Atlas** computer in 1962 by a team led by **Tom Kilburn** (1921–2001) at the University of Manchester in the United Kingdom. The system used paging across a hierarchy of decreasingly faster storage devices. Virtual memory is now available in practically all computer systems.

FURTHER READING

Carr, Richard W. *Virtual Memory Management*. Ann Arbor, Mich.: UMI Research Press, 1984.

Patterson, David, and John Hennessy. *Computer Architecture: A Quantitative Approach*. San Mateo, Calif.: Morgan Kaufmann, 1990; 2nd ed., San Francisco, 1996.

Sumner, Frank. "The Atlas Computer." In R. Rojas and Ulf Hashagen, eds., *The First Computers*. Cambridge, Mass.: MIT Press, 2000.

—*Margarita Esponda*

Virtual Reality

Virtual reality (VR) uses **graphics** to place a user inside a three-dimensional computer-generated environment. Within this environment, the user can move and interact with virtual objects in real time. The computer responds by adjusting the scene to reflect the user's actions. For example, a user can "walk through" virtual space by controlling actions in real space.

VR implementations range from simple monitor displays with **mouse** and **keyboard** input to control action in the virtual space, to immersive headset systems with full body trackers. Other variations include flight simulators and video games where the windows of the cockpit are high-resolution computer screens; cave-type systems in which the computer scene is projected on the floor, walls, and ceiling, and the user is tracked within the room; boxes displaying the computer scene on stereo cameras that the user looks into and manipulates to control virtual movement; immersive desks that allow the user to hand-manipulate a virtual scene on a slanted table; augmented reality, where information is projected onto a transparent screen in a headset, allowing the real world to be enhanced through the added graphics; and telepresence, where remote cameras and microphones immerse the user in another real location.

The degree of realism within the virtual scene is determined by several factors. Stereo systems present both a left- and right-eye view to the user, which is helpful for focusing on close objects. This is generally accomplished with either two display devices, one for each eye, as in the headset, or by shutter or polarized glasses and interlaced scene projection used in desktop and cave-type systems. Three-dimensional sound is incorporated into most VR. Tactile devices that allow the sensation of touching a real object to match the virtual object have been shown to increase realism greatly. Gloves with tracking devices can permit the user to interact more naturally with virtual objects.

Although the elements of present VR systems have been evolving since the military introduced flight simulators following World War II, only recently have computing power, memory and storage, graphics **hardware**, and **software** refinements allowed VR to develop outside the military or research institutions. **Ivan**

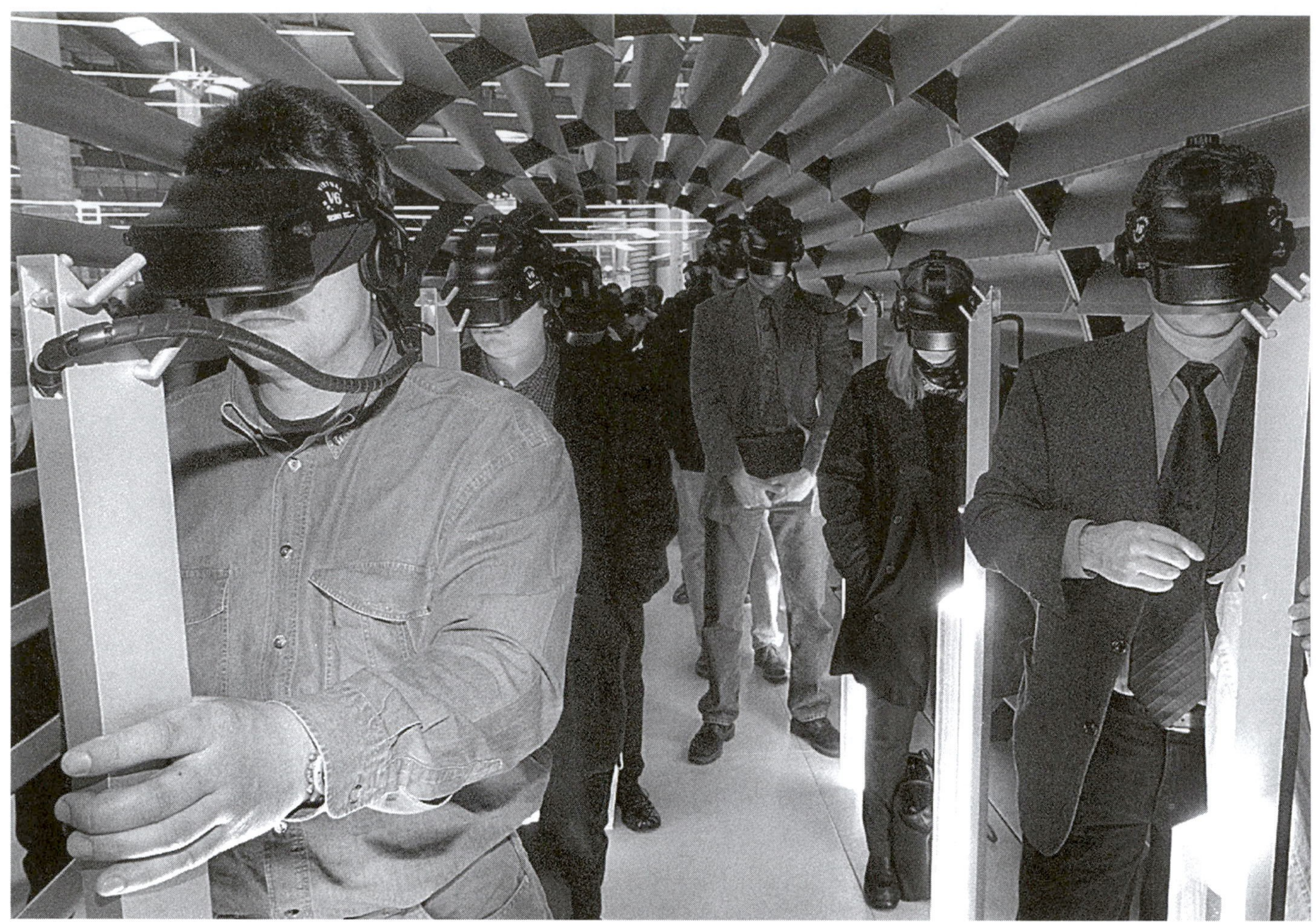

Virtual reality helmets at the CeBit fair in Hanover, Germany, 18 March 1999. (©AFP/CORBIS)

Sutherland (1938–) invented the head-mounted VR display in 1965, but the processing power needed to generate stereo images in real time was nonexistent. In the 1970s, computerized flight simulators became common. The gaming industry followed closely with action games and add-ons such as Mattel's Power-glove, which was designed at NASA's Ames Research Center. Both Hollywood and research institutions were regularly using graphics interactively by the 1980s.

VR hardware and software systems have found a variety of uses in medicine, business, and entertainment, and some systems are commercially available for home computers. Several proposals exist for three-dimensional modeling standards, such as VRML (**Virtual Reality Modeling Language**), a software platform for the development of virtual worlds. Although there are still technical problems with realism in virtual worlds, the promise of VR is becoming more real than ever.

Further Reading

Durlach, Nathaniel I., and Anne S. Mayor, eds. *Virtual Reality: Scientific and Technological Challenges.* Washington, D.C.: National Academy Press, 1995.

Heim, Michael. *Virtual Realism.* New York: Oxford University Press, 1998.

Vince, John. *Essential Virtual Reality Fast: How to Understand the Techniques and Potential of Virtual Reality.* New York: Springer-Verlag, 1998.

—*Dorothy Strickland*

Virtual Reality Modeling Language

Virtual Reality Modeling Language (VRML) was the first file format widely available for describing interactive three-dimensional (3D) objects capable of being downloaded on the **World Wide Web**. It was important in opening up the possibilities of virtual reality in **cyberspace**. Using VRML whole virtual worlds can be developed in which the user can explore interacting with objects.

The VRML version 1.0 specification, released on 26 May 1995, was created by the graphics workstation company **Silicon Graphics, Inc.** It was based on the company's Open Inventor file format; Open Inventor was an object-oriented toolkit for the development of interactive 3D graphics applications. VRML 2.0, released on 6 August 1996, added significantly more interactive capabilities. It was designed by Silicon Graphics' VRML 1.0 team with help from Sony Research and Mitra, an **Internet** systems and information consultant. VRML 2.0 was reviewed by the VRML-moderated discussion group (*www-vrml@wired.com*). Subsequently, it was adopted and endorsed by a number of companies and individuals. In 1997, the Virtual Reality Modeling Language ISO/IEC 14772-1:1997 international standard, sometimes referred to as VRML97, was issued. In 2000, a revised version, ISO/IEC 14772:200x, was drafted.

Most **browsers** have not recognized the VRML MIME (Multipurpose Internet Messaging Extensions) type directly. A number of VRML viewers have been developed as stand-alone programs and Web browser plug-ins, including Cosmo and VRwave. Probably the most widely used and consistently available viewer has been Cosmo Player, originally developed by Silicon Graphics.

VRML has been supported by collaborative efforts, notably the VRML Consortium Inc. The Web 3D Consortium has provided coordinated support for VRML activities. VRML has been important in initiating virtual reality on the Web, but there is now significant competition. In particular, **Java** 3D, providing 3D graphics support in the Java programming language that underpins much of the Web, has threatened VRML's lead.

FURTHER READING

Carey, Rikk, and Gavin Bell. *The Annotated VRML 2.0 Reference Manual.* Reading, Mass.: Addison-Wesley, 1997.

The VRML Consortium Incorporated. *The Virtual Reality Modeling Language.* International Standard ISO/IEC 14772-1:1997, 1997. *http://www.vrml.org/Specifications/VRML97*

Web 3D Consortium. *The VRML Repository.* *http://www.web3d.org/vrml/vrml.htm*

—*Jonathan Bowen*

Viruses

Computer viruses are programs that do at least two things: search for new hosts to infect, and make copies of themselves. Many also have the ability to hide from and combat the attacks of antivirus programs. Some computer scientists insist that a true computer virus must attach itself to another program; they define those that self-replicate without attaching to programs as **worms**. The distinction between worms and viruses is largely academic: Both can spread like wildfire and cause great damage.

In theory, there are countless ways to wreak havoc in a computer. In practice, however, virus coders have concentrated on just a few avenues of attack: attachment to program files; infection of the disk boot sector; and attachment to macros that may be embedded in documents such as text files, databases, and **spreadsheets**.

Viruses did not become common "in the wild" (in other words, outside a computer science laboratory) until 1987. From that time forward, most viruses have attacked **DOS** and **Windows** computers. Many early viruses were simple infectors of executable programs. The more primitive ones simply overwrite part of a program and damage it; more sophisticated infectors attach themselves to a program without harming the code.

Here's how the virus MINI-44.ASM works. (The extension ASM indicates that it is written in assembly language.) This is one of the tiniest known viruses, measuring only 44 bytes. Its life cycle begins when an infected program is loaded into the computer memory. The first thing the virus does is take control of the computer by running before any of the other program code can be executed. Next, MINI-44.ASM uses a DOS service routine to get the **operating system** to search for executable files and return these data to the virus. It then tells DOS to open a file, or victim program, and overwrites part of the victim's executable file with its own code. It ends the infection process by closing the program file. MINI-44.ASM continues this process until it doesn't find any more uninfected files in the current directory. It destroys every program it infects because it overwrites a portion of each victim's code.

A *companion virus* is one step up in complexity. It resides in its own file instead of inserting itself into a victim program. It renames the victim program and takes its name for itself. For example, if the victim file has the extension "exe," the virus may give itself the same name with the extension "com." This takes advantage of the fact that DOS, given the choice of running a program with an extension of "com" versus "exe," will run the "com" program. When the virus starts up, it launches the program with the "exe" extension. The user, seeing the victim program running normally, will not realize that two programs have been launched instead of one. Boot sector viruses take advantage of the fact that starting the computer from an infected floppy or hard disk always runs a special program in the boot sector, which can contain a virus.

Some viruses are able to hide. A powerful criterion for hiding is that a virus should not cause noticeable harm; if it did, it would motivate antivirus companies to discover ways to detect them. The most dangerous kind of virus is one that waits a long time before doing something destructive. Some viruses wait for a certain date to do their damage—for example, the Michelangelo virus of 1992, which became activated on the artist's birthday—while others wait for the victim to perform a certain action that triggers a destructive payload. For instance, *macro viruses* travel as attachments to **electronic mail**; these viruses are activated when the user opens an infected attachment. Some viruses hide in **RAM** (memory resident) and rewrite themselves to disk only when the computer is shut down.

Viruses can even enter computers through **World Wide Web** servers. Many Web sites use languages such as **Java** and Active X, which automatically download and run programs on the victim computer. Mark D. LaDue wrote one of the first viruses that could be transmitted from the Web by a Java program. Upon infection of a **Unix** system, it displays the ironic message, "Java is safe, and Unix viruses do not exist."

Not all viruses are harmful. Some are merely humorous, such as the Hantavirus Pulmonary Syndrome: Every Saturday it flips computer graphics to their mirror images. Others are helpful, such as Cruncher, released in 1993, which compresses executable files to save disk space, or Potassium Hydroxide, which will encrypt and decrypt files at the user's command. **Artificial life** researchers are interested in viruses because they are forms of "life" invented by human beings that can leave the laboratory and thrive in the wild.

Antivirus programs defend computers by scanning them for known classes of viruses. However, no antivirus program can exist that will defend against all possible viruses. This dismaying knowledge is based on mathematical research in automata theory first published by **John von Neumann** (1903–57) in 1948 and elaborated upon by Fred B. Cohen in his doctoral dissertation of 1986. The task of determining if a program can do harm is, in mathematical terminology, undecidable. The best antivirus researchers can do is analyze and program defenses for each new class of virus they encounter.

FURTHER READING

Artificial Life. MIT Press Journals.

Cohen, Fred, B. *A Short Course on Computer Viruses*. Hudson, Ohio: ASP, 1990; 2nd ed., New York: Wiley, 1994.

———. *It's Alive!: The New Breed of Living Computer Programs*. New York: Wiley, 1994.

Denning, Peter, ed. *Computers Under Attack: Intruders, Worms, and Viruses*. New York: ACM Press, 1990.

Hoffman, Lance. *Rogue Programs: Viruses, Worms, and Trojan Horses*. New York: Van Nostrand Reinhold, 1990.

Ludwig, Mark A. *The Giant Black Book of Computer Viruses*. Show Low, Ariz.: American Eagle Publications, 1995; 2nd ed., 1998.

Shoch, J. F., and J. A. Hupp. "The 'Worm' Programs: Early Experience with a Distributed Computation." *Communications of the ACM*, Mar. 1982, pp. 172–180.

Slade, Robert. *Robert Slade's Guide to Computer Viruses: How to Avoid Them, How to Get Rid of Them, and How to Get Help*. New York: Springer-Verlag, 1994.

—*Carolyn Meinel*

Vision, Computer

Sight is an extremely effective way of gathering information; research into computer vision (or *machine vision*) aims to produce machines that can use humanlike perception with similar effect. But visual perception is immensely complex. A large area of the human brain has evolved to process visual information, and although machine vision has been notably successful at certain carefully prescribed tasks, researchers are still a long way from developing a general-purpose visual system as good as the one in the human brain.

Machine vision draws heavily on **artificial intelligence** and pattern recognition using **neural networks**, but understanding the psychology of human visual perception and the physiology of the eye and brain have proved equally important in making computers that can see. Indeed, a major stimulus for the development of machine vision was the publication in 1982 of *Vision*, a seminal book by British psychologist David Marr (1945–80), which proposed that the human brain might construct representations of the real world by analyzing an image through a series of mathematical and computational processes.

But the central problem of computer vision—constructing a useful computer model of the visual world—turns out to be immensely complex. For example, only part of an image is useful for a given task, but how does a machine know which part? Objects must be picked out against their background, but how does the machine know which is which? When an object moves or rotates, how can the machine be sure that it is the same object? The human visual system makes all this seem deceptively easy.

The "physiology" of machine vision—the hardware it uses in place of the human eye—turns out to be one of the simpler problems. Where the retina recognizes the color and brightness of light passing into the eye, computer vision systems use charge-coupled display (CCD) devices such as those in digital cameras and scanners to digitize an image and feed it into a computer for processing. But just as the eye is only the first stage of our perception, so the greatest challenges of computer vision are concerned with developing **software** for analyzing images once they have been scanned in.

The apparent complexity of machine vision has been tackled by breaking it into a number of distinct areas that mirror aspects of human vision studied by psychologists. Objects can be picked out from their background by detecting edges and boundaries or grouping together areas of similar colors or visual textures (optical patterns such as the crisscross lines made by blades of grass). Binocular (two-perspective, stereo) vision, the degree of focus of different objects, and differences in visual texture can be used to provide information about the relative distances (depth) of different objects. Objects can be recognized and classified either by comparing them against stored representations (templates) of similar objects, by picking out distinctive features, or by using neural networks (collections of interconnected units operating in parallel that can recognize patterns after repeated training). Moving scenes can be understood by processing what is known as an optical flow—the way the visual world appears to wash around you, for example, when you walk down the street. These techniques are the reverse of those used to produce realistic computer graphics and animations and there is a considerable, productive overlap between computer graphics and computer vision.

One of the most ambitious (albeit distant) goals of computer vision research is to produce a replacement visual system to relieve various kinds of human blindness. The Retinal Implant Project run by Massachusetts Institute of Technology (MIT) and Massachusetts Eye and Ear Infirmary has already completed successful trials of a miniaturized "artificial retina" based on a silicon CCD sensor. Less ambitious goals have produced highly effective machine vision systems for limited applications. These include automated face recognition systems for analyzing security videos, guidance systems for industrial robots, and a wide variety of systems that can inspect the quality of manufactured goods. Machine vision systems have found particularly important applications in medical diagnosis and imagery where doctors require considerable training and patience to produce consistently accurate results. Tests of a machine vision system at Kurt Rossman Laboratories at the University of Chicago, which can detect early signs of breast cancer by examining images from scans, showed that it could increase the detection of tumors that would otherwise have been missed by around 50 percent.

Future applications of machine vision are likely to focus on developing specific solutions to specific problems, such as computerized vehicle guidance systems that increase the safety of motoring by warning drivers of potential hazards. But general-purpose computer vision systems are also being developed. The COG humanoid robot in development at the **MIT Artificial Intelligence Laboratory** includes a humanlike head and two "eyes." Designed very much along human lines, these are gray-scale cameras with a wide field of vision and two motors that scan them both horizontally and vertically around a room at the same speed as human eyes. Such sophisticated mimicry does not guarantee humanlike perception, however. It will be many years before computers can understand the optical illusions and tricks of the light that millions of years of evolution have allowed humans to process, quite literally, in the blink of an eye.

FURTHER READING

Ballard, Dana H., and Christopher M. Brown. *Computer Vision.* Englewood Cliffs, N.J.: Prentice Hall, 1982.

Cipolla, Roberto, and Alexander Pentland, eds. *Computer Vision for Human-Machine Interaction.* New York: Cambridge University Press, 1999.

Computer, Vol. 13, No. 5, 1980. Special edition on machine perception for industrial applications.

Giger, Maryellen L., and Charles A. Pelizzar. "Advances in Tumor Imaging." *Scientific American*, Sept. 1996.

Horn, Berthold. *Robot Vision.* Cambridge, Mass.: MIT Press, 1986.

Jain, Ramesh, Rangachar Kasturi, and Brian Schunck. *Machine Vision.* New York: McGraw-Hill, 1995.

Low, Adrian. *Introductory Computer Vision and Image Processing.* London and New York: McGraw-Hill, 1991.

Marr, David. *Vision: A Computational Investigation into the Human Representation and Processing of Visual Information.* San Francisco: Freeman, 1982.

Schoon, Nicholas. "Caught on Camera." *New Scientist*, 25 Sept. 1999.

—*Chris Woodford*

Visual Basic

Visual Basic is a powerful programming language and environment designed specifically to facilitate the creation of **Windows**-based applications. **Microsoft** first released Visual Basic in April 1991. By June 1998, Visual Basic was in version 6.0 and held the distinction of being the most popular rapid application development (RAD) prototyping tool for Windows-based systems programming.

Visual Basic is based on the **BASIC** (Beginners All-Purpose Symbolic Instruction Code) programming language and was one of the first **software** development products to utilize a graphical drop-and-drag environment for the creation of user **interfaces**. Instead of using layout grids and other tools to determine the placement of on-screen text and controls, the Visual Basic development environment enables programmers to visually place these controls (e.g., buttons, text boxes, and drop-down menus) visually in desired locations on the user interface. A series of properties associated with each control can be specified to define appearance and behavior.

Visual Basic is classified as an event-driven programming language. This means that different pictures, text boxes, buttons, and other controls on the screen can respond to events initiated by the program user. Examples of events include moving the cursor over a certain area, typing text, pressing a key, and clicking the mouse. Visual Basic code modules can be constructed to respond to these events.

In addition to its event orientation, Visual Basic also provides constructs for object-oriented programming. A programmer can use existing objects or create new ones. Controls are an example of a class of Visual Basic objects. Each object has a predefined set of behaviors, called *properties*, and perform a predefined set of actions, called *methods*. When a specific object, such as a button, is placed on a user interface, an instance of a class or specific object is created.

Visual Basic programs are constructed of forms—visual representations of the user interface (windows)—and modules. Modules contain the programming code, which is activated by user-initiated events. Modules can be associated with a particular form, or they can be independent and used to control the sequence of forms, define global variables, or provide functions.

Since its launch in 1991, Visual Basic's approach to programming has become the norm for programming languages. Many other visual programming environments are being developed using the same concepts.

FURTHER READING

Shelly, G. B., and T. J. Cashman. *Microsoft Visual Basic 6 Complete Concepts and Techniques.* Cambridge, Mass.: Course Technology, 1999.

—*Roger McHaney*

VLSI See Very Large Scale Integration.

VMS

VMS is a proprietary **operating system** (OS) that originated at the **Digital Equipment Corporation** (DEC) in the late 1970s. When in the mid-1980s DEC was the second-largest computer company in the world, VMS was the leading OS for its most popular products, then called **minicomputers**. **Compaq Computer Corporation** acquired DEC in 1998, and the OS is now available from Compaq under the OpenVMS trademark. OpenVMS remains a supported OS in the year 2000, with a reputation for reliability, comprehensive documentation, and technical excellence.

DEC released version 1.0 of VMS in 1978 for the first of its extremely successful VAX line of computers, the first 32-bit commercial machines. By 1984, VMS included sophisticated security, networking, and clustering abilities, many of which remain unavailable in other operating systems 15 years later. To compete more effectively with **Unix** rivals, Version 5.5 implemented the entire Portable Operating System Interface (POSIX) standard programming interface in 1991; this made OpenVMS a candidate for a range of U.S. government contracts that previously could be filled only by Unix machines.

The next year, 1992, DEC released the new AXP **central processing unit** (CPU) architecture with VMS. As 2000 begins, OpenVMS is at release 7.2 as the property of Compaq, which acquired DEC in 1998. Note that OpenVMS is merely a new marketing label for VMS; there is no technical difference between VMS and OpenVMS.

Structurally, VMS most resembles **IBM**'s OS/400, for the latter is also a proprietary midrange OS designed in parallel with its underlying **hardware** and noted for its high level of reliability. In the marketplace, however, the Unix OS has been VMS's principal competitor in its traditional niches of scientific computing, industrial control, and database hosting. Like traditional Unix, a command-line interface (CLI) is most common for VMS users. The most common application languages for VMS development are DCL (the VMS "shell"), **Fortran**, **BASIC**, and **C**. Among VMS's many attractions is that different languages are compatible in object format. This means that it is straightforward to code different parts of an application using Fortran and C, for example, and have them work together correctly.

Although there have been several projects to host VMS on less expensive hardware than the VAX and AXP (now called Alpha) CPUs, none of these moved beyond the point of laboratory experimentation. One footnote to VMS's legacy is that the Microsoft **Windows NT** (and later Windows 2000) OS recruited several designers and took many ideas from VMS.

FURTHER READING

Holmay, Patrick, and James F. Peters III. *The VMS User's Guide.* Bedford, Mass.: Digital Press, 1990; 2nd ed., published under the title *The OpenVMS User's Guide*, Boston: Digital Press, 1998.

Miller, David Donald. *Open VMS Operating System Concepts.* Boston: Digital Press, 1997.

—*Cameron Laird*

Von Neumann Architecture

Von Neumann architecture is the basic arrangement of the **hardware** associated with **digital computers** since the advent of the first stored program machines in the late 1940s. The name has been controversial, since **John von Neumann** (1903–57), the brilliant Hungarian mathematician, was just a consultant to the team of engineers that built the **ENIAC** in 1944–45.

The ENIAC team realized that their machine's design made it difficult to program and that this would be an obstacle to widespread adoption of computer technology. They came to the conclusion that storing the program, together with the data, in memory would make the machine more flexible and easy to use. Von Neumann volunteered to write a report of the discussions and his **"First Draft of a Report on the EDVAC"** was soon circulating widely. Although von Neumann was not the sole intellectual source of the ideas contained in the report, the term *von Neumann architecture* stuck and is still used today.

The von Neumann architecture consists of five main parts: an arithmetic and control unit, a memory, and input/output devices. Since the processor is usually faster that memory, the connection between both is typically called the *von Neumann bottleneck*. Stored programs are considered a main feature of the von Neumann architecture, and usually von Neumann architectures are sequential—that is, every instruction in executed in turn.

John Backus (1924–) coined another term, the *von Neumann style of programming*. This refers to the fact that data have to be moved between processor and memory explicitly by the programmer. This can lead to errors and poor productivity.

As can be seen, the term *von Neumann architecture* is used in many different senses, but usually refers to (1) the **stored program** concept, (2) sequential machines and (3) computers with separate processor, memory and input/output. The term *non-von Neumann architecture* is also used; it can refer to parallel machines, functional machines (e.g. **LISP** machines), or machines in which processing and memory are not clearly separated.

Further Reading

Backus, John W. "Can Programming Be Liberated from the von Neumann Style? A Functional Style and Its Algebra of Programs." *Communications of the ACM*, Vol. 21, 1978, pp. 613–641.

Hurd, Cuthbert. "Early IBM Computers: Edited Testimony." *Annals of the History of Computing*, Vol. 3, No. 1, 1981, pp. 163–182.

Von Neumann, John. "First Draft of a Report on the EDVAC." In *Papers of John von Neumann on Computers and Computer Theory*. Cambridge, Mass.: MIT Press; Los Angeles/San Francisco: Tomash Publishers, 1987, pp. 17–82.

—*James Tomayko and Raúl Rojas*

Von Neumann, John

1903–57

Hungarian–U.S. Mathematician and Scientist

John von Neumann (Neumann Janos in Hungarian) was one of the most outstanding mathematicians and logicians of the twentieth century. He made significant contributions to pure mathematics, quantum physics, meteorology, game theory for economics, and to the theory and practice of high-speed computing machines and their programming. He was associated with the earliest all-electronic computers in the United States: the **ENIAC**, the **EDVAC**, and the **IAS machine**. Von Neumann's enthusiasm and logical design efforts helped set a strong mathematical and scientific foundation for the development of the modern computer.

John von Neumann grew up in an environment that encouraged intellectual activity and curiosity. At extended lunches and dinners, family members were encouraged to make scholarly or literary presentations. Intellectual achievement was held in high esteem not just at home but in much of the middle-class community in Budapest. At school, John stood out as particularly intelligent, and his schoolmaster arranged for him to be tutored by mathematicians from Budapest University, who were amazed at the brilliant solutions John proposed for the problems they posed him.

In 1926, when von Neumann was at the University of Göttingen in Germany, again the atmosphere was intellectually vibrant. Werner Heisenberg (1901–76) had just developed the matrix approach to quantum mechanics, which was soon challenged by the wave formulation of Erwin Schrödinger (1887–1961). In the midst of the debate, von Neumann and others drew the logical conclusion that since both theories were arriving at the same results, there must be different ways of saying the same thing. Von Neumann went on to show that both the Heisenberg and Schrödinger formulations of quantum mechanics satisfy the same set of axioms, and therefore the wave and particle descriptions are equivalent at the mathematical level.

World War II was a turning point in the development of important new technologies such as radar and computing. By then von Neumann had been in the United States for almost a decade, was a naturalized citizen, and was much in demand by U.S. government agencies involved with the war effort. He was consulted on the solution of ballistics, detonation, and aerodynamics problems and worked at Los Alamos on the atomic bomb project. He was intimately involved with problems that needed massive calculations for their solution and therefore required computing machines.

In 1943, von Neumann visited England and saw its most advanced computational equipment. On a train ride with his host, he wrote down how to interpolate intermediate values for a calculation on that equipment. It was perhaps his first translation of a mathematical procedure into instructions for machine solution. Upon his return, he surveyed the advanced computing machinery in the United States that could be used for the numerical solution of complex problems. He was directed to **Howard Aiken**'s (1900–73) **Harvard Mark I**, **George Stibitz**'s (1904–95) work on relay computers at **Bell Labs**, and similar work at Columbia University. It was only by accident that he learned of **J. Presper Eckert**'s (1919–95) ENIAC (Electronic Numerical Integrator and Computer), the first large-scale electronic computer. Von Neumann immediately appreciated the improvement such a machine represented for solving problems that he was encountering in his war-related work.

The ENIAC was just then entering its preliminary testing. It was to be an enormous machine using over 17,000 **vacuum tubes** for its circuitry. Being all electronic, it promised 1000 times faster calculations than that of any previous computer. Von Neumann was too late to influence its design. Instead, he was appointed as a consultant to the **Moore School** project so he could be involved in planning the use of the ENIAC and in discussions already begun about its successor, the EDVAC (Electronic Discrete Variable Arithmetic Computer). The ENIAC was "programmed" externally by setting switches and replugging circuits for each new problem. When it was operational, von Neumann helped devise a way to speed up the ENIAC's setup by programming it using its over 3000 function table switch settings, eliminating the need for replugging. The first problem solved by the ENIAC was suggested and arranged for by von Neumann and helped the Los Alamos Laboratory decide the feasibility of building a fusion bomb.

Von Neumann brought to his meetings at the Moore School his knowledge of the many projects under way and his sense of the importance of high-speed calculations. He foresaw that numerical solutions to problems would lead to insights for mathematicians; therefore, computers would be research tools. Von Neumann devoted enormous amounts of his prodigious energy to working out in great detail logical control of the EDVAC. His presence seems also to have led to a more formal approach to technical issues. Minutes of the technical meetings were now taken and distributed, and von Neumann took on gathering up the thinking of the group and generating a report. His 101-page "**First Draft of a Report on the EDVAC**" was distributed to the Moore School staff and others at the end of June 1945. It was the first public documentation concerning electronic high-speed computers.

John von Neumann, Hungarian mathematician and physicist. (©Bettmann/CORBIS)

"First Draft" presented detailed arguments for the axiomatic design features that have characterized computers ever since. To achieve the full speed of a computer, instructions must be fed to units of the machine as fast as the data can be processed. Thus the computer has to be fully automatic. All numerical information and numerically coded instructions must be given in exhaustive detail so that the calculation can be carried out without further human intervention. For mathematical and scientific precision only digital (not analog) technology should be considered. Whatever the technology, it would be based on two-state elements, and thus internally all numbers would be represented by binary digits. Logically, the necessary units of a high-speed computer would be a central arithmetic unit wired to carry out the basic arithmetic operations; a central control unit to sequence the operations properly based on the coded instructions and feedback from the ongoing processes; as large a primary fast access memory as possible to store both numerical and instructional data; input and output units; and a secondary memory or outside recording medium.

Von Neumann's highest principle was simplicity of construction and of programming. Therefore, all processing should be sequential, not parallel, so as to require the fewest basic elements. Also, for simplicity, a clock pulse should synchronize processing. It is no trivial matter to conceive how all this could work together at the million pulse per second clock rate that was needed. By working out the functions of each unit and their interrelationships, von Neumann set a logical foundation upon which to base the engineering details.

Among the other contributions of "First Draft" was von Neumann's choice of brain cell–like idealized elements for the logical design rather than vacuum tubes. Such generalization—combining electronic computing and the insights from the human nervous system—was central to his thinking. He conceived of both the computer and the brain as essentially logic machines. For von Neumann, computer design was a scientific question first, with engineering design an important second. His design was thus independent of the technology and operated on a more theoretical and rigorous level. Also, because von Neumann was a user as well as a developer of computers, he brought to his design the need of mathematicians for high precision and for the largest possible memory capacity. Because scientists and mathematicians are always asking new questions and might require unexpected uses for a computer, von Neumann argued for the greatest generality, which he called "all purpose." He worked out in the report a set of basic instruction codes to achieve such flexibility. Also, in a supplementary letter he presented the coded instructions for the solution of a sample problem, a sort and merge routine. This was the first published program written for a stored program computer.

Von Neumann wanted to ensure that a computer would be developed that could be used as a research tool by mathematicians and scientists. He was concerned that if a government lab developed a computer it would be for its own limited purpose, and if there was commercial development it would be linked to past products and practices and not have a fresh start. Von Neumann had been at the Institute for Advanced Study (IAS) in Princeton, New Jersey, since his appointment there as a Fellow in 1933. As the war was ending, von Neumann conceived of developing such a computer at the institute. He argued that a computer for scientists should be developed in an institute devoted to pure research and it would have many imitators. Based on his arguments and his prestige, he won the approval of the institute and found funding, including from the U.S. Army and Navy. His military funders accepted that the computer would have military value even though its use was restricted to experimental scientific research.

The IAS computer, as it became known, was designed by von Neumann with the assistance of Herman Goldstine (1913–) and Arthur Burks (1915–), with whom he had worked at the Moore School. The design followed and expanded the concepts from "First Draft," incorporating a newer memory technology. Similar to a **cathode ray tube**, the new device allowed for random or equal speed rather than sequential access to all 163,840 of its memory locations. Because of this memory device, the designers were able to relax von Neumann's principle of strict serial processing. In the IAS computer the 40 binary digits of each number were processed simultaneously. The result was greater speed of operation.

Goldstine, Burks, and von Neumann signed, at the latter's suggestion, a notarized pledge that any patentable ideas they generated in their work on the IAS computer would belong to the public domain. Then in a series of reports, they presented detailed analysis of the basic logical design known today as the **von Neumann architecture**. The reports also set out the general principles for writing instructions for such machines. Von Neumann and Goldstine described the flow diagramming technique they invented to deal with the complexity that results as the computer executes the coded orders. They worked out some examples and discussed a programming methodology based on a library of written subroutines. Via these reports, which were sent to about 175 institutions and people in several countries, von Neumann and his colleagues helped launch computer science and made possible the rapid transfer of advanced computer technology.

Even before the IAS was completed, with von Neumann's encouragement and the help of these reports, some related machines were designed at Los Alamos, the RAND Corporation (the JOHNNIAC), three other U.S. government laboratories, the University of Illinois, and at **IBM** (the 701). Other early computers based on the IAS computer where built in Australia, Israel, Germany, Sweden, and the Soviet Union. Widespread copying of the IAS computer was its great achievement.

Combining his mathematical intuition with his work on actual computing machines and his reading in neurophysiology, von Neumann began to construct a general theory of information processing. His theory sought to understand biological as well as artificial autonomous information processing systems, which he called *automata*. The striking similarity between neurons, which react to combinations of stimuli in an all-or-nothing way, and the logical circuits out of which computers were built led von Neumann to search for a general logical and mathematical description of all automata. In this search he raised the questions of how reliable systems can be built out of unreliable components and what logical organization is sufficient for an automaton to be able to reproduce or repair itself. He even sought to understand how an automaton can reproduce itself in such a way that the product would be more advanced. Unfortunately, von Neumann never completed his automata theory: He died at age 53 from cancer.

It is no accident that the design of practically all current computers is referred to as von Neumann architecture. Rather, it is a tribute to the intelligence and enthusiasm with which von Neumann developed and championed computers as all-purpose scientific tools. His insights into the similarity of biological and artificial information processing systems has set the foundation for even more breakthroughs in the future.

BIOGRAPHY

John von Neumann. Born 28 December 1903, in Budapest, Hungary. Studied at the Lutheran Gymnasium in Budapest. Ph.D. in chemistry from Technische Hochschule in Zürich, 1926; Ph.D. in mathematics, University of Budapest, 1926. Rockefeller Fellow, Göttingen, Germany, 1926. Privatdozent, Berlin, 1927–29. Mathematics faculty, Princeton University, 1930–3. Fellow, Institute for Advanced Study 1933–57. Consultant to U.S. government agencies, 1940–57. Wrote "First Draft of a Report on the EDVAC," 1945. Director, Electronic Computer Project, IAS, 1946–52. President, American Mathematical Society, 1951–53. Member, US Atomic Energy Commission, 1955–57. Recipient of numerous honors and awards, including Distinguished Civilian Service Award, 1947; Presidential Medal of Freedom, 1956; Albert Einstein Commemorative Award, 1956; and Enrico Fermi Award, 1956. Died 8 February 1957 in Washington, D.C.

SELECTED WORKS

Von Neumann, John. *The Computer and the Brain.* New Haven: Yale University Press, 1958.

———. *Theory of Self-Reproducing Automata.* Edited and compiled by Arthur W. Burks. Urbana: University of Illinois Press, 1966.

———. "First Draft of a Report on the EDVAC." Reprinted (in part) in Brian Randell, ed., *Origins of Digital Computers: Selected Papers.* Berlin and New York: Springer Verlag, 1982. Reprinted with corrections in *IEEE Annals of the History of Computing*, Vol. 15, No. 4, 1993, pp. 28–75.

FURTHER READING

Aspray, William. *John von Neumann and the Origins of Modern Computing.* Cambridge, Mass.: MIT Press, 1990.

Goldstine, Herman H. *The Computer: From Pascal to von Neumann.* Princeton, N.J.: Princeton University Press, 1993.

Stern, Nancy B. *From ENIAC to UNIVAC: An Appraisal of the Eckert-Mauchly Computers.* Bedford, Mass.: Digital Press, 1981.

—*Jay Robert Hauben*

VRML See Virtual Reality Modeling Language.

WAIS

WAIS is an acronym for *wide-area information servers* (or service); it is an **Internet** search tool that is based on the Z39.50 standard. Z39.50 is an **American National Standards Institute** (ANSI)/NISO standard communications protocol for searching and retrieving bibliographical data in online databases. Z39.50 is used on the Internet to search the online public access catalogs (OPACs) of library holdings. It is also sometimes used to link disparate OPACs and form a single united OPAC.

The **parallel processing** search **algorithms** on which WAIS is based were developed in the 1980s at **Thinking Machines Corporation**. WAIS was designed from the beginning to retrieve information from multiple indexed document sources. Its designers recognized that such documents may be stored in many different places. The emphasis on searching and the ability to query many different data sources simultaneously are why WAIS is often the indexer (or **search engine**) running in the background for the **World Wide Web**.

WAIS works on the client–server principle. A WAIS client program enables the user's computer to contact a WAIS server, submit a search query, and receive a response to that query. The user enters a search argument and may choose which databases should be used to complete the search; the client then accesses all the servers on which the databases are distributed. The results provide a description of each text that meets the search requirements. The user can then retrieve the full text. The databases themselves are not searched for the requested phrase; it is an index for each database that is searched. This index is created by people and may contain all the words in all the items contained in the database, or as many as required.

WAIS provides relevancy ranking to help the user decide which of the items returned will be the most useful. WAIS assigns a number to each document to rank them according to the number of times a word appears in the search phrase. The formula also takes into account where the term appears in the document.

WAIS can be accessed via telnet, a specific WAIS client, or the Web. Most WAIS-indexed databases are now available through the Web, and most Web users will find that the abundance of server files and search engines already available on the Web will make WAIS superfluous. However, librarians, medical researchers, and others may find some specialized information available through WAIS that is not currently available elsewhere.

FURTHER READING

Franks, Mike. *The Internet Publishing Handbook: For World-Wide Web, Gopher and WAIS.* Reading, Mass.: Addison-Wesley, 1995.

Gilster, Paul. *Finding It on the Internet: The Essential Guide to Archie, Veronica, Gopher, Wais, WWW (Including Mosaic), and Other Search and Browsing Tools.* New York: Wiley, 1994.

—*Manuel Sanromà*

WAN

See Wide Area Network.

Wang, An

1920–90

U.S. Inventor and Businessman

An Wang made important contributions to the development of computer memory, desktop electronic calculators, and the use of **minicomputers** in business. From 1951 until 1981, and again for a brief time in the mid-1980s, he served as president of **Wang Laboratories**, a firm he founded to market his inventions.

Wang studied electrical engineering with an emphasis on communications at Chiao-Tung University in his native city of Shanghai. He spent World War II in inland China designing radio equipment for the Chinese army to use in its fight against Japan. After the war, Wang did graduate work at Harvard. Unwilling to return to a China now governed by Communists, Wang went to work for **Howard Aiken** (1900–73) at the Harvard Computation Laboratory.

Aiken and his associates had operated the **Harvard Mark I** computer during World War II and gone on to build several other large computing devices. Aiken's early computers used electromagnetic relays and mechanical components, but for his fourth and last machine, he planned to use **vacuum tubes**. At Aiken's request, Wang set out to develop a way to record information magnetically and to retrieve it without mechanical motion. Wang realized that a small, doughnut-shaped ring of ferromagnetic material could be magnetized in either of two directions, and hence represent the binary digit 0 or 1. An electrical current traversing the ring would be able to read the magnetization. Wang envisioned a set of cores arranged in series, with the current generated by one core used to magnetize the next one. In 1950, Wang and Harvard associate Way Dong Woo published a description of this work. Jay W. Forrester (1918–) of the Massachusetts Institute of Technology (MIT) soon envisioned a more efficient way of arranging magnetic cores, which was used in the **Whirlwind** computer built at MIT. Magnetic core memory would become standard on computers of the early 1960s.

Wang took out a patent for magnetic cores and left Harvard to set up his own business, Wang Laboratories. He continued to think about other small-scale applications of digital electronics and took on a variety of consulting contracts for digital equipment. In 1956, after considerable legal wrangling, Wang sold his patent rights for magnetic core memory to **IBM** for U.S.$400,000. In the mid-1960s, he invented a transistorized logarithmic calculating instrument that made it possible to carry out routine arithmetic electronically both rapidly and at relatively low cost. With this invention, Wang was ready to enter a larger commercial market, manufacturing desktop electronic calculators that were much faster than conventional adding machines and much cheaper than contemporary computers. The machines initially sold for U.S.$6500, and were used in schools, laboratories, and engineering firms.

Wang also supervised construction of a later calculator, introduced in 1969 and sold as the Wang 700, that found considerable application in business, particularly automobile dealers. However, foreseeing the advent of smaller, cheaper hand-held calculators, Wang decided in 1971 to withdraw entirely from the calculator business and focus the attention of Wang Laboratories on the manufacture of word processors and small computers.

Difficulties with Wang Laboratories' first attempt to build a small computer had led Wang to acquire a **software** company, PHI, Inc., in 1968. Both the first Wang computer actually sold to customers, the 3300 **BASIC**, and an early word processor proved unsuccessful. In about 1973, the company introduced a small computer for business use, the Wang 2200, which sold for U.S.$8000 and operated using BASIC programs. It was the firm's first successful computer, and encouraged development of a more complicated system of networked computers, each workstation equipped with its own **microprocessor**.

The Wang Word Processing System, introduced in 1976, transformed the company. It was designed specifically to be accessible to secretaries and business users rather than the hobbyists who purchased many contemporary **microcomputers**. In 1977, the company introduced a **minicomputer**, the Wang VS, which also proved highly successful. By this time Wang Laboratories had a considerable staff of hardware and software engineers for product development. However, until about 1981, Wang himself still spent more than half his time directly managing research and development at the company. He devoted less time to financial, marketing, and sales planning and even less on functions relating to public, corporate, and staff relations.

In the 1980s, Wang began thinking about new leadership for Wang Laboratories. In 1983, he placed his son Fred in charge of research and development and named a longtime employee, John Cunningham, as president of the company. Difficulties at the firm led An Wang to resume the presidency in 1985, and the following year he named Fred Wang as president. Unfortunately, neither the products initiated under the new leadership nor the style of management proved adequate to keep Wang Laboratories a growing concern. By August 1989, growing losses at Wang Laboratories persuaded An Wang to fire his son and hire an outsider to run the company he had founded. By this time, Wang himself was suffering from fatal esophageal cancer.

BIOGRAPHY

An Wang. Born 7 February 1920 in Shanghai, China. Studied at Shanghai Provincial High School; undergraduate degree, Chiao-Tung University, Shanghai; 1940. Master's degree in communications engineering, Harvard University, 1946; Ph.D. in engineering and applied physics, Harvard University, 1948. Harvard Computation Laboratory, 1948–51. Founded Wang Laboratories, 1951. Awarded the U.S. government's Medal of Liberty, 1986. Resigned as president of Wang Laboratories, 1983, resumed duties, 1985, resigned again, 1986. Elected into National Inventors Hall of Fame, 1988. Died 24 March 1990 in Boston, Massachusetts.

SELECTED WRITINGS

Wang, An. "Pulse Transfer Controlling Devices." U.S. patent 2,708,722. Filed 21 Oct. 1949, issued 17 May 1955.

Wang, An, with Eugene Linden. *Lessons: An Autobiography.* Reading, Mass.: Addison-Wesley, 1986.

Wang, An, and Way Dong Woo. "Static Magnetic Storage and Delay Line." *Journal of Applied Physics*, Vol. 21, Jan. 1950.

FURTHER READING

Gardner, W. D. "An Wang's Early Work in Core Memories." *Datamation*, Mar. 1976, pp. 161–164.

Kenney, Charles C. *Riding the Runaway Horse: The Rise and Decline of Wang Laboratories.* Boston: Little, Brown, 1992.

Salton, Gerard. "Howard Aiken's Children: The Harvard Computation Laboratory and Its Students." *Abacus*, Vol. 1, No. 3, Spring 1964, p. 28.

Weiss, Eric. "An Wang, Obituary." *Annals of History of Computing*, Vol. 15, No. 1, 1993, pp. 60–69.

—*Peggy Aldrich Kidwell*

Wang Laboratories

Wang Laboratories introduced large numbers of people to the possibility of electronic calculators and then to **word processing** and computing more generally. At the same time, the company provided jobs for thousands, particularly in the state of Massachusetts, and trained executives who now occupy positions at a wide range of high-technology companies.

Founded in 1951 in Boston, Massachusetts by **An Wang** (1920–90), Wang Laboratories first made magnetic cores, which Wang had invented and patented while working at Harvard's Computation Laboratory under **Howard Aiken** (1900–73). Other early products of the company included a digital device for the U.S. Air Force that measured the cloud ceiling, a digital tachometer to measure revolutions per minute, and a digital machine to count red and white blood cells. In 1962, the company built a machine called the Linasec for justifying lines of text for printing and publishing companies. An Wang also developed an interest in electronic calculators. Transistorized Wang desktop calculators sold quite widely in the mid-1960s—first the LOCI (logarithmic calculating instrument), then the Wang 300 series, and then the programmable Wang 700 series. The company went public in 1967 and soon thereafter acquired the software firm Philip Hankins, Inc. In the 1970s, the firm moved away from the calculator business, which increasingly was dominated by inexpensive handheld calculators, and began to build word processors, **minicomputers**, and **microcomputers**. Wang placed particular emphasis on providing networked workstations for business use. In the late 1980s, stiff competition from **IBM**, **Apple**, and a host of other vendors, combined with An Wang's withdrawal from active management of the firm, led to financial difficulties. By 1993, Wang Laboratories was bankrupt. In fiscal 1994, revenues were down from U.S.$2.5 billion to a third of that and the number of employees had decreased from 20,000 to 5300.

In the late 1990s, under the leadership of Joseph Tucci (1947–), the company has placed increasing emphasis on revenues from installation, training, and network services for desktop computers. Wang bought up several service companies, including Olsy, the computer services unit of the Italian firm **Olivetti**. To suggest its new orientation, the company took the name Wang Global. However, profits proved elusive, and in 1999 Wang Global merged with the Dutch firm Genetronics.

During its best years, Wang computers were synonomous with business automation and word processing. However, like other minicomputer companies, Wang was unable to keep up with the software offered for stand-alone personal computers, leading to its eventual demise.

FURTHER READING

Kenney, Charles C. *Riding the Runaway Horse: The Rise and Decline of Wang Laboratories.* Boston: Little, Brown, 1992.

Wang, An, with Eugene Linden. *Lessons: An Autobiography.* Reading, Mass.: Addison-Wesley, 1986.

—*Peggy Aldrich Kidwell*

Watson, Thomas, Jr.

1914–93

U.S. Industrialist

Described by *Fortune* magazine as "the world's greatest capitalist," Thomas J. Watson, Jr., was the dynamic industrialist who steered **IBM** to world domination of the computer industry from 1946 until his retirement in 1971.

After being fired in 1914 as general sales manager of the National Cash Register (NCR) Corporation, Thomas J. Watson, Sr. (1874–1956) joined the Computing-Tabulating-Recording (C-T-R) Corporation. Watson became president of C-T-R within a year of joining; C-T-R changed its name to International Business Machines, or IBM in 1924. It was Watson who stressed the central importance of the customer; placed an emphasis on engineering, research, and education; borrowed the company motto "Think" from NCR (because he said failure to think had cost the world millions of dollars); put his salesmen in regulation dark suits; and established a pioneering program of employee benefits not as an incentive but as a reward for efforts he considered his workers had already made.

In October 1937, Thomas J. Watson, Jr. joined his father's company as a salesman in downtown Manhattan. His corporate career was curtailed, however, by the outbreak of war. In 1940, he enrolled in the U.S. Army Air Corps, served as a B-24 pilot, and achieved the rank of lieutenant colonel by the end of the war. Watson returned to IBM in 1946. Within six months, he was promoted to vice-president and became a member of the board. Almost immediately, his influence began to change the company. In 1947, he hired Eliot Noyes (1910–77) as IBM's chief design consultant. Noyes, with the help of designer Paul Rand (1914–96) and numerous influential architects, established the corporate identity that made IBM one of the best-known and most valuable brands in the world, and made IBM's products and buildings a distinctive hallmark of corporate America.

By 1952, Watson had become president of IBM, second in command to his father. Their intense rivalry was certainly a motivating factor, as Watson confided to the *Wall Street Journal* in 1986 when he revealed that his ambition had been to prove that he could "run on the same race track" as his father. But the two men had dramatically different visions for IBM. Watson, Jr., believed that the future lay in making electronic computers for the corporate market; at a sales conference in 1949 (only two years after the invention of the **transistor**), he had predicted the complete replacement of mechanical computing devices by electronics within the decade. Watson, Sr., was reluctant to invest in the factories needed to make the new machines, and he is often (unfairly) remembered by his probably apocryphal 1943 remark: "I think there's a world market for about five computers."

The rivalry ended in 1956 when Watson, Sr. reluctantly retired after 42 years in charge of IBM; he died six weeks later. As president and chief executive officer, Watson, Jr., immediately embarked on a full-scale reorganization of the company, creating six decentralized divisions and devolving more power to his executives. His biggest success was the introduction in April 1964 of the **IBM mainframe** computer, the System/360. This "scalable" machine could grow to meet its customers needs, was compatible across different models, and became the cornerstone of IBM's dominance of corporate computing throughout the 1960s and 1970s. Another important milestone was the decision in 1969 to "unbundle" IBM's products. Before this time, IBM had offered its customers packages (bundles) of **hardware**, **software**, and services. Largely as a result of numerous antitrust actions by the U.S. government, which centered on allegations that the company's dramatic growth had led to an unfair monopoly, IBM was forced to sell these items separately. This decision, possibly more than any other, contributed to the massive growth of the computer industry on the back of IBM's success.

Although Watson steered IBM through its most dramatic period of growth, his success came at some personal cost. In 1970, he suffered a heart attack, and he stepped down as chief executive officer of IBM the following year, commenting: "This is a very sentimental moment for me. I am stepping down from a job I have valued more than anything in my life outside of my own family." He stayed on as chairman of the executive committee of IBM until 1979, and remained on the board of directors until 1984, but from 1979 until 1988 followed a distinguished second career as the U.S. Ambassador to the Soviet Union under Presidents Jimmy Carter (1924–) and Ronald Reagan (1911–).

When Watson became chief executive officer of IBM in 1956, the company employed 72,500 people and had a gross revenue of U.S.$892 million. By the time he stepped down in 1971, the workforce had nearly quadrupled to 270,000 and the revenue had grown a thousandfold, to U.S.$8.3 billion. The difference was more than a matter of numbers: Watson's achievement had involved nurturing IBM from a medium-scale maker of mechanical calculating and tabulating machines, against his father's inclination, into the world's biggest manufacturer of electronic computing equipment.

Watson's success was due partially to sheer force of will and partially to the tremendous competition he felt with his father. It could be argued that there was also an element of luck—that IBM had simply had the good fortune to be in the computing business at a time when the world discovered the value of computers. But this would be a misinterpretation of the way in which Watson transformed IBM. It was Watson's vision and determination that enabled IBM to create, exploit, and ultimately dominate the global market for corporate computers.

Like his father, Watson believed strongly that a corporation would be successful only if its culture were rooted in firmly held business values and beliefs. In 1962, Watson declared that the "philosophy, spirit, and drive" of a corporation contribute more to its success than economic or technological factors. The values of Watson and his father have always been very much in evidence at IBM. Once a year, the corporation's employees are still required to sign their agreement with a detailed statement of values, known as the IBM Business Conduct Guidelines. Some critics have argued that the corporation's entrenched culture was one of the main reasons behind its problems after the 1980s. Indeed, at one point in the early 1990s it appeared that IBM would be broken up into a number of much smaller entities, which would then be run or sold off as separate companies. But when Louis V. Gerstner, Jr., (1942–) was appointed chief executive officer in 1993, one of his first decisions was that IBM should remain a single company that could continue to meet the varied computing needs of its customers, thus reaffirming the importance of Watson's original vision.

BIOGRAPHY

Thomas Watson, Jr. Born 8 January 1914 in Dayton, Ohio. Educated at Brown University, receiving a B.A. in 1937. Joined IBM as a trainee salesman in Manhattan, October 1937. Joined U.S. Army Air Corps in 1940, rising to the rank of lieutenant colonel. Rejoined IBM in 1946 and appointed vice-president and board member six months later, then president in 1952; became chief executive officer (CEO) on the death of his father, Thomas Watson, Sr., in 1956; retired as CEO in 1971, remained an active board member until 1985. Served as U.S. Ambassador to the Soviet Union, 1979–1988. Retired from IBM in 1985, but remained chairman emeritus. Recipient of many honors and awards from business and trade organizations. The Watson Institute for International Studies, at Brown University, is named in his honor. Died 31 December 1993 in Greenwich, Connecticut.

FURTHER READING

Mills, D. Quinn, and G. Bruce Friesen. *Broken Promises: An Unconventional View of What Went Wrong at IBM.* Cambridge, Mass.: Harvard Business School Press, 1996.

Watson, Thomas J., Jr., and Peter Petre. *Father, Son, & Co.: My Life at IBM and Beyond.* New York: Bantam Books, 1990.

—*Chris Woodford*

Wearable Computers

A wearable computer is any one of a number of small, wearable devices that provide the functionality of a **personal computer** but that differ in physical form and function from a portable computer. Many computer scientists believe that wearable computers herald the next generation of computing devices and applications.

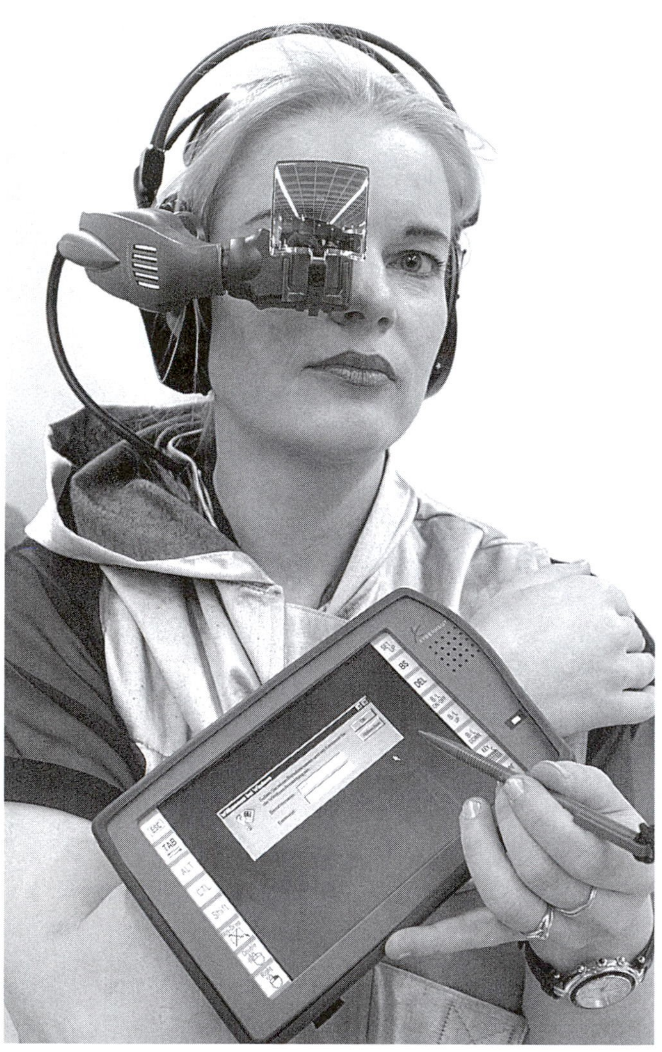

Astrid Ullsperger of the German Klaus Steilmann Institute demonstrates a wearable computer with virtual reality visor and forearm touchscreen in May 2000. (©AFP/CORBIS)

Unlike notebook computers, which are miniature versions of desktop systems, a wearable computer is a fully functional information device that is small enough to be worn without interfering with any normal user activities. It is always on and readily available, providing constant access to the **Internet** or to a specific network or information system. It is user configurable and has all of the processing power of a home computer. Wearable computers function more as auxiliary devices that can augment the human senses and intellect without detracting from the user's primary task—unlike conventional computers, where the computer itself is the focus of user attention. Wearable computing assumes that the user will be doing the computing simultaneous with doing something else that is the primary task.

As yet there is no generic design for a wearable computer. However, such devices typically consist of an input system that is either voice activated and/or **keyboard** controlled. For example, the Twiddler is a small, portable, one-handed "chorded" keyboard for such devices, a processing unit, that may be attached to the belt or worn as a backpack, and a display device, such as a small, head-mounted display.

For optimal ergonomic design, a wearable computer needs to be small but still functional, light weight, usable in heat and cold, have a minimum number of cables, be easily powered, and be easy to put on and take off. When wearable computer designs have these embedded in clothing, other factors, such as the size of the clothing, become important if the computers are to be used by a number of people. Wearable computers that are belt mounted can be used in turn by a number of people.

Wearable computers have been developed for specific applications, such as military operations, and for inventory control in warehousing. Future applications may include information-rich situations such as the maintenance of complex machinery, financial management, and medical operations. However, to date most wearable computers are still prototypes that are under development. Several organizations are developing wearable computers: Boeing is investigating wearable computers for manufacturing and maintenance, the **MIT Media Laboratory** has created wearable assisted-living devices, and Carnegie Mellon University has developed 13 generations of wearable computers for various applications.

FURTHER READING

Baber, C., D. J. Haniff, and S. I. Woolley. "Contrasting Paradigms for the Development of Wearable Computers." *IBM Systems Journal*, Vol. 38, No. 4, 1999, pp. 551–565.

—*Alan Hedge*

Web Caching

Web caching is a technique to improve **World Wide Web** page response times and reduce network **bandwidth**. Similar in operation to memory and disk **caches**, a Web cache stores frequently accessed content on a local server. Requests for popular pages can be served directly from the cache, resulting in faster delivery and wide-area-network bandwidth savings.

Caching originated in 1994 at the CERN laboratories. The CERN Hypertext Transfer Protocol (HTTP) server was the first Web caching application. Around this time, **firewalls** were becoming increasingly popular. Firewalls usually include application-layer gateways, or *proxies*, to control the passage of traffic between the internal network and the outside world. It made sense for the proxy to store, or cache, the HTTP responses for possible future use.

Web caching is effective because some Web sites are more popular than others, and people share some common interests. A *cache hit* occurs when someone requests a page that was previously requested by someone else and stored. For a typical Web cache, 30 to 40 percent of requests result in cache hits. Some **Internet service providers** pay metered rates for bandwidth, so cache hits translate into significant cost reductions. Hit ratios increase as the number of cache users increases because more people are likely to visit the same Web sites.

The HTTP describes many aspects of Web caching. It defines headers and algorithms that caches use to decide whether or not a particular response can be stored for reuse. It also defines a consistency and validation model to ensure that users receive up-to-date information.

In addition to improving response times and reducing bandwidth, Web caches also used to provide additional features and services. Most products have the ability to block requests to sites with objectionable content (e.g., pornography). Caches can also be used to "anonymize" Web traffic and protect privacy. Some products offer various translation features, such as reducing image size and quality for faster downloads, or perhaps translating text from one language to another. Some products also have the ability to detect viruses in downloads.

Web caching is widely accepted today, but it was more controversial in the past. Still, a few important issues remain. Some people feel that caching violates copyright laws. A number of recently written laws seem to provide exceptions for caching in computer networks. Dynamic content is another potential problem. In the past, Web caches were known to some dynamically generated pages and serve them as cache hits. These days, it is less of a problem because content providers use the latest HTTP features to prevent caching of dynamic pages.

FURTHER READING

Chankhunthod, Anawat, Peter B. Danzig, Chuck Neerdaels, et al. "A Hierarchical Internet Object Cache." *Proceedings of the USENIX Annual Technical Conference.* Berkeley, Calif.: USENIX Association, 1996, pp. 153–163.

Wessels, Duane, and K. Claffy. "ICP and the Squid Web Cache." *IEEE Journal on Selected Areas in Communication*, Vol. 16, No. 3, Apr. 1998, pp. 345–357.

—*Duane Wessels*

Whirlwind

The Whirlwind computer was a creation of Massachusetts Institute of Technology (MIT)'s Project Whirlwind, an ambitious plan to create a computerized flight simulator to train pilots in the final years of World War II. The design and construction of the Whirlwind required innovations in technology that had a great impact on the future of computers.

The project, led by Jay Forrester (1918–), ran from 1946 to 1955 at MIT. At first, it seemed headed for disaster. The complexity of the original task—building an analog computer to support flight simulation—was vastly underestimated, and the cost and size of the computer skyrocketed after the decision to switch to largely unknown digital technology. It reached the point where it was dominating the U.S. Navy's research and development budget. After the Soviet Union exploded its atomic bomb in 1949, the focus of the project changed from flight simulation to air defense, to counter the threat of Russian nuclear bomber attacks. Now under Air Force sponsorship, the Whirlwind computers eventually became the hearts of **SAGE** (Semi-Automatic Ground Environment) control stations. SAGE could detect attacking aircraft, scramble interceptors, guide the fighters to targets, and even conduct fire control.

These many tasks required innovations that rapidly improved the utility of computers. The most important was the use of the machine as a real-time controller, presaging aircraft and spacecraft flight control systems as well as **embedded systems** in automobiles, household appliances, and consumer electronics. Forrester's team also developed the most truly stable mass memory, based on the polarization of ferrite cores. Core memory was still in widespread use in some critical military and space systems as late as the 1990s, due to its robustness and persistence of data even when power is cut off. Other innovations attributed to Whirlwind included a graphic display, lightpen, data communication over phone lines, remote interaction with the machine, air traffic control functions, tools for producing large-scale **software**, and pattern recognition.

FURTHER READING

Everett, Robert R. "Whirlwind." In N. Metropolis, J. Howlett, and Gian-Carlo Rota, eds., *A History of Computing in the Twentieth Century*. San Diego, Calif: Academic Press, 1980, pp. 365–384.

Forrester, Jay W. *Collected Papers of Jay W. Forrester*. Cambridge, Mass.: Wright-Allen Press, 1975.

Pugh, Emerson W. *Memories That Shaped an Industry: Decisions Leading to IBM/360*. Cambridge, Mass.: MIT Press, 1984.

Redmond, Kent C., and Thomas M. Smith. *Project Whirlwind: The History of a Pioneer Computer*. Bedford, Mass.: Digital Press, 1980.

—*James Tomayko*

Wide Area Networks

Wide area networks (WANs) are typically networks of networks. The term refers to a collection of technologies that allow entities to communicate seamlessly across countries, continents, and the globe. The **Internet** is comprised of numerous WANs.

WANs use a wide variety of techniques and rules of communication to achieve end-to-end global connectivity, including a substrate of networking technologies such as leased high-speed lines or an ATM (**asynchronous transfer mode**) network. This substrate is then exploited by both data networks and conventional telephony, so that it is impossible to know exactly how a particular set of data is being carried from one point of the global network to the other. For example, voice telephony may be carried on top of an Internet connection, which in turn may be using both a conventional high-speed data link and an ATM network. Similarly, an exchange of data packets may be carried directly over leased telephone lines which are used to interconnect the nodes of a private packet network. A variety of technologies may be used to reach the end users of a WAN, including **local area networks** (LANs) such as **Ethernet**, **token rings**, or low-speed telephone connections using **modems**.

Two very important considerations in the deployment and use of WANs are standards and tariffs. Standards relate to the set of technical rules that allow networks of different types to be connected to each other to create a seamless networking infrastructure. They permit networking equipment from various manufacturers to operate together and exchange traffic without altering the contents, which are of essence to the end users. The strong relationship between networking and standards goes back to the earlier days of the telephone industry and of telephone operating companies, when most such operating companies were either government monopolies or de facto monopolies that were highly regulated by governments. Modern deregulation of the telecommunications industry does not seem to have impaired the functioning of international standards bodies such as the **International Telecommunications Union** (ITU).

Tariffs relate to the financial charges that are levied on the traffic carried by networks. Since the wave of telecommunications deregulation over the last 15 to 20 years, tariffs have become very varied and negotiable, to the point where many end users are lost in the complex charging policies offered by networking operators.

Traditionally, operators of WANs and the manufacturers of WAN equipment have been separate entities, although before deregulation, telecommunication equipment manufacturers were heavily influenced by the small number of customers they could choose from. The deregulation of telecommunications has created a boom in the information technology industry that is still far from being over.

FURTHER READING

Fdida, Serge, and Raif Onvural, eds. *Data Communications and Their Performance: Proceedings of the IFIP Working Group 6.3 on Performance of Computer Networks.* London: Chapman and Hall, 1996.

Gelenbe, Erol, ed. *System Performance Evaluation: Methodologies and Applications.* Boca Raton, Fla.: CRC Press, 2000.

Gelenbe, Erol, and G. Pujolle. *Introduction to Queueing Networks.* New York: Wiley, 1987; 2nd ed., 1998.

—*Erol Gelenbe and G. A. Marin*

Wiener, Norbert

1894–1964

U.S. Mathematician

Norbert Wiener named and helped create the science of **cybernetics** in the 1940s and 1950s. Cybernetics makes use of generalized concepts of communication, control, and the feedback of information to study both living and nonliving systems.

Wiener was a child prodigy who fulfilled the high expectations of his father, the Harvard linguist Leo Wiener (1862–1939). He completed a Harvard Ph.D. in mathematical logic at the age of 18, and after temporary jobs and travel in Europe where he met mathematicians Bertrand Russell (1872–1970), G. H. Hardy (1877–1947), and David Hilbert (1862–1943), he began his lifelong work at the Massachusetts Institute of Technology (MIT) in 1919. Wiener's work in the 1920s concentrated on stochastic processes and "random walks," such as the Brownian motion observed of particles buffeted by molecules in a fluid. Wiener's interests were always broad, and at MIT in the 1930s encompassed work with **Vannevar Bush** (1890–1974) on analog computers and exchanges with J. B. S. Haldane (1892–1964) on biology.

During World War II, Wiener worked on both practical and theoretical aspects of antiaircraft systems. One outcome of this work was a contribution to mathematics, the at-first secret report *Extrapolation, Interpolation, and Smoothing of Stationary Time Series* (1949), which established Wiener alongside the Russian A. N. Kolmogoroff (1903–87) as a major contributor to the theory of the prediction of stationary time series. With the engineer Julian Bigelow he devised a mathematical account of the problem of using limited information to predict the future location and motion of aircraft. A core concept in this analysis was feedback: the cycle of information involved in predicting position, receiving more information via radar, predicting a new position, adjusting the gun controls, and so completing the loop. In particular, *negative feedback,* in which incoming information was used to correct the deviation between direction and goal, was a concept of general importance to self-governing goal-oriented systems. Wiener saw in this example principles that could be general-

Norbert Wiener lecturing at Massachusetts Institute of Technology, circa 1958. (©Bettmann/CORBIS)

ized and employed to discuss the purposelike behavior of both machines and living creatures. Antiaircraft guns were the exemplar case on which was based the science of cybernetics.

Wiener debated these issues in the early 1940s with a friend at Harvard, the Mexican physiologist Arturo Rosenblueth (1900–70). Wiener and Bigelow were excited to hear from Rosenblueth of certain physiological conditions marked by uncontrollable oscillations that might be considered as cases of defective or excessive feedback. Through Rosenblueth, Wiener's ideas reached two other scientists, Chicago neuropsychiatrist **Warren McCulloch** (1898–1969) and the logician Walter Pitts (1923–69), who were seeking mathematical formulations to describe nervous systems. They had devised a model of the neuron by analogy to the electromechanical relays. (Relays were at that moment being used by **Howard Aiken** (1900–73) in the United States and **Konrad Zuse** (1920–95) in Germany to construct sophisticated calculating machines). By 1945 a loose group of scientists, including Wiener, McCulloch, Pitts, Rosenblueth, **John von Neumann** (1903–57), Bigelow, and Rafael Lorente de Nó (1902–90) had committed to further developing this unified cybernetic vision. Later social scientists, such as Gregory Bateson (1904–80), joined the research.

The Macy Foundation funded a serious of conferences that provided an unusual institutional framework within which the interdisciplinary subject of developed. The group first called itself the Conference for Circular Causal and Feedback Mechanisms in Biological and Social Systems, but on Wiener's insistence changed it to the simpler Conference on Cybernetics. Wiener had derived the word in 1947 from the Greek for "steersman," thus embodying the key concepts of steering, purpose, and feedback. However, *cybernetique* had been used by André-Marie Ampère (1775–1836) as early as 1834 in reference to the art of governing. Ten conferences were eventually held between 1946 and 1953.

In the postwar years, Wiener eschewed research of direct military relevance and concentrated instead on three areas: physiology with Rosenblueth and Pitts; collaboration with Jerome Wiesner (1915–94) on medical research, developing prosthetic devices to replace lost senses or lost limbs; and working on a coherent synthesis of the cybernetic insights. In 1948 Wiener published ***Cybernetics or Control and Communication in the Animal and the Machine***. *Cybernetics* received some criticism, especially from mathematicians suspicious that accuracy and rigor were lost in writing a popular account on a scientific subject. *Cybernetics* was a wide-ranging but contradictory book, a bestseller despite mathematical chapters, bubbling with ideas—from the reformation of the life sciences to a call to move to a society not based on a market for labor. *Cybernetics* is perhaps best understood as an attempt by an ambitious but interdisciplinary subject to claim the status and legitimacy denied it by the traditional disciplines. Its significance is therefore broader and cultural rather than as a narrow contribution to learning.

As a field, cybernetics' significance to the history of computing also works on several levels. First, it contained a vision that encompassed both machines and living organisms, and which centered on information, communication, and control rather than concepts, such as energy, derived directly from physics. The emphasis was firmly on considering humans, say, as being a component like any other in a system, as being like machines rather than vice versa. As the historian Paul Edwards (1957–) notes, the theory of feedback control had a double-face: it described not only how mechanisms could predict future positions, but also how their human controllers could do the same, or, given enough information about the human element, why they failed. Second, cybernetics articulated and publicized terminology, including *information*, *message*, *feedback*, and *control*, which could be used to discuss a wide range of subjects. Such language was picked up and applied in subjects as diverse as political theory, economics, management, and anthropology. Third, cybernetics was closely related to other theoretical developments in the 1940s and 1950s, in particular **Claude Shannon**'s (1916–2001) information theory (especially in its statistical treatment of information, entropy, and noise).

Wiener himself drew upon cybernetic ideas in further popular books, to discuss politics, religion, and science policy. In *The Human Use of Human Beings* (1950), communication was cast as the central phenomenon of society, which was therefore open to cybernetic analysis. The Soviet Union, which Wiener characterized by its rigid system and poor internal communication, was therefore akin to a defective cybernetic system. (Soviet reaction to cybernetics swung from rejection under Stalin as a capitalist science, to acceptance as a theory consistent with dialectical materialism in the late 1950s.) Capitalist societies did not escape Wiener's criticisms of rigidity either. In *God and Golem, Inc.* (1964), Wiener reflected on the perils of creation, but commented in passing that he was neither pro- nor anti-communist but antirigidity. Wiener's thoughts on science policy and the philosophy of technology were published posthumously in the *Invention: The Care and Feeding of Ideas* (1993).

Biography

Norbert Wiener. Born 26 November 1894 in Columbia, Missouri. B.A. in mathematics from Tufts College, 1909; M.A. from Harvard, 1912; Ph.D., also from Harvard, with a dissertation on mathematical logic, 1913. Army service, 1915–19. Professor of mathematics, Massachusetts Institute of Technology, from 1919–60. Promoted to associate professor, 1930; to full professor, 1932; to professor emeritus, 1960. Publications include *Cybernetics* (1948), *God and Golem, Inc.* (1964), *Invention* (1993). Died 18 March 1964 in Stockholm, Sweden.

Selected Writings

Wiener, Norbert. *Cybernetics*. New York: Wiley, 1948; 2nd ed., Cambridge, Mass.: MIT Press, 1961.

———. *Ex-Prodigy*. Cambridge, Mass: MIT Press, 1964.

———. *God and Golem, Inc.: A Comment on Certain Points Where Cybernetics Impinges on Religion*. Cambridge, Mass.: MIT Press, 1964.

———. *I Am a Mathematician: The Later Life of a Prodigy*. Cambridge, Mass.: Victor Gollancz, 1964.

———. *The Human Use of Human Beings: Cybernetics and Society*. Boston: Houghton Mifflin, 1950; 2nd ed., New York: Avon Books, 1970.

———. *Invention: The Care and Feeding of Ideas*. Cambridge, Mass.: MIT Press, 1993.

Further Reading

Edwards, Paul N. *The Closed World: Computers and the Politics of Discourse in Cold War America*. Cambridge, Mass.: MIT Press, 1996.

Heims, Steve J. *John von Neumann and Norbert Wiener: From Mathematics to the Technologies of Life and Death*. Cambridge, Mass.: MIT Press, 1980.

—*Jon Agar*

Wilkes, Maurice V.

1913–

British Computer Scientist

Maurice Wilkes led the team that constructed the Electronic Delay Storage Automatic Calculator (**EDSAC**), the first full-scale electronic stored-program computer, in 1949. The EDSAC team developed many important early techniques of programming, and the first commercial office computer, the LEO, built by Lyons & Co. in 1951, was based on the EDSAC. Wilkes built up the Computing Laboratory at Cambridge University, moving on in 1980 to act as a consultant for **Digital Equipment Corporation** and **Olivetti**.

The boyhood hobby of amateur radio introduced Wilkes to electrical engineering, a background he shared with many other scientists of his generation. At Cambridge he kept abreast of the subject, alongside his formal education in mathematics. Wilkes combined the two in his postgraduate research, an investigation of the ionosphere using long-wave radio waves, at the radio group of the Cavendish Laboratory, under J. A. Ratcliffe. His research demanded the solution of difficult differential equations, which led him to use and eventually take charge of the physical chemistry department's Differential Analyzer, an **analog computer**.

Just before the outbreak of World War II, Wilkes was mobilized to work on army radar, including operational research issues. After the war, Wilkes was appointed as head of Cambridge University's Mathematical (later Computer) Laboratory. Encouraged by Manchester University mathematician Douglas Hartree (1897–1958), an expert on numerical methods who had witnessed the **Harvard Mark I** and the **ENIAC**, Wilkes attended the famous **Moore School** course on electronic computers in 1946. He met **John Mauchly** (1907–80), **J. Presper Eckert** (1919–95), and Herman Goldstine (1913–), and he became familiar with the stored-program concept and ideas of how to store electronic data.

Wilkes began sketching a design for a stored-program computer while still in Philadelphia and continued on the long ocean journey home to the United

Kingdom. The crucial practical problem for all the early stored-program computers was the memory, and Wilkes was greatly assisted when the Cambridge physicist Thomas Gold (1920–) presented him with a feasible means of storing data in the form of electrical pulses passed and delayed through tanks of mercury. This delay line method was demonstrated in 1947, and its importance is reflected in the name of the EDSAC itself. Also in 1947, the Mathematical Laboratory began a partnership with Lyons & Co., the firm that had visited many of U.S. computer projects before hearing of the EDSAC. In return for £3000 and the loan of personnel, Wilkes' team undertook to assist Lyons build their own computer, the Lyons Electronic Office (LEO). The EDSAC ran its first program, computing a table of squares, on 6 May 1949, one of the first electronic stored-program computers to operate. It was demonstrated at the influential conference on high-speed calculating machines held in Cambridge in June 1949.

The historical significance of the EDSAC also lies in the development of software techniques. First, rather than adopt the difficult method of direct programming, Wilkes and his colleagues, especially David J. Wheeler, developed the method of higher-order symbolic notation in which coding was made much easier. The process of programming, however, involved repeating many sections of code. To make programming more efficient, the Cambridge team argued, it was better to preserve these repeated segments elsewhere and call them up as and when required: That way, code had to be written only once and was less prone to errors. A subroutine library was started; by the end of 1950, the library contained 80 subroutines. Wilkes proposed subroutine assembly and free addresses, now called *floating addresses,* to make subroutines easier to use.

Wilkes, Wheeler, and Stanley Gill (1926–75) wrote the first textbook on programming, *The Preparation of Programs for an Electronic Digital Computer*, published in 1951; a second edition followed in 1957. The historian Martin Campbell-Kelly (1945–) has described this book as a highly significant historical event because it provided the first accessible model of a how a symbolic programming system could be constructed. The Cambridge techniques strongly influenced programming on other early machines, notably the **Whirlwind** at Massachusetts Institute of Technology and the ILLIAC at the University of Illinois, among many others.

Under Wilkes the Cambridge University Mathematical Laboratory became a center of expertise in programming. The EDSAC and EDSAC 2 were applied in important scientific research, including the Nobel–prize winning determination of the structure of large organic molecules. The EDSAC was followed by a second machine, the EDSAC 2, which used ferrite-core memories rather than mercury delay lines, and again demonstrated new ideas, such as microprogramming and a read-only memory, although by the time it was fully operational in 1958, the lead had been taken by the United States.

Wilkes contributed to the professional organization of computer science, assisting in the creation of the British Computer Society (BCS, 1957) and the **International Federation for Information Processing** (IFIP, 1960).

BIOGRAPHY

Maurice Vincent Wilkes. Born 26 June 1913 in Dudley, England. Educated at King Edward VI School, Stourbridge, 1930. Entered Cambridge University, 1931, taking the Mathematical Tripos, and receiving a Ph.D. in mathematics, 1937. Worked on radar during World War II at the Coastal and Anti-Aircraft Defense Experimental Establishment, the Air Defense Research and Development Establishment, and the Telecommunications Research Establishment. Head of the Cambridge University computing laboratory, 1946-80, during that time he led the team that built the EDSAC, an electronic stored-program computer completed in 1949. Subsequently, a senior consulting engineer with Digital Equipment Corporation, 1980–86, and Olivetti, 1986–present. Elected Fellow of the Royal Society, 1956.

SELECTED WRITINGS

Wilkes, Maurice. *Memoirs of a Computer Pioneer*. Cambridge, Mass.: MIT Press, 1985.

———. "The Genesis of Microprogramming." *Annals of the History of Computing*, Vol. 8, No. 2, 1986, pp. 115–126.

Wilkes, Maurice, David J. Wheeler, and Stanley Gill. *The Preparation of Programs for an Electronic Digital Computer*. Cambridge, Mass.: Addison-Wesley, 1951; 2nd ed., New York: Addison-Wesley, 1957.

FURTHER READING

Campbell-Kelly, Martin. "Programming the EDSAC: Early Programming Activity at the University of Cambridge." *Annals of the History of Computing*, Vol. 2, 1980, pp. 7–36.

Lavington, Simon. *Early British Computers: The Story of Vintage Computers and the People Who Built Them.* Bedford, Mass.: Digital Press, 1980.

—*Jon Agar*

Williams Memory Tube

The Williams memory was invented by Sir Frederic Williams at Manchester University in 1947. Williams modified a **cathode-ray tube** to paint dots and dashes on the fluorescent screen, creating a memory device with electronic speed. **IBM** used a similar technology for the IBM 701, one of its first commercial computers. The Williams memory tube was soon replaced by **flip-flops** and core memories.

At the onset of the computer age, providing enough memory for stored-program computers was a difficult technical challenge. To be effective, a stored-program computer requires high-speed memory to store both instructions and data. Numerous approaches were tried at the time, including **vacuum tube** flip-flop circuits, mercury acoustic delay lines, an electrostatic storage device called the selectron, the barrier grid tube, and the Williams memory.

The Williams memory tube consists of a cathode-ray tube (CRT, like those used in television sets), to store charge at discrete locations, organized as an array on the face of the CRT. The CRT operates with an electron beam directed toward the face of the tube. Before striking the fluorescent coating, the beam passes between two pairs of plates, one pair for horizontal and one pair for vertical deflection. The voltage on each pair of plates can deflect the beam to any desired position on the CRT face.

When the electron beam in the CRT hits the fluorescent coating on the inside face of the tube with sufficient velocity, it produces secondary electrons and visible light. Someone watching the face of the tube sees a luminous dot. Using the beam, luminous points or dashes can be painted in the screen. The dots can be interpreted as zeros, the dashes as ones.

Williams tube, 1947. (Courtesy of the Computer Museum History Center)

To read the data, a watch glass with a conductive and transparent coating is placed over the face of the tube and is connected electrically to a video amplifier. The voltage of the output signal from the video amplifier determines whether the position selected by the beam is charged or uncharged.

The Williams memory system for the IBM 701 had a memory cycle time of 12 microseconds (μs), meaning that the contents of an address can be read or written in 12 μs. The IBM 701 used 72 Williams tubes with 1024 bits stored on the face of each tube for a total of 2048 words of 36 bits in each word. Each 36-bit word can be read, written, or regenerated in 12 μs.

The tubes were not without their problems. The charge stored on the face of the CRT can leak off, in a period of milliseconds; therefore, each address must be regenerated before the charge is lost. Another problem associated with the Williams memory is that continually reading and writing an address can cause the secondary electrons produced to discharge the adjacent address. The number of times that an adjacent address can be interrogated before discharging the contents of the first address is called the *read-around ratio*. The ratio achieved for the IBM 701 was 400. This very difficult goal was achieved by very careful design of the deflection amplifiers and the power supplies that supplied power to the deflection amplifiers.

FURTHER READING

Croarken, Mary. *Early Scientific Computing in Britain.* Oxford: Oxford University Press, 1990.

Lee, J. A. N. *Computer Pioneers.* Los Alamitos, Calif.: IEEE Computer Society Press, 1995.

—*Joseph Logue*

Windows and Windows NT

Windows and Windows NT are the names of the **operating systems** (OSs) marketed by **Microsoft** for the IBM **personal computer** (PC) and compatible computers. First delivered in 1985, Windows has gone through several major releases during its lifetime—the latest release of the product is Windows 2000. Millions of copies of both operating systems are sold each year; Microsoft's revenue from all Windows platforms was around U.S.$7 billion in 1999.

The history of Windows goes back to the Lisa, a machine shipped in 1983 by **Apple Computer**. The IBM PC was introduced in 1981, and the operating system, **DOS**, was text-based—that is, instructions had to be typed in a command line. The Lisa, however, was more like modern computers in that it used a **graphical user interface** (GUI) with multiple windows and used a **mouse** as a pointing device.

The GUI proved popular, and since IBM and Microsoft were not offering a GUI for the PC, other companies started selling add-ons for DOS. This was the case of VisiOn a GUI written in 1983 by programmers working for the company VisiCalc, and of GEM (Graphics Environment Manager) announced by Digital Research in 1984. However, GEM was not compatible with older PC **software** and gained little acceptance in the PC world. Only Atari would later adopt GEM for its own line of personal computers. IBM also introduced in 1985 a kind of multitasking add-on for DOS called TopView, which was text based but allowed users to switch between DOS applications. (This was a new feature because DOS let the user run only a program at a time; if another program was needed, the first had to be closed.) Finally, there was also a multitasker for DOS called DESQview, sold by Quarterdeck Office Systems with a functionality similar to that of TopView.

In November 1985, Windows 1.0 finally shipped. It had been announced three years earlier by Microsoft but had gone through several delays. It still had many significant shortcomings; the application windows could not be overlapped, and the **fonts** and **graphics** did not look as crisp on the screen as in the **Macintosh**. Significantly, DOS programs had to be rewritten for the new system. Few companies incurred the trouble of doing so, and therefore, for several years afterward, the most important applications were still DOS programs.

In the following two years, programs appeared that would increase the appeal of Windows. The first was PageMaker, a desktop publishing software with WYSIWYG capabilities; WYSIWYG stands for What You See (on the screen) Is What You Get (out of the printer). The other program was Excel, Microsoft's **spreadsheet**; already available for the Macintosh, it was ported to the IBM PC to challenge the market dominance of Lotus 1-2-3. Around this time, IBM and Microsoft decided to work on different versions of the operating system of the future. While IBM introduced and continued developing OS/2, Microsoft made a strong commitment to Windows, releasing version 2.0 in 1987, but without entirely removing the shortcomings of 1.0.

The first really popular version of Windows, release 3.0, was shipped in 1990. Competitors had already developed alternatives, such as DR-DOS from Digital Research, a system called GEOS 1.0, and IBM OS/2 with the new presentation manager. However, Windows 3.0 was better because it looked much more like the Macintosh: It offered overlapping windows, better fonts, and better disk management. Also, Microsoft started signing vendors to offer computers with Windows preinstalled, in this way effectively bundling the OS to the **hardware**.

At the same time that Microsoft was readying Windows 3.0, the company was already thinking about its follow-up, the New Technology (NT) system with the code name "Chicago," which would later became Windows NT. Microsoft raided the software industry, contracting the most talented software engineers, as for example David Cutler from **Digital Equipment Corporation**. Initially, NT would be based on the approach followed when working with

IBM on OS/2. But in 1991, the decision was taken of giving NT the look and feel of Windows. It was initially planned that the new operating system would be **microprocessor** independent, programming everything in **C**, but this approach was abandoned when NT and Windows were fused in Windows NT. Finally, in early 1993, Windows NT was released. It was geared for the server market and the first version was named 3.1 to avoid starting from 1.0, which would suggest that the system was still unreliable.

In 1995 Windows 95 was launched to great fanfare. Using a song from the Rolling Stones ("Start Me Up") as a theme, the new operating system made its debut. Windows had equaled the Macintosh at last. It had taken Microsoft 10 years to reach the quality level of the Apple product, but in the meantime Apple had barely improved the operating system of the Mac. Windows 95 also included support for **TCP/IP**, dial-up networks, and scalable fonts. Just a year later, Microsoft shipped Windows NT 4.0 with the same user interface as Windows 95 and a staggering 16 million lines of code. Microsoft's strategy concentrated on displacing **Unix** in the research and corporate market with Windows NT.

After Windows 95, two major releases of Windows followed, Windows 98 and Windows 2000. Whereas the 98 version was just an interim solution, the 2000 version represents the fusion of parts of the original Windows with NT. It is intended to bring both worlds together, providing better networking and security features. In Windows 2000 the user has to log on in the computer, even if it is his home computer, providing a password. System files cannot be modified by all users, providing in this way a shield against intruders or computer viruses. Although the security features of Windows have been widely criticized and its vulnerability to viruses is well known, Microsoft will try to close the security holes in future releases.

Nathan Myhrvold (1969–), chief technology officer at Microsoft, has noted that software behaves like a gas, filling all the available memory if given a chance. This is certainly true for Windows NT, which over the years has doubled in size every two years. In 1998, Windows NT was estimated to have 20 million lines of code, and for Windows 2000 there are contradictory accounts that set the size of the system between 35 and 60 million lines of code. As a point of comparison, the free operating system **Linux** has an estimated size of 5 million lines of code, including all its utilities.

The main difference between an operating system such as Windows and one such as Solaris, sold by **Sun Microsystems**, is the different philosophy. Windows is a *client-oriented operating system*—each user has a full copy of the system in his or her machine. Every time a new release of the OS is distributed, or if a patch has to be installed, every machine in a corporation has to be serviced. This can become a logistical nightmare. **Unix** (and its Solaris variation) are *server-centered* systems, where the operating system resides on a powerful server. The clients start the operating system through the network and if a patch or new version of the OS becomes available, only the server has to be upgraded.

However, PCs are much cheaper than workstations, and Windows has become the dominant OS. Large corporations need to manage all machines linking them in a coherent network, so Microsoft's strategy has been to provide NT for servers and Windows for clients. Windows 2000 should be the first step toward the fusion of both operating systems.

The market share of the various operating systems available has been changing over time, but Microsoft's market share is around 95 percent in the IBM PC world. If the Macintosh computers are included, Microsoft market share still remains near 90 percent. Only in the case of the Windows version for handheld computers (Windows CE) has Microsoft been unable to grab a significant portion of the market—here the OS of the PalmPilot **personal digital assistant** still dominates. One significant statistic is that the market share of the Microsoft browser increased to 75 percent in 1999, while Netscape's Navigator fell to less than 25 percent. Since Microsoft has integrated the browser with the OS, this dominance in the browser market serves to cement Microsoft's overall hegemony in the software sector.

Statistical forecasts see the market share of the Mac OS and Unix falling below 2 percent and 1 percent in 2001, respectively. The only alternative operating system whose market share is expected to increase is Linux, with 5 percent of the market in 2001.

FURTHER READING

Edstrom, Jennifer, and Marlin Erler. *Barbarians Led by Bill Gates: Microsoft from the Inside.* New York: Henry Holt, 1998.

Gates, Bill. *The Road Ahead*, rev. ed. New York: Penguin Books, 1996.

Glenn, Walter. *How to Use Microsoft Windows 2000.* Indianapolis, Ind.: Sams, 2000.

Manes, Stephen, and Paul Andrews. *Gates: How Microsoft's Mogul Reinvented an Industry—And Made Himself the Richest Man in America.* New York: Doubleday, 1993; Simon and Schuster, 1994.

Zachary, Pascal. *Show-Stopper! The Breakneck Race to Create Windows NT and the Next Generation at Microsoft.* New York: Free Press; Toronto: Maxwell Macmillan Canada; New York: Maxwell Macmillan International, 1994.

—*Raúl Rojas*

Wired

Wired Ventures pioneered electronic magazine publishing in the 1990s. The company has been credited with largely inventing what has become known as *wired culture* through its magazine *Wired* and its companion **World Wide Web** site *HotWired.*

Wired Ventures was formed in October 1992 by Louis Rossetto (1949–) and his partner, Jane Metcalfe (1961–), who had published a pioneering electronic publishing journal called *Electric Word* in Amsterdam in the late 1980s. Returning to the United States in 1991 with an idea for a magazine that would become *Wired*, they initially failed to find investors. But Nicholas Negroponte (1943–), director of the **MIT Media Laboratory**, offered to supply the U.S.$75,000 they needed to produce a pilot edition and became one of *Wired* magazine's first contributors. After attracting venture capital investment in late 1992, Rossetto and Metcalfe were able to publish the first issue of *Wired* in January 1993 to a circulation of 1000 readers. Despite rapidly gaining readers (*Wired*'s circulation would reach 300,000 in its first three years), the company lost nearly U.S.$1 million in its first year of business.

Given Rossetto's interest in electronic publishing, it was not long before he began putting into practice some of the ideas that *Wired* was exploring. After experimenting with **electronic mail** articles and content distributed through **America Online**, he was prompted to launch a *Wired* Web site toward the end of 1993 when two Japanese readers starting circulating *Wired* articles on their own Web server. The result was HotWired, launched in October 1994, one month before **Netscape** Navigator was released. HotWired became the model of the Web site magazine. It pioneered the use of the banner advertisement, initially by selling space to blue-chip advertisers such as **IBM** and Volvo. Free site membership was designed to build a loyal community of readers, and the use of distinctive magazine brands within HotWired, such as WebMonkey for Web developers and the irreverent Suck.com column, drew different readers to different parts of the site.

Both *Wired* and HotWired drew attention, praise, and numerous awards for Rossetto and his colleagues. But the company was still not making a profit and failed several times to go public in 1996. However, that year did bring two more notable successes. In May 1996, HotWired launched an Internet search engine called HotBot that would win dozens of awards for its user-friendly interface. In November, HotWired launched Wired News, its daily technology roundup.

Rossetto stepped down from Wired Ventures in July 1997 and by November of that year, Wired Digital (the part of Wired Ventures devoted to electronic publishing) had laid off 20 percent of its staff. In May 1998, *Wired* magazine and Wired Digital were split off from one another. *Wired* was sold to international magazine publisher Condé Nast Publications for around U.S.$75 million. Wired Digital continued to trade as a separate company until October 1998, when it was bought by the Lycos search engine and **portal** company for U.S.$83 million.

FURTHER READING

Brockman, John. *Digerati: Encounters with the Cyber Elite.* San Francisco: HardWired Books, 1996.

Reid, Robert. *Architects of the Web: 1,000 Days That Built the Future of Business.* New York: Wiley, 1997.

—*Chris Woodford*

Wireless Application Protocol

The Wireless Application Protocol (WAP) is a platform-independent technology that allows mobile computers and cellular telephones to access the **Internet**. The phenomenal growth in wireless Web phones, **personal digital assistants** (PDAs), and other hand-held devices has provided the momentum behind WAP. Datacomm Research estimates that 350 million of these devices will be shipped by 2003. Wireless data subscribers are projected to increase 1400 percent from 2000 to 2003, according to Cahner's In-Stat Group.

Accessing Internet content is a particular challenge for hand-held devices because of their small screens, low memory and power, and differing platform technologies, and also for wireless networks, because of their low **bandwidth** and high latencies. These limitations keep some older Internet protocols, such as Hypertext Markup Language (**HTML**), from working efficiently and effectively for mobile Internet-based communications.

Before WAP, mobile users could access the Web via such technologies as the UP Browser, by Unwired Planet (now Phone.com), which ran on AT&T PocketNet CDPD (cellular digital packet data) phones. WAP, on the other hand, is designed to address small devices' technical limitations and work with a variety of wireless platforms. WAP offers a scalable, extensible protocol stack that handles security, the establishment of sessions, and other aspects of mobile communications.

Internet access via hand-held devices was possible before WAP, but the technologies never took off commercially, WAP was designed to solve some of the problems caused when small, low-powered devices on different platforms try to use low-bandwidth wireless network technology to access services or data-intensive content via the Internet. A number of different protocols accomplish this. Key protocols include WTP and WLTS. WTP manages transactions by facilitating requests and responses between a user agent, such as a WAP microbrowser, and an application server for such activities as browsing and **electronic commerce** transactions. Wireless Transport Layer Security (WTLS) secures, authenticates, and encrypts data transmissions between the WAP gateway and mobile devices. In **wireless networks**, which frequently experience considerable latency, this can greatly slow response time.

WAP works with the major wireless network technologies used in different parts of the world, including CDMA (code-division multiple access), GSM (global system for mobile communication), and TDMA (time-division multiple access). WAP also supports the major **operating systems** used with hand-held devices, including Epoc, JavaOS, PalmOS, and Windows CE.

A number of WAP-enabled devices are on the market. The first was Nokia's 7100 phone, released in November 1999. Ericsson and **Motorola** have recently introduced WAP-enabled phones. Vendors are rolling out such WAP-enabled applications as browsers and corporate clients, as well as e-mail, calendar, and extranet programs. WAP-based e-commerce applications are also appearing, particularly in Europe, where the use of GSM as a continent-wide wireless standard has led to faster overall wireless adoption than in the United States, which uses several standards.

Deutsche Bank, Swiss Handelsbank, and other European banks are starting to use WAP to give customers with hand-held devices real-time access to account information. In some parts of Scandinavia, insurance companies are using WAP to let customers adjust coverage and handle other transactions. Finland's Sonera Oy company has even rolled a WAP-enabled soft-drink machine that lets users purchase beverages via WAP-enabled mobile telephones and charges purchases to the user's phone bill. Meanwhile, Webraska, a French startup, has released an application that generates maps and real-time traffic reports via WAP-enabled phones.

Ultimately, WAP will support **multimedia**, potentially an important consideration for the technology's future. Video, in particular videophones, will be a major WAP multimedia application. As bandwidth improves there will also be a proliferation of video **electronic mail** devices from manufacturers such as Nokia and Ericsson. The WAP Forum, an industry organization comprised of leading WAP manufacturers and software developers, is working on a formal standardization with a number of standards bodies: the European Computer Manufacturers' Association (ECMA), the European Telecommunications Standards Institute (ETSI), the Internet Engineering Task Force (IETF), the Telecommunications Industry Association (TIA), and the World Wide Web Consortium. WAP will have a large number of users—at least for a couple of years, until more mainstream protocols, such as HTML and Extensible Markup Language (**XML**), can be used effectively with mobile devices.

FURTHER READING

Buckingham, Simon. *Data on WAP.* Alpharetta, Ga.: Mobile Lifestreams, 20009.

Mann, Steve. *Programming Applications with the Wireless Application Protocol: The Complete Developer's Guide.* New York: Wiley, 2000.

Van der Heijden, Marcel, and Marcus Taylor, eds. *Understanding WAP: Wireless Applications, Devices, and Services.* Norwood, Mass.: Artech House, 2000.

Wireless Application Protocol Forum Staff. *Official Wireless Application Protocol.* New York: Wiley, 1999.

—*Neal Leavitt*

Wireless Networks

Wireless networks do not use a cable to convey information from one computer to another — the information is sent using a radio or an infrared link. New problems arise with this type of network, such as the mobility of the users and interference during radio communication. The types of protocols used in the physical layer of wireless networks is therefore very different from those used in cable-based networks.

When messages are transmitted in a wireless **local area network** (LAN) they can collide with messages from other users since the communication medium is shared. One solution, allocating fixed time slots for each computer, cannot be used when the number of computers in the network is changing dynamically. A better solution is to allow all users to send information at the same time but using different frequencies. To avoid blocking one frequency by a single user, the sender hops from one frequency to another in pseudorandom fashion. The receiver knows the **algorithm** used to change frequencies and tracks the sender so that the entire message can be received. This technique, called *frequency hopping spread spectrum* was developed by military agencies to circumvent espionage. When this approach is used within the civil radio band, there are some rules that have to be followed and there are a minimum number of frequencies that have to be used during hopping. The purpose of this is to make a sender appear as random noise in the background in such a way that other senders are not affected.

In the direct sequence spread spectrum approach, each bit (a 1 or a -1) is converted into a pseudorandom sequence of several bits, which can be transmitted over different frequencies. The receiver knows what to expect and can check if the pseudorandom sequence is present. Other participants in the network detect the sequence as random noise and are not affected. Many senders can be active at the same time, since the pseudorandom sequence used by each is different, and the sum of many such messages cancels statistically. There are different wireless LAN adapter cards on the market, operating in frequency ranges that do not require a special license: 902 to 928 megahertz (MHz), and at 2.4 to 2.484 gigahertz (GHz). This range is called the *industrial, scientific, and medical band* (ISM).

Wireless LANs can also be built using microwave senders. However, the main use of microwaves is to interconnect buildings in a restricted geographical area. Since a directed antenna and a line of sight are required, microwaves cannot be used in all circumstances. A similar option is the use of satellites, which are used to relay information at high speed to end users, while the uplink (the information from the user to the network) is transmitted at a slower rate. In some cases, a satellite relays information directly to a user (who has a satellite dish at home) and the information from the user to the network is sent through a conventional modem.

Apple Computer introduced the first personal computers with bundled wireless links in the late 1990s. Using the AirPort, a product developed in a collaboration with Lucent Technologies, it is possible to start a wireless home local area network in which several computers and **laptops** share devices. AirPort runs at a speed of 11 megabits per second (Mbps) and is based in the IEEE 802.11 Direct Sequence Spread Spectrum (DSSS) standard.

The latest development in the field of wireless networks has to do with short-range communication. Bluetooth, a novel wireless interconnection standard developed by Ericsson, will eliminate the cables not only between computers and printers, keyboard, and mouse, but also between portable computers and embedded processors. The sheer explosion in the number of embedded processors used in many appliances and computer equipment has led to a cabling nightmare that the Bluetooth initiative addresses directly. Bluetooth operates in the 2.4 GHz range and communication can be established within 10 meters of each device (100 meters with optional amplifiers).

Harald Bluetooth, a tenth-century Viking king, was selected as patron of the standard because he unified Denmark and Norway, much as the new Bluetooth will unify computer communication. Fittingly, it was Ericsson, a Swedish company, who started investigating the possibility of short-range radio communication in 1994. In 1997, Ericsson representatives approached manufacturers of computer equipment, and in February 1998, five promoters (Ericsson, **IBM**, Nokia, **Toshiba**, and **Intel**) formed a special-interest group to promote the new technology. Lucent, **Microsoft**, **3Com**, and **Motorola** joined the group shortly thereafter. Ericsson expects Bluetooth to become the fastest-growing wireless standard ever. Bluetooth is based on fast frequency hoping with a raw throughput of 1 Mbps and single-chip implementations already exsist.

The first decade of the twenty-first century will witness two main developments in the computer industry: the widespread introduction of embedded processing in all types of appliances, in cars, and at home; and the dominance of wireless networks for the "last mile" of network connectivity at home, in the office, and when traveling. In the world of the future we will have pervasive, seamless, anytime, everywhere wireless networking.

FURTHER READING

Geier, James T. *Wireless LANs: Implementing Interoperable Networks.* Indianapolis, Ind.: Macmillan Technical, 1999.

Miller, Brent, and Chatschick Bisdikian. *Bluetooth Revealed.* Upper Saddle River, N.J.: Prentice Hall, 2000.

Santamaría, Asunción, and F. J. Lopez-Hernandez. *Wireless LANs: Standards and Applications,* Norwood, Mass.: Artech House, 1999.

—*Raúl Rojas*

Wirth, Niklaus

1934–

Swiss Computer Scientist

Niklaus Wirth will be remembered primarily as a prolific and successful designer of imperative programming languages. **Pascal**, **Modula-2**, and **Oberon** were all his creations. He was also a leader in the **structured programming** movement, and his languages helped in the quest for more understandable programs.

After obtaining a degree in electrical engineering from Swiss Federal Institute of Technology (ETH) in Zurich in 1959, Wirth studied at Canada's Laval University and completed an M.Sc. degree in 1960. At the University of California–Berkeley, Wirth worked toward his doctorate, which he obtained in 1963, under the supervision of Harry D. Huskey (1916–), an early computer pioneer. From 1963 to 1967, Wirth taught as an assistant professor at the newly created Computer Science Department at Stanford University, then at the University of Zurich. In 1968 he was appointed full professor of computer science at ETH Zurich.

The first programming languages that Wirth worked on in the 1960s were the PL360 language and, in conjunction with the IFIP Working Group 2.1, a version of **ALGOL** called ALGOL-W. The original and elegant ALGOL 60 programming language, popular in Europe, was developed into the much more complicated ALGOL 68, which was never successful. Disagreements within the ALGOL 68 working group helped lead indirectly to what is probably Wirth's greatest contribution to programming language design: Pascal.

Wirth developed Pascal between 1968 and 1970. The language was designed originally as a teaching tool to promote good programming practice in the structured programming style of **Edsger Dijkstra** (1930–). It, together with its derivatives, have been used in this role ever since, as well as being used for serious programming development projects. Pascal incorporated all the standard control structures of structured programming; the "go to" statement was retained but discouraged. Wirth also included in-built data structures such as arrays, files, records, sets, and even user-defined types. Overall, Pascal was designed to be simple. Indeed, one of the beauties of the language was that Wirth was able to develop an elegant **compiler** for Pascal in the language itself.

Building on Dijkstra's structured programming ideas, Wirth systematized program development by stepwise refinement in the early 1970s. Later in the 1970s, Wirth developed his initial version of the Modula programming language as a research exercise aimed at demonstrating that an **operating system** for a personal workstation could be written entirely in a high-level language. Modula was based on Pascal with the addition of modules and concurrent processes. The module features helped in the design, interfacing, and structuring of larger programs.

Wirth worked on the subsequent and much more widely used Modula-2 language between about 1979 and 1981. The concept of concurrent processes was removed from Modula-2. Like Pascal, Modula-2 was widely used as a teaching language. Modules enabled interfaces between different parts of a large program to be well defined. A system module could allow access to low-level facilities. Wirth also included very strong typing in Modula-2, which can help in reducing errors. Modula-2 was the programming language used in Wirth's Lilith personal computer system.

Later, a less widely used **object-oriented** version of Modula-2 called Modula-3 was developed at **Digital Equipment Corporation** and **Olivetti**, in consultation with Wirth. Wirth also developed a language with some object-oriented features named Oberon. This project was launched in 1985 by Wirth with Jürg Gutknecht. The main work was undertaken between 1985 and 1989. Oberon had many of the features of Modula-2, but some unneeded aspects were removed. Other features were added, such as type extensions. This project was originally targeted toward in-house-built **hardware**, and this drove the language design, but ported versions of the Oberon language and system were made available for a number of commercial platforms.

Wirth's main contributions to computer science have been in the area of software engineering and its tools, especially concerning programming languages, although he also has experience in digital hardware design. During his career, he designed a series of important imperative programming languages. Of these, Pascal has had the most lasting influence, embodying many of the ideas of structured programming, of which he has been a great proponent.

BIOGRAPHY

Niklaus Wirth. Born 15 February 1934 in Switzerland. Undergraduate studies in Department of Electrical Engineering at ETH Zurich, 1954–58. Degree in electrical engineering, Swiss Federal Institute of Technology (ETH), Zurich, 1959. M.Sc. degree, Laval University, Quebec, Canada, 1960. Ph.D. in electrical engineering from University of California, Berkeley, 1963. Assistant professor, Computer Science Department, Stanford University, 1963–67. Appointed professor of computer science at ETH Zurich, 1968. Head of the Institute of Computer Systems at ETH, 1990. Retired 1 April 1999. Recipient of numerous honors and awards, including honorary doctorates from Universities of York, Linz, Laval, Masaryk, Novosibirsk, and Pretoria, the Open University and École Polytechnique Fédéral, Lausanne; the 1984 Turing Award for developing a sequence of innovative computer languages; and the 1987 Computer Pioneer Award from the IEEE Computer Society.

SELECTED WRITINGS

Wirth, Niklaus. "The Programming Language Pascal." *Acta Informatica*, Vol. 1, 1971, pp. 35–63.

———. "The Design of a PASCAL Compiler." *Software—Practice and Experience*, Vol. 1, No. 4, 1971, pp. 309–333.

———. *Systematic Programming: An Introduction*. Englewood Cliffs, N.J.: Prentice Hall, 1973.

———. "On the Composition of Well-Structured Programs." *Computing Surveys*, Vol. 6, No. 4, 1974, pp. 247–259.

———. *Algorithms + Data Structures = Programs*. Englewood Cliffs, N.J.: Prentice Hall, 1976.

———. "Recollections about the Development of Pascal." *History of Programming Languages Conference (HOPL-II)*, Preprints, Cambridge, Mass., 20–23 Apr. 1993. *ACM SIGPLAN Notices*, Vol. 28, No. 3, 1993.

Wirth, Niklaus, and Jürg Gutknecht. *Project Oberon: The Design of an Operating System and Compiler*. New York: ACM Press; Wokingham, Berkshire, England, and Reading, Mass.: Addison-Wesley 1992.

Wirth, Niklaus, and Kathy Jensen. *PASCAL: User Manual and Report.* Berlin and New York: Springer-Verlag, 1974; 4th ed., 1991.

FURTHER READING

Bergin, Thomas J., and Richard G. Gibson, eds. *History of Programming Languages II.* New York: ACM Press; Reading, Mass.: Addison-Wesley, 1996.

Böszörményi, Làszló, Jürg Gutknecht, and Gustav Pomberger, eds. *The School of Niklaus Wirth: The Art of Simplicity.* San Francisco: Morgan Kaufmann, 2000.

—*Jonathan Bowen*

Women and Computer Science

Women have played key roles in computer science (CS) since its inception—be it by funding projects, by designing machines, or by programming them. Indeed, during World War II, programmers were almost all women; they were called *calculators* or *computers*. It was only later that the terms came to represent machines. However, despite their leadership roles, women continue to be underrepresented in **computer science**. Many current programs are addressing this issue and are mentioned here.

From the very beginning of the CS field, women have made their mark, especially in the realm of what we now call **software**. **Augusta Ada Byron Lovelace** (1815–52) wrote and published comments about the **Analytical Engine**—conceived by **Charles Babbage** (1791–1871) as the first automatic calculating device—as a general-purpose programming machine. Through her notes, Lovelace described the operations necessary for automating the process of solving mathematical problems with what we now call conditional branching and loop concepts, and she wrote the world's first published program. She even described the use of the machine for programming music. Her work was highly regarded by Babbage and other mathematicians of her time, and she continues to be highly regarded today. The U.S. Department of Defense's high-level programming language **Ada** is named in her honor.

After Lovelace, women continued to be innovators of programming. The world's first programmers of the first electronic computing machine, the **ENIAC**, were six women: Kay Mauchly Antonelli, Jean Jennings Bartik, Betty Snyder Holberton, Marlyn Wescoff Meltzer, Frances Bilas Spence, and Ruth Lichterman Teitelbaum. Given only the **hardware** schematics of the ENIAC, they programmed the machine to calculate ballistic tables during World War II. By tracing the logical flow of instructions and data, they were able to rewire all 20 of ENIAC's signed 10-decimal-digit memory positions and its 6000 switches and cables to perform the desired operations.

The most famous of the early woman programmers was **Grace Murray Hopper** (1906–92), an admiral in the U.S. Navy who programmed the first large-scale digital computer, the **Harvard Mark I**. Hopper's first task was to design and implement a program that computed the coefficients of the arctangent series. In 1949 Hopper joined the newly formed Eckert-Mauchly Corporation, where BINAC and **UNIVAC I**, the first commercial computers, were developed. Hopper supervised the department that developed the first compiler, A-0, and its successor, A-2. Also employed at Eckert-Mauchly during that period was one of the ENIAC programmers, Betty Holberton, who developed the C-10 instruction code, **keyboards**, control console, and the first sort–merge generator for UNIVAC I.

Women had a large role to play in developing the business programming language **COBOL**. Hopper wrote Flow-Matic, which was the only implemented business data processing language in use at the time. Flow-Matic was a key innovation since it was used as a model for COBOL. Hopper partially supervised the industry-wide COBOL Short Range Committee, which initially included three women: Holberton, Mary K. Hawes, and Jean E. Sammet. Through COBOL, Hopper led the way in the standardization of programming languages; the first program able to run successfully on two different machines, the RCA 501 and the UNIVAC II, was written in COBOL.

In the early days of computing, women were also actively involved in all levels at the U.S. National Bureau of Standards (NBS, now known as the National Institute for Standards and Technology (NIST). The NBS played a key role in producing some of the world's first stored-program machines and in

WOMEN IN COMPUTER SCIENCE

In the 1980s and 1990s, women continued to make valuable contributions to the computing community—a few leading lights are described here. Additional biographies of women leaders in computer science and information technology can be found online at the Women in Technology International (WITI) Hall of Fame (*http://www.witi.com/center/witimuseum/halloffame/index.shtml*).

- Fran Allen of IBM is a pioneer in the field of compiler optimization and was the first woman to become an IBM Fellow.
- Carol Bartz is chief executive officer of Autodesk, the fourth-largest PC software company in the world.
- Anita Borg is the founder and director of the Institute for Women and Technology (IWT), founder of the Grace Hopper Conferences, founder of Systers, and was awarded the EFF (Electronic Frontier Foundation) Award.
- Judy Estrin founded three successful networking companies: Bridge Communications (which became part of 3Com), Network Computing Devices, and Precept Software; she is now the current chief technology officer of Cisco Systems, a world leader in data networking.
- Thelma Estrin, a pioneer in bioengineering, helped design and develop the first large-scale computer in Israel (the WEIZAC), set up the first computer facility in a medical school (the Data Processing Laboratory), and developed one of the first analog-to-digital conversion systems. Estrin was also the first woman member of the board of directors of the Aerospace Corporation and the first woman to be elected to the IEEE board of directors.
- Adele Goldberg was a co-inventor of Smalltalk (inventing the object-oriented paradigm for programming) and was chair and founder of ParcPlace Systems.
- Shafrira Goldwasser pioneered work in theoretical computer science in computation theory, computational number theory, and cryptography. She won the Gödel prize of theoretical computer science and the ACM Hopper Award for her achievements.
- Barbara J. Grosz is credited with helping to establish the field of computational modeling of discourse. Grosz is a Fellow of the American Association for the Advancement of Science (AAAS) and a founding fellow and former president of the American Association of Artificial Intelligence (AAAI).
- Anita Jones, a researcher in computer software systems, was the director of Defense Research and Engineering for the U.S. government and former chair of the CS department at the University of Virginia.
- Barbara Simons is the current president of the Association of Computing Machinery (ACM), founder of USACM, and recipient of the CPSR Norbert Wiener Award for Professional and Social Responsibility in Computing and the Electronic Frontier Foundation Award for her influential contributions to the empowerment of people in the use of computers.

starting the field of numerical analysis. Gertrude Blanch and Ida Rhodes were key members of the Math Tables Project, which was the first computing program at the NBS. Mina Rees, from the Office of Naval Research (ONR), was highly influential in procuring funds for the NBS to develop their computing machines—such as the SEAC, one of the first stored program machines—and in establishing the field of numerical analysis. Ruth Haueter Cahn was part of the engineering team that developed the circuits and logic of the SEAC machine. Finally, Ethel Marden, Florence Koons, and Rhodes were part of the programming team that first programmed the SEAC and UNIVAC. In fact, the first program of the SEAC was written by Ethel Marden, who also became the first woman to be appointed a division chief at NBS.

In contemporary times, many women are in leadership positions in the CS and technology community (see boxed item). However, in the late 1990s only 2 percent of technology company chief executive officers were women. Recent data from the U.S. Department of Education show that at the turn of the century, women received only 29 percent of the bachelor's degrees awarded in computer science in the United States, 26 percent of the master's degrees, and 12 percent of the doctoral degrees in U.S. and Canadian universities. The last decade has witnessed an alarming decline of women graduating with degrees in computer science: for instance, there was a 24 percent drop at the B.S. level since the 1980s. Meanwhile, other science and engineering fields have seen increasing percentages of women participants.

It is not clear exactly why the percentages of women in CS are decreasing, especially when the number of positions in information technology (IT) are increasing rapidly. The number of unfilled jobs will only increase: According to the U.S. Bureau of Labor Statistics, the demand for workers in the IT field will grow to more than 1 million by 2005.

The declining numbers are probably due to a multitude of issues, where the whole effect is much greater than the sum of its parts. Girls may be turned off from computing at early ages if their first interaction with computers is through "shoot'em up" video games, the bulk of which are aimed at boys. Girls and young women may also be reluctant to pursue CS because of the "nerd" stigma that is often associated with the field, or precisely because CS is perceived to be a male-dominated field. To counteract these trends, many organizations that specialize on women in technology are trying to provide mentoring and role model programs. Such programs help young women to imagine themselves as a CS or IT professional and receive the support they need to scale the academic and professional ladder. In addition, some companies have recently developed computer games aimed at the girl market, such as Purple Moon, Broderbund, the Learning Company, Girl Games, and Her Interactive; it is too early to tell if these products have made an impact.

In the past, universities have been criticized for—subtly or unsubtly—discouraging women from pursuing CS majors. To counteract this, some universities have recently improved their CS curriculum to better reflect women's interests and learning styles; many have been highly successful at retaining their female students. Another factor behind the low percentages of women in CS may be similar to experiences in other male-dominated fields like engineering—a feeling of isolation caused by being one of a few women in their entire class, department, or company.

Numerous organizations and programs exist with the goal of increasing the numbers of women in computing and IT fields. For example, the Association for Computing Committee on Women in Computing (ACM-W) is very active in bringing more women to the computing community around the world. The Computing Research Association Committee on the Status of Women in Computing Research (CRAW) focuses on increasing the numbers of women in academic research. The Institute of Women and Technology (IWT) looks at ways to bring more women into technology in all phases in design, development, and use of technology. The Grace Hopper Celebration of Women in Computing is a national conference designed to encourage girls and women in computing by highlighting women's achievements in CS. Systers is an electronic community that brings together and provides community in CS for more than 2500 women around the world. Finally, the Ada Project is a web-based clearinghouse of information on women in computing.

FURTHER READING

Amann, Dick, and Dick Smith. *The Forgotten Women of Computer History*. Stow, Mass.: Programmed Studies, 1978.

Camp, Tracy. "The Incredible Shrinking Pipeline." *Communications of the ACM*, Vol. 40, No. 10, 1997, pp. 103–110.

Freeman, Peter, and William Aspray. "The Supply of Information Technology Workers in the United States." Report by the Computing Research Association, 1999.

Fritz, W. Barkley. "The Women of ENIAC." *IEEE Annals of the History of Computing*, Vol. 18, No. 3, 1996.

Gürer, Denise. "Pioneering Women in Computer Science." *Communications of the ACM*, Vol. 38, No. 1, 1995, pp. 45–54.

———. "Women's Contributions to Early Computing at the National Bureau of Standards." *IEEE Annals of the History of Computing*, Vol. 18, No. 3, 1996, pp. 29–35.

Kim, Eugene Eric, and Betty Alexandra Toole. "Ada and the First Computer." *Scientific American*, Vol. 280, No. 5, 1999, pp. 66–71.

National Science Foundation. "Women, Minorities, and Persons with Disabilities in Science and Engineering." *Report NSF99338*. Washington D.C.: National Science Foundation, 1998.

Toole, Betty Alexandra, ed. *Ada, the Enchantress of Numbers: A Selection from the Letters of Lord Byron's Daughter and Her Description of the First Computer*. Mill Valley, Calif.: Strawberry Press, 1992.

—Denise Gürer

Word Length

In general, a *word* is a group of **bits** that are treated as a unit for some purpose. The word length of a computer is usually the size of its accumulator register(s), most often expressed in bits, but sometimes in characters. Up until the mid-1950s, the word was also the smallest unit of transfer between computer memory and the processor; since then, most computers have been able to transfer partial words (*bytes*).

On the **ENIAC** (1945) the accumulators could hold 10 decimal digits plus the sign. Subsequent **vacuum tube** and **transistor** computers had word sizes varying from the 12 bits of the PDP-5 and PDP-8 (1963 and 1965) up to the 72 bits (12 characters) of the **UNIVAC** I (1951). There were all sorts of sizes in between, not all of them being even numbers: the BINAC (1949) was 31 bits, the SEAC (1950) was 45 bits, and the Bendix G-15 (1954) was 29 bits. The most common word size for scientific computers during the vacuum tube and transistor eras was the 36 bits of the **IBM** 701/704/709/7090/7094 family and the UNIVAC 1103/1105/1107 series. On these computers, character data were stored as six 6-bit characters per word.

Besides marking the beginning of the transition from transistors to **integrated circuits**, the 1964 introduction of the IBM 360 system also established 32 bits as the dominant word size for large computers. Other computer companies used larger sizes, such as the 36 bits of the UNIVAC 1108, General Electric 6000 series, and **Digital**'s DECSystem 10 and 20, the 48 bits of the **Burroughs** large-scale computers, and the 60 and 64 bits used by **Control Data Corporation**. At this time, characters (bytes) also grew from 6 bits to 7 (**ASCII** code) or 8 (Extended ASCII and **EBCDIC** codes).

The **minicomputers** of the 1960s used word sizes of 12 or 18 bits, but introduction of the PDP-11 in 1970 marked the shift to 16-bit words (and 8-bit characters), the size that was most common during the 1970s. Digital's introduction of the **VAX** at the end of 1978 moved the standard up to 32. The same sort of progression occurred with **microprocessors**. **Intel**'s 4004 of 1971 had just a 4-bit word, but word sizes grew to 8 bits with introduction of the Intel 8080 in 1974 and to 16 bits with the Intel 8086 and **Motorola** 68000 at the end of the 1970s. The jump to 32 bits was made by the Intel 80386 in 1985. In the late 1990s, 64-bit architectures were introduced by Digital (**Compaq**) with the Alpha chip and by Intel.

Besides their word size, computer processors can also be described by the way in which they store multibyte integers within a word. The term *big-endian* is used where the most significant byte is stored at the beginning of the word—that is, the value is stored "big end first." *Little-endian* describes the opposite approach, where the least significant byte (the little end) goes at the beginning of the word. The little-endian approach was used on the PDP-11 and VAX and in Intel microprocessors. Most processors, including the IBM 370 family, the PDP-10, the **Unisys** 1100/2200 and A series, the Motorola microprocessor families, and many of the various **reduced instruction set computer** designs are big-endian.

FURTHER READING

Tomek, Ivan. *Introduction to Computer Organization.* Rockville, Md.: Computer Science Press, 1981.

Weik, Martin H. *A Third Survey of Domestic Electronic Digital Computer Systems.* Aberdeen, Md.: Ballistic Research Laboratory, 1961.

—*George Gray*

Word Processing

Word processing involves using a computer to write or edit text documents. Unlike a typewriter, which prints letters onto a page when the keys are pressed, a word processor allows the text to be edited and formatted before it is printed out. The first word processors were pieces of **hardware** (electronic typewriters with memories), but the **microcomputer** revolution of the 1970s popularized inexpensive word processing software and made it cost-effective for people to buy a **personal computer** (PC) and **printer** just to write and edit documents. Today, word processors have all but replaced typewriters in businesses and homes.

Conceptually, word processors are much the same as typewriters. Words are typed at the **keyboard** (or dictated, using a microphone and **speech recognition** software) and they appear immediately on a blank screen that represents a sheet of paper. But word processors differ from typewriters in the extra features they offer. Text can be cut from one part of a document and pasted in elsewhere. A particular string of characters can be searched for and replaced with a different string. Different parts of the document can be laid out in different **fonts**, and sophisticated word processors allow precise control over the ultimate formatting of the final document (such as where images appear in the text, whether boxes of text should be shaded, and so on). In this, word processors are not so very different from **desktop publishing** software, and the difference between the two has become increasingly blurred.

Different word processors do, however, work in different ways. The least sophisticated allow editing of **ASCII** text (simple, unformatted text that uses a least-common-denominator set of letters and symbols understood by almost all computers) and not much more; one familiar example is the Notepad editor packaged with **Windows**. More advanced ASCII editors offer other features. For example, Xedit, an ASCII editor widely used on **IBM mainframes**, allows users to write highly sophisticated programs called *macros* to carry out commonly performed tasks. Today's best-known PC word processors, such as Microsoft Word and Corel WordPerfect, operate on the principle of "what you see is what you get" or WYSIWYG, where what appears on the screen resembles very closely what appears on paper when the document is printed. They achieve this by embedding control codes (hidden strings of characters that switch formatting styles on and off) in between sections of ordinary text.

Not all word processors use the WYSIWYG principle. Some involve defining or marking up different parts of a document with visible ASCII control words called *tags*, which are interpreted only when the document is printed out or displayed on the screen. For example, a tag such as <p> is inserted to indicate the start of a new paragraph, and <table> may indicate a text table. Most markup languages—such as the **HTML** (Hypertext Markup Language) and **XML** (Extensible or Extended Markup Language) used to structure Web pages—conform to a standard set of rules known as Standard Generalized Markup Language (SGML). The main advantage of markup languages is their extreme flexibility. Unlike a Microsoft Word file, a document tagged in SGML or HTML does not have a rigidly defined appearance. The tags indicate only the structure of the document; the appearance can be changed by changing the way that tags are processed when the document is printed or displayed. This means that SGML documents originally produced for printed output can rapidly be converted to electronic formats or searched more precisely than documents produced in formats such as Word.

Word processors with their QWERTY keyboards are visibly descended from the manual typewriter designed in 1867 by Christopher Latham Sholes (1819–90), a U.S. inventor from Milwaukee, Wisconsin. The first word processor may well have been a pneumatic machine called the Autotypist, developed by the Shulz Company in 1936, which stored documents on punched paper tape and recalled them rather like a player piano. The gradual convergence of typewriters and computerized word processors owes much to **IBM**'s development of electric typewriters in the 1920s and 1930s. But the term *word processing* was not invented until 1964, when IBM used it to describe its Magnetic Tape/Selectric Typewriter (MT/ST). This used magnetic tape to store and retrieve documents and offered a choice of fonts.

By this time, mainframe computers were also being used to manipulate text. In 1962, **Ivan Sutherland** (1938–) developed the first mainframe word processor, which featured search and replace, automatic wrap-around at the end of lines, and programmable macros. A system called Type Justifier-2 (TJ-2), running on the **Digital Equipment Corporation** (DEC) PDP-1 computer, was being used at Massachusetts Institute of Technology (MIT) by 1963. It allowed rudimentary formatting of text, including justification (insertion of spaces to make the right margin even) and centering. During the 1960s, experiments with **hypertext** (a method of structuring text not as a continuous scroll but as a collection of independent linked modules) spawned several advanced word processors. These included the Hypertext Editing System, used to develop documentation for the Apollo space program in the late 1960s. Most of these editors used a principle known as *line editing*, in which a command line displayed at the bottom of the mainframe terminal could be used to edit documents one line at a time. Later mainframe editors, such as IBM's Xedit, allowed any number of changes to be made anywhere on the screen, but these changes were registered and stored only when a key such as ENTER was pressed, causing the modified screen image to be sent back from the terminal to the mainframe.

The world's first dedicated word processor was the Wang 1200, a **minicomputer** launched in 1972. Wang's machines dominated the market until the arrival of inexpensive microcomputers in the late 1970s, which could store long documents on **floppy disks**. Unlike today's PCs, microcomputers were based on largely incompatible proprietary **operating systems** and hardware; a program designed for one machine would not run on another, so each computer needed its own word processor. Thus, the **Altair 8800** ran the first microcomputer word processor, Electric Pencil, written by Michael Shrayer; the hugely successful **Apple II** ran a word processor called Apple Writer, launched in 1979. Fortunately, a standard microcomputer word processor did eventually emerge when Seymour Rubenstein and Rob Barnaby of Micropro International Inc. released WordStar in 1979. This was ported to (rewritten for) a variety of different machines, and eventually ran on both **CP/M** (an early microcomputer disk operating system) and **DOS**.

Until the early 1980s, word processors were very much text editors dedicated to manipulating simple ASCII files. The output from the printer usually bore little resemblance to what was displayed on the screen, depending on the type of printer used; and professional-looking documents, such as books and magazines, still required specialist typesetting equipment. All that changed with the popularization of the graphical user interface following the introduction of the Apple Lisa and **Macintosh** computers. This led to WYSIWYG word processors such as MacWrite for the Macintosh and Microsoft Word for both Macintosh and PC, and ignited the laser-printed revolution known as desktop publishing (DTP).

Today's word processors and DTP programs are faster and more sophisticated, but they are fundamentally the same as they were in the mid-1980s. However, another word processing revolution has been taking place thanks to the success of the **World Wide Web** and the markup languages (such as HTML) on which it is based. HTML can trace its roots to the SGML language developed by Charles Goldfarb (1940–) at IBM in the late 1970s and early 1980s. SGML was based on IBM's earlier text formatting languages DCF (Document Composition Facility), also known as SCRIPT/VS, and GML, which stands for Generalized Markup Language, but also intentionally credits its inventors, Charles Goldfarb, Ed Mosher, and Ray Lorie.

One of the first markup languages of this kind was RUNOFF, developed by Jerome Saltzer (1939–) at MIT in the early 1960s. It involved inserting formatting commands preceded by a period into the text (such as ".ctr" to center text and ".sp 2" to leave two blank lines). RUNOFF became popular on DEC machines and evolved into Digital Standard Runoff (DSR) and VAX Document, and spawned other systems called roff and troff (popular **Unix** text processors). These early markup systems used a two-stage process. First, text was marked up using an editing program. Later, the marked-up text was turned into a printer-ready file by a formatting program that used considerable processor time and therefore typically ran in batch (offline).

Although contemporary markup languages are seldom used for everyday word processing, they are commonly used to prepare technical documentation and multi volume reference books such as dictionaries. IBM, reputedly the world's second largest publisher, uses SGML to produce its technical manuals simultaneously as books, **CD-ROMs**, and HTML. CALS (Computer-aided Acquisition and Logistic Support), used by the US Defense Department to produce documentation from 1987 onward, was another early application of SGML. The recent emergence of WYSIWYG HTML Web page editors, such as Microsoft FrontPage and Netscape Composer, and e-mail programs that exchange richly formatted HTML instead of unformatted ASCII, has led to an increase in the use of HTML markup for word processing (though mainly for documents designed to be read on the screen).

Ultimately, word processing is important not just because it enables documents to be written and edited more easily. By shifting the currency of information from paper to electronic media, word processors have made it easier for blind and otherwise disabled people to create and exchange information the same as anyone else. In an age when television and telephones had all but killed off written communication, word processors have empowered people to communicate their thoughts more logically and more professionally. It is no exaggeration to suggest that what Gutenberg's printing press did for society as a whole, word processors have since done for individuals. Even more revolutionary is the way information is created and stored in electronic files that can be converted to a variety of printed and online formats.

On the other hand, many—often incompatible—systems have been developed in the short history of word processing. Paper documents hundreds of years old and stone tablets very much older can still be read, albeit sometimes with difficulty. Yet how many word-processed documents written during the last 30 years have become inaccessible simply because the systems that produced them have now become obsolete? How many more will be lost by the difficulties of maintaining information in electronic form? Word-processed information seems far more convenient and robust than information committed to paper, but librarians designing the digital libraries of the future and others still have questions over the durability of electronic information.

FURTHER READING

Biermann, Alan. *Great Ideas in Computer Science: A Gentle Introduction*. Cambridge, Mass.: MIT Press, 1996.

Goldfarb, Charles. *The SGML Handbook*. Oxford: Clarendon Press, 1990.

Kinkoph, Sherry. *How to Use Microsoft Word 2000*. Indianapolis, Ind.: Sams, 1999.

Myers, Brad. "A Brief History of Human–Computer Interaction Technology." *ACM Interactions*, Vol. 5, No. 2. Mar. 1998, p. 44.

Parker, Roger C. *Desktop Publishing and Design for Dummies*. Foster City, Calif.: IDG Books, 1995.

Romano, Frank. *Digital Media: Publishing Technologies for the 21st Century*. Torrance, Calif: Micro Publishing Press, 1996.

Rothenberg, Jeff. "Ensuring the Longevity of Digital Documents." *Scientific American*, Jan. 1995, p. 24.

—*Chris Woodford*

Workflow Software

Workflow software is the generic term used to refer to integrated systems capable of encompassing all phases of office work. Instead of employees exchanging paper files, workflow systems allow them to exchange electronic files. All transactions are monitored through all stages, so that the state of a certain work unit can be assessed immediately. Installing these systems at corporations is not an automatic process, and therefore workflow systems require an associated activity called *business process reengineering* (BPR).

In every office, work is organized in a pipeline. One office worker receives a document, processes it, and sends it to the next worker in the line. Much time is lost, not in the actual processing of the document, but in the physical exchange of paper. Also, in many cases it is uncertain which phase the document has reached. Workflow software automatizes the exchange process, making office workers more productive. The workflow software industry has now become a multibillion dollar business.

Workflow analysts distinguish between material, information, and human processes. The purpose of workflow systems is to make information processes faster and to provide tools (e.g., videoconferencing, meetings calendar) for the human processes in a business.

Three types of workflow are usually distinguished: image-based, form-based, and coordination-based systems. *Image-based workflow processes* are optimized by transferring documents to a digital file and moving them through the organization. Many banks, for example, do not move paper checks across their branches but rather, a digital image of the check. *Form-based workflow systems* make entering data into forms more efficient by avoiding paper. Forms are displayed on screens and are filled in, for example, at hospitals or car rental agencies. *Coordination-based workflow systems* try to facilitate collaboration of several persons through the various stages of a task.

Typically, a business process reengineer has to go through three steps in order to reorganize the information processing at a business. First, all the persons involved in the process are interviewed and a map of the interactions between them and of the transaction flow is created. This is actually a difficult task, because the structure of a company is rarely documented, it just "exists." Next, the processes are broken down into meaningful, manageable pieces that can be analyzed individually. Finally, a new information processing graph is sought, which can fulfill the same task more efficiently, that is, in less time and with less work. For all these steps of the evaluation process, special software can be used to assist the evaluator in determining the old and new workflow structures.

At this point, the business engineer has to assess the technological options available and design a new integrated system, capable of implementing the new workflow. There are many commercial packages that can be selected for this task.

The Workflow Management Coalition is a nonprofit organization of software vendors and users interested in developing standards for the interoperability of workflow systems. In this way, different companies could connect their systems together to avoid having to go back to paper at the company's boundary.

FURTHER READING

Dogac, Asuman, ed. *Workflow Management Systems and Interoperability*. Berlin: Springer-Verlag, 1998.

Schäl, Thomas. *Workflow Management Systems for Process Organisations*. Berlin: Springer-Verlag, 1998.

—*Raúl Rojas*

World Intellectual Property Organization

The World Intellectual Property Organization (WIPO) is an intergovernmental organization within the United Nations system that is responsible for the promotion of the protection of intellectual property throughout the world. In early 2000, more than 170 countries were members of WIPO.

WIPO is dedicated to helping to ensure that the rights of creators and owners of intellectual property are protected worldwide and that inventors and authors are recognized and rewarded for their ingenuity. There are two main forms of intellectual property: industrial property, chiefly in inventions, trademarks, industrial designs, and appellations of origin; and copyright, chiefly in literary, musical, artistic, photographic, and audiovisual works. WIPO carries out many tasks related to the protection of both forms of intellectual property.

The need for international protection of intellectual property first became evident when foreign exhibitors refused to attend the International Exhibition of Inventions in Vienna in 1873 because they were afraid their ideas would be stolen and exploited commercially in other countries. Ten years later, the Paris Convention for the Protection of Industrial Property was convened to develop the first major international treaty designed to help people obtain protection for their intellectual creations in countries other than their own. The treaty addressed industrial property rights, known as inventions (patents), trademarks, and industrial designs. In 1886, international copyright protection was addressed by the Berne Convention for the Protection of Literary and Artistic Works.

Both the Paris and the Berne Conventions established international bureaus to carry out their activities, and in 1893, these two organizations combined into the United International Bureaux for the Protection of Intellectual Property, the predecessor to WIPO. In 1960, the organization moved to Geneva to be closer to the United Nations, and in 1970, underwent a series of structural reforms to become WIPO, which became an agency of the United Nations in 1974.

Today, WIPO administers a total of 21 international treaties that define international intellectual property law or simplify the international protection process by providing for a single registration or filing that has effect in all countries that are parties to the treaty. WIPO also provides assistance to developing countries in establishing effective intellectual property protection systems by training officials dealing with intellectual property and assisting them in establishing effective administrative procedures.

Copyright is the legal mechanism by which most **software** developers protect their right to control the distribution and use of the software they have developed; therefore, WIPO's efforts to ensure consistency in definition and enforcement of copyright law among its members is of great significance to the international software industry.

With the great expansion of the **Internet** for commercial and personal use in the 1990s, the need arose to ensure that intellectual property law provided adequate protection for software and information distributed electronically. WIPO drafted the World Intellectual Property Organization Copyright Treaty (WCT) to ensure that copyrighted works remain protected when transmitted online and that there are prohibitions in law against measures that would defeat copyright protection mechanisms.

The discussions surrounding the draft of the treaty were highly controversial, with parties such as online service providers arguing that the proposed wording would potentially make them liable for copyright infringements by their customers over which they had no control. Others argued that the prohibitions against measures to defeat protection mechanisms would prevent legitimate attempts to "crack" security systems in order to determine their vulnerability.

A final version of the treaty, which attempted to deal with the concerns that were raised, was adopted on 20 December 1996. For the treaty to become effective internationally, it must be ratified by 30 nations, each of which must modify its copyright protection laws as needed to conform to the provisions of the treaty. As of mid-2000, the WCT had been ratified by more than 20 countries.

WIPO is headquartered in Geneva, Switzerland, with a coordinating office in New York City. In early 2000, it had a staff of 690 from 75 countries.

Further Reading

Convention Establishing the World Intellectual Property Organization. Washington, D.C.: U.S. Government Printing Office, 1967.

Beier, Friedrich-Karl, and Gerhard Schricker, eds. *GATT or WIPO: New Ways in the International Protection of Intellectual Property,* Symposium at Ringberg Castle, 13–16 July 1988. Cambridge, England: VCH, 1989.

World Intellectual Property Organization. *WIPO: World Intellectual Property Organization, General Information.* Geneva: WIPO, 1987.

http://www.wipo.int

———. *World Intellectual Property Organization Copyright Treaty.* Washington, D.C.: U.S. Government Printing Office, 1997.

—*Luanne Johnson*

World Wide Web

The World Wide Web is often confused with the **Internet**, presumably because in recent years most Internet traffic has been Web traffic. However, the Internet had developed long before the Web was created; it is one of various applications that use the Internet: including **electronic mail**, **Usenet** discussion groups, videoconferencing, and chat programs. Whereas the Internet is a network of computers, the Web is a network of text documents, sounds, pictures, and videos. This information is not held in one computer and not even in one place. It is distributed all over the world, but it appears on the screen of the user's computer as if it was all there, right at the user's fingertips.

The Web consists of information resources, called *documents*, and connections between them, called *links*. Documents are usually referred to as *Web pages*. Each Web page has a networkwide address, which is called a *Unified Resource Locator* (URL). Each link points at the URL of a document. Documents and links together form a non-hierarchical web of information.

In the early 1990s, **Tim Berners-Lee** (1955–) and his colleagues at CERN, a particle physics laboratory in Switzerland, developed and promoted the concept of an open, universally accessible network of computer-held information. Since then the World Wide Web, also called WWW, W3, or simply "the Web," has grown exponentially from less than 100 Web servers in 1992 to more than 1 million estimated servers in 1995 and it is still growing. Indeed, the Web has developed into a worldwide information resource and communication tool that dominates the daily lives of many people.

Although other formats are possible, most Web pages are written in **hypertext**, basically text with hyperlinks. In the Web pages links often show as colored and underlined words. These links can lead from any section of a document to other sections of the same document or to all or part of another document. Since documents do not need to be texts and can be sounds, movies, or pictures, the term *hypermedia* is often applied to these multimedia-type Web pages. Picture documents especially come in all sorts of formats (e.g., GIF and **JPEG** files). To provide universal access, the designers of the Web endowed it with the ability to negotiate quite a variety of document formats.

Hypertext and hypermedia documents are prepared using markup languages. The markup language developed particularly for the Web is **HTML** (Hypertext Markup Language). HTML allows the document to be described in terms of its structure and its links, but not its format. **XML** (Extensible Hypertext Markup Language), an extension of HTML, has been developed to overcome some of the deficiencies of HTML.

For the links to become operational and document information to be sent and understood by all Web applications, the Web uses a set of rules called the Hypertext Transfer Protocol (HTTP). The most remarkable feature of HTTP is its universality. It not only negotiates various document formats, it also understands a number of other protocols, such as **FTP**, **telnet**, and **Gopher**, and can translate back and forth between them. For instance, FTP documents are represented as text with links, Gopher information is represented either as plain text or as a menu with hyperlinks.

To view and read Web pages users need a program called a **browser**. The browser lets the reader follow the hyperlinks in a Web page and allows direct jumps to any URL. It helps navigate the Web by way of various tools, such as keeping a list of visited Web sites and creating bookmarks for Web pages to which the user may want to return.

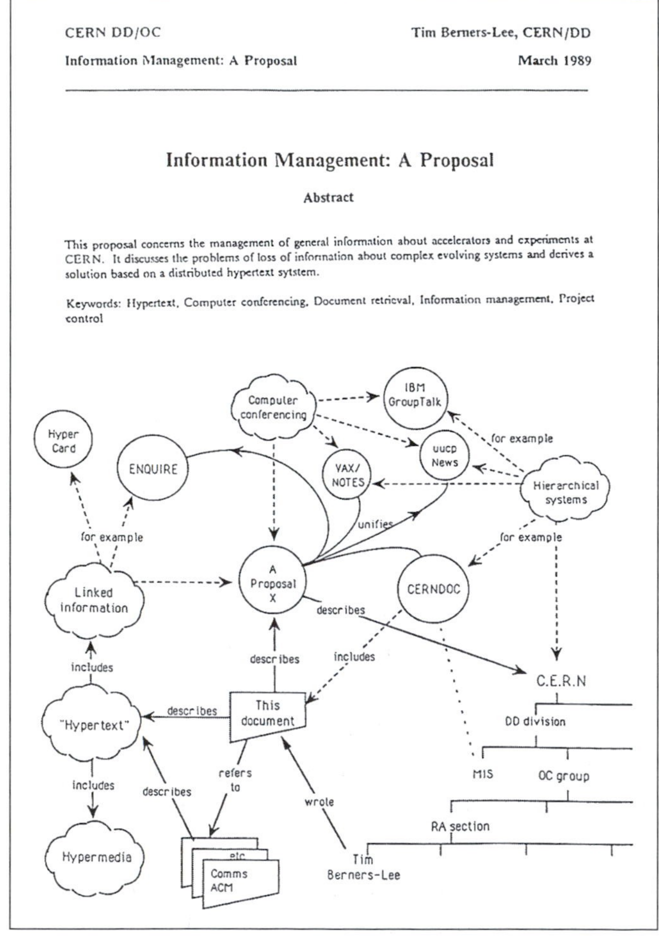

CERN DD/OC — Tim Berners-Lee, CERN/DD

Information Management: A Proposal — March 1989

Information Management: A Proposal

Abstract

This proposal concerns the management of general information about accelerators and experiments at CERN. It discusses the problems of loss of information about complex evolving systems and derives a solution based on a distributed hypertext sytstem.

Keywords: Hypertext, Computer conferencing, Document retrieval, Information management, Project control

Berners-Lee proposal for the World Wide Web. (Courtesy of the Computer Museum History Center)

Using the Web as a reader (i.e., viewing Web pages by using a browser), is called running a *client*. A client is a program that asks for information, receives it, and displays it on the screen of the user's computer. The information provider on the other side has to run a program called a *server*. In theory, every Web user could run a Web server, but in practice it tends to be organizations, companies, individual experts, and Internet service providers who run Web servers. Employees, group members, and subscription holders often merely add Web pages to these Web servers.

Since anyone can publish on the Web and anyone can read the published Web pages (access provided), there seems no limit to the uses to which the Web can be put. However, the unlimited freedom of the Web comes with some downsides and unresolved problems. These are issues of usability, data security, and privacy as well as social, ethical and legal issues. On the user's side, the endless network structure of the Web can become confusing for the user and can cause problems of disorientation. Also, the quality and trustworthiness of the information are not always apparent. Besides, servers can place files, called **cookies**, on the client's machine, which are open to misuse by other electronic visitors. Although these cookies can contain sensitive and private data, the user has practically no control over the content.

Furthermore, organized crime and other villains have discovered the Web. Whereas parents are more worried about documents with violent and pornographic content, the police are concerned with criminal activities on the Net, including the interception and selling of credit card details and the dissemination and organization of extremist activities. Another major problem of the Web is related to copyright laws, which vary across countries. Thus, the Web has numerous and multiple problems.

However, the Web also has quite a number of positive effects on how we live, learn, and work. Of course, the foremost use of the Web is communication via documents. No matter where the information is located physically, the Web enables people to read it whenever and wherever they need it. This particularly benefits users who operate on a more global scale. Companies, organizations, and individuals present themselves to a worldwide audience on the Web. Learning materials on the Web enable pupils and students to learn independently from time and place. For instance distance learning, having been around for ages, started developing explosively with the emergence of the Web. The Web also provides a medium for cooperation across locations. Working groups can be distributed all over the world and still can almost instantly share and exchange information via the Web. Most prominently, the Web provides them with the means for reading and commenting on each other's work and for writing texts with multiple concurrent authors.

Electronic commerce has played an important role in the extreme growth of the Web. Nowadays, virtual bookstores, supermarkets, pharmacies, and so on, take orders via the Web and ship the ordered goods to the user. Newspapers and brokers sell their services on the Web. Hotel rooms, flights, and concert tickets can be booked online, games can be played online. There is virtually no service or product that cannot be sold on the Web. However, there is one security issue particularly related to e-commerce. Currently, payment on the Web includes using a credit card. Although the transmission of credit card details is fairly safe, the placement of cookies can jeopardize these safety measures. Alternative forms of payment including electronic cash and micropayments, are being developed but have not yet left the status of pilot projects.

Today, e-commerce generates huge revenues for companies and individuals. When in the early 1990s Berners-Lee and his CERN colleagues developed the Web, they had not foreseen this development, but they also did not exclude it. However, neither Berners-Lee nor any of his colleagues nor CERN registered any patents or claimed any financial benefits from their development. Beyond that, they devoted much of their free time to the development and promoted the Web as a common information space for everybody. Thereby they made the Web what it is today: an open and universal network of information through which we communicate and interact by sharing information.

Further Reading

Berners-Lee, Tim, with Mark Fischetti. *Weaving the Web: The Original and Ultimate Destiny of the World Wide Web by Its Inventor.* San Francisco: HarperCollins, 1999.

Evan, Tim. *10 Minute Guide to Html 3.2.* Indianapolis, Ind.: Ave, 1996.

Gunn, Angela. "Why the Web Sucks." *Seattle Weekly,* 5–11 Aug. 1999.

Karpinski, Richard. *Beyond HTML.* Berkeley, Calif.: Osborne McGraw-Hill, 1996.

Laudon, C. Kenneth, and Jane Price Laudon. *Business Information Systems: A Problem-Solving Approach.* Fort Worth, Texas: Dryden Press, 1998, Chaps. 7–9.

Nielsen, Jakob. *Designing Web Usability: The Practice of Simplicity.* Indianapolis, Ind.: New Riders, 1999.

—*Elke Dunker*

World Wide Web Consortium

The World Wide Web Consortium (W3C) is an international association of industrial and service companies, research laboratories, educational institutions, and organizations of all sizes that share a compelling interest in the long-term evolution and stability of the **World Wide Web**.

W3C is a nonprofit organization funded partly by commercial members; its activities, however, remain vendor neutral. W3C also receives the support of governments that consider the Web the platform of choice for a global information infrastructure. W3C was originally established at the Laboratory for Computer Science of the Massachusetts Institute of Technology (MIT/LCS) in collaboration with the Centre Européene pour la Recherche Nucléaire (CERN), birthplace of the Web, with support from the U.S. Defense Advanced Research Projects Agency (DARPA) and the European Commission (EC).

The W3C is currently located at three host institutions on three continents: in North America, at the MIT/LCS; in Europe, at France's Institut National de Recherche en Informatique et en Automatique (INRIA); and in Asia, at Japan's Keio University (KEIO).

W3C is not a legal entity. W3C contracts and details of membership are established between each member company and the host institutions. Host institutions pledge that no member will receive preferential treatment within W3C and that individual contracts will remain confidential.

The W3C was founded in 1994, a year of intense activity for development of the Web. In March, **Marc Andreessen** (1972–) and colleagues left the National Center for Supercomputing Applications (NCSA) to form Mosaic Communications Corp., later called **Netscape**. In June, European commissar Martin Bangemann (1934–) issued his report to the European Commission on the Information Society, and CERN's first Web server registered a load 1000 times greater than that of three years earlier. In July a MIT/CERN agreement to start a W3 organization was announced in Boston by Bangemann. In September, **Tim Berners-Lee** (1955–) joined the MIT/LCS, and in October, W3C was formally founded. Later, in December, CERN decided not to continue Web development, and in an agreement with the European Commission and INRIA, transferred its role to the latter. INRIA became the consortium's second host institution in April 1995. In August 1996, Keio University joined MIT and INRIA in becoming the third site to host W3C.

The W3C team consists of a chairman, a director, and staff. The current W3C chairman is Jean-François Abramatic, who is responsible for managing the general operation of the consortium and chairing the advisory committee and board. The director of W3C is Tim Berners-Lee, the leading architect for the technologies developed at the consortium. He approves recommendations and activity proposals and designates group chairs.

The advisory committee (AC) consists of one representative from each member organization. It reviews proposals and annual plans, assesses W3C's progress, and suggests future direction. The advisory board (AB) is elected by the AC to provide guidance on strategy, management, legal matters, process issues, and conflict resolution. It ensures that W3C remains responsive to the needs of its members and to those of entities outside W3C (notably other standards bodies).

When W3C decides to become involved in an area of Web technology or policy, it initiates an activity in that area. An activity means that W3C resources (people, time, money, etc.) are dedicated to work in that area. Generally, an activity is carried out by one or more groups. W3C activities are reviewed at each AC meeting, which are held biannually. Each activity's progress is described by an activity statement, which is updated before the AC meetings. This list is also revised before the AC meeting.

All W3C technical reports and software are made available free of charge to the general public. This policy is part of the membership agreement and stems from the W3C's core goal of keeping the Web as one. Moreover, to ensure that its results are acceptable to the general public and to promote trial implementations, W3C may call for public comments about working drafts and software releases.

Any organization or company can become a member by signing a membership agreement with the W3C and paying the annual fees. The W3C has approximately 400 members.

FURTHER READING

Robischon, Noah. "The End of the Monolithic Browser." *Time*, 3 Jan. 1995.

Lohr, Steve. "His Goal: Keeping the Web Worldwide." *New York Times*, 18 Dec. 1995.

—*Manuel Sanromà*

Worm

A worm is a computer program that propagates autonomously from one computer to other computers in a network, infecting and using them as a new starting point for further propagation. A worm is different from a **virus** in that it does not attach itself to a program or to a boot diskette. A worm can exist only as long as the infected computer continues running.

Like so many elements of personal computing, the worm was conceived at the **Xerox Palo Alto Research Center** (PARC). In 1978, John Shoch and David Boggs developed a short program to search PARC's network of 200 Alto computers for idle processors. However, the worm spiraled out of control and had the unintended effect of invading networked computers, creating a security threat. Shoch borrowed the term *worm* from the science fiction book *The Shockwave Rider*, by John Brunner (1934–95), in which an omnipotent "tapeworm" program runs amuck through a network of computers.

The most famous example of such an intruder is the Internet Worm, which is said to have infected 5 percent of the **Internet** hosts in 1988. The program was written by Robert Morris, Jr., a graduate student at Cornell University. It was sent via **electronic mail** using conventional **Unix** utilities. Started on 2 November, the worm began traveling the net faster than it could be deleted from host machines, so that many computers had to be taken off the network. This was actually a programming error because the worm created too many replicas of itself in the same machine, eventually overwhelming the **operating system**. This helped to detect the worm early, but the damage was nonetheless significant. By 4 November the code had been decompiled by specialists and it was clear that the program did not modify any system files.

The Internet worm exploited several security holes in some versions of the Unix operating system. The most significant was a **back door** left by the creators of the mailing protocol. To service the mailer, the code included a **debugging** option that allowed a remote user to execute commands in the machine receiving an electronic mail message. Robert Morris knew of this back door and let his worm execute in a remote computer. The worm started by finding the names of other hosts connected to the Internet. This is easy to do in many Unix systems since the relevant information is stored in public files with a standard name. The worm also checked users' passwords against a list of common passwords (first names, sports teams, etc.). Once a user account had been cracked, the worm sent a small *bootstrap program* to be executed by the compromised account and close the connection. The bootstrap program (also called a *vector*) then called back the original sender, retrieved all worm source code, compiled it, and executed it in the new host. A new infection cycle could then be started with the list of hosts found in this machine.

The size of the threat posed by worms in the networked age was driven home in the spring of 2000 when the "Love Bug" traveled around the world, crippling networks large and small, in a matter of hours. The Love Bug vaulted itself across the Net in the form of e-mail with the subject line "ILOVEYOU." When the attachment to the e-mail was opened, the worm invaded users' address books and sent itself to everyone in the contact lists. Thus the worm exploited not one but two security flaws—one in Microsoft's Outlook e-mail manager, and another in the minds of thousands of unsuspecting users who opened the e-mail attachment thinking that they had received a love letter from an admirer.

Other types of network intruders include viruses, **Trojan horses**, and logic bombs. *Logic bombs* are programs that run in the background waiting for a specific date or set of conditions in order to wreak havoc in the host machine. Most logic bombs are the work of disgruntled insiders.

FURTHER READING

Cohen, Frederick B. *A Short Course on Computer Viruses.* New York: Wiley, 1994.

Denning, Peter, ed. *Computers Under Attack: Intruders, Worms, and Viruses.* Reading, Mass.: Addison-Wesley, 1990.

Hiltzik, Michael A. *Dealers of Lightning: Xerox PARC and the Dawn of the Computer Age.* New York: Harper Business, 1999.

Smith, George. *The Virus Creation Labs: A Journey into the Underground.* Show Low, Ariz.: American Eagle, 1994.

—*Raúl Rojas*

Wozniak, Steve

1950–

U.S. Computer Engineer and Teacher

Steve "Woz" Wozniak is best known as the designer of the **Apple II**, the world's first easy-to-use **microcomputer**. After founding **Apple Computer** with **Steve Jobs** (1955–) in 1976, Wozniak continued to work for the company until 1985. He has also been involved in a number of other educational and charity projects and currently devotes much of his time to working as an elementary school teacher.

Wozniak always seemed destined to become a great scientist or engineer. At Homestead High School in

Los Altos, California, he excelled in math and science, became the president of the electronics club, and was building computer electronic projects by the fifth grade. After dropping out of his electronics and **computer science** studies at the University of California at Berkeley in 1971, Wozniak went to work as a hardware engineer for one of **Silicon Valley**'s oldest and most prestigious companies, **Hewlett-Packard**.

Wozniak was also a keen electronics hobbyist in his spare time. By the mid-1970s, he was regularly attending meetings of the **Homebrew Computer Club** in Palo Alto, California. The launch, in 1975, of a primitive computer kit called the **Altair 8800** by MITS Inc., proved a turning point, both for Wozniak and the computing world. Although Wozniak had been tinkering with computer projects for years, it was the Altair that finally persuaded him to make a microcomputer of his own.

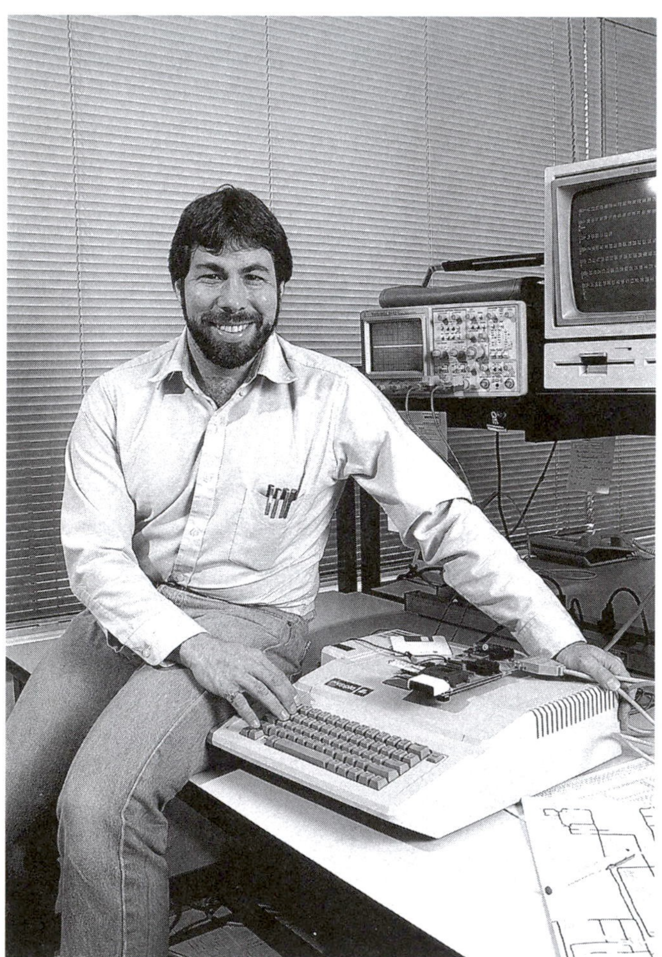

Steve Wozniak with the Apple II computer in Cupertino, California, May 1986. (©Roger Ressmeyer/CORBIS)

Instead of using the **Intel** 8800 **microprocessor** favored by the Altair, he adopted the much cheaper **Motorola** 6502, which subsequently became very popular in other microcomputers at that time. This decision began a long relationship between Apple and Motorola but also, almost arbitrarily, set Apple computers apart from the industry-standard Intel PCs that would dominate the personal computing world in the years to come. It was not just the choice of processor that distinguished the **Apple I** from the Altair. Where the Altair had to be programmed by flicking tiny switches on its case, the Apple I had a typewriter-style **keyboard**; where the Altair produced its output on a row of flashing light-emitting diodes, the Apple I could be connected up to a standard television set.

When Wozniak showed off his machine at the Homebrew club, his friend Steve Jobs immediately recognized a business opportunity. To raise capital, Jobs sold his Volkswagen bus and Wozniak sold his programmable calculator, and together they formed Apple Computer in June 1976, assembling computers in a garage belonging to Steve Jobs's parents. As Wozniak wrote later, moneymaking played no part in this adventure: "Our first computers were born not out of greed or ego but in the revolutionary spirit of helping common people rise above the most powerful institutions."

Wozniak was soon starting work on what would be an even more successful machine, the Apple II, the world's first real home computer and the machine that would take Apple from the Jobs's garage onto the Fortune 500 list of the world's top companies. From the **BASIC** language interpreter (the **software** that turns English-like programming commands into instructions that a microprocessor can understand) and the color video display to the **floppy disk** drive that eventually made the machine such a success with small businesses, the innards of the Apple II were almost entirely the design of Steve Wozniak. The Apple II inspired other companies to produce microcomputers of their own, notably the Radio Shack TRS-80, the Commodore PET, and eventually, the IBM **personal computer** (PC), which began an industry standard. But it was Wozniak's Apple II that really gave birth to the personal computer revolution.

After a serious plane crash in 1981, Wozniak took an extended leave from Apple to get married, return to college at Berkeley, and pursue a number of personal projects, including two financially unsuccessful music festivals. After resigning from Apple in 1985, he founded CL-9 (Cloud Nine Inc.), an electronics company manufacturing remote control devices for domestic appliances, but it ceased trading in 1987. More recently, Wozniak has been closely involved in educational and charity activities, notably helping to set up educational links between the United States and the former Soviet Union. In 1991, he realized a long-held ambition to teach electronics and computing to students between the fifth and eighth grades. Today, he devotes much of his time to inspiring young people to feel the same enthusiasm for electronics and computing that drove him to create two of the world's first and most influential microcomputers.

BIOGRAPHY

Stephen Gary Wozniak. Born 11 August 1950 in San Jose, California. Dropped out of University of California–Berkeley, 1971. Worked as hardware engineer at Hewlett Packard, 1973–76. Apple Computer cofounder and vice president, 1976–85. Designed Apple I, 1976, and Apple II, 1977. B.S. in electrical engineering and computer science, University of California–Berkeley, 1982. U.S. music festivals, 1982–83. Resigned from Apple, 1985. Received National Technology Medal, 1985, and numerous honors and awards from community groups. Founder and president of CL-9, 1985–87. From 1990 onward, worked on numerous educational and charity projects, including collaborations between the United States and the former Soviet Union.

FURTHER READING

Carlton, Jim. *Apple: The Inside Story of Intrigue, Egomania, and Business Blunders*. New York: Harper Business, 1998.

Levy, Steven. *Hackers: Heroes of the Computer Revolution*. Garden City, N.Y.: Anchor Press/Doubleday, 1984.

Pitta, Julia. "A Teacher from the Apple." *Forbes*, 3 June 1996, p. 138.

—*Chris Woodford*

Xanadu

Xanadu is a grand design for a universal system of digital data access and storage. It was conceived in 1960 by Theodor H. Nelson (1940–), while he was a student; he described Xanadu as "an ideal and general model for all computer use, based on sideways connections among documents and files."

In 1965, Nelson presented his first paper about Xanadu and coined the terms ***hypertext*** and *hypermedia*, so common today. In the book *Dream Machines* (1974) Nelson described his system in more detail. Hyperlinks are central to his vision of how to structure literary information. He writes about hypergrams (branching diagrams), hypermaps (with transparent overlays), and branching movies. Nelson's dream of intertwined information owes much to the *memex* of **Vannevar Bush** (1890–1974), which was described in his paper "**As We May Think**," and which Nelson reprinted in his own book.

Nelson's Xanadu has never been well understood, since Nelson himself is rather ambiguous and his writing style sometimes resembles the great extrapolations of **Marshall McLuhan** (1911–80). Nelson admitted: "The project is well known, but not well understood. Its greatest aspiration, a universal instantaneous hypertext publishing network, has not been generally understood at the technical level and has created various false impressions. One publication, for example, referred to it as 'a database-to-be the size of the world'—a very muddled description." Although Nelson has remained optimistic about the eventual success of Xanadu, the final release date was moved from 1976 to 1988, then to 1991, and it has still not been completed. Several companies have tried to develop Xanadu into a product: Xanadu Operating Company (1981), Autodesk (1988), Xanadu Australia (1993), and Xanadu America (1994). Some cynics have dismissed Xanadu; in a ***Wired*** magazine profile, Xanadu was termed "the longest running vaporware project in the history of computing." However, Xanadu genuinely seems to have anticipated some current developments, like the **World Wide Web**, groupware, and virtual organizations.

Since Xanadu has not been delivered, some of Nelson's ideas have been published in the form of proposals to enhance Internet hyperlinks. This is the case with *transclusion*, a new tag for the Web that would make it possible to insert a reference to a portion of another text in a Web page. Only a link to the referenced portion has to be inserted (stating, for example, that the second page of a book should be included). *Transpublishing* means that the moment someone opens a home page, he or she obtains, for example, quotes from another proprietary page. The text of the other page has not really been included in the page the person opened but only their *transclusion*, that is, the reference to them. Since the work quoted was not copied to the page that was opened but only to the person's screen, no copyright is infringed. This could make it possible, for example, to send the contents of an online newspaper through a filter that would quote only text and omit the advertisement banners.

Nelson chose the name Xanadu for the palace Shan-Du mentioned by Marco Polo (c. 1254–c. 1324) in his autobiography and for the Xanadu mentioned by Samuel Taylor Coleridge (1772–1834) in his poem *Kubla Khan*. Like the original Xanadu, Nelson's vision appears to be more mythical than actual.

FURTHER READING

Nelson, Theodor H. *Computer Lib: Dream Machines*. Redmond, Wash.: Microsoft Press, 1987.

———. *Literary Machines 93.1.* Sausalito, Calif.: Mindful Press, 1992.

Project Xanadu. "Project Xanadu Homepage." 25 Jan. 2000. *http://www.xanadu.net/*

Sanders, Craig. "Xanadu." *Desktop Magazine,* Aug. 1994. *http://www.xanadu.com.au/xanadu/desktop.html*

Wolf, Gary. "The Curse of Xanadu." *Wired,* 3.06, June 1995. *http://www.wired.com/wired/archive/3.06/xanadu_pr.html*

—Raúl Rojas

Xerox

Xerox is a Stamford, Connecticut–based maker of copiers and other office equipment, whose revenues totaled more than U.S.$19 billion in 1999. Its most famous contribution to the history of computing was surely the **Xerox Palo Alto Research Center** (PARC), where many of the foundational elements of **personal computers** and networking were developed.

Xerography, a dry process for making clean duplicates of images and text, was invented by Chester Carlson (1906–68) in 1938. In 1946, the Halloid company of Rochester, New York brought the first electrophotographic copier to the market. In 1960, with the new name Xerox Corporation, it released the 914 copier, which revolutionized both copying and the way offices and people handle paperwork. Gone were carbon paper and carbon copies, in favor of fast, endlessly perfect "Xerox" copies. An industry was born and Xerox led it.

This has proved to be both a blessing and a curse. Although Xerox has poured hundreds of millions of dollars into noncopier research and is responsible for countless innovations unrelated to copier technology, it may be Xerox's fate to be remembered mainly as "the Copier Company."

The company has tried since the early 1970s to be more than that, focusing its efforts on its world-class research facility, Xerox PARC (the company now has other research centers around the world). Scientists at PARC invented the first text processing system to incorporate a **local area network**, a **mouse**, and a windows **interface** (the Xerox Star). It was not a mainstream product under Xerox's aegis, but in the early 1980s it was popular in large corporations, the federal government (including the White House), and research facilities. This intelligent combination of features formed the basis for the **Macintosh** and Microsoft's **Windows** (as well as much litigation). PARC is also given credit for the **Ethernet**, invented by PARC scientist **Robert Metcalfe** (1946–), perhaps the most important local area network technology today, as well as important contributions in printing, type fonts and electronic layout, document management, and collaboration.

In the 1990s, Xerox created a new business with its successful invention of the DocuTech line of integrated printing systems, capable of high-volume high-resolution printing, but also of combining digital files and scanned text and images and integrating finished output with cover stock into brochures, booklets, and even hardback books. Entire new businesses, based on on-demand printing for student reading, low-volume scientific books, and the creation of documents in one geography with distribution prior to printing, were the result.

Xerox has never been concerned that paper will disappear as the digital age advances, but rather that digital data (and their storage and distribution) will become more important. They have sought to be involved in that market as well, with a strong attempt to reposition the company from the Copier Company to the Document Company. This has included entry into new digital-focused markets such as collaboration and document management software (DocuShare) and intellectual property protection (ContentGuard, a joint venture with **Microsoft**).

FURTHER READING

Hiltzik, Michael A. *Dealers of Lightning: Xerox PARC and the Dawn of the Computer Age.* New York: Harper Business, 1999.

Smith, Douglas K., and Robert C. Alexander. *Fumbling the Future: How Xerox Invented, Then Ignored, the First Personal Computer.* New York: Morrow, 1988.

—Amy Wohl

Xerox Palo Alto Research Center

Xerox is a name that most people do not associate with **personal computers**, but scientists employed by Xerox's Palo Alto Research Center (PARC) invented the concept of personal computers—along with bit-mapped displays, laser printing, the **graphical user interface**, and much more. Although Xerox developed these technologies, it did not market most of them as consumer products.

Xerox's original decision to set up the now legendary PARC was based on a variety of factors. Xerox had evolved from obscurity in 1959 to a monopoly leadership position in the copier industry in 1968. That year, Xerox revenues surpassed the billion dollar mark and the company became, along with **IBM**, one of America's leading office products companies. Simultaneously, Peter McColough (1922–) became chief executive officer and tried to diversify the company into other noncopier markets. McColough coined the phrase *architecture of information* to describe his vision of Xerox's future.

PARC was started by Jack Goldman, Xerox's chief scientist. Its original organizational structure was broken down into three areas of research: the General Science Laboratory (GSL), the Systems Science Laboratory (SSL), and the Computing Science Laboratory (CSL). Xerox was able to recruit top computer researchers due to an exodus from defense-sponsored research in the early 1970s, caused largely by political pressures from the Vietnam War. Xerox hired a former Defense Department project manager, Bob Taylor (1931–), and he then recruited the following researchers: Peter Deutsch, Chuck Geschke, Bill English, Butler Lampson, Ed McCreight, **Robert Metcalfe** (1946–), Jim Mitchell, Jim Morris, Charles Simonyi, Bob Sproull, Larry Tesler, and Chuck Thacker. These were people who built the first interactive computer systems, the first intellectual augmentation systems, and the first packet-switching networks.

In Taylor's vision for PARC, CSL would work on developing and building basic computer **hardware** and operating system software. The operating system is the **software** that organizes the information in the computer and mediates between the bare machine and the user's application programs. The applications would be identified and developed by SSL to run on the CSL-designed computer systems. Taylor's emphasis on "one person, one computer" made for important philosophical and technical differences with the collaborative computing approach pioneered by **Douglas Engelbart** (1925–).

Outside the Xerox Palo Alto Research Center. (Courtesy of Xerox)

To head the SSL team, Taylor recruited **Alan Kay** (1940–). Kay wanted to develop a machine called the Dynabook, a small computer with a high-resolution display screen that utilized a graphical computer language. While Kay's team developed the Smalltalk programming language, the CCSL team worked on the hardware for the new **Alto computer**. The researchers made use of **multitasking**, a technique that enables a computer to execute a number of processes at the same time. They also developed the bit-mapped screen, the digital mouse, the laser **printer**, and the client–server model for networking computers.

In 1976, after the Alto had been built, designed, and tested, Xerox decided not to market the computer; some observers have speculated that Xerox executives did not understand what they had, while others suggest that the Alto was simply too far ahead of its time. In the years that followed, a number of PARC researchers left and started their own companies or went to work for preexisting companies. **Apple Computer**, for example, is one company that benefited tremendously from innovations that began at Xerox PARC. Technologies started at PARC but later marketed by other companies include bit-mapped display screens, **mouse**- and icon- based computing, laser printer, drawing tablets, **Ethernet** office networking, computer animation, "What you see is what you get" (WYSIWYG) **word processing**, the **Smalltalk** language, and the Postscript language.

In 1981, Xerox introduced the user-friendly Star computer system that utilized many of the Alto technologies. However, it failed in the marketplace because it was not compatible with other computer systems and it did not offer a full range of application software. Additionally, IBM released its own personal computer, which quickly dominated the business arena.

Despite these product failures, PARC continued to invent the "office of the future." During the mid-1980s, PARC researchers developed a project called Media Space to explore collaborative work split between Palo Alto, California and Portland, Oregon. Media spaces enable the two-way transmission of auditory and visual information via a projection screen. Screens located in central places at each research site create media spaces in which people can interact with each other as an extension of physical space.

Another concept developed at PARC is ubiquitous computing. Ubiquitous computing is integrating computers into physical spaces. People wear active badges that make every computer they sit down at appear to be their own system. The badge sends information via infrared signals to the computer to identify the user. The user's personal interface and data files appear on the computer screen.

Since its inception, PARC has been doing pioneering research on **human–computer interaction** and

Children play with an Alto computer, created at Xerox PARC. (Courtesy of Xerox)

the social impact of computing. In the 1990s, Xerox developed a number of research centers around the globe and it began reinventing itself. PARC, under the direction of John Seely Brown, began devoting its research efforts to the digital document and the standards, protocols, and services defining the future of the Internet.

FURTHER READING

Gaver, W. W. "The Affordance of Media Spaces for Collaboration." *ACM 1992 Conference on Computer-Supported-Cooperative Work, Sharing Perspectives*, 31 Oct.–4 Nov. 1992, Toronto, Ontario, Canada. New York: Association for Computing Machinery.

Hiltzik, Michael A. *Dealers of Lightning: Xerox PARC and the Dawn of the Computer Age*. New York: Harper Business, 1999.

Jacobson, Gary, and John Hillkirk. *Xerox American Samurai*. New York: Macmillan, 1986.

Segaller, Stephen. *Nerds 2.0.1.: A Brief History of the Internet*. New York: TV Books, 1998.

Smith, Douglas K., and Robert C. Alexander. *Fumbling the Future: How Xerox Invented, Then Ignored, the First Personal Computer*. New York: Morrow, 1988.

—*Susan B. Barnes*

XML

A markup language defines a syntax to add formatting or semantic information to a plain text. The Extensible Markup Language (XML) is a Web standard to define grammars of markup languages. XML resulted from efforts to extend the Hypertext Markup Language (**HTML**) and was standardized in 1998 as a recommendation of the **World Wide Web Consortium**.

With XML, one develops a grammar called *document type definition* (DTD), which defines the elements of a markup language and rules on how they can be combined. It can then be used to validate the syntactical correctness of a document, for automatic processing and interchange among applications, to use with syntax-driven tools such as XML editors, and for displaying documents in browsers. Languages defined with XML distinguish the markup elements from ordinary text by placing them in angle brackets, such as in 'obey the speed limit of <speed>60</speed>!'. The text '60' is enclosed by the start and end tags of the 'speed' element.

A DTD contains definitions of elements and possible attributes that can be used with an element. '<!ELEMENT speed ANY>' defines the above '<speed>' element and states that it can enclose any kind of text. After a definition '<!ATTLIST speed unit (mph|kmh) #IMPLIED>' one can use an attribute 'unit' with possible values of 'mph' or 'kmh' as in '<speed unit="kmh">60</speed>'. Element specifications can include a rule about which kind of information it may enclose. With a definition '<!ELEMENT person name, phone*, fax?>', the '<person>...</person>' element must enclose a '<name>' element, any number of '<phone>' elements, and zero or one '<fax>' elements.

XML allows it to define and standardize application-domain-specific markup languages. This is enabling for the seamless interchange of information augmented with semantic information represented as markup. A variety of markup languages have developed—for the exchange of business data (XML-EDI), for example, or for wireless information systems (WAP/WML). It is important to note that only the syntax of a markup language is specified with XML; the definition of the semantics of elements is left to other mechanisms and free text descriptions.

FURTHER READING

Bray, Tim, Jean Paoli, and C. M. Sperberg-McQueen, eds. *Extensible Markup Language (XML) 1.0*. W3C Recommendation, 1998.

Connolly, Dan, ed. "XML: Principles, Tools, and Techniques." *World Wide Web Journal*, Vol. 2, No. 4, 1997.

—*Robert Tolksdorf*

X-Windows

The X-Windows system is a **graphical user interface** (GUI) developed at the Massachusetts Institute of Technology (MIT) in the mid-1980s. The X system was designed to be platform independent and network based, in the spirit of MIT's Project Athena. With X, the programmer can write an application in a

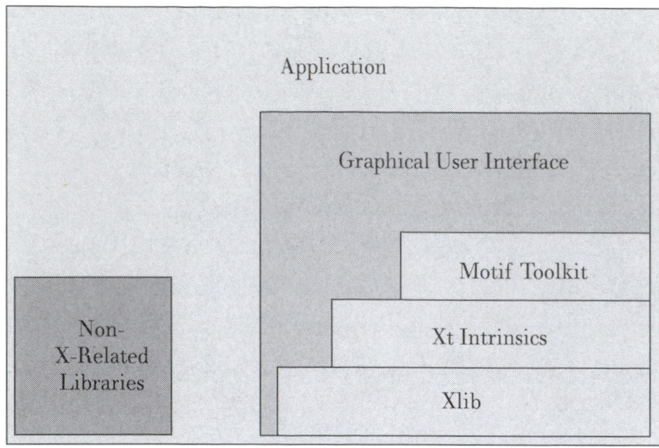

Programming model, illustrating the relationships between the application program and the various parts of the X system.

single language and run this program on different machines with little or no modification. Moreover, applications can actually run programs on one computer and have the results displayed on another (or several) computer's terminal. The computer can be a similar model or an entirely different one altogether. The possibilities are endless.

The X-Window system is primarily the graphical interface development system for the **Unix** operating system (including **Linux**). Proprietary windows systems for **personal computers** (PCs) (such as Microsoft **Windows**) and the **Macintosh** still dominate, but X-Window display–client **software** is available for such platforms.

The window environment is built on top of a computer's **operating system**. It controls how windows are displayed and how events—invoked by mouse selection keystrokes, and so on—are processed. The general term for the housekeeping of windows is *window management*. Two key components are usually provided by a windowing environment: the window manager and toolkit libraries. The window manager basically defines the *look and feel* of a particular toolkit: how the interface appears on the screen and how the user interacts with the interface via the computer. However, with ever-increasing windowing needs, the basic window manager and related system and common application needs have grown into a common desktop environment (CDE) providing a whole suite of tools.

X is network oriented, and applications need not be running on the same system as the one supporting the display. The program that controls each display is known as the *server*: a local program that controls our *display*. The display may be available to other systems across the network. The server acts basically as a go-between between user programs, called *clients* or applications, and the resources of the local system.

The client and server are connected by a communication path called the *connector*. This is performed by a low-level (**C** language) interface known as *Xlib*, the lowest level of the X-system software hierarchy or architecture. Many applications can be written using Xlib alone. However, the main task of Xlib is to enable clients and servers to interact via special forms of messages (defined by the X Protocol).

An application program in X will usually consist of two parts: the graphical user interface, written in one or more of Xlib, Xt, or Motif, and the **algorithmic** or functional part of the application, where the input from the interface and other processing tasks are defined. The figure illustrates the relationships between the application program and the various parts of the X system.

In general, it will be difficult and time consuming to write complex GUI programs only in Xlib. Many higher-level subroutine libraries, called *toolkits*, have been developed to remedy this problem. There are usually two levels of toolkits above Xlib:

1. *X Toolkit (Xt) Intrinsics.* These are parts of the toolkit that allow programmers to build new interface components (referred to as *widgets*). Toolkits implement a set of user interface features or application environments, such as menus, buttons, or scroll bars. If such widgets are used properly, they will simplify the X programming process and help preserve the *look and feel* of the application, which should make it easier to use.
2. *Third-Party Toolkits* (such as Motif). X allows extensions to the Xt Intrinsics toolkit. Many software houses have developed custom features that make the GUI's appearance attractive, easy to use, and easy to develop. Motif, one such toolkit, is a widely accepted set of user interface guidelines developed

by the Open Software Foundation (OSF) around 1989 that specifies how an X-Window system application should look and feel.

In early 1996, OSF merged with X/Open to form the Open Group. The Open Group continues development and support on the X-Window system, Motif, CDE, and other technologies.

FURTHER READING

Johnson, Eric F., and Kevin Reichard. *Power Programming Motif.* New York: MIS Press, 1993.

Open Software Foundation. OSF/Motif Series (*Programmer's Guide, Programmer's Reference, Motif Style Guide, Motif User's Guide, Motif Widget Writer's Guide, AES/User Environment Volume*). Upper Saddle River, N.J.: Prentice Hall, 1995.

X Window System User's Guide, Vols. 0–8. Cambridge, Mass.: O'Reilly, 1988.

—*David Marshall*

Yahoo!

Yahoo! Inc. is a U.S.-based corporation built up around a site on the **World Wide Web** that acts as a guide to thousands of other sites. Originally "Jerry and David's Guide to the World Wide Web," Yahoo! has always been one of the Web's most visited sites. Since its creation in early 1994, it has evolved into one of the best-known **Internet** brands and is expected to become one of the world's most influential media corporations in the future.

There are two main ways of finding relevant information using the Web. Internet **search engines** such as AltaVista and Hotbot suggest Web sites based on a set of keywords that users type in. Yahoo! is the best-known example of the other approach, the Web directory. Reputedly short for "Yet Another Hierarchical Officious Oracle," Yahoo! arranges tens of thousands of Web sites in a comprehensive (but intuitively easy to understand) hierarchy or tree structure based on 14 top-level categories such as Business and Economy, News and Media, and Entertainment. Users work their way down the tree structure until they find sites that offer the information they want. Where search engines are based on scanning Web pages and using statistical methods to guess what users might be looking for, Yahoo! is a human-crafted method of structuring knowledge, more like the methods used in libraries. Thus, whereas a keyword search for "Apple" using a search engine would mix up hits for **Apple Computer**, the rock musician Fiona Apple, and the fruit from trees, Yahoo! makes a clear distinction between "Computers and Internet," "Entertainment," and "Society and Culture," offering different links to "Apple" in each category.

Yahoo! began life in April 1994 as a part-time project for Stanford University Ph.D. students Jerry Yang (1969–) and David Filo (1966–). Yang's family had emigrated to California from Taiwan when he was 10, and he later graduated from Stanford in electrical engineering. Louisiana-born Filo had graduated from Tulane University, New Orleans, in 1988 and attended Stanford for his Master's degree. Both were enthusiastic users of the Internet even before Mosaic (the user-friendly Web **browser** developed by **Marc Andreessen** [1972–]) prompted the explosive growth of the Web in 1993. Filo and Yang regularly swapped lists of their favorite Web sites; in spring 1994 they decided to combine their lists. The subsequent reorganization of the lists into categories, and a reorganization of the categories into a hierarchy, led to a forerunner of Yahoo! known as "Jerry's Guide to the World Wide Web." The site—originally hosted on Yang's Stanford server, *akebono.stanford.edu*, named for a favorite Hawaiian Sumo wrestler—was soon attracting hundreds of hits (and suggestions for other links) from other Web users, and was renamed Yahoo! What had begun as an after-hours project was clearly serving an important need: helping people to make sense of the ever-expanding universe of information that the Web had become.

Making sense of the Web rapidly became a full-time job for the two Ph.D. students, and by fall 1994 they found themselves with a difficult choice: Either they could rein-in Yahoo! and concentrate on their degrees, or they could work on Yahoo! full time. Taking a sabbatical from Stanford (now extended indefinitely), they chose the second option and began discussions with commercial partners around November 1994. Discussions were held with London-based news agency Reuters, but Yahoo!—as a business, rather than as a student project—needed to generate revenue to be of more than passing interest. Yang and Filo persuaded Tim Brady, a Harvard Business School student, to write a business plan for Yahoo! over the winter of 1994–95. Meanwhile, the site grew from a simple list of links into a full-scale database attached to a Web server.

By the spring of 1995, the Yahoo! partners were holding discussions with **Silicon Valley** venture capital firms (financial companies willing to back high-risk startups in return for owning a significant percentage of the business). They soon attracted the interest of Sequoia Capital, a company noted for backing winners, including Apple Computer, games maker Atari, and database developer Oracle. Others interested in acquiring Yahoo! included the giant **America Online** (AOL) corporation, then a proprietary information network (a kind of private Internet with paying subscribers). In March 1995, AOL offered Yang and Filo the difficult choice between accepting a takeover or facing tough competition from a rival service that AOL threatened to set up if Yahoo! turned it down. Yang and Filo stuck to their guns, also rejecting an offer from Andreessen to become part of **Netscape Communications**, but accepting Netscape's offer to host Yahoo! on its servers when it outgrew those provided by Stanford University.

By April 1995, Sequoia had agreed to finance Yahoo! With this investment, Yang and Filo set about building Yahoo! both as a service and as a business. They hired Tim Brady as director of marketing and appointed Srinija Srinivasan as "Ontological Yahoo!"—the person responsible for arranging and developing Yahoo!'s unique hierarchical classification. An army of professional Web surfers, some of them experienced librarians, was later hired to check submissions and further build the all-important hierarchy.

Meanwhile, Yang and Brady started to implement the company's business plan. Having ruled out charging users to access Yahoo! and charging site owners for their listings (both of which would have simply driven traffic onto rival sites), they settled on the idea of effectively giving away their product for free and selling advertising instead. By August 1995, a redesigned Yahoo! site was carrying an improved classification system, a news service provided by Reuters, and advertisements, sold initially to a handful of sponsors for U.S.$20,000 per month. Advertisements were controversial, because the Internet community was largely drawn from the academic community at that time, and commercialism was considered by some to undermine the community spirit.

Most significant of these additions, however, was the news service, because it marked the beginning of Yahoo!'s transition from a simple search site into what is now known as a **portal**: a gateway to the Internet that offers news, weather, stock information, **electronic mail** access, and a variety of constantly updated features tailored to its users. Portals lie somewhere between search engines and daily newspapers, and in some circles it is believed that they may replace both in the future. Jerry Yang had always conceived Yahoo! as a media property, such as *Time* magazine or the *Wall Street Journal*, not "just another" website. Logically, this meant developing Yahoo! as a magazine might develop: adding more content to attract more users, who would attract more advertisers, who would pay for more content. The news service was swiftly followed by weather, stock reports, and other up-to-the-minute information. A massive investment by Japanese-owned publishing group Softbank (owner of the Ziff-Davis corporation, which publishes many computer books and magazines) made it logical for Yahoo! to develop further in this direction (e.g., by launching a Ziff-Davis magazine called *Yahoo! Internet Life*).

By 1996, Yahoo!'s success was sufficiently assured for it to go public. Its initial public offering (IPO) on April 12 valued the company at around U.S.$850 million, with Yang and Filo owning around U.S.$130 million each. Since then, Yahoo! has continued to develop along broadly similar lines: recruiting more and more professional surfers to keep its hierarchy up to date; strengthening the Yahoo! portal by adding additional services, such as travel news, online auctions, and an **electronic commerce** shopping mall; and building awareness of the Yahoo! brand. As well as continuing to develop the worldwide site, Yahoo! has launched versions tailored to local regions. There are some 20 country-specific Yahoo!s and a number of others serving distinct communities, such as New York and the San Francisco Bay area.

In May 1999, Yahoo! vastly increased its content by purchasing, for U.S.$4.6 billion, the gigantic *Geocities.com* Web site community, estimated to provide free home pages to around 30 million people. Far from being put out of business by AOL, as Yang and Filo had once feared, the acquisition of Geocities made Yahoo! one of AOL's most serious rivals. All told, Yahoo! now serves an estimated worldwide audience of around 100 million people.

Unlike newer companies which have piggybacked onto the growth of the Internet, and traditional companies such as Wells Fargo and Barnes and Noble, which have reoriented themselves around electronic trading, Yahoo! has been both the principal engineer and the chief beneficiary of its own success. Like Netscape (and its predecessor Mosaic), Yahoo! played a vital role in transforming the World Wide Web from a quirky academic research tool into an indispensable, easy-to-access universe of information. And like Netscape, it helped to break the dominance of closed, proprietary information networks such as AOL, **CompuServe**, and **Prodigy**, which were forced to integrate their services with the open Internet. But unlike Netscape, a brand relatively constrained to the mechanics of delivering the Internet to its users, Yahoo! is a more pliable media brand that links people and their interests to the increasingly divergent content of the Web. All this makes Yahoo! one of a handful of dominant Web sites and positions it to become of the world's leading corporations as the Internet becomes increasingly central to the global economy.

FURTHER READING

Lynch, Clifford. "Searching the Internet." *Scientific American*, Mar. 1997, p. 44.

Reid, Robert. *Architects of the Web: 1000 Days That Built the Future of Business*. New York: Wiley, 1997.

—*Chris Woodford*

Y2K Problem

The term Y2K is a nickname for the "Year 2000," with the K referring to *kilo* or *thousand*, hence (Y)ear 2(1000). The Y2K problem (or **bug**) was one of data ambiguity. It is common practice to refer to a year by only two digits (e.g., "68" refers to 1968) but when the century rollover approached, all kinds of system malfunctions were predicted, since "00" would be interpreted by computers as 1900. The greatest reprogramming effort in history was undertaken.

The seeds of this problem were planted in the 1960s. As computers became more accessible, it became feasible for governments and companies to utilize them in labor-intensive activities such as accounting, manufacturing, and inventory processes. Although computing costs were declining, computers were still incredibly expensive in terms of both internal processing memory and external data storage. All programs had to balance the format of data representation against the cost of storing and processing that representation.

Simply put, each **bit** of data cost money to both process and store. Any reduction in the number of bits used to store a particular piece of information reduced the cost of data storage and data entry, and possibly (depending on the computing cost of interpreting the data representation) also reduced the processing cost.

One obvious area where a reduction in data storage costs was easily achieved was in the representation of dates. Computers were programmed to store the date in the format dd/mm/yy: that is, two digits for the day (dd), two digits for the month (mm), and two digits for the year (yy). To save storage space we ignored the two digits of century data, largely because in day-to-day calculations it was practically a constant. It would only pose a problem when the century indicator changed from "19" to "20"—a rare (in the minds of most programmers) calendrical event.

It should be noted there are several obvious variations on this date format. Others include yy/mm/dd, mm/dd/yy, and yy/ddd, where ddd represents the day of the year (e.g., 00/035 is 4 February 2000). What they all have in common is the truncation of the information necessary to indicate the century to which the data item belongs.

To understand the implications of this little compromise, we must look at one of the most basic, and most common, business process calculations performed by the computer . The calculation to determine how much time has passed from one event to the next: for example, calculating someone's age. If you were born on 23 January 1955 and ask the computer how old you are, it subtracts your birth date from the current date. So it will perform a calculation similar to 96 55 (remember that it has only two digits for the year information) and provides the answer of 41 years old.

On 1 January 2000, the calculation would be exactly the same. Subtract the birth year from the current year, 00 − 55 and the computer would state that you are -55 years old. This type of miscalculation affects every type of time calculation that includes dates from both the 1900s and the next century.

The computer industry was well aware of the problems posed by this widely adopted compromise. There was no doubt that the ambiguous nature of the de facto two-digit year standard would cause processing errors. Although some people thought the problem would make itself known throughout 1999 and 2000, others disagreed—they believed the problem would fix itself as software was replaced in the normal course of business.

Highlighting the issues, the *IBM Systems Journal* published an article in 1986 by B. G. Ohms entitled "Computer Processing of Dates Outside the Twentieth Century." The article provides several solutions to the general problem, including the specific solution known as *windowing*, which was ultimately chosen as the de facto standard to solve the problem in the late 1990s. The windowing solution proposed by Ohms is one that allows the programmer to make assumptions about the date in question. If a two-digit year is less than a chosen pivot date, for example 50, it is assumed to lie in the next century; otherwise it is assumed to reside in the 1900s. This meant that the program would interpret "25" as 2025 while "55" would be interpreted as 1955.

What is particularly interesting about the Ohms article is that it assumes, without argument, evidence, or examples, that the reader is intimately aware of the difficulties associated with the ambiguous nature of the two-digit representation of the year. Clearly, this was not the case, as even the committees responsible for setting standards for the computing industry were ignorant of the problem. In the first edition of the ISO (**International Organization for Standardization**) 8601 document, they make it clear that the century indicator can be omitted the date representation if the date element refers to the current century.

Although the ISO standard makes literal sense, and if followed precisely, it would have served to avoid the Y2K problem, programmers ignored the reality that the phrase *current century* does not apply to any data item stored for any period of time. In short, the current century changes. The current century is not a constant that applies to any data.

The Year 2000 problem began to make itself known in the banking industry in the early 1970s. Mortgages were often designed with closing dates 25 to 30 years in the future. Because of this, financial institutions were first to encounter the Y2K bug and also to begin addressing it.

There were numerous other examples of the Y2K problem in the years leading up to 2000, the most noticeable to consumers, had they paid close attention, was in the area of credit cards. Credit cards were typically issued with three-or four-year expiry cycles. Cards issued in 1996 and 1997 would therefore have expiry dates in the year 2000 or 2001. For security reasons a simple validity check was standard operating procedure. Was the expiry date "less than" the current date? If the year of the expiry date was "00," then since "00" is less than "96" or "97" the card was rejected as expired.

The credit card companies found a simple workaround to this problem—they reduced the renewal cycle from three or four years to two and three years, forcing an increased number of cards to expire in 1999. Until the necessary changes could be made to both hardware and software, this was the simplest solution. This practice was continued by some companies until the early months of 1999.

Ultimately the Y2K problem was solved using a variety of techniques. The most obvious solution was to expand all years from two to four digits; although that was the cleanest solution to the problem, it was also the most expensive. The more common solution was the windowing technique described above. Another, more esoteric solution was to take advantage of a peculiarity of the Gregorian calendar. It has been observed that the calendar repeats every 28 years, meaning that 1972 has exactly the same calendar as 2000. If dates were time-shifted backward (or forward) by 28 years before any calculations took place, and then shifted again in reverse, the results of this mathematical manipulation bypassed the Y2K problem. This method, although more complicated than either windowing or expansion, was used by companies that had left themselves little time to implement the more commonly accepted solutions.

By mid-1999, it was estimated that some U.S.$300 billion had been spent worldwide to avoid the Y2K problem. The net result of this worldwide effort was that nothing significant in the way of system failures was experienced.

Toward the end of 1999, Y2K became a sociological phenomenon. Predictions of mass system failure arose from all types of prognosticators. The Y2K issue was picked up by survivalists, the extreme religious right, and those partial to conspiracy theories. The predictions of failure included the accidental unleashing of nuclear missiles, the meltdown of nuclear reactors, total loss of the telecommunications networks, global blackouts, the failure of the entire oil industry, and the collapse of governments. These predictions were totally at odds with predictions from the computer industry itself. Given the work and effort invested in solving the problem throughout the 1990s, infrastructure problems were deemed very unlikely. The expectation was that while there would be numerous problems, they would all be solvable in either hours or possibly days. Ultimately, these less apocalyptic predictions by the computer industry provided a better and more accurate picture of what happened as we entered the year 2000.

Given the surprisingly smooth transition an inevitable question was raised: Was all the effort really necessary? The final committee report published by the U.S. Senate on 29 February 2000 addressed this specifically with the following statement: "The U.S. spent an estimated U.S.$100 billion on the Y2K problem, and the positive results domestically were not unexpected. Several factors contributed to a relatively uneventful rollover. In addition to the unprecedented level of effort undertaken by most organizations, the sharing of information, focus on supplier interrelationships, and attention to contingency planning all contributed to a smooth transition."

FURTHER READING

de Jager, Peter, and Richard Bergeon. *Countdown Y2K: Business Survival Planning for the Year 2000.* New York: Wiley, 1998.

International Organization for Standardization. *ISO 8601: Data Elements and Interchange Formats, Information Exchange, Representation of Dates and Times.* Geneva: ISO, 1988.

Ohms, B. G. "Computer Processing of Dates Outside the Twentieth Century." *IBM Systems Journal,* Vol. 25, No. 2, 1986.

U.S. Senate Special Committee on the Year 2000 Technology Problem. S.Prt. 106-xx, *Y2K Aftermath: Crisis Averted, Final Committee Report,* 29 Feb. 2000.

—Peter de Jager

Z

Zadeh, Lotfi

1921–

Iranian–U.S. Computer Scientist

Lotfi Zadeh developed the concept of **fuzzy logic**, a theory that is likely to leave a permanent mark on the evolution of science and engineering in the latter half of the twentieth century and into the twenty-first. Zadeh has also played an influential role in the evolution of education in electrical engineering and **computer science** in the United States.

The son of Azerbajani parents, Zadeh received a bachelor's degree in electrical engineering from the University of Teheran in 1942 and moved to the United States in 1944 to pursue graduate studies at the Massachusetts Institute of Technology, where he earned his master's degree in 1946. Also that year, Zadeh's parents moved to the United States and settled in New York. To be with them, he took a position as an instructor in electrical engineering at Columbia University, where he received a Ph.D. degree in 1949. He was appointed an assistant professor, rising to full professor in 1957. In 1959, he joined the University of California at Berkeley as a professor in electrical engineering and subsequently he was the founding chair of Berkeley's Department of Electrical Engineering and Computer Science in 1967, a department that is one of the world's leading centers of education.

The second half of the twentieth century saw the emergence of complex human-made systems that typically include sensors and actuators, mechanical, electromechanical, and electronic components, and that use mathematical models built into analog and **digital computers** to perform complex tasks such as piloting aircraft, guiding a missile, or controlling manufacturing processes. It thus became necessary to develop compact and comprehensive mathematical representations of complex systems for purposes of analysis, engineering design, and real-time control. These needs gave rise to the new scientific field of optimal control theory, and later to the broad field of mathematical systems.

Zadeh's early contributions to mathematical systems theory and to control system theory placed him in the front ranks of contributors in these fields. He codeveloped what has come to be known as the Z-transform method for the analysis of sampled-data systems. He developed a theory of time-varying systems, and his seminal book on linear system theory with Charles A. Desoer (1926–) is widely viewed as a classic in its field. He also made important contributions to the theories of filtering and prediction.

The exact quantitative techniques which typically form the basis of mathematical systems theory have serious limitations. The various simplifying assumptions that are needed to develop analytically or numerically tractable representations are often impossible to justify or verify. The system parameters that one needs to insert into a model are themselves known only in an imprecise manner. Furthermore, the design approaches based on some form of optimization can often be inapplicable because the optimization criteria that can be used are hard to characterize and do not easily relate to the underlying practical issues and needs.

Conventional **artificial intelligence** (AI), which is based largely on deductive logic and predicate calculus, provides another approach to the control of complex human-made systems. This has given rise to the wide use of expert systems that capture some form of human expertise. These methods tend to be computationally quite slow, so that other techniques are also needed to link qualitative reasoning, often used to describe the desirable properties of a system, to the quantitative aspects that emerge when a system or its components are observed with the help of numerically based sensing systems. *Fuzzy logic* provides an answer to some of these issues.

Lotfi Zadeh is widely known as the inventor and "father" of fuzzy logic. The concept of fuzzy logic has received attention in practically all fields of science, engineering, as well as in linguistics, psychology, economics, and in many other fields within the social sciences and humanities. Although the idea formalizes the natural concept of approximate reasoning, it was met with fierce resistance in some quarters for many years. Fuzzy logic has now become a standard tool in the repertoire of methods that are used in engineering fields such as operations research, systems engineering, and problem solving in artificial intelligence. Recent theoretical results, which show that fuzzy logic can be used to approximate continuous functions on a compact set, have served to reconstruct the links between mathematical systems theory, fuzzy logic, **neural networks**, and other areas of computational intelligence.

Zadeh was and continues to be a vocal proponent of the integration of electrical engineering and computer science. A new direction in his work relates to what he calls the computational theory of perceptions. Zadeh is also an advanced amateur photographer specializing in portraiture of prominent personalities. His portraits include those of Alexander Kerensky (1881–1970; the premier of Russia just before the October Revolution), Richard Nixon (1913–94), Harry Truman (1884–1972), **Claude Shannon** (1916–2001), Aldous Huxley (1894–1963), and many others. His multilingual and multicultural background, his long experience in the world of science and engineering, and his life in major international centers such as Berkeley and New York have shaped his very broad humanistic perspective on the role of science and engineering in society.

Biography

Lotfi Asker Zadeh. Born 4 February 1921, in Baku, Azerbaijan. B.S. in electrical engineering from the University of Teheran, 1942; M.S. in electrical engineering from Massachusetts Institute of Technology, 1946; Ph.D. in electrical engineering from Columbia University, 1949. Professor, Columbia University, 1949–59. Professor of electrical engineering at University of California–Berkeley, 1959–present; founding chair of Berkeley's Department of Electrical Engineering and Computer Science, 1967. Visiting professor at MIT, 1963, 1968; visiting member of the Institute for Advanced Studies at Princeton, 1956. Currently, professor in the Graduate School at Berkeley and director of the Berkeley Initiative in Soft Computing. Recipient of numerous honors and awards, including Congress Award from the International Congress on Applied Systems, Research and Cybernetics, 1980; Outstanding Paper Award from the International Symposium on Multiple-valued Logic, 1984; Honda Prize, 1989; Berkeley Citation, from the University of California at Berkeley, 1991; IEEE Richard W. Hamming medal, 1992; and Grigore Moisil Prize for Fundamental Research, 1993.

Selected Writings

Zadeh, Lotfi A. "Fuzzy Sets." *Information and Control*, Vol. 8, 1965, pp. 338–353.

———. "A Computational Approach to Fuzzy Quantifiers in Natural Languages." *Computers and Mathematics*, Vol. 9, No. 1, 1983, pp. 149–184.

———. "From Computing with Numbers to Computing with Words—From Manipulation of Measurements to Manipulation of Perceptions." *IEEE Transactions on Circuits and Systems*, Vol. 45, 1999, pp. 105–119.

Zadeh, Lotfi A., and Charles A. Desoer. *Linear System Theory: The State Space Approach*. New York, McGraw-Hill, 1963.

Further Reading

Zadeh, Fay. *My Life and Travels with the Father of Fuzzy Logic*. Albuquerque, N.M.: T S I Press, 1998.

—*Erol Gelenbe*

Z1, Z2, Z3, and Z4

From 1936 to 1945 in Berlin, the German inventor **Konrad Zuse** (1910–95) built some of the earliest computers: the machines Z1 (1936–38), Z2 (1940), Z3 (1938–41), and Z4 (1941–45). The Z1 was a mechanical device, whereas the Z3, which had the same logical structure, was built using electrical telephone relays. The Z2 was an intermediate prototype in which the memory consisted of mechanical components and the processor was made of relays. The Z4 was also a relay machine—a "better Z3" in the sense that it had a much greater memory and the instruction set was enlarged to handle more operations.

All machines used the **binary system** internally for the arithmetic operations. Numbers were entered in decimal notation and the processor took care of transforming from the decimal to the binary system. After computing the result using binary arithmetic, it was transformed from binary to decimal and was displayed using lamps.

The Z1, Z3, and Z4 worked with **floating-point** numbers, numbers written as an exponent and a mantissa, as in 1.5×2^3. Zuse wanted his machines to be used for engineering and business computations and developed an internal numerical representation that strongly resembles the floating-point format of today's **Institute of Electrical and Electronics Engineers** (IEEE). Each number was stored using three fields: the sign of the number, the exponent of the number in two's-complement notation, and the mantissa of the number. The number 2.0, for example, was stored as a positive sign, binary exponent 1 and mantissa 1.0 (i.e., $2 = 1.0 \times 2^1$). The processor of the Z1, Z3, and Z4 thus consisted of two main components, one for handing the exponent of a number and one for handling the mantissa.

The three main machines (the Z2 was just an experimental prototype) shared a common architecture, with three main components: the memory, the processor, and the program. The memory (64 words for the Z1 and Z3, 1024 for the Z4) was used to store floating-point numbers. The processor operated on them using two internal registers, R1 and R2. The program commands were stored on a punched tape and they were read sequentially. The instructions were executed by the control unit, and the I/O console allowed the user to enter decimal numbers through a keyboard or read decimal results from lamps.

The clear separation between memory and processor, not present in machines such as the **ENIAC** or the **Harvard Mark I**, makes the Z1 and Z3 forerunners of what later was to be called **von Neumann architecture**. However, the program was not stored in memory, mainly because all machines had so few addressable memory locations. Zuse had thought of stored-program architectures but did not pursue the idea further.

The instruction set of the Z1 and Z3 consisted of the following operations: (1) addition, (2) subtraction, (3) multiplication, (4) division, (5) square root, (6) read a number from the keyboard to a register, (7) display the number in register R1, (8) store a number in memory, and (9) load a number from memory . Before doing any computation, numbers were read from the numerical **keyboard** to registers R1 and R2. Once the registers were loaded, addition, subtraction, multiplication, or division could be performed. The result was stored again in register R1. The time required by the Z3 for multiplication was 3 seconds. According to Zuse, the Z1 and Z3 were almost equally fast. The Z3 used 2000 relays—600 for the processor and 1400 for the memory.

Using the instruction set shown above, it is possible to process any arithmetical formula of the type used in engineering applications. However, the instruction set does not provide a conditional branching instruction, so it is relatively difficult, although not impossible, to perform more complex computations. Also, the punched tape can be bound to form a loop, so that iterative calculations are possible. Instructions were punched on the tape using an 8-bit code. Zuse's machines could be driven by the program stored in the tape or could be used with direct human input, much like modern pocket calculators.

The processor registers R1 and R2 could also be loaded with numbers stored in memory. Adding two numbers stored at memory locations X and Y and storing the result in memory location Z, consisted of the following sequence of operations: first, load R1 with the number stored in address X; then load R2 with the number stored in address Y; perform the addition; and finally, store the result in address Z. It is not difficult to see how more complex programs could be written for these machines.

Zuse avoided having to use many **logic gates** for the processor by using a control unit that worked as microsequencer, one for each command in the instruction set. A microsequencer consisted, in the case of the Z3, of a rotating arm that advanced one step in each cycle of the machine. A clock (a rotating motor) provided the clock cycles needed to synchronize the machine. In the case of the Z3, the operating frequency was about 5 hertz. At each cycle, the rotating arm in a microsequencer activated the circuits necessary for the operation at hand.

For example, in the case of multiplication, repeated addition and shifting of binary numbers were needed. The 18 partial operations needed were all started by a microsequencer with 18 contacts for the rotating arm. The microsequencer can be thought of as a hardwired program that implemented more complex instructions from atomic binary operations. Modifying the internal operation of the machine therefore consisted only in rewiring these microsequencers, without having to modify the rest of the processor. This resulted in a very efficient and flexible architecture, as was shown thereafter, when the instruction set of the Z3 was expanded for the Z4.

The Z4 would become the computer that Zuse had in mind from the beginning. It was built under contract for the German Airspace Research Office. The main difference between it and the Z3 was the larger memory (1024 addresses). However, using relays for the memory was out of the question, since this would have made the Z4 too bulky. Zuse developed a mechanical memory using the same types of components first used in the Z1. The final size of the larger memory was less than 1 cubic meter. The processor, on the other hand, was made of relays, and although it had the same basic structure as the processor of the Z3, it made more instructions available for the programmer. It was possible, for example, to multiply a number by 10, to shift a binary number, to calculate the reciprocal of a number, and so on.

All these extra instructions did not demand a fundamental change in the architecture of the machine, only that more microsequencing units be included in the machine. Multiplication by 10 was already effectively present as atomic operation in the Z3 (and was necessary to transform a number from the binary to the decimal notation) but was hidden from the programmer. In the Z4 many hidden instructions were made visible to the programmer, in this way increasing the usefulness of the machine. The main difference between the Z4 and Zuse's previous machines was the inclusion of conditional branching in the Z4, which enabled more sophisticated calculations to be performed.

After World War II the Z4 was moved from Berlin to Bavaria, where it stayed in a barn for almost four years. Eduard Stiefel from the Technical University of Zürich heard of the machine and after visiting Zuse, decided to rent the computer for his university. He asked Zuse to include conditional branching in the instruction set, a second punched tape for numbers, and to use a typewriter to print out the results. The machine was refurbished and conditional branching was added. The new instruction worked in the following way: When the contents of **register** R1was negative, the control unit skipped all following instructions until a special code ("start") was found in the punched tape. In this way it was possible to jump over sequences of instructions (i.e., those constituting the not-taken branch of a conditional instruction in the source code).

A detailed comparison of the numerical **algorithms** used by Zuse for the floating-point calculations in his machines with algorithms used in modern machines shows that they are almost identical. For division, Zuse used the approach now known as non-restoring division. Square rooting was done using a similar method based on the division algorithm.

During the years 1941–49 Zuse developed plans for other machines and even applied for patents for some of them. He designed a logarithmic machine, in which numbers were stored as binary logarithms. He also designed the circuits for a device that he called a "logic machine," in which each memory word consisted of a single bit. The processor could only perform atomic logic operations (conjunction, disjunction, and negation) and a program was a sequence of such atomic operations. Perhaps the most surprising device he thought of was a machine that would be a front-end for the Z4: Formulas would be typed in a keyboard, using the standard mathematical notation, and the machine would transform them into assembler code for the Z4. This "Planfertigungsgerät," which was never completed, would have been a hardware **compiler**.

FURTHER READING

Rojas, Raúl, and Ulf Hashagen, eds. *The First Computers: History and Architectures.* Cambridge, Mass.: MIT Press, 1999.

Zuse, Konrad. *The Computer: My Life.* Berlin: Springer-Verlag, 1993.

—*Raúl Rojas*

Zuse, Konrad

1910–95

German Inventor

Konrad Zuse is popularly recognized in Germany as the inventor of the computer. He built a mechanical device, which he called Z1, in the living room of his parents' apartment in Berlin. The construction of the Z1, the first programmable binary computing machine in the world, began in 1936 and finished in 1938.

As part of his civil engineering studies at the Technical University Berlin–Charlottenburg, Zuse learned to perform repetitive static calculations—for example, those needed to determine the stress on materials of structures such as bridges. Static calculations were performed by filling out forms on which all necessary formulas had been preprinted. Zuse started considering the possibility of automating this task. The engineer had to fill in the data and follow the prescribed computational path—surely a machine could do this work.

With his parents' financial help, he began to build the automaton which until that point had only existed in his imagination. Some friends assisted by working for him; others gave him small amounts of money so that he could finish what would become the Z1. This might be the most important difference between Zuse and other computer inventors working at the time: While in the United States, scientists such as **John Atanasoff** (1903–95) and **Howard Aiken** (1900–73) had the resources of universities or companies at their disposal, Zuse was working alone. The entire design of the machine was his own work.

Ignorant of the internal structure of any type of calculator built at the time, Zuse started from scratch and developed an entirely new kind of mechanical construction. Whereas contemporary desktop calculators were based in the decimal system and used rotating mechanical components, Zuse decided to use the **binary system** and metallic plates that could move in only one direction—that is, they could only shift position. These plates were all that was needed for a binary machine, but some other obstacles had to be surmounted. It was not only necessary to design the complete logical description of the machine and then wire it accordingly; the mechanical components posed an additional formidable challenge since every movement of one logical gate had to be coupled with the movement of the other gates. Linear shifts of the components had to be transformed to linear shifts in different layers of the machine, or shifts in perpendicular directions. From today's perspective, the mechanical design of the machine was much more challenging than the logical structure. Nobody except Zuse understood exactly how the machine worked, although many of his friends helped in cutting the hundreds of metallic plates needed for the apparatus.

The Z1 was operational in 1938. It was demonstrated to several people, computing the determinant of a 3 by 3 matrix. The mechanical Z1 proved that the logical structure of the machine was sound; now an electronic or electrical realization, using telephone relays, could be contemplated. Helmut Schreyer, an electronic engineer and friend of Zuse, suggested the

Konrad Zuse, German engineer and inventor. (Courtesy of the Computer Museum History Center)

use of **vacuum tubes**. Schreyer, in fact, adopted this as a Ph.D. project and developed some vacuum-tube circuits for the electronic machine. Zuse himself was not convinced that vacuum tubes should be used. They promised extremely fast calculations, but he thought that vacuum-tube machines could not be made to perform as reliably as relays or even mechanical components. Zuse had already been contemplating the possible uses for his machine, and his goal was the development of a programmable replacement for mechanical desktop calculators, for use at large or medium-sized companies. Clearly, the machines had to be both resilient and fault-tolerant.

Nevertheless, Schreyer and Zuse showed some of the electronic circuits to a small group at the university in 1938. When asked how many vacuum tubes would be needed for a computing machine, they replied that 2000 tubes and several thousand other components would be necessary. The most complex vacuum circuits at the time used no more that some hundred tubes. The university audience left in disbelief—surely the power necessary to keep the machine working would be excessive. A few years later, the **ENIAC** would show to the world that vacuum-tube machines were indeed expensive, but entirely feasible.

The start of World War II had immediate consequences for Zuse; he was called to serve in the army. With the help of Kurt Pannke, a constructor of mechanical calculators, Zuse tried to obtain a transfer to Berlin in order to continue his work on the next computing machine. Helmut Schreyer, who worked as an engineer at the university, also tried to obtain Zuse's discharge. He offered the military command to build an automatic air defense machine that could be operational in two years: By way of reply, he received a sardonic reminder that the war would be won in much less time. Ultimately, Zuse was transferred to the Henschel airplane factory, to make the calculations needed for the stability of the "flying bombs" (now called *cruise missiles*) being built in Berlin.

Zuse started working for the "special section F" at the Henschel factory in 1940. During this time he developed two machines that could automatically measure some parameters of missile wings, transform the analog measurement into a digital number, and compute a formula based on these values. This could well have been the first analog–digital converter built for subsequent digital calculations. In 1940, he also built the machine Z2, which used an integer processor built out of relays but had a mechanical memory. The machine helped Zuse convince the German Airspace Research Office (DLV in German) to partially finance development of Z3, which would be built using only relays. The Z3 was operational in 1941: It had the same logical design as the Z1, but with electrical components.

Zuse continued working for the Henschel factory, but started his own business in 1941. The Zuse Ingenieurbüro und Apparatebau, Berlin was the first company founded with the sole purpose of developing computers. The success with the Z3 brought Zuse a contract with the DLV to develop a still larger computer, the Z4. This machine had a very similar design to the Z3, but would have 1024 memory words instead of only 64. The machine was built and was almost ready in 1945, when Berlin was occupied by Russian troops. Zuse flew with the Z4 to southern Germany, where he was later stationed. Some British and U.S. military experts interviewed Zuse and inspected the machine after the war, but Zuse was not among the scientists who finished their careers working for the Allies.

After the war, Zuse continued working on two main projects: the development of an algorithmic language, which he called the ***Plankalkül*** (calculus of programs); and starting his company again. The Plankalkül can be considered to be the first high-level programming language conceived at the time, although no compiler or interpreter was ever written for it. Zuse's company was revived after Eduard Stiefel, from the Technical University of Zürich, saw the refurbished Z4 in operation and decided to rent it for his university. The Z4 was installed in Zürich in 1950 and was the first commercial computer in operation, some months before the first **UNIVAC** was delivered in the United States.

Zuse's company (with the new name Zuse KG) flourished after the war and many other machines were built. They were all numbered progressively according to their introduction (i.e., Z5, Z11, Z22, Z23, etc.). The dominance of the U.S. computer industry in Europe, as well as the late adoption of a fully electronic design, brought the Zuse KG in financial difficulties. The company was sold in 1962 to Brown Boveri and Co., and later to **Siemens**. Production of the Zuse series of computers was eventually stopped.

In retrospect it can be said that Konrad Zuse's greatest achievement was the development of a family of fully digital **floating-point** programmable machines, which were built in almost total intellectual isolation from 1936 to 1945. His dream was to create a small computer for business and scientific applications, and he worked singlemindedly for many years to achieve this objective. Zuse's machines were undoubtedly smaller than the early U.S. computers, especially the **Harvard Mark I** and the **ENIAC**. However, from the point of view of modern computer architecture, they were more elegant and "canonical." A floating-point **microprocessor** built today using a few thousand transistors would probably have a structure similar to that of the Z3.

Zuse's patent application of 1941 for the computing machine Z3 was ultimately refused in 1967 by a German judge, who declared it to lack "inventiveness." The long delay between application and decision was due initially to the war and its aftermath. Then when the patent application was finally reconsidered in the 1950s, the established computer companies fought against it with every means available to them. The result was a protracted and costly legal battle that Zuse eventually lost.

Zuse always considered himself the true inventor of the computer, and his public statements on this subject demonstrated some bitterness about his lack of recognition abroad. In the United States, his name was almost totally unknown during the 1960s and 1970s, except in the academic communinty. It was not until the 1980s and 1990s that more information about his work became available for the general public in countries other than Germany.

BIOGRAPHY

Konrad Zuse. Born 22 June 1910 in Berlin, Germany. Studied at the Braunsberg High School in Braunsberg and later at the Technische Hochschule Berlin–Charlottenburg, 1927–34; civil engineering degree, 1935. Z1 computer completed, 1938. Served in German army, 1940. Founded company, Zuse Ingenieurbüro und Apparatebau, Berlin (later called Zuse KG), and completed Z3 computer, 1941. Z4 installed at University of Zurich, 1954. Recipient of many honors and prizes from international associations and universities as well as from the German government. Zuse KG liquidated in 1962. Died 18 December 1995 in Hühnfeld, Germany.

SELECTED WRITINGS

Zuse, Konrad. *The Computer: My Life*. Berlin: Springer-Verlag, 1993.

FURTHER READING

Rojas, Raúl. "Konrad Zuse's Legacy: The Architecture of the Z1 and Z3." *Annals of the History of Computing*, Vol. 19, No. 2, 1977, pp. 5–16.

—*Raúl Rojas*

BIBLIOGRAPHY

CONTENTS

ARTIFICIAL INTELLIGENCE AND ROBOTICS

Adam, Alison. *Artificial Knowing: Gender and the Thinking Machine*. London: Routledge, 1998.

Albus, James S. *Brains, Behavior, and Robotics*. New York: McGraw-Hill, 1981.

Arbib, Michael A. *The Metaphorical Brain: An Introduction to Cybernetics as Artificial Intelligence and Brain Theory*. New York: Wiley-Interscience, 1972.

———. *The Metaphorical Brain 2: Neural Networks and Beyond*. New York: Wiley, 1989.

Avouris, Nicholas M., and Les Gasser, eds. *Distributed Artificial Intelligence: Theory and Praxis*. Dordrecht, The Netherlands, and Boston: Kluwer Academic, 1992.

Bailey, James. *After Thought: The Computer Challenge to Human Intelligence*. New York: Basic Books, 1996.

Barfield, Woodrow, and Thomas A. Dingus, eds. *Human Factors in Intelligent Transportation Systems*. Mahwah, N.J.: Lawrence Erlbaum Associates, 1998.

Barr, Avron, and Edward A. Feigenbaum, eds. *The Handbook of Artificial Intelligence*. Reading, Mass.: Addison-Wesley, 1989.

Berkeley, Edmund C. *Giant Brains: Or Machines That Think*. New York: Science Editions, 1961.

Bishop, Christopher M. *Neural Networks for Pattern Recognition*. Oxford: Clarendon Press; New York: Oxford University Press, 1995.

Bloomfield, Brian P., ed. *The Question of Artificial Intelligence: Philosophical and Sociological Perspectives*. London and New York: Helm Publishing, 1987.

Boden, Margaret A., ed. *The Philosophy of Artificial Intelligence*. Oxford and New York: Oxford University Press, 1990.

———. *Artificial Intelligence*. San Diego, Calif.: Academic Press, 1996.

Bolles, R. C., H. Bunke, and H. Noltemeier, eds. *Intelligent Robots: Sensing, Modeling, and Planning*. Singapore, and River Edge, N.J.: World Scientific, 1997.

Bonabeau, Eric, Marco Dorigo, and Guy Theraulaz. *Swarm Intelligence: From Natural to Artificial Systems*. New York: Oxford University Press, 1999.

Bond, Alan H., and Les Gasser, eds. *Readings in Distributed Artificial Intelligence*. San Mateo, Calif.: Morgan Kaufmann, 1988.

Bourbakis, Nikolaos G., ed. *Artificial Intelligence and Automation*. Singapore, and River Edge, N.J.: World Scientific, 1998.

Bradshaw, Jeffrey M., ed. *Software Agents*. Menlo Park, Calif.: AAAI Press; Cambridge, Mass.: MIT Press, 1997.

Cannon, Walter B. *The Wisdom of the Body*. Birmingham, Ala.: Classics of Medicine Library, 1989.

Cassell, Justine, Joseph Sullivan, Scott Prevost, and Elizabeth Churchill, eds. *Embodied Computational Agents*. Cambridge, Mass.: MIT Press, 2000.

Cawsey, Alison. *The Essence of Artificial Intelligence*. London and New York: Prentice Hall, 1998.

Charniak, Eugene, and Drew MacDermott. *Introduction to Artificial Intelligence*. Reading, Mass.: Addison-Wesley, 1986.

Copeland, J. *Artificial Intelligence: A Philosophical Introduction*. Oxford, and Cambridge, Mass.: Blackwell, 1993.

Cox, I. J., and G. T. Wilfong, eds. *Autonomous Robot Vehicles*. New York: Springer-Verlag, 1990.

Crevier, Daniel. *AI: The Tumultuous History of the Search for Artificial Intelligence*. New York: Basic Books, 1993.

Crick, Francis. *The Astonishing Hypothesis: The Scientific Search for the Soul*. New York: Scribner; Toronto: Maxwell Macmillan Canada; New York: Maxwell Macmillan International, 1994.

Damasio, Antonio R. *Descartes' Error: Emotion, Reason, and the Human Brain*. New York: Bard/Avon, 1998.

Dechert, Charles R. *The Social Impact of Cybernetics*. Notre Dame, Ind.: University of Notre Dame Press, 1966.

De Latil, Pierre. *La Pensée Artificielle*. Paris: Librairie Gallimard, 1956. *Thinking by Machine: A Study of Cybernetics*. Translated by Y. M. Golla. Boston: Houghton Mifflin, 1957.

Dennett, D. C. *Darwin's Dangerous Idea: Evolution and the Meanings of Life*. New York: Simon and Schuster, 1995.

Drescher, Gary L. *Made-Up Minds: A Constructivist Approach to Artificial Intelligence.* Cambridge, Mass.: MIT Press, 1991.

Dreyfus, Hubert L. *What Computers Still Can't Do: A Critique of Artificial Reason.* Cambridge, Mass.: MIT Press, 1992.

Duda, Richard O., and Peter E. Hart. *Pattern Classification and Scene Analysis.* New York: Wiley, 1973.

Dyson, George B. *Darwin Among the Machines: The Evolution of Global Intelligence.* Reading, Mass.: Perseus Books, 1998.

Ennals, J. R. *Artificial Intelligence: Applications to Logical Reasoning and Historical Research.* Chichester, West Sussex, England: Ellis Horwood; Chichester, West Sussex, England, and New York: Halsted Press, 1985.

Feigenbaum, Edward A., and Julian Feldman, eds. *Computers and Thought: A Collection of Articles.* Malabar, Fla.: R.E. Krieger, 1981.

Fischler, Martin, and Oscar Firschein. *Intelligence: The Eye, the Brain, and the Computer.* Reading, Mass.: Addison-Wesley, 1987.

Gardner, Howard. *The Mind's New Science: A History of the Cognitive Revolution.* New York: Basic Books, 1985.

Genesereth, Michael R., and Nils J. Nilsson. *Logical Foundations of Artificial Intelligence.* Los Altos, Calif.: Morgan Kaufmann, 1987.

Goldberg, David E. *Genetic Algorithms in Search, Optimization, and Machine Learning.* Reading, Mass.: Addison-Wesley, 1989.

Goldberg, Ken. *The Robot in the Garden: Telerobotics and Telepistemology in the Age of the Internet.* Cambridge, Mass.: MIT Press, 2000.

Graubard, Stephen R., ed. *The Artificial Intelligence Debate: False Starts, Real Foundations.* Cambridge, Mass.: MIT Press, 1988.

Gray, Chris Hables, ed. *The Cyborg Handbook.* New York: Routledge, 1995.

Halacy, Daniel S. *Bionics: The Science of "Living" Machines.* New York: Holiday House, 1965.

Haugeland, J. *Artificial Intelligence: The Very Idea.* Cambridge, Mass.: MIT Press, 1985.

———. *Mind Design: Philosophy, Psychology, Artificial Intelligence.* Montgomery, Vt.: Bradford Press, 1981.

Hertz, John, Anders Krogh, and Richard G. Palmer. *Introduction to the Theory of Neural Computation.* Redwood City, Calif.: Addison-Wesley, 1991.

Hofstadter, Douglas R. *Metamagical Themas: Questing for the Essence of Mind and Pattern.* New York: Basic Books, 1985.

Holland, John H. *Adaptation in Natural and Artificial Systems: An Introductory Analysis with Applications to Biology, Control, and Artificial Intelligence.* Ann Arbor, Mich.: University of Michigan Press, 1975; 2nd ed., Cambridge, Mass.: MIT Press, 1992.

Jones, Joseph L., Bruce A. Seiger, and Anita M. Flynn. *Mobile Robots: Inspiration to Implementation.* Wellesley, Mass.: Peters, 1993; 2nd ed., Natick, Mass., 1999.

Kortenkamp, David R., Peter Bonasso, and Robin Murphy, eds. *Artificial Intelligence and Mobile Robots: Case Studies of Successful Robot Systems.* Menlo Park, Calif.: AAAI Press; Cambridge, Mass.: MIT Press, 1998.

Kosko, Bart. *Neural Networks and Fuzzy Systems.* Englewood Cliffs, N.J.: Prentice Hall, 1992.

Kurzweil, Raymond. *The Age of Spiritual Machines: When Computers Exceed Human Intelligence.* New York: Viking/Penguin, 2000.

Lajoie, Susanne P., and Martial Vivet, eds. *Artificial Intelligence in Education: Open Learning Environments: New Computational Technologies to Support Learning, Exploration and Collaboration.* Amsterdam, and Washington, D.C.: IOS Press; Tokyo: Ohmsha, 1999.

Leonard, Andrew. *Bots: The Origin of New Species.* San Francisco: Hardwired, 1997.

Luger, George F., and William A. Stubblefield. *Artificial Intelligence and the Design of Expert Systems.* Redwood City, Calif.: Benjamin-Cummings, 1989; 3rd ed., published under the title *Artificial Intelligence: Structures and Strategies for Complex Problem Solving*, Harlow, Essex, England, and Reading, Mass.: Addison-Wesley, 1998.

MacCorduck, Pamela. *Machines Who Think.* San Francisco: W.H. Freeman, 1979.

Marr, David. *Vision: A Computational Investigation into the Human Representation and Processing of Visual Information.* San Francisco: W.H. Freeman, 1982.

Maturana, Humberto R., and Francisco J. Varela. *The Tree of Knowledge: The Biological Roots of Human Understanding.* Boston: New Science Library, distributed in the United States by Random House, 1987; rev. ed., Boston and New York: Shambhala, distributed in the United States by Random House, 1992.

Minsky, Marvin. *The Society of Mind.* New York: Simon and Schuster, 1986.

Minsky, Marvin L., and Seymour Papert. *Perceptrons: An Introduction to Computational Geometry.* Cambridge, Mass.: MIT Press, 1988.

Moravec, Hans. *Mind Children: The Future of Robot and Human Intelligence.* Cambridge, Mass.: Harvard University Press, 1988.

Morecki, Adam, and Józef Knapczyk, eds. *Basics of Robotics: Theory and Components of Manipulators and Robots.* Vienna and New York: Springer-Verlag, 1999.

Nilsson, N. J. *Principles of Artificial Intelligence.* Palo Alto, Calif.: Tioga Publishing, 1981.

Nwana, Hyacinth S., and Nader Azarmi, eds. *Software Agents and Soft Computing: Towards Enhancing Machine Intelligence: Concepts and Applications.* Berlin and New York: Springer-Verlag, 1997.

Pearl, Judea. *Probabilistic Reasoning in Intelligent Systems: Networks of Plausible Inference.* San Mateo, Calif.: Morgan Kaufmann, 1988.

Pinker, Steven. *The Language Instinct.* New York: William Morrow, 1994.

Reeves, Byron, and Clifford Nass. *The Media Equation: How People Treat Computers, Television, and New Media Like Real People and Places.* New York: Cambridge University Press, 1996.

Rich, Elaine. *Artificial Intelligence.* New York: McGraw-Hill, 1983; 2nd ed., with Kevin Knight, New York: McGraw-Hill, 1991.

Robinson, W. S. *Computers, Minds, and Robots.* Philadephia: Temple University Press, 1992.

Rojas, Raúl. *Neural Networks.* Berlin and New York: Springer-Verlag, 1996.

Rumelhart, David E., James L. McClelland, and the PDP Research Group. *Parallel Distributed Processing: Explorations in the Microstructure of Cognition.* Cambridge, Mass.: MIT Press, 1986.

Russell, Stuart J., and Peter Norvig. *Artificial Intelligence: A Modern Approach.* Englewood Cliffs, N.J.: Prentice Hall, 1995.

Schank, Roger C., and Robert P. Abelson. *Scripts, Plans, Goals, and Understanding: An Inquiry into Human Knowledge Structures.* Hillsdale, N.J.: Lawrence Erlbaum Associates; New York: distributed by the Halsted Press Division of John Wiley and Sons, 1977.

Schraft, Rolf Dieter, and Gernot Schmierer. *Service Robots: Products, Scenarios, Visions.* Natick, Mass.: Peters, 2000.

Shapiro, S., ed. *Encyclopedia of Artificial Intelligence.* New York: Wiley, 1987; 2nd ed., 1992.

Simon, Herbert A. *The Sciences of the Artificial.* Cambridge, Mass.: MIT Press, 1969; 3rd ed., 1996.

Sutton, Richard S., and Andrew G. Barto. *Reinforcement Learning: An Introduction.* Cambridge, Mass.: MIT Press, 1998.

Webber, Bonnie L., and Nils J. Nilsson, eds. *Readings in Artificial Intelligence.* San Francisco: Morgan Kaufmann, 1981.

Weizenbaum, J. *Computer Power and Human Reason.* San Francisco: W.H. Freeman, 1976.

Wiener, Norbert. *Cybernetics, or Control and Communication in the Animal and the Machine.* New York: Wiley, 1948; 2nd ed., Cambridge, Mass.: MIT Press, 1961.

Winograd, Terry, and Fernando Flores. *Understanding Computers and Cognition: A New Foundation for Design.* Reading, Mass.: Addison-Wesley, 1986.

Winston, Patrick Henry. *Artificial Intelligence.* Reading, Mass.: Addison-Wesley, 1977; 3rd ed., 1993.

Zeki, S. *A Vision of the Brain.* Oxford: Blackwell, 1993.

COMPUTER GRAPHICS, ANIMATION, AND DESIGN

Abrash, Michael. *Power Graphics Programming.* Carmel, Ind.: Que Corporation; Springfield, Oreg.: Programmer's Journal, 1989.

Adams, J. Alan, and Leon M. Billow. *Descriptive Geometry and Geometric Modeling: A Basis for Design.* New York: Holt, Rinehart and Winston, 1988.

Ammeraal, Leendert. *Computer Graphics for Java Programmers*. Chichester, West Sussex, England, and New York: Wiley, 1998.

———. *Programming Principles in Computer Graphics*. Chichester, West Sussex, England, and New York: Wiley, 1986; 2nd ed., 1992. Series title: *Wiley Professional Computing*.

Anand, Vera B. *Computer Graphics and Geometric Modeling for Engineers*. New York: Wiley, 1993.

Angel, Edward. *Interactive Computer Graphics: A Top-Down Approach with Open GL*. Reading, Mass.: Addison-Wesley, 1997; 2nd ed., 2000.

Baker, Robin. *Designing the Future: The Computer Transformation of Reality*. New York: Thames and Hudson, 1993.

Banchoff, Thomas F. *Beyond the Third Dimension: Geometry, Computer Graphics, and Higher Dimensions*. New York: Scientific American Library, distributed by W.H. Freeman, 1996.

Birtwistle, Graham, ed. *AI, Graphics, and Simulation*. La Jolla, Calif.: Society for Computer Simulation, 1985.

Bowyer, Adrian, and John Woodwark. *A Programmer's Geometry*. London and Boston: Butterworths, 1983.

Brinkmann, Ron. *The Art and Science of Digital Compositing*. San Francisco: Morgan Kaufmann; San Diego, Calif.: Academic Press, 1999.

Casti, John. *Would-Be Worlds: How Simulation Is Changing the Frontiers of Science*. New York: Wiley, 1997.

Conger, Sue A., Richard O. Mason. *Planning and Designing Effective Web Sites*. Cambridge, Mass.: Course Technology, 1998.

Cubitt, Sean. *Digital Aesthetics*. London, and Thousand Oaks, Calif.: Sage Publications, 1998.

Curtis, Hillman. *Flash Web Design: The Art of Motion Graphics*. Indianapolis, Ind.: New Riders Publishing, 2000.

Devlin, Keith. *Life by the Numbers*. New York: Wiley, 1998.

Egerton, P. A., and W. S. Hall. *Computer Graphics: Mathematical First Steps*. London and New York: Prentice Hall Europe, 1998.

Foley, James D., and Andries van Dam. *Fundamentals of Interactive Computer Graphics*. Reading, Mass.: Addison-Wesley, 1982; 2nd ed., published under the title *Computer Graphics: Principles and Practice*, by James D. Foley et al., Reading, Mass.: Addison-Wesley, 1990.

Foley, James, et al. *Computer Graphics: Principles and Practice*. Reading, Mass.: Addison-Wesley, 1996.

Freeman, Herbert, ed. *Interactive Computer Graphics*. Los Alamitos, Calif.: IEEE Computer Society Press, 1980.

Garcia, Mario R. *Redesigning Print for the Web*. Indianapolis, Ind.: Hayden Books, 1997.

Glassner, Andrew, ed. *An Introduction to Ray Tracing*. London: Academic Press, 1989.

———. *Graphics Gems*. Boston: Academic Press, 1990.

Gomes, Jonas, and Luiz Velho. *Image Processing for Computer Graphics*. Translated by Silvio Levy. New York: Springer-Verlag, 1997.

Gonzalez, Rafael C., and Paul Wintz. *Digital Image Processing*. Reading, Mass.: Addison-Wesley, 1977; 2nd ed., 1987.

Hamlin, J. Scott. *Effective Web Animation: Advanced Techniques for the Web*. Reading, Mass.: Addison-Wesley, 1999.

Henderson, Kathryn. *On Line and on Paper: Visual Representations, Visual Culture, and Computer Graphics in Design Engineering*. Cambridge, Mass.: MIT Press, 1999.

Jones, Gerald E. *Font Secrets and Solutions*. San Francisco: SYBEX, 1994.

Kerlow, Isaac Victor. *The Art of 3-D: Computer Animation and Imaging*. New York: Van Nostrand Reinhold, 1996; 2nd ed., New York: Wiley, 2000.

Krause, Kai, ed. *In Your Face: The Best of Interactive Interface Design*. Rockport, Mass.: Rockport Publishers; distributed by North Light Books, Cincinnati, Ohio, 1996.

Kyng, Morten, and Lars Mathiassen, eds. *Computers and Design in Context*. Cambridge, Mass.: MIT Press, 1997.

Lathrop, Olin. *The Way Computer Graphics Work*. New York: Wiley, 1997.

Laurel, Brenda, ed. *The Art of Human–Computer Interface Design*. Reading, Mass.: Addison-Wesley, 1990.

Levkowitz, Haim. *Color Theory and Modeling for Computer Graphics, Visualization, and Multimedia Applications.* Boston: Kluwer Academic, 1997.

Maeda, John, and Paola Antonelli. *Design by Numbers.* Cambridge, Mass.: MIT Press, 1999.

Marsh, Duncan. *Applied Geometry for Computer Graphics and CAD.* London and New York: Springer-Verlag, 1999.

Mortenson, Michael E. *Computer Graphics: An Introduction to the Mathematics and Geometry.* New York: Industrial Press, 1989; 2nd ed., published under the title *Mathematics for Computer Graphics Applications*, 1999.

Niederst, Jennifer. *Web Design in a Nutshell: A Desktop Quick Reference.* Beijing, and Sebastopol, Calif.: O'Reilly, 1999.

Pilling, Jayne, ed. *A Reader in Animation Studies.* London: Libbey, 1997.

Rogers, David F. *Procedural Elements for Computer Graphics.* New York: McGraw-Hill, 1985; 2nd ed., Boston: WCB/McGraw-Hill, 1998.

Rogers, David F., and J. Alan Adams. *Mathematical Elements for Computer Graphics.* New York: McGraw-Hill, 1976; 2nd ed., 1990.

Salomon, David. *Computer Graphics and Geometric Modeling.* New York: Springer-Verlag, 1999.

Spool, Jared M., et al. *Web Site Usability: A Designer's Guide.* San Francisco: Morgan Kaufmann, 1999.

Stollnitz, Eric J., Tony D. DeRose, and David H. Salesin. *Wavelets for Computer Graphics: Theory and Applications.* San Francisco: Morgan Kaufmann, 1996.

Todd, Stephen, and William Latham. *Evolutionary Art and Computers.* London, and San Diego, Calif.: Academic Press, 1992.

Tufte, Edward R. *Envisioning Information.* Cheshire, Conn.: Graphics Press, 1995.

Vince, John. *Essential Computer Animation Fast: How to Understand the Techniques and Potential of Computer Animation.* London and New York: Springer-Verlag, 2000.

———. *Computer Graphics.* London: Design Council, 1992.

Watt, Alan H. *Fundamentals of Three-Dimensional Computer Graphics.* Wokingham, Berkshire, England, and Reading, Mass.: Addison-Wesley, 1989.

———. *3D Computer Graphics.* Reading, Mass.: Addison-Wesley, 1993; 3rd ed., 2000.

Watt, Alan, and Fabio Policarpo. *The Computer Image.* Harlow, Essex, England, and Reading, Mass.: Addison-Wesley, 1998.

Watt, Alan H., and Mark Watt. *Advanced Animation and Rendering Techniques: Theory and Practice.* New York: ACM Press; Wokingham, Berkshire, England, and Reading, Mass.: Addison-Wesley, 1992.

COMPUTER MUSIC

Appleton, Jon H. *21st-Century Musical Instruments: Hardware and Software.* Brooklyn, N.Y.: Institute for Studies in American Music, Conservatory of Music, Brooklyn College of the City University of New York, 1989.

Backus, John. *The Acoustical Foundations of Music.* New York: W.W. Norton, 1969; 2nd ed., 1977.

Baggi, Denis, ed. *Readings in Computer-Generated Music.* Los Alamitos, Calif.: IEEE Computer Society Press, 1992.

Bateman, Wayne. *Introduction to Computer Music.* New York: Wiley, 1980.

Bates, John. *The Synthesizer.* Oxford: Oxford University Press, 1988.

Cary, Tristram. *Dictionary of Musical Technology.* New York: Greenwood Press, 1992.

Chadabe, Joel. *Electric Sound: The Past and Promise of Electronic Music.* Upper Saddle River, N.J.: Prentice Hall, 1997.

Chamberlin, Hal. *Musical Applications of Microprocessors.* Rochelle Park, N.J.: Hayden Publishing, 1980; 2nd ed., 1985.

Cope, David. *New Music Composition.* New York: Schirmer Books, 1977.

———. *The Algorithmic Composer.* Madison, Wis.: A-R Editions, 2000.

Davis, Deta S. *Computer Applications in Music: A Bibliography, Supplement 1.* Madison, Wis.: A-R Editions, 1992.

Desain, Peter, and Henkjan Honing. *Music, Mind, and Machine: Studies in Computer Music, Music*

Cognition, and Artificial Intelligence. Amsterdam: Thesis, 1992.

Deutsch, Herbert A. *Electroacoustic Music: The First Century.* Miami, Fla.: Belwin Mills, 1993.

Dobson, Richard. *A Dictionary of Electronic and Computer Music Technology: Instruments, Terms, Techniques.* Oxford and New York: Oxford University Press, 1992.

Dodge, Charles, and Thomas A. Jerse. *Computer Music: Synthesis, Composition, and Performance.* New York: Schirmer Books, 1985; 2nd ed., New York: Schirmer Books; London: Prentice Hall International, 1997.

Emmerson, Simon, ed. *The Language of Electroacoustic Music.* New York: Harwood Academic; London: Macmillan, 1986.

Haus, Goffredo, ed. *Music Processing.* Madison, Wis.: A-R Editions, 1993.

Karl, John H. *An Introduction to Digital Signal Processing.* San Diego, Calif.: Academic Press, 1989.

Lee, William F. *Music in the 21st Century: The New Language.* Miami, Fla.: CPP/Belwin, 1994.

Manning, Peter. *Electronic and Computer Music.* Oxford: Clarendon Press; New York: Oxford University Press, 1985; 2nd ed., 1994.

Marsden, Alan, and Anthony Pople, eds. *Computer Representations and Models in Music.* London and New York: Academic Press, 1992.

Miranda, Eduardo Reck. *Computer Sound Synthesis for the Electronic Musician.* Oxford and Boston: Focal Press, 1998.

Matthews, Max V., ed. *Sound Examples: Current Directions in Computer Music Research.* Cambridge, Mass.: MIT Press, 1989.

Moore, F. Richard. *Elements of Computer Music.* Englewood Cliffs, N.J.: Prentice Hall, 1990.

Oppenheim, Alan V., and Ronald W. Schafer. *Discrete-Time Signal Processing.* Englewood Cliffs, N.J.: Prentice Hall, 1989; 2nd ed., Upper Saddle River, N.J., 1999.

Pellman, Samuel. *An Introduction to the Creation of Electroacoustic Music.* Belmont, Calif.: Wadsworth, 1994.

Roads, Curtis, ed. *Composers and the Computer.* Los Altos, Calif.: Morgan Kaufmann, 1985.

———. *The Music Machine: Selected Readings from Computer Music Journal.* Cambridge, Mass.: MIT Press, 1989.

Roads, Curtis, and John Strawn, eds. *Foundations of Computer Music.* Cambridge, Mass.: MIT Press, 1985.

Schrader, Barry. *Introduction to Electro-acoustic Music.* Englewood Cliffs, N.J.: Prentice Hall, 1982.

Wick, Robert L. *Electronic and Computer Music: An Annotated Bibliography.* Westport, Conn.: Greenwood Press, 1997.

CORPORATIONS AND LABORATORIES

Asakura, Reiji. *Revolutionaries at Sony: The Making of the Sony Playstation and the Visionaries Who Conquered the World of Video Games.* New York: McGraw-Hill, 2000.

Bashe, Charles J., Lyle R. Johnson, John H. Palmer, and Emerson W. Pugh. *IBM's Early Computers.* Cambridge, Mass.: MIT Press, 1986.

Bunnell, David. *Making the Cisco Connection: The Story Behind the Real Internet Superpower.* New York: Wiley, 2000.

Campbell-Kelly, Martin. *ICL: A Business and Technical History.* Oxford: Clarendon Press; New York: Oxford University Press, 1989.

Carlton, Jim. *Apple: The Inside Story of Intrigue, Egomania, and Business Blunders.* New York: HarperCollins, 1998.

Carroll, Paul. *Big Blues: The Unmaking of IBM.* New York: Crown Publishing, 1993.

Chposky, James, and Ted Leonsis. *Blue Magic: The People, Power, and Politics Behind the IBM Personal Computer.* New York: Facts On File, 1988.

Cortada, James W. *Historical Dictionary of Data Processing Organizations.* New York: Greenwood Press, 1987.

———. *Before the Computer: IBM, NCR, Burroughs, and Remington Rand and the Industry They Created, 1865–1956.* Princeton, N.J.: Princeton University Press, 1993.

Cusumano, Michael A., and Richard W. Selby. *Microsoft Secrets: How the World's Most Powerful Software Company Creates Technology, Shapes Markets, and Manages People.* New York: Free Press, 1995.

Cusumano, Michael A., and David B. Yoffie. *Competing on Internet Time: Lessons from Netscape and Its Battle with Microsoft.* New York: Free Press, 1998.

Dell, Michael, with Catherine Fredman. *Direct from Dell: Strategies That Revolutionized an Industry.* New York: Harper Business, 1999.

Fisher, Franklin M., James W. McKie, and Richard B. Mancke. *IBM and the U.S. Data Processing Industry: An Economic History.* New York: Praeger, 1983.

Garfinkel, Simson. *Architects of the Information Society: 35 Years of the Laboratory for Computer Science at MIT.* Cambridge, Mass.: MIT Press, 1999.

Heller, Robert. *The Fate of IBM.* London: Little, Brown, 1994.

Hiltzik, Michael A. *Dealers of Lightning: Xerox PARC and the Dawn of the Computer Age.* New York: Harper Business, 1999.

Ichbiah, Daniel, and Susan L. Knepper. *The Making of Microsoft: How Bill Gates and His Team Created the World's Most Successful Software Company.* Rocklin, Calif.: Prima Publishing, 1991.

Jackson, Tim. *Inside Intel: Andy Grove and the Rise of the World's Most Powerful Chip Company.* New York: Dutton, 1997.

Jacobson, Gary, and John Hillkirk. *Xerox: American Samurai.* New York: Macmillan, 1986.

Kenney, Charles. *Riding the Runaway Horse: The Rise and Decline of Wang Laboratories.* Boston: Little, Brown, 1992.

Kunkel, Paul. *Digital Dreams: The Work of the Sony Design Center.* New York: Universe Publishing, 1999.

Lewis, T. G. *Microsoft Rising—And Other Tales of Silicon Valley.* Los Alamitos, Calif.: IEEE Computer Society Press, 1999.

Linzmayer, Owen W. *Apple Confidential: The Real Story of Apple Computer, Inc.* San Francisco: No Starch Press, 1999.

Lundstrom, David E. *A Few Good Men from Univac.* Cambridge, Mass.: MIT Press, 1987.

Mercer, David. *IBM: How the World's Most Successful Corporation Is Managed.* London: K. Page, 1987; rev. ed., London: Kogan Page, 1988.

Moody, Fred. *I Sing the Body Electronic: A Year with Microsoft on the Multimedia Frontier.* New York: Viking, 1995.

Moritz, Michael. *The Little Kingdom: The Private Story of Apple Computer.* New York: William Morrow, 1984.

Oldfield, Homer R. *King of the Seven Dwarfs: General Electric's Ambiguous Challenge to the Computer Industry.* Los Alamitos, Calif.: IEEE Computer Society Press, 1996.

Olsen, Kenneth H. *Digital Equipment Corporation: The First Twenty-Five Years.* New York: Newcomen Society in North America, 1983. Series title: *Newcomen Publication*, No. 1179.

Packard, David. *The HP Way: How Bill Hewlett and I Built Our Company.* New York: Harper Business, 1995.

Pugh, Emerson W. *Memories That Shaped an Industry: Decisions Leading to IBM System/360.* Cambridge, Mass.: MIT Press, 1984. Series title: *History of Computing.*

———. *Building IBM: Shaping an Industry and Its Technology.* Cambridge, Mass.: MIT Press, 1995. Series title: *History of Computing.*

Quittner, Joshua, et al. *Speeding the Net: The Inside Story of Netscape and How It Challenged Microsoft.* New York: Atlantic Monthly Press, 1998.

Rodengen, Jeffrey L. *The Spirit of AMD: Advanced Micro Devices.* Ft. Lauderdale, Fla.: Write Stuff Enterprises, 1998.

Rose, Frank. *West of Eden: The End of Innocence at Apple Computer.* New York: Viking, 1989.

Sheff, David, and Eddy Andy. *Game Over: How Nintendo Zapped an American Industry, Captured Your Dollars, and Enslaved Your Children.* New York: Random House, 1993.

Smith, Douglas K., and Robert C. Alexander. *Fumbling the Future: How Xerox Invented, Then Ignored, the First Personal Computer.* New York: William Morrow, 1988.

Stauffer, David. *It's a Wired, Wired World: Business the AOL Way.* Dover, N.H.: Capstone Press, 2000.

Stross, Randall E. *The Microsoft Way: The Real Story of How the Company Outsmarts Its Competition.* Reading, Mass.: Addison-Wesley, 1996.

Swisher, Kara. *AOL.Com: How Steve Case Beat Bill Gates, Nailed the Netheads and Made Millions in the War for the Web.* New York: Crown Publishing, 1999.

Tsang, Cheryl D. *Microsoft First Generation: The Success Secrets of the Visionaries Who Launched a Technology Empire.* New York: Wiley, 2000.

Wagner, Richard. *Inside Compuserve*, 3rd ed. Indianapolis, Ind.: New Riders Publishing, 1995.

Wallace, James. *Overdrive: Bill Gates and the Race to Control Cyberspace.* New York: Wiley, 1997.

Wildes, Karl L., and Nilo A. Lindgren. *A Century of Electrical Engineering and Computer Science at MIT, 1882–1982.* Cambridge, Mass.: MIT Press, 1985.

Zell, Deone. *Changing by Design: Organizational Innovation at Hewlett-Packard.* Ithaca, N.Y.: ILR Press, 1997.

CRYPTOGRAPHY AND ENCRYPTION

Abadi, Martín, and Roger Needham. *Prudent Engineering Practice for Cryptographic Protocols.* Palo Alto, Calif.: Digital Systems Research Center, 1994.

Adams, Carlisle, and Steve Lloyd. *Understanding Public-Key Infrastructure: Concepts, Standards, and Deployment Considerations.* Indianapolis, Ind.: Macmillan Technical Publishing, 1999.

Bacard, André. *The Computer Privacy Handbook.* Berkeley, Calif.: Peachpit Press, 1995.

Baker, Stewart Abercrombie, and Paul R. Hurst. *The Limits of Trust: Cryptography, Governments, and Electronic Commerce.* The Hague, The Netherlands, and Boston: Kluwer Law International, 1998.

Bauer, Friedrich Ludwig. *Decrypted Secrets: Methods and Maxims of Cryptology*, 2nd rev. and extended ed. Berlin and New York: Springer-Verlag, 2000.

Beckett, Brian. *Introduction to Cryptology and PC Security.* New York: McGraw-Hill, 1997.

Bellare, Mihir, ed. *Advances in Cryptology—CRYPTO 2000*, proceedings of the 20th Annual International Cryptology Conference, Santa Barbara, Calif., Aug. 20–24, 2000. Berlin and New York: Springer-Verlag, 2000

Beutelspacher, Albrecht. *Cryptology: An Introduction to the Art and Science of Enciphering, Encrypting, Concealing, Hiding, and Safeguarding Described Without Any Arcane Skullduggery but Not Without Cunning Waggery for the Delectation and Instruction of the General Public.* Transformation from German into English, succored and abetted by J. Chris Fisher. Washington, D.C.: Mathematical Association of America, 1994. Series title: *MAA Spectrum.*

Biham, Eli, and Adi Shamir. *Differential Cryptanalysis of the Data Encryption Standard.* New York: Springer-Verlag, 1993.

Brands, Stefan A. *Rethinking Public Key Infrastructures and Digital Certificates: Building in Privacy.* Cambridge, Mass.: MIT Press, 2000.

Campbell, Duncan, and Steve Connor. *On the Record: Surveillance, Computers and Privacy—The Inside Story.* London: Michael Joseph, 1986.

Diffie, Whitfield, and Susan Landau. *Privacy on the Line: The Politics of Wiretapping and Encryption.* Cambridge, Mass.: MIT Press, 1998.

Dr. Dobb's Essential Books on Cryptography and Security. San Mateo, Calif.: Miller Freeman, 1999.

Electronic Frontier Foundation. *Cracking DES: Secrets of Encryption Research, Wiretap Politics and Chip Design.* Sebastopol, Calif.: Electronic Frontier Foundation; distributed by O'Reilly, 1998.

Enge, Andreas. *Elliptic Curves and Their Applications to Cryptography: An Introduction.* Boston: Kluwer Academic, 1999.

Feghhi, Jalal, and Peter Williams. *Digital Certificates: Applied Internet Security.* Reading, Mass.: Addison-Wesley, 1999.

Garfinkel, Simson. *PGP: Pretty Good Privacy.* Sebastopol, Calif.: O'Reilly, 1995.

Goldreich, Oded. *Modern Cryptography, Probabilistic Proofs, and Pseudorandomness.* Berlin and New York: Springer-Verlag, 1999.

Gurak, Laura J. *Persuasion and Privacy in Cyberspace: The Online Protests over Lotus Marketplace and the Clipper Chip.* New Haven, Conn.: Yale University Press, 1997.

Hoffman, Lance J., ed. *Building in Big Brother: The Cryptographic Policy Debate.* New York: Springer-Verlag, 1995.

Joyner, David, ed. *Coding Theory and Cryptography: From Enigma and Geheimschreiber to Quantum Theory.* Berlin and New York: Springer-Verlag, 2000.

Knudsen, Jonathan. *Java Cryptography*. Sebastopol, Calif.: O'Reilly, 1998.

Koops, Bert-Jaap. *The Crypto Controversy: A Key Conflict in the Information Society*. Boston: Kluwer Law International, 1999.

McCurley, Kevin S., and Claus Dieter Ziegler, eds. *Advances in Cryptology, 1981–1997: Electronic Proceedings and Index of the CRYPTO and EURO-CRYPT Conferences, 1981–1997*. Berlin and New York: Springer-Verlag, 1998.

Menezes, Alfred J., Paul C. van Oorschot, and Scott A. Vanstone. *Handbook of Applied Cryptography*. Boca Raton, Fla.: CRC Press, 1997.

Newton, David E. *Encyclopedia of Cryptology*. Santa Barbara, Calif.: ABC-CLIO, 1997.

Nichols, Randall K., Daniel J. Ryan, and Julie J. C. H. Ryan. *Defending Your Digital Assets: Against Hackers, Crackers, Spies and Thieves*. New York: McGraw-Hill, 2000.

Schneier, Bruce. *Applied Cryptography*, 2nd ed. New York: Wiley, 1995.

Schneier, Bruce, and David Banisar, eds. *The Electronic Privacy Papers: Documents on the Battle for Privacy in the Age of Surveillance*. New York: Wiley, 1997.

Sebag-Montefiore, Hugh. *Enigma: The Battle for the Code*. London: Weidenfeld and Nicolson, 2000.

Singh, Simon. *The Code Book: The Evolution of Secrecy from Mary, Queen of Scots, to Quantum Cryptography*. New York: Doubleday, 1999.

Smith, Michael. *Station X: The Codebreakers of Bletchley Park*. London: Channel 4 Books, 1998; New York: TV Books, 1999.

Van Tilborg, Henk C. A. *Fundamentals of Cryptology: A Professional Reference and Interactive Tutorial*. Boston: Kluwer Academic, 2000.

Zimmermann, Philip. *PGP Source Code and Internals*. Cambridge, Mass.: MIT Press, 1995.

CYBERCULTURE

Arbib, Michael A. *Computers and the Cybernetic Society*. New York: Academic Press, 1977; 2nd ed., Orlando, Fla., 1984.

Arms, William Y. *Digital Libraries*. Cambridge, Mass.: MIT Press, 2000.

Aronowitz, Stanley, Barbara Martinsons, and Michael Menser, eds. *Technoscience and Cyberculture*. New York: Routledge, 1996.

Balkin, J. M. *Cultural Software: A Theory of Ideology*. New Haven, Conn.: Yale University Press, 1998.

Barglow, Raymond. *The Crisis of the Self in the Age of Information: Computers, Dolphins, and Dreams*. New York: Routledge, 1994.

Barrett, Edward, ed. *Sociomedia: Multimedia, Hypermedia, and the Social Construction of Knowledge*. Cambridge, Mass.: MIT Press, 1992.

Barry, John A. *Technobabble*. Cambridge, Mass.: MIT Press, 1991.

Bell, David, and Barbara M. Kennedy, eds. *The Cybercultures Reader*. London and New York: Routledge, 2000.

Benedikt, Michael, ed. *Cyberspace: First Steps*. Cambridge, Mass.: MIT Press, 1991.

Beniger, James R. *The Control Revolution: Technological and Economic Origins of the Information Society*. Cambridge, Mass.: Harvard University Press, 1986.

Bennahum, David S. *Extra Life: Coming of Age in Cyberspace*. New York: Basic Books, 1998.

Brook, James, and Iain A. Boal. *Resisting the Virtual Life: The Culture and Politics of Information*. San Francisco: City Lights, distributed by Subterranean Co., Monroe, Oreg., 1995.

Bukatman, Scott. *Terminal Identity: The Virtual Subject in Postmodern Science Fiction*. Durham, N.C.: Duke University Press, 1993.

Bynum, Terrell Ward, and James H. Moor, eds. *The Digital Phoenix: How Computers Are Changing Philosophy*. Oxford, and Malden, Mass.: Blackwell, 1998.

Cairncross, Frances. *The Death of Distance: How the Communications Revolution Will Change Our Lives*. Boston: Harvard Business School Press, 1997.

Calcutt, Andrew. *White Noise: An A–Z of the Contradictions in Cyberculture*. New York: St. Martin's Press, 1999.

Castells, Manuel. *The Power of Identity*. Malden, Mass.: Blackwell, 1997.

Cavallaro, Dani. *Cyberpunk and Cyberculture: Science Fiction and the Work of William Gibson.* London, and New Brunswick, N.J.: Athlone Press, 2000.

Cherny, Lynn. *Conversation and Community: Discourse in a Social MUD.* Cambridge: Cambridge University Press, 1999.

Chesebro, James W., and Donald G. Bonsall. *Computer-Mediated Communication: Human Relationships in a Computerized World.* Tuscaloosa, Ala.: University of Alabama Press, 1989.

Cotton, Bob, and Richard Oliver. *The Cyberspace Lexicon: An Illustrated Dictionary of Terms from Multimedia to Virtual Reality.* London: Phaidon Press, 1994.

Coyne, Richard. *Technoromanticism: Digital Narrative, Holism, and the Romance of the Real.* Cambridge, Mass.: MIT Press, 1999.

Crang, Mike, Phil Crang, and Jon May, eds. *Virtual Geographies: Bodies, Space and Relations.* New York: Routledge, 1999.

Currie, Wendy. *The Global Information Society.* Chichester, West Sussex, England, and New York: Wiley, 2000.

Damer, Bruce. *Avatars! Exploring and Building Virtual Worlds on the Internet.* Berkeley, Calif.: Peachpit Press, 1998.

Denning, Peter J., ed. *Talking to the Machine: Computers and Human Aspiration.* New York: Copernicus, 1998.

Dertouzos, Michael L. *What Will Be: How the New World of Information Will Change Our Lives.* San Francisco: Harper*Edge*, 1997.

Dery, Mark. *Flame Wars: The Discourse of Cyberculture.* Durham, N.C.: Duke University Press, 1994.

———. *Escape Velocity: Cyberculture at the End of the Century.* New York: Grove Press, 1996.

Dibbell, Julian. *My Tiny Life.* New York: Henry Holt, 1998.

Dixon, Joan Broadhurst, and Eric J. Cassidy, eds. *Virtual Futures: Cyberotics, Technology and Post-human Pragmatism.* London and New York: Routledge, 1998.

Dodsworth, Clark, Jr., ed. *Digital Illusion: Entertaining the Future with High Technology.* New York: ACM Press; Reading, Mass.: Addison-Wesley, 1998.

Doheny-Farina, Stephen. *The Wired Neighborhood.* New Haven, Conn.: Yale University Press, 1996.

Dolce, Joe. *Product Design 5.* New York: Library of Applied Design, PBC International, 1992.

Donnelly, Denis P., ed. *The Computer Culture: A Symposium to Explore the Computer's Impact on Society.* Rutherford, N.J.: Fairleigh Dickinson University Presses, 1985.

Drucker, Susan J., and Gary Gumpert, eds. *Real Law @ Virtual Space: Communication Regulation in Cyberspace.* Creskill, N.J.: Hampton Press, 1999.

Druckrey, Timothy, ed. *Electronic Culture: Technology and Visual Representation.* New York: Aperture, 1996.

Ducatel, Ken, Juliet Webster, and Werner Herrmann, eds. *The Information Society in Europe: Work and Life in an Age of Globalization.* Lanham, Md.: Rowman and Littlefield, 2000.

Dyson, Esther. *Release 2.0: A Design for Living in the Digital Age.* New York: Broadway Books, 1997.

Ebo, Bosah L., ed. *Cyberghetto or Cybertopia: Race, Class, and Gender on the Internet.* Westport, Conn.: Praeger, 1998.

Featherstone, Mike, and Roger Burrows, eds. *Cyberspace/Cyberbodies/Cyberpunk: Cultures of Technological Embodiment.* London, and Thousand Oaks, Calif.: Sage Publications, 1996.

Gibson, William. *Neuromancer.* New York: Ace Books, 1984; London: Victor Gollancz, 1985.

Gordo-Lopez, Angel J., and Ian Parker, eds. *Cyberpsychology.* Basingstoke, Hampshire, England: Macmillan; New York: Routledge, 1999.

Hafner, Katie, and John Markoff. *Cyberpunk: Outlaws and Hackers on the Computer Frontier.* New York: Simon and Schuster Trade, 1991.

Hakken, David. *Cyborgs @ Cyberspace? An Ethnographer Looks to the Future.* New York: Routledge, 1999.

Harcourt, Wendy, ed. *Women @ Internet: Creating New Cultures in Cyberspace.* London and New York: Zed Books, 1999.

Harraway, Donna. *Simians, Cyborgs and Women: The Reinvention of Nature.* London: Free Association, 1990, 1991; New York: Routledge, 1991.

Harris, Craig, ed. *Art and Innovation: The Xerox PARC Artist in Residence.* Cambridge, Mass.: MIT Press, 1999.

Hayles, N. Katherine. *How We Became Posthuman: Virtual Bodies in Cybernetics, Literature, and Informatics.* Chicago: University of Chicago Press, 1999.

Heim, Michael. *The Metaphysics of Virtual Reality.* New York: Oxford University Press, 1993.

Herman, Andrew, and Thomas Swiss, eds. *The World Wide Web and Contemporary Cultural Theory.* New York: Routledge, 2000.

Hiltz, Starr Roxanne. *Online Communities: A Case Study of the Office of the Future.* Norwood, N.J.: Ablex Publishing, 1984.

Holmes, David, ed. *Virtual Politics: Identity and Community in Cyberspace.* London, and Thousand Oaks, Calif.: Sage Publications, 1997.

Horn, Stacy. *Cyberville: Clicks, Culture, and the Creation of an Online Town.* New York: Warner Books, 1998.

Johnson, Steven. *Interface Culture: How New Technology Transforms the Way We Create and Communicate.* San Francisco: Harper*Edge*, 1997.

Jones, Steven G., ed. *CyberSociety 2.0: Revisiting Computer-Mediated Communication and Community.* Thousand Oaks, Calif.: Sage Publications, 1998.

Jordan, Tim. *Cyberpower: The Culture and Politics of Cyberspace and the Internet.* London and New York: Routledge, 1999.

Kolko, Beth E., Lisa Nakamura, and Gilbert B. Rodman, eds. *Race in Cyberspace.* New York: Routledge, 2000.

Leary, Timothy Francis, et al. *Chaos and Cyber Culture.* Berkeley, Calif.: Ronin Publishing, 1994.

Lunenfeld, Peter. *Snap to Grid: A User's Guide to Digital Arts, Media, and Cultures.* Cambridge, Mass.: MIT Press, 2000.

Lunenfeld, Peter, ed. *The Digital Dialectic: New Essays on New Media.* Cambridge, Mass.: MIT Press, 1999.

Makimoto, Tsugio, and David Manners. *Digital Nomad.* New York: Wiley, 1997.

Manovich, Lev. *The Language of New Media.* Cambridge, Mass.: MIT Press, 2000.

Mansell, Robin, and Uta Wehn, eds. *Knowledge Societies: Information Technology for Sustainable Development.* Oxford and New York: Oxford University Press, 1998.

Margolis, Michael, and David Resnick. *Politics as Usual: The Cyberspace "Revolution."* Thousand Oaks, Calif.: Sage Publications, 2000.

Martin, William J. *The Global Information Society.* Brookfield, Vt.: Gower, 1995.

McLuhan, Marshall. *Understanding Media: The Extensions of Man.* New York: McGraw-Hill, 1964.

———. *The Gutenberg Galaxy: The Making of Typographical Man.* New York: NAL, 1969.

McLuhan, Marshall, and Quentin Fiore. *The Medium Is the Massage: An Inventory of Effects.* New York: Random House, 1940.

Negroponte, Nicholas. *Being Digital.* New York: Alfred A. Knopf, 1995.

Nelson, Theodor H. *Computer Lib: Dream Machines,* rev. ed. Redmond, Wash.: Tempest Books of Microsoft Press, 1987.

Perelman, Michael. *Class Warfare in the Information Age.* New York: St. Martin's Press, 1998.

Rattray, Gregory J. *Strategic Warfare in Cyberspace.* Cambridge, Mass.: MIT Press, 2001.

Rawlins, G. *Moths to the Flame: The Seductions of Computer Technology.* Cambridge, Mass.: MIT Press, 1996.

Rheingold, Howard. *The Virtual Community: Homesteading on the Electronic Frontier.* New York: Harper Perennial, 1994.

Rifkin, Jeremy. *The End of Work: The Decline of the Global Labor Force and the Dawn of the Post-market Era.* New York: Putnam, 1995.

Robins, Kevin, and Frank Webster. *Times of the Technoculture: From the Information Society to the Virtual Life.* London and New York: Routledge, 1999.

Schroeder, Ralph. *Possible Worlds: The Social Dynamic of Virtual Reality Technology.* Boulder, Colo.: Westview Press, 1996.

Shenk, David. *Data Smog: Surviving the Information Glut.* San Francisco: Harper*Edge*, 1997.

Slouka, Mark. *War of the Worlds: Cyberspace and the High-Tech Assault on Reality.* New York: Basic Books, 1995.

Smith, Marc A., and Peter Kollock, eds. *Communities in Cyberspace*. London and New York: Routledge, 1999.

Stone, Allucquere Rosanne. *The War of Desire and Technology at the Close of the Mechanical Age*. Cambridge, Mass.: MIT Press, 1995.

Sudweeks, Fay, Margaret L. McLaughlin, and Sheizaf Rafaeli, eds. *Network and Netplay: Virtual Groups on the Internet*. Cambridge, Mass.: MIT Press; Menlo Park, Calif.: AAAI Press, 1998.

Taylor, Paul. *Hackers: Crime in the Digital Sublime*. New York: Routledge, 1999.

Turkle, Sherri. *The Second Self: Computers and the Human Spirit.* New York: Simon and Schuster, 1984.

———. *Life on the Screen: Identity in the Age of the Internet.* New York: Simon and Schuster, 1995.

Valovic, Thomas S. *Digital Mythologies: The Hidden Complexities of the Internet*. New Brunswick, N.J.: Rutgers University Press, 2000.

Wilson, Mark I., and Kenneth E. Corey, eds. *Information Tectonics: Space, Place, and Technology in an Electronic Age*. Chichester, West Sussex, England, and New York: Wiley, 2000.

ELECTRONIC COMMERCE

Aldrich, Douglas F. *Mastering the Digital Marketplace: Practical Strategies for Competitiveness in the New Economy.* New York: Wiley, 1999.

Amor, Daniel. *The E-Business (R)evolution: Living and Working in an Interconnected World.* Upper Saddle River, N.J.: Prentice Hall, 2000.

Angell, Ian O. *The New Barbarian Manifesto: How to Survive the Information Age*. London, and Dover, N.H.: Kogan Page, 2000.

Applegate, Lynda M., et al. *Business and the Internet.* Boston: Harvard Business School Publishing, 1999.

Bishop, Bill. *Global Marketing for the Digital Age*. Lincolnwood, Ill.: NTC Business Books, 1999.

Bonorris, Steven. *Digital Money: Industry and Public Policy Issues*. Washington, D.C.: Institute for Technology Assessment, 1997.

Brynjolfsson, Eric, and Brian Kahin, eds. *Understanding the Digital Economy.* Cambridge, Mass.: MIT Press, 2000.

Buzzell, Robert D., ed. *Marketing in an Electronic Age*. Boston: Harvard Business School Press, 1985.

Camp, L. Jean. *Trust and Risk in Internet Commerce*. Cambridge, Mass.: MIT Press, 2000.

Carnoy, Martin, et al. *The New Global Economy in the Information Age*. University Park, Pa.: Pennsylvania State University Press, 1993.

Carpenter, Phil. *eBrands: Building an Internet Business at Breakneck Speed*. Boston: Harvard Business School Press, 2000.

Chissick, Michael, and Alistair Kelman. *Electronic Commerce: Law and Practice*, 2nd ed. London: Sweet and Maxwell, 2000.

Cohan, Peter S. *The Technology Leaders: How America's Most Profitable High-Tech Companies Innovate Their Way to Success*. San Francisco: Jossey-Bass, 1997.

———. *Net Profit: How to Invest and Compete in the Real World of Internet Business*. San Francisco: Jossey-Bass, 1999.

Coyle, Diane. *Weightless World: Strategies for Managing the Digital Economy*. Cambridge, Mass.: MIT Press, 1998.

Currie, Wendy. *The Global Information Society.* New York: Wiley, 2000. Series title: *Wiley Series in Information Systems.*

Doernberg, Richard L., and Luc Hinnekens. *Electronic Commerce and International Taxation*. The Hague, The Netherlands, and Boston: Kluwer Law International, 1999.

Dordick, Herbert S., Helen G. Bradley, and Burt Nanus. *The Emerging Network Marketplace*. Norwood, N.J.: Ablex Publishing, 1981.

Downes, Larry, and Chunka Mui. *Unleashing the Killer App: Digital Strategies for Market Dominance*. Boston: Harvard Business School Press, 1998.

Evans, Philip, and Thomas S. Wurster. *Blown to Bits: How the New Economics of Information Transforms Strategy*. Boston: Harvard Business School Press, 2000.

Figallo, Cliff. *Hosting Web Communities: Building Relationships, Increasing Customer Loyalty, and Maintaining a Competitive Edge*. New York: Wiley, 1998.

Huff, Sid L., et al. *Cases in Electronic Commerce*. Boston: Irwin/McGraw-Hill, 2000.

Leadbeater, Charles. *The Weightless Society: Living in the New Economy Bubble*. New York: Textere, 2000.

Lee, Chong-Moon, William F. Miller, Marguerite Gong Hancock, and Henry S. Rowen, eds. *The Silicon Valley Edge: A Habitat for Innovation and Entrepreneurship.* Stanford, Calif.: Stanford University Press, 2000.

Levine, Rick, et al. *The Cluetrain Manifesto: The End of Business as Usual.* Cambridge, Mass.: Perseus Books, 2000.

Schiller, Dan. *Digital Capitalism: Networking the Global Market System.* Cambridge, Mass.: MIT Press, 1999.

Southwick, Karen. *Silicon Gold Rush: The Next Generation of High-Tech Stars Rewrites the Rules of Business.* New York: Wiley, 1999.

Tapscott, Don, Alex Lowy, and David Ticoll, eds. *Blueprint to the Digital Economy: Creating Wealth in the Era of E-Business.* New York: McGraw-Hill, 1998.

Treese, G. Winfield, and Lawrence C. Stewart. *Designing Systems for Internet Commerce.* Reading, Mass.: Addison-Wesley, 1998.

GENERAL HISTORY

ACM Turing Award Lectures: The First Twenty Years, 1966 to 1985. New York: ACM Press; Reading, Mass.: Addison-Wesley, 1987.

Aspray, William. *John von Neumann and the Origins of Modern Computing.* Cambridge, Mass.: MIT Press, 1990.

Aspray, William, and Philip Kitcher, eds. *History and Philosophy of Modern Mathematics,* Minneapolis, Minn.: University of Minnesota Press, 1988.

Auzenne, Valliere Richard. *The Visualization Quest: A History of Computer Animation.* Rutherford, N.J.: Fairleigh Dickinson University Press, 1994.

Berkeley, Edmund C. *Giant Brains: Or Machines That Think.* New York: Wiley, 1949; New York: Science Editions, 1961.

Bird, Peter J. *LEO: The First Business Computer.* Wokingham, Berkshire, England: Hasler, 1994.

Bleackley, Beverley J., and Jean LaPrairie. *Entering the Computer Age: The Computer Industry in Canada, the First Thirty Years.* Agincourt, Ontario, Canada: published in association with Datacrown by the Book Society of Canada, 1982.

Brand, Stewart. "SPACEWAR: Fanatic Life and Symbolic Death Among the Computer Bums." *Rolling Stone,* Vol. 7, Dec. 1972. *http://www.baumgart.com/rolling-stone/spacewar.html*

Bronson, Po. *The Nudist on the Late Shift.* New York: Random House, 1999.

Caminer, David, John Aris, Peter Hermon, and Frank Land. *LEO: The Incredible Story of the World's First Business Computer.* New York: McGraw-Hill, 1998.

Campbell-Kelly, Martin, and William Aspray. *Computer: A History of the Information Machine.* New York: Basic Books, 1996.

Cardwell, Donald. *The Norton History of Technology.* New York: W.W. Norton, 1995.

Ceruzzi, Paul E. *A History of Modern Computing.* Cambridge, Mass.: MIT Press, 1998.

———. *Reckoners: The Prehistory of the Digital Computer, from Relays to the Stored Program Concept, 1935–1945.* Westport, Conn.: Greenwood Press, 1983.

Cortada, James W. *The Computer in the United States: From Laboratory to Market, 1930 to 1960.* Armonk, N.Y.: M.E. Sharpe, 1993.

Cringely, Robert X. *Accidental Empires: How the Boys of Silicon Valley Make Their Millions, Battle Foreign Competition and Still Can't Get a Date.* Reading, Mass.: Addison-Wesley, 1992; rev. and expanded ed., New York: Harper Business, 1996.

———. *Triumph of the Nerds,* written and presented by Robert X. Cringely. New York: Ambrose Video, 1996. Three videocassettes.

Dunham, William. *The Mathematical Universe: An Alphabetical Journey Through the Great Proofs, Problems, and Personalities.* New York: Wiley, 1994.

Glass, Robert L., ed. *In the Beginning: Recollections of Software Pioneers.* Los Alamitos, Calif.: IEEE Computer Society Press, 1998.

Goldstine, Herman. *The Computer from Pascal to von Neumann.* Princeton, N.J.: Princeton University Press, 1972.

Gomes-Casseres, Benjamin. *International Trade, Competition, and Alliances in the Computer Industry.* Boston: Division of Research, Harvard Business School, 1992.

Greenia, Mark W. *History of Computing: An Encyclopedia of the People and Machines That Made Computer History*. CD-ROM. Antelope, Calif.: Lexikon Services, 2000.

Hendry, John. *Innovating for Failure: Government Policy and the Early British Computer Industry*. Cambridge, Mass.: MIT Press, 1989. Series title: *History of Computing*.

Herz, J. C. *Joystick Nation: How Videogames Ate Our Quarters, Won Our Hearts, and Rewired Our Minds*. Boston: Little, Brown, 1997.

Kaplan, David A. *The Silicon Boys and Their Valley of Dreams*. New York: William Morrow, 1999.

Kline, Morris. *Mathematical Thought from Ancient to Modern Times*. New York: Oxford University Press, 1972.

Lavington, Simon. *A History of Manchester Computers*. Manchester, Lancashire, England: NCC Publications, 1975.

———. *Early British Computers: The Story of Vintage Computers and the People Who Built Them*. Bedford, Mass.: Digital Press, 1980.

Levy, Steven. *Hackers: Heroes of the Computer Revolution*. Garden City, N.Y.: Anchor Press/Doubleday, 1984.

Lewis, Michael. *The New New Thing: A Silicon Valley Story*. New York: W.W. Norton, 2000.

Lewis, Ted G. *Microsoft Rising—And Other Tales of Silicon Valley*. Los Alamitos, Calif.: IEEE Computer Society Press, 1999.

Licklider, J. C. R. "The Man–Computer Symbiosis." *IRE Transactions on Human Factors in Electronics*, Vol. 1, Mar. 1960, pp. 4–11. *http://memex.org/licklider.pdf*

Licklider, J. C. R., Robert Taylor, and E. Herbert. "The Computer as a Communication Device." *International Science and Technology*, Apr. 1968. *http://memex.org/licklider.pdf*

Lindgren, Michael. *Glory and Failure: The Difference Engines of Johann Müller, Charles Babbage and Georg and Edvard Scheutz*. Translated by Craig G. McKay. Cambridge, Mass.: MIT Press, 1990.

McCartney, Scott. *ENIAC: The Triumphs and Tragedies of the World's First Computer*. New York: Walker, 1999.

Metropolis, Nicholas, ed. *A History of Computing in the Twentieth Century*. San Diego, Calif.: Academic Press, 1980.

Moreau, René. *The Computer Comes of Age: The People, the Hardware, and the Software*. Translated by J. Howlett. Cambridge, Mass.: MIT Press, 1984.

Palfreman, Jon, and Doron Swade. *The Dream Machine: Exploring the Computer Age*. London: BBC Books, 1991.

Pugh, Emerson W., Lyle R. Johnson, and John H. Palmer. *IBM's 360 and Early 370 Systems*. Cambridge, Mass.: MIT Press, 1991.

Randell, Brian, ed. *The Origins of Digital Computers: Selected Papers*. Berlin and New York: Springer-Verlag, 1973; 3rd ed., 1982.

Rao, T. R. N., and Subhash Kak, eds. *Computing Science in Ancient India*. Lafayette, La.: Center for Advanced Computer Studies, University of Southwestern Louisiana, 1998.

Raymond, Eric S., ed. *The New Hacker's Dictionary*. Cambridge, Mass.: MIT Press, 1991; 3rd ed., 1996.

Redmond, Kent C., and Thomas M. Smith. *From Whirlwind to MITRE: The R&D Story of the SAGE Air Defense Computer*. Cambridge, Mass.: MIT Press, 2000.

Riordan, Michael, and Lillian Hoddeson. *Crystal Fire: The Birth of the Information Age*. New York: W.W. Norton, 1997.

Rojas, Raúl, and Ulf Hashagen, eds. *The First Computers: History and Architectures*. Cambridge, Mass.: MIT Press, 2000.

Sale, Tony. *Colossus 1943–1996*. Cleobury Mortimer, Shropshire, England: M&M Baldwin, 1998.

Shannon, Claude E., and Warren Weaver. *The Mathematical Theory of Communication*. Urbana, Ill.: University of Illinois Press, 1949.

Shurkin, Joel. *Engines of the Mind: A History of the Computer*. New York: W.W. Norton, 1984.

Siegfried, Tom. *The Bit and the Pendulum: From Quantum Computing to M Theory—The New Physics of Information*. New York: Wiley, 2000.

Stern, Nancy B. *From ENIAC to UNIVAC: An Appraisal of the Eckert–Mauchly Computers*. Bedford, Mass.: Digital Press, 1981. Series title: *Digital Press History of Computing Series*.

von Neumann, John. "First Draft of a Report on the EDVAC." Moore School of Electrical Engineering, University of Pennsylvania, Philadelphia, June 30, 1954. Reprinted in *Annals of the History of Computing*, Vol. 15, No. 4, 1993.

———. *The Computer and the Brain*. New Haven, Conn.: Yale University Press, 1958; 2nd ed., 2000.

Williams, Michael, R. *A History of Computing Technology*. Englewood Cliffs, N.J.: Prentice Hall, 1985; rev. ed., Los Alamitos, Calif.: IEEE Computer Society Press, 1997.

Hardware and Architecture

Ashenden, Peter J. *The Designer's Guide to VHDL*. San Francisco: Morgan Kaufmann, 1996.

Burks, Alice R., and Arthur W. Burks. *The First Electronic Computer: The Atanasoff Story*. Ann Arbor, Mich.: University of Michigan Press, 1989.

Dasgupta, Subrata. *Computer Architecture: A Modern Synthesis*. New York: Wiley, 1989.

Englander, Irv. *The Architecture of Computer Hardware and Systems Software*. New York: Wiley, 1996.

Flynn, Michael J. *Computer Architecture: Pipelined and Parallel Processor Design*. Boston: Jones and Bartlett, 1995.

Freiberger, Paul, and Michael Swaine. *Fire in the Valley*. Berkeley, Calif.: Osborne/McGraw-Hill, 1984; 2nd ed., New York: McGraw-Hill, 2000.

Goldberg, Adele, ed. *A History of Personal Workstations*. New York: ACM Press; Reading, Mass.: Addison-Wesley, 1988. Series title: *ACM Press History Series*.

Hennessy, John L., and David A. Patterson. *Computer Architecture: A Quantitative Approach*. San Francisco: Morgan Kaufmann, 1990.

Hill, Mark D., Norman P. Jouppi, and Gurindar Sohi. *Readings in Computer Architecture*. San Francisco: Morgan Kaufmann, 2000.

Hillis, Daniel W. *The Connection Machine* Cambridge, Mass: MIT Press, 1985.

Kawasaki, Guy. *The Macintosh Way*. Glenview, Ill.: Scott, Foresman, 1990.

Koren, Israel. *Computer Arithmetic Algorithms*. Englewood Cliffs, N.J.: Prentice Hall, 1993.

Leighton, Frank Thomson. *Introduction to Parallel Algorithms and Architectures: Arrays, Trees, Hypercubes*. San Mateo, Calif.: Morgan Kaufmann, 1992.

Lenoski, Daniel E., and Wolf-Dietrich Weber. *Scalable Shared-Memory Multiprocessing*. San Francisco: Morgan Kaufmann, 1995.

Linzmayer, Owen W. *The Mac Bathroom Reader*. San Francisco: SYBEX, 1994.

Lynch, Nancy A. *Distributed Algorithms*. San Francisco: Morgan Kaufmann, 1997.

Milutinović, Veljko. *High-Level Language Computer Architecture*. New York: Computer Science Press, 1989.

Newrock, Melody. *Here Come the Clones! The Complete Guide to IBM PC Compatibles*. New York: Micro Text, 1984.

Patterson, David A., and John Hennessey. *Computer Architecture: A Quantitative Approach*. San Mateo, Calif.: Morgan Kaufmann, 1990; 2nd ed., San Francisco, 1996.

Przybylski, Steven A. *Cache and Memory Hierarchy Design: A Performance-Directed Approach*. San Mateo, Calif.: Morgan Kaufmann, 1990.

Rutland, David. *Why Computers Are Computers: The SWAC and the PC*. Philomath, Oreg.: Wren Publishers, 1995.

Silc, Jurij, Borut Robic, and Theo Ungerer. *Processor Architecture: From Dataflow to Superscalar and Beyond*. Berlin and New York: Springer-Verlag, 1999.

Stallings, William. *Computer Organization and Architecture: Principles of Structure and Function*. New York: Macmillan, 1987; 5th ed., published under the title *Computer Organization and Architecture: Designing for Performance*, Upper Saddle River, N.J.: Prentice Hall, 2000.

Tanenbaum, Andrew S. *Structured Computer Organization*, 4th ed. Upper Saddle River, N.J.: Prentice Hall, 1999.

Walker, John, ed. *The Autodesk File: Bits of History, Words of Experience*, 3rd ed. Thousand Oaks, Calif.: New Riders Publishing, 1989.

Weste, Neil H. E., and Kamran Eshragian. *Principles of CMOS VLSI Design: A Systems Perspective*. Reading, Mass.: Addison-Wesley, 1985; 2nd ed., 1993.

HUMAN–COMPUTER INTERACTION

Adler, Paul S., and Terry A. Winograd, eds. *Usability: Turning Technologies into Tools*. New York: Oxford University Press, 1992.

Baecker, Ronald M., and William A. S. Buxton, eds. *Readings in Human–Computer Interaction: A Multidisciplinary Approach*. Los Altos, Calif.: Morgan Kaufmann, 1987.

Baecker, Ronald M., Jonathan Grudin, William A. S. Buxton, and Saul Greenberg, eds. *Readings in Human–Computer Interaction: Toward the Year 2000*, 2nd ed. San Francisco, Calif.: Morgan Kaufmann, 1995.

Banks, William W., and Jon Weimer. *Effective Computer Display Design*. Englewood Cliffs, N.J.: Prentice Hall, 1992.

Beaudouin-Lafon, Michel, ed. *Computer Supported Co-operative Work*. Chichester, West Sussex, England, and New York: Wiley, 1999.

Benyon, David, Diana Bental, and Thomas Green. *Conceptual Modeling for User Interface Development*. London and New York: Springer-Verlag, 1999.

Bergman, Eric, ed. *Information Appliances and Beyond: Interaction Design for Consumer Products*. San Francisco: Morgan Kaufmann, 2000.

Bodker, Susanne, ed. *Through the Interface: A Human Activity Approach to User Interface Design*. Hillsdale, N.J.: Lawrence Erlbaum Associates, 1991.

Bowers, John M., and Steven D. Benford. *Studies in Computer Supported Cooperative Work: Theory, Practice and Design*. Amsterdam and New York: North-Holland, 1991.

Cantoni, Virginio, et al., eds. *Human and Machine Perception 2: Emergence, Attention, and Creativity*. New York: Kluwer Academic/Plenum Publishers, 1999.

Card, Stuart K., Thomas P. Moran, and Allen Newell. *The Psychology of Human–Computer Interaction*. Hillsdale, N.J.: Lawrence Erlbaum Associates, 1983.

Carroll, John M., ed. *Interfacing Thought: Cognitive Aspects of Human–Computer Interaction*. Cambridge, Mass.: MIT Press, 1987.

———. *Designing Interaction: Psychology at the Human–Computer Interface*. Cambridge and New York: Cambridge University Press, 1991.

———. *Making Use: Scenario-Based Design of Human–Computer Interactions*. Cambridge, Mass.: MIT Press, 2000.

Cipolla, Roberto, and Alex Pentland, eds. *Computer Vision for Human–Machine Interaction*. Cambridge and New York: Cambridge University Press, 1998.

Downton, Andy, ed. *Engineering the Human–Computer Interface*. London and New York: McGraw-Hill, 1991.

Edwards, Alistair D. N., ed. *Extra-ordinary Human–Computer Interaction: Interfaces for Users with Disabilities*. Cambridge and New York: Cambridge University Press, 1995.

Elzer, P. F., R. H. Kluwe, and B. Boussoffara, eds. *Human Error and System Design and Management*. London and New York: Springer-Verlag, 2000.

Faulkner, Christine. *The Essence of Human–Computer Interaction*. London and New York: Prentice Hall, 1998.

Head, Alison J. *Design Wise: A Guide to Evaluating the Interface Design of Information Resources*. Medford, N.J.: CyberAge Books, 1999.

Hix, Debra, and H. Rex Hartson. *Developing User Interfaces: Ensuring Usability Through Product and Process*. New York, Wiley, 1993.

Kajler, N., ed. *Computer–Human Interaction in Symbolic Computation*. With a foreword by Dana S. Scott. Vienna and New York: Springer-Verlag, 1998.

Laurel, Brenda. *The Art of Human–Computer Interface Design*. Reading, Mass.: Addison-Wesley, 1990.

Liu, Z.-Q., and S. Miyamoto, eds. *Soft Computing and Human-Centered Machines*. New York: Springer-Verlag, 2000.

Marsh, Jonathon P., Barbara Gorayska, and Jacob L. Mey, eds. *Humane Interfaces: Questions of Method and Practice in Cognitive Technology*. Amsterdam and New York: Elsevier, 1999.

Newman, Dan. *Talk to Your Computer: Speech Recognition Made Easy*. Berkeley, Calif.: Waveside, 2000.

Noyes, Janet M., Jan Noyes, and Chris Baber. *User-Centered Design of Systems*. London and New York: Springer-Verlag, 1999.

Palanque, Philippe, and Fabio Paternò, eds. *Formal Methods in Human–Computer Interaction.* London and New York: Springer-Verlag, 1998.

Pfleger, S., J. Gonçalves, and K. Varghese, eds. *Advances in Human–Computer Interaction: Human Comfort and Security.* Berlin and New York: Springer-Verlag, 1995.

Picard, Rosalind W. *Affective Computing.* Cambridge, Mass.: MIT Press, 1997.

Raskin, Jef. *The Humane Interface: New Directions for Designing Interactive Systems.* Reading, Mass.: Addison-Wesley, 2000.

Sasse, M. Angela, and Chris Johnson, eds. *Human–Computer Interaction: INTERACT '99.* Burke, Va.: IOS Press, 1999.

Shapiro, Dan, Michael Tauber, and Roland Traunmuller, eds. *The Design of Computer Supported Cooperative Work and Groupware Systems.* Amsterdam and New York: Elsevier, 1996.

Shneiderman, Ben. *Designing the User Interface: Strategies for Effective Human–Computer Interaction.* Reading, Mass.: Addison-Wesley, 1987; 3rd ed., Addison-Wesley Longman, 1998.

Smith, David E., ed. *Knowledge, Groupware, and the Internet.* Boston: Butterworth-Heinemann, 2000.

Suereth, Russell. *Developing Natural Language Interfaces: Processing Human Conversations.* New York: McGraw-Hill, 1997.

Vaske, Jerry J., and Charles E. Grantham. *Socializing the Human–Computer Environment.* Norwood, N.J.: Ablex Publishing, 1990.

Wooffitt, Robin, et al. *Humans, Computers, and Wizards: Analyzing Human (Simulated) Computer Interaction.* London and New York: Routledge, 1997.

INFORMATION TECHNOLOGY

Allouche, José, and Gerard Pogorel. *Networks, Machines, and Portfolios: Technology Decision-Making in Large Corporations.* Milan, Italy: Angeli, 1990.

Batt, Chris. *Information Technology in Public Libraries*, 6th ed. London: Library Association Publishing, 1998.

Bauer, Martin, ed. *Resistance to New Technology: Nuclear Power, Information Technology and Biotechnology.* Cambridge and New York: Cambridge University Press, 1995.

Bell, Simon. *Learning with Information Systems: Learning Cycles in Information Systems Development.* London and New York: Routledge, 1996.

Beniger, James R. *The Control Revolution: Technological and Economic Origins of the Information Society.* Cambridge, Mass.: Harvard University Press, 1986.

Best, David P., ed. *The Fourth Resource: Information and Its Management.* Aldershot, Hampshire, England, and Brookfield, Vt.: Aslib Gower, 1996.

Billings, Bruce H. *China and the West: Information Technology Transfer from Printing Press to Computer Era.* Long Beach, Calif.: Intertech Press, 1997.

Black, Sandra E., and Lisa M. Lynch. *How to Compete: The Impact of Workplace Practices and Information Technology on Productivity.* Cambridge, Mass.: National Bureau of Economic Research, 1997.

Bloomfield, Brian P., Rod Coombs, and David Knights, eds. *Information Technology and Organizations: Strategies, Networks, and Integration.* Oxford and New York: Oxford University Press, 1997.

Boisot, Max H. *Information and Organizations: The Manager as Anthropologist.* London: Fontana/Collins, 1987.

———. *Information Space: A Framework for Learning in Organizations, Institutions, and Culture.* London: Routledge, 1995.

———. *Knowledge Assets: Securing Competitive Advantage in the Information Economy.* Oxford and New York: Oxford University Press, 1998.

Boland, Richard J., Jr., and Rudy A. Hirschheim, eds. *Critical Issues in Information Systems Research.* Chichester, West Sussex, England, and New York: Wiley, 1987.

Borghoff, Uwe, and Remo Pareschi, eds. *Information Technology for Knowledge Management.* Berlin and New York: Springer-Verlag, 1998.

Borgman, Christine L. *From Gutenberg to the Global Information Infrastructure: Access to Information in the Networked World.* Cambridge, Mass.: MIT Press, 2000.

Borgmann, Albert. *Holding On to Reality: The Nature of Information at the Turn of the Millennium.* Chicago: University of Chicago Press, 1999.

Bresnahan, Timothy F., Erik Brynjolfsson, and Lorin M. Hitt. *Information Technology, Workplace Organization, and the Demand for Skilled Labor: Firm-Level Evidence.* Cambridge, Mass.: National Bureau of Economic Research, 1999.

Brooking, Annie. *Corporate Memory: Strategies for Knowledge Management.* London and New York: International Thomson Business Press, 1999.

Brosnan, Mark J. *Technophobia: The Psychological Impact of Information Technology.* New York: Routledge, 1998.

Bryson, Jo. *Managing Information Services: An Integrated Approach.* Aldershot, Hampshire, England, and Brookfield, Vt.: Gower, 1997.

Butler, Meredith A., and Bruce R. Kingman, eds. *The Economics of Information in the Networked Environment.* Washington, D.C.: Association of Research Libraries, 1996.

Button, Graham. *Technology in Working Order: Studies of Work, Interaction, and Technology.* London and New York: Routledge, 1993.

Castells, Manuel. *The Informational City: Information Technology, Economic Restructuring, and the Urban–Regional Process.* Oxford, and Malden, Mass.: Blackwell, 1999.

Connors, Michael. *The Race to the Intelligent State: Charting the Global Information Economy into the 21st Century.* Oxford: Capstone, 1997.

Coppock, Terry, ed. *Information Technology and Scholarship: Applications in the Humanities and Social Sciences.* Oxford: Oxford University Press, 1999.

Cronin, Blaise, ed. *Information Management: From Strategies to Action.* London: Aslib, 1985.

———. *Information Management: From Strategies to Action 2.* London: Aslib, the Association for Information Management, 1992.

Cronin, Blaise, and Elisabeth Davenport. *Elements of Information Management.* Metuchen, N.J.: Scarecrow Press, 1991.

Davenport, Thomas H., and Laurence Prusak. *Information Ecology: Mastering the Information and Knowledge Environment.* New York: Oxford University Press, 1997.

Davis, Gordon Bitter, and J. David Naumann. *Personal Productivity with Information Technology.* New York: McGraw-Hill, 1997.

Falling Through the Net: Defining the Digital Divide: A Report on the Telecommunications and Information Technology Gap in America. Washington, D.C.: U.S. Department of Commerce, National Telecommunications and Information Administration, 1999.

Finnegan, Ruth, Graeme Salaman, and Kenneth Thompson, eds. *Information Technology: Social Issues.* Sevenoaks, Kent, England: Hodder and Stoughton, in association with the Open University, 1987.

Galliers, Robert D., and Walter R. J. Baets, eds. *Information Technology and Organizational Transformation: Innovation for the 21st Century Organization.* Chichester, West Sussex, England, and New York: Wiley, 1998.

Gandy, Anthony, and Chris Chapman. *Information Technology and Financial Services: The New Partnership.* Chicago: Glenlake Publishing, distributed by Fitzroy Dearborn, 1997.

Gardner, Christopher. *The Valuation of Information Technology: A Guide for Strategy Development, Valuation, and Financial Planning.* New York: Wiley, 2000.

Garson, G. David, ed. *Social Dimensions of Information Technology: Issues for the New Millennium.* Hershey, Pa.: Ideas Group Publishing, 2000.

Goonatilake, Susantha. *Merged Evolution: Long-Term Implications of Biotechnology and Information Technology.* Newark, N.J.: Gordon and Breach, 1999.

Green, Eileen, Jenny Owen, and Den Pain, eds. *Gendered by Design? Information Technology and Office Systems.* London: Taylor and Francis, 1993.

Hussain, Khateeb M., and Donna Hussain. *Information Technology Management.* Oxford and Boston: Butterworth-Heinemann, 1997.

Information Technology Industry Council. *Information Technology Industry Data Book,*

1960–2008. Washington, D.C.: ITIC, Industry Statistics Programs, 1998.

Kemerer, Chris F., ed. *Information Technology and Industrial Competitiveness: How IT Shapes Competition.* Boston: Kluwer Academic, 1998.

Lubbe, Sam. *IT in Developing Countries: An Assessment and Practical Guideline.* Hershey, Pa.: Ideas Group Publishing, 1999.

Mansell, Robin, and Uta Wehn, eds. *Knowledge Societies: Information Technology for Sustainable Development.* Oxford and New York: Oxford University Press, published for and on behalf of the Commission on Science and Technology for Development, United Nations, 1998.

Milligan, Peter, and Patrick Corr, eds. *New Frontiers of Information Technology: Proceedings, Short Contributions,* 23rd Euromicro Conference, Budapest, Hungary, Sept. 1–4, 1997. Los Alamitos, Calif.: IEEE Computer Society Press, 1997.

Schön, Donald A., Bish Sanyal, and William J. Mitchell, eds. *High Technology and Low-Income Communities: Prospects for the Positive Use of Advanced Information Technology.* Cambridge, Mass.: MIT Press, 1999.

Tzafestas, S. G., ed. *Advances in Manufacturing: Decision, Control, and Information Technology.* New York: Springer-Verlag, 1999.

Williams, Brian K., Stacey C. Sawyer, and Sarah E. Hutchinson, eds. *Using Information Technology: A Practical Introduction to Computers and Communication,* 3rd ed. Boston: Irwin/McGraw-Hill, 1999.

Wilson, Mark I. and Kenneth E. Corey, eds. *Information Tectonics: Space, Place, and Technology in an Electronic Age.* Chichester, West Sussex, England, and New York: Wiley, 2000.

NETWORKING AND INTERNET

Abbate, Janet. *Inventing the Internet.* Cambridge, Mass.: MIT Press, 1999. Series title: *Inside Technology.*

Andrews, Paul. *How the Web Was Won: Microsoft from Windows to the Web: The Inside Story of How Bill Gates and His Band of Internet Idealists Transformed a Software Empire.* New York: Broadway Books, 1999.

Antonelli, Cristiano, ed. *The Economics of Information Networks.* Amsterdam and New York: North-Holland, distributed in the United States and Canada by Elsevier Science, 1992.

Baran, Paul. "On Distributed Communication Networks." In *Rand Memoranda,* Vols. 1–11. Santa Monica, Calif.: Rand Corporation, Aug. 1964. *http://www.rand.org/publications/RM/baran.list.html*

Berners-Lee, Tim, with Mark Fischetti. *Weaving the Web: The Original Design and Ultimate Destiny of the World Wide Web by Its Inventor.* New York: HarperCollins, 1999.

Bolt Beranek and Newman, Inc. *A History of the ARPANET: The First Decade.* Arlington, Va.: Bolt Beranek and Newman, 1981.

Buckingham, Simon. *Data on WAP.* Alpharetta, Ga.: Mobile Lifestreams, 1999.

Byrnes, Philippe. *Protocol Management in Computer Networking.* Boston: Artech House, 2000.

Cameron, Debra. *Internet 2: The Future of the Internet and Next-Generation Initiatives.* Charleston, S.C.: Computer Technology Research Corporation, 1999.

Cerf, Vinton, and Robert Kahn. "A Protocol for Packet Network Interconnection." *IEEE Transactions on Communication Technology,* Vol. 22, May 1974, pp. 627–641.

Christensen, Ward, and Randy Seuss. "Hobbyist Computerized Bulletin Boards." *Byte,* Nov. 1978, p. 150.

Comer, Douglas. *The Internet Book: Everything You Need to Know About Computer Networking and How the Internet Works,* 2nd ed. Upper Saddle River, N.J.: Prentice Hall, 1997.

Everard, Jerry. *Virtual States: The Internet and the Boundaries of the Nation-State.* London and New York: Routledge, 2000.

Gardner, Robert, and Dennis Shortelle. *From Talking Drums to the Internet.* Santa Barbara, Calif.: ABC-CLIO, 1997.

Gelenbe, Erol, ed. *System Performance Evaluation: Methodologies and Applications.* Boca Raton, Fla.: CRC Press, 2000.

Gelenbe, Erol, and G. Pujolle. *Introduction to Queueing Networks.* Chichester, West Sussex, England, and New York: Wiley, 1987; 2nd ed., 1998.

Gellersen, Hans-W., ed. *Handheld and Ubiquitous Computing: Proceedings of the First International Symposium, HUC '99*, Karlsruhe, Germany, Sept. 27–29, 1999. Berlin and New York: Springer-Verlag, 1999.

Gibson, David V., George Kozmetsky, and Raymond W. Smilor, eds. *The Technopolis Phenomenon: Smart Cities, Fast Systems, Global Networks.* Lanham, Md.: Rowman and Littlefield, 1992.

Gilder, George. *Telecosm: How Infinite Bandwidth Will Revolutionize Our World.* New York: Free Press, 2000.

Golden, James R. *Economics and National Strategy in the Information Age: Global Networks, Technology Policy, and Cooperative Competition.* Westport, Conn.: Praeger, 1994.

Graham, Gordon. *The Internet: A Philosophical Inquiry.* London and New York: Routledge, 1999.

Grant, Gail L. *Understanding Digital Signatures: Establishing Trust over the Internet and Other Networks.* New York: McGraw-Hill, 1998.

Grenier, Ray, and George Metes. *Enterprise Networking: Working Together Apart.* Bedford, Mass.: Digital Press, 1992.

Hafner, Katie, and Matthew Lyon. *Where Wizards Stay Up Late: The Origins of the Internet.* New York: Simon and Schuster, 1996.

Handel, Rainer, Manfred N. Huber, and Stefan Schroder. *ATM Networks: Concepts, Protocols, and Applications*, 2nd ed. Harlow, Essex, England, and Reading, Mass.: Addison-Wesley, 1994; 3rd ed., 1998.

Harasim, Linda, ed. *Global Networks: Computers and International Communication.* Cambridge, Mass.: MIT Press, 1993.

Harrison, Teresa M., and Timothy D. Stephen, eds. *Computer Networking and Scholarly Communication in Twenty-First-Century University.* Albany, N.Y.: State University of New York Press, 1996.

Hauben, Michael, and Rhonda Hauben. *Netizens: On the History and Impact of USENET and the Internet.* Los Alamitos, Calif.: IEEE Computer Society Press, 1997. *http://www.columbia.edu/~hauben/netbook*

Krol, Ed, and Mike Loukides, eds. *The Whole Internet User's Guide and Catalog.* Sebastopol, Calif.: O'Reilly, 1992; 2nd ed., 1994.

Leiner, Barry M., Vinton G. Cerf, David D. Clark, et al. "A Brief History of the Internet." 20 Feb. 1998. *http://www.isoc.org/internet-history/brief.html*

Levy, Stephen. *Hackers: Heroes of the Computer Revolution.* New York: Dell Publishing, 1984.

Mann, Steve. *Programming Applications with the Wireless Application Protocol: The Complete Developer's Guide.* New York: Wiley, 2000.

Metcalfe, Robert M. *Packet Communication.* San Jose, Calif.: Peer-to-Peer Communications, 1996.

Moschovitis, Christos, et al. *History of the Internet: A Chronology, 1843 to Present.* Santa Barbara, Calif.: ABC-CLIO, 1999.

Naughton, John. *A Brief History of the Future: The Origins of the Internet.* London: Weidenfeld and Nicolson, 1999; New York: Overlook Press, 2000.

Quittner, Joshua, and Michelle Slatalla. *Speeding the Net: The Inside Story of Netscape and How It Challenged Microsoft.* New York: Atlantic Monthly Press, 1998.

Randall, Neil. *The Soul of the Internet: Net Gods, Netizens and the Wiring of the World.* London and Boston: International Thomson Computer Press, 1997.

Reid, Robert H. *Architects of the Web: 1,000 Days That Built the Future of Business.* New York: Wiley, 1997.

Segaller, Stephen. *Nerds 2.0.1: A Brief History of the Internet.* New York: TV Books, 1998.

Spencer, Henry, and David Lawrence. *Managing Usenet.* Sebastopol, Calif.: O'Reilly, 1998.

Stallings, William. *Data and Computer Communications.* New York: Macmillan; London: Collier Macmillan, 1985; 6th ed., Upper Saddle River, N.J.: Prentice Hall, 2000.

———. *Local and Metropolitan Area Networks*, 6th ed., Upper Saddle River, N.J.: Prentice Hall, 2000.

Stoll, Clifford. *The Cuckoo's Egg: Tracking a Spy Through the Maze of Computer Espionage.* New York: Pocket Books, 1990.

Telleen, Steven L. *IntraNet™ Methodology: Concepts and Rationale.* Sunnyvale, Calif.: Amdahl Corporation, 1995.

Valovic, Thomas. *Corporate Networks: The Strategic Use of Telecommunications*. Boston: Artech House, 1993.

van der Heijden, Marcel, and Marcus Taylor, eds. *Understanding WAP: Wireless Applications, Devices, and Services*. Boston: Artech House, 2000.

Wireless Application Protocol Forum. *Official Wireless Application Protocol*. New York: Wiley, 1999.

Wolinsky, Art. *The History of the Internet and the World Wide Web*. Berkeley Heights, N.J.: Enslow Publishers, 1999. Series title: *The Internet Library*.

PEOPLE

Amann, Dick, and Dick Smith. *Forgotten Women of Computer History*. Stow, Mass.: Programmed Studies, 1978.

Austrian, Geoffrey. *Herman Hollerith: Forgotten Giant of Information Processing*. New York: Columbia University Press, 1984.

Barsky, Robert F. *Noam Chomsky: A Life of Dissent*. Cambridge, Mass.: MIT Press, 1997.

Caddes, Carolyn. *Portraits of Success: Impressions of Silicon Valley Pioneers*. Palo Alto, Calif.: Tioga Publishing, distributed by William Kaufmann, Los Altos, Calif., 1986.

Campbell-Kelly, Martin, ed. *Babbage: Passages from the Life of a Philosopher*. Piscataway and New Brunswick, N.J.: Rutgers University Press, 1994.

Cohen, I. Bernard. *Howard Aiken: Portrait of a Computer Pioneer*. Cambridge, Mass.: MIT Press, 1999.

Cohen, I. Bernard, and Gregory W. Welch, eds. *Makin' Numbers: Howard Aiken and the Computer*. Cambridge, Mass.: MIT Press, 1999.

Gates, Bill. *Bill Gates Speaks: Insight from the World's Greatest Entrepreneur*. Compiled by Janet Lowe. New York: Wiley, 1998.

Glass Robert L., ed. *In the Beginning: Personal Recollections of Software Pioneers*. Los Alamitos, Calif.: IEEE Computer Society Press, 1998.

Heims, Steve J. *John von Neumann and Norbert Wiener: From Mathematics to the Technologies of Life and Death*. Cambridge, Mass.: MIT Press, 1980.

Hodges, Andrew. *Turing: A Natural Philosopher*. London: Phoenix, 1997.

Hyman, Anthony H. *Charles Babbage: Pioneer of the Computer*. Oxford: Oxford University Press, 1982.

Lee, J. A. N., ed. *International Dictionary of Computer Pioneers*. Chicago and London: Fitzroy Dearborn, 1995.

MacHale, Desmond. *George Boole: His Life and Work*. Dublin: Boole Press, 1985.

Macrae, Norman. *John von Neumann*. New York: Pantheon Books, 1992.

Manes, Stephen, and Paul Andrews. *Gates: How Microsoft's Mogul Reinvented an Industry and Made Himself the Richest Man in America*. New York: Doubleday, 1993.

Marchand, Philip. *Marshall McLuhan: The Medium and the Messenger*. Cambridge, Mass.: MIT Press, 1998.

Moody, Fred. *The Visionary Position: The Inside Story of the Digital Dreamers Who Are Making Virtual Reality a Reality*. New York: Times Business, 1999.

Morgan, Christopher. *Wizards and Their Wonders: Portraits in Computing*. New York: ACM/The Museum, 1997.

Murray, Charles J. *The Supermen: The Story of Seymour Cray and the Technical Wizards Behind the Supercomputer*. New York: Wiley, 1997.

Nyce, James M., and Paul Kahn, eds. *From Memex to Hypertext: Vannevar Bush and the Mind's Machine*. Boston: Academic Press, 1991.

Rifkin, Glenn, and George Harrar. *The Ultimate Entrepreneur: The Story of Ken Olsen and Digital Equipment Corporation*. Chicago: Contemporary Books, 1988; updated, Rocklin, Calif.: Prima Publishing, 1990.

Ritchie, David. *The Computer Pioneers: The Making of the Modern Computer*. New York: Simon and Schuster, 1986.

Ross, G. MacDonald. *Leibniz*. Oxford and New York: Oxford University Press, 1984.

Shasha, Dennis, and Cathy Lazere. *Out of Their Minds: The Lives and Discoveries of 15 Great Computer Scientists*. New York: Springer-Verlag, 1997.

Slater, Robert. *Portraits in Silicon*. Cambridge, Mass.: MIT Press, 1987.

Spencer, Donald. *Great Men and Women of Computing*. Ormond Beach, Fla.: Camelot, 1996; 2nd ed., 1999.

Stein, Dorothy. *Ada: A Life and a Legacy*. Cambridge, Mass.: MIT Press, 1985.

Turing, Sara. *Alan M. Turing*. Cambridge, England: Heffer, 1959.

Wang, An, with Eugene Linden. *Lessons: An Autobiography*. Reading, Mass.: Addison-Wesley, 1986.

Wilkes, Maurice V. *Memoirs of a Computer Pioneer*. Cambridge, Mass.: MIT Press, 1985.

Wilson, Mike. *The Difference Between God and Larry Ellison: Inside Oracle Corporation*. New York: William Morrow, 1997.

Young, Jeffrey S. *Steve Jobs: The Journey Is the Reward*. Glenview, Ill.: Scott Foresman, 1988.

POLITICS, ETHICS, AND LAW

Abramson, Jeffrey B., F. Christopher Arterton, and Gary R. Orren. *The Electronic Commonwealth: The Impact of New Media Technologies on Democratic Politics*. New York: Basic Books, 1988.

Alexander, Cynthia J., and Leslie A. Pal, eds. *Digital Democracy: Policy and Politics in the Wired World*. Toronto and New York: Oxford University Press, 1998.

Arterton, F. Christopher. *Teledemocracy: Can Technology Protect Democracy?* Newbury Park, Calif.: Sage Publications; Washington, D.C.: Roosevelt Center for American Policy Studies, 1987.

Band, Jonathan, and Masanobu Katoh. *Interfaces on Trial: Intellectual Property and Interoperability in the Global Software Industry*. Boulder, Colo.: Westview Press, 1995.

Becker, Ted, and Christa Daryl Slaton. *The Future of Teledemocracy*. Westport, Conn.: Praeger, 2000.

Bellamy, Christine, and John A. Taylor. *Governing in the Information Age*. Buckingham, England, and Bristol, Pa.: Open University Press, 1998.

Bennett, Colin J., and Rebecca Grant, eds. *Visions of Privacy: Policy Choices for the Digital Age*. Toronto, Ontario, Canada: University of Toronto Press, 1999.

Bradley, Stephen P., Jerry A. Hausman, and Richard L. Nolan, eds. *Globalization, Technology, and Competition: The Fusion of Computers and Telecommunications in the 1990s*. Boston: Harvard Business School Press, 1993.

Brown, Geoffrey. *The Information Game: Ethical Issues in a Microchip World*. Atlantic Highlands, N.J.: Humanities Press International, 1990.

Bynum, Terrell Ward, Walter Maner, and John L. Fodor, eds. *Teaching Computer Ethics*. New Haven, Conn.: Research Center on Computing and Society, 1992.

Cavazos, Edward A., and Gavino Morin. *Cyberspace and the Law: Your Rights and Duties in the Online World*. Cambridge, Mass. and London: MIT Press, 1994.

Clapes, Anthony Lawrence. *Softwars: The Legal Battles for Control of the Global Software Industry*. Westport, Conn.: Quorum Books, 1993.

Cooper, Jonathan. *Liberating Cyberspace: Civil Liberties, Human Rights, and the Internet*. London, and Sterling, Va.: Pluto Press, 1999.

Couch, Carl J. *Information Technologies and Social Orders*. New York: Aldine de Gruyter, 1996.

Danziger, James N., William H. Dutton, Rob Kling, and Kenneth L. Kraemer. *Computers and Politics: High Technology in American Local Governments*. New York: Columbia University Press, 1982.

DeCew, Judith Wagner. *In Pursuit of Privacy: Law, Ethics, and the Rise of Technology*. Ithaca, N.Y.: Cornell University Press, 1997.

Denning, Dorothy E., and Peter J. Denning, eds. *Internet Besieged: Countering Cyberspace Scofflaws*. New York: ACM Press; Reading, Mass.: Addison-Wesley, 1997.

Doern, G. Bruce. *Global Change and Intellectual Property Agencies: An Institutional Perspective*. London and New York: Pinter, 1999.

Dunlop, Charles, and Rob Kling, eds. *Computerization and Controversy: Value Conflicts and Social Choices*. Boston: Academic Press, 1991; 2nd ed., Rob Kling, ed., San Diego, 1996.

Dutton, William H., ed. *Society on the Line: Information Politics in the Digital Age*. Oxford and New York: Oxford University Press, 1999.

Forester, Tom, and Perry Morrison. *Computer Ethics: Cautionary Tales and Ethical Dilemmas in Computing*. Oxford, and Cambridge, Mass.: Blackwell, 1990; 2nd ed., Cambridge, Mass.: MIT Press, 1994.

Friedman, Batya, and Terry Winograd, eds. *Computing and Social Responsibility: A Collection of Course Syllabi.* Palo Alto, Calif.: Computer Professionals for Social Responsibility, 1990.

Gill, Karamjit S., ed. *Information Society: New Media, Ethics and Postmodernism.* London and New York: Springer-Verlag, 1996.

Godwin, Mike. *Cyber Rights: Defending Free Speech in the Digital Age.* New York: Times Books, 1998; New York: Random House, 2000.

Granstrand, Ove. *The Economics and Management of Intellectual Property: Towards Intellectual Capitalism.* Cheltenham, Gloucestershire, England, and Northampton, Mass.: Edward Elgar Publishing, 1999.

Grossman, Lawrence K. *The Electronic Republic: Reshaping Democracy in the Information Age.* New York: Viking, 1995.

Grossman, Wendy M. *Net.wars.* New York: New York University Press, 1997.

Hague, Barry N., and Brian Loader, eds. *Digital Democracy: Discourse and Decision Making in the Information Age.* London and New York: Routledge, 1999.

Harper, Christopher. *And That's the Way It Will Be: News and Information in a Digital World.* New York: New York University Press, 1998.

Hill, Kevin A., and John E. Hughes. *Cyberpolitics: Citizen Activism in the Age of the Internet.* Lanham, Md.: Rowman and Littlefield, 1998.

Hirst, Paul Q. *Associative Democracy: New Forms of Economic and Social Governance.* Cambridge: Polity Press, 1994.

Johnson, Deborah G. *Computer Ethics.* Englewood Cliffs N.J.: Prentice Hall, 1985; 2nd ed., 1994.

Jonas, Hans. *The Imperative of Responsibility: In Search of an Ethics for the Technological Age.* Translated by Hans Jonas. Chicago: University of Chicago Press, 1984.

Kahin, Brian, and Charles Nesson, eds. *Borders in Cyberspace: Information Policy and the Global Information Infrastructure.* Cambridge, Mass.: MIT Press, 1997.

Kelleher, Denis, and Karen Murray. *IT Law in the European Union.* London: Sweet and Maxwell, 1999.

Lessig, Lawrence. *Code and Other Laws of Cyberspace.* New York: Basic Books, 1999.

Lipschultz, Jeremy Harris. *Free Expression in the Age of the Internet: Social and Legal Boundaries.* Boulder, Colo.: Westview Press, 2000.

Litan, Robert E., and William Niskanen. *Going Digital! A Guide to Policy in the Digital Age.* Washington, D.C.: Brookings Institution Press; Cato Institute, 1998.

Loader, Brian, ed. *The Governance of Cyberspace: Politics, Technology and Global Restructuring.* London and New York: Routledge, 1997.

———. *Cyberspace Divide: Equality, Agency, and Policy in the Information Society.* London and New York: Routledge, 1998.

Margetts, Helen. *Information Technology in Government: Britain and America.* London and New York: Routledge, 1999.

Miles, Sarah. *How to Hack a Party Line: The Democrats and Silicon Valley.* New York: Farrar, Straus and Giroux, 2001.

McChesney, Robert W., Ellen Meiksins Wood, and John Bellamy Foster, eds. *Capitalism and the Information Age: The Political Economy of the Global Communication Revolution.* New York: Monthly Review Press, 1998.

National Research Council, ed. *The Digital Dilemma: Intellectual Property in the Information Age.* Washington D.C.: National Academy Press, 2000.

Parker, Donn, Susan Swope, and Bruce N. Baker. *Ethical Conflicts in Information and Computer Science, Technology and Business.* Wellesley, Mass.: QED Information Sciences, 1990.

Perritt, Henry H. *Law and the Information Superhighway: Privacy, Access, Intellectual Property, Commerce, Liabilty.* New York: Wiley, 1996.

Perrolle, Judith A. *Computers and Social Change: Information, Property and Power.* Belmont, Calif.: Wadsworth, 1987.

Preece, Jennifer. *Online Communities: Designing Usability and Supporting Sociability.* New York: Wiley, 2000.

Robinett, Jane, and Ramon Barquin, eds. *Computers and Ethics: A Sourcebook for Discussions.* Brooklyn, N.Y.: Polytechnic Press, 1989.

Schon, Donald A., Bish Sanyal, and William J. Mitchell, eds. *High Technology and Low-Income Communities: Prospects for the Positive Use of Advanced Information Technology.* Cambridge, Mass.: MIT Press, 1998.

Selnow, Gary W. *Electronic Whistle-Stops: The Impact of the Internet on American Politics.* Westport, Conn.: Praeger, 1998.

Slatalla, Michele, and Joshua Quittner. *Masters of Deception: The Gang That Ruled Cyberspace.* New York: HarperCollins, 1996.

Sterling, Bruce. *The Hacker Crackdown: Law and Disorder on the Electronic Frontier.* New York: Bantam Books, 1992. *http://www.lysator.liu.se/etexts/hacker*

Stichler, Richard N., and Robert Hauptman, eds. *Ethics, Information, and Technology: Readings.* Jefferson, N.C.: McFarland, 1998.

Sussman, Gerald. *Communication, Technology, and Politics in the Information Age.* Thousand Oaks, Calif.: Sage Publications, 1997.

Tsagarousianou, Roza, Damian Tambini, and Cathy Bryan, eds. *Cyberdemocracy: Technology, Cities and Civic Networks.* London and New York: Routledge, 1998.

Walch, James. *In the Net: An Internet Guide for Activists.* London and New York: Zed Books, distributed in the United States by St. Martin's Press, New York, 1999.

Woo, Jisuk. *Copyright Law and Computer Programs: The Role of Communication in Legal Structure.* New York: Garland Publishing, 2000.

SOFTWARE AND PROGRAMMING

Alic, John A., Jameson R. Miller, and Jeffrey A. Hart. *Computer Software: Strategic Industry.* Bloomington, Ind.: Indiana Center for Global Business, School of Business, Indiana University, 1991.

Baecker, Ronald M., ed. *Readings in Groupware and Computer-Supported Cooperative Work: Assisting Human–Human Collaboration.* San Mateo, Calif.: Morgan Kaufmann, 1993.

Bergin, Thomas J., and Richard G. Gibson. *A History of Programming Languages II.* New York: ACM Press; Reading, Mass.: Addison-Wesley, 1996.

Booch, Grady. *Object Oriented Design with Applications.* Redwood City, Calif.: Benjamin-Cummings, 1991.

Borenstein, Nathaniel. *Programming As If People Mattered: Friendly Programs, Software Engineering, and Other Noble Delusions.* Princeton, N.J.: Princeton University Press, 1991.

Brooks, Frederick P., Jr. *The Mythical Man-Month: Essays on Software Engineering.* Reading, Mass.: Addison-Wesley, 1982.

Brookshear, J. Glenn. *Computer Science: An Overview,* 5th ed. Reading, Mass.: Addison-Wesley, 1997.

Casavant, Thomas L., and Mukesh Singhal. *Readings in Distributed Computing Systems.* Los Alamitos, Calif.: IEEE Computer Society Press, 1994.

Christian, Gram, and Gilbert Cockton, eds. *Design Principles for Interactive Software.* London: Chapman and Hall, 1996.

Coffman, Edward G., Jr., and Peter J. Denning. *Operating Systems Theory.* Englewood Cliffs, N.J.: Prentice-Hall, 1973.

Coulouris, George F., Jean Dollimore, and Tim Kindberg. *Distributed Systems: Concepts and Design.* Wokingham, Berkshire, England, and Reading, Mass.: Addison-Wesley, 1983; 2nd ed., 1994.

Dahlbom, Bo, and Lars Mathiassen. *Computers in Context: The Philosophy and Practice of Systems Design.* Cambridge, Mass.: NCC Blackwell, 1993.

Date, C. J. *An Introduction to Database Systems.* Reading, Mass.: Addison-Wesley, 1999.

Davenport, Thomas H. *Mission Critical: Realizing the Promise of Enterprise Systems.* Boston: Harvard Business School Press, 2000.

Davis, Alan M. *Software Requirements: Objects, Functions, and States.* Englewood Cliffs, N.J.: Prentice Hall, 1993.

DiBona, Chris, Sam Ockman, and Mark Stone, eds. *Open Sources: Voices from the Open Source Revolution.* Beijing, and Sebastopol, Calif.: O'Reilly, 1999.

Dijkstra, Edsger. *A Discipline of Programming.* Englewood Cliffs, N.J.: Prentice Hall, 1976.

Dunne, Paul E. *Computability Theory: Concepts and Applications.* New York: Ellis Horwood, 1991.

Floyd, Christiane, et al. *Out of Scandinavia: Alternative Approaches to Software Design and System Development.* Hillsdale, N.J.: Lawrence Erlbaum Associates, 1989.

Ford, Neville J. *Computer Programming Languages Made Simple.* Upper Saddle River, N.J.: Prentice Hall, 1990.

Friedman, Andrew L., and Dominic S. Cornford. *Computer Systems Development: History, Organization and Implementation.* Chichester, West Sussex, England, and New York: Wiley, 1989.

Genette, Gerard. *The Architext: An Introduction.* Translated by Jane E. Lewin. Berkeley, Calif.: University of California Press, 1992.

Kernighan, Brian W., and Dennis M. Ritchie. *The C Programming Language*, 2nd ed. Upper Saddle River, N.J.: Prentice Hall, 1989.

Knuth, Donald Ervin. *The Art of Computer Programming*, Vols. 1–3, 3rd ed. Reading, Mass.: Addison-Wesley, 1997.

Koza, J. R. *Genetic Programming: On the Programming of Computers by Means of Natural Selection.* Cambridge, Mass.: MIT Press, 1992.

Lerner, Joshua, and Jean Tirole. *The Simple Economics of Open Source.* Cambridge, Mass.: National Bureau of Economic Research, 2000.

Meissner, Gerd. *SAP: Die heimliche Software-Macht.* English: *SAP: Inside the Secret Software Power.* Translated from the German by Jürgen Ulrich Lorenz. London and New York: McGraw-Hill, 2000.

Qualls, Bill. *Mainframe Assembler Programming.* New York: Wiley, 1998.

Raymond, Eric S. *The Cathedral and the Bazaar: Musings on Linux and Open Source by an Accidental Revolutionary.* Beijing, and Cambridge, Mass.: O'Reilly, 1999.

Ritchie, D. M. *The Evolution of the Unix Time-Sharing System.* Lecture Notes in Computer Science, No. 79: *Language Design and Programming Methodology.* New York: Springer-Verlag, 1980.

Shaw, John Crossley. *JOSS: A Designer's View of an Experimental On-Line System.* Santa Monica, Calif.: RAND Corporation, 1964.

Silberschatz, A., and James Lyle Peterson. *Operating System Concepts.* Reading, Mass.: Addison-Wesley, 1983; 5th ed., with P. B. Galvin, New York: Wiley, 1999.

Stroustrup, Bjarne. *The C++ Programming Language*, 2nd ed. Reading, Mass.: Addison-Wesley, 1991.

Tanenbaum, Andrew S. *Modern Operating Systems.* Englewood Cliffs, N.J.: Prentice Hall, 1992.

Taylor, Dave. *Global Software: Developing Applications for the International Market.* New York: Springer-Verlag, 1992.

Wang, Yingxu, and Graham King. *Software Engineering Processes: Principles and Applications.* Boca Raton, Fla.: CRC Press, 2000.

Wayner, Peter. *Free for All: How Linux and the Free Software Movement Undercut the High-Tech Titans.* New York: Harper Business, 2000.

Wexelblat, Richard, ed. *History of Programming Languages.* New York: Academic Press, 1981.

Wills, Linda, and Philip Newcomb, eds. *Reverse Engineering.* Boston: Kluwer Academic, 1996.

Wirth, Niklaus. *Systematic Programming: An Introduction.* Englewood Cliffs, N.J.: Prentice Hall, 1973.

———. *Algorithms + Data Structures = Programs.* Englewood Cliffs, N.J.: Prentice Hall, 1975.

Yourdon, Edward, and Larry L. Constantine. *Structured Design: Fundamentals of a Discipline of Computer Program and Systems Design.* Englewood Cliffs, N.J.: Prentice Hall, 1979.

Zachary, G. Pascal. *Show-stopper! The Breakneck Race to Create Windows NT and the Next Generation at Microsoft.* New York: Free Press; Toronto, Ontario, Canada: Maxwell Macmillan Canada, 1994.

Appendix One
Computers Outside United States as of 1955

Country	Institution	Computer	Date[a]
Belgium	Bell Telephone Manufacturing, Antwerp	Unnamed	1954
Britain	Government Code & Cypher School, Bletchley Park	Colossus	1943
	Elliott Brothers Ltd.	152[b]	1947
	Cambridge University	EDSAC	1949
	Manchester University	Mark I	1949
	London University, Imperial College	ICCE[b]	1950
	National Physical Laboratory	Pilot ACE	1950
	Atomic Energy Authority, Harwell	Unnamed[b]	1951
	Lyons & Company	LEO I	1951
	Ferranti Ltd.	Mark I	1951
	London University	APE(R)C	1952
	Elliott Brothers Ltd.	Nicholas	1952
	Elliott Brothers Ltd.	Eccles	1953
	Manchester University	Transistor prototype	1953
	Ministry of Supply, Malvern	MOSAIC	1953
	Royal Aircraft Establishment	RASCAL (never completed)[b]	1953
	Telecommunications Research Establishment	TREAC	1953
	Elliott Brothers Ltd.	401	1954
	Ferranti Ltd.	Mark I[b]	1954
	Manchester University	MEG	1954
	Power-Samas Company	PCC[b]	1954
	British Tabulating Machine Company	HEC 1200	1954
	Elliott Brothers Ltd.	WREDAC	1955
	Elliott Brothers Ltd.	402	1955
	English Electric Company	DEUCE	1955
	Manchester University	MV950 prototype	1955
	Ferranti Ltd.	Pegasus	1955
	Atomic Energy Authority, Harwell	CADET	1955
Czechoslovakia	Research Institute for Mathematical Machines	SAPO	1951–58
Denmark	Regnecentralen	DASK	1953–58
East Germany	Carl Zeiss Firm, Jena	Oprema[b]	1955
France	Machines Bull	Gamma 2	1951
	Machines Bull	Gamma 3	1952
	Société d'Electronique et d'Automatisme	CUBA	1952
	Société d'Electronique et d'Automatisme	CAB 2000	1955
Israel	Weizmann Institute, Rehovot	WEIZAC	1955
Italy	Instituto Nazionale per le Applicazioni del Calcolo, Rome	FINAC	1955
	University of Pisa	CEP	1955–61

Country	Institution	Computer	Date[a]
Japan	Tokyo University	Statistical Relay Computer[b]	1939–51
	Tokyo University	TAC	1952–59
	ETL	Mark I[b]	1952
	ETL	Mark II[b]	1955
Netherlands	Mathematisch Centrum	ARRA I[b]	1951
	Mathematisch Centrum	ARRA II	1953
	Post-Telephone-Telegraph Laboratory	PTERA	1953
	Fokker Airplane Works, Amsterdam	FERTA	1955
Norway	University of Oslo	NUSSE	1953
Sweden	Matematikmaskinnamnden	BARK[b]	1950
	Matematikmaskinnamnden	BESK	1954
Switzerland	Eidgenossische Technische Hochschule, Zurich	ERMETH	1954–57
U.S.S.R.	Ukrainian Academy of Science	MESM	1950
	—	BESM I	1952
	—	M1	1952
	—	M2	1953
	Ministry for Machine Building	STRELA	1953
	Ministry for Precise Mechanics	URAL 1	1954
	—	M3	1955
West Germany	Zuse	Z3[b]	1941
	Zuse KG	Z4[b]	1950
	Zuse KG	Z5[b]	1953
	Max-Planck-Institute	G1	1953
	Max-Planck-Institute	G2	1954
	Technische Hochschule, Munich	PERM	1950–56
	Technische Hochschule, Darmstadt	DERA	1955

[a] *Dates are intended to represent when the machine first attained effective operation, which in many cases is difficult to date exactly.*

[b] *Does not meet all requirements of a general-purpose, digital, electronic, stored-program calculating system.*

SOURCE : William Aspray, "International Diffusion of Computer Technology, 1945–55," *Annals of the History of Computing*, Vol. 8, No. 4, Oct. 1986.

Appendix Two
U.S. Electronic Digital Computers as of 1955

Manufacturer	System[a]
Argonne National Laboratory	ORACLE
Barber-Colman Company	BAR-COL DEC DIG
Bendix Aviation Corporation	BENDIX-D12, BENDIX-G15
Burroughs Corporation	BUR-E101, UDEC-I, UDEC-II
ElectroData Corporation	DATATRON
Electronics Corporation of America	MAGNEFILE-B, MAGNEFILE-D
Ferranti Electric, Inc.[b]	FERRANTI MARK-I, FERRANTI MARK-II, PEGASUS
General Electric Company	OARAC
Haller, Raymond, and Brown	AN/UJQ-2(XA-1)
Harvard Computation Laboratory	ADEC
Hogan Laboratories	CIRCLE
Hughes Aircraft Company	HUGHES ACC MOD-III
Institute for Advanced Study	IAS
International Business Machines Company	CPC, 604, 607, 608, 650, 701, 702, 704, 705, NORC
Laboratory for Electronics, Inc.	TIM-II
Librascope Company	LGP-30
Logistics Research, Inc.	ALWAC-III
Los Alamos Scientific Laboratory	MANIAC, MANIAC-II
Marchant Research, Inc.	MINIAC
Massachusetts Institute of Technology	WHIRLWIND-I
Mellon Institute of Industrial Research	MELLON INSTITUTE-DIG
Monroe Calculating Machine Company	MONROBOT-III, MONROBOT-V, MONROBOT-VI-MU
Mountain Systems, Inc.	MODAC-404, MODAC-410, MDP-MSI-5014

Manufacturer	System[a]
National Bureau of Standards	DYSEAC, SEAC, SWAC
National Cash Register Company	NCR-CRC-102A, NCR-CRC-102D, NCR-303, WHITESAC (CRC-106)
Naval Research Laboratory	NAREC
Oak Ridge National Laboratory	ORACLE
Olivetti Corporation of America	OLIVETTI-GBM
Pennsylvania State University	PENNSTAC
Radio Corporation of America	RCA-BIZMAC
Rand Corporation	JOHNNIAC
Raytheon Manufacturing Company	RAYDAC, RAXCOM
J.B. Rea Company, Inc.	READIX
Sperry Rand Corporation (including Engineering Research Associates)	UNIVAC, UNIVAC-II, LOG LARC, UNIVAC-SCIENTIFIC (ERA-1101) UNIVAC-SCIENTIFIC (ERA-1103, ERA-1103A) UNIVAC-SCIENTIFIC (ERA-1102)
Technitrol Engineering Company	TECHNITROL-180
Teleregister Corporation	BAEQS, MAGNETRONIC RESERVISOR, TELE REGISTER SPEDDH
Underwood Corporation	ELECOM-50, 100, 120A, 125, 125FP, ORDFIAC
U.S. Air Force Missile Test Center	FLAC
University of California, Berkeley	CALDIC
University of Illinois	ILLIAC, ORDVAC
University of Michigan	MIDAC
University of Pennsylvania	EDVAC, ENIAC
University of Wisconsin	WISC
Wang Laboratories	WEDILOG

[a] *The spelling, capitalization, and punctuation in this table are as given in Weik (1955).*

[b] *Imported computer systems.*

SOURCE: Compiled from William Aspray, "International Diffusion of Computer Technology, 1945–55," *Annals of the History of Computing*, Vol. 8, No. 4, Oct. 1986; and Martin H. Weik, *A Survey of Domestic Electronic Digital Computing Systems*, Ballistics Research Laboratory Report 971, Aberdeen Proving Ground, Aberdeen, Md., Dec. 1955.

INDEX

Page numbers in **boldface** indicate main entries; those in *italics* indicate illustrations.

B

C

D

E

F

I

M

N

S

T

U

V

W

X

Y

Z

Contributors

Agah, Arvin University of Kansas, United States

Agar, Jon University of Manchester, United Kingdom

Anderberg, Anthony Yahsbam Systems, United States

Asaro, Peter University of Illinois at Urbana-Champaign, United States

Ashrafuzzaman, Mohammad Xcert International, Inc., Canada

Ball, Guy D. Calculator Historian, United States

Barnes, Susan Fordham University, United States

Barsky, Robert Université du Québec à Montréal, Canada

Bekey, George University of Southern California, United States

Bell, Gordon Microsoft Corporation, United States

Berthold, Michael University of California, Berkeley, United States

Bowen, Jonathan P. South Bank University, United Kingdom

Brinning, Jenna L. Freie Universität Berlin, Germany

Broukhis, Leonid A. Software Engineer, United States

Brunskill, David A. Staffordshire University, United Kingdom

Campbell-Kelly, Martin University of Warwick, United Kingdom

Cantu-Paz, Erick Lawrence Livermore National Laboratory, United States

Casner, Stephen Packet Design, Inc., United States

Cawsey, Alison Heriot-Watt University, United Kingdom

Chin, Amita Goyal Virginia Commonwealth University, United States

Chlamtac, Imrich University of Texas at Dallas, United States

Cohen, I. Bernard Harvard University, United States

Cranor, Lorrie Faith AT&T Labs-Research, United States

Cronin, Blaise Indiana University, United States

Darius, Frank Technische Universität Berlin, Germany

de Jager, Peter de Jager & Company Limited, United States

Deane, John CSIRO, Australia

Dornan, Andy Network Magazine, United States

Duncker, Elke Middlesex University, United Kingdom

Duquenoy, Penny Middlesex University, United Kingdom

Earnest, Les Stanford University, United States

Eckstein, Peter Author, United States

Edwards, John TeleworkNetwork, Inc., United States

Ekert, Artur Oxford University, United Kingdom

Esponda, Margarita Freie Universität Berlin, Germany

Fey, Dietmar Universität-GH Siegen, Germany

Fields, Bob Middlesex University, United Kingdom

Fine, Thomas A. Harvard-Smithsonian Center for Astrophysics, United States

Flower, Joe What If, United States

Friedland, Gerald Freie Universität Berlin, Germany

Gelenbe, Erol University of Central Florida, United States

Gey, Steven G. Florida State University, United States

Gintar, Kimberly Author, Germany

Glass, Robert L. *Journal of Systems and Software*, United States

Gloye, Alexander Freie Universität Berlin, Germany

Goldwasser, Samuel M. Engineering Consultant, United States

Goodman, Seymour E. University of Arizona, United States

Grad, Burt Burton Grad Associates, Inc., United States

Gray, George DeKalb Technical College, United States

Gray, Richard Trintech, Inc., United States

Grier, David Alan George Washington University, United States

Gurer, Denise 3Com, United States

Gustafson, John Sun Microsystems, United States

Hauben, Jay Robert Amateur Computerist Newsletter, United States

Hauben, Michael Author, United States

Hauben, Ronda Author, United States

Hedge, Alan Cornell University, United States

Heide, Lars Syddansk Universitet, Denmark

Hodges, Andrew Wadham College, Oxford University, United Kingdom

Hull, Richard Brunel University, United Kingdom

Hunter, Christopher D. University of Pennsylvania, United States

Johnson, Luanne Software History Center, United States

Jones, Matt Middlesex University, United Kingdom

Jones, Roger Bishop Roger Bishop Jones Limited, United Kingdom

Kaplan, Erez Software Engineer, Israel

Keahey, Kate Los Alamos National Laboratory, United States

Kelley, Paul L. Tufts University, United States

Kernighan, Brian Bell Labs, United States

Kidwell, Peggy National Museum of American History, Smithsonian Institution, United States

Kim, Eugene Eric *Dr. Dobb's Journal*, United States

Koops, Bert-Jaap Tilburg Universiteit, the Netherlands

Koren, Israel University of Massachusetts, United States

Koulopoulos, Thomas M. The Delphi Group, United States

Kuittinen, Petri University of Arts and Design (Helsinki), Finland

Laird, Cameron Phaseit, Inc., United States

Larmouth, John University of Salford, United Kingdom

Leavitt, Neal Leavitt Communications, United States

Logue, Joseph C. IBM Fellow (Retired), United States

Marshall, David Cardiff University, United Kingdom

Maurer, Hermann Graz University of Technology, Austria

McHaney, Roger Kansas State University, United States

Meenakshisundaram, Ramachandran Openlink Financial, Inc., United States

Meinel, Carolyn M/B Research, United States

Metzlar, Alle Teacher/Author, the Netherlands

Mitchell, David Software Consultant, United States

Morelos-Zaragoza, Robert Sony Computer Science Laboratories, Inc., Japan

Morreale, Patricia Stevens Institute of Technology, United States

Moschovitis, Christos J. P. The Moschovitis Group, United States

Muller, Chris Software Consultant, United States

Murphy, Gary Lawrence TeleDynamics Communications, Inc., Canada

Napper, Brian University of Manchester, United Kingdom

Neil, Stephanie Thomas Publishing Company, United States

Nelson, Mark Cisco Systems, Inc., United States

Orzech, Dan Author, United States

Pascoe, R.S.V. Northern Territory University, Australia

Paterson, Tim Paterson Technology, United States

Peirce, Michael Trinity College, Ireland

Pimentel, Andy D. University of Amsterdam, the Netherlands

Platt, Allan B. Netcafé Internet Consulting Services, United States

Poole, Hilary W. The Moschovitis Group, United States

Reiter, Mike Bell Labs, United States

Roache, Christina Author, United States

Robson, Gary Author, United States

Rogers, Juan D. Georgia Institute of Technology, United States

Rojas, Raúl Freie Universität Berlin, Germany

Rojas-Esponda, Tanja Steglitzer Gymnasium, Germany

Russel, Gordon Napier University, United Kingdom

Sander, Oliver Konrad Zuse Zentrum für Informationstechnik Berlin (ZIB), Germany

Sanromà, Manuel University of Tarragona, Spain

Schneier, Bruce Counterpane Internet Security, Inc., United States

Schoenherr, Steven E. University of San Diego, United States

Schroeder, Michael City University London, United Kingdom

Schwerk, Thomas Freie Universität Berlin, Germany

Shapiro, Stuart Consultant, United States

Shea, Virginia Author, United States

Shields, Paul Nortel Networks; The Business Mac, United States

Stallings, William Author, United States

Stein, Bob VisiBone, United States

Stone, Dan Ancept, Inc., United States

Strickland, Dorothy Rutgers University, United States

Swartzlander, Earl University of Texas at Austin, United States

Tolksdorf, Robert Technische Universität Berlin, Germany

Tomayko, James Carnegie Mellon University, United States

Törn, Aimo Åbo Akademi, Finland

Van der Spiegel, Jan University of Pennsylvania, United States

Van Vleck, Tom Multician, United States

Varga, Akos Siemens, Hungary

Voisard, Agnes Freie Universität Berlin, Germany

Wagner, Gerd Freie Universität Berlin, Germany

Wessels, Duanne Packet Pushers, United States

Whitten, David Department of Veterans' Affairs, United States

Williams, Michael R. University of Calgary, Canada

Wirth, Niklaus Eidgenössische Technische Hochschule Zürich, Switzerland

Woehr, Jack J. *Dr. Dobb's Journal*, United States

Wohl, Amy D. Wohl Associates, Inc, United States

Woodford, Chris Author, United Kingdom

Wright, Tom Microcosm, United States

Wu, Wei-ju SESA AG, Germany

Yaroslavtsev, Michael Pluris, Inc., United States

Yee, Danny University of Sydney, Australia

Yost, Jeffrey R. Charles Babbage Institute, United States

Ziring, Neal U.S. Government, United States